THE CONFUCIAN PERSUASION

STANFORD STUDIES IN THE CIVILIZATIONS OF EASTERN ASIA
Editors: Arthur F. Wright, George Sansom, John D. Goheen,
Thomas C. Smith, Robert H. Brower, Mary Clabaugh Wright

*Volumes published under the auspices of the Committee on
Chinese Thought of the Association for Asian Studies*

Arthur F. Wright, ed., *Studies in Chinese Thought* (Chicago, 1953)
John K. Fairbank, ed., *Chinese Thought and Institutions* (Chicago, 1957)
David S. Nivison and Arthur F. Wright, eds., *Confucianism in Action* (Stanford, 1959)
Arthur F. Wright, ed., *The Confucian Persuasion* (Stanford, 1960)
Arthur F. Wright and Denis Twitchett, eds., *Confucian Personalities* (Stanford, 1962)

THE CONFUCIAN PERSUASION

Edited by

ARTHUR F. WRIGHT

With Contributions by

JAMES F. CAHILL	YUJI MURAMATSU
TSE-TSUNG CHOW	DAVID S. NIVISON
JOSEPH R. LEVENSON	EDWIN G. PULLEYBLANK
HISAYUKI MIYAKAWA	ROBERT RUHLMANN
FREDERICK W. MOTE	ARTHUR F. WRIGHT

STANFORD UNIVERSITY PRESS · STANFORD, CALIFORNIA

Stanford University Press
Stanford, California
© 1960 by the Board of Trustees of the
Leland Stanford Junior University
Printed in the United States of America
Original edition 1960
Last figure below indicates year of this printing:
78   77   76   75   74   73   72   71   70   69

Preface

This volume is the fourth in a series of symposia devoted to the principal traditions of Chinese thought as these have influenced the cultural life and institutional development of China. These studies are a sequel to *Confucianism in Action,* edited by David S. Nivison and Arthur F. Wright (Stanford, 1959), and both volumes grew out of the 1957 and 1958 conferences on Chinese thought sponsored by the Committee on Chinese Thought of the Association for Asian Studies.

The Committee began its explorations of the problems of Chinese thought in 1951, and two volumes were published with generous support from the University of Chicago Program of Comparative Studies of Cultures and Civilizations directed by Milton Singer and the late Robert Redfield. These were *Studies in Chinese Thought* (Chicago, 1953), edited by Arthur F. Wright, and *Chinese Thought and Institutions,* (Chicago, 1957), edited by John K. Fairbank. The Committee now plans a fifth symposium to be devoted to biographical studies of Confucians whose lives reveal the relation between their creeds and their patterns of behavior.

The emphasis in the symposia is upon two aspects of the Confucian tradition. One is the operational force of Confucianism: how it has affected individual lives and the evolution of institutions. The other is its pattern of growth and change: the complex ways in which it has been adapted to the shifting needs of the Chinese through twenty-five centuries of their history. As a result of this emphasis we have unfortunately been obliged to slight the formal aspects of Confucian thought and the rich traditions of classical scholarship—subjects which demand far more varied and disciplined study than has thus far been given them in the West.

The problem interests of this volume, like those of its predecessor and possible sequel, have been dictated by two considerations: the desirability of enlisting the talents of scholars in many disciplines, and the possibility of reconnoitering periods on which little organized knowledge was available. (For example, Mr. Mote's study of the intellectual history of the period of Mongol dominion is the first on that subject to appear in a Western language.) Briefly, we have sought ways to arrive at a deeper understanding of Chinese civilization and to make the most effective use of existing scholarly talents.

In thus conceiving its task, the Committee has not "commissioned" research papers or sought to draw scholars away from their established concerns. Rather, our aim has been to provide intellectual stimulation and to bring together in our conferences scholars with convergent or overlapping interests. With the assistance, since 1957, of a generous grant from the Rockefeller Foundation, we have also been able to provide research and secretarial assistance, travel and fellowship funds for foreign scholars, and occasional grants-in-aid for research. Our work has been further facilitated by the support of the Chairman's activities first at Stanford and now at Yale University. We should also like to acknowledge the fellowship assistance given to Professor Muramatsu by the Committee on East Asian Studies at Stanford and the friendly and efficient attention given our problems by the Stanford University Press.

The Committee is indebted to many others for sympathetic encouragement and assistance. Among them are Professor Mary C. Wright; Dr. Francis X. Sutton of the Ford Foundation and Professor Richard Rudner of Michigan State University, who served as outside critics at our 1957 and 1958 conferences, respectively; Dr. Kai-yu Hsü, now of San Francisco State College, who was our faithful rapporteur at both conferences; Mrs. Mary H. Johnson and Mrs. Rosaline Schwartz, efficient and helpful secretaries to the Committee; and Dr. Susan Han Marsh and Mr. Jonathan Spence, who have prepared the Index.

A. F. W.

Yale University
June 6, 1960

Contents

Contributors

JAMES F. CAHILL received his training in Oriental languages at the University of California in Berkeley, and took his doctorate in Fine Arts at the University of Michigan, with a thesis on the Yüan dynasty painter Wu Chen. He has also studied at Kyoto University. He is now on the staff of the Freer Gallery of Art, Washington, D.C., where he also teaches at American University. His chief interest is in Chinese painting.

TSE-TSUNG CHOW received his B.A. from the Central University of Political Sciences in China, the M.A. and Ph.D. in political science from the University of Michigan. He worked as editor-in-chief of the *New Understanding* monthly and other magazines, and taught at colleges in Chungking during World War II. He served as secretary to the President of the Republic of China from 1945 to 1947. He is now research fellow at Harvard University and sometime lecturer at Harvard and Columbia. He has written several volumes in Chinese and some poetry, and was co-author of *Election, Initiative, Referendum and Recall: Charter Provisions in Michigan Home Rule Cities* (1958). His most recent book is *The May Fourth Movement: Intellectual Revolution in Modern China* (1960).

JOSEPH R. LEVENSON received his Ph.D. from Harvard, where he was a member of the Society of Fellows. He is now Associate Professor of History at the University of California. His research has been primarily in the field of Chinese intellectual history. He is the author of *Liang Ch'i-ch'ao and the Mind of Modern China* and *Confucian China and Its Modern Fate: The Problem of Intellectual Continuity.*

HISAYUKI MIYAKAWA was graduated from Kyoto University in 1935 and did his graduate work in East Asian History at the same university. He is now Associate Professor of East Asian History at Okayama University. In 1957–58 he did research at Stanford University as a Fellow of the Committee on Chinese Thought. His research interests are in the institutional and religious history of the period A.D. 200–600. Among his publications are *Rikuchō Shūkyōshi* ("The Religious History of the Six Dynasties Period") (1948) and *Rikuchōshi Kenkyū* ("Studies in the History of the Six Dynasties") (1956).

FREDERICK W. MOTE took his B.A. in Chinese history at the University of Nanking in 1948, and did further work in Chinese history in the graduate schools of Peking National University and Nanking University. He received his Ph.D. from the University of Washington in 1954, did postdoctoral research at the Hoover Institute, in Kyoto, and at National Taiwan University, and taught Chinese at Leiden on a Fulbright exchange lectureship in 1955–56. Since 1956 he has been Assistant Professor of Oriental Studies at Princeton. His research interests are in late Yüan and early Ming history, and he has a book on the intellectual history of the fourteenth century ready for publication.

YUJI MURAMATSU was graduated from Hitotsubashi University in 1933, and since 1951 has been Professor of Chinese History and Political Economy at that institution. He came to the United States in 1957 as a Traveling Fellow of the Tokyo Seminar on Modern China and did research at Harvard and Stanford. In 1958–59 he was a research fellow of the Committee on East Asian Studies, Stanford University. He is the author of *Chūgoku Keizai no Shakai-taisei* ("The Social Framework of Chinese Economics") (1949) and of numerous articles on modern Chinese history.

DAVID S. NIVISON obtained his professional training in Far Eastern languages at Harvard, receiving the doctorate there in 1953. For a number of years he has been teaching at Stanford, where he is now Associate Professor of Philosophy and Chinese. He is the author of several articles dealing with modern Chinese intellectual history and of a forthcoming volume on the eighteenth-century philosopher of history Chang Hsüeh-ch'eng.

EDWIN G. PULLEYBLANK graduated in Classics from the University of Alberta in 1942. After war work in which he began the study of Japanese and Chinese, he went to the School of Oriental and African Studies, London, in 1946 on a Chinese Government Scholarship. In 1948 he was appointed to the staff of the School as a Lecturer in Classical Chinese. In 1951 he received the degree of Ph.D. from London University for his thesis, *The Background of the Rebellion of An Lu-shan*, subsequently published in the London Oriental Series. Since 1953 he has been Professor of Chinese at Cambridge University.

ROBERT RUHLMANN was trained in classical and medieval humanities at Paris, in Chinese at Paris and Peking. He spent the years 1946 to 1953 in Peking. Since 1954 he has been teaching Chinese at the Ecole Nationale des Langues Orientales Vivantes in Paris, and Chinese literature at the Chinese Institute of the Sorbonne. His major interest is the history of Chinese fiction, drama, and folklore as materials for the study of Chinese thought. He has published translations from the *Kuo Yü*, from the *San Kuo Chih*, and from modern Chinese fiction.

THE CONFUCIAN PERSUASION

Arthur F. Wright

INTRODUCTION

One of the problems that have long troubled students of China is: What aspects of this extraordinary civilization may be understood to be in some meaningful sense "Confucian"? With the passage of time, the advances of modern scholarship, and the collapse of the Confucian tradition, we are beginning to find this question less difficult to answer. We can no longer accept the judgment of the great Chinese scholars of the past that everything—or at least everything of value—in Chinese culture was somehow part of the Confucian tradition and that all the rest was flotsam and jetsam, historical accident, or the aberrant intrusion of alien influences. The truth is far more complicated.

In presenting a second symposium on Confucianism, we have attempted a further exploration of the interrelations of Confucianism and the civilization it dominated for so many centuries. The papers deal with a wide range of ideas, and with manifestations of social and cultural behavior scattered across two millennia. They are, in a sense, case studies. Each paper seeks to clarify some of the complexities of the Confucian tradition itself, to point out how it has interacted with other traditions in given circumstances, and to show how it has changed in response to the demands of new defenders or new times.

We have given this volume the title *The Confucian Persuasion,* following Marvin Meyers' apt definition of a persuasion as "a matched set of attitudes, beliefs, projected actions: a half-formulated moral perspective involving emotional commitment."[1] The rebels, the statesmen, the emperors and peasants, who move across our pages—for all their variety of aims and settings—share certain common assumptions. The historians, the connoisseurs of painting, the leaders of mass rebellions, tend to invoke the same values and to partake of a common moral perspective. They are not systematic thinkers, but men of thought and action. Each, in his way, is selecting and adapting inherited ideas to the peculiar complexities of his time and milieu.

Thus the present volume shares with its predecessor, *Confucianism in Action,* an interest in the interrelations of Confucian ideas and the behavior of individuals and groups. Yet—with some exceptions—the men in these new studies are less methodical in their invocation of Confucian ideals, and their realms of action are more diverse, than the social and political activists who figure in our earlier volume. What the protagonists in these new studies share is neither a philosophy nor an ideology; it is rather certain common attitudes and beliefs; it is indeed a half-formulated moral perspective involving emotional commitment. This is the Confucian persuasion.

The Confucian tradition, from which the Confucian persuasion drew its attitudes, ideals, and emotional commitments, was a variegated and ever-changing thing. Yet certain radical continuities underlie this multiplicity. These are discussed in the pages of *Confucianism in Action,* but it may be useful to recall some of them here. One continuing element is a belief in the eternal truth and universal validity of the founder's vision of perfected men living in a stable and harmonious sociopolitical order. The vision, it is believed, becomes beclouded for later men as they improvise solutions to their problems, come to mistake means for ends, or are blinded by the false claims of competing traditions. But the true and eternal vision remains, and it remains in the Confucian Classics, always there to be rediscovered and applied— an infallible solution to the problems of any time or milieu. At the center of this vision, perennially rediscovered and refurbished, is the ideal of a moral order, perceived by Confucius and validated by sages and historians down the centuries. The moral order is viewed as a set of true and invariable norms for the conduct of life in society. Elaborated in the *li,* the codified rules of social behavior, the Confucian norms find their perfect embodiment in the well-ordered patriarchal family, which is the microcosm of the order that should prevail in state and society.

For the moral order to prevail, it must be understood and exemplified by enlightened rulers and ministers who live according to its norms and spread it through wise measures of education and social control. The values implicit in the Confucian vision are those of harmony, stability, and hierarchy. Moral force is held to be superior to coercion, and morally perfected men are the only ones entitled to manage the affairs of society and the state. Desirable change draws society peacefully back toward the ancient moral order. Undesirable change is violent, precipitated by uncultivated men; it is a sequence of random improvisations which will lead society away from the moral order and into chaos and ruin. This vision and these values and the attitudes and habits of thinking associated with them persist, and we shall see their traces in all the studies presented in this volume.

In introducing certain of the themes which appear in these essays,

I have sought at the same time to speculate on some problems which seem to me central to our understanding of the Confucian tradition as a whole: How does variety develop and change occur? What accounts for the tradition's capacity for survival and self-renewal? How has it propagated its ideals and values? How has it dealt with protest and dissent? And, finally, what factors in the tradition itself hastened its ultimate collapse and fragmentation?

VARIETY AND CHANGE

Variety in Confucianism seems to me to take two main forms: permanent mutations and temporary adjustments. The permanent mutations derived from long-term changes in Chinese society, from the demands of its institutional growth; such mutations may be thought of as altering the components, the balance of elements, in the Confucian persuasion. The temporary adjustments were made in response to the particular needs of an individual or a group; they may be thought of as differences of emphasis, the stressing of one component of the tradition at the expense of all others. Let me illustrate these mutations and variations by reference to the papers in this volume.

The first type of change is seen with great clarity in Mr. Mote's paper. As a consequence of major social and political changes beginning in the late T'ang and continuing through the Sung, the content of one of the Confucian moral norms, "loyalty," was radically altered. From its earlier meaning as an obligation tempered by moral judgment, it was redefined as a blind and unquestioning allegiance to a superior. This shift and others related to it occurred under the pressure of an increasingly centralized and despotic monarchy. Thereafter, one who consciously or unconsciously invoked the value of "loyalty" invoked an altered component of the Confucian persuasion.

The second type of variation, brought about by men who find one or another element in the tradition especially suited to their needs, is illustrated by Mr. Miyakawa's colonizers of South China, who persistently appealed to the "civilizing mission" of Chinese culture and of the Confucian gentleman as its ideal instrument. Centuries later, as Mr. Mote shows us, Chinese intellectuals obliged to live under the harsh alien rule of the Mongols had recourse to a strain in the tradition which sanctioned a dignified withdrawal from active life. In another age and sphere of activity, Mr. Cahill's artists and critics found in the philosophy of later Confucianism values for the creation and judgment of works of art and a rationale for the role of "gentlemen painters" in society.

The range is wide, yet each rationale is embedded in a common matrix of thought and feeling, the Confucian vision of morally perfected men in a perfected society. Indeed, each owes its intellectual and emotional appeal to the persisting authority of that vision. We next consider how and why the vision persisted, and what spurred men of every generation to try to make it a reality.

One of the paradoxes of Confucianism's survival is that if it had ever achieved the total dominance of Chinese thought and life to which it aspired, it might well have withered and died of inanition. Indeed, it may actually have owed its long life to the challenge of rival ideas. Consider, for example, its response to the challenge of Buddhism; it borrowed wholesale the ideas of its rival, and having digested what it borrowed, it recast its own thought and ethics in a synthesis that spelled the eventual doom of Buddhism as a separate system. In Mr. Pulleyblank's paper, we see the beginnings of this Confucian rally in the late T'ang. The men he speaks of knew that they lived in an age of crisis, that the future of their civilization and their society was gravely in doubt. They were strikingly open-minded in their explorations of ideas and programs from several rival traditions, and when they returned to the Confucian Classics, they saw them with fresh eyes and interpreted them in an unconsciously eclectic spirit. Such periods of challenge, doubt, and experiment repeatedly brought new vigor to the Confucian tradition and help to explain its phenomenal powers of survival and self-renewal.

But we may well wonder why the Sung synthesis that emerged was a "Confucian" one. How had certain key elements of the Confucian tradition survived the long ages of Buddhist dominance, and why did they now come to form the core of a new synthesis? One partial answer is that Confucian learning had been kept alive in certain literate families; scriptural continuity had somehow been maintained. This was not the preservation of learning for learning's sake; rather, such families felt themselves responsible for safeguarding and transmitting the unchallengeable moral truths laid down in the Classics—truths that were infallible guides to the conduct of life and that might, in more propitious times, regain their dominance in society as a whole. The sixth-century scholar-official Yen Chih-t'ui lived much of his life under "barbarian" dynasties, in an age when Buddhism permeated the life and culture of all China. In his volume of instructions for his family, he commended Buddhism as more profound than any native tradition. Yet, in the same book, he asserts the primacy of Confucian morality:

Influence for moral betterment proceeds from those above to those below; it extends from the elder generation to the younger. This is why, when the father is not kind, the son is not filial; when the elder brother is not friendly, the younger is not respectful; when the husband is unjust, the wife is not obedient. When the father is kind and the son is refractory; when the elder brother is friendly and the younger is rude; when the husband is just and the wife is insolent, then these are people who are naturally evil, and they must be subjected to punishment, since they are not to be changed by counsel and guidance. When severe floggings are abolished in the home, misbehavior will immediately appear among the children. "If punishments are not properly awarded, the people do not know how to move hand or foot." [*Analects*, XIII, 3.] The gentleness tempered with severity used in governing the household is indeed like that which is required in governing the state.[2]

For Yen Chih-t'ui, as for countless others who lived in the age of Buddhist dominance, Confucian ethics remained the infallible guide for life in the patriarchal family, and the family remained the microcosm of the well-ordered state. The persistence of this nexus of moral ideas and patterns of behavior helps further to explain Confucianism's capacity for survival and self-renewal.

Another factor in the survival of Confucianism is the range of ideas it accommodated. We shall speak of varieties of dissent and protest later in this Introduction, but here we shall note some recurrent differences of view between professed Confucianists on the nature of man, on the essence of the Confucian ideal order, and on the means of realizing that order in later times when the sage-kings and Confucius had become a distant and revered memory.

Sentimentalists within the tradition could and did advocate a literal return to the "way of former kings." The unfortunate Fang Kuan, described by Mr. Pulleyblank, even attempted the revival of "classical" warfare with ox-drawn chariots, only to be disastrously defeated. Others, like some of the pre-modern enthusiasts for the "well-field" system discussed by Mr. Levenson, felt that the reconstitution of the land system and other institutions of Confucius' own day were necessary to the remaking of society in accord with the founder's vision. In contrast to such men, but still ardently "Confucian," were the tough-minded scholars and statesmen who held that time had wrought irreversible changes and that antique institutions were gone beyond recall. The historian and statesman Tu Yu discussed by Mr. Pulleyblank is the polar opposite of Fang Kuan, for Tu Yu admired the state planners of the Legalist tradition; he applauded their draconian measures designed to ensure the wealth, power, and stability of the state. Yet Tu Yu remained within the Confucian tradition. He did not follow the Legalists in making the power of the state the end; rather, he asserted that authoritarian controls are the means to the reconstitution of a society in accord with the broad principles laid down by the Confucian sages. Men of every age who called themselves Confucians argued in their writings and in their struggles over state policy about means; they differed, too, in their interpretations of the Confucian dream as they perceived it through the Classics. Invariably they deplored the lack of unanimity among themselves, but the clash of views over means and ends drove men to think, argue, and plan, and thus saved the tradition from stagnation.

The millennial argument among Confucians over ends and means was heightened by the perennial clash between conscience and authority. Confucians as thinkers and statesmen were often at odds with a monarchy whose symbols and actions paid scant heed to Confucian ideals. When things got bad enough, men could protest and remonstrate; or they could withdraw from the public sphere and thus dramatize their disapproval of the monarch or his court. Most men compromised, as most men will, but the bolder spirits protested, struggled, and were exiled, tortured, or killed. In this way the moral dilemmas—ends versus means, the ideal versus reality, conscience versus authority —were dramatized in the life of each generation, and men were driven to seek out and reinterpret the moral imperatives of the original Confucian vision. Moral thought was thus saved from devolving into academic conversation about "the good," and the moral core of the Confucian vision was never forgotten or submerged. More than this, Confucian morality demanded that the standards of good conduct be assiduously cultivated within and tirelessly spread among one's fellow men. This brings us to the next major problem in the development of the Confucian tradition.

THE PROPAGATION OF MORALITY

Educated men of innumerable generations imbibed with their studies of the Classics a sense of their obligation to spread the principles of morality in whatever sphere of life they found themselves. It is no accident that the historian of Chinese politics finds all questions of state policy—domestic reform, foreign policy, matters of court precedence and succession, legal enactments, and military measures—argued in terms of moral principles. Disdained by ruthless monarchs, thwarted by palace intrigue, circumvented by eunuch power, undone by venality in their own ranks, China's bureaucrats nevertheless persisted in their efforts to infuse the politics of the realm with the principles of Confucian morality. In the founding of schools and academies, the building of memorials to the virtuous, the patronage of classical studies, and in countless other ways, officials in their public roles responded to the imperative to spread Confucian principles. Papers in the present volume deal with this imperative as it is revealed in the work of historians, painters, colonizers, and the writers and manipulators of popular fiction.

In my study of the stereotype of the "bad last" ruler, we find a demonstration of the historian's concern with the moral dynamic in human affairs. History illustrated the working out of moral principles in the affairs of men and provided for posterity positive and negative exemplars, models for later men to follow or abjure. When we find a historian transforming a personality of a "last ruler" into a stereotyped model of badness, we must not imagine that this was solely because the historian was the servant of a succeeding dynasty. Rather, such a historian saw political failure as a form of moral failure: the ruler who presided over the fall of a dynasty *must have been* thoroughly evil. This bias then governed the selection of evidence and the writing of the final account from which later men were to take warning. Similarly, "good first" rulers are judged "good" because political success and an opportunity to reconstitute a harmonious moral order cannot fall to the unworthy. Thus the failings of dynastic founders are minimized, and these men appear as shining exemplars for posterity.

Confucian historians and early Chinese painters shared one fundamental concern: to create models—in words, or in lines and pigments—which would inspire men and mold their conduct. Mr. Cahill quotes the typical moralistic view of painting expressed by the eighth-century writer Chang Yen-yüan: "Paintings are the means by which events are preserved in a state in which they serve as models for the virtuous and warnings to the evil." This naïve didacticism found its parallels in early writings about poetry and the other arts. But its limitations as a basis for the judgment of painting were obvious, and Mr. Cahill traces the slow growth of a more sophisticated theory under the successive influences of neo-Taoism, Buddhism, and the new Confucianism of the eleventh century and after. Briefly, this theory held that the quality of a painting lay in the character of the artist. Obviously a painting of a bamboo such as the one reproduced as a frontispiece to this volume does not *represent* virtue as the ancient portraits of worthies had sought to do. Rather, if it is to be judged favorably, it should reflect the perfection of the character of the artist, and this perfection—perceived in the painting—in turn inspires the beholder to try to attain a comparable perfection. In a new context and with a new vocabulary the centrality of moral perfection was reiterated, and painting was raised above the status of avocation or artisanship; it became instead a means of expressing the attributes of the Confucian perfected man and of inspiring others to cultivate his qualities.

If the histories preserved the moral lessons of the past and illustrated the working of the moral principles of the Classics, they did so only for the upper class, which had the education to read them and the motivation to master their contents as preparation for an official career. Similarly, the works of the gentleman painters could only inspire those with long training and experience in the arts. Different means had to be used when the elite responded to its self-imposed obligation to spread the moral teachings of Confucianism among the masses.

Through the centuries the elite developed many tactics for spreading Confucian moral teachings in the population as a whole. Again and again, for example, we hear of local officials feasting the aged and the filial, inflicting public chastisement on moral deviants, and awarding prizes to diligent students of the Classics. When we turn to Mr. Miyakawa's account of the Confucianization of South China, we find all these and many other devices for mass propaganda, and we are reminded of two special characteristics of Confucianism which help to explain its age-long influence on Chinese life. One of these is an ideology of Chinese dominance over other peoples, a rationale of a civilizing mission at once moral and cultural. The other is an ability to make use of strains of other traditions to supplement the Confucian arsenal of suasive and emotional appeals.

Most of the colonial officials described by Mr. Miyakawa felt that the sinicization of the conquered aborigines depended first on the "reform of customs," and second on a commitment to the moral ideas of the Classics. It is significant that the reform of family customs had first place because, as we have noted, the hierarchized paternalistic family remained always the indispensable unit for learning, teaching, and spreading the principles of Confucian morality. Once the sinicization of family customs had been begun, the establishment of schools with a classical curriculum followed immediately, and rewards of status and wealth were given to those of aborigine ancestry who did well in the new schools. Thus the solid advantages of adopting Chinese ways and studying the Confucian classics were dramatically demonstrated. We see in the strategy and tactics of the early colonizers many of the same measures perennially used by Chinese administrators to rehabilitate areas of China that had been devastated by war and invasion.

For all their successes in these realms, Confucians recognized certain limitations of their doctrine and made free use of elements from other traditions. Gernet has recently pointed to the Confucian interpretation of Buddhism. Not only did court and officialdom sanction Buddhism's moral restraints and such other elements of Buddhist doctrine as were consonant with Confucian morality, but they actively sought to capitalize on the fervor of Buddhist belief in the interests of a Confucian moral order.[3] As a seventeenth-century official put it:

When the people are at peace, they are governed and live according to the rules of conduct (*li*), but when troubles arise, punishments must be used. When these penalties are not sufficient to control the people, the sanctions of religion must be employed, for men are frightened of spiritual forces which they cannot see nor hear. We know that Buddha lived in ancient times, and we may employ his teaching, with that of Lao Tzi, even though we do not use their names, to reinforce the doctrines of Confucius.[4]

Mr. Miyakawa's colonial officials took a similar view. They recognized that Confucian moral teaching would strike the rude peoples of South China and later Formosa as somewhat dry, lacking in colorful pageantry and emotional appeal. They therefore introduced Buddhist ceremonies to supply the missing element. In other instances they simply insinuated Confucian moral teachings into a folk religion that already offered the sanctions and satisfactions of religion.

The use of religion is but one example of Confucian manipulation of popular culture in the interests of Confucian values. In their origins, the popular repertories of dramatists and storytellers were independent of Confucianism. Their purpose was to entertain, and they drew far larger crowds, we may suppose, than public banquets for the aged and filial, or for successful examination candidates. The mass audience of the storytellers and dramatists tempted Confucian officials to use these media for the propagation of approved morality. The compiler of an early-seventeenth-century collection of short stories puts the case clearly:

Now the cultivated minds of this world are few, the rustic ears many; and fiction lends itself more to the popularizer than the stylist. Make a trial of the storytellers of today, with their extempore descriptions: they will gladden you, startle you, make you weep for sorrow, make you dance and sing; some will prompt you to draw your sword, others will make you want to bow in reverence, or strangle yourself, or give money. The coward will be made brave, the profligate pure, the miser generous, the dullard ashamed. Although a man from his childhood days intone the *Analects of Confucius* or the *Classic of Filial Piety*, he will not be moved so swiftly or so profoundly as by these storytellers. Can such results be achieved by anything but popular colloquial writing?[5]

Mr. Ruhlmann discusses the moral-didactic uses of story and drama, and he points to the manipulation of repertories by Ming and Ch'ing officials, to the homilies, often in doggerel, that introduced the incidents in a popular tale, to the officially managed apotheosis of a popular hero such as Kuan-yü into an epitome of virtues deemed desirable by state and officialdom. Yet it is clear from Mr. Ruhlmann's study that fiction, like the popular culture of China as a whole, had a dynamic life of its own which could not be made wholly subservient to the values of the elite.

Thus, for example, the *hao-han*, "bravos," were a type beloved by popular audiences through many centuries. The rugged independence of such men, their bold directness in rescuing the oppressed and chastising the oppressors, created a character model that was the very opposite of the desired type of submissiveness exemplified by the "twenty-four filial sons." The full-blooded heroes of fiction provided vicarious satisfaction for the nonconformist impulses of millions who were doomed to live humdrum lives within the bonds of established custom and morality.

Again, the tales of blood brotherhood dramatize an egalitarian faithfulness within a band of outlaws—a model of behavior for rebels rather than for dutiful and prudent subjects. Yet, as Mr. Ruhlmann shows, these deviant models are often presented in contexts that affirm a whole cluster of Confucian values. For example, the band of bravos celebrated in *Water Margin* are united under the slogan *T'i t'ien hsing tao*, "Accomplish the Way for Heaven!" This slogan challenges an existing authority which subverts the Confucian ideal of government, and appeals to the moral sanctions that justify the replacement of an evil ruler by one who will reconstitute the moral order. We shall return to this theme in discussing Mr. Muramatsu's history of rebel ideologies.

The presence in innumerable plays and stories of what Mr. Ruhlmann calls the adviser type of hero—urbane, calculating, accomplishing by stratagem what force would never achieve—serves to reiterate the Confucian ideal of the supremacy of moral-intellectual power in the affairs of men. No play or story challenges the principle of gentry dominance of society, and none makes a case for the merchant—the despised object of upper-class abuse and repression. Wherever a moral judgment of a "bad last" ruler appears in popular legend and story, it is basically the same as that found in the Confucian histories. Chinese officialdom was plainly powerless to prevent the growth of independent, sometimes rebellious, hero-identifications, but popular entertainments generally supplied a heavy dosage of Confucian morality. More than mere indoctrination was involved. Why? The fact is that no other course was possible. Neither a play nor an incident in life itself "made sense" except in terms of the moral values that were the common property of educated elite and illiterate masses: For all the great gulf in their tastes and styles of life, the two classes shared a common moral perspective, and the Confucian persuasions by which they lived and judged their fellow-men were remarkably similar.

TOLERANCE OF PROTEST AND DISSENT

The adaptability, the suppleness, and the inner variety of the Confucian tradition have been discussed as ways of accounting for its survival. We next consider certain varieties of dissent and protest that it not only tolerated but sanctioned or actually encouraged. In the papers by Messrs. Nivison, Mote, and Muramatsu, we find three varieties of dissent, ranging from relatively mild criticism to outright rebellion. Each of these papers calls our attention, once more, to the inner variety of the tradition and also to its limits: the boundaries beyond which one could not go without entering the camp of a competing tradition.

Mr. Nivison's study of the traditions of protest against the examination system again calls attention to certain persisting tensions between ideal and reality. One fundamental difficulty was that a system of state examinations was incompatible with the true moral order that had prevailed in antiquity, when men of virtue were recognized, recommended, and employed and a natural hierarchy of virtue prevailed. Some critics urged a return to the simpler social order that would make possible the revival of that hierarchy. Others—and they were more numerous—felt that the moral golden age was gone beyond recall, and sought to reform the system so that it would turn out men of intellectual vigor and moral independence. These critics railed against the succession of formal literary requirements that strangled originality and brought success to memorizers, parroters, and the products of cram schools.

For all the variety of dissent discussed by Mr. Nivison, some views are notably absent. No one maintained that certain men were innately capable of perfecting themselves and governing others, or that a long period of study and reflection could be dispensed with. Certain figures in the Taoist tradition inclined toward this view; those of the Confucian persuasion never did. Again, no one believed that the examinations and the selection of officials should be based solely on mastery of the practical affairs of government, on evidence of ability to operate the machinery of the state. The Legalists consistently favored the selection of officials on this basis, for they distrusted personal morality and private standards of value; but the Confucians of imperial China, though heir to much of the machinery of the Legalist state, clung to a morality that was partly independent of the state.

They strove, in effect, to be sages. And it is this standard, embedded

in the persisting dream of a balanced moral order, that distinguishes
Confucian criticism of the examination system. The system is denounced as deflecting men from the pattern of study and reflection that
would reveal to them the essentials of the moral order and perfect their
characters. It is criticized as encouraging literary fripperies at the expense of moral truths. Worst of all, it puts "study" on the market and
makes fame and preferment the goal rather than moral value; men
are corrupted by the very institution which is supposed to foster moral
worth.

But in none of these protests are the moral norms themselves challenged. In none are they regarded as anything less than essential to
the cultivation of men for public roles. In none is it suggested that
the Classics are not the prime repository of the essential moral truths.
Many things may be questioned, but there is no questioning the primacy
of moral principles. Similarly, Confucian critics never challenged the
principle of monarchy, the necessity of a hierarchized society, or the
central importance of a familistic morality. In short, this sort of tradition of dissent allowed men freedom to talk about what was important
in the Confucian heritage without in any sense challenging the prevailing institutional order to which the fortunes of the Confucians were
indissolubly bound.

When the whole of China fell to the Mongols in 1279, Chinese
institutions came under the control of Kublai Khan and his successors—
harsh masters who had scant regard for the Chinese heritage and its
values. What was the fate of the Confucians in this grim age? In
answering this question, Mr. Mote's study points up further elements
of adaptability in the Confucian tradition, further ways to account for
its capacity to survive in great adversity. Specifically, Mr. Mote discusses two clusters of Confucian ideas which had a powerful influence
on the Confucian literati through the long dark years of Mongol dominance: voluntary and involuntary eremitism.

The first was the classical rationale for not following an official
career. The authoritative sanctions for voluntary withdrawal were to
be found in the writings of Confucius and Mencius—great teachers who
themselves had failed to find official employment in the decaying feudal
order of the late Chou period. Their stand was unambiguous: when
times are unpropitious for the public employment of virtuous men,
and when one fails to find an upright prince whom one can serve with
honor, then withdrawal is the only course open to a man of integrity.
The Mongol rulers were scarcely "upright princes," and the classical
sanction for withdrawal was accordingly invoked without hesitation
by Confucian intellectuals who found it impossible to come to terms

with the regime. This poem by the sensitive Confucian scholar Liu Yin is one such invocation:

> Those who uphold *tao* [ethics] frequently are led to follow a
>   solitary course.
> This practice has existed since Chou and Ch'in times.
> The solitary course of the recluse moreover merits approval;
> What kind of person would weakly submit to defiling himself?
> . . . .
>
> In a degenerate final age,
> Is it not meaningless to possess Confucian rank and office?

The specifically Confucian quality of this renunciation is its moral rationale. A Confucian's withdrawal is not like that of the Taoist, who actually prefers an unencumbered life in pursuit of the *Tao* or the chimera of longevity; nor is it like that of the Buddhist, who seeks in retirement the one spiritual reality he acknowledges in a world of illusion. In his proud withdrawal, the Confucian devotes himself to the study of the great principles of the sages and spreads them by example and instruction among his fellow men. Then, in more propitious times to come, those principles will not have been perverted or lost but will be ready for men to use once again to put the world in order.

Involuntary eremitism, by contrast, is interpreted by Mr. Mote as occasioned by a shift in the tone and temper of Confucian orthodoxy from the Sung onward. The classical notion of a loyalty based on moral discrimination was partially replaced by a new concept of blind subservience to the ruling house, a shift seen by Mr. Mote as part of the adaptation of Confucian values to an increasingly centralized and authoritarian state. The new loyalty had a corollary which is succinctly stated by Ssu-ma Kuang: "The servitor serves his ruler, and will die in preference to serving another." For many Confucians of the early years of Mongol rule, this meant that even when they needed official emoluments for the support of their parents (a Confucian obligation), and even if they hoped to moderate Mongol rule through official service, the moral imperative was to withdraw and, as it were, become involuntary recluses. That this newer imperative had great force may be seen in the careers of some Confucians of the early Ming who, though they had served the hated Mongols under duress, refused to serve their successors.

These two kinds of withdrawal, each with its own rationale, serve to underline the political passivity of the Confucians in this period. And, as Mr. Mote tells us, these men did not rally to the dissident movements which developed in the late years of Mongol rule. They preserved and cultivated morality. They awaited the coming of wise and

enlightened government which might employ them or their descendants, but they did little or nothing to bring it nearer. Such passivity
may perhaps be interpreted as characteristic of scholar-officials under
the later authoritarian dynasties, but there is much in earlier Confucianism which helps to explain it. When we look back to the upheavals
that accompanied the fall of the Ch'in and the rise of the Han in the
years 208–202 B.C., we find no Confucian activists, no Confucian leaders
of rebellion against the hated Ch'in regime. The Confucian scholars
tried to ride out the storm, to wait for the emergence of a victor—a
"just prince" to whom they could give their allegiance. The victor, the
Han founder, was a plebian man of action who in his years of desperate
struggle had developed a visceral hatred of the pious Confucians. Yet
he soon had need of their services, and one of them helped him rationalize the necessary shift in his views. "The Confucians," said Shu-sun
T'ung, "are difficult to associate with in vigorous action [i.e., the seizure
of power], but one may usefully associate with them in preserving and
consolidating [what has been won]."[6] Perhaps this very aloofness from
violent political change helps to account for the survival of Confucians
and their tradition, even as their political specialization in "preserving
and consolidating" made them the inevitable beneficiaries of any new
political order. But their dissociation from political violence was neither
opportunistic nor fortuitous. Ultimately it was sanctioned by the classical Confucian concepts of the morality and the mechanics of a transfer
of power. We may explore this set of concepts by reference to Mr.
Muramatsu's account of the history of Chinese rebel ideologies.

When we proceed from the traditions of protest discussed by Mr.
Nivison and the ideologies of withdrawal analyzed by Mr. Mote to
rebel ideologies, we move from the elite social level to the level of
the illiterate masses. The break, however, is not as sharp as it might
at first appear. First of all, Confucian theory invested the "people"
with an important political role. "Heaven sees as the people see, and
Heaven hears as the people hear," and by these and other classical
statements, the people—not the educated elite—are authorized to gen-
erate the violence which will wrest the Heavenly Mandate from a decadent house and make way for a new order. But, as Mr. Muramatsu
shows us, the "people" in the sense of peasant cultivators seldom, particularly in the later dynasties, took the initiative in organizing mass
rebellion. Instead, leadership came from an ever-changing but ever-
present middle group—sorcerers, monks, soldiers of fortune, disaffected
merchants—who shared many of the ideas and the values of the educated Confucian elite. If not all these leaders were of the Confucian

persuasion, many of their slogans and ideologies assumed the general acceptance of that persuasion in society at large.

Let us look at some of the themes of rebel ideologies which suggest values shared by rulers, officials, rebel leaders, and their followers, and point to some that are linked to the Confucian persuasions of different generations. Rebels again and again appealed to Confucian principles of political morality. The famed slogan "Accomplish the Way for Heaven!" means that the rebels have a sacred obligation to strike down the unworthy and, in keeping with Heaven's will, raise up the just. Li Tzu-ch'eng's title "Great General Claiming Justice for Heaven" reiterates just such a moral bid for supreme power. Loyalty to a defunct ruling house, a concept with a powerful hold on the elite (as we have seen in discussing Mr. Mote's paper), is widely enough diffused in later dynasties to figure in the slogans and ideologies of rebel movements as well. And when, from the Sung onward, demands for economic reforms enter into rebel ideologies, the slogans echo the Confucian utopian phrases which figure in the solemn memorials of reforming officials.

Chinese rebels began to invoke a racialist patriotism rather late in Chinese history, and perhaps only as cultural self-consciousness was fostered by the decline of great families and vastly increased social mobility. When such slogans do appear, they are not wholly new. They may be viewed as a new form of the classical ideology of Chinese superiority outlined in Mr. Miyakawa's paper. Now, in a new context, that ideology becomes the property of the masses as well as the elite, and its new universality gives it for the first time potency as a rallying cry for rebels.

Rebel movements repeatedly appeal to the close interrelation of natural and human events, an idea that became part of imperial Confucianism in Han times. Confucian scholars were ever ready and willing to provide their rulers with signs and omens demonstrating that they were functioning effectively as social and cosmic pivots. But this omen lore, with its supporting theories of yin-yang and five-element symbolism, was a double-edged sword: rebels could use it to strengthen their challenge to the reigning dynasty. Rural sorcerers manipulated for their rebel masters the same symbol system that Confucian officials drew on for their imperial patrons, and for the same purpose: to demonstrate that supernatural powers favored the cause of their employers. The repeated use of this symbolism by both groups testifies to their conviction that it was acceptable and persuasive among the people as a whole.

Of course, there is much in rebel lore that is either sub-Confucian or drawn from competing traditions. Among the sub-Confucian elements are belief in spirits and in mediums who assure their aid, belief in practices that assure invulnerability to arrows (and later, bullets), and blind faith in the charisma of a heroic leader. Such beliefs, as Mr. Muramatsu shows, are interwoven with elements from foreign religions: faith in the saving power of Bodhisattvas, in the efficacy of Buddhist or Manichean regimens, in the imminence of the end of the world, and a new beginning. The Confucian tradition, as we have noted was lacking in animating faiths, heady and moving symbolism, colorful cult practices—things that gave potential rebels courage to take the desperate step from which there was no turning back. While the basic rationale of rebellion was unequivocally Confucian, and rebels relied on the widespread acceptance of this rationale, other traditions provided the impetus to rebel. Yet looking back at the successful rebel movements of twenty centuries, one is struck by the fact that for all the rebels' promises of a new heaven and a new earth, the moment they were successful, they invariably summoned the Confucians to set about "protecting and consolidating," with the result that the socio-political order resumed its slow evolution under their guiding hands.

THE END OF A TRADITION

In a tradition's end, as in its origins and growth, there are clues to its basic character, signs that help us understand its long persistence and repeated revivals. The papers in this volume do not deal directly with the final collapse of the monarchy with which Confucianism had such a long and uneasy partnership, but in the papers by Mr. Levenson and Mr. Chow we see some of the ways in which men of the late Ch'ing and the Republic contributed to the erosion of the Confucian tradition. These men no longer lived by Confucian ideas but manipulated them for what residual authority they had in a desperate effort to find a formula for China's survival in the modern world.

Under the pressure of political collapse and social chaos, articulate Chinese of the twentieth century appealed to new and foreign ideals: progress, democracy, science, and nationalism. Politicians like Sun Yat-sen and Chiang Kai-shek exhorted their people to follow the ancient moral norms of Confucianism, but the aim was to make men loyal, hard-working citizens of a militant national state, not contented subjects of a serenely balanced moral order existing under a benevolent prince. The words they used were the same, but in the new context, their meaning was totally changed.

In Mr. Chow's paper, we follow the break-up of the Confucian tradition at the hands of the intellectuals and the youth of modern China. He presents the successive phases of the effort to modernize Confucianism and then discusses the subsequent all-out attack on the tradition as a whole. In K'ang Yu-wei's effort to promote Confucianism as a state religion, we see a clear admission that the teachings of the Sage were no longer all-sufficient for the needs of modern China. From presiding over a civilization, Confucius was now to be reduced to presiding over "morals" in the Western sense, and his church was to have only the limited powers enjoyed by the Church of England in modern Britain. When K'ang's disciple Liang Ch'i-ch'ao asserted, "I love Confucius, but I love truth more," he denied a principle that had been at the core of Confucianism for two millennia: that the Classics shaped by Confucius contained all the truth, all that was needed for men and society to find their way to perfection.

Perhaps the most devastating effects were wrought by those who "discovered" in the Confucian tradition what was being forced on them by the Westerners and the Westernizers, thus distorting and devaluing one element of the tradition after another. Mr. Chow cites Lu Hsün's bitter comment on this process:

There is a favorite technique used by those who know the old literature. When a new idea is introduced, they call it "heresy" and bend all their efforts to destroy it. If that new idea, by its struggle against their efforts, wins a place for itself, they then discover that "it's the same thing as was taught by Confucius."

Among the men who argued about the *ching-t'ien* or "well-field system" in the twentieth century, a few employed this "favorite technique." But most of the polemicists described by Mr. Levenson were bent on revolutionary change. The well-field system, as recorded in the Classics, was but one counter in a furious controversy over the desirable rate and direction of sweeping change. Some argued, like Russian socialists invoking the ancient *mir*, that the well-field system had been an early indigenous form of socialism, and that China could become a socialist state without total subservience to foreign models. Others maintained that the well-field system was pure "feudalism," and thus represented a stage in social development—a stage that put China on the universal Marxist escalator of progress. None of the polemicists argued—as so many Confucians had—that a literal restoration of the system was possible or desirable, and not for a moment did anyone suggest that it was a viable way back to the whole harmonious and balanced order which was the dream of the ancient sages and of those who followed them. In Mr. Levenson's terms, they invoked this ancient idea, not because it was true, or a key to the perfect society, but because it was *Chinese* and helped a little to assuage their outraged pride at having to borrow wholesale from the West.

Whatever was left undone by the defenders of the tradition, or by those who sought in it balm for their national pride, was accomplished by the all-out attack that began in 1915. There was no longer any denying China's inferiority to the Western powers, and partisans of various Western panaceas now openly pointed to Confucianism to explain the political and social collapse that was there for all to see. The accusations were sweeping: for ages Confucianism had smothered creativity; it was the natural ally of despotism and the enemy of democracy; it had fostered the submission of women, the subjugation of the young by the old, the tyranny of officials; it had preached passivity and resignation, attitudes that must be obliterated if China were to fight her way to equality with the nation-states of the West. New critical studies of the Classics stripped the ancient texts of their old authority, and a whole generation of more or less scholarly "antiquity doubters" used the solvents of anthropology, sociology, and historical and textual criticism to reduce the sages' dicta to mere data.

When most of the heated controversy over Confucianism had spent itself against the crumbling defenses of the traditionalists, there was a disposition to find something good in Confucius and his followers. He was spoken of as a rather agreeable old gentleman, a great educator, perhaps even a Chinese Socrates. But his authority as the supreme teacher of all men for all time was gone, and the Confucian tradition was dispersed. Fragments of Confucianism lived on among antiquarians, and in the practices of more conservatives families; its proverbial sayings came readily to the lips of statesmen and demagogues; but its wholeness and integrity as a tradition were gone forever. Men no longer lived by a Confucian persuasion.

Hisayuki Miyakawa

THE CONFUCIANIZATION
OF SOUTH CHINA

The Chinese people, the principal molders of East Asian history, were frequently under the domination of northern peoples, and frequently in collision with peoples to the south. Social and commercial contact, and later intermarriage, between the Chinese and these surrounding peoples led to the interchange and compounding of cultures, and gradually to the increasing ascendancy of Chinese Confucian civilization with its superior creative powers and its impressive assimilative capacity. The alien tribes, originally racially and culturally distinct from the Chinese of the Central Plain (Chung-yüan), were ultimately incorporated by blood and domicile into the Chinese, who themselves were enriched as a result. Of course this civilization was not immune to the vicissitudes of time; generally speaking, however, the Chinese preserved their distinctive cultural forms, and in the long run assimilated the peoples who surrounded them.

It should be noted here that relations between the Chinese and their neighbors differed from north to south. The peoples to the north were nomads or large-scale hunters, who, though few in number, were able to conquer the agricultural masses of China by military force. When they came into contact with the technically, intellectually, and economically superior Chinese culture, however, they were compelled to adopt it, and a policy of sinification was then put into effect by their rulers. When the northern peoples felt that the adoption of Chinese civilization would endanger their own existence as independent ethnic groups, or when they were acquainted with another superior civilization as well (as were the Mongols, who had had contact with various western peoples before conquering China proper), the sinification policy was not always pressed forward; but in general they became devoted admirers of Chinese Confucian culture and established their bases on Chinese territory as Confucian states.

In the southern regions the Chinese encountered peoples who subsisted by hunting, primitive agriculture, or fishing, and whose productive techniques were inferior to their own. These peoples were not
particularly warlike; more important, they were unacquainted with the
cavalry tactics which had so overawed the Chinese in their battles with
the northerners. Nor was the numerical superiority of the invaders so
marked as to create serious problems of integration. The southward
migration of the Chinese proceeded smoothly, hindered only by their
susceptibility to subtropical diseases, and the racial stocks and ways
of life of the southern tribes were incorporated into the Chinese community.

Confucian concepts of the forms appropriate to social actions (*li*)
played an important role in this process of sinification, as did Confucian
ideas concerning government and education. Although there were differences among the tribes, all who studied Confucianism and honored
its mores could be viewed as members of Chinese society.

Confucianism, however, did not confine itself solely to universal
ethical teachings. It also fostered a kind of nationalistic feeling which
gave rise to what was in fact a racist doctrine, and revealed the existence of certain tensions between the Chinese and their barbarian rivals
or rulers.[1]

CONFUCIANISM AS A RELIGION

A sinocentric cultural doctrine (a product of pride in the superiority of Chinese racial institutions and the wish to extend them to the
gentiles if possible) and a stress upon universal ethics were elements
that had been present in Confucianism since the beginning. They were
of no practical importance, however, until the first centuries of the
Christian era—the period in which the resistance of both southern and
northern peoples checked the political expansion of that perfect Confucian state, the Later Han empire, and Chinese Confucian culture was
inexorably modified by internal contradiction and external opposition.

The religious situation in eastern Asia at this time can be regarded as
parallel to that of the Hellenistic period in western Asia and the Mediterranean region,[2] and the trends manifested by Confucianism as a
religion can be compared to the universalistic aims and foreign evan-
gelism characteristic of post-exilic Judaism. In eastern Asia, however,
there was no clear-cut evolution from a national religion to a world
religion, such as was seen in the West. Moreover Confucianism, unlike
Judaism, did not develop into a religion by itself alone, but had to be
supplemented by outside spiritual forces from Buddhism and Taoism.
The Chinese literati, who were or should have been the bearers of Con-

fucian culture at this time, labored to preserve their aristocratic status and maintain the rites of Confucianism in their homes, but at the same time adopted Buddhism, and occasionally Taoism, as more profound spiritual foundations. This simultaneous acceptance of the Three Teachings, as they are commonly known, gave a special character to later Chinese culture.

Like Confucianism, Taoism played a role in the civilization of foreign tribes, but neither was a missionary religion in the full sense of the term. Buddhism was by nature the most universal of the three, but its refusal to recognize the existence of a Supreme Being entirely apart from mankind denied it the compelling evangelistic drive of Christianity; moreover, the tolerance of other religions, which has been regarded as one of its chief strengths, was in this respect a weakness, allowing it to become merged with alien faiths and to be altered by the peculiarities of individual nations. The Chinese, then, had no contact with a purely monotheistic world religion until recent times. Hence their persistent "sinocentrism," a point of view which, as we have seen, was generous toward peoples who resembled the Chinese or sought to imitate them, but preserved a strong element of racial solidarity beneath the surface. The core of this civilization was Confucianism—basically a system of ethics for the present world, but also functioning as a religion through its doctrines of the rites (*li*) and of righteousness (*i*).

CONCEPTS OF BARBARIANS IN EARLY CONFUCIAN DOCTRINE

How was the barbarian regarded by the early Confucian school, and especially by Confucius himself? I shall quote several passages referring to the barbarians from the text of the *Analects*.

"The Master said, 'The rude tribes of the east and north have their princes, and *are not like the states of our great land which are without them.*'"[3] (The italicized clause, which Legge translated according to Chu Hsi's commentary, should be replaced by "are still not equal to China with its anarchy," following the earlier commentary by Ho Yen, who died in the year 249, before the unprecedented invasions of the barbarians into China.)

The *Lun-yü Cheng-i* ("Standard Commentary on the *Analects*," by T'ang scholars) explains this passage as follows: "The rites and righteousness prevail in China, but not among barbarians even when they have established chieftains. China did not lose her rites and righteousness even during the interregnum (877–864 B.C.) after the banishment of King Li of Chou."

"The Master said, extolling the merit of a Ch'i statesman, Kuan Chung (?–645 B.C.): 'But for Kuan Chung, we should now be wearing our hair unbound and buttoning the lappets of our coats on the left side.' "[4]

The "Standard Commentary" explains as follows: "But for him, China might have sunk into a barbarous state, with neither monarch-like monarch nor subject-like subject."

There are two criteria by which the difference between the civilized and the barbarous may be judged: the political (monarchy or anarchy) and the cultural (rites and righteousness or their absence). If we take the two criteria in combination, the following four situations are possible:

(1) China with monarchy and also with rites and righteousness.
(2) China without monarchy (a step toward barbarization).
(3) Barbarians with monarchy and without rites and righteousness.
(4) Barbarians with neither monarchy nor rites and righteousness.

China never forfeits her fundamental culture, the rites and righteousness, as long as she remains China. Consequently Sino-barbarian relations are generally of four types. Let me illustrate. When the Chou state flourished with her monarchy and culture, there were barbarians without monarchy and culture—combination of (1) and (4). The unification of China into a powerful empire in the third century B.C. was closely connected with the concurrent unification of the north; the Han and Hsiung-nu relationship is a combination of (1) and (3). Thereafter the situation changed dramatically. China lost her unity, but her culture survived. The turbulent period from the Three Kingdoms to the end of the Western Chin saw a new combination: China without monarchy and with culture, and barbarians with neither, (2) and (4). Soon after, the barbarians established a monarchy—the Northern Wei— while the Chinese south barely managed to maintain a monarchy of its own.

Returning to the main issue, a problem may arise: What does a Confucian elite do when China forfeits her own territory? The answer is suggested in the *Analects*: "The Master said, 'My doctrines make no way. I will get upon a raft, and float about in the sea. He that will accompany me will be Yu, I dare to say.' "[5] Thus a Confucian may go among the barbarians when China becomes so degenerate as to suffocate a Confucian-minded man.

When Confucius "was wishing to go and live among the nine wild tribes of the east, someone said, 'They are rude. How can you do such a thing?' The Master said, 'If a superior man dwelt among them, what rudeness would there be?' "[6] Wherever a superior man resides, he can instruct those about him to conduct themselves in accord with the rites and righteousness.

Confucius admitted that China might sometime leave the right path;

in such cases, he said, what a righteous man should do is to leave China and uphold the true doctrine among the non-Chinese. This is the fundamental idea behind the seemingly antisocial and egoistic conduct of the hermits and recluses in the subsequent periods of anarchy and decadence. But if the non-Chinese among whom he dwells are no more than wild beasts, how can a Confucian-minded man even maintain his virtue, inasmuch as Confucian virtues consist solely in human relations? A disciple of Confucius gave his views on this question. Tzu Hsia consoled his colleague Ssu-ma Niu, who had no brothers, saying, " 'Let the superior man never fail reverentially to order his own conduct, and let him be respectful to others and observant of propriety:—then all within the Four Seas will be his brothers. . . .' "[7]

How did the ancient Chinese come to have a concept of the four seas? Without doubt they knew the East China Sea, and the *Chuang-tzu* referred to a South Sea and a North Sea in the famous metaphor of its first page. But where could Tzu Hsia have got the idea of the West Sea, since nothing of the sort was known until the first century A.D., when Kan Ying discovered a West Sea that can probably be equated with the eastern Mediterranean? Without pursuing this question, we note simply that the Four Seas were undoubtedly outside of the nine provinces which the civilized Chinese occupied. So Tzu Hsia meant that all people, whether they were barbarians within the surrounding seas or Chinese within the boundaries of the nine provinces, would become brothers to a Confucian if he made known to them the rites and righteousness.

Confucian ethics ought to be observed even when a Confucian lives among savages. Fan Ch'ih asked about perfect virtue. "The Master said, 'It is, in retirement, to be sedately grave; in the management of business, to be reverently attentive; in intercourse with others, to be strictly sincere. Though a man go among rude, uncultivated tribes, these qualities may not be neglected.' "[8] Tzu Chang asked how a man should conduct himself so as to be everywhere appreciated. "The Master said, 'Let his words be sincere and truthful, and his actions honorable and careful; such conduct may be practiced among the rude tribes of the south or the north.' "[9]

The above are the minimum requirements for a Confucian who happens to live in a barbarous district where he has none of the amenities of civilized life. Though barbarians surround him, menace him, urge him to discard his refined, Confucian ways, he should stand his ground. These sayings of Confucius suggest comparison with Jesus' statement: "Behold, I send you forth as sheep in the midst of wolves: be ye therefore wise as serpents, and harmless as doves."[10]

Did Confucius anticipate the turbulent days when Chinese rulers would lose virtue, barbarians would invade the Central Plain, and Confucians would have to live under an alien yoke in a rude and uncongenial environment? This must remain in the realm of speculation. But the later history of Confucianism was much as Confucius had prophesied. And it was in part this moral energy of Confucianism which drove the Chinese people to expand their own culture to the newly developed areas in the south and to other parts of eastern Asia. Finally, Confucius remarked, "In teaching there should be no distinction of race [*lei*]."[11] (Legge translated the last word "classes," but it has a wider range of meaning than social class.) This important remark means, to my mind, that in principle Confucianism may be propagated to the foreign tribes as well as to the lower classes in Chinese society. The universalist bent of this saying gave an impetus to Confucians to assimilate different peoples and cultures into Chinese civilization.

Let us now turn to the sayings of Mencius. In discoursing with a Mohist, Hsü Hsing, Mencius said: "I have heard of men using the doctrines of our great land to change barbarians, but I have never yet heard of any being changed to barbarians. . . . Now here is this shrike-tongued barbarian of the south, whose doctrines are not those of the ancient kings. You turn away from your Master and become his disciple."[12]

Confucius had remarked that moral practice was something more than daily custom and should not be neglected by a superior man even among barbarians. Mencius went a step further and affirmed the Confucian's responsibility to change the barbarian way of life. He said: "'It is said in *The Book of History*, "As soon as King T'ang began his work of executing justice, he commenced with [the dominion of] Ko. The whole empire had confidence in him. When he pursued his work in the east, the rude tribes in the west murmured. So did those in the north, when he was engaged in the south. Their cry was—'Why does he make us last?' " ' "[13] In saying this, Mencius combined moral principle with cultural influence, and even with political subjugation. Mencius quoted the verse from *The Book of Poetry*: "He smote the barbarians of the west and the north; he punished Ching and the Hsü; and no one dared to resist us." He said that these father-deniers and king-deniers would have been smitten by the Duke of Chou.[14] Though Mencius alluded to the "heresies" of Yang Chu and Mo Ti, it is clear that he deemed barbarian anarchy justifiably subject to punitive attack by a Confucian king.

These teachings of Confucius and Mencius were reflected in the policies of subsequent Chinese dynasties toward southern peoples. I shall illustrate this in subsequent sections.

SOCIETAL CONTACTS BETWEEN CHINESE AND NON-CHINESE

Societal contacts between Chinese and non-Chinese may be analyzed from two points of view, namely (1) who were the political rulers and who the ruled, and (2) who were the cultural assimilators and who the assimilated. Combining the two leads us to consider the following four relationships:

(1) The Chinese as the political rulers and the cultural assimilators of the non-Chinese. This was the ordinary situation in Chinese contacts with southern peoples.

(2) The Chinese as the political rulers of the non-Chinese but the culturally assimilated, as in the Kao-ch'ang state founded by Chinese in the northwest frontier area.[15] Instances of such relationships between the Chinese and the southerners will be discussed below.

(3) The Chinese as the politically ruled but the cultural assimilators. This was the usual situation in Chinese contacts with northern peoples, notably in the time of Hsiao-wen Ti (reigned 471–99) of the Northern Wei dynasty. Chin Shih-tsung's (reigned 1161–89) policy of "conserving the national spirit" and the uncompromising attitude of the Mongols toward Chinese civilization are examples of reaction on the side of barbarians and are characteristic of modern ages.

(4) The Chinese as the politically ruled and the culturally assimilated. This occurred with certain minority groups: for example, Chung-hang Yüeh, who surrendered to the Hsiung-nu and became their adviser,[16] and the Chinese who were settled in the Six Garrisons (*liu-chen*) during the time of the Northern Wei.[17] No doubt there were relationships of this sort between the Chinese and the southern peoples as well.

The following discussion will be concerned primarily with Chinese relations with southern peoples. Of the four relationships listed above, the first is the classic type in the south, although it is likely that it was preceded by instances of the second and fourth.

CHINESE MINORITIES BARBARIZED
AND RESISTING BARBARIZATION

Ch'in Shih Huang-ti (reigned 246–210 B.C.) established the first milestone in the southward movement of the Chinese in 243 B.C. when he opened up the area of modern Kwangtung, Kwangsi, and North Vietnam, established the commanderies of Nan-hai, Kuei-lin, and Hsiang-chün, and sent out men who had been sentenced to banishment and transport to live among the natives.

In the time of Erh-shih Huang-ti (reigned 209–208 B.C.), an independent state was established by one Chao T'o, whose home of record

was in Chen-ting (Cheng-ting, Hopei), but who had long lived in
Kwangtung. He called himself Wu Wang of Southern Yüeh. Lu Chia, a
commissioner from Han Kao-tsu, came to remonstrate with Wu Wang in
196 B.C., saying, "You are Chinese. The graves of your relatives, brothers
and cousins, as well as your ancestral graves are at Chen-ting. Will you
now turn against natural instincts, abandon your cap and sash, and vie
with the Son of Heaven from this small land of Yüeh?" Chao T'o acknowledged his fault, saying, "As a result of living among the southern
barbarians, I have been remiss in showing you the proper courtesies."[18]

Chao T'o was by no means an ardent exponent of Confucianism.
Moreover, the time was not ripe for general approval of Confucianism
in China. Chao T'o had seen no need for honoring the Confucian rites
and ceremonies until the Confucianist Lu Chia reproved him for ruling
a southern people in accordance with their own customs instead of those
of China.

Let us further examine the attitudes of the Chinese minorities dwelling among the southern barbarians. Chang Shu, a man of superior abilities who lived at Tieh-yü (Ta-li hsien, Yunnan) during the Former Han
period, was so distressed by the illiteracy of the natives that he is said
to have studied under Ssu-ma Hsiang-ju and returned home to instruct
his villagers.[19] Similarly, during the reign of Shun Ti (reigned 126–44)
in the Later Han period, Ch'en Lin, the governor of Ts'ang-wu (Kwangsi), said, "Though my house is on an island in the sea [Hainan], I shall
refrain firmly from adopting the usages of the southern barbarians."[20]
In the time of Huan Ti (reigned 147–167), Yin Chen of Wu-lien in
Tsang-k'o Commandery (Kweichow) said in self-criticism, "Because I
was born upon the wild frontiers, I am ignorant of the rites and righteousness." He studied Confucian Classics and works on prognostication
and divination under Hsü Shen and Ying Feng at Ju-nan (Ju-nan hsien,
Honan), and returned home to teach, whereupon, it is said, "there was
learning in the southern regions for the first time." He eventually became intendant of Ching Province.[21]

These examples show that during the Han period there was a Chinese minority in the south that strove to maintain Chinese ways and
pursue Confucian studies, though surrounded by barbarians. On the
other hand, it is said of Chuang Ch'iao, the Ch'u general in the Warring
States period who subdued Yunnan and established the state of Tien,
that "he changed his robes and followed their habits." Chuang was himself the offspring of a Ch'u family descended from southern barbarians,
and he had almost no ties with Confucianism. Actually, however, he
was unable even to preserve the culture of Ch'u, which was more nearly
Chinese than that of Yunnan. Although we enter the realm of legend

here, another example of how Chinese customs were altered by those of barbarians is perhaps to be found in the story of Chou Wen Wang's uncle, T'ai-po, who is said to have imitated the usages of Wu by letting his hair hang loose and tattooing his body.[22]

A more passive instance of attachment to the Chinese way of life is provided by the story of Ch'en Hsiu, a governor of Yü-chang (Kiangsi) during the Later Han period. Ch'en ordinarily kept his seat mats rolled and refused to receive guests, claiming that the customs of the commandery were not in order, but he treated Hsü Chih and Li Chui with special courtesies when they visited him. This shows that a small number of Chinese literati, living among southern peoples unacquainted with the rites, were able to maintain "proper" relationships only among themselves.[23]

OPENING AND CONTROL OF THE SOUTH BY LOCAL CONFUCIAN OFFICIALS

The power of the nomads restricted northward expansion by the Chinese dynasties of the Central Plain, as did the unsuitability of the northern climate for agriculture. Consequently, it was inevitable that Chinese dynasties should move southward, despite the heat and the danger of endemic diseases. Commanderies and prefectures were established in every part of South China, and military subjugation was followed by the appointment of governors and other officials, whose mission was to bring their areas under Chinese dynastic administration. Chekiang, the land of Wu and Yüeh in the Spring and Autumn period, was the first area into which the culture of the Central Plain penetrated. Szechwan was next to become a part of the Chinese homeland, after the Ch'in destroyed the ancient kingdoms of Pa and Shu.[24] Because the South Sea trade made Kwangtung particularly interesting to the Chinese, Hupeh and Hunan were settled and developed as early as Han times in order to facilitate access to Kwangtung ports. From these three areas, serving as bases in the east, west, and center, respectively, the regions to the southeast and southwest—Kiangsi, Fukien, Yunnan, Kweichow and Kwangsi—were brought under Chinese control. This was a gradual process, however; the development of the last three is very recent.

After the upsurge of Confucianism under Han Wu Ti (reigned 140–87 B.C.), all local officials were literati trained in Confucian studies; and even military men esteemed such learning. Actually, however, the techniques of the Legalists were employed in government and in the administration of the laws. This difference or tension between the more permissive and the more coercive strains in Han policy and administration is reflected in the paired categories of biographies of officials found in the three histories which deal with the Han dynasty. The harsher, more legalistic type of official (*k'u-li*) was in this period the servant of the centralizing power of the Han house, while the gentler, more humane type (*hsün-li*) was associated with local elites and sought to develop local cultures centrifugally in accord with Confucian ideals. Both strains in policy and both types of officials are to be seen in the subjugation and development of the south in this period.

Among the officials in the *Hou Han Shu* is Ti-wu Lun, who became governor of K'uai-chi in A.D. 53. In his new post he found that the common folk worshiped many false deities, relied heavily upon divination, and dissipated the material assets of their farms by constantly offering sacrifices of oxen. Previous governors had been unable to control the shamans, who deceived the people by telling them, "If you eat the flesh of the ox without offering any to the deities, you will fall sick and appear to be dying, lowing like an ox." Ti-wu Lun finally eliminated such customs by issuing prohibitory orders punishing shamans who deceived and frightened ignorant men with their stories of demon deities, and penalizing peasants who unlawfully sacrificed their plow oxen.

Although the use of plow oxen had been known in the Central Plain at least since Spring and Autumn times, the south had been unacquainted with it. Consequently, there was a surplus of fertile but uncultivated land and a constant shortage of food; this is clear from Wang Ching's biography in the *Hou Han Shu*. Wang Ching became governor of Lu-chiang (Anhwei) in A.D. 83.

Whereas the stern Ti-wu Lun employed legalistic measures in his war against the shamans, the milder Sung Chün undertook to establish a school while he was the chief official of Ch'en-yang (Ch'en-ch'i hsien, Hunan). In Chiu-chiang, where Sung Chün went as governor, there was a group of shamans at Mount T'ang and Mount Hou in Chün-ch'iu Prefecture (east of Ho-fei hsien, Anhwei). Like the K'uai-chi shamans who took the people's property on religious pretexts, they seized peasant men and women every year to serve the gods, calling them brides and bridegrooms, but not allowing them a married life. This custom was prohibited by Sung Chün.

Because Confucianism was put forward as a substitute for shamanism, it became necessary to establish schools and to teach Confucian marriage and burial rites to the natives. In the commandery of Kuei-yang (Pin hsien, Hunan), the inhabitants were strongly influenced by the customs of the adjacent Chiao Province, and knew nothing of ritual rules. When Wei Sa became governor of the commandery, sometime after A.D. 26, he encouraged school education, instituted the rites of marriage, and within a year transformed the area's customs. According to the *Tung-kuan Han-chi,* Wei's successor Tz'u Ch'ung encouraged the people to plant mulberry trees for sericulture and hemp for the manufacture of sandals.[25] In this way Confucian culture was bolstered by agricultural and technical improvements.

It is said that Hsi Kuang, a governor of Chiao-chih (North Vietnam) at the end of the Former Han period, educated both the Chinese citizenry and the barbarians under his jurisdiction, leading them gradually toward the rites and righteousness. The equally famous Jen Yen, governor of the more remote Chiu-chen (Central Vietnam), seeing that his people habitually looked to Chiao-chih for food supplies (they gained their livelihood by hunting and fishing and were unacquainted with the ox), made them prosper by directing them to manufacture agricultural implements of iron.

REFORM OF SOUTHERN MARRIAGE AND FAMILY SYSTEMS

An important way in which Confucianism civilized the southern natives was by improving their marriage systems. The Lo-yüeh (people of Vietnam), for example, observed no ritual marriage laws, but mated indiscriminately according to their fancies, ignorant of the nature of the father-son relationship and the duties of husband and wife. Jen Yen sent orders to the districts under his jurisdiction, requiring all men from twenty to fifty and all women from fifteen to forty to decide upon spouses in keeping with their age. Officials were ordered to use part of their stipends to aid those who were too poor to defray the cost of getting married. As a result, more than two thousand persons were married simultaneously. Favorable weather that year produced a good harvest, and for the first time couples who had children recognized them as their own. Everyone said, "It is Mr. Jen who has given these children to us," and there were many who named their children Jen.[26]

Jen Yen's innovation, which might be called compulsory official marriage, was an effort to establish a patriarchal society by imposing monogamy on the promiscuous south. In a memorial submitted to the throne in the year 231, Hsieh Tsung of the Three Kingdoms state of Wu said of Jen, "He instituted matchmaking offices for their sake, and made them acquainted with marriage."[27]

T'ao Chi, an intendant of Chiao Province in the time of the Three Kingdoms state of Wu, is credited with a similar achievement: "The barbarians of the area were unacquainted with the rites and ceremonies. Men and women beguiled each other, coupled hastily (*pen-sui*), and produced children whose fathers could not be ascertained. When T'ao

Chi arrived at his post, he taught them the ways of marriage, instructed them in the obligations of fathers and sons, and established schools and colleges." Thus he transformed the region.[28]

Hsieh Tsung's memorial of 231 also says: "Since ancient times it has been the custom in the settlements of Chu-yai (Hainan Island) for the inhabitants to gather in fields during the eighth month, where the men and women look for likely mates and become husband and wife. Even mothers and fathers cannot abolish this practice. In the two districts of Mi-leng in Chiao-chih (Hanoi) and Tu-p'ang in Chiu-chen,[29] it is usual for a younger brother to marry the widow of an older brother. Even the local officials cannot prevent it." Hsieh Tsung further said, "Give local chief officials strong authority to rectify this," and voiced approval of such measures as Jen Yen's establishment of matchmaking offices.

Confucianism condemned marriage forms which involved promiscuity, polygamy, or the levirate. It sought to increase the father's authority over the family, and to introduce stable monogamous marriage. The introduction of iron farm implements, ox-drawn plows, and other new agricultural techniques from China increased the role of the male in agricultural operations; and the corresponding improvement in agricultural production, by making it possible to feed the gradually increasing Chinese population, abetted the development of family units. To consolidate these socio-economic advances, it became necessary to indoctrinate the people with Confucian ethics; to teach them the distinction between father and son and the order of elder and younger.

Ch'en Lin, a governor at Ts'ang-wu during the Later Han period, has been mentioned earlier. Ch'en was an earnest official who taught the people filial piety and fraternal love. On one occasion, a man whose father had been murdered before his birth was condemned to death for obtaining revenge on the murderer. Aware that the man had no heir, Ch'en allowed his wife to visit him in prison so that she might bear him a son. It is said that the people praised the vastness of Ch'en's mercy, and that Heaven rewarded him by making his descendants flourish.[30]

In the time of Ho Ti (89–105), the Kuei-yang governor Hsü Ching instituted regulations for mourning periods and marriages. While on a tour to Lei-yang (Heng-yang tao, Hunan), Hsü observed that a resident of the prefecture named Chiang Chün had brought suit against his younger brother in a quarrel over property. He thereupon sought a judgment against himself from a higher office, asserting that he was to blame for not having brought enlightenment to the brothers. As a result, the brothers were reconciled.[31]

Our discussion so far has been restricted primarily to the activities

of individual local officials. Before proceeding further it will be useful
to consider the schools established by these local officials as a part of
their policy of encouraging Confucianism, schools that must surely have
brought about the gradual increase of learned adherents of Confucianism in the south.

When the local officials established schools, they first enrolled boys
from the families of subordinate officials. Wen Weng of the Former Han
period, whose fame in the history of the development of Szechwan ranks
next to that of Li Ping of Ch'in, established a school at Ch'eng-tu at a
time when, as a result of Ch'in misrule, the school system of the country
at large was deteriorating. In addition to enrolling boys from officials'
families in the school, he dispatched to Ch'ang-an eighteen men of
superior talent, Chang Shu among them, who studied the Seven Classics
under learned doctors and returned home to teach. This was during the
reign of Wen Ti (179–157 B.C.). It was claimed that Shu (Ch'eng-tu)
learning could be compared to that of Ch'i and Lu, home of Confucianism, and that the literary studies inaugurated at Pa and Han-chung
(Nan-cheng, Shensi) were the models for those that were undertaken
later in the prefectures and states of the empire.[32]

A later Han governor of Kuei-yang, Luan Pa, went so far as to order
officials of very inferior position to study at a school that he founded.
He examined these men and promoted them according to their abilities.[33]

The minor local officials who studied at schools established by cen-
trally appointed officials were for the most part natives of the areas in
question. They mastered the Confucian learning and took the lead in
upholding the marriage and burial ceremonies fostered by the governors, establishing a basis upon which local Confucian studies could continue by themselves. It is said that because Confucian learning was encouraged by Chang Pa, a governor of K'uai-chi during the Later Han
period, the people in the commandery who vied with one another in
ardent study of the Classics were numbered by the thousand, and on the
roads and highways only the sound of lute strings and the chanting of
books could be heard. Such students of Confucianism were granted
appointments to office when the opportunity arose. Chang Pa gave employment to all commandery inhabitants of distinguished attainments,
among them the scholar Ku Feng.[34] Thus the influence of the local officials persisted until later ages, and a few Confucians existed even among
the southern barbarians. When Ch'e Chün from Nan-p'ing (Hunan)
met Lu Sun in debate, he so impressed the assembled ministers of Wu
that they said, "Are there such rare men in the southern barbarian commandery of Wu-ling?"[35]

It was not only local officials who encouraged Confucianism; there were also scholars wandering through the south who instituted private schools. One of the first to do so was Pien Shao of the Later Han period, who taught students at Tzu-t'ung (Tzu-t'ung hsien, Szechwan), and is said never to have had fewer than a hundred students.[36]

THE ADOPTION OF CHINESE DRESS

It appears that the first step toward inculcating the principles of Confucianism was to prevail upon the native peoples to adopt Chinese dress. Hsieh Tsung says in his memorial, "Men and women of Jih-nan Commandery seem unashamed of their naked bodies." He also states that Jen Yen obliged the natives to wear caps and sandals. It is said that Ku Yung, a governor of Yü-lin (Kuei hsien, Kwangsi) who subjugated more than 100,000 Wu-hu barbarians in A.D. 170, made the conquered people accept caps and sashes.[37] Similarly, Tz'u Ch'ung's reason for teaching his subjects to manufacture sandals was simply that he wished them to provide themselves with footgear and abandon the old custom of walking barefoot. So the inculcation of Confucian usages paralleled technological development.[38]

COMPROMISE WITH BUDDHISM AND TAOISM;
NEW SUCCESSES IN THE SOUTH

As is indicated by the following two examples, during the last years of the Later Han era and the Three Kingdoms period (a time of great interest from the standpoint of religious history), the charisma of a local Chinese chief official was not necessarily Confucian. Chang Chin, intendant of Chiao Province (from about 201 to 205) abandoned Chinese precepts, read "false and vulgar Taoist books" (Tao-shu), and administered his region wearing a red turban. Sun Ts'e, in a denunciation of a popular Taoist practitioner named Han Chi, said of Chang Chin: "Formerly, Chang Chin of Nan-yang (Hupeh) became intendant of Chiao Province. He ignored the teachings of the ancient sages and abolished the laws of the Han dynasty. He wore a red turban, played on the lyre, burned incense, and read false and vulgar books, which he believed to promote culture. Eventually he was killed by southern barbarians (nan-i)."[39]

Similarly, when Shih Hsieh (137–226), who was favorably inclined toward Confucianism (as a disciple of Liu T'ao of the Ku-wen school), was governor of Chiao-chih, he was saluted by scores of the Hu barbarians with burning incense every time he left or arrived at his office. Chang Chin was well disposed toward the doctrines of Buddhism and Taoism, while Shih Hsieh was honored by foreigners (apparently followers of Buddhism) with ceremonies such as were performed in honor of Buddhas and kings in India.[40] It is apparent that local officials did not always exert a purely Confucian influence upon their communities. Even a foreign religion could be substituted for Confucianism if it were capable of serving the official system.

I have discussed above how Confucian governors and scholars endeavored to propagate Confucian doctrine and culture in frontier territories during Han times. The policy of Confucianization began to have considerable success toward the end of the Later Han period, when a great change—both political and intellectual—took place, and Confucianism, gradually losing its vigor, had to be supplemented by other spiritual energies, those of Buddhism and Taoism.

During this time of rapid change the activities of the southern peoples, as well as those of the western, northern and eastern "barbarians," became more important than ever before. Recent studies in China have given us new information about the southern tribes that played a significant role in this confused period.[41]

The most noteworthy of these tribes was the northernmost, the Lin-chün Man; their territory extended over Shensi, southern Honan, and much of Szechwan, Hupeh, Hunan, and Anhwei. They had the white tiger as a totem and were called by different names according to their localities in contemporary Chinese accounts. The branch that occupied Szechwan was called Pa-ti; many of its members accepted Wu-tou-mi tao, a variety of religious Taoism.

Their contact with the Chinese became closer toward the end of the Six Dynasties. They were so far tamed and sinicized that they were registered as Chinese commoners belonging to commanderies and prefectures. An example of their sinification is given in the biography of Hsieh Shen:[42]

"It was the custom of the Man people to live apart from their parents who were still alive when they married." Judging this custom most deplorable from the standpoint of Confucian ethics, Shen personally exhorted them to conduct themselves in accordance with filial piety and parental benevolence. He also sent local officials under his jurisdiction to admonish the people to this effect. "Thus a cultural transformation was effected, and among the barbarians there was sinification of customs." It should be noticed that Shen mentioned parental benevolence as a counterpart of filial piety, since in general Confucianism stresses the latter more than the former.

As early as the third century the western branch of the Lin-chün Man had been assimilated to Chinese culture to such a degree that they shared the provincial loyalties of the local Chinese. It is recorded that

Li T'e, a military commander of the Ti tribe, regarded himself as a fellow villager of Chao Hsin, a Chinese official.[43]

In the Sui and T'ang period, the Lin-chün Man retreated to Szechwan, Kweichow, Hunan, and Kiangsi. There some of the Lin-chün Man tribes lived together with the P'an-hu Man, who led an agricultural life with domesticated animals and had the dog as their totem.[44]

Chu-ko Liang, chancellor of the Shu-Han state, made an expedition in 225 into the southernmost parts of Szechwan, Kweichow, and Yunnan, penetrating to the very borders of Burma. As a result of this expedition, a number of southern people called Nan-i were appointed as officials of Shu-Han.[45] A Nan-i chieftain, Ts'uan Hsi, appeared in history at this time. The Ts'uan clan was descended from the Pai tribe, which, under the Ch'in and Former Han dynasties, had moved south to Lake Tien-ch'ih (Yunnan) about the beginning of the Christian era. Lake Tien-ch'ih is located in the land of the Kun-ming tribe. A recent study has revealed that the White (Pai) Man and the Black (Wu) Man of the T'ang are the descendants of the Pai and the Kun-ming, respectively, and the ancestors of the present Pai-tsu (White tribe) and Hui or Nahsi, both living in Yunnan as minority groups.[46]

Such foreign tribes, after being pacified by military force, were made subject to severe laws that aroused their resentment. Other sources of resentment were the ruthless methods employed by Chinese officials to seize the wealth of the south, and clashes produced by differences in customs.

After Chu-ko Liang's expedition, the Shu-Han state endeavored strenuously, but not always successfully, to control the southern barbarians of southwestern Szechwan, Yunnan, and Kweichow. Chang I, the governor-general of Lai-hsiang (Ch'ü-ching hsien, Yunnan), enforced the laws so strictly that he alienated the natives and brought on the rebellion of the Great Chieftain Liu Chou.[47] On the other hand, Chang's successor Ma Chung was so popular that he was actually worshiped by the southern barbarians; and the barbarians thought so highly of Wang Ssu—another Shu-Han official—that they participated in his funeral rites and later treated his descendants as their flesh-and-blood brothers.[48] The attitude of the native southern subjects was conditioned by the individual character of the local official. The saying "governors, but no government" may well be applied to the situation.

That individual influence was actually effective in bringing about the submission of southern barbarians is shown by the story of the barbarian Meng Huo, who said "My lord is a heavenly god" after he had been "seven times released and seven times captured" by Chu-ko

Liang.[49] When influential leaders were also sponsors of Confucianism, the workings of the doctrine appeared to the natives in the light of a religious faith, something to replace their long-held shamanistic beliefs. Accordingly, Confucian education became a responsibility of local officials, on a par with military subjugation, legalistic control, and an economic policy designed to encourage agriculture.

CONFUCIAN CIVILIZATION IN THE SOUTH
DURING THE SIX DYNASTIES PERIOD

From Han times on, Confucian local officials who surrounded themselves with Confucian literati were frequently praised for their governmental achievements by the inhabitants of the south, including the barbarians. In the Six Dynasties period, schools were established and superior talents fostered by Fan Hsüan of Eastern Chin and Chang Wan of Liang at Yü-chang, and by Yü Po of Eastern Chin at P'o-yang (Kiangsi). When Hsiao Hsiu of Liang was governor-general of Ching, Hsiang, and other provinces, he established schools and "summoned the recluses."[50] Since this "summoning of the recluses" meant that scholars learned in the Confucian arts were brought together from their scattered retreats and given recognition, it was in effect a stimulus to the sinification of the southern barbarian regions.

Of particular note as an improvement of customs was Ku Hsien-chih's prohibition of "washed-bone burials" when he was governor of Heng-yang (Hsiang-t'an hsien, Hunan) during the Southern Ch'i period. It was the custom of the "mountain people" (*shan-min*) to attribute sickness to ancestral curses. In order to remove a curse they broke into the offending ancestor's tomb, opened the coffin, and washed the bones in water. This was called "exorcising evil influences." Ku Hsien-chih explained to these people the differences between the living and the dead and the lack of causal connections between them. In this way the custom was reformed.[51]

During the Six Dynasties period, Confucianism in the south seems to have been fostered by gentry families coming in from the north to settle. Speaking of the development of Fukien, the *Chiu-kuo Chih* ("Record of Nine States") says, "During the time of the Yung-chia disturbances [307–312], the eight families entered Min [i.e., Fukien]. Unrest in the Central Plain caused them to fear difficulties and long for peace; and yet they were unable to go toward the north to get on in the official circles. Consequently, one seldom hears of famous officials among the Six Dynasties." According to the *Pa-min T'ung-chih*, Cheng Lu's study was located at Hsing-haufu (P'u-t'ien hsien, Fukien) as early as the Liang and Ch'en periods, and the *T'ang Shih-tao Chih* ("A T'ang To-pography of the Ten Districts") tells us that many "robe and cap" gentry families gathered at Ch'üan-choufu (Chin-chiang hsien, Fukien) when the Chin capital was removed to the south.[52]

In the Six Dynasties period, there were relatively few of the milder, more permissive officials (*hsün-li*) depicted in the *Hou Han Shu*—men who sought, as faithful officers of a Confucian state, to provide the southern natives with a Confucian education. Nevertheless, on the whole, the sinification of the south appears to have gone forward during that time, thanks on the one hand to the gradual increase of immigrant gentry families, and on the other to the groundwork of Confucian learning laid before the end of the Han period.

The trend toward local autonomy which was characteristic of the Six Dynasties period was strong in the south as well as the north. Single families tended to wield actual authority as local officials for several generations, governing and civilizing the barbarian peoples. For four generations, five descendants of Shih Hsieh of Wu and T'ao Chi of Chin ruled over Chiao Province.[53] There is also the example of the Feng family, which governed Kwangtung from the Six Dynasties period to the T'ang.

Feng Yung, a descendant of Feng Hung of the Northern Yen dynasty (409–36), was born into a branch of the family that had settled at P'an-yü (Kwangtung). When he became intendant of T'eng Province (T'eng hsien, Kwangsi) during the Liang period, he effectively pacified the natives "with rites and righteousness, and with authority and trustworthiness." Drawing men of letters to his side, he composed poems and songs with them, and by these methods civilized the barbarians, until the strings of the lute and the chanting of books were heard daily in the land of the banana and lichee. When Feng toured the lands under his jurisdiction, the southern barbarian chieftains burned incense and played music wherever he went, and one after another those who spied his banner came to greet him. On such occasions, it was his custom to warn his subordinates, "I, Chief Elder Feng (Feng Tu-lao), have come. Do not allow evil acts to involve you in crime." Under these conditions, the people dwelling in barbarian caves rejoiced in their occupations, and several decades elapsed without a military disturbance.

Although Feng Yung's forefathers had been local officials in the south, their orders had been disregarded because they were men whose homes were elsewhere. Consequently, Yung married his son Pao, the governor of Kao-liang (En-p'ing hsien, Kwangtung), to a daughter of the Hsi family, a powerful native clan in the commandery. Thereupon the Li tribe submitted to him and obeyed his laws and orders.[54]

T'ANG CONFUCIANISM IN THE SOUTH

In the T'ang period, there is the example of Ch'en Cheng and his descendants, who governed Chang Province (Yün-hsiao hsien, later Lung-ch'i hsien, Fukien). Before the Tsung-chang era (668–69), Chang Province was an underdeveloped area still in the stage of military pacification. However, Ch'en Cheng's assistant, Hsü T'ien-cheng, was a man of broad learning and literary ability, who always had a classical work in his hands during respites from his task of military administration. Hsü educated Cheng's grandson Hsiang so carefully that Hsiang's father Yüan-kuang said to him: "You are not a knight of the lance and halberd, but an accomplished Confucian scholar of the Court of General Affairs!" Hsiang later rose in the examination system, took the Doctor of Classics degree, and established a study at Sung-chou (Hunan), the newly established provincial capital, where he offered instruction in the Classics, to the benefit of public morals. After Yüan-kuang's death in battle, Hsiang succeeded to his father's post and devoted himself wholeheartedly to military campaigns and educational activities.[55] The story of how the Ch'en family strove to pacify and administer Chang Province for four generations, from Cheng to Hsiang's son Feng, does not appear in the two T'ang histories, but may be found in the *Chang-chou Fu-chih,* ch. 24.

During the T'ang dynasty's administration of the south, Chinese and barbarians lived together and intermarried, especially in the Ling-nan area;[56] and when life became difficult, some Chinese were sold into slavery right along with the barbarians.[57] Moreover, from the Southern Dynasties period on, the prosperity brought to the ports of Kwangtung by the South Sea trade had resulted in the appearance of large numbers of corrupt local officials.

What is particularly to be noted in the present connection, however, we find stated in the *Kuang-tung T'ung-chih*: that whereas in pre-T'ang times those who were exiled to Ling-nan were all sent in the status of commoners, in T'ang times the area became a land to which officials were demoted. It is in this period that the term "degraded official" (*che-huan*) first appears. Among the men of this sort who moved into the area there were people like Teng Wen-chin, who provided lodging and food for over a thousand such exiles, assigning the braver ones to guard duties.[58] K'ung K'uei gave official employment to the descendants of men who had been exiled to the south for crime.[59] Ch'ang Kun, a worker in the development of Fukien, encouraged studies among the villagers and urged official careers upon "accomplished commoners" (*hsiu-min*), men who were versed in literature and practiced in official business, but who had not dared to seek office. In this way, careers were opened to men who later became well known in the central government, such as Ou-yang Chan.[60] Two instances of improvement of local customs are afforded by Wei Chou, intendant of Yung Province (Ling-ling hsien, Hunan), who prohibited the wild carousals that had accompanied marriage ceremonies and ended the practice of extortion by gangs of juvenile miscreants;[61] and Liu Yü-hsi, who, as military adjutant of Lang Province (Ch'ang-te hsien, Hunan), reformed the shaman songs of the barbarians, composing new verses for them in the style of the *Ch'u Tz'u*.

In the introduction to his "Bamboo Branch Poems" (*Chu-chih Tz'u*), Liu Yü-hsi (772–842) says:

The songs of barbarians are different from one another, but they are all musical. In the first moon, I came to Chien-p'ing [Wu-shan hsien, Szechwan]. I saw the village children sing "The Bamboo Branch" in groups, playing on short flutes, beating a drum to keep time. The singers raised their sleeves and danced with an upward glance. The more variations the song had, the more people praised it. I found them in accord with "feather" [a scale] of "Yellow bell" [C-flat] [*huang-chung chih yü*] of Chinese music. The last phrase is acute and strong like the Wu notes. Though unrefined and confused, the notes of the song can express continuous emotions like the love songs of Ch'i [Honan] and Pu [Shantung] districts. When the great Ch'u poet Ch'ü Yüan was banished to Hunan, he heard the country song to invoke gods and regarded it as fearfully crude. So he composed the Nine Songs for them. Up to the present, the inhabitants of Hunan use these songs when they dance and beat drums in festivals. So I have composed the nine chapters of "The Bamboo Branch" and made the good singers sing them.[62]

The texts of his nine songs treat of such subjects as the Szechwan landscape, peasants burning off new fields (*shao-yü*), dancers and waitresses in a country town. The *Ch'u Tz'u* poems of Ch'ü Yüan came from the shaman songs of the ancient Ch'u state. The great poet altered some words of these songs and introduced cultivated and Confucian ideas. A millennium afterwards, the T'ang poet again altered some vulgar points of the country songs. The peculiar tones of these ancient religious songs may have remained through later ages.

When Confucian teachings were expounded, fitting ceremonies, such as the *shih-tien* offering, were performed. The ritualism accompanying such ceremonies delighted the southerners. We may cite here the case of Wang I-fang, who was degraded to the post of assistant (ch'eng) in Chi-an Prefecture, Tan Province (Ch'ang-chiang hsien, Kwangtung), early in the T'ang era. Lecturing upon the Classics for the benefit of youths from families of southern barbarian chieftains, Wang performed the *shih-tien* offering, complete with music, songs, and proper ordering of the participants' ascent to and withdrawal from the ceremonial place. It is said that the barbarian chieftains who watched were delighted.[63]

The religious atmosphere of the Confucian rites impressed the native peoples as superior to the primitive songs and dances of shamanism. For them Confucianism was not only a system of learning and a bearer of culture, but a religion rivaling and excelling shamanism. It cannot be said, however, that Confucianism Confucianized the southern peoples solely by functioning as a religion. Its religious function was supported by the military and political power of Chinese dynasties, and by local officials and literati. Its limited influence did not extend beyond a superior minority among the governed, and even with them its success was only gradual.

Another shamanistic practice, the curing of disease by prayer without the use of medication, continued until later ages, but it too was attacked, both by the court and by local officials. An example of shamanistic sway over matters connected with disease comes from the reign of Te-tsung (780–804). Imperial inspector Li Te-yü found that the people of Che-hsi (west of the river Ch'ien-t'ang, Chekiang) believed so implicitly in spells and goblins that they completely abandoned leprous relatives. Li attempted to reform this inhuman practice by selecting wise villagers to admonish offenders, and by instituting appropriate laws.[64] He acted in the name of Confucian family morals, which do not sanction abandoning the sick, although to the extent that effective medical care was not available he probably increased the danger of the spread of leprosy within the family.

Under the T'ang dynasty there were also such local officials in the south as Yang Ch'eng, who combined the humanism of Confucianism (e.g., his prohibition of the presentation of slaves as tribute) with the strict justice of the Legalists.[65] The T'ang was also a period during which the strength of Buddhism increased in the south, although the power of the shaman spells was slow to decline.

SUNG CONFUCIANISM IN THE SOUTH

With the coming of the Sung period, the influence of Confucianism at last became firmly established in the south. But the combat with shamanism still continued. For example, an edict issued by Sung T'ai-tsung in 985 reads: "The customs of the Ling-nan ('South of the Peaks') area . . . , including the sacrifice of human beings in demon worship and the failure to summon physicians in case of sickness, . . . should be reformed by careful instruction."[66] Chou Chan, governor of Jung-chou, had ancient Chinese medical treatises carved on stone in order to teach the local inhabitants how to treat illnesses; he also forbade shamans to practice their cures.[67] In this connection, we may note here that the "Household Regulations" of Ch'en Ch'ang-ch'i, a magistrate at

Ku-t'ien (Min-hai tao, Fukien) during the Sung period, condemns the use of shamanistic spells as inconsistent with benevolence, righteousness, rites, and music.

The moral influence of Chu Hsi was very great, and his *Wen-kung Chia-li* regulated the lives of the literati in Fukien and all its surrounding provinces. Local gazetteers compiled in modern times to record the customs of the various areas speak of the south as "the land of enlightenment," "close to antiquity," and "resembling the homeland of Confucius."

One way Chu Hsi contributed to the reinvigoration of Confucianism in South China was by stressing the scholar's integrity and the necessity of maintaining sexual separation. When he was an official at T'ung-an (Amoy, Fukien) he noticed women walking on the streets with their faces uncovered. So he issued a regulation to the effect that a woman should hide her face with patterned cloth when she was out of doors. People came to call the cloth "the lord's covering" (*kung-tou*). When he became an official in Ch'üan and Chang provinces, which were notorious for their frequent cases of abduction, he advised the women there to attach wooden blocks to their shoes so that they made noise in walking. These were called wooden-block shoes (*mu-t'ou li*).[68]

These measures taken by Chu Hsi are based upon the high consequence assigned to the sense of shame (*lien-ch'ih*) in Confucian doctrine. If it is proper to say that Christianity attaches importance to the sense of guilt and Buddhism to the sense of pain, Confucianism stresses the sense of shame. For this reason women were kept in seclusion, and acquiesced in their inferior position in the community. The local records compiled in the Ch'ing period provide further evidence that female seclusion was thought to conform to good custom.

At Shan-yin Prefecture (Chekiang), one could overhear Confucian songs sung and Confucian texts recited from house to house. The women there never conducted themselves frivolously. Even the wives of brothers and cousins did not see each other.[69] Among all counties (*hsiang*) of Hsia-men (Amoy) Prefecture, T'a-t'ou county was most noted for strictness of sexual seclusion. The women observed decorum faithfully, and were ashamed to see male guests.[70]

It was said that the good customs of Ch'eng Prefecture (southwest of Ningpo, Chekiang) originated in the women's apartments. The distaff culture there was most elaborate. The women abstained from attractive clothes and were assiduous in female occupations. The distinction between the inner (woman) and the outer (man) sides was very clear.[71]

We shall not consider in detail the Confucianization process in the Yüan and Ming periods. It suffices to note that during these periods the *t'u-ssu* system—the use of aboriginal chiefs for local control—was firmly established in the southern frontier areas of China, and that Chinese migration into the south proceeded without interruption.[72]

THE CH'ING CONFUCIANIZATION OF FORMOSA

After 1683, when the Manchu government wrested Formosa from the control of the Cheng family, which in turn had expelled the Dutch force, Confucian doctrine as prescribed in the Four Books and Five Classics, reconfirmed by several edicts issued by Manchu emperors, was imposed upon this undeveloped territory. The educational regulations of the White Deer Cave (Po-lu Tung), a private school founded by Chu Hsi, were applied in the Confucian schools established in Formosa by the Manchu government.[73]

Lan Ting-yüan (1680–1733), whose cousin Ting-chen (1664–1730) was engaged in overcoming the Formosan bandit Chu I-kuei around the year 1721, got firsthand information from him about affairs in Formosa and wrote many essays on policy for the administration of this island. In a letter to one of his friends, he stated, "Founding schools and transforming popular customs in Taiwan are essential to military preparedness." He wrote in one of his official letters that the difficulty in pacifying Taiwan lay not in economic but in educational problems:

We should establish schools and show respect for leading Confucian scholars. We should organize a number of private schools from the main towns to the countryside, and invite men of character as teachers. The Sixteen Maxims of the K'ang-hsi Emperor should be expounded on the first day and the middle day of each month to guide and instruct people. At each house door, the teaching should be carried on by inscribing the eight characters, viz., filial piety [*hsiao*], fraternal love [*ti*], faithfulness [*chung*], sincerity [*hsin*], propriety [*li*], righteousness [*i*], integrity [*lien*], and sense of shame [*ch'ih*]; we can thus expect to reform the customs of both the intellectuals and the common people. This is the urgent business of today!

In his discussion on Taiwan affairs with an official named Wu, he says:

The Taiwan people do not know how to study. Most of the applicants for government examinations are immigrants from the mainland; few of them are capable of composing a good essay. We must build many private schools to encourage scholarship. . . . At the prefectural capital [*fu-ch'eng*], an academy [*shu-yüan*] should be established. . . . We should select students of excellent character, wide learning, and ambition, and we should nominate them as students in the district school. We should invite learned scholars from the mainland and ask them to lecture on the proper forms of behavior between father and son, sovereign and subject, the elder and the younger; on the relationship between body and mind; on nature [*hsing*] and life [*ming*]. We should let people know that wisdom is attained only by those who perform their filial and fraternal duties and conduct themselves faithfully and in a trustworthy manner.

Having no access to edification, the Taiwan people never talk about faithfulness and truthfulness, nor do they even hear about proper filial and fraternal conduct. We should arrange a series of moral lectures; assemble the gentry and men of honor at the public meeting house and give them explanations of the Ten Thousand Character Exposition of the Sacred Edict of K'ang-hsi, and tell them stories of good and evil exemplars of ancient and modern times, to awake the dull perception of the ignorant. These lectures should be given at any city, town, village, or hamlet . . . where people gather, . . . to instruct and enlighten ignorant men and women and make them realize the happiness of doing good. Only thus may we expect to improve the customs.[74]

The worship of Confucius was celebrated in Confucian schools (*ju-hsüeh*), where preliminary examinations were held for advanced candidates for the civil service examinations. The *shih-tien* ceremony was held twice every year on fixed days in the middle months of spring and fall. In 1745, the Emperor ordered that the high-ranking officials of the provinces, both civil and military, should hold services at the shrines of Confucius, burn incense, and pay homage. In Taiwan, not only the government officials but also some distinguished laymen advocated setting up an organization for the worship of Confucius, to be called the Cultural Sage Society (*wen-sheng hui*).

The propagation of Confucianism among the villagers was effected by lectures (*hsüan-chiang*) on the Sixteen Maxims. Even in the remote Pescadores Islands, Confucianism was expounded in such lectures on the first and sixteenth days of each month. On these occasions the governor assembled subordinate officers at the meeting hall of the Ma-tsu (sea goddess) shrine, where the tablet inscribed with the Sacred Edict was placed on the incense table. The attendants carried out the ceremony of three kneelings and nine kotowings, then sat together in two groups, one on the east side, the other on the west. Two of the sixteen chapters were read loudly, first in the official language and then in local dialect. The lecture could be heard by the people outside the shrine.

It must be noted that the lectures were not purely Confucian. Other elements were added to enhance their effect. The text of the eighth chapter reads, "Lecture on laws to caution the ignorant and the obstinate." In his Commentary on the Broadened Instruction, Yeh Shih-cho provided some pictures showing the five punishments (*wu-hsing*). This introduces a legalist element in the lecture. Sometimes Taoist books, such as *Kan-ying p'ien* and *Yin-chih wen*, were expounded on these occasions.

People were encouraged by the government to hold formal discussions among themselves on certain moral books (*shan-shu*), with a view to augmenting the effect of the official lectures. In these popular lectures, the principle of the Sacred Edict was fully maintained, but was explained in vernacular phrases in the more readily understandable terms of Buddho-Taoist doctrines of retribution. The Society for the Extension of Felicity (*fu-chang she*), which was founded by the gentry of Hsin-chu Prefecture in 1884, promoted such instruction. Its members occasionally worshiped deities and burned incense at an altar in the lecture room. Moral books of all kinds were widely distributed free of charge, the expenses being met by voluntary contributions from the gentry.[75] The principal themes of such books were this-world ethics, fidelity to family religion, and denouncing superstition. We can see in this how Confucianism had added to its effectiveness among the people by the ancillary use of other teachings.

I shall now consider how Confucianism influenced the Takasago tribes, the aborigines of Taiwan. To those who were already civilized, called "shou-man," Confucianism was taught at the village school (*she-hsüeh*) by teachers (*she-shih*). In the nineteenth century, their sinification progressed so remarkably that the practice of segregated education was discontinued. Toward the end of the Ch'ing period, Wu Kuang-liang dictated thirty-two articles based in principle on the Sacred Edict, to be used in sinicizing the natives. Wu's articles encouraged such Confucian values as filial piety, adoption of Chinese dress, proper marriage customs, and ancestor worship.

The uncultivated tribes (*sheng-man*) had their own concept of ancestor worship. With the purpose of earning welcome to the eternal residence of their ancestors, these tribes practiced head-hunting. Needless to say, the Chinese government tried to exterminate this custom. At that time, negotiations between Chinese and the aborigines were entrusted to the chieftain (*t'ou-mu*) and the interpreter (*t'ung-shih*) or manager (*tung-shih*). Among Chinese officials who worked to suppress head-hunting, the case of the interpreter Wu Feng (1699–1769) is noteworthy. He sacrificed himself in the cause of Confucian humanism, presumably following a saying of Confucius: "The determined scholar and the man of virtue will not seek to live at the expense of injuring their virtue. They will even sacrifice their lives to perserve their virtue complete."

The sources differ on the dates and details of his life. The most authentic record tells us that he was born in Chang district, Fukien, and migrated to Taiwan in his boyhood. There he carried on trading with the wild tribe of Mount A-li, who were most savage and practiced head-hunting on a large scale. After he was appointed interpreter in 1722, he tried to eradicate this practice by repeatedly issuing strict bans, but without success. Finally, he determined to sacrifice his life in an effort to attain his goal. One day he told the tribesmen that he would permit them to cut off only one head, that of a man wearing a vermilion robe and a red cap who would be found riding a horse near the community center early the next morning. On the following day, the tribe held a head-hunting ceremony. They did not fail to find the man. When they killed him and cut off his head, they found to their astonishment that the man was Wu Feng himself. During his forty-eight years of service he had won their absolute devotion and admiration by his cordial friendliness and upright impartiality. The Mount A-li tribesmen repented heartily, and their head-hunting ceased.

According to a different tradition passed down in this tribe, their ancestors killed Wu Feng by accident, mistaking him for one of his cruel subordinates. The tribe suffered from smallpox after Wu Feng's death, and believed that the wrath of his spirit caused it. So they ceased to hunt human heads thereafter.

This exceptional deed of Wu Feng was officially commended by the Japanese governor's office in 1913. His biography was edited by official order and entitled "The Interpreter Wu Feng Who Sacrificed His Life to Preserve Virtue" (Tsūji Go Hō).[76]

CONCLUSION

Wei Yuan, in his *Sheng-wu Chi,* says, "Below Heaven there are states with walled cities, nomadic states, and maritime states." Confucianism arose in a state with walled cities, converted nomadic peoples, and finally, supported by the military and political power of the Confucian state and the economic power of the agricultural Chinese people, extended its scope to maritime states abutting on the southern ocean.

Even today, however, shamanistic practices have not been eradicated wholly in the south, where the strength of Buddhism and Taoism can be regarded as a manifestation of old beliefs in an altered guise. Confucianism was unable to gain sole possession of the hearts of the people because it stressed relations between one individual and another, instead of relations between the individual and the Absolute. It failed to give satisfaction to flights of the spirit. At the same time, Buddhism and Taoism were unable to triumph over it, in spite of their apparent satisfaction of this spiritual need, because they did not fit smoothly into the positive transition to Chinese society. At about the time that Confucianism reached the coast of South China, Christianity was introduced from beyond the sea; a new faith, which was to seek to create a new crisis in the spiritual history of the Chinese.

Arthur F. Wright

SUI YANG-TI:
PERSONALITY AND STEREOTYPE

Yang Kuang (569–618), who ruled as Yang-ti of the Sui, is of interest to the student of Chinese history and civilization in a number of ways. First of all, he is an interesting historical figure in his own right. He was the second and last ruler of a dynasty which successfully brought to an end China's longest period of disunity and laid many of the institutional foundations of the empires that followed; a gifted and brilliant man whose fate it was to bring himself and his empire to spectacular ruin. Second, he has his place in the history of Chinese political thought, as the "bad last" ruler *par excellence,* one in a long sequence of negative exemplars reaching back to Chou Hsin, the last ruler of Shang, and Chieh, the last king of Hsia. In this role he has been stereotyped by the conventions of moralistic history; his personality and behavior have been reduced to a collection of attributes and qualities which later monarchs would do well to study and abjure. Third and last, he figures as a perennial stock villain in folk myth and popular literature—a wretch whose spectacular vices long titillated the readers of fiction and sent thrills of horrified delight through peasant audiences gathered round storytellers and rural dramatic troupes.

These three roles suggest the principal divisions of this paper. First, I shall attempt to sift the evidence and present an interpretation of the historical personality of Yang-ti; a more detailed study will appear at a later date. Second, I shall analyze Yang-ti as the political stereotype of the depraved last ruler. Third, I shall attempt to describe the stock villain, the Yang-ti of popular myth and story.

An undertaking of this kind is beset by many problems. It is not easy to discern historical reality behind the moralistic ornament and evaluative verbiage of Confucian historical writing. To come up (in this instance) with something resembling a human being of the sixth and early seventh century, we must read between the lines, sensing the orthodox historian's subtle suppressions of evidence, some of them conscious, some probably unconscious. Buddhist writings and fragments of unofficial literature help us. So do some of the insights of modern psychology. But the fact remains that the basic source for this period, the *Sui-shu*, was written under the succeeding dynasty of T'ang, which specifically ordered its official historians to record the history of the Sui in such a way as to explain its dramatic fall from the heights of power and unequivocally justify the T'ang succession. The closeness of these historians to the events they recorded made a fair appraisal of the Sui not only difficult but politically dangerous. Yet we should not regard these men as time-serving fabricators of evidence. Two principles of Chinese historiography operated to make their writing of history something far more complex than an opportunistic response to political pressure. One was the historian's obligation to write an accurate account, for only from such an account could posterity learn the lessons of history. The other was the assumption that historical truth, when told, would automatically carry a moral message; when a historian rejected an item that did not support his moral convictions, he felt that he was merely sifting out an item of untruth. It is in histories written from this point of view that we seek the historical personality of Yang-ti.

The political stereotype is easier to discern than the historical personality. The stereotype emerges in the final judgments which the T'ang historians pass on this ruler; it is reiterated in political essays and discussions, in memorials to the throne, in all writings which generalize about the rise and fall of dynasties and about the sorts of men who bring dynasties to ruin. It is fully intelligible only when placed within the traditional characterology of the bad last ruler. We shall attempt to see the stereotype within that context.

The popular figure can be built up out of the tales and stories which have been read and drawn on from the early T'ang until yesterday. Here too some attention must be paid to the literary conventions which governed the formation of the type. What did a popular audience expect of its villains, especially of its imperial villains? Was the purpose in presenting Yang-ti as villain wholly to entertain or partly for moral instruction? Further, we must recognize that the purpose in various literary presentations varied with the changing times and the shifting outlook of various writers.

When we have seen something of these three avatars of Yang-ti, we may ask what the relations among them were. What can we say about the relation of political stereotype to historical personality? Did the political stereotype—the particular property of the literate elite—

pass over unchanged to become the stock villain of popular tales? Or did the popular figure—or the sources for its portrayal—influence the work of the historians and moralists? These questions bear on the fundamental question of the relations between elite and peasant cultures within Chinese civilization. Perhaps this study may at least help in the exploration of this broader problem.

THE PERSONALITY OF SUI YANG-TI

Yang Kuang, the future Yang-ti, was born in 569, the second son of a twenty-eight-year-old Northern Chou official and his non-Chinese wife. The unexpected and meteoric rise of his father, who proclaimed himself emperor of a new dynasty in 581, need not be described here,[1] except in terms of its probable effects on the formation of the child's character. In the first place the Yang family came suddenly to imperial power in a time of great tension and uncertainty, emerging through a nightmare sequence of murder, treachery, and intrigue. They were uneasy of their imperial honors, fearful lest a sudden turn of fortune's wheel should displace them, suspicious of old friends and trusted advisers, avid of supernatural reassurances from all sources: Buddhist monks, Taoist adepts, sycophantic courtiers. Perhaps more important, their rise to power immediately made their children key political pawns in the predatory struggle for power and wealth which went on around the throne.

Their father, burdened by the herculean tasks of reuniting a China that had been culturally and politically divided for nearly three centuries, was wracked by insecurity. On more than one occasion he flew into a rage and beat an official senseless in the throne hall. He regularly sought spiritual solace from Buddhist monks, and was relentless in his demand for favorable portents. He was intensely parsimonious; he would not permit himself or his family to enjoy the luxuries of supreme power lest the gods who had raised them up should jealously strike them down.[2] He threw himself into state affairs, great and small—drudgery which was an anodyne to his fears and his sense of hubris. Further, his dependence on his strong-minded wife—which makes him the most notoriously henpecked emperor in Chinese history—also suggests his basic insecurity. All these traits made him a suspicious, tyrannical, and fickle parent; and none of his defects were offset by the character of his consort.

The Empress Tu-ku was the daughter of a Toba noble who had served the Northern Chou, fallen into disfavor, and been obliged to commit suicide.[3] The future empress saw at first hand the horrors of the Northern Chou court under the mad ruler Yü-wen Pin (among other things, his savagery at one point threatened the life of her daughter). From that time on she was close to her husband at each hazardous stage of his rise to power, and she remained his close confidante until her death in 602. She was in some respects a typical northern woman of the period: harsh, puritanical, a fanatical monogamist, a sharp and economical household manager;[4] she was also meddlesome, vindictive, and insanely jealous. Chao I considers her the most jealous of the palace women of Chinese history.[5] She meddled constantly in her children's affairs, spying upon their private lives, criticizing their extravagance, censuring their habits, intervening whenever she detected any deviation from her rigid standards. Her second son, Yang Kuang, was her darling, the special object of her cloying solicitude, the beneficiary of her jealous intrigues.

These two neurotic parents dominated the youth of the future Yang-ti and of his brothers and sisters. Both parents were devout Buddhists; their children were given Buddhist childhood names (*hsiao-tzu*).[6] Sutra readings took place daily at the palace; the princes all had their clerical mentors, and became patrons of temples or of pious works.[7] The young Yang Kuang, it is said, was handsome, perceptive, impulsively generous to his attendants, fond of study, and good at literary composition.[8] Although this description smacks of the biographical cliché, Yang Kuang did indeed display an impressive literary virtuosity in later life, and something of the other qualities as well. We know nothing of his early reading or intellectual interests, but we may infer from his later writings that he developed a wide acquaintance with Chinese literature and Buddhist scriptures.

His political apprenticeship began early in 581 when, at the age of twelve, he was made Prince of Chin and governor of Ping-chou—a post with general responsibility for the defense of the northern frontier.[9] His father appointed trusted older men to guide the young prince. In the same year the emperor sought a bride for him among the royal princesses of the small southern satellite state of Liang.[10] The oracles dictated the choice, but the young prince was married to a woman he came to love and respect. She is said to have been studious, literary, and of compliant disposition, and to have been esteemed by her father-in-law the emperor.

This marriage to a southern princess was perhaps Yang Kuang's first introduction to the culture of South China. Nature and history had combined, by the last quarter of the sixth century, to produce a culture south of the Yangtse which was strikingly different from that of the north. The land was green and beautiful, the climate benign; living was easier than it was in the dry plains of the north. The Chinese who had settled there in the centuries of disunion had developed a way of life which was more leisurely, more elegant, and more sensuous than the life of the north under its succession of barbarian overlords.[11] And despite centuries of political weakness and ineptitude, the southern dynasties claimed "legitimate" descent from the great Empire of Han and proprietorship of all the orthodox traditions in literature, music, and the arts. The culture of the south proved irresistibly attractive to Yang Kuang—the son of parents whose values and manners epitomized the harsh uncouth culture of the north. Yang Kuang's fondness for southerners and southern ways later became almost an obsession, very like the perennial Northern European infatuation with the culture of the Mediterranean world.[12]

Like some of the Germanic rulers he resembled, he participated in the conquest of the region he had come to love. In 589 he moved in a command position with the Sui forces toward the long-planned conquest of the Ch'en, the last of the "legitimate" dynasties of the south. So far as we know, this was the prince's first trip into the Yangtse valley and below; it may well have had a strong influence on the development of his character and his policies. When the Ch'en empire fell to the northern invaders, the tasks to be faced were formidable: first, military occupation and pacification; second, the integration of the southern areas and populations into the new ecumenical empire of Sui. In 591 the young prince succeeded his brother Chün as viceroy of the south, with his capital at Yang-chou.[13] There he began the work of mollifying southern opinion, of governmental reorganization—of, in short, making the rich areas of the south an integral part of the Sui empire—an enterprise which was to occupy him for the next nine years.

One of his first acts as viceroy was to summon to his capital Chih-i, the founder of the T'ien-t'ai sect and the outstanding southern Buddhist leader of the time. There, on December 14, 591, in the midst of a splendid assembly of monks, the young prince knelt to receive from the great monk the "Bodhisattva vows" for lay Buddhists, and the religious name of Ts'ung-chih p'u-sa, "Bodhisattva of Absolute Control."[14] In Yang Kuang's continuing relations with Chih-i and the clerical communities of the south, strands of personal and political interest on both sides are interwoven with religious feelings and aspirations. The prince, as the representative of Sui power, was interested in reassuring southern Buddhists, both lay and clerical, who had recently been loyal subjects of the old Ch'en dynasty. As I have shown elsewhere, it was Sui policy to use Buddhism to knit together the long divergent polities and societies of north and south; the viceroy's acts were consistent with that policy. The southern clerics, for their part, saw in the prince a powerful patron and a rising political figure whose favor might be of long-term importance for their faith.

Yang Kuang became the donor and patron of temples and shrines, the sponsor of innumerable pious projects. His discipleship to Chih-i and his successors at T'ien-t'ai is fully recorded in the pages of the *Kuo-ch'ing Pai-lu*. Through the ornate rhetoric of these documents glimmers something of Yang Kuang's Buddhist faith. He appears to have been widely read in Buddhist literature, and particularly versed in the Lotus sutra; he was committed to the Mahayana vision of salvation and to the T'ien-t'ai interpretation of it. He recognized the deep conflict between Buddhist religious ideals and the exercise of power in a worldly kingdom. At the same time he could visualize himself as a Buddhist ruler, commanding the reverence and loyalty of all the Buddhists of the realm. When his master presented him with a Bodhisattva chaplet, he wrote in his letter of thanks:

As to the making of the present chaplet, its conception appears to be derived from divine will, and its design is comparable to a work of Maudgāl-yayāna. The wonder of its workmanship excels the artistry of the mason of Ying. . . . A chaplet does honor to the wearer. With formal solemnity, I fitted it to my head; kneeling to receive it, I wore it upon my head. As I looked in a hand mirror, and walked back and forth, it seemed to flatter my homely face; adding grace, it changed my appearance. . . .[15]

He goes on in this letter and elsewhere in these documents to pledge himself to uphold and spread the teachings of Buddha both in private life and in the exercise of power. In all these expressions, there is a mixture of sentiment and calculation: sincere religious feelings linked to a deep self-love; a genuine regard for the great cleric who was his master compounded with a desire to win over southern Buddhists and demonstrate his religious zeal for the benefit of his pious parents.

His tenure as viceroy was thus a period of deepening association with Buddhism. But he by no means neglected the southern traditions of Confucianism and Taoism. He drew to his southern capital representatives of both and displayed himself as an impartial patron of all the best in the culture of the south.[16] These years as viceroy undoubtedly strengthened his ties with the south and with southerners; many of the palace confidants of his viceregal days accompanied him to Ch'ang-an when he became crown prince and then emperor, and the official appointments of his reign—as well as his later preference for southern generals—may be explained in part by the alliances that he formed in these years.

While he must have given close attention to the immense work of reconstruction and reorganization which ultimately transformed the south into a productive and loyal part of the Sui empire, he did not neglect his relations with his parents in Ch'ang-an. It is said that when he went to take leave of his mother just before starting for his new post in 591, he found her in a rage at the extra-marital activities of the crown prince, whom she suspected of poisoning his consort; and that she became maudlin over her favorite son's departure for a distant post. This interview, say the chroniclers, left Yang Kuang with the impression that it would be possible to eliminate his elder brother and replace him as crown prince.[17] In the distant south he could live as he pleased, far from his parents' suspicious prying. And, in his frequent visits back to report to the emperor, he was a model of pious and proper deportment. His earnest patronage of Buddhism in the south, his devotion to the noted cleric Chih-i, his many public wishes for the well-being of his parents, his frugal and decorous behavior in Ch'ang-an, all served to ingratiate him further with the emperor and empress.

It is hard to say just what touched off Yang Kuang's imperial ambitions. The environment in which he grew up, the adulation of his mother, the self-serving flattery of his courtiers whose fortunes were tied to their master's, all were calculated to induce an inflated view of himself and his destiny. From his success as a viceroy he may have concluded that no one could be better qualified to carry on the dynasty his father had founded. His ambition was certainly fed by the flattery and prognostications of the learned and pious men who graced his viceregal court; after all, the testament of the great Chih-i had placed in him the hope of a vast, peaceful Buddhist state; had he not seen himself in a mirror wearing the divine chaplet of a Bodhisattva sent him by his master?[18] Moreover, his actual prospects were grim; an able and popular imperial prince had a very limited life expectancy once an elder brother succeeded to the throne, and the alternative to liquidation-through-intrigue was civil war.

It seems clear that he saw himself as a man endowed with unusual gifts, a man with proven military and administrative abilities, a man of culture who could knit together with understanding the north from which he came and the south which he had come to love; and above all as a man of imagination and vision—not a prudent bureaucratic drone like his father—who could expand and glorify the Sui until the imperial name echoed throughout the known world. It is a measure of his ambitions that he likened himself to the great and ruthless Han Wu-ti (ruled 140–87 B.C.), who brought his dynasty to the zenith of power in eastern Asia. Such a self-image explains many of the steps and stratagems in Yang Kuang's pursuit of power. His artistic sensibility and imagination are clues to both the strengths and the weaknesses of his imperial policies. Lasswell, in discussing *homo politicus*, says, "Indeed, self-deception is perhaps the rule, for the political personality with a strong artistic component possesses a florid imagination which dramatizes his personal history and subordinates all reality to ambitious plans."[19] Yang Kuang's self-image was the product of this sort of imagination, of flattery, and of cumulative successes. It dissolved disastrously under the impact of adversity.

To return to our narrative, the year 600 was a critical one in the life of Yang Kuang's father, the reigning emperor. In July he completed a full sexagenary cycle of life—to his own surprise and that of most of his subjects.[20] But he did survive, and a week after his birthday, his third son Chün was poisoned—an event which caused the father little remorse and possible relief at the disappearance of a potential rival. Late in the year Yang Kuang's long intrigues against Yung, the crown prince, finally bore fruit; Yung was degraded, and he and his family were reduced to the rank of commoners. On December 13 Yang Kuang was proclaimed crown prince, and with the new year, a new era was proclaimed—Jen-shou, "Benevolent Longevity," symbolizing the end of the crisis and the beginning of long years of benevolent rule by the aging emperor.

The new crown prince moved to the capital with his southern wife and entourage. There he built a mansion near the beautiful lake in the southeast corner of the city. Nearby he built the Jih-yen temple and invited there many of the leading southern clerics who had graced the viceregally supported temple in Yang-chou.[21] In his new temple he sponsored sutra readings, Buddhist scholarship, and religious observances. In these years the emperor and empress became ever more deeply involved in Buddhist activities, and it was necessary for the crown prince to make seemly displays of piety. The vow he made about this time to give a maigre feast for one thousand monks at Mount T'ien-t'ai contains passages which are blatant flattery of his parents:

Your disciple has happily been able to rely on a most fortunate destiny . . . I was born in a Buddhist family. The Emperor and Empress instructed me in the womb with kindness and benevolence. They are possessed of the love which Candrākadīpa showed to his eight royal sons, of the stimulating power for goodness which Mahābhijñā Jnānābhibhu manifested to his sixteen śrāmanera sons. . . .[22]

After Yang Kuang became crown prince, his father increasingly depended on him for the conduct of state affairs. The chronicles say that whenever the old man went to his summer palace to escape the heat, he ordered the crown prince to take charge.[23] In September of 602, the empress died; Yang Kuang had lost his most consistent partisan supporter, the emperor his lifelong confidante. The filial and dutiful crown prince ordered the monks of his Jih-yen temple to hold special services in her memory.[24] A late source says that the prince publicly showed unbearable grief at his mother's death but privately ate, drank, and joked as usual.[25] Here is the hypocritical, unfilial ingrate painted by the moralistic historians of later times (see below), a picture to be viewed with skepticism.

On January 27, 603, the emperor degraded his fourth son on evidence of black magic manufactured by Yang Kuang's henchmen. Another potential rival was out of the way, and Yang Kuang was drawing nearer to the imperial position. In the summer of 604 the emperor fell ill, and Yang Kuang's moment was at hand. The "Annals" of the *Sui-shu* baldly state that the emperor died and the prince succeeded to the imperial position in the Jen-shou palace,[26] but several biographies hint at dark intrigues.[27] The emperor's favorite, the lady Hsüan-hua of the defunct Ch'en ruling house, reported to the dying emperor that the crown prince had improperly accosted her. The old man rallied, it is said, and sent an order summoning the deposed crown prince Yung, presumably with the idea of reinstating him; but Yang Kuang and his henchman Yang Su intercepted the message. At that point another of Yang Kuang's men, Chang Heng, entered the sickroom and ordered the lady Hsüan-hua and the other attendants to leave the room. Shortly thereafter they heard that the emperor had died. The palace attendants were suspicious of foul play and feared for their lives. Yang Kuang continued his pursuit of the lady Hsüan-hua and used the collective fears of the palace attendants to force her to submit to him. That night he had his way with her.

We can never know the truth; we can only judge the extent to which these alleged acts fit in with our other information on Yang Kuang's behavior. Clearly this behavior suggests the belated resolution of an Oedipus complex. Do we find other symptoms of such a complex in other known behavior of Yang Kuang? Again, is the forcing of a daughter of the defunct "legitimate" dynasty of Ch'en to be interpreted, as Balazs has suggested, as supercompensation for the northern prince's feeling of social and cultural inferiority?[28] To take the second question first, I think not. I have suggested that Yang Kuang's emotional identification with the south sprang in part from his disgust with the uncouth and overbearing ways of his parents. If this is correct, there is something to be said for the oedipal interpretation. Moreover, it seems more than likely that Yang Kuang resented his father. He was his mother's adored favorite. He clandestinely and later openly cultivated habits of the sort his father despised: sensuous indulgence, high living, aesthetic pleasures. And in many of his policies he reversed his father's altogether: for example, his tolerance of Confucianism, his political favoring of southerners over northerners, his development of imaginative and often extravagant plans for the glorification of the dynasty at home and abroad. Our evidence is incomplete, but what we do know suggests the possibility of an oedipal drive.

Yang Kuang ascended the throne as Yang-ti of the Sui on August 21, 604. In discussing the events of his reign, we shall be concerned only with those which shed light on the development and disintegration of Yang-ti's personality. Immediately on his accession he took steps to rehabilitate Confucian education and to set up an examination system.[29] In doing this he reversed his father's harsh anti-Confucian measures of the year 601, but spiting his father was far from being his main motive. He had, rather, two political purposes, both designed to broaden and strengthen the basis of imperial power. One was to curb the power of the great entrenched northern—particularly northwestern—families on whom his father had almost exclusively depended. The other was a corollary: to enfranchise the southern gentry and the gentry of the northeast, whose scholarly traditions would favor them in an examination system.[30] The total effect would be to redress the balance of power between northerners and southerners—also between those of non-Chinese and those of Chinese stock—and assure the emperor of a wider and more diversified pool of competent officials. There is preliminary evidence that there was a trend toward this diversification during Yang-ti's reign.[31] With Yang-ti Buddhism continued to contribute to both the miranda and the credenda of state and dynasty, but Confucianism was revived as the body of knowledge whose acquisition gave access to power.

Another measure early in the new reign was the building of an eastern capital at Loyang. The city had been a Han capital, later became one of the capitals of the Western Chin, and was to be the eastern capital of the T'ang; it was culturally important and a significant center of trade; and it had been, as recently as the period 494–577, the political and military hub of the rich and populous east China area. Moreover, it was distant from the estates of the northwestern gentry whose power Yang-ti was seeking to curb, and more accessible than Ch'ang-an to the east China gentry and the southerners whom Yang-ti favored. There were, therefore, sound reasons for Yang-ti's desire to build here a new and magnificent capital which would be a symbol and a center of Sui power.[32] He proceeded to recruit corvée labor—even as his father had done for the construction of his new capital at Ch'ang-an, and the building of the city, the palaces, and the imperial parks was completed at high speed. The *Sui-shu* tells us that four or five laborers out of ten died under the intense pressure of the work,[33] a result of the emperor's impatience to occupy his new and impressive capital.

The greatest of the new emperor's building projects was the improvement and extension of the canal system which his father had begun to link together the new empire. The southward extension from the new eastern capital at Loyang to a point near the head of Hang-chow bay was the most ambitious part of the project, though much of the route utilized natural watercourses. Again masses of corvée labor were used, and by 605 the emperor was able to make a progress by barge to Chiang-tu (Yang-chou), his "Yangtse capital," where he had long served as viceroy. The spectacular luxury of the imperial flotilla is roundly denounced by the moralists and lovingly embroidered by the storytellers, but this and subsequent progresses were, as Balazs has pointed out, sound political acts. They were demonstrations of Sui power and wealth along a waterway which served to link together the long disunited areas of north and south;[34] they were tangible evidence of the ruler's concern for the recently incorporated southern areas whose culture and people he found so appealing. And, as the T'ang use of these canals was to show, they were vital links between the economically expanding south and the seats of political power in the north. In building them Yang-ti displayed what appears to us to be remarkable political and economic vision. But Confucian historians of later years—interested only in a stable, balanced agrarian economy—saw all Yang-ti's building projects as acts of vainglorious profligacy, a reckless and pointless ravaging of the full treasury and the bulging granaries left by his father. Here, as in so many other cases in Chinese history, policies necessary to the vigorous and expansive exercise of imperial power are condemned by gentry officialdom as violations of their principles and their interests.

In 607 Yang-ti turned to another of the classic concerns of vigorous Chinese rulers: the western and northern frontiers. He began to open up contact with the peoples of Central Asia, and followed up his first overtures by sending out military expeditions, establishing military colonies, and asserting political power among the leaders of steppe tribes. Thus was developed a costly "full forward" policy along the steppe frontiers, designed to free the empire of the barbarian incursions which had plagued the preceding reign. Another frontier measure was the reconstruction of the Great Wall, a common move in the early years of a new dynasty. The chroniclers of Yang-ti's reign dolefully report that of the million laborers conscripted for this work, more than half died.[35] Despite the appalling human costs of all these programs of building and expansion, each one was well calculated to assert and solidify the power of the dynasty.

The attempt to bring the kingdom of Koguryō (northern Manchuria and northern Korea) to full submission was, of course, the beginning of Yang-ti's downfall. Yet it was not an altogether foolish project: a dynasty bent on expansion clearly could not tolerate a threatened subversive alliance between the king of Koguryō and the Eastern Turks—an alliance which would have menaced all the northern marches and routes of trade. Yang-ti planned his expedition against Koguryō with great care and led his armies to initial victories in the valley of the Liao River. It was no doubt in the hopeful summer months of 612 that Yang-ti composed this poem celebrating the campaign:

> East of the Liao, north of the Sea, we will kill the monstrous beast,
> And the wind-driven clouds are clearing for ten thousand *li*.
> Now we should smelt down our weapons, disperse our horses and cattle,
> And return in triumph to feast in the ancient capital.
> Those in front will sing, those behind will dance, rousing our martial ardor,
> And with libations in the ancestral hall we shall doff our warrior's garb.
> Would anyone judge that we have vainly marched ten thousand *li* away
> Or returned empty-handed to the five plains?[36]

Yet the autumn came without success, and the unhappy ruler returned to his capital, not for a triumph, but to deal with serious economic and political difficulties. Perhaps at this point he should have given up the effort to chastise Koguryō and concentrated wholly on relieving the mounting distress within the empire, but such a move would have been out of character for this ambitious, imaginative, and supremely egotistical monarch. He now needed success to rehabilitate his reputation and his self-esteem. Twice more he imposed special tax levies, raised conscripts, commandeered supplies, and marched to the northeast. In the course of the third campaign, which ended in the autumn of 614, rebellions broke out all over the empire, and Yang-ti's regime was in dire straits.[37]

Under the impact of these disasters and of a narrow escape from capture by the Eastern Turks in the autumn of 615 the emperor's personality disintegrated. His judgment and decisiveness deserted him. He expressed his frustration in murderous rages against his advisers, in orgies of self-pity, in sensuous indulgence, and finally in a last burst of extravagant display: the ordering of a new imperial flotilla in 616. He turned his back on problems he now found too great to solve, left Ch'ang-an for Loyang, and shortly thereafter sailed in splendor down the canal to his beloved Yang-chou.

Through the year 617 the emperor watched the country sink into civil war, as rival claimants to the succession arose throughout the land. He was haunted by dreams, wracked by fears of impending doom, and filled with the bitterness of defeat. There is no evidence that his Buddhist faith helped reconcile him to the loss of his worldly kingdom or caused him to question his lifelong pursuit of power and glory. Even the soft beauty of spring in his lovely Yangtse capital no longer had its old power to please and comfort him. Everything spoke with the voice of doom. In the spring of 618, he wrote this poem:

> I seek to return but cannot get away.
> When, in sober fact, I face such a spring as this,
> The songs of the birds spur on our toasting,
> But the plum blossoms make mock of our company.[38]

In this same tragic spring the poet-emperor was murdered and his empire passed to the rising house of T'ang. Yet, as we shall see in the following sections, the death of this man was but the beginning of the two other lives he was to have: as a political stereotype and as a figure in popular mythology.

SUI YANG-TI AS A POLITICAL STEREOTYPE

The transmutation of the historical personality of Yang-ti into a political stereotype may be considered under several aspects. First, it is the work of historians, moralists, political thinkers, and officials motivated by various conscious and unconscious drives. They viewed the past as a rich repository of experience, as a collection of situations whose causes, configurations, and effects would serve the living as a guide to action; they viewed the past also as a continuum within which certain moral principles operated, permanent and universal principles laid down by the sages. The past could only teach its lessons if the moral dynamics of history were pointed out, abstracted from the manifold of events, hammered home by argument and illustration. One of the most persuasive ways to present such lessons was to exemplify in certain historical figures the virtues or vices which governed the course of human events.

In doing this the tendency was to paint in black and white, to strip the subject of all characteristics that blurred the positive or negative image, to portray events as a simple continuum in which the subject's basic personal qualities were decisive.

Other factors also helped shape the image, notably literary and historiographical conventions and existing historical stereotypes. By Yang-ti's time, Chinese history numbered half a dozen or more rulers—

from the remote last ruler of the Hsia to the last emperor of the Ch'en—
dead but a decade or so—whose fatefully evil behavior had already been
abstracted from the record and related to simplified versions of the
path to political disaster. These figures were described in metaphor
and allusions which linked the earlier and later figures together in a
single literary nexus. When the historians of the early T'ang set to work
on Yang-ti, the fall of the Ch'en and the character of its last ruler had
been shaped to the established pattern in the memory of living men.

Finally, as we have seen, there were specific political pressures
upon the early T'ang historians that affected the ultimate stereotyping
of Yang-ti. At the inception of most new dynasties there is an urgent
need to find sanctions, to formulate an ideology in support of the regime.
And one of the time-honored ways of sanctioning a new dynasty is to
write a history of the defunct regime, showing it to be corrupt, in-
effectual, and tyrannical, a rule whose disruptions of the interrelated
natural and human orders has produced signs of Heaven's displeasure,
of Heaven's wish to see the political mandate pass to another house.

Early T'ang historians shared with their imperial masters a deep
interest in explaining the fall of the Sui in such a way as to justify its
displacement by the T'ang. Discussions between the Emperor T'ai-
tsung and Wei Cheng, the head of the commission for the compilation
of the Sui history, reveal this common interest and suggest the political
atmosphere in which the historian worked. In a memorial of 636 Wei
Cheng presented a rousing indictment of the iniquities of Yang-ti and
sounded many of the notes that we shall find reiterated in the histories;
he followed the indictment with a strikingly contrasted picture of the
wise beneficence of the new dynasty.[39] On another occasion Wei Cheng
gave a still more impassioned denunciation of Yang-ti, and the emperor
reminded his official that some of the blame for the Sui's iniquities
devolved upon its ministers who failed in their duty to remonstrate.[40]
This interchange again suggests the tension that existed in the historian's
task: paint the last ruler in darkest hues, for a last ruler must have been
immoral, and his immorality sanctions the new dynasty; but do not go
so far as to distort history and destroy its didactic value.

In sum, the stereotyping process was constrained by a historical
tradition which approved a stress on the moral dynamic in human affairs
but disapproved the fabrication and distortion of evidence. It was
molded by a millenial political myth which stressed the quintessential
virtue or vice of a ruler as a prime historical force. It was stimulated
by the immediate demands of a regime which required both historical
and moral justification.

Perhaps before turning to an analysis of the growth of the Yang-ti stereotype, we should ask what sort of a class bias influenced those who developed it. Clearly the power and material interests of the gentry-literati had been favored by many of Yang-ti's policies: the reinstitution of the examination system, the revival of the Confucian curriculum,[41] the building of a new capital that was geographically more accessible to the sons of educated families. Thus he was negatively judged and ultimately stereotyped by those whose class interests he had favored. In seeking to explain this apparent anomaly, we would refer to a theme that has become increasingly clear in recent studies: the endemic tension between monarchy and bureaucracy. The gentry-literati needed the monarchy, and the monarchy was dependent on skills which the gentry-literati alone possessed. Yet in ethos the two were perenially at odds. The prudential economic thought of the gentry clashed with the more expansive ideas of a vigorous monarch; the gentry were bitterly critical of the pomp and display by which the monarchy asserted the power and greatness of the dynasty; the court always seemed to gentry families flamboyant and improvident, always tainted with immorality, always at odds with the gentry's ideal of a frugal, wise, judicious and self-denying exercise of kingly power. These and related attitudes constitute the class bias of the interpretations we shall consider.

Traditional Characterology of a Bad Ruler

It may help us to understand the force of traditional models in the stereotyping of Yang-ti if we consider some earlier representatives of the type. One of the earliest and most important of these was Chou Hsin, the last ruler of the Shang, which was traditionally brought down by the virtuous house of Chou in the twelfth century B.C.[42] In most respects the stereotype finds its complete expression in this early exemplar. The accompanying paradigm of the behavioral attributes of Chou Hsin can serve as a basis for the analysis of later figures in the same sequence, including Yang-ti.

The vices presented in this outline have, of course, ramifying relationships to other Chinese values and attitudes. These vices are also interrelated, sometimes in an obvious fashion, sometimes more subtly. For example, the ruler's desire for conspicuous consumption and extravagant construction works is often stimulated by his favorite and opposed by an "upright minister" who gives a lecture on the frugality and prudence of ancient sage kings, the suffering of the people and its probable consequences, etc. The upright minister is promptly and cruelly executed for his pains, and a vicious sycophant replaces him. In such a sequence the characteristics we have numbered A,1,2,3, B,2,3, and C,5 are all closely linked in something like a causal nexus whose

STEREOTYPE OF THE BAD-LAST RULER

Shu-ching and *Shih-chi* references for the stereotype of Chou Hsin*

	Shu-ching	Shih-chi
A. Tyranny (the abuse of supreme political power)		
1. Neglect or abuse of upright officials	284, 285 291, 295 303	201–2
2. Favoritism toward sycophants and corrupt officials	303, 468 513	203
3. Callousness toward the suffering of the masses	468	200–201
(a) Unreasonable and unseasonable exactions of taxes and labor		
(b) Harsh laws and cruel punishments	284	201
(c) The flouting of good laws	295	
B. Self-indulgence (unrestrained use of supreme power and wealth for self-gratification)		
1. Drunkenness	471	199
2. Passion for rare and expensive goods: clothing, food, etc.		200
3. Elaborate and extravagant construction: palaces, pleasure pavilions, gardens, carriages, boats, etc.	284	
4. Pleasure before work, sloth	468, 513	199
C. Licentiousness (sex-linked behavior of disapproved kinds)		
1. Lust, sexual overindulgence	284	199
2. Orgies, "unnatural" sex acts		200
3. Sadism	285	
4. Promotion of lascivious music		200
5. Blind infatuation with a favorite	295	199
D. Lack of personal virtue (i.e., flouting of established norms of interpersonal relations and of retions with supernatural powers)		
1. Unfilial behavior	294	
2. Unbrotherly behavior	294	
3. Improper conduct toward wife	294	
4. Improper treatment of paternal and maternal relatives	303	
5. Lack of ceremonial respect to Heaven, the spirits, and ancestors	286, 295 303	204–5
6. Addiction to sorcery and "heretical" religious practices		

* The page numbers in the right-hand columns are first to James Legge, *The Chinese Classics*, Vol. II, and second to Edouard Chavannes, *Les Mémoires historiques de Se-ma Ts'ien*, Vol. I. A few subheadings have been added for vices that are not specified but implied.

starting point is a sort of undifferentiated "badness" of character in the ruler. To take another example, licentiousness (C) leads to absorption in pleasure and neglect of duty (B,4) and also to the trespasses numbered D,1–4; sometimes the upright remonstrator protests the licentious conduct of his master and is killed (A,1).

The weight given to licentiousness as a dynamic in the process of personal and dynastic ruin might seem to the historian of the West—or of the Middle East—to be somewhat excessive. Fully to explain this weighting would take us far afield, but the traditional Chinese view of sex helps us to understand it. Sexual intercourse is approved for procreation only. The sexually demanding woman is believed to sap the vitality of the male. Male energy, whether physical or intellectual, is dissipated by sexual indulgence; the male becomes depleted and unfit to play his role in life.[43] Thus, in the case of a ruler, sexual overindulgence undermines his moral stamina, his judgment in state affairs, his ability to perform all the complex ritual and practical duties of his exalted office. His position entitles him to take his pleasure with the most attractive women of the empire, but in the stereotype, he is usually the victim of a *femme fatale*—an unprincipled and demanding favorite who lures and seduces him to the utter depletion of his energies. She is in many ways the analogue of the "fox women" of the popular stories who lure men to their ruin. It is the duty of the righteous succeeding regime to execute her, and this is usually a part of the story.

It will be noted in our outline that nearly all the evil characteristics of Chou Hsin which appear in the *Shu-ching* are found in Ssu-ma Ch'ien's account of the fall of the Shang. There is a sharp contrast, however, in the tone of the two characterizations. The *Shu-ching* documents, whatever their varying dates may be, reflect in their colorful rhetoric the urgent need of the Chou to justify itself; Ssu-ma Ch'ien is far enough from the events to adopt the sober circumstantial moralizing tone which dominates the standard histories which were to follow.

The historians of the Han were not agreed on how to interpret the fall of the unifying empire of Ch'in, to whose drastic measures of centralization and reorganization the Han owed so much. They were somewhat awed by Ch'in Shih Huang-ti's accomplishments, though they found his cruelty, ruthlessness, and anti-traditionalism abhorrent.[44] Ssu-ma Ch'ien and Chia I placed much of the blame for bringing the empire to ruin on literally the *last* ruler, Prince Tzu-ying, who held the shadow of power against a host of enemies for a mere three months. This view was attacked by Pan Ku, at the invitation of the Emperor Hsiao-ming (reigned A.D. 58–75). Pan Ku accepts what he says is a widespread tradition that Ch'in Shih Huang-ti was the instigator of all the evils, but that Erh-shih Huang-ti carried them to extremes. For all this lack of agreement, the picture of the second—and last effective ruler—of the Ch'in which emerges from the *Shih-chi* is presented within the conventions of the traditional characterology of the bad-last ruler. It is his misdeeds that reduce the Ch'in empire to ruin. Erh-shih Huang-ti is explicitly credited with all the defects under heading A in our outline, and with all the ones under B except drunkenness and sloth. Derelictions under C are implied but not specified, and the absence of the favorite, the *femme fatale*, is notable. Category D is represented by unbrotherly behavior and by failure to respect the ancestral altars.[45]

Perhaps the most striking thing about this characterization is that the regimes of two totalitarian monarchs—new in Chinese history—added no new categories to the characterology in the *Shu-ching*. This suggests that the relative effectiveness of institutional means for the realization of evil designs is of little weight in the allocation of blame.

We now pass over some seven hundred years and consider a ruler who was transmuted into a bad-last stereotype by the Sui dynasty itself: the last emperor of the Ch'en, whose dynasty was extinguished by the Sui in its conquest of the south in 589. In the spring of 588, the Sui emperor issued an edict specifying twenty crimes committed by the Ch'en ruler. Then, as part of his "psychwar" preparation for the attack on the south, he ordered 300,000 copies made and broadcast throughout the area south of the Yangtse.[46] Three aspects of this move are of interest to us here. First, despite the extensive use which the early Sui made of Buddhism to provide sanctions for their regime, the content of this communication is wholly within the Confucian tradition; this suggests that this tradition continued to provide the ideology of political transition even in a dominantly Buddhist age. Second, it is important to note that the northerners, despite their mixed culture and the thinness of their Confucian learning, recognized the usefulness of this segment of the Confucian tradition for accomplishing their ends. Third, the mass propaganda use of the edict indicates that the Sui leadership believed that the traditional arguments would be accepted by large elements of the southern population—not proof, perhaps, but surely presumptive evidence that the tradition was widely accepted. Finally, we note with interest that the characterology of bad-last rulers was not wholly the work of historians working after the fact but played a role in actual political-ideological struggle.

The Sui denunciation gives the Ch'en ruler nearly all the characteristics specified in our outline. He executes the worthy and those who speak truthfully (A,1). The worthies fly into hiding while the mean get their way (A,1,2). Soldiers are forced to manual labor in hunger and cold; his levies of all kinds are unceasing and even fall on women and children (A,3a). He extinguishes blameless families; he uses the punishment of slicing and cruelly exterminates the good and the talented (A,3b). His flouting of all good laws and established mores (A,3c) is clearly implied throughout. There is drunkenness in the women's apartments, and drinking which turns the day into night, i.e., the days are spent sleeping off the excesses of the night (B,1). There is limitless indulgence in jeweled clothing and costly foods (B,2). He ruthlessly uses forced levies to build his palaces, and work never stops (B,3). He pursues his pleasures night and day; from dawn to dusk he attends to no business of state (B,4). His concubines are numbered in the tens of thousands (C,1). He cuts out men's livers and drains off their blood (C,3). His drinking bouts are accompanied by lascivious music (C,4). His blind infatuation with a single favorite does not figure in this document, but the *femme fatale* is identified in the course of the Sui conquest, and despite Yang Kuang's wish to have her for his harem, the stern Kao Chiung has her executed, citing the precedent that King Wu of the Chou executed the favorite of the last Shang king.[47] We find no specific details on the Ch'en emperor's lack of familial virtues, but he outrages heaven with his evil deeds and worships demons to seek their help (D,5,6), and the graves of the dead are violated (D,5). In heaven and earth, in the world of beasts and of men, there are monstrous occurrences which testify to his neglect of the proper observances; he is wildly contumacious toward the five elements and insolently ignores the three principles of heaven, earth, and man.[48]

The attribution to the last ruler of the Ch'en of most of the elements of the traditional characterology of the "bad last" ruler demonstrates its continuing vitality in the Sui period. Yet it is interesting to note that the Sui were not so carried away by their rhetoric as to execute this "monster," who was comfortably pensioned off. Nor did this portrait long survive the ideological demands that had given rise to it. By the time the Ch'en history was in final form, the T'ang had succeeded the Sui, and its historians were not interested in blackening the character of a ruler who had been overwhelmed by the Sui conquest.[49]

Yang-ti as Stereotype

These examples may have suggested the conventions within which the historical Yang-ti was transmuted into a stereotype. It remains for us to consider how this was done. The first and authoritative transmutation was accomplished by the authors of the *Sui-shu* writing, as we have seen, under the pressure of the new T'ang ruling house. Let us first see how the complexity of Yang-ti's character and the momentous events of his reign were simplified and moralized in the three summations of these events in the *Sui-shu* (here referred to as texts I, II, and III).[50] The letter and number combinations below once again refer to our outline of the stereotype.

Category A is amply filled out by the authors of the *Sui-shu*. A,1: "He dismissed remonstrating officials in order to conceal his faults"; "He slaughtered the loyal and the good" (I). "He became estranged from his brave officers in the field and was suspicious of the loyal and the good at court" (II). Category A,2 is mentioned or implied in many passages: "Cunning officials exploited the people so that they could find no way to live" (I). A,3,a: "The army standards stretched out for ten thousand *li*; the tax levies became ever more numerous"; "The disgruntled soldiery was urged on again and again, and construction work never ceased" (I). A,3,b and A,3,c: "Those who received gifts from him were not aware of their merit; those who were killed by him did not know what their crime was" (I). "Then he took harsh measures to harass the people; he made punishments more severe therewith to threaten the people; he used troops and brute force to control them" (I).

The general theme of self-indulgence (B) is presented as a corollary of an immense vanity, an insatiable lust for self-glorification. Describing the last doomed court at Yang-chou, the historians say, "No one gave a thought to the uprisings; they flapped their silly wings and played out their long night revelries" (I). Elsewhere in the *Sui-shu* we are given a picture of Yang-ti at the end as a maudlin drunk,[51] but in the appraisals we are considering, drunkenness (B,1) is relatively unstressed. The passion for rare and expensive goods (B,2) is only hinted at. Naturally, Yang-ti's elaborate construction work, B,3, is fully stressed. "Construction work was unceasing" (I). "Thus he ordered canals dug and roads built; the former were shaded by willow trees and the latter decorated with gilded arms . . . Mountains were cut open and valleys filled up. Boats sailed on the canals to the sea. The people's resources were exhausted, and there was no limit to the corvée and frontier military service" (II). The theme of "pleasure before work," Category B,4, is brought in only in connection with the last years of the dynasty: the accusation is not that Yang-ti was slothful but that his vanity produced a frenetic energy which drove him and his regime to undertakings which were beyond their resources.

Category C, "Licentiousness," is rather understressed. "He wantonly indulged in licentiousness," and did so clandestinely so as to keep his mother's favor (I). But we find no reference to orgies, unnatural sex acts, sadism, or lascivious music (C,2,3,4), and no *femme fatale*.

Category D, the flouting of established norms of relations with men and gods, is far less elaborated for Yang-ti than for earlier stereotypes. "He slaughtered his blood relatives" (I) serves to suggest defects D,1,2,4, but given the strong suspicion of patricide and connivance in fratricide in the historical accounts themselves, this range of vices is rather strikingly understressed. On the other hand, text III achieves the ultimate simplification of the Sui collapse by attributing it to Yang-ti's loss of virtue: "One man lost virtue, and the world collapsed into ruin." It is also said that "his teaching violated the four cardinal virtues [propriety, righteousness, integrity, morality]," but there is no mention whatever of D,5 or D,6. (The record shows that he maintained in fact a full ceremonial calendar.) Again he is not accused of addiction to sorcery or "heretical" religious practices (D,6).

Thus the T'ang historians lay particular stress on Yang-ti's tyranny and self-indulgence as factors in the downfall of the Sui and only touch on the other two principal categories of our outline. In fact, their appraisal, in deviating significantly from the traditional stereotype, is occasionally close to the conclusions which a modern rationalistic historian might reach; certainly this appraisal is far more "rational" than the historical estimates of earlier bad-last rulers.

Nonetheless, the writers of the *Sui-shu* explicitly fit Yang-ti into the tradition of bad-last rulers. Note in the following passage from text II the favorable estimates of the two fathers which serve to emphasize the vice and folly of the two sons:

As to the Sui dynasty's achievements and shortcomings, its preservation and destruction, these are generally analogous to those of the Ch'in. Shih-huang [of the Ch'in] unified the country; so did Kao-tsu [Sui Wen-ti]. Erh-shih [of the Ch'in] tyrannically used force and harsh punishments. Yang-ti wantonly indulged in malevolent cruelty. In both cases their ruin began with the uprisings of rebels, and they lost their lives at the hands of commoners. From beginning to end, they are as alike as the two halves of a tally.

This is an excellent example of the way all the variations and differences, all the special features of a given regime, can be disregarded in the interests of making a didactic moral point. Clearly, throughout all these estimates, we see a tension—a conflict—between the urge toward moralistic simplification within the traditional characterology and the demands of specific historical data. The conflict is not resolved in these estimates, and they are thus made up of two distinguishable strata—one produced by the first urge and the other molded by historical knowledge.

In another respect the authors of the *Sui-shu* come very close to one important point made in our analysis of the historical personality of

Yang-ti; they identify the crisis point in his life and his regime and stress the rapid disintegration of both after that point. At one point text II suggests that it was only after his narrow escape from capture by the Turks in 615 that his spirit broke. Elsewhere the same text sees his abandonment of his two northern capitals as the crisis point. "Yang-ti's spirit was stripped and his courage gone." And then they suggest that his flight southward was following the pattern of the Chin, which abandoned the north and fled to the Yangtse valley in 317. The general tendency throughout is to begin the full development of the bad-last ruler characterology from the northeastern campaigns or from one of the other two points in time mentioned above. In some cases, to be sure, the "good" policies of the earlier part of his reign are forgotten and the "badness" is projected back over the whole period— notably in the matter of legal enactments, which were unusually mild in the early years and became increasingly draconian as the crisis deepened.[52] Nonetheless, the identification of a turning point in Yang-ti's career brings the T'ang estimate close to what a sifting of the evidence reveals.

At still another point the estimates agree with what a critical sifting of the evidence has shown: in their emphasis on Yang-ti's enormous vanity, what we might call his delusively inflated self-image. Text II puts it this way:

He considered that owing to his mighty deeds all creation would instantly obey him, that he was the great prince whose merit was higher than that of the ancient exemplars. He needed no "outside" relatives to win the succession, nor help from subordinates to gain power. In stature he compared favorably with Chou and Han rulers. Ten thousand generations hence there would be none to equal him. From high antiquity onward there had been only one such prince.[53]

In later historical writings Yang-ti appears again and again. My impression is that the stereotype survives almost as a cliché and that the variations suggested in the *Sui-shu* estimates tend to drop away. In Chao I's discussion of the Prince of Hai-ling (ruler of the Chin, 1149–61) Yang-ti is used as a kind of crude standard of "badness." Chao I remarks that although Yang-ti killed his father and his brothers (assertions not to be found in the *Sui-shu*), the Prince of Hai-ling killed several hundred members of his own house. Yang-ti was not this bad! Again, the massive conscriptions of the Prince of Hai-ling for his campaign against the Sung equaled the exactions of Yang-ti for his expeditions against Koguryŏ; here they are equally "bad." Finally, both were murdered by their own subordinates. Chao I adds that Shih Hu of the Later Chao (ruled 334–49) was the most immoral (*wu-tao*) ruler prior to Yang-ti and the Prince of Hai-ling.[54] Chao I is writing "notes" and not organized essays, but it is odd that he should not have mentioned the long line of depraved rulers prior to the fourth century A.D., some of whom we have considered. For him the criterion of "badness" is Yang-ti, and it is as this bald stereotype that Yang-ti appears in the literati's essays and memorials of the 1,300 years from his fall to the end of the Chinese empire.

SUI YANG-TI AS A STOCK VILLAIN

If the moralized political image just described was the particular property of the elite, Yang-ti as a stock villain had a broader clientele: readers of short stories and tales of the remarkable, town and village storytellers, rural dramatic troupes, and, eventually, the novel-reading audiences of the eighteenth and nineteenth centuries. Our knowledge of the historical sociology of Chinese fiction is so imperfect that we cannot say with certainty when, or in what form, the popular image began to take shape. But since palace gossip, retailed and embroidered as it spread through the empire, lies behind the fictionalized accounts of more recent emperors, we may reasonably suppose that the earliest tales of Yang-ti's character and activities were based on just such gossip, possibly supplemented by eyewitness accounts from those who had returned from the wars or from the capitals. The basic elements of a good story were all there: a high-born and handsome leading man who climbed the heights of power and descended dramatically to a tragic end; family intrigue which linked the lowliest Chinese family to the highest; the splendor of great deeds which linked the listener through wish-fulfillment fantasy with the protagonist; scenes of luxury and sensuality. And behind this high drama were the presiding fates, who lent a touch of solemnity and pointed the moral lesson without which many of the audience might have felt unsatisfied. The fates in this case were heaven—that amorphous deity which yet sent disaster to the tyrannical and the unrighteous—and the prevailing moral norms of Chinese society: not deities, not divine laws, yet somehow working for those who adhered to them and against those who did not.

The storytellers' tales, for a number of reasons, went unrecorded for centuries.[55] For the early years, we have only the *ch'uan-ch'i* tales, written down in a rather loose-jointed classical style for the entertainment of the literate. No canons of historiography restrained the authors; their purpose was solely to entertain. The *ch'uan-ch'i* stories dealing with Yang-ti's reign seem to me to be relevant materials for the early popular image in two respects. First, it appears to be from these stories that later storytellers and novelists drew much of their material for vernacular fiction dealing with Yang-ti; it is in these stories that the stereotyped "bad ruler" mentioned in much of later fiction begins to take shape. It seems likely, therefore, that there was a considerable overlap in content between the *ch'uan-ch'i* stories and the lost tales of the oral tradition, since both presumably derived from recent memories of great events. The Sui lived on in the palaces, the canals, the cities which dotted the landscape; it lived on in collective memories in which the differences between elite and folk levels may well have been slight.

The editors of the imperially commissioned "Catalogue of the Four Treasuries Collection" comment disparagingly on three of the collections of anecdotes we shall consider. They point out anachronisms and errors, and they say disdainfully, "They are close to vulgar *ch'uan-ch'i* tales and, it goes without saying, are utterly unreliable."[56] Since it is the "vulgar" image of Yang-ti that we seek in these stories, this comment is reassuring.

Reverting once again to the outline on p. 62, we shall summarize the content of four works by T'ang and Sung writers: *Mi-lou Chi* (MLC), *Hai-shan Chi* (HSC), *K'ai-ho Chi* (KHC), and *Ta-yeh Shih-i Chi* (TYC).[57] Many of the stories in these collections describe how good and evil omens were borne out by events. In some stories Yang-ti is a rather incidental figure; in a good many others, the prognostications have to do with his own fall, and he emerges as superstitious, volatile, and subject to black moods. Another large category of anecdotes is concerned with the misdeeds of Yang-ti's officials, particularly Yang Su (HSC) and Ma Shu-mou, who was in charge of the building of the Pien section of the Grand Canal (KHC). These men are represented as corrupt, rapacious, and fiendishly cruel—even worse, it would seem, than their imperial master.

Our Category A, "Tyranny," is filled, and with florid detail. Officials who protested the fiendish exactions of Ma Shu-mou were flogged (KHC). Ho-jo Pi, advising against the plan to rebuild the Great Wall, cites the ills that befell the Ch'in regime in their work on it. The emperor becomes angry with the remonstrator; Ho-jo is put under house arrest and commits suicide (KHC). Category A,3, "Callousness toward the suffering of the masses," is still more fully developed: perhaps one-fourth of the stories describe the people's ills under Yang-ti's tyranny. The lament of a veteran of the Koguryŏ campaign disturbs the emperor's repose aboard his barge; his song tells of near-starvation in the northern campaigns; now the man is forced to pull the imperial barge. Everyone in the country is hungry; he has not a grain of his daily ration; the canal towpath stretches out 3,000 *li* ahead; surely he will die alone far from home (HSC). The emperor exacts a flotilla of five hundred large canal boats from people in the Huai and Yangtse valleys; families assigned a quota of one boat are bankrupted, family members are pilloried and flogged and finally sell their children to meet the demands (KHC). Yang-ti is enraged at the discovery of shallow stretches in the Grand Canal; he orders that the people living opposite the shallows be tied up and buried alive, head first, in the banks of the canal. Fifty thousand are buried alive (KHC).

All the headings of category B, "Self-indulgence," are represented with stories, stories replete with vivid, sometimes titillating, detail. A reference to Yang-ti's visiting his harem when drunk (TYC) is the sole mention of drunkenness in these texts, although elsewhere we read of his physician's warning him against excessive drinking (MLC). But the emperor's passion for rare and expensive goods is recounted in detail. For example, the sun-shades over the bows of the imperial barges were woven in Central Asia of the eyelashes of a rare animal and the threads of young lotus root; the sails were embroidered, and the tow ropes were made of silk (TYC). To please the emperor's fancy, his women daily received a huge quantity of costly eyebrow paint imported from Persia (TYC).

Yang-ti's extravagant building projects are given full treatment. The building of the canal is presented as a personal whim, to give him easy and luxurious transport to the place he found most pleasurable, Yang-chou (KHC). The *K'ai-ho Chi*, as the name suggests, deals largely with the cost of this project in lives and treasure. (According to this text, Yang-ti had trees planted along the watercourse to keep the sun off the beautiful girls who were recruited to pull the barges.) The building of the Western Plaisance (Hsi-yüan) is described in detail: a million conscripted laborers were at work at one time fashioning its artificial lakes, its four artificial seas, its artificial mountains, and its sixteen courtyards, and stocking it with birds, animals, plants, and flowers (HSC). The *Mi-lou Chi* is rich in detail on extravagant construction and on the lascivious conduct of Yang-ti. For the Mi-lou was the "Maze Pavilion," so named because of its intricate labyrinth of secret rooms and secret passages, designed to ensure the emperor privacy for his carnal pleasures. It was built of precious materials on a magnificent scale—"a thousand doors and ten thousand windows." Several tens of thousands of laborers managed to complete it in a year, and the treasury was totally depleted.

The licentiousness (C) of the emperor in this sumptuous setting is described in loving detail. He stocked the pavilion with several thousand girls of good family and sometimes stayed there a month at a time. One of his ministers designed a "virgin car" which apparently held the victims' hands and feet while they were deflowered by the lustful Yang-ti. The walls of the palace were hung with pornographic pictures, but these were replaced with polished bronze screens which mirrored what went on in the imperial bed. Yang-ti resorted to aphrodisiacs, and was able to take "several tens" of women each day. All these passages of the *Mi-lou Chi* conjure up scenes of vast luxury and sensuous indulgence. Singing and music are mentioned, but the use of "lascivious music"—perennial object of the Confucian moralist's disapproval—is scarcely mentioned. The storyteller was not interested in the moral effects of music.

In these four texts no *femme fatale* appears to hasten Yang-ti's doom. He has a succession of favorites, but his historical empress appears in many scenes as an object of his indulgence or sometimes as a jealous wife. It appears to be only in later stories that the empress takes on the attributes of the *femme fatale*—sapping Yang-ti's vitality, spurring him to folly, leading him to final disaster.[58]

Turning to category D, "Lack of personal virtue," we find that these texts are virtually silent. The one account of the death of Wen-ti (HSC) does not accuse Yang Kuang of patricide. There is no mention of his role in the liquidation of his brothers, nor are there references—good or bad—to his religious and ceremonial observances.

The storytellers are not really concerned with moral dynamics in the historical process. At the end of the *Mi-lou Chi*, T'ang T'ai-tsung appears on the scene, comments that the Maze Pavilion has been built of the flesh and blood of the people, and orders it burnt down. This, says the text, bears out the prophetic lines in a popular song and a poem of Yang-ti's which had been previously recounted. "Hence one knows that the rise and fall of dynasties is never accidental." This is far different from the laboring of the moral dynamic in the historical accounts; it really says no more than that coming events cast their shadows before them, or that a person with a sharp eye for signs and portents can know what is to come.

This shift of emphasis—the relative underplaying of the moral dynamic and the relative neglect of Yang-ti's defects of "personal virtue"—is understandable enough: it is hard to make an entertaining story out of unfilial or unbrotherly behavior, or out of the neglect of proper ceremonial conduct. Moreover, the moral dynamic may have been far less persuasive with the lower classes, or the lower levels of the elite, than it was with officials, historians, and political thinkers.

Common sense also explains the great emphasis on Yang-ti's tyranny.

The tyranny stories are what we would call "tear-jerkers"; they are designed to evoke a quick response from those who share the experience of living under an autocratic bureaucracy. The waste, the corruption, the oppressive officials, the fads and follies of the supreme autocrat—all these are part of the real-life experience of the people who read these stories, and this serves to make them both interesting and believable.

The emphasis on self-indulgence and licentiousness is a different matter. The ordinary Chinese who heard the storytellers' versions of these stories, or who in later times became literate enough to read vernacular versions of them, led hard-working, impoverished, self-denying lives; they were constrained by the state, by the straitjacket of convention, by the pressure of the family. What better escape than into the perfumed halls of Yang-ti's sumptuous palaces to consort for an hour with beautiful and compliant damsels? This combination of verisimilitude and wish-fulfillment fantasy often occurs in Chinese fiction. As a tyrant—whether operating directly or through his minions—Yang-ti was eminently believable. As a cultivated debauchee, he provided vicarious satisfaction for many suppressed desires.

It should be clear by now that the stereotyped "bad last" ruler of the historians was not by any means reproduced in the early popular writings about Yang-ti.

In the seventeenth century and after, the early fictional accounts were drawn upon, elaborated, and collected in books which reached a far broader literate audience than ever before. One of these books is the *Sui Yang-ti Yen-shih* ("A Colorful History of Sui Yang-ti").[59] It is written in a style close to the vernacular, and its colorful dialogues are far more intelligible to a popular audience than the semi-classical speeches in the earlier stories. Its forty dramatic incidents were admirably suited for serialized storytelling or for use as the basis of popular dramatic skits. In content the *Sui Yang-ti Yen-shih* is an elaborated compendium of all the themes of the earlier fictionized accounts, with particular development of the sex interest. One writer on Chinese fiction says that the "Colorful History" sold very widely, and that thanks to its incorporation of the lurid stories of the *Mi-lou Chi*, Yang-ti became, among the common people, the most familiar example of an extravagant and corrupt monarch.[60] The "Colorful History" contains the poetical introductions that are so familiar in modern popular fiction, and these occasionally make a feeble effort to point the moral lesson of the incidents they introduce. But the purpose of the work was to entertain a popular audience, and in doing this it spread a stereotype in which spectacular extravagance and sexual license are far more emphasized than violations of ritual, moral, and political norms.

A somewhat more sober account of Yang-ti appears in the *Sui T'ang Yen-i*, which dates from the late seventeenth century.[61] Its author tells us that he drew on earlier tales but also on the accounts in the histories. He made extensive use of the *Sui Yang-ti Yen-shih*,[62] but he omitted much of its titillating detail and replaced the more lurid descriptions with euphemisms. Moreover, his introductory passages and asides are more explicitly moral in intent. In short, the *Sui T'ang Yen-i* is clearly more "respectable" than the "Colorful History." Nevertheless, its utterly black image of Yang-ti is clearly derived from the popular tradition. The "toning down" of the Yang-ti story in the *Sui T'ang Yen-i* was in part, perhaps, a reflection of the increasingly puritanical mores encouraged by official neo-Confucianism or perhaps also a reaction against the vogue of pornographic fiction that had produced the *Chin-p'ing Mei* and the "Colorful History." Its more respectable tone may also have served to protect authors and readers from the government censors and book-burners of the late seventeenth and eighteenth centuries. The *Sui T'ang Yen-i* certainly carried the popular image of Yang-ti into many a gentry and city household where the *Sui Yang-ti Yen-shih* would have been regarded as too salacious for family reading.

In another novel of the sixteenth or the seventeenth century—a novel which may have been influenced by the revival of popular Taoism—Yang-ti is shown as having a cosmically evil influence:

The next day he [the Venerable Teacher] takes possession of his Sun Palace where he gives audience to his subjects. Suddenly from the north an atmosphere of dissatisfaction reaches the heavens. The Venerable Teacher discusses it with his followers. The cause is the misrule of Emperor Yang of Sui. The evil influence of the cosmos fills heaven and the subjects of the Supreme Ruler start a rebellion.[63]

There can be little doubt that the *ch'uan-ch'i* accounts and their successors influenced the elite image just as the historical records influenced the popular image. It is worth noting that Ssu-ma Kuang, in the compilation of the *Tzu-chih T'ung-chien*, specifically instructed his staff not to be afraid to draw upon such anecdotes and tales as were consistent with an accepted historical version of a given event.[64] In the *T'ung-chien's* account of Yang-ti's reign a number of these works were consulted; in some cases their versions were rejected, but in others they unquestionably colored the final narrative.[65] Moreover, despite their moral strictures against fiction, the literati read it avidly; and one might speculate that when, from the eighteenth century on, they referred to the misrule of Yang-ti in a memorial to the throne, the image presented in the *Sui Yang-ti Yen-shih* and the *Sui T'ang Yen-i* was as likely to be in their minds as the image found in the *Sui-shu*. It would be too much to say that the elite and popular images of Yang-ti fused into a single myth, but it is certain that the two images, influencing each other, have drawn closer together during the thirteen centuries since the death of Yang-ti.

The myth of Yang-ti persists in the People's China today, and there it has been further embroidered with the demonology of vulgar Marxism. In a small popular volume called "Talks on Chinese History," the chapter concerning Yang-ti is headed: "Yang-ti Builds the Canal to View the Hortensia Flowers."[66] Here are the familiar stories, partly from the histories, more from the stories and novels. Extravagance, licentiousness, and oppression of the people are laid out in well-worn clichés, and the new Marxist terms of opprobrium are added. Yang-ti becomes a "feudal autocrat," and a particularly oppressive representative of this reprehensible type.

A work with some scholarly pretensions is Han Kuo-ch'ing's *Sui Yang-ti*, published by the Hupeh People's Publishing House in 1957. The treatment is an incredible mishmash of Communist clichés and uncritical retailing of accounts from popular stories and the "feudal ruling class" histories. The author's Marxism has apparently failed to liberate him from the old mythology of bad-last rulers or from the stereotyped image of Yang-ti that was the joint product of the interests of the elite and the popular imagination. Here is his final judgment:

Yang-ti had the animal courage and the ambition of Ch'in Shih-huang-ti and Han Wu-ti, but his abilities were not the equal of theirs; he was as cruelly tyrannical as Chieh [the last ruler] of Hsia and Chou [the last ruler] of Shang, but in treachery and coldbloodedness he exceeded them. He had all the extravagance and fantastic licentiousness of Tung-hun Hou of the Ch'i and Hou-chu of the Ch'en [last rulers of the Southern Ch'i and Ch'en respectively], but their extravagant palaces [named] did not approach the grand scale of Yang-ti's Western Plaisance and Maze Pavilion. Yang-ti was truly a grand composite of ancient Chinese rulers. But he had few of their good points, while their treachery and cruelty, their licentiousness and extravagance, were all embodied in him. Therefore we say that his achievement was slight and his guilt was heavy; his goodness little, his evil great. He constituted a barrier to social development [!] He was *the* tyrannical ruler [*pao-chün*] of Chinese history, *the* criminal oppressor of the people.[67]

Of the three problems discussed in this essay—Yang-ti the personality, Yang-ti the political stereotype, and Yang-ti the villain of story and drama—the first must be the object of more intensive research, of study that proceeds in close relation with a deepening scholarly understanding of Chinese psychology and historiography. The third, which has been largely exploratory in this paper, could only be fully developed if other figures from Chinese history and folklore were subjected to similar study and if the techniques of such study were perfected through testing and progressive refinement. The second, the genesis and evolution of a political stereotype, likewise deserves far fuller treatment than has been attempted here. For example we can now only speculate as to when and how the authority of such politically motivated stereotyping began to wane; there is evidence that those who analyzed the fall of dynasties from the Sung onward tended to do so in somewhat more "rational" terms and, when moralizing, to point the finger of blame toward the bad last minister or servitor and not to the monarch himself.[68] Did this reflect the increasingly despotic character of the Chinese throne and its consequent immunity from moralistic criticism? Yet those who have observed the Chinese Communist demonography of Chiang Kai-shek might wonder whether the authority of the "bad last ruler" image has been altogether dissipated. Rather it would appear to be one of those elements in the Confucian tradition that lingers on with a semblance of vitality long after the system which gave it point has been fragmented and dispersed.

Edwin G. Pulleyblank

NEO-CONFUCIANISM AND NEO-LEGALISM IN T'ANG INTELLECTUAL LIFE, 755–805

The Yüan-ho period (A.D. 806–20) is looked upon as the second flowering of the T'ang dynasty, a time of partial recovery after the K'ai-yüan and T'ien-pao (713–55) glories had been cut short by the disastrous events of the rebellion of An Lu-shan (713–55). In particular it is the time associated with the *ku-wen* movement for the reform of the content and style of prose writing, and with the beginnings of the revival of Confucian philosophy which culminated in Sung Neo-Confucianism. If one were looking for the era of greatest and most significant intellectual activity, it would, however, be more appropriate to turn one's attention to the preceding Chen-yüan period (785–805), for it was under the autocratic and miserly Te-tsung (780–805), one of the most individual and forceful of T'ang emperors, who was also one of the greatest patrons of literature of his line, that activity was most vigorous. A galaxy of young men, whose maturity came in the reign of his grandson Hsien-tsung (805–20), congregated in Ch'ang-an seeking fortunes by their talents and spending leisure hours in discussions on political and economic as well as ethical and metaphysical problems. In the fields of prose writing and philosophy, the best known names are those of Han Yü and Liu Tsung-yüan, but they are only two among a numerous crowd. Some, such as Liu Yü-hsi, Lü Wen, and Li Ao, left writings which have survived; others we know only through references in the histories or in the writings of friends. This is a focal period in Chinese intellectual history, for it represents the high point of enthusiasm and hope among the literati for a rejuvenation of the T'ang dynasty, before the successive setbacks and disappointments of the early ninth century brought disillusionment.

During Te-tsung's reign, in spite of the many unsolved problems that still beset the state, some degree of stability and order seemed to have been established, and there was hope that a genuine restoration might be possible. It was this that gave point to discussions on fundamental issues. New institutions were taking shape—a new basic system of taxation and other fiscal devices, modifications in the structure of the bureaucracy—which were to have a long history into and through the Sung period. There was plenty to stimulate and occupy the minds of would-be statesmen.

A few of these men are well known. Han Yü and Li Ao have received attention mainly as precursors of the Sung Neo-Confucians, but judgments of them are mostly based on views of Ou-yang Hsiu or Chu Hsi. To understand them properly, it is necessary to put them in the context of their own time. Moreover, Confucianism was by no means the only philosophy in vogue. Throughout this period men were not overly concerned by the demands of orthodoxy; indeed Han Yü's authoritarian exclusiveness, his one real claim to originality as a thinker, was quite exceptional. As always, men turned to the Classics for inspiration, but they turned also to Buddhism, Taoism, and the ancient Legalist writers. A new critical spirit was abroad which made men seek in the Classics for interpretations consonant with reason rather than merely consistent with the orthodox commentaries. It may be true to say that the culmination of all this came in Sung, but the immediate significance was for its own time and it is surely a mistake to look only at what the Sung thinkers three hundred years later found to be significant.

I have attempted in what follows to outline in a preliminary way the important intellectual developments of the half-century following the An Lu-shan rebellion.

CONSEQUENCES OF THE AN LU-SHAN REBELLION

A brief account of the half-century from 755 to 805 will set the stage and bring out some of the main political and economic problems which, even when not overtly occupying the attention of writers, lay in the background of their thinking.

The first impulse of the rebellious armies which moved rapidly down in the winter of 755–56 from the Peking region to take the Eastern Capital, Lo-yang, was checked for a while at the T'ung-kuan. Loyal uprisings along the rebels' line of communications and the invasion of Hopei from Shansi through the T'u-men Pass by Kuo Tzu-i's imperial army seemed on the way to defeating the rebels when, in the summer of 756, the collapse of the T'ung-kuan left the way to Ch'ang-an unguarded. Hsüan-tsung abandoned his court and fled westward. At Ma-wei post-station, west of Ch'ang-an, his mutinous bodyguard killed the Chief Minister Yang Kuo-chung and forced the emperor to put to death his favorite, Yang Kuo-chung's cousin, Yang Kuei-fei. Hsüan-tsung then went on to Ch'eng-tu in Szechwan, but the Crown Prince proceeded northwest to Ling-wu where he assumed the imperial dignity and began gathering forces to restore the fortunes of his house. Helped by an Uyghur contingent, and by the murder of An Lu-shan at the beginning of 757 which destroyed the coherence of the rebels, before the year's end the new emperor Su-tsung recaptured first Ch'ang-an and then Lo-yang. The T'ang forces did not, however, have the strength to push their victory to completion, and the rebels were able to re-form, first under An Lu-shan's son, An Ch'ing-hsü, then under his general, Shih Ssu-ming, and finally under Shih Ssu-ming's son, Shih Ch'ao-i. For several years the war moved inconclusively back and forth in the Yellow River plain. Finally, at the end of 762, with the aid of a second Uyghur intervention, the T'ang armies were able to defeat Shih Ch'ao-i decisively. Abandoned by his supporters, he tried to flee northward to the land of the Khitans, but was treacherously slain by one of his own men.

This marked the official end of the rebellion, but the country was far from pacified. On the west, the aggressive Tibetans had occupied large areas left undefended by the recall of frontier armies to fight the rebels. In 763 they even advanced on Ch'ang-an and forced the emperor to flee east to Shan-chou. They entered the city and attempted to set up a puppet emperor. Though they soon withdrew and did not repeat their past success, they remained a constant menace and large armies had to be stationed on the western frontier to guard against their raids. On the north, the Uyghurs were nominally the allies and restorers of the dynasty, but their friendship was almost as oppressive as the enmity of the Tibetans. Their soldiers disturbed the peace with impunity in Ch'ang-an, and foreign merchants under their protection evaded Chinese control.[1]

In the northeast, peace was only restored by allowing rebel generals to retain control of their territories as T'ang military governors. Although they were too undisciplined and divided among themselves again to menace the dynasty, they were effectively independent of T'ang authority and combined against any major attack by the central government. They ran their own internal affairs and paid no taxes to the center, except for occasional "tribute" to solicit favors. They were conscious of an analogy with the "feudalism" of the Ch'un-ch'iu (722–481 B.C.) period, and the language of feudalism was commonly used of them.[2]

In large parts of the rest of China, conditions were not much more favorable for centralized control. Imperial armies raised to fight the rebels and now stationed throughout the country were almost as untrustworthy as the former rebels in Ho-pei. Generals attempted to emulate their fellows in Ho-pei and establish independent satrapies. Soldiers were unruly and might assassinate or drive out a commander who was too strict a disciplinarian or too niggardly with his largesse. The suppression of militarism and the restoration of civil government were vital tasks, but, although a certain measure of success was gradually achieved in part of the empire, the problem was not successfully solved until the Sung dynasty two hundred years later.

The central government itself was in an unhealthy state. Great numbers of bureaucrats had either gone over to the rebels or been scattered far and wide, and Su-tsung, when he had retaken the capitals, had at first to make do with such officials as had followed him to Ling-wu. Later, others came from Hsüan-tsung's court in Ch'eng-tu and elsewhere, but it is not surprising that Su-tsung relied heavily on those he knew best, his eunuchs. He had lived in seclusion at his father's court, constantly afraid of being suspected of involvement in plots, real or imagined, against his father's throne.[3] He can have had little contact with the literati or indeed with any but men like Li Fu-kuo, the former eunuch stable boy[4] who was at his side on the flight northwest from Ma-wei to Ling-wu and came to wield immense power over the court after the return to Ch'ang-an. Although Li Fu-kuo himself fell from power in 762, his place was taken by others. Eunuchs had previously been used as messengers between the inner palace and the ministers. Now this practice was institutionalized by the setting up of the *Shu-mi Yüan,* a eunuch secretariat which gradually assumed advisory and ultimately executive functions.[5]

If civil officials were mistrusted, the military were under even graver suspicion, and the emperors turned naturally to eunuchs to act as their eyes and ears in keeping watch. The system of eunuch supervisors (*chien-chün*)[6] was extended to all armies under imperial authority, both in the provinces and at the capital. In the course of time, eunuch supervisors supplanted altogether the regular commanders in the Palace Armies, and this was the basis for their dominance over the court, which was to last until the end of the dynasty. In the provinces the friction and suspicion between eunuch supervisors and generals were frequently a source of trouble and aggravated the problem of militarism.

The rebellion resulted in great financial difficulties for the central government. Cut off from most of its tax-producing area, Su-tsung's court struggled painfully to gather resources for war. Financial exhaustion prevented the mustering of effort necessary to bring the war to a close and this in turn increased the financial exhaustion. A series of desperate fiscal expedients including forced loans from merchants,[7] sale of offices and Buddhist and Taoist ordination certificates,[8] and the minting of token coinage[9] was resorted to. When peace nominally came in 762, most of North China was in ruins and still overrun with armies. Furthermore, the loss of life and the migrations caused by the war had completely upset the local registers of population, which were the basis of taxation.

The south was relatively unscathed, but even the prosperous Chiang-nan area had felt the ravages of war in 760–61 when a dissident general from Huai-hsi (northern Anhwei) invaded the southern Kiangsu area.[10] He was subdued only by armies from the north, and these caused at least as much damage by pillaging as the rebels. In 762, when communications with the capital were somewhat improved, Yüan Tsai, as tax commissioner, tried to collect eight years of back taxes in Chiang-nan and Huai-nan, and to register the many fugitives who had invaded those regions. These harsh measures led to peasant uprisings, which once again required the importing of armies from the north to suppress them.[11]

In 762, Liu Yen was appointed Commissioner for Revenue, Salt and Iron, Transport and Taxation for the eastern half of the empire, a post which he held with short intervals until 780. He was undoubtedly a genius. By a tactful and farsighted policy he was able to encourage the economic recovery of the areas under his authority and, at the same time, to make their tax yield the financial foundation of the T'ang government. He did this, first, by restoring the transport canal system from the Yangtze to Lo-yang and Ch'ang-an and, second, by applying and perfecting the salt monopoly, which in 758 had been introduced as a war measure by Ti-wu Ch'i. He paid less attention to the registration of the people and the restoration of direct taxes. Much of his success was due to his skill as an administrator. He was meticulous in his own work and managed to get the same standard from his subordinates. Many of the financial experts of the latter part of the century were men whom he had recruited into his service and trained.[12]

The reform of direct taxation had to wait till the beginning of Te-tsung's reign in 780, when Yang Yen, Liu Yen's great rival, introduced his Two Tax (*liang-shui*) reform. This abolished the old system of taxation in kind, which had been levied on a head tax basis in connection with the Equal Field (*chün-t'ien*) system of land-holding and in accordance with registration of households in the districts of their origin. Instead, all direct taxes were calculated in money and grain, and were based on household classification by wealth and on the land actually under cultivation. Moreover, tax quotas were established for each locality on the basis of past receipts, and no effort was made to levy taxes, as previously, at standard rates throughout the empire. This reform finally recognized the decrepitude of the old system and was a rationalization of practices which had grown up in chaotic fashion during its decay. In turn, it soon gave rise to evils and abuses that called forth much criticism.[13]

Liu Yen and Yang Yen were personal enemies. Both had originally been friends of Yüan Tsai, the brilliant but corrupt Chief Minister of Tai-tsung, but Liu was instrumental in Yüan's downfall in 777. Yang Yen in turn brought about Liu Yen's banishment and death in 780. Lu Ch'i, who caused Yang Yen's defeat and death soon after, was reputedly taking revenge for Liu Yen.[14] It has been suggested that the feud arose from differences in economic theory reflected in Liu Yen's use of indirect taxes and development of regional economy as opposed to Yang Yen's emphasis on direct taxation and centralized control.[15] Although personalities and factional rivalries must be given a large share of the blame, especially for the later repercussions of the feud, there does seem to have been a divergence of viewpoint, as we shall see when considering the economic ideas of Lu Hsüan-kung and Tu Yu.

There were of course other problems of government in the reigns of Tai-tsung and Te-tsung besides fissiparous militarism, eunuch influence, and economic policy. The minds of the literati were exercised particularly by the examination system and by the growing complexities of the bureaucratic system in which they found themselves enmeshed. In this period we also perceive the beginnings of a number of institutions which did not form part of the regular T'ang system; for example, a formalized system of recommendation and sponsorship as a supplement to other methods of appointing officials.[16] The Han-lin Academy is no longer—as it was under Hsüan-tsung—simply an office within the palace where the emperor kept such experts in chess, calligraphy, juggling, or literary composition as he might wish to have close at hand. Rather, it becomes a small informal body of confidential advisers who sometimes wield greater influence than the titular Chief Ministers.[17] Its development, like that of the eunuch secretariat, follows a pattern occurring frequently in Chinese institutional history, whereby, when there is antagonism or lack of confidence between the emperor and the bureaucracy, new informal bodies of advisers appear close to the throne, only in turn to be institutionalized and lose their intimate character.

This, without going into details, is a sketch of some of the main developments in the second half of the eighth century. Now let us turn to some of the thinkers and writers of this period.

From the time An Lu-shan unleashed his armies on North China and took Ch'ang-an, the great clans and lesser houses of the northeast (*Kuan-tung*) were thrown into confusion. Some individuals made their way to the courts of Hsüan-tsung at Ch'eng-tu, or to that of Su-tsung at Ling-wu. Some organized resistance in the rear of the rebels. Others fell into rebel hands and collaborated willingly or unwillingly with their captors. Still others took refuge in the hills. But as time went on and prospects of peace and order returning to the Yellow River plain became more remote, more and more made their way south to the peaceful lands across the Yangtze, as in the Yung-chia period (307–12) when North China fell to the barbarians.[18] There is no way of estimating the size of this movement, but it is clear from the frequency with which it is referred to in biographies that it must have involved very considerable numbers. The common people were on the move too, but how many of them, as distinct from the great clans and their adherents, were able to escape the ravages of war, famine, and pestilence, and arrive safely in the south can only be conjectured.

The immigrants settled in various places in central China. One of the principal escape routes was through Nan-yang and the Han River, and some stopped at places in Hu-pei such as the present Hankow. Others went farther east and south into Kiangsi, and many more came, whether by that route or more directly, to the ancient cities of the Wu-Yüeh region—Jun-chou (Chen-chiang) Su-chou, Ch'ang-chou, Hang-chou, etc.

We can, today, only speculate on the economic aspects of this movement. It is probable that many of the clans were able to bring some part of their wealth with them and to use it to establish themselves in the south, which was at the beginning of its great expansion. Others may have been able to return later and recover their property in the north. For very many, however, it must have meant impoverishment. What is evident is that for some time there was a large aggregation of unemployed educated men in the south unable because of the war to find places in the regular bureaucracy. They were frequently recruited to the staffs of local military governors or to the newly established Salt Commission. Among these displaced literati we find the beginnings of the intellectual movements that reach their high point at the end of the century.

The rebellion itself and the challenges it presented were no doubt directly responsible for one of the most striking characteristics of post-rebellion thought in contrast to the immediately preceding period—

its seriousness, its involvement in the world, its concern, even when dealing with theoretical problems, for application to the present day— its activist (*yu-wei*) tone. In the fetid political atmosphere prevailing before the rebellion, characterized by the oppressive dominance of Li Lin-fu and by the dangerous power struggle between Yang Kuo-chung and An Lu-shan, men of character had tended to seek to maintain their personal integrity through withdrawal from the world or, at least, in the individualistic cultivation of such things as poetry, fine writing, or philosophy. After 755, we seem to find a new spirit of social concern—even among those of a Taoist turn of mind.

There is, for example, Yüan Chieh (719–72), an aristocrat who before the rebellion had held aloof from political life and written satirical attacks from a Taoist point of view on the world's degenerate state. When the rebels took Lo-yang, he was first forced to flee with his family to the south and was then drawn willy-nilly into official employment.[19] Or we may think of the Taoist writer, Liu Shih, who managed to spend the war years in retirement in the region of Nan-ch'ang (Kiangsi). Even he was acutely aware of the troubles of the time, and he wrote not only about the pleasures of his country retreat, but also about the sufferings of the peasants sold into slavery because of want, an evil which seems to have touched the consciences of scholar-officials from this time onward in a way that it had not done previously.[20]

Similar patterns can be found in other biographies of the period. More common perhaps were the men who had held office or would have looked naturally to an official career, but were cast adrift and given both the leisure and the stimulus to think about the problems of their time. For some the reaction was shock and pain—as in Tu Fu's poems in which private griefs are universalized to express the torment of society. But in the comparative quiet and safety of the lower Yantze region, groups of young men soon began to congregate, interspersing their drinking parties with discussions on how to reform the world, and scholars began to seek in the Classics and ancient philosophers, or in a revitalized literature, ways to bring order, peace, and moral regeneration.

For instance, there were the so-called "Four K'uei" at Shang-yüan (present Nanking), one of whom was Han Hui, the elder brother of Han Yü.[21] Han Yü's father, Han Chung-ch'ing, happened to be a magistrate of Wu-ch'ang when the rebellion broke out, so he had no need to flee from the north. When, in 757, he was about to be transferred to the magistracy of P'o-yang, the poet, Li Po, who had been in that region for several years, composed an inscription praising his government of Wu-ch'ang.[22] What happened to him thereafter until his death in 770[23] is not clear. The Han family later possessed an estate (*pieh-yeh*) at Hsüan-ch'eng.[24] Judging by the analogies in other family histories of the time, I suspect that it may have been acquired by Han Chung-ch'ing during the rebellion period. At any rate, the eldest son, Han Hui, and his companions, Ts'ui Tsao, Lu Tung-mei, and Chang Cheng-tse, are said to have been sojourning at Shang-yüan in the Yung-t'ai period (765) where they "loved to discuss plans for settling the affairs of the world (*ching-chi*) and considered themselves capable of serving as ministers to princes." Unfortunately no writings have survived to tell what sort of plans they discussed. But Han Hui was later associated, along with Yang Yen, in the regime of the Chief Minister, Yüan Tsai, in whose downfall they were implicated in 777;[25] Ts'ui Tsao was a close friend of Liu Yen and was himself later a financier.[26] It is therefore not difficult to suppose that the *ching-chi* discussed by the "Four K'uei" may have had its modern meaning of "economics." In addition, Han Hui was deeply interested in another topic that was in the air, the reform of literature, an interest he was to pass on to his younger brother.[27]

THE KU-WEN MOVEMENT

The best known intellectual movement of the second half of the eighth century is undoubtedly the *ku-wen* movement for the reform of prose style. There had been criticisms of the empty euphuism of the parallel-prose style even before the beginning of the T'ang dynasty and advocacy of a return to a simpler style modeled on Chou and Han writers;[28] but it is only in the post-rebellion period that we find these ideas taking on the character of a movement. Some northern scholars exiled in Chiang-nan formulated the principles of literary composition and stressed the importance of a reformed prose for moral regeneration and the revival of the Confucian tradition which Han Yü developed and propagandized with a brilliance that left his forerunners in the shade.

The central figure in the initial period was Li Hua, already a celebrated writer in the reign of Hsüan-tsung. He had held a number of not very high offices, and when the rebellion broke out he was Omissioner of the Left. In the summer of 756, the T'ung-kuan fell and the court fled westward in panic. Li Hua, instead of going to join the exiled emperor, went to seek his mother who was living in rebel-controlled territory in southern Ho-pei. He was captured by the rebels and forced to take office under them. When the capitals were retaken the following year, he was tried for collaboration and was only saved from a severe penalty by the intervention of Liu Chih (of whom more will be said presently). He was given a minor post at Hang-chou. Soon after, his mother died and he retired. For the rest of his life he took no office but settled on a farm at Ch'u-chou (Huai-an Hsien in Kiangsu). He suffered from ill health and, according to Tu-ku Chi who wrote a preface to his works, was so poor that the younger members of his family had to work in the fields. He himself eked out his income by composing tomb inscriptions for the gentry of the region.[29]

Li Hua and his friends Hsiao Ying-shih and Chia Chih had already, before the rebellion, in the words of Tu-ku Chi, "advocated the style of middle antiquity (i.e., Chou and Han) in order to enlarge the influence of literature."[30] Unfortunately Li's early writings were already lost when Tu-ku Chi wrote, and it would be difficult to judge whether there was development in his later years. His mood and that of his friends before the rebellion seem to have resembled Yüan Chieh's. They sought relief for a corrupt world through a reform of literature which would present the true way of the ancients. Apparently it was while he was in retirement that Li Hua influenced others to try to revive the ancient style and started the movement which dominated literary discussions during the next half-century.

Li's friend Hsìao Ying-Shih, a descendant of the Southern Liang ruling house, was a proud-spirited man who held office for only a few brief periods and who, it was once said, even dared on one occasion to show disrespect to Li Lin-fu. He anticipated post-rebellion interest in the *Spring and Autumn Annals* and in the later problem of the legitimate line of successsion (*cheng-t'ung*), for he wrote, or at least projected, a continuation of that work from Han to Sui in which he expressed judgments on men and events and, in particular, made the line of legitimacy pass directly from Liang to Sui, bypassing Ch'en. Allegedly, he gathered disciples around him who treated him as their master.[31]

During the rebellion, he fled south like so many others, was for a time in Shan-nan (Hupei), and then farther east. Probably at this time he acquired an estate near Lake P'o-yang. He died at the age of 52 in 768. His son, Hsiao Ts'un, was a friend of Han Hui, and Han Yü, when a boy, knew him.[32] Ts'un was intimate with the *ku-wen* writer Liang Su and the historian Shen Chi-chi, and had a career as a financial official.

Another close friend of Li Hua was Li Hsün, a son of the great historian Liu Chih-chi (661–721), author of the *Shih-t'ung*, and a brother of Liu Chih who was instrumental in saving Li Hua's life. A student of the Classics, Hsün wrote a work called the *Liu shuo*, which, according to Li Hua, was aimed at "harmonizing men's minds by means of the Six Classics." Since the work is now lost, we have no way of telling how this was to be brought about, but it is interesting evidence of the beginnings of the revival of Confucian studies even before the rebellion.[33]

Although such men as Yüan Chieh, Li Hua, and Hsiao Ying-shih were all affected by the rebellion and reacted to it, they had matured during the pre-rebellion period. Their ideas for reform of scholarship, literature, and morals were originally prompted by revulsion from the world and, as we have seen, tended to be idealistic and impractical. They were aristocrats, and several of them had been content to live in retirement on their estates rather than to seek office. Too, with the exception of Hsiao Ying-shih, they were northerners, and, as Lo Ken-tse suggests,[34] part of their protest may have been the traditional adherence of the north to classical studies and its objection to the florid literature of the south, which had been invading the T'ang court since the beginning of the dynasty.

After the rebellion, the young men who followed in their footsteps and took inspiration from their ideas were in a quite different position. It was no longer sufficient to hold oneself aloof and perfect oneself in retirement. The disordered state of the world cried out for practical remedies; many of the scions of aristocratic houses were forced as never before to seek employment and to use scholarship and literary craftsmanship either to attract the notice of provincial governors or to seek office at court through the examination system. Dwelling in the south and coming under direct influence of the southern cultural tradition, some of the displaced northerners modified their protest from a simple, negative, purist reaction to a creative synthesis which, in the field of belles-lettres, eventually produced a rich and supple free prose style and, in the field of philosophy, drew on southern forms of Buddhism to supply a metaphysical grounding for a revived Confucianism.

Possibly this modification can already be seen in Li Hua's later works, and it is clear in the writings of Tu-ku Chi. Tu-ku Chi came from an illustrious northern family and shared his family's strong interest in Taoism. As a young man, in the years before the rebellion, he attracted attention as a writer and met Li Hua and Fang Kuan. He passed the examination in the Taoist Classics in 754. During the rebellion he fled to Chiang-nan and established his home at Su-chou, where he served for a short time under the Military Governor of Chiang-huai and was later summoned to court and appointed Omissioner of the Right. In this position he is said to have remonstrated sharply on various abuses. After holding other offices at the capital, he went in 768 to be Prefect of Hao-chou (near Feng-yang Hsien in Anhwei). From then until his death in 777, he served in the lower Yangtze region. In 771 he became Prefect of Shu-chou (Ch'ien-shan Hsien in Anhwei), and finally, in 774, he became Prefect of Ch'ang-chou, the title by which he was posthumously known.[35]

Like his friend and master, Li Hua, he practiced and advocated *ku-wen* and gathered disciples. He associated with other leading figures and was regarded as the leader of the movement. According to the modern critic Lo Ken-tse, he was less uncompromising than Li Hua in his demands for simplicity of diction and for rejection of all but the canonical works as models.[36] His greatest pupil was Liang Su, who occupied a pivotal position in the history of *ku-wen* before Han Yü. But before considering Liang Su, let us turn to certain other intellectual trends which were developing in the south in the post-rebellion period.

THE NEW CRITICISM OF THE SPRING AND AUTUMN ANNALS

Parallel to the main literary and philosophical movement leading to *ku-wen,* we find a new trend in criticism of the Confucian Classics which arose in reaction to the orthodoxy established by the standard commentaries (*Wu ching cheng-i*) in the reign of T'ai-tsung.[37] As on other occasions in the history of Chinese thought, it began with a new school of interpretation of the *Spring and Autumn Annals.*

Tan Chu (725–70), the founder of this school, was of northern origin. He had not yet held office when the rebellion broke out in 755, but was then sojourning in Chiang-nan. Because of the troubles in the north, he did not return. He was appointed to minor posts (perhaps by the local military governors?) first at Lin-hai Hsien (Chekiang) and then at Tan-yang Hsien in Jun-chou (Kiangsu). At the end of his second period of appointment, in 761, he retired and settled permanently in Jun-chou. During the next ten years, until 770, he worked on his commentary to the *Spring and Autumn Annals.* In that year Chao K'uang, who was the person principally concerned with the publishing and transmitting of Tan's work, was serving on the staff of Ch'en Shao-yu, Military Governor of Hsüan-she (southern Anhwei), and passed through Jun-chou on official business. There he met Tan Chu and became interested in his work. In the same year Tan Chu died, at the age of forty-seven. Later that year Chao was transferred, along with the Military Governor, his superior, to Che-tung (northern Che-kiang). Tan Chu's son Tan I and Lu Ch'un, who was later sometimes referred to as Chao K'uang's disciple but who seems to have been a direct disciple of Tan Chu, copied out Tan Chu's writings and took them to Chao K'uang, who edited them. Lu Ch'un then prepared the work, known as the *Ch'un-ch'iu t'ung-li,* for publication and wrote a preface dated 775.[38]

There are only meager details available about Chao K'uang. He is known to have been Prefect of Yang-chou (Yang-hsien in Shensi) (presumably later than his post under Ch'en Shao-yu) and he wrote a long critique of the examination system, in which, among other interesting remarks, he expresses his dislike of the standard commentaries on the Classics and his desire that classical studies concern themselves with the "general meaning" (*ta-i*) of the texts rather than with mere questions of punctuation and textual criticism.[39]

Lu Ch'un, like most of his surname, came from Su-chou. Liu Tsung-yüan states that he was a friend and disciple of Tan Chu, so he must have begun his studies before the latter's death. According to his biography Lu first received employment on Ch'en Shao-yu's staff when the latter was Military Governor at Yang-chou (773–84). It is possible that Lu received the appointment through Chao K'uang's influence in order that the two might work together on Tan Chu's posthumous papers.[40]

Later he was at Ch'ang-an where he held a number of offices, finally being made Doctor in the University of the Sons of State (*Kuo-tzu po-shih*). It was no doubt in this capacity that he was able to propagate his ideas among the young intellectuals. Besides advocating the works of Chao K'uang and Tan Chu, he also wrote his own commentary on the *Annals*. In the latter part of Te-tsung's reign he was serving in the provinces, but his works circulated in the capital and had great influence. He returned to Ch'ang-an in 804 and found himself the revered teacher of an important coterie.

Before the time of Tan Chu, students of the *Spring and Autumn Annals* had generally followed the tradition of one or another of the three commentaries established in the Han period—Kung-Yang, Ku-liang, or Tso—and though they might supply deficiencies in their favored commentary by reference to the others, there was little or no attempt to make any fundamental criticism of the accepted opinions about them. Tan Chu, however, proposed to reject the authority of all three commentaries and return directly to the Classic itself to establish on a rational basis the rules of "praise and blame" which Confucius had used in editing it. He thought that all three commentaries had been orally transmitted at first and only after several generations written down by later disciples. Moreover, in the case of the Tso commentary, the tradition of Confucius' teaching had been greatly amplified, partly at the beginning by Tso Ch'iu-ming's drawing on the chronicles of various other states, and partly at the time of writing down by the addition of material from heterogeneous sources such as family biographies of leading figures, books of divination, collections of anecdotes, and proposals of the School of Politicians, etc., so that it was difficult to sort out true from false. Chao K'uang went further and rejected the tradition that identified the author of the Tso commentary with Tso Ch'iu-ming. He declared that the *Kuo-yü* and the *Tso-chuan* were different in style (*wen-t'i*) and had such discrepancies that they could not be by the same author.[41]

It is difficult for us to understand the interest which the dry, crabbed chronicle of Lu aroused among Chinese literati, but we can, I think, appreciate the excitement with which young men learned of such a radical and "modern" critical approach to a canonical work. One can hardly find a parallel in Europe before the Homeric criticism of Bentley and his successors at the end of the seventeenth century. It is not merely that scholars dared to call tradition into question; others such as Wang Ch'ung and Liu Chih-chi had done this before. But we have only to compare Tan Chu, Chao K'uang, and Lu Ch'un with Liu Chih-chi half a century earlier, to see the difference. Liu Chih-chi was as bold or bolder in his attack, for he would even call Confucius to account; but he was frequently partial and prejudiced, and he dealt haphazardly with individual points.[42] Most remarkable in the School of Tan Chu is the cool, detached, and methodical rationality with which they attempted to get at the truth. No doubt by our standards they did not go far enough in questioning tradition; we must remember, however, that they stood at the very beginning of the critical scholarship which eventually flourished under Sung. Several leading Sung scholars acknowledged their debt to these three men, whom, in the opinion of the late nineteenth-century critic P'i Hsi-jui, they did not surpass in the justness of their judgment.[43] And such a modern scholar as Professor William Hung has found Chao K'uang's arguments relevant to his discussion of the *Spring and Autumn Annals* and its commentaries.[44]

There was, it is true, an ambivalence in their critical approach of which they were unaware. Their purpose was to get behind the distortions of tradition to the true meaning of the Sage, and they assumed this to be perfectly consonant with their own highest principles of rationality. Thus we find in them, and in the criticism of such a follower of theirs as Liu Tsung-yüan, a mixture of judgments based on critical historical arguments and of unhistorical, *a priori* judgments about what must be true. The unquestioned assumption about the agreement between the real ideas of the Classics and the metaphysical ideas being developed during the T'ang and Sung was unjustified, so that there were bound to be conflicts in the thought of later men, if not in the initiators of the critical movement. During the Sung we find the two tendencies differently emphasized in different thinkers. The unhistorical side finally won out, for Neo-Confucianism in its Chu Hsi synthesis used the interpretation of the Classics as the vehicle for expounding its new metaphysical system. Before this happened, however, criticism had made many solid gains and established a basis from which the Ch'ing philologists could once again react against subjective interpretation of the Classics and try to get a more objective idea of what they really were and really said.

One further remark about Tan Chu, Chao K'uang, and Lu Ch'un is worth making. In contrast to the *ku-wen* writers, who were mostly aristocrats, none of these initiators of the new critical approach to the Classics belonged to the great ruling families. Their personal backgrounds are obscure, but we may safely surmise that they belonged to the stratum of the literati which depended entirely on the examination system for entrance into official position. Chao K'uang's views on the examinations are set out at length in the *T'ung-tien* and are referred to below. As we shall see, he criticized the existing system not with a view to abolishing it and reverting to a dependence on recommendation, which was the nostalgic view of some aristocrats, but in order to put substance and meaning into the Confucian curriculum and to ease the candidates' financial burdens.

What can be inferred from this difference in social background is not clear. Both classical studies and training in literary composition were largely directed toward passing the civil service examinations. It may be that new men were comparatively free from family traditions of classical scholarship and so able to look at problems with a fresh eye; on the other hand, the tradition of letters as the avocation of aristocratic courtiers may have played a part. It seems to me no mere coincidence that both movements developed at a time when enforced leisure and remoteness from the capital diverted energies from the scramble for office.

T'IEN-T'AI BUDDHISM

In Buddhism new movements were also developing. Though we are concerned here mainly with the Chinese classical tradition, it would be misleading to give the impression that at this period Buddhism had lost its hold on the minds of the secular learned, or was kept apart in the monasteries without influence on the world outside. Indeed, a substratum of Buddhist ideas is often to be presumed even when not explicitly present, and it is well known that as Neo-Confucian metaphysics developed it drew directly on Buddhism.

At Ch'ang-an, official Buddhism with its elaborate and costly ceremonies was now dominated by the newly introduced Tantric School;

but in the provinces, and mainly in the south, there were other more significant developments. This was the period of the great movement started by Fa Chao (active 766–805) for the spread of the Pure Land teachings among the people.[45] More limited and sophisticated in appeal, the Ch'an and T'ien-t'ai Sects were philosophically opposites but alike in their tendency to assimilate Buddhism to Chinese intellectual tradition.[46] Of the two, Ch'an has the more perennial interest, but T'ien-t'ai is the more immediately relevant to the present discussion. The syncretism of this sect, which sought to harmonize sectarian divisions within the faith by treating them not as mutually exclusive but as forming a hierarchy of "levels," prepared the way for finding the truths of Buddhist metaphysics in Confucian texts as well. Several of the early T'ang Neo-Confucians were lay followers of this sect, and the influence of its metaphysics can be seen clearly in their writings.

The T'ien-t'ai Sect was indeed undergoing a rejuvenation under its ninth patriarch Chan-jan (711–82) which amounted to a second founding. His lay surname was Ch'i and he came from a family with a tradition of secular learning. From the age of about twenty, he studied Buddhism under the preceding patriarch Tso-ch'i, and began to gather disciples as a "scholar in retirement" (ch'u-shih), but it was not until after 742 that he became a monk. He wrote prolifically, expounding T'ien-t'ai doctrines and confuting opponents, and gained great fame.[47] It is perhaps no more than coincidence that his period of influence coincided with the flight of northern scholars to the south and with the ku-wen movement, but one wonders whether there may not have been some reciprocal stimulus. It seems legitimate to suppose that his great success resulted at least partly from the attention he attracted among these refugee scholars and the encouragement they gave him. Li Hua and Liang Su were followers of both him and his disciple Yüan-tsao.[48] Later, Liu Tsung-yüan was called a disciple in the fourth generation.[49]

THE RETURN TO THE NORTH UNDER TE-TSUNG

With the accession of Te-tsung (780–805) we find the center of intellectual life moving back from the provinces to Ch'ang-an. Already, under Tai-tsung (763–79), members of coteries in the southeast had been drawn into political life at the capital. We have already mentioned Han Yü's elder brother Han Hui, who achieved some fame in the south in 765, came to Ch'ang-an and became involved in the downfall of Yüan Tsai in 777. Clearly the patronage of the leaders of the ku-wen movement was used by men of talent in the Yangtze region as a means, first, to get employment under one of the military governors or financial commissioners of the region and, then, to get valuable recommendations for passing the examinations and obtaining posts in the central bureaucracy, which still remained the ultimate goal of all men of ambition. Thus we find Tu-ku Chi saying farewell to a Mr. Liu and commending him to the financier Han Hui (not Han Yü's brother) who, he says, has already been instrumental in the advancement of several other friends.[50] When Ts'ui Yu-fu, a close friend of Tu-ku Chi and Li Hua, and a strong supporter of the *ku-wen* movement, became Chief Minister in 779–80, he immediately filled a great many offices with personal acquaintances.[51] He defended this on the ground that it was only by personal knowledge that he could vouch for their ability and character. We note with interest that he is in no way condemned for this by the T'ang historians. Rather, Ts'ui's rival, whom he supplanted, is criticized for having rigidly kept to the examination procedures in making appointments.

This throws an interesting light on contemporary criticisms of the examination system (discussed by Mr. Nivison elsewhere in this volume) and also on the development of a formalized system of sponsorship, the beginnings of which we see at the same period.[52] Candidates protested against the narrow formalized curriculum they were forced to submit to, and against the exhausting, costly, long-drawn-out, and, for the majority, ultimately frustrating ordeal of the examination system. They looked back to an idealized past in which true merit had allegedly been recognized and brought forward by simpler procedures. Their attitude to patronage, however, differed according to whether they were successful in obtaining it or not. Men of good family background, who found it relatively easy to make good connections, were naturally more inclined to see the virtues of direct recommendations. Those who found in the examination system, however arduous, their only hope of advancement were more inclined to lay stress on the impartiality of the examiners, but even they saw nothing reprehensible in trying to attract attention of influential persons by sending examples of their writing. What would be currying favor when done by a "small man" would only be obtaining just recognition of merit when done by a true gentleman.

Examiners in their turn were anxious to make their names illustrious by selecting young men of authentic talent, and evidently relied on such extracurricular aids to their judgment as much as on the formal examination essays. They regarded this as in no way impairing their impartiality. To the outsider and the disappointed candidates, the line between such practices and favoritism or even corruption must often have seemed finely drawn. Yet, as contemporary critics of the examinations maintained, an all-round estimate of a candidate's talents and accomplishments by a man of discernment was more reliable than mechanical results obtained in formalized and impersonal examinations.

The most illustrious examiner during the twenty-five years of Te-tsung's reign probably was Lu Hsüan-kung (Lu Chih),[53] administrator of the doctoral examinations in Chen-yüan 8 (792). This was an *annus mirabilis* in which not only Han Yü but also several other noted writers who were his friends, such as Ou-yang Chan,[54] and Li Hua's nephew Li Kuan,[55] and future statesmen such as Li Chiang[56] and Ts'ui Ch'un,[57] received their degrees. In making his choice, Lu Hsüan-kung is said to have relied especially on the recommendations of Tu-ku Chi's disciple Liang Su, who had since 789 been in Ch'ang-an serving as Han-lin Scholar and tutor to the imperial princes.

Lu Hsüan-kung has an important place in intellectual history. A southerner from the prominent Lu clan of Su-chou, he was a statesman who, after passing the *chin-shih* degree in 773, had risen to prominence as a Han-lin Scholar during Te-tsung's exile in Feng-hsiang in 783, where he had been in charge of composing edicts. Since that time he had been an important adviser of the emperor. Lu Hsüan-kung was not himself a *ku-wen* writer; indeed, he was a most elegant practitioner of the balanced prose style. But in his attitude to politics he was a Confucian moralist and his writings—though somewhat long-winded— are full of substance. Unfortunately, his private writings have not been preserved; although we know a good deal about his views on public matters, we know comparatively little about his personal relationships.

As a statesman he was a conservative who advocated ancient moral precepts but nevertheless had a realistic view of practical matters. He is noted for the way in which he opposed Te-tsung's desire for personal rule. For example, though a Han-lin Scholar, he memorialized against the encroachments this palace organ was making on the functions of the regular bureaucracy.[58] He is represented as the paragon of Confucian constitutionalists, and was obviously considered the leader and patron of that element in the literati.

Liang Su,[59] Lu Hsüan-kung's adviser on examination candidates, came from a northern family which had been forced to flee south at the time of the An Lu-shan rebellion and had in consequence "somewhat come down in the world."[60] He also studied extensively in all fields of learning—Classics, philosophers, history, Taoism, and Buddhism—and he attracted the notice of Li Hua and Tu-ku Chi by his brilliant writings. He was a lay follower of the T'ien-tai Sect and wrote the *Chih-kuan t'ung-li*,[61] an exposition of *chih-kuan* meditation, one of the principal tenets of the sect. Of this work the *Sung Kao-seng chuan* says, "The Han-lin Scholar Liang Su therefore alone wielded a mighty

brush and achieved words of extraordinary virtue. . . . When we examine Scholar Liang's discourse we find conclusions and arguments
equally cogent. Who but this man could move great Confucians?"[62]
Ts'ui Yüan-han,[63] the Confucian who composed Liang's epitaph, compared this work to the Great Appendix to the *Book of Changes*. Nothing illustrates more clearly how little philosophical conflict between
Confucianism and Buddhism was felt at this period—until Han Yü came
along with his intransigent attitude.

After his arrival in Ch'ang-an in 789, Liang Su was the acknowledged
leader of the new stylistic movement, and hopeful young men hastened
to pay him court and study under his direction. Lü Wen, who studied
the *Spring and Autumn Annals* under Lu Ch'un, was Liang Su's pupil
in literary composition.[64] Han Yü, then at the capital trying to take his
chin-shih degree, does not appear to have been personally a student
of Liang Su, but, according to his biography, "he went around with
the followers of Tu-ku Chi and Liang Su."[65] Han Yü himself, in a letter
written ten years later when he held the post of Doctor in the Ssu-men
Academy and was seeking similar favor for some of his own protégés,
referred to Liang Su's part in presenting his name and those of other
examination candidates.[66]

Liang Su's death and the fall of Lu Hsüan-kung in 794 did not bring
to an end the interest in *ku-wen* and in revitalized Confucian studies
among the examination candidates during the last years of Te-tsung's
reign, nor is there any reason to suppose that examiners were unsympathetic. Candidates who were unsuccessful, or had to wait for some
time to pass, naturally complained of unfairness, but one must take
such murmurings with a grain of salt.[67] After all, only a few could be
chosen each year from the many applicants. Of those who were chosen,
many made their mark later. The examiners who followed Lu Hsüan-
kung are for the most part praised in the histories. Ku Shao-lien[68]
(793–94 and 798), who followed Lu Hsüan-kung and under whom Liu
Tsung-yüan took his *chin-shih,* is not an outstanding figure but his apparent hostility to Pe'i Yen-ling suggests he probably supported Lu
Hsüan-kung. Kao Ying[69] (799–801) was noted for his uprightness as an
examiner, and Ch'üan Te-yü[70] (802–3 and 805), a writer of considerable
fame, later received Han Yü's praise for his conduct as an examiner,[71]
a significant tribute, for Han Yü had been concerned during Ch'üan's
period of examining with getting his own candidates through. Only
Lü Wei (795–97),[72] who had connections with P'ei Yen-ling, is hos-
tilely treated in his biography, but since his son Lü Wen was a student
of Liang Su and Lu Ch'un, and a close friend of Liu Tsung-yüan, it is
unlikely that Lü Wei was prejudiced against the "new thought."

Among the young men themselves two groups stand out. There were those who from about 803 onward constituted a "brains trust" for the faction headed by Wang Shu-wen, Wang P'ei, and Wei Chih-i, which took power and came to grief in 805 under Shun-tsung. Liu Tsung-yüan, Liu Yü-hsi,[73] Lü Wen, Li Ching-chien,[74] Han Yeh,[75] Han T'ai,[76] and Ch'en Chien[77] are among the most prominent of them. The rival group included Han Yü and his followers.

Liu Tsung-yüan's group was probably more influenced by Tan Chu's school of classical studies than by the *ku-wen* movement proper. Liu says of himself, "I practiced literature for a long time, but I despised it in my heart and did not work at it. I looked upon it as no more than a special skill such as in chess. So when I was at Ch'ang-an I did not try to make a name by this means. My intention was to apply myself to practical affairs and make my way that of reforming the age and affecting people."[78] He describes how his interest in the *Spring and Autumn Annals* was aroused by hearing a discussion at the house of his brother-in-law P'ei Chin in Ch'ang-an. He heard P'ei and a certain Mr. Yüan arguing with Lü Wen and Han Yeh on the meaning of a passage in the *Annals*. It came to him as a revelation that the ancient significance of the work which had long been hidden was being laid bare. Later, at Han T'ai's house, he saw a copy of Lu Ch'un's works.[79] Finally, when Lu Ch'un returned to Ch'ang-an in 804, Liu Tsung-yüan and his friends were able to talk directly with the man they looked on as their master.

The influence of this school of interpretation can be seen in Liu Tsung-yüan's own critical works. Sometimes his argument recalls Tan Chu's views on the transmission of the commentaries to the *Spring and Autumn Annals*. This resemblance is to be seen in Liu's essays on the authenticity of *Wen-tzu, Yen-shih ch'un-ch'iu, Kang-ts'ang-tzu,* and *Ho-kuan-tzu,* and in his discussion of the *Analects* (which, he argues, cannot have been composed by Confucius' own disciples but was probably put together by the disciples of Tseng-tzu).[80] More often, however, his criticism of ancient works is ethical and rationalistic. Old stories are criticized for the conduct that is portrayed in them, judged on a timeless basis, without taking into account any relativity of standards. This is the spirit pervading his critical attack on the *Kuo-yü* (*Fei Kuo-yü*) which he composed during his exile.[81] The spirit is one of independence, of unwillingness to accept tradition blindly; but the impulse is toward a rationalistic ethic for his own time rather than toward what we would think of as objective historical scholarship, aimed at understanding the past in its own terms.

Liu Tsung-yüan and his friends must have shocked people by their boldness. In a letter to Lü Wen about the *Fei Kuo-yü*, Liu relates the comment that a man named Lu had made about his friend Li Ching-chien's *Critique of Mencius* (*Meng-tzu p'ing*). "It is certainly well done. But did the ancients in writing books attack their predecessors like that?" Liu observed, "His intention was to make clear the Way. It was not to attack Mencius."[82]

Liu Tsung-yüan's group seems to have remained eclectic in its thought. However fervently the value of the Classics was discussed, there did not seem to be a need felt to reject non-Confucian schools of thought. For example, we find Liu Tsung-yüan, Li Ching-chien, and Lü Wen showing great interest in Tuan Hung-ku, an advocate of Legalist doctrines.[83] This again shows that their main concern was to construct a valid philosophy, not to preserve an orthodoxy.

By contrast Han Yü, who like other advocates of *ku-wen* emphasized *wen* as the means of expressing the Way, adopted an attitude of militant Confucian orthodoxy. There was little in Han Yü's specific ideas either on literature or on philosophy that had not already appeared in the writings of his predecessors. Interest in such works as the *Doctrine of the Mean,* the *Great Learning,* and the *Book of Changes* as sources of a Confucian metaphysics was by now a commonplace. The idea that the line of succession of Confucian teaching had been broken was expressed also by others, notably Lü Wen.[84] Han Yü's innovation lay in actually assuming the role of teacher in the line of Mencius. According to both his own account[85] and that of Liu Tsung-yüan,[86] this pretension brought him ridicule and, although he did get a devoted group of followers, was responsible for his ill success in getting into office. After futile attempts to get a post through the Placement Examinations in 793 and 795, he gave up and took service under military governors at Pien-chou and Hsü-chou. Only in 802 did he get a post at Ch'ang-an as a Doctor in the Ssu-men Academy. In 803, he at last won entry into political office; he became an Examining Censor as a colleague of Liu Tsung-yüan, who was his junior in years and had had a much smoother start to his career. Liu Yü-hsi, who had taken his *chin-shih* degree in 793, was in the same office along with Liu Tsung-yüan, but had since then been serving at Yang-chou on the staff of the Military Governor. This Military Governor, who was none other than Tu Yu, one of the most learned scholars of the age and a distinguished statesman, also came to Ch'ang-an in 803, and it is now time to say something about him.

POLITICAL AND ECONOMIC THOUGHT—TU YU

Besides the new ideas in belles-lettres, scholarship, and metaphysics, there was in the post-rebellion period much thought devoted to practical matters of government and to questions of economic policy. Indeed, two of the most notable productions of the second half of the eighth century were Su Mien's *Hui-yao* and Tu Yu's *T'ung-tien,* both encyclopedic works of institutional history which provided models for later continuations and imitations. The *Hui-yao,*[87] out of which grew the existing *T'ang Hui-yao,* was limited in scope for it dealt only with the T'ang dynasty. But the idea of providing a classified digest of important official documents was a most useful one, to which many generations of students have been immensely indebted. Unfortunately we are not well informed about Su Mien, although his brother Su Pien was an important financial official in the latter years of Te-tsung's reign.[88] The Su family were scholars, and the family library was reputed to be the most extensive private collection in the empire. There are scattered personal comments by Su Mien preserved in the *T'ang Hui-yao* from which we can deduce that, like his contemporary Tu Yu, he was concerned to explain the troubles that had befallen the dynasty in terms of economic and institutional history.[89] His views, however, were traditional and much less interesting than those of Tu Yu, who is seldom mentioned in the history of Chinese philosophy but whose independence and originality deserve close attention.

Tu Yu's *T'ung-tien* was inspired by, and based on, a previous institutional encyclopedia known as the *Cheng-tien,* written by the son of the historian Liu Chih-chi, Liu Chih,[90] who was, as already mentioned, instrumental in saving Li Hua's life. Liu Chih's work has not survived, but there are a number of lengthy quotations from it[91] and we have other indications of his way of thinking. The Japanese scholar Kanai Yukitada[92] credits him with considerable understanding of the problems of his time, especially of the examination system and of the development of centralized bureaucracy. I find it hard to agree. His ideas are not without interest, but, like others of his contemporaries, he was a would-be statesman prevented by the political situation from taking an active part in affairs, expressing his frustration in theorizing insufficiently controlled by reality. His chance eventually came, only to end most ingloriously.

Liu Chih had already made a name for himself by his discussions on government policies in the years 734–35 when he held the office of Administrator in the Left Chien-men Guard. His memorial against Chang Chiu-ling's proposal to allow private coinage of money is noteworthy; Tu Yu considered it to be one of the best expositions of the problems of currency that had ever been made. During Li Lin-fu's dictatorship, Liu Chih dropped out of sight as a politician, but it was at that time that he wrote the *Cheng-tien.* He was greatly admired by Fang Kuan, another scholar official, who had achieved limited fame as a provincial administrator before the An Lu-shan rebellion but had failed to advance to high office at the capital. Opportunity came for both of them when, after having protested vainly against the disastrous policy of seeking battle with the An Lu-shan forces at the T'ung-kuan,[93] they joined the emperor on his flight to Szechwan in 756. The old emperor rewarded Fang Kuan's loyalty by making him Chief Minister, and Liu Chih played the role of confidential adviser. One of Fang Kuan's first acts was to persuade the emperor to divide the empire into regions and put a son in charge of each.[94] This must have been Liu Chih's suggestion, for we know that he was strongly in favor of restoring the ancient "feudal" system of the Chou period and regarded it as a great mistake that T'ai-tsung had not persisted in his plan to establish the T'ang empire on this basis. The policy proved to be a costly fiasco; the only prince to go to his post ("fief"), Prince Lin, who was sent to the south, promptly made plans to set up an independent empire based on the Yangtze, and had to be put down by an expeditionary force.[95]

Later Fang Kuan was sent to join the new emperor, Su-tsung, at Feng-hsiang; he enjoyed such high favor that in spite of being a civil official, he was put in charge of the army and allowed to plan the campaign against the rebels. Once again he adopted a plan based on literal imitation of "the way of the former kings"; he went into battle with chariots drawn by oxen. The result was a disastrous defeat in which the imperial army suffered 40,000 casualties. Liu Chih was Fang Kuan's staff officer (*ts'an-mou*) for this operation and, as Kanai surmises, it is extremely likely that he was responsible for the fanciful tactics.[96] Although we do not possess any of Liu's writings on war, we know that, apart from the probable inclusion of a section on war in the *Cheng-tien,* he wrote two works on military theory.[97] Fang Kuan did not immediately lose office because of this disaster, but his influence not unnaturally declined. He ceased to attend to affairs of state and gave himself over to pleasure in the company of his scholar associates. They remained in power long enough to protect Li Hua in the collaboration trials after the recapture of the two capitals, but in the middle of 758 they were all dismissed to provincial posts,[98] and Liu Chih died soon after.[99]

At this time Tu Yu[100] was a young man living amid the intellectual ferment of the lower Yangtze, but it was somewhat later that Liu Chih's book came to his notice, or, at any rate, that he conceived the idea of enlarging it. As a thinker, Tu Yu stands apart from most of his contemporaries. He has been called a Legalist. Whether or not this is an altogether fitting description, he has undeniable Legalist affinities. His appreciation of political planners and his belief that one should not attempt to imitate antiquity but should adapt the essential truths of older writings to the needs of the present are qualities which are usually associated, if not necessarily with pure Legalism, at least with the Legalist pole within Confucianism. His views as expressed in his encyclopedic history of governmental institutions, the *T'ung-tien*, have a refreshing down-to-earthness and practicality combined often with a clear insight into the nature of contemporary problems and their historical background.

Tu Yu came from an aristocratic northwestern family. Although a man of great learning, he did not practice belles-lettres and was almost ostentatious in referring to his lack of literary ability. He entered service through *yin* privilege and was made an Administrator (*ts'an chün*) in Chi-nan Commandery (Li-ch'eng in Shantung). The time must have been just before the rebellion of An Lu-shan. His next post was in the south at Shan-hsien (Sheng-hsien in Chekiang). By his knowledge of the law he attracted the notice of his father's old friend Wei Yüan-fu,[101] the Prefect of Jun-chou, who made him his Legal Administrator (*Ssu-fa ts'an chün*). We have no precise dates for Tu's appointments in the southeast nor any information about how he came there, but it is likely that he was originally a refugee. It is, of course, possible that he received his appointment at Shan-hsien before the rebellion broke out, but the ten-year interval before the first recorded date, 765, is rather long, and it is probable that there was a period of unemployment in the first part of it. Significantly his career thereafter was in the service of a governor in the region where refugees were congregating.

When Wei Yüan-fu was made Inspector of Che-hsi (with headquarters at Jun-chou) in 765,[102] Tu Yu remained on his staff. At this time he began the *T'ung-tien*, working on it from 766 to 801 before presenting it to the emperor.[103] Although his completed work belongs to the end of the eighth century and made its impact then, we are no doubt right to think of it primarily as a product of the post-rebellion period.

Tu Yu had a distinguished career as an official mainly in the provinces. His one important service in Ch'ang-an was in 780 when Yang Yen became Chief Minister and initiated his financial reforms. Yang summoned Tu Yu to the capital and entrusted him with various financial offices, in particular the management of supplies for military operations then under way. Finally he was put in charge of the Public Revenue Department. While in this office he attempted a rationalization of some of the miscellaneous functions that this department had accumulated since the rebellion. He also seems to have been partly responsible for an effort to raise emergency revenues by forced loans on merchants.

When Lu Ch'i drove Yang Yen from power, in 782, Tu Yu was also dismissed and for the next twenty years served mostly in provincial posts. In 789 he became Military Governor of Huai-nan, an important province at the lower end of the Transport Canal—a post which his patron Wei Yüan-fu had once held. Except for a break after his mother's death, he occupied this post until 803, when he was summoned to court and made a titular Chief Minister with the high honorific rank of Ssu-k'ung. Now sixty-eight years old, an elderly and distinguished statesman, he published his *Li-tao yao-chüeh* in ten chapters, a work consisting of thirty-three essays on political science which seem to have corresponded in the main to the discussions on various topics scattered through the *T'ung-tien*.[104]

Tu Yu was certainly a law specialist, whether or not he can be called a Legalist in a strict sense. His admiration for the Legalist planners of antiquity, including, for instance, Lord Shang who laid the foundations for the rise of Ch'in, could hardly have been countenanced by a strict Confucianist.[105] He admired Legalist statesmen for the way they developed institutions suited to the conditions of their own days, untrammeled by the imitation of past models; ancient books should be consulted for the basic principles they propounded rather than for ideal patterns. He himself valued the economic ideas of *Kuan-tzu,* but speaking of that work, he remarked: "Whenever one consults the books of the ancients, it is because one wishes to reveal new meanings and form institutions in accordance with present circumstances. Their Way is inexhaustible. How much more are plans for contrivances and expedients subject to a thousand changes and ten thousand alterations. If one imitates in detail, it is like notching a boat to mark a spot . . ."[106]

This may seem a self-evident principle, but it was not understood by a great many of the restorers of antiquity. The historian Liu Chih-chi had been opposed to mechanical imitation of past models in historiography.[107] Nevertheless, as we have seen, his son Liu Chih was sometimes a literalist concerning the ways of former kings; nor was he alone in this. A good deal of the impetus toward the revival of Confucianism came from ritualists who believed that regeneration could only be achieved by literal adherence to the precepts of the Rites. Liu Tsung-yüan tells the story of a Mr. Sun who brought ridicule on himself by trying to restore the practice of announcing at court the coming of age, "capping," of sons. When he presented his bamboo tablet and said to the assembled courtiers, "The capping of my son so-and-so is completed," the Governor of the Capital stood in his path and, trailing the tablet behind him, angrily said, "What has it to do with me?"—to the great amusement of the assembly.[108]

Tu Yu was not bemused by any such phantoms of the past. Chu Hsi called his *Li-tao yao-chüeh* "a book that makes the past wrong and the present right."[109] Tu's introduction to the section on barbarians in the *T'ung-tien* gives an idea of his views on the progressive development of world history. He attributes China's advancement compared with the surrounding peoples to its central geographical position and favorable conditions of life: "The people's nature is mild, and their wits are intelligent. The products of the earth are abundant, and its creatures multiply after their kind. Therefore it gave birth to sages and worthies who, one after another, gave forth laws and teaching. According to the needs of their times, they remedied evils and adapted things to profit and use." He goes on to explain that in the Three Dynasties (Hsia, Shang, and Chou) the country was divided into warring states until Ch'in suppressed the feudal lords and established bureaucratic government. Nor was this the end of the story, for population had increased through the Han, Sui, and T'ang, and the achievement of peace and increase of population were the proper objectives of government.

He criticizes the Taoist picture of a golden age of simplicity before the creation of social institutions. While he sympathizes with the Taoists' satire on the degenerate sophistication of civilized life, he feels that their view of antiquity is unrealistic. He maintains that the ancient Chinese lived very much like the barbarians—and he proceeds to list customs such as living in caves or in the open and failure to practice clan exogamy, which were recorded of the ancient Chinese and were also known among the barbarians of his own day.[110]

In thus giving a positive value to the social institutions invented by the sages, Tu Yu's position agrees with that of a Confucian like Han Yü in the "Yüan tao." It differs in (1) substituting an environmental explanation for the element of magic or mystique in the sages, (2) making progress continuous and cumulative, and including such men as Shang Yang and even Ch'in Shih-huang-ti among its agents, (3) adopting a purely materialistic criterion for judging human welfare. Confucius had given due importance to the people's livelihood, but his followers tended to talk about more spiritual things. Whereas the *ku-wen* reformers wanted to use literature as a means of promoting "civilizing transformation" or "culture" (*chiao-hua*), a favorite expression of theirs, Tu Yu says bluntly, "The beginning of the Way of Good Government lies in putting into practice civilizing transformation; the basis of civilizing transformation lies in bringing about a sufficiency of food and clothing."[111]

One subject on which Tu Yu differs most noticeably from his model Liu Chih is "feudalism" (*feng-chien*). As we have seen, Liu Chih, before the An Lu-shan rebellion, strongly advocated this institution hallowed by association with the sage kings. Afterward, with the military governors often likening themselves to the "feudal lords" of the Chou dynasty, the faults of the *feng-chien* system became obvious. Yet *feng-chien* terminology was constantly used in a literary way of the military governors, and some optimistic literati may have felt comforted by the historical analogy. They may even have looked to the perfecting of a *feng-chien* system like that of Chou as a solution to the dynasty's difficulties. For Tu Yu at least the issue was clear. The *feng-chien* system did not, he says, originate by a deliberate act on the part of the sages. It was the result of custom. The original feudal lords were not chosen by the Son of Heaven but were simply the chiefs of small communities. Originally these were very numerous, but the numbers were reduced in successive dynasties until Ch'in abolished them altogether.

Liu Chih and others before him had advocated a *feng-chien* system as a defense for the imperial house, since if the ruler enfeoffed his sons there would be support in the country when any other family attempted to usurp. The long duration of Chou in comparison to Ch'in was offered as proof. Tu Yu does not directly refute this argument. He says that if the criterion is to be the duration of the royal house, then feudalism may be the answer, but there will be war and the population will be sparse; if the criterion is the populousness of the people, then there must be a bureaucratic system of provincial government. "To set up feudal kingdoms benefits one house. To arrange commanderies benefits all the people." And he adds, "All laws and ordinances that are established must decay. It is only a question of estimating how long they will go on doing harm [before they can be reformed]."[112] To find a Chinese scholar in imperial times stating so frankly that there can be a contradiction between the interests of the ruling house and those of the people is remarkable.

Those who know Liu Tsung-yüan's works will have no difficulty seeing in this discussion the inspiration of the "Feng-chien lun" ("Discourse on Feudalism"). Liu, like Tu, treats "feudalism" not as a perfect institution deliberately conceived by the ancient sages, which the ancient kings had been unable to do away with all at once, but as an unfortunate result of society's natural evolution. Liu's essay is even more remarkable than Tu's, for he gives a more fully worked out theory of society's origins. Rulers first arose, neither as divinely inspired sages nor as men of superior endowment produced by the favorable environment of the Central Land, but as the result of conflict and struggle which led people to submit to those who could settle their disputes. This happened first on a small local scale; then the conflicts of localities and groups led to the formation of larger and larger political units until the whole empire had been brought under one man. The influence of Hsün-tzu's conception of men's desires giving rise to conflict as the prime factor necessitating social organization is obvious and explicitly acknowledged, but Liu Tsung-yüan goes much further than Hsün-tzu in giving human society a naturalistic origin instead of looking on ancient institutions as the deliberate creations of sages, of men with more than normal intelligence and vision. Liu's account of feudalism's evils and its breakdown follows and elaborates Tu Yu's argument.[113]

Tu Yu's ideas on the selection of officials and on economics are of great interest. The problem of the examinations intimately affected all bureaucrats and would-be bureaucrats. The examination system was sufficiently new—in its Sui-T'ang form—so that both its detailed workings and its basic principles were matters of debate. Scarcely anyone writing on it fails to adopt a critical tone, but there are differences in the criticisms, often only subtle nuances, that stem from different interests and outlooks. The debate is, of course, reflected in the "Treatise on Examinations" in the *New T'ang History*.[114] There is much more material in the relevant chapters of the *T'ung-tien*, and a full translation of these would be of great interest.

Tu Yu, who had entered office through hereditary privilege and had no literary pretensions, was among those who thought the examination system had opened the door much too wide and accepted men for accomplishments irrelevant to the business of government. He would have tried rigorously to reduce the number of official posts at the capital and leave it to senior officials to appoint their own staffs or make recommendations.[115]

Critics who were more closely identified with literature and classical scholarship were more inclined to emphasize the hardships of the candidate under the existing system. For instance, Chao K'uang, already mentioned as a follower of Tan Chu's school of classical studies, appreciated the relative equality of opportunity provided by a centralized examination system and proposed a scheme whereby candidates would write their essays in the provinces to be forwarded to the capital for grading. He also wished to limit the opportunities for non-scholars to get official posts without examination, and to ensure that those who did get in were grounded in classical studies.[116] Lu Hsüan-kung did not think the examination system had opened the door too wide. He told Te-tsung on one occasion that, although the Empress Wu (under whom the examination system had for the first time brought a considerable number of new men into the bureaucracy) had no doubt gone too far in making advancement easy, her arrangements for the judgment of character and achievement had in fact brought many good officials to the top. Unlike Tu Yu, he felt that under Te-tsung it had become too difficult to enter officialdom.[117]

Lu proposed to introduce into the system of promoting officials a formal procedure of recommendations by the heads of bureaus who would then be held responsible for their protégés and receive merit or demerit on the basis of the grades the protégés received in the annual examination of merit. This is not the place to discuss fully the T'ang beginnings of the sponsorship system, which was to play an important role in the Sung.[118] To Lu Hsüan-kung it seems to have commended itself as a public procedure for avoiding the evils of secret favoritism. When complaints were made that sponsorship meant favoritism, the emperor wished to entrust all promotions to Lu Hsüan-kung as Chief Minister, but Lu would not accept this responsibility. He defended his plan, which was, however, rescinded.[119]

The conflict between literatus and aristocrat is again to be seen in the contrast between the economic ideas of Lu Hsüan-kung and Tu Yu. Lu Hsüan-kung is famous for his memorials criticizing Yang Yen's tax reforms of 780;[120] whereas Tu Yu, who had been associated with Yang Yen, continued to take a favorable view of the measures. A full understanding of the differences in the theoretical outlook of Tu Yu and Lu Hsüan-kung would require an intensive study of their backgrounds in earlier Chinese economic thought, particularly as found in the *Kuan-tzu*, for clearly the two men shared many basic conceptions. Both had the same physiocratic ideal of a basically agrarian and equalitarian economy, and they drew on the same or similar maxims to illustrate their points. Yet there were profound differences of emphasis.

Lu's economic theory was conservative and traditional. He admitted that after the rebellion of An Lu-shan the fiscal situation of the country had become thoroughly unsound and in need of reform, but he maintained that to remedy present evils Yang Yen should have restored rather than eliminated the fundamentally good system instituted by the founders of the dynasty and based on principles hallowed in antiquity. He attacked the principle of taxing property and production rather than levying equal taxes on all individuals and households. It would take too long to discuss all his ideas in detail, but in general they favor relaxation of state interference to let the economy find its own harmony, and intervention only to suppress abuses such as the encompassment of small holdings in large estates (*chien-ping*) or to ensure stability in times of need by use of granaries. He was particularly opposed to Te-tsung's tendency to rely on unscrupulous financial officials who would raise money by all kinds of extralegal means. This stand finally brought about his downfall, for Te-tsung was determined to enrich himself, and when it came to a showdown in 794, he preferred P'ei Yen-ling to Lu Hsüan-kung.[121]

Tu Yu, on the other hand, argued that it was of the highest importance for the state to see that the people were all settled on the land and registered in localities, and he expressed his admiration for statesmen of the past such as Kao Chiung of the Sui[122] and Yü-wen Jung of the K'ai-yüan period (713–42)[123] who had sought to effect this. He distinguished them from other officials who had devised unscrupulous schemes for enriching the treasury.

Tu Yu praised Yang Yen's reform primarily from this point of view —because it reduced somewhat the chaos into which the registers had fallen and increased the number of people accounted for on the rolls.[124] Lu Hsüan-kung, however, although he wanted the people settled on the land, was with those who felt that it was best to foster conditions that would make them content and felt that coercive methods would be self-defeating. These different viewpoints reflect the contrast between Hsün-tzu's view that human nature is naturally bad and must be coerced, and Mencius' view that man is naturally good and will respond to good treatment.

On a more theoretical level there appears to be a difference in Tu Yu's and Lu Hsüan-kung's views on the proper basis of taxation which reflects their different attitudes to Yang Yen's reform. As already mentioned, Lu advocated taxation on the basis of the individual person and household and decried the principle of taxes based on production or property. But Tu Yu is at pains to argue that in ancient times good systems of taxation were always based on land and not on men.[125]

Tu Yu shows his Legalist bias in his attitude to merchants; he stresses the primacy of agriculture but, like the Legalist-minded great officials of the "Discourses on Salt and Iron" in the Han Dynasty,[126] shows little sympathy for commerce. Mainly his references to it emphasize the necessity of curbing the merchants' tendencies to exploit the economic weakness of the peasants, to accumulate fortunes and upset the equilibrium of society. He does not condemn the extraordinary levies on merchants made in the An Lu-shan rebellion, commenting, "It was the proper thing in a time of emergency."[127] He was himself partly responsible for a similar measure in 782.[128] With this attitude we may perhaps contrast the view expressed in 822 by Han Yü on a proposal to change the organization of the salt monopoly by having officials instead of merchants handle distribution and sales. Han Yü did not exactly praise the salt merchants but he recognized their position as a vested interest cooperating with the state.[129] Any difference of attitude toward merchants among the literati was, to be sure, a matter of nuance, but I think one may see here a difference between the lofty and distant contempt expressed by aristocrats like Tu Yu and the more realistic evaluation of merchants by Confucians of less exalted ancestry.

THE REFORM PARTY OF WANG SHU-WEN

The year 803, in which Tu Yu came to the capital and became a titular Chief Minister, is an important one, for just at this time a reform party with the Crown Prince as its center begins to be active in political affairs, evidently in the expectation that he would soon succeed his father. There was widespread resentment of various abuses that had grown up in the latter years of Te-tsung's reign as a result of his increasingly autocratic and personal rule. His autocratic temper, combined with his avarice, led him to treat the bureaucracy with suspicion and to rely on favorites who used unscrupulous methods to fill the treasury (and their own pockets). These dissatisfactions were combined with a wish to strike radically at the cankers of eunuch influence and militarism which had been undermining the state for the past half-century.

The leaders of the reform group were two men of the Crown Prince's personal entourage, Wang Shu-wen and Wang P'ei, and a Secretary in the Ministry of Civil Office, Wei Chih-i, who had once been a Han-lin Scholar and was now the leader of the liberal element in the bureaucracy. These three gathered around them a number of the most brilliant young men at Ch'ang-an, including, as we have seen, Liu Tsung-yüan and other followers of the *ku-wen* movement in literature and of the new critical movement in scholarship.

In 805 Te-tsung died, Shun-tsung succeeded to the throne, and for a short time the group controlled the government. Unfortunately for their plans, Shun-tsung had shortly before suffered a stroke, making him an invalid unable to speak. This misfortune and the opposition from eunuchs, military governors, and more conservative members of the bureaucracy ensured their downfall after only a few months. The abdication of the emperor in favor of his son, posthumously known as Hsien-tsung, was engineered, and the members of the reform group were convicted of seditious conspiracy and banished to lowly offices in the remote south.[180]

The most severely dealt with were Wang Shu-wen and Wang P'ei, men of undistinguished family background and no connections; they have both been vilified in the official histories. Wang P'ei[181] was a calligrapher from Hang-chou—a man of ugly appearance with a southern accent which made him ridiculous in the eyes of the northern literati. Wang Shu-wen,[182] who came from nearby Yüeh-chou (Shao-hsing), had initially won the favor of the Crown Prince as an expert in the game of *wei-ch'i* but had more claims to scholarship. Wang Shu-wen was put to death after being exiled; this may also have been the fate of Wang P'ei, who is not heard of again. Wei Chih-i[183] came from an aristocratic family and his connections protected him for a time, but in the end he was banished to the most pestilential place in the empire, Hainan island, where he eventually died.[134] Liu Tsung-yüan and the other lesser criminals were also banished, but not quite so far. In 815 they were pardoned to the extent that they were made prefects of *chou*, but they were sent to remote spots.[135]

The Crown Prince seems to have played an active part in gathering these men around him. If we may trust the biography of Wei Chih-i in the *Old T'ang History*, Wei was first introduced in 785 to Wang Shu-wen by the Crown Prince.[136] There is evidence that in the early years of Te-tsung's reign the Crown Prince, already a grown man, had at his court leading Buddhist monks debating on conflicts of doctrine,[137] and we note that Liang Su for a time held the post of Reader to him.[138] If we could discover more about the Crown Prince's personality and his entourage during his father's reign, we might be in a better position to understand the events of his own reign.

The reformist aims of the group seem clear. In general, their official condemnation as a seditious faction was accepted thereafter, but already during the Sung, Hung Mai expressed doubts. He pointed out that during their brief period of power they had executed a number of highly commendable measures, including: (1) steps to curb the oppressive behavior of the eunuchs, procuring goods for the palace in the markets of the capital, (2) steps to prevent the youths of the eunuch-controlled palace stables from terrorizing the streets, (3) abolition of the monthly "tribute" from the Salt and Iron Commission, (4) drastic reduction of the number of singing girls in the palace, (5) the recall of good officials such as Lu Hsüan-kung who had been exiled during the latter years of Te-tsung's reign and kept in distant regions by the ten-year lack of amnesties. Furthermore, if their attempt to deprive the eunuchs of control of the Palace Armies (which was turned into the most serious evidence against them) had succeeded, later tragedies would have been prevented.[139] The Ch'ing historians Wang Fu-chih[140] and Wang Ming-sheng[141] later expressed similar views, and, in recent times, several scholars studying the period have adopted this point of view.[142]

In retrospect we can see that their aim was to reform and strengthen the central government, and, not surprisingly, they incurred the inveterate hostility of the main body of military governors whom they failed to placate. What might seem less understandable at first sight is the opposition from within the ranks of the bureaucracy. Liu Tsung-yüan attributed it to consternation at seeing young men suddenly promoted to high office, and to the envy and disappointment of those who could not share in their good fortune. I think that this was undoubtedly true. Although there was antagonism between eunuchs and bureaucrats, eunuchs had by now become part of the established order, and relations of mutual dependence and benefit existed between individual bureaucrats and eunuchs. To the conservative-minded, the existing system was no doubt more tolerable than government by upstarts who might threaten their hard-won positions.

The Wang Shu-wen group is indeed a classic example of what is often called a "faction" (*p'eng-tang*). In another volume in this series Mr. Nivison discusses "faction" as a recurrent problem in Chinese political theory.[143] It was generally held that any combination was *ipso facto* wrong. Officials ought to "stand alone" (*tu-li*) and express their honest views for the benefit of the emperor. In the Sung period there were some who held that it was proper for superior men to join forces, but even if this were admitted, it could only be on the basis of ethical principles, not of detailed policies. For men to combine and plan privately to try to effect policies would be to subvert the hierarchy of authority flowing down from the emperor.

In practice of course this did not mean that men "stood alone." Officials who in fact did so were an eccentric few who might win reputations for their Confucian virtue but were unlikely to rise rapidly on the bureaucratic ladder. To get ahead one had, not to combine with one's colleagues, but to curry favor with persons of influence. An infinitely complicated web of one-to-one personal relationships took the place of definable interest groups and parties with programs. No doubt it is often possible to distinguish different interests expressing themselves now in one way, now in another, but it is extremely difficult in practice to correlate interests and personal groupings continuing over any length of time.

Such a situation in political life, which is of course not at all restricted to China, naturally tends to a conservative maintenance of the *status quo*. However strongly a person might feel that certain reforms ought to be made, as long as he remained isolated and dependent for advancement on his superiors, he would be likely to find it advisable to curb his ardor and avoid antagonizing vested interests. By the time he had raised himself to a position of influence, he had become part of the system and was unlikely to try to alter it. It is no accident, therefore, that when we do find reformist movements, they are often initiated close to the throne outside the regular bureaucratic procedures, and often incur the stigma of "faction," not distinguished in the eyes of Chinese historians from other factional groupings of a purely personal character.

It is in the light of such considerations that we must, I think, judge the role of Tu Yu in the affair. It has, so far as I know, never been suggested that he had anything to do with the reform group. On the contrary, he was apparently involved in arranging for the abdication of Shun-tsung, which sealed its ruin; we know that in his role as elder statesman Tu Yu conveyed the abdication document from Shun-tsung to his son.[144] The fact that during the reform group's period of power Tu Yu was made Commissioner for Public Revenue and Salt and Iron, and given general authority over state finances, is explained away by the statement that he was merely a figurehead for Wang Shu-wen, who, as his deputy, kept the real power in his own hands.[145] Yet it seems to me there is good reason to think that even if Tu Yu was never personally in the intimate counsels of the group, his ideas were influential among them and he was looked upon as a source of leadership and inspiration. Though he never seems to have been a particularly forceful man in practical affairs, in contrast to his daring as a thinker, Tu Yu's eminence and prestige were such that he could hardly have been used against his will by Wang Shu-wen. There is every reason for thinking that he would have approved of the aims of the group, though he, like other senior statesmen, may have been shocked, or found it politic to be shocked, by the "excesses" and rash and hasty actions of the group when it became clear that they had taken on more than they could handle.

As to the ideological influence of Tu Yu on the group, it should be noted that one of the young men, Liu Yü-hsi, had been for a long time on his staff in Huai-nan and came with him to Ch'ang-an. The publication of the *T'ung-tien* in 801 and the collection of essays from it, the *Li-tao yao-chüeh* in 803, seems to have caused a considerable stir in intellectual circles: Ch'üan Te-yü praised it fulsomely;[146] and we have seen that Liu Tsung-yüan's "Feng-chien lun" was certainly derived from Tu Yu. Later, while in exile, Liu expressed views about government economic policy closely resembling those of Tu Yu.[147]

Furthermore it seems to me not impossible that Han Yü's "Yüan tao" ("Inquiry into the Way") may also owe something to Tu Yu's discussion about the development of civilization. The dates of this and other related philosophical works by Han Yü are not known precisely, but the first probable reference to them is in the year 805, and it seems to me likely that they were the product of his period of exile from the winter of 803 to the winter of 805, coming immediately after his short period in the censorate along with Liu Tsung-yüan and Liu Yü-hsi in the latter part of 803.[148]

That Han Yü and his friends were actively discussing philosophical problems around this time seems to be indicated by Liu Tsung-yüan's "T'ien shuo," in which he expresses his view of the indifference of heaven to human affairs.[149] The essay purports to be a record of a conversation between himself and Han Yü, and is referred to by Liu Yü-hsi in terms which also imply this. If we accept this, the occasion cited must have been either before 794, when Liu Tsung-yüan, only in his twenty-second year, left Ch'ang-an on a two-year visit to his uncle in Pin-chou to the west,[150] or after 801, when Han Yü returned to Ch-'ang-an after serving on the staffs of military governors in the east since 795.[151] I think the latter period is much more probable. Liu Yü-hsi at some time after 805 wrote his "T'ien lun" as a development of Liu Tsung-yüan's essay.[152] It is not necessary to suppose that he was present at the conversation between Han Yü and Liu Tsung-yüan, but his interest in the matter suggests that he may have been. At any rate, he came to Ch'ang-an along with Tu Yu in 803, and Han Yü later referred to his intimacy with the two Lius at this time.[153]

The association with Tu Yu need not mean that the Wang Shu-wen group is to be regarded as pro–Yang Yen and anti–Liu Yen, for they included in their number Ch'en Chien, who had once been on Liu Yen's staff and had written a eulogy of him and his policies.[154] Moreover, one of the first acts of Shun-tsung's reign was to rehabilitate Lu Hsüan-kung and other victims of the tyranny of Te-tsung's later years. Probably that old factional dispute had died out.

Han Yü's personal involvement with the reform group is both interesting and important. Though he was a personal friend of Liu Tsung-yüan and Liu Yü-hsi, he does not seem to have been brought into the censorate as their colleague in 803 by the Wang Shu-wen party. Indeed, shortly before his appointment he wrote an obsequious letter of flattery to Te-tsung's corrupt and brutal favorite, Li Shih,[155] and, embarrassing as the suggestion is to those who see him as a model Confucian, it is not impossible that this was what brought about his appointment. He did not last long in the censorate, for a few months later he and two others were suddenly expelled to govern counties in the south.[156] The occasion for this expulsion seems to have been a memorial they sent drawing attention to the people's distress that resulted from the current drought,[157] and it has been assumed by traditional commentators that Li Shih, who had been collecting taxes as usual, was offended and brought about their dismissal. Others have pointed out, however, that Han Yü himself doubted that the memorial was the actual reason for their dismissal, for he seemed to blame it on Wang Shu-wen. He even suggested that his friends Liu Tsung-yüan and Liu Yü-hsi might have revealed private conversations. Although he did not long hold a grudge against them, he continued to feel hatred for their leaders, in whose downfall he exulted.[158]

Wang Shu-wen and Wei Chih-i probably were responsible for the expulsion in 803 from the capital of others whom they suspected of opposition to them,[159] and if they regarded Han Yü as unreliable—as they may well have done, especially if he was friendly with Li Shih—they may have seized a pretext to get rid of him. Control of the censorate was particularly important for a group seeking to take over the government.

There was certainly a sharp difference in ideas between Han Yü's "conservative" ku-wen movement and the "radical" school which was dominant at the end of Te-tsung's reign. In contrast to the interest of Liu Tsung-yüan and his associates in the new classical scholarship, Han Yü seems to have concerned himself very little with it. When he meets Lu T'ung, a follower of the Tan Chu school of criticism of the Spring and Autumn Annals, he is mainly interested in him as a recluse and a poet, and his comments on his scholarship, although appreciative, are made from the outside and show nothing of Liu Tsung-yüan's fervor.[160] Later he confessed to an adherent of the Kung-yang school of interpretation that he had paid little attention to such matters since preparing for his chin-shih examination.[161] Chinese critics recognized that Han did not show anything like the critical acumen displayed by Liu Tsung-yüan;[162] nor are his contributions to philosophy impressive. Most of the new ideas in this field attributed to him were already current among the ku-wen writers, and it is only because of his literary eminence and his efforts as a propagandist that they are known through him. It seems reasonable to suppose that it was this mediocre attainment in scholarship, though not in literary composition, that made people look askance at his setting himself up as a teacher and at his claim to renew the broken line of Confucian tradition.

Although Han Yü's advocacy of the teacher-pupil tradition and adoption of the role of teacher have been regarded as important points in his favor, in contrast to Liu Tsung-yüan's rejection of this role,[163] from a modern point of view this judgment should probably be reversed. The authoritarian character of the Confucian teacher-pupil relationship has had a baneful influence on the development of scholarship in the Far East. Liu Tsung-yüan's attitude is both exceptional and enlightened. He refused to claim the superiority that qualified him to be a teacher of others; instead he invited prospective pupils to come and engage in free discussion with him for their mutual benefit.

Han Yü compensated for his weakness in metaphysics and Confucian scholarship by a nationalistic rejection of Buddhism that contrasted sharply with the eclectic attitude of the earlier ku-wen movement. Their political attack on this "foreign intrusion" may have fostered in Han Yü and his followers an attitude of acceptance toward the existing political order, which Liu Tsung-yüan and his "radical" friends regarded as urgently in need of reform. The disciples who acknowledged Han Yü's leadership are not particularly distinguished but they seem to have maintained this opposition to Buddhism. We find Sun Ch'iao protesting at the restoration of Buddhism after its suppression in 845.[164]

There have been efforts to give a sociological interpretation of the contrasting positions of Han Yü and Liu Tsung-yüan. Marxist writers have tried to show that Han Yü represented the large landowners while Liu represented the small.[165] This is far too crude. It is not at all easy to see in the affair of 805 any correlation between social background and political alignment. Professor Ch'en Yin-k'o's view that the factional struggles of the following reigns reflect the conflict of interest between hereditary privilege of the aristocracy and the aspirations of new men has recently been subjected to severe criticism.[166] This latter question must be left aside. Yet one may note the apparently paradoxical fact that in the general development of thought in the post-rebellion period, persons of aristocratic (mainly north-western) background were frequently rationalistic and unorthodox in their political thinking, while the new literati coming up through the examinations system, with whom the future lay, were more inclined to a moralistic traditionalism.

CONCLUSION

This essay has tried to place in perspective the thought, mainly the political thought, of the half-century following the An Lu-shan rebellion. I have been especially struck by the way the most significant intellectual movements can be traced back to the refugee scholars who congregated in the lower Yangtze region during the rebellion period. The next generation developed further the ideas of their predecessors and, carrying the movement back to Ch'ang-an, tried, if my picture is correct, to apply themselves to a renaissance of the dynasty. The defeat of Wang Shu-wen's party in 805, which strengthened the power of the eunuchs and removed from political life some of the most ardent spirits, must have discouraged would-be reformers. The way eunuchs were able, thereafter, to murder one emperor after another added to the gloom, no doubt. In 835 came the disaster of the Sweet Dew incident. A plot against the eunuchs which had the connivance of Emperor Wen-tsung was discovered by the eunuchs; many officials were massacred and the three Chief Ministers were put to death as traitors. It is small wonder that the literati retreated more and more into the consolations of poetry and belles-lettres, and into Taoism.

If the philosophy of the period I have discussed was attempting to deal with a particular historical situation, it was also, in a wider sense, attempting to deal with the problems of the evolving bureaucratic impe-

rial system. It is therefore not surprising that when the Confucian literati again came into their own in the Sung dynasty they should have to
some degree started where the T'ang thinkers stopped. Han Yü became
the patron saint of a new *ku-wen* movement and is in the direct line of
Neo-Confucian philosophy. Liu Tsung-yüan, on the other hand, was
appreciated for his descriptions of scenery but was not valued as a
thinker.

Yet, more radical, rationalistic types of thinking did not disappear,
and it is perhaps legitimate to think of the reform movements of Northern Sung, culminating in Wang An-shih, as in some sense corresponding
to the abortive movement of Wang Shu-wen's party in 805. In the Sung,
too, we find the "Legalist" tradition drawn upon and introduced in Confucian dress, perhaps more covertly than in T'ang and with more sophistication. No doubt the specific problems and aims of the eleventh century were quite different from those of the ninth, but it may be possible
to see an underlying similarity in the mood which inspired both, and in
the type of opposition both aroused.

One might also broach the question whether it was inevitable in the
Chinese situation that rationalism should always come off second best in
the contest with traditional moralism. It is possible that the kind of clear-
sightedness toward the traditional mystique of Chinese society we find
in Tu Yu or Liu Tsung-yüan came too close to undermining the foundations of that society. If the emperor system was to be maintained—and
there was no conceivable alternative in anyone's mind—it was perhaps
necessary to buttress and maintain its mystique with the kind of authoritarianism that Chu Hsi and his followers preached. It is, however, a
fallacy in history to suppose that what in fact happened was necessarily
the only thing possible. In more favorable circumstances it is conceivable that the stultification of the Ming might have been avoided. But
we shall understand what did happen better by trying to understand
those who attempted to stand in the way of history and deflect it into
another course.

James F. Cahill

CONFUCIAN ELEMENTS
IN THE THEORY OF PAINTING

In most modern studies of Chinese painting, there has been a curious lack of reference to Confucian thought as a force in the creation of art and in the formulation of art theory. Such infrequent mentions of it as one encounters tend to be brief and unsympathetic. For Confucianism is reserved the doctrine that painting, by depicting exemplary themes, can serve as a didactic tool or a moralizing influence; all those views which involve the communication of intuitive knowledge, the operation of an aesthetic sense, or the embodiment of individual feeling are attributed to the working of Taoist and Buddhist ideas and attitudes. Similarly in matters of style: it is sometimes suggested that the Confucian temperament, when it found graphic expression, produced a dry academicism, while Taoism and Ch'an Buddhism fostered the more spontaneous, "untrammeled" styles.

The neglect and distortion of the role of Confucianism in the arts probably results in part from an extension into aesthetics of the unfortunately widespread view of the Confucian tradition as "inherently reactionary and sterile . . . in the political and social sphere,"[1] or from a supposition that its rationalist bent denied it any place in what are essentially non-rational processes, the production and appreciation of works of art. In addition, the more immediate appeal of Taoism and Buddhism—especially Ch'an Buddhism—to the modern Western mind has led to a concentration of attention upon Taoist and Buddhist elements in art as in other areas of Chinese culture. Added to these causes is the profound and protracted impact of one school of Japanese art-historical scholarship, itself strongly influenced by Zen Buddhist attitudes and tea-cult aesthetic, upon pioneer Western studies of Chinese art. Fenollosa, seeing the Chinese through Japanese eyes, announced that "a very large part of the finest thought and standards of living that have gone into Chinese life, and the finest part of what has issued therefrom in literature and art, have been strongly tinged with Buddhism."[2] Arthur Waley, at an early and still somewhat incautious stage in his distinguished career as an Orientalist, revealed a similar dependence on Japanese attitudes when he wrote: "it is in the language of Zen that, after the twelfth century, art is usually discussed in China and Japan."[3] We must assume that Waley had not yet acquainted himself with Sung and later Chinese art literature when he made this statement; because to have made it after having done so would be quite impossible.

The lack of any sound basis in Chinese art theory for such pronouncements has not diminished their effect on Occidental thinking. The fact that the great majority of painters who were philosophically committed at all (at least of those whose broader beliefs can be ascertained), and the majority of poets and calligraphers as well, were Confucian scholars, is unnoticed or ignored; or else it is supposed that when these scholars wrote and painted, they were somehow transformed into Taoists and Buddhists, and that when they thought and theorized about art, they renounced their basic beliefs and turned to the rival systems for guidance.

Joseph Levenson, for example, considering the Ming dynasty development of *wen-jen hua,* "literati painting" or painting done by scholar-amateurs, asks: "How could Ming Confucian intellectuals . . . reject the theory of painting which they associated with learning, and prize instead an anti-intellectual theory of mystical abstraction from civilized concerns? One might expect that Confucian traditionalists . . . would feel an affinity with an academic northern aesthetic and oppose the southern Ch'an . . . "[4] Levenson's association of *wen-jen hua* theory with Ch'an ideals seems to be based chiefly on the famous analogy drawn by Tung Ch'i-ch'ang (1555–1636), a leading late Ming spokesman for the literati painting movement, between the "northern and southern schools" of painting and the two branches of Ch'an. But the main outlines of *wen-jen hua* theory had been established some five centuries before Tung's time; and his analogy does not, in any event, require any close connection between literati painting and Ch'an.[5]

A characterization of literati painting by Alexander Soper may serve to represent another class of statements about painting of this school, which suppose it to have affinities with Taoism: "The 'literary man's style' of painting became the implacable enemy of the Academy and all its ways, the enemy of all organization, training, and planning; almost the exponent in art of a free, untrammeled Taoism, protesting against Confucian punctiliousness and formality."[6]

Among the relatively few contributions toward a more correct assessment of the influence of Confucian thought on art is the writing of Victoria Contag, who has sought to relate the Chinese artists' modes of representing a "second reality," especially within the literati painting school, to Neo-Confucian theories of knowledge.[7] Stimulating and convincing as I find her arguments, I do not intend here to follow her example and move between philosophy and painting proper. I shall instead confine myself to the exploration of possible instances of dependence upon Confucian ideas, not in the practice of painting but in the theory of it. I shall be concerned especially with the Sung dynasty *wen-jen hua* theorists' treatment of two problems: the function of painting, and the nature of expression in painting. But we must give some preliminary consideration to the ways in which these same problems were dealt with before the emergence of *wen-jen hua* theory, and to some Chinese notions about the other arts. In doing so, we shall begin to work toward a definition of what is specifically Confucian in Chinese art theory and criticism.

It is not easy to determine what views of painting prevailed during the Han and Six Dynasties periods, since so little writing on the subject has survived from these periods, and so little of that is pertinent to the broad questions proposed above. The earliest references to painting in extant literature seem to assign to it three main functions: the illustrative, the magical, and the moral. The first two, which are not of much concern to us here, since they play no important part in the later theorizing, may be illustrated with quotations from the *Lun Heng* by Wang Ch'ung (second century A.D.):

Popular legends, though not true, are impressively portrayed, and by these artistic representations, even wise and intelligent men are taken in.

By making pictures of dragons the duke of She succeeded in bringing down a real dragon.

The district magistrates of our time are in the habit of having peach-trees cut down and carved into human statues, which they place by the gate, and they paint the shapes of tigers on the door screens . . . These carvings and paintings of images are intended to ward off evil influences.[8]

Chang Yen-yüan, ninth-century author of *Li-tai Ming-hua Chi* ("Record of Famous Painters of Successive Dynasties"), draws upon Han dynasty and later sources in presenting the third, the moralistic view of painting. He cites the portraits of eminent and virtuous men which were painted on the walls of the Cloud Terrace and Unicorn Pavilion in the Han dynasty, and comments: "For to see the good serves to warn against evil, and the sight of evil serves to make men long for wisdom." He quotes the words of Ts'ao Chih (192–232) describing how people seeing pictures of noble rulers "look up in reverence," while those who see paintings of degenerate rulers are "moved to sadness."

Chang concludes: "From this we may know that paintings are the means by which events are preserved in a state in which they serve as models [for the virtuous] and warnings [to the evil]."[9]

The narrowness of these views of painting, and the probable reason for their early abandonment, lies in their failure to make any allowance for aesthetic value; a picture was successful to the degree that its subject was well chosen and convincingly portrayed. The often quoted remark of Han Fei-tzu, that "dogs and horses are difficult [to paint] and demons and divinities easy . . . because dogs and horses are things generally and commonly seen," whereas no one can reasonably dispute the painter's portrayal of demons,[10] implies such an absence of aesthetic criteria: exempt from criticism based on the verisimilitude of his picture, the painter of imaginary subjects should find his task "easy," since no other standard of judgment is to be applied to his work.

But there was no denying the wide variations in both style and artistic quality between one picture and another, variations for which these concepts of painting were helpless to account. One can imagine the perplexity of the Han dynasty Confucian scholar who happened to be endowed with an aesthetic sense, and found himself preferring a good picture of an unelevating subject to a bad one with a noble theme. Morality and art: what is the relationship between the two, and how are they to be reconciled? A problem which could not but concern the ethically-minded Confucianists, and which, in various later periods, was to trouble them in its relation to literature. Han Yü (768–824), who was "far more concerned with content than with elegance of language,"[11] was nonetheless suspected by the severe Chou Tun-i, an eleventh century Neo-Confucianist, of being too interested in style, not enough in doctrine. "Literary style is a matter of *art*," writes Chou, "whereas morals and virtue [*tao-te*] are the matters of real substance. If one is sincere about these substantial matters and uses art, then the beauty of one's writing will be loved; loved, it will be transmitted." Style for Chou Tun-i was only an ornament to ethical and moral content which made this content easier to assimilate; for him, "literature is the vehicle of Tao."[12] Some such means of justifying the elements of style and beauty in painting may have occurred to the Han dynasty scholars; the literature of the time gives us no clue.

Whether or not because of this inherent weakness, the notion that painting derives moral value from moral subject matter was fairly short-lived. By the time of Chang Yen-yüan, as we shall see when we come to consider Chang's own ideas (as distinct from those which he quotes or alludes to), it was invoked from the past in a somewhat ceremonious manner, but practically ignored in actual judgments of painters and paintings. Therefore, to offer this view of painting as if it were the sole contribution of Confucianism to painting theory, as some writers have done, is quite misleading. We can only say that it appears to have been the dominant Confucian view in the Han dynasty; what later Confucians thought about painting is what we shall try to determine later in this paper.

It is in the succeeding Six Dynasties period that serious discussions of painting are first composed, and new theories put forth which seek to enlarge the function of painting beyond that of simple representation. In the small corpus of critical and theoretical writing on the subject which survives from this period, we may distinguish two more or less distinct (although overlapping and not contradictory) notions about the nature and purpose of the art.

The first conceived of painting as the creation of *images*, symbolic abstractions of natural form and phenomena, analogous to the hexagrams of the *I-ching* ("Book of Changes") or to the graphs of the written language. A fifth century artist, Wang Wei, begins his essay on landscape painting by quoting a letter from his contemporary, Yen Yen-chih, who states that painting "is not to be practiced and accomplished merely as a craft; it should be regarded as of the same order as the images of the *Changes*."[13] Seen in this way, painting becomes a means of understanding and interpreting natural phenomena.

The other, historically more important view of painting in the Six Dynasties regarded it as the embodiment of the artist's feeling toward the thing depicted; the painter imbues his pictures of natural objects or scenes with some expression of his emotional responses to what he sees. If he is successful, the person who sees his picture will respond to it in a like way. The essay on landscape painting by Tsung Ping, a contemporary of the fifth-century Wang Wei quoted above, opens with a statement, typical for the period, of the ideal man's response to nature: "The sage, harboring the Tao, responds to external objects; the wise man, purifying his emotions, savors the images of things." Further on in his essay, Tsung explains the application of this response to painting: "Now, if one who considers the right principle to be *response to his eyes and accord with his heart* perfects his skill in keeping with this principle, then all eyes will respond to, and all hearts be in accord with [his paintings]."[14]

Although these two concepts are here treated as separate, they need not be. The one operation could, of course, serve as a means of accomplishing the other; the artist might embody his personal vision of the world and his understanding of it in his mode of transforming visual impressions into "images." But there was an element of Taoist mysticism as well, and perhaps of even older Chinese beliefs, involved in this notion of "response." The objects of nature, whether or not animate in the usual sense, were considered to be animated by spirit, or "souls" (*shen*). The human soul responds to these in a spiritual accord (*shen-hui*), which is the source of the sensitive man's profound feeling toward nature—or, if these "souls" have been captured by an equally sensitive artist, toward a picture of nature.

The closest philosophical affinities of both the above-mentioned theories seem to be with the school of Neo-Taoism, the strongest current of thought in this period. The view of paintings as abstractions of visual impressions into "images," symbolizing the configurations of the physical world, has its roots in the cosmological speculations of the Neo-Taoist school, and especially in its theory of the creation and significance of images.[15] The other view, that which sees painting as the embodiment of the artist's feeling toward his subject, is based upon what Fung Yu-lan terms the "sentimentalist" branch of the school,[16] wherein a deliberate savoring of physical sensations, and an intensification and refinement of one's emotional responses to them, overcame for a time the old warnings against attachment to sensible objects. That romantic movement whose adherents figure in the anecdotes of the *Shih-shuo Hsin-yü* seems also to have given rise to the earliest painting of natural scenery for its own sake in China, and to the belief that painting can serve as a substitute for that scenery by evoking the same feelings which the actual scene would evoke.

Something which corresponds to this latter view appears in literary theory of the time. The early-sixth-century *Wen-hsin Tiao-lung*, for example, describes how the poet is deeply moved by the changing aspects of the world, and continues: "And so the poet's response to things starts up an endless chain of associations; he lingers among myriad images, immerses himself in sights and sounds. He captures in words the spirit of things, depicts their appearance," calling forth a corresponding response in the reader of his poem.[17]

It is interesting to see how these ideas fared, and what others arose, in the T'ang dynasty, when Confucianism regained its dominance in government and society and the leading writers were Confucian scholars. The most important T'ang treatise on painting, Chang Yen-yüan's *Li-tai Ming-hua chi* opens with a fanfare of high-sounding generalities, meant to impress upon the reader the metaphysical and moral value of the art of painting:

Now painting is a thing which accomplishes the purpose of civilizing teaching and helps to maintain the social relationships. It penetrates completely the divine permutations of Nature and fathoms recondite and subtle things. Its merit is equal to that of any of the Six Arts of antiquity and it moves side by side with the Four Seasons. It proceeds from Nature itself and not from human invention.[18]

This introduction includes, as we have seen, a formal exposition of the moralistic, "elevated subject-matter" view of painting, with quotations from early writings. One might be tempted to concentrate upon this introduction, with all its echoes of Confucian ethical doctrine, in seeking to characterize the Confucian tone of Chang's book. But to do so would be a mistake, I think; for there is little indication in the rest of the book that Chang himself took very seriously the ideas he presents in his introduction. William Acker, who translated the first portion of the book, along with two earlier critical texts, says of such conventional references as Chang's: "Painting must be fitted into the Confucian scheme of the universe, and its uses demonstrated in terms of traditional Chinese thought.[19] Having discharged their responsibilities as Confucians in their prefatory remarks, he suggests, the critics go on to discuss individual painters and their works in quite different terms. They express admiration for vigorous or elegant brushwork, for noble conceptions, for brilliant stylistic innovations.

What is significantly absent from Chang Yen-yüan's own opinions, as they are stated or reflected in the main body of his book, is any reflection of that Six Dynasties view described above according to which a painting conveys the emotional response of the artist to the depicted object. In his treatment of the Sui dynasty painter Chan Tzu-ch'ien, Chang quotes the opinion of an early T'ang Buddhist monk, which includes the phrase *ch'u-wu liu-ch'ing*, "Aroused by things of the world he consigned his emotions to them"—that is, embodied his feelings about them in pictures of them.[20] But nowhere does Chang himself adopt this theory of expression. A possible reason for Chang's rejection of it, I think, is that its implications of *attachment to material objects* made it unacceptable to the Confucian literatus. This possibility will be further considered below.

There are scattered indications in *Li-tai Ming-hua Chi* that Chang, dissatisfied both with the Six Dynasties view of painting (with its overtones of Taoist mysticism) and with the older Confucian view which attached moral value to paintings by virtue of the subjects they portrayed, was working toward a new concept by which a Confucian humanist approach could be applied to his judgments of artistic quality, a concept which would also be in harmony with traditional Confucian attitudes toward the other arts. He begins to touch on the relationship between the artist and his work. "From ancient times," he writes, "those who have excelled in painting have all been men robed and capped and of noble descent, retired scholars and lofty-minded men . . ."[21] Two centuries later, this same observation was to be made to support one of the basic tenets of *wen-jen hua* theory. Nobility in a painting, the literati theorists were to insist, can only be a reflection of nobility in the man; the man is revealed in his works. Chang Yen-yüan's comments on the landscapist Yang Yen (late eighth century) contain the earliest statement I know in the painting literature of this notion of "seeing the man in his works":

He was polished and elegant in his bearing, vigorous and energetic in his spirit and feeling. He was good at landscapes; his works were lofty and unusual, refined and strong . . . When I look at the late Mr. Yang's landscape pictures, I see in imagination what he was as a man—his imposing stature and unconventionality.[22]

But Chang fails to develop the idea further. In another passage he takes up the fundamental Confucian problem of aesthetic quality vs. moral significance, making the same distinction between *te* (virtue) and *i* (art) as Chou Tun-i, quoted above, was to make for literature. He writes:

I, Yen-yüan, consider that the classical statement, "the perfection of virtue is primary, and the perfection of art follows afterward"[23] is a doctrine which disdains the man who has art but lacks virtue. But the princely man "follows the dictates of loving-kindness and seeks delight in the arts."[24] . . . Here, the Master esteems virtue and art equally. So, if someone lacks virtue but at least attains art, then even though he labor as hard as a menial servant, what cause is there for regret in this?[25]

From Chang's remarks, we see that the problem of the relative importance of "virtue" and "art," in the artist, in the creative process, and in the finished work, was a persisting one. In fact, Chang drew this distinction from the Classics, where it was made for music and ceremonial; Chou Tun-i later drew upon the same source. But Chang, as a critic of painting, is faced with (and ignores) a problem with which Chou was not troubled: what *is* moral significance, "virtue," in painting? Literature can state moral truths directly; painting cannot, except perhaps by its choice of subject; and as Acker remarks of the critics who make much of virtue, "there is no suggestion anywhere that they would have placed a bad portrait of Confucius above a good painting of an Imperial Concubine, merely because of the former's power to inspire emotions of reverence."[26]

The *wen-jen hua* theorists of the Northern Sung period were to arrive at a solution of this problem by finding for painting a means other than descriptive by which it might communicate the ineffable thoughts, the transient feeling, the very nature, of an admirable man, and so contribute to the moral betterment of those who see it. Before going on to this development, however, I should like to consider the occurrence of related ideas in the theory of the other arts: music, literature, and calligraphy.

The notion of art as communication, or as a revelation of the nature of the artist, appears earlier in other arts than it does in painting. Literature, as an extension of the basic verbal mode of expressing thought and feeling, is understandably the first to be treated in this way. In the *Lun Heng* we find the following observations:

The *I-ching* says that the feelings of a sage appear from his utterances . . . When he has expressed himself in writing, his true feeling shines forth in all its splendour.

The greater a man's virtue, the more refined is his literary work.[27]

The sixth-century *Shih P'in* says of the works of T'ao Ch'ien (365–427): "Whenever we look at his writings we see, in imagination, the virtue of the man."[28] And in the *Wen-hsin Tiao-lung,* about the same period, we are told that "although the period of a writer may be far removed in time, so that no one can see his face, yet if we look into his literary works, we seem immediately to see his mind."[29]

In speaking of literature as a revelation of thought and feeling, the writers of the above passages were probably not referring only—or even primarily—to straightforward statement or description of particular ideas and emotions. What is implicitly contained in a piece of writing, they felt, is likely to be more profound and meaningful than what is explicitly stated. In critical discussions of poetry and other literary forms, one finds frequent references to conceptions which "go beyond the literal meaning of the words." From early times, it was recognized that direct prose discourse is not always adequate to convey all that the writer might conceive and experience. The "Great Commentary" (*Ta-chuan*) to the *I-ching* says: "Writing cannot express words completely, and words cannot express thought completely."[30] It goes on to advance the notion that images and symbols can be used to embody ideas too abstruse for verbal statement. One of the Neo-Confucian philosophers, the eleventh-century Hsieh Liang-tso, writes:

The words of the sage are near and familiar, but his meaning is nonetheless far-reaching; for words have a limited capacity, while his meaning is inexhaustible. The words, being limited, can be investigated through commentaries; but the meaning, being inexhaustible, must be grasped with the spirit. It is like becoming acquainted with a man: yesterday you knew only his face, today you know his mind.[31]

The expression of what is either too subtle or too strong for direct verbal statement is one of the functions of art within the Confucian system. Both poetry (considered as a spontaneous outburst of song) and music are said to come forth when emotion becomes too intense and language, used in the ordinary way, will no longer suffice for its expression. The "Great Preface" ("Ta-hsü") to the *Shih-ching* says: "The feelings stir within one, and are embodied in speech. When speech is insufficient, one sighs and exclaims them. When sighs and exclamations are insufficient, one makes songs of them."[32]

An almost identical statement is applied to music at the end of the "Record of Music" ("Yüeh-chi") section of the *Li-chi*.[33] Chu Hsi (1130–1200), the leading figure in Neo-Confucianism, echoes this theory of poetry when he writes:

Someone asked me, "Why is poetry composed?" I answered, "Man is born in a state of tranquillity; that is his innate nature. He responds to things and is moved; that is the desire of his nature. Now, when he has such desire, he cannot be without thought, nor can he, when he thinks, be without speech. When he speaks, then what he cannot completely express in words comes out in sighing and singing; and this overflow always has a spontaneous music and rhythm, which the poet cannot restrain. This is why poems are made."[34]

The only function of the ordinary man's expressions of emotion, presumably, is the one suggested by the passages above: catharsis, the discharging of feelings which, if pent up, might becloud the mind. When the superior man sets forth his feelings, however, another purpose is served, and one which gives art a moral value in the Confucian system. If the manifold facets of the mind, the character, the exemplary qualities, of the superior man can be communicated in a work of art, then those qualities may be perceived by others and implanted in them. The "Record of Music" presents this view at length, making such statements as "Music displays the virtue [of the composer]" and "When notes that are correct affect men, a corresponding correct spirit responds to them [from within]." The superior man, it says, "makes extensive use of music in order to perfect his instructions."[35] The continuation of the conversation quoted above from the writing of Chu Hsi contains a clear statement of this idea of art serving as "instruction" by embodying the superior man's responses:

He then asked, "If this is so, what is the value of poetry as instruction?" I answered, "Poetry is the product of man's response to external things, embodied in words. Now, what the mind responds to may be either corrupt or correct; therefore, what is embodied in words may be either good or bad. But the sages above us respond only to what is correct, so that their words are all worthy of serving as instruction."[36]

Besides serving as "instruction," the artistic creations of superior men also fulfill another Confucian desideratum, that of fostering a community of spirit and a continuity of basic values within the literati tradition. The scholar who comes to understand his predecessors by reading their literary works or savoring their calligraphy and painting comes also to feel a kinship with them; another dimension, an extension into the past, is added to his sense of communion with men of like mind. Mencius saw literature as a means of nourishing such feelings of affinity:

The scholar whose virtue is most distinguished in the kingdom will make friends of all the other virtuous scholars of the kingdom. When the scholar feels that his friendship with all the virtuous scholars of the kingdom does not suffice, he proceeds to consider the men of antiquity. Reciting their poems, reading their writings, how can he help but come to know what they were as men?[37]

With the recognition of the long-established importance of these beliefs about the function of art, we begin to see why a new concept of painting was required in order that painting might attain a respectable status in the Confucian system. The weakness of the early moralist view which depended upon nobility of subject matter ("to see the good serves to warn against evil") was discerned already in the Han dynasty by Wang Ch'ung:

People like to see paintings. The subjects reproduced in these pictures are usually men of ancient times. But would it not be better to be informed of the doings and sayings of these men than to contemplate their faces? Painted upon a bare wall, their shapes and figures are there; the reason why they do not act as incentives, is that people do not perceive their words or deeds. The sentiments left by the old sages shine forth from the bamboos and silks, where they are written, which means more than mere paintings on walls.[38]

Elsewhere he writes that "the doings and sayings of worthies and sages, handed down on bamboo and silk, transform the heart and enlighten the mind . . . " His low opinion of painting was based on the failure of that art, as he saw it, to "transform" and "enlighten." *Wen-jen hua* theory overcomes this objection, as we shall see, with a new concept of the source of expression in painting, according to which the import of the picture is primarily dependent not upon its subject, but upon the mind of its maker.

To understand how it was possible to regard painting as capable of conveying human thought and feeling without depending upon the outward associations of its subject matter, we may look a bit further into theories of the other arts. Although poetry and music are treated as intimately related in the early Chinese literature, the modes of expression they depend upon differ in one fundamental way: in poetry, thought or emotion *can* be stated explicitly, although with an inevitable loss of nuance and often to the detriment of the poem as a work of art; whereas music can only symbolize it, suggest it, evoke it, always by non-descriptive, "abstract" means. However, a recognition of the inadequacy of direct verbal expression led the theorists to the view that purely formal means, dependence upon those artistic devices which distinguish the poem from the prose statement, were in some cases preferable in literature as well, having an immediacy denied to intellectualized discourse and allowing the communication of intuitive truths which cannot be presented in rational terms.

The theory of calligraphy is especially revealing in this connection, since the forms of calligraphy, like those of music, do not represent anything (the text written being more or less irrelevant to the work as calligraphy) and must rely on their inherent qualities without referring directly to anything in everday sensory experience. The earliest extant essay on calligraphy, the "Fei Ts'ao-shu" ("Polemic against the 'Grass' [cursive] Script") by Chao I of the late Han dynasty, already recognizes calligraphy as revealing not only the skill but also the nature and character of the writer—a recognition which was not to be accorded to painting until much later:

Now, of all men, each one has his particular humours and blood, and different sinews and bones. The mind may be coarse or fine, the hand may be skilled or clumsy. Hence when the beauty or ugliness of a piece of writing must depend both upon the mind and the hand, can there be any question of making [a beautiful writing] by sheer force of effort?[39]

By the Six Dynasties period, calligraphy was seen as a means of communicating the ineffable, functioning (as Wang Wei, in the same period, considered painting to function) in a symbolic way, as an abstraction of natural form, analogous to the hexagrams of the *I-ching*. Wei Heng, a Chin dynasty calligrapher, writes: "[The calligrapher] observes [and utilizes] the images of things to convey his thoughts; these are such as cannot be expressed in words."[40]

T'ang dynasty developments in the application of these ideas to calligraphy may be illustrated with quotations from two Confucian scholars of the period: Chang Huai-kuan, an eighth-century appointee to the Han-lin Academy; and the great littérateur and precursor of Neo-Confucianism Han Yü. Chang's essay entitled "I Shu" ("Discourse on Calligraphy") contains the following:

Cliffs and canyons compete for breath-taking effect, mountains and rivers strive respectively for height and depth. One gathers, as in a bag, these myriad phenomena, brings them into order as a single image. This one lodges in calligraphy in order to give rein to one's varied thought, or commits to calligraphy to release one's pent-up emotions.

Calligraphy and written documents, if they are of the highest order, all have a profound import through which the intent of the writer is revealed. Looking at them makes one understand him fully, as if meeting him face to face . . . Reading the words of the sages of the past is not the same as hearing them speak in person, but in appreciating the calligraphy of former masters, one can never exhaust their profound conceptions.

Of the Chin dynasty calligrapher Wang Hsi-chih:

When we look at his complete calligraphy, we lucidly perceive the aim and spirit of his whole life, as if we were meeting him face to face.[41]

In the first paragraph quoted above, we encounter for the first time the notion of "lodging," which was later to occur frequently in literati discussions of painting. To speak of "lodging," or embodying, one's thoughts and emotions in the work of art was a common way of describing the process of artistic expression. The final lines of *Wen-hsin Tiao-lung,* for example, are: "If my writing indeed conveys my mind, then my mind finds lodging." We shall encounter other uses of the term as we proceed, and its meaning will become more clear.

Han Yü, believing with Chang Huai-kuan in the capacity of calligraphy to manifest human feelings, applies to this art the concept of catharsis, mentioned above as one of the Confucian justifications for artistic creation: by allowing the writer to release his pent-up emotions, it forestalls the unseemly operation of those emotions in other directions, and so enables him to preserve his composure. For, as Hsün-tzu had said about music, "Man cannot be without joy, and when there is joy, it must have a physical embodiment. When this embodiment does not conform to right principles, there will be disorder."[42] Calligraphy, as well as good music, was evidently thought to "conform to right principles." Han Yü writes:

If a man can give lodging to his skill and knowledge, so that they respond sensitively to his mind but without damming up his energy, then his spirit will be whole and his character will be firm. Although external things come [into his cognizance], they will not adhere to his mind.

He then cites examples of people who have been fond of particular things or activities—food, wine, chess—and goes on:

These things they enjoyed to the end of their days, insatiably. How could they have leisure for other desires? The late Chang Hsü was good at the grass script; he did not develop other talents. Joy and anger, distress and poverty, sorrow, contentment and ease, resentment, longing, intoxication, dejection and unrest—anything which moved his mind he inevitably expressed in his grass script. He looked at things, saw mountains and rivers, cliffs and valleys . . . all the transmutations of events and objects in the world. The enjoyable, the awesome, all were given lodging in his calligraphy.[43]

The idea of embodying individual response and emotion in music or calligraphy was acceptable to these Confucians; the embodiment of it in painting, through representation of the stimulus of that emotion, evidently was not. Other T'ang dynasty Confucian writers, like Chang Yen-yüan, avoid presenting painting in such terms. I should like to suggest—and some quotations will be introduced below to support the suggestion—that the problem of *non-attachment* is involved here. Expressing emotion through the portrayal of whatever had inspired that emotion implied a dwelling on that thing, and on the state of mind it had evoked. Confucian writings cautioned, on the contrary, that one should allow one's mind to rest only lightly upon the things it comes into contact with, never to become captivated by them; the mind must always preserve a degree of aloofness. Expression in music and calligraphy entailed no description or representation of the original stimulus of feeling; it was not a matter of being moved by something one encountered and externalizing one's response in a picture of, or a poem about, that thing. The images of a representational art remained bound to the object of representation. The forms of a non-representational art were not so bound, could be invested with a more general import, and so could serve to reveal the nature and thought of the person who composed them.

The case of painting was complicated by the ambivalence of its very substance, its lines, forms, colors, textures: they might portray material things, but might also serve as somewhat independent expressive means, undergoing quasi-arbitrary mutations which had little or nothing to do with their descriptive function. Literary evidence indicates that as early as the T'ang dynasty, unorthodox kinds of brushwork which had previously been employed only in calligraphy were introduced into painting, not so much because they served better to reproduce the visible features of anything as for their inherent interest and their efficacy in displaying the temperament of the artist. This development in painting style evidently preceded, and perhaps to some extent stimulated, the emergence of the *wen-jen hua* concept. Technical innovations in art are not, ordinarily, the work of its critics; the expressive potentialities of brush and ink had to be expanded in fact before they could be expanded in theory.

A shifting of emphasis from the subject of the picture to its formal elements was thus facilitated; and as this shift went on, painting and calligraphy drew closer to becoming, in principle, a single art.[44] The way was opened for the evolution of *wen-jen hua*, and the recognition of painting, within the Confucian order, as a means by which the individual man could communicate to others the workings of his mind.

Although anticipations of some features of *wen-jen hua* theory can be discovered in pre-Sung writings (e.g., in Chang Yen-yüan's remarks about Yang Yen, quoted above), the formulation of this theory as a coherent body of doctrine did not take place until the late eleventh and early twelfth centuries. It was accomplished chiefly by members of a coterie of artists and critics, of which Su Shih, or Su Tung-p'o (1036–1101), was the central figure. Some of these men reveal in their writings an interest in Taoism and Ch'an Buddhism, but it generally goes no further than was normal for the somewhat eclectic Neo-Confucians They were, like most major figures of the *wen-jen hua* movement in later times, Confucian literati. Su Tung-p'o was fascinated, during various periods of his life, with Buddhist mysticism and Taoist alchemy, and objected to the stern morality of some Neo-Confucian philosophers;[45] but he also wrote commentaries on the Confucian Classics, expressed a deep admiration for Chou Tun-i,[46] and always preserved a thoroughly Confucian concern for human society.

The fundamental contention of the *wen-jen hua* theorists was that a painting is (or at least should be) a revelation of the nature of the man who painted it, and of his mood and feelings at the moment he painted it. Its expressive content therefore depends more upon his personal qualities and his transient feeling than upon the qualities of the subject represented. A man of wide learning, refinement, and noble character will, if he adds to these attributes a moderate degree of acquired technical ability, produce paintings of a superior kind.

To support this belief, it was necessary to suppose—sometimes in spite of the evidence, one feels—that the great painters of the past had all been what Chang Yen-yüan claims they were, "retired scholars and lofty-minded men." Chang himself stopped short of basing his critical judgments consistently upon this somewhat questionable criterion; the painter whom he praises above all others, Wu Tao-tzu, was a professional artist of no notable scholarly status. Su Tung-p'o, however, professed to prefer the works of the T'ang poet-painter Wang Wei (699–759) to those of Wu Tao-tzu; the latter, "for all his surpassing excellence, must still be discussed in terms of painting skill, while Wang Mo-chieh [i.e., Wang Wei] achieved his effects beyond the visual image."[47]

Kuo Jo-hsü, the late eleventh-century author of *T'u-hua Chien-wen Chih* and a leading spokesman for the *wen-jen hua* viewpoint, elaborates on Chang Yen-yüan's observation:

I have . . . observed that the majority of the rare paintings of the past are the work of high officials, talented worthies, superior scholars, or recluses living in cliffs and caves; of persons, that is, who "followed the dictates of loving-kindness and sought delight in the arts."[48] . . . Their elevated and refined feelings were all lodged in their paintings. Since their personal quality was lofty, the "spirit consonance" [of their paintings] could not but be lofty.[49]

Mi Yu-jen, son of another member of the Su Tung-p'o coterie, the painter and connoisseur Mi Fu (1051–1107), borrows the words of the Han dynasty Confucian Yang Hsiung in setting forth the view of painting as communication:

Yang Hsiung considered writing to be the "delineation of the mind." Unless a person has a firm grasp of *li* [principle], his words cannot attain [a high level of wisdom]. In this regard, painting, as a form of discourse,[50] is also a "delineation of the mind." In these terms it is understandable that all [outstanding artists] in the past should have been the glories of their respective ages. How could this be anything that the artisans for hire in the market place could know about?[51]

What Yang Hsiung had written is this: "Speech is the voice of mind; writing is the delineation of the mind. When this voice and delineation take form, the princely man and the ignoble man are revealed."[52] Kuo Jo-hsü also quotes these lines, prefacing them with the flat statement: "Painting is the equivalent of writing." Both calligraphy and painting he regards as "prints of the heart [mind]"; the painter's conception, he says, "arises in feeling and thought, and is transferred to silk and paper."[53]

It will be clear from these examples, which are typical of Sung dynasty *wen-jen* statements about painting, that literati painting theory is based upon, and completely in harmony with, the Confucian ideals of the arts which we have outlined above. As a worthy activity for the literatus who wishes to "seek delight in the arts" and to manifest his mind, painting is now a means of self-cultivation; and the products of this activity, as embodiments of the admirable qualities of cultivated individuals, serve a Confucian end in conveying those qualities to others. Along with literature and calligraphy, painting helps to maintain a desirable continuity within the great humanist tradition of the Confucian scholars, perpetuating feelings and awarenesses which would otherwise perish with the men who felt them.

A few qualifications should be made here. Obviously, not all good painters were sages or paragons of virtue; nor were all men of noble character good painters. No critic of any consequence ever judged a picture according to what he knew about the moral worth of the artist. A literati critic was likely, on the other hand, to consider the admirable qualities which he perceived in the picture to be reflections of admirable qualities in the man who produced it. The notion of "the man revealed in the painting" was used, that is, to account for excellence in art, not to determine it.

Also, one finds fewer explicit references to morality in the Sung dynasty discussions of painting than in some of the earlier writings on art quoted above. In Sung and later times, the men most admired were not those who merely exemplified the simple virtues. Such men were accorded their eulogies in the appropriate sections of the biographical compilations (Filial Piety, Unswerving Loyalty, etc.), but scarcely noticed otherwise. The Ideal Man, for the later periods in China, was a more complex figure, a richer personality; and the desire of later ages was to understand him, see him in all his richness and complexity. Treasured and transmitted were anecdotes reporting his behavior and sayings in various circumstances; his surviving literary productions; and, as revelations of even subtler facets of his mind than these could preserve, his calligraphy and paintings.

The transition from the romantic theory of expression, in which the artist's response to his subject determines the emotional content of the work, to the *wen-jen hua* theory in which the expression was less dependent upon subject matter, may be further illustrated with two short and syntactically parallel phrases which were applied to artists of the sixth and eleventh centuries. The first, used by an early T'ang writer in speaking of Chan Tzu-ch'ien, has already been quoted: "Aroused by things of the world, he consigned his emotions to them" (*ch'u-wu liu-ch'ing*). The second occurs in the comments on Wen T'ung, a painter of bamboo and a close friend of Su Tung-p'o, which appear in the early-twelfth-century catalog *Hsüan-ho Hua-p'u*: "Wen T'ung availed himself of natural objects in order to lodge his exhilaration" (*t'o-wu yü-hsing*).[54]

The ways in which these phrases differ reveal the change in attitude toward subject matter in painting. Response to particular objects or scenes in nature is no longer the stimulus of that emotion which impels one to artistic creation; instead, the painter "avails himself of things" (*t'o-wu*), or as other writers have it, "borrows things" (*chia-wu*), as vehicles for conveying feelings having no necessary connection with those things. *Ch'ing*, "emotion," has given way to *hsing*, "exhilaration." *Hsing*, in art theory, denoted an undefined intensity of feeling which, embodied in a work of art, could instill in that work a quality of subtle excitement without suggesting an unseemly display of strong and particularized emotion.

Even more interesting is the replacement of *liu* (rendered as "consigned" but more properly "to deposit, leave behind") by *yü*, "to lodge." Both *yü* and the closely related, often interchangeable *chi* are favored by the *wen-jen hua* writers for describing the embodiment of personal feeling in art; the combination *chi-hsing*, "lodging exhilaration," is especially common. Teng Ch'un, for example, writing of an early Sung landscapist in his *Hua Chi* (1167), speaks of works in which the painter has "lodged his exhilaration, pure and remote—true gentleman's brush-

work!"[55] These terms do not appear in T'ang or pre-T'ang texts on painting; they are, I think, bound up with the *wen-jen hua* concept of artistic
expression.

Su Tung-p'o seems to have considered the "lodging of one's mind"
as a means of dispersing emotion, somewhat as did Han Yü. He writes
the following of calligraphy, but might as well have written it of painting:

The traces of brush and ink are committed to that which has form [i.e., the
writing itself]; and what has form must then be subject to corruption. But if,
even though it does not achieve non-being, one can enjoy oneself with it for
the moment, in order to give lodging to one's mind, forget the sorrows of
one's declining years, then it is a wiser pastime than gambling at chess.

Nevertheless, to be able to maintain one's inner equilibrium without making
use of external diversions is the highest achievement of the sages and worthies.
But only Yen-tzu [Yen Hui, the favorite disciple of Confucius] could achieve
that.[56]

Behind some part of *wen-jen hua* theory, I believe, lie Neo-Confucian attitudes toward the emotions and toward the proper modes of
response to material things. Fung Yu-lan contrasts the Taoist insistence
on non-attachment to the view of the Neo-Confucians, who "argue
that there is nothing wrong with the emotions *per se;* what is important
is simply that they should not be a permanent part of the person who
sometimes expresses them." One's essential composure must not be
disturbed; unbalance is to be avoided. The *Chung-yung*, a text highly
esteemed and often quoted by the Neo-Confucians, says:

While there are no stirrings of pleasure, anger, sorrow, or joy, the mind may
be said to be in a state of equilibrium. When these feelings have been stirred,
and they act in their due degree, there ensues what may be called a state of
harmony.[57]

Fung, quoting this passage, comments: "All such feelings are natural,
and so must be allowed expression. But at the same time we must keep
them ordered by means of 'instruction,' and must regulate their expression so that it will be neither too extreme nor too restrained."[58] A good
part of *wen-jen hua* aesthetic is, in fact, a "regulation of expression" in
terms of painting, aimed at ensuring that the artist does not commit the
artistic equivalents of those excesses in human conduct against which
the Confucians warn. The literati painters' theory of expression, by
divorcing the import of the picture from that of whatever it represents,
lessened the danger of "over-attachment." The same attitude operated,
I believe, in both philosophy and art: the perfect man responds to
natural stimuli, but is not permanently affected by them, because they
do not alter his essential self; the scholar-painter makes use of natural

objects only to "lodge his mind," not allowing them, or his feelings toward them, to dictate the import of his pictures.

Tung Yu, the early-twelfth-century author of *Kuang-ch'uan Hua-pa*, a series of colophons written for paintings, points out that the painter should rely primarily upon what is within himself, rather than upon what he sees outside. Tung tells the familiar story of how Wu Tao-tzu painted a landscape of a place he had visited without depending upon sketches, and comments: "The theorists say that hills and valleys are formed within the painter's breast; when he wakes, he issues them forth in painting. Thus the things leave no traces in him, whereas involvement would arise out of actual perception."[59]

The term *yü-i*, which in *wen-jen hua* writings has the sense of "lodging one's conceptions," is also used for "resting one's thoughts lightly upon" something, giving it one's passing attention. The two senses are not, I think, totally unrelated. Neither "lodging one's conceptions" in pictures or things nor "resting one's thoughts" on them implies any abiding concern with those things. Su Tung-p'o, composing a dedicatory inscription for his friend Wang Shen's "Precious Painting Hall" (Pao-hui T'ang), employs the same antithesis of the verbs *yü* and *liu* as we saw in the parallel phrases quoted above, to contrast a "lodging" or "resting" of attention with a more permanent "depositing" or "fixing." His argument adheres completely to the Neo-Confucian position, even making the standard distinction between that and the Taoist view. He writes:

The princely man may rest (*yü*) his thoughts on objects, but may not fix (*liu*) his thoughts on objects. If he rests his thoughts on them, then even subtle things will suffice to give him pleasure, and even extraordinary things cannot become afflictions [obsessions] to him. If, however, he fixes his thoughts on them, even subtle things will be afflictions, and not even extraordinary ones a pleasure. Lao-tzu says: "The five colors confuse the eye, the five sounds dull the ear, the five tastes spoil the palate . . ."; but the sage never really renounces these [sensual objects], for he merely rests his thoughts on them.

Now, of all enjoyable things, painting and calligraphy are best suited to giving men pleasure without at the same time influencing them. But if one's thoughts become fixed inextricably in things, this will lead to unspeakable disaster.

Su Tung-p'o tells how he himself has owned many notable examples of painting and calligraphy, but has allowed them to leave his hands without begrudging them. He comments:

It is like clouds and mists passing before my eyes, or the songs of birds striking my ears. How could I help but derive joy from my contact with these things? But when they are gone, I think no more about them. In this way, these two things [painting and calligraphy] are a constant pleasure to me, but not an affliction to me.[60]

The painter, by deriving the forms of his paintings from his own mind, can escape being "involved" with material things; the collector, avoiding over-attachment to the objects he owns, can prevent them from becoming "afflictions" to him. Tung Yu was once accused by a Ch'an Buddhist monk of encouraging such over-attachment to paintings by writing in praise of them. The two were discussing a " Grove of Pines" picture owned by the Ch'an master, whose name was Hui-yüan. Hui-yüan said:

The enjoyment of things weakens one's will; for one cannot forget one's love for them. This is another kind of corruption. You, moreover, write about these [paintings]; how can you escape increasing people's emotional attachments, multiplying their involvements?

Long ago, the master Hsüan-lan attained a "beyond-mind method" [hsin-wai fa]; he forgot himself and also forgot external things. He retained [liu] no resentment or desire. Chang Tsao once painted [the walls of Hsüan-lan's] house, doing old pines, thinking that these would be beautiful to look upon. Fu-tsai heard of this, and composed an encomium; Wei Hsiang made a poem to be attached to it. In a later age, these were called the "Three Nonpareils." Next day, Hsüan-lan saw them and plastered them over, saying, "They had no business scabbing up my walls!"

This is to say, why should such things be retained in the breast even though they be good? It's all the worse when one is stuck to a single thing and can't break loose from it!

Tung Yu replied:

If a person is sincere (ch'eng) within, he is released from such attachments, and although things be ever so numerous, revealing their images and baring their forms, they cannot become involvements to him. He who is cultivated within his mind is fixed and quiet, like still, deep water; since he does not offer a target for things, they cannot leave their barbs in him.[61]

However unsatisfying, or even irritating, this answer may have been to Hui-yüan, it is exactly the reply which a good Confucian should have returned to such a Buddhist outburst.[62] If you are so "uncultivated" that you must be afraid of your responses, it suggests, go and live in a monastery, or a cave; we Confucianists cultivate our minds and remain in the world. The key word in Tung's answer is ch'eng, "sincerity"—in the Sung period, a kind of summation of the Confucian virtues. "Sagehood is simply a matter of sincerity," writes Chou Tun-i. "Sincerity is the foundation of the five virtues, and the source of all virtuous conduct."[63]

It was the Confucian virtues, in wen-jen hua theory, which regulated the creation of paintings as well as the enjoyment of them. A painting done by a cultivated man was a reflection of his sincerity. To understand how it was so, we may consider a few more of the tenets of wen-jen hua.

Non-purposefulness; spontaneity. In the ideal creative act the painter creates as Heaven does, spontaneously, without willfulness. Su Tung-p'o reports a conversation between his friend Wen T'ung and a guest who argued that painting was not "in accord with the Tao," since the painter, through human activity, usurps the creative powers of Heaven. Wen answered:

But the Tao is what I love! I am quite unattached to bamboo . . . At the beginning, I saw the bamboo and delighted in it; now I delight in it and lose consciousness of myself. Suddenly I forget that the brush is my hand, the paper in front of me; all at once I am exhilarated, and the tall bamboo appears, thick and luxuriant. How is this in any way different from the impersonality of creation in nature?[64]

According to Mi Fu, the T'ang calligrapher Yen Chen-ch'ing criticized the writing of some of his famous predecessors as having "too much of purposeful activity, lacking the air of blandness, of something accomplished by Heaven."[65] This desirable quality of "blandness" will be considered later. While there are undoubtedly traces here of the Taoist concept of *wu-wei*, "non-activity," and perhaps of the Ch'an practice of empty-mindedness in meditation as well, such ideas were by this time so thoroughly assimilated into Confucian thought that the Sung scholars had no need to turn to other sources for them. Chou Tun-i begins the third section of his *T'ung Shu* with the words "Sincerity is non-acting" (*ch'eng wu-wei*). Ch'eng Hao, another Neo-Confucian philosopher who was contemporary with Su Tung-p'o, stresses the importance of emptying the mind:

Denying outer things and affirming inner ones is not as good as forgetting both outer and inner. When both are forgotten, one's mind is cleansed and uncluttered; uncluttered, it will be concentrated; concentrated, it will be clear. Once one's mind is clear, how can any further response to external things become an involvement?[66]

For the notion of non-purposefulness, the *Chung-yung* again supplies classical authority: "He who possesses sincerity is he who, without any effort, hits what is right, and apprehends, without the exercise of thought; he is the sage who naturally and easily embodies the right way."[67]

Creation as transformation; li (principle). Huang T'ing-chien (1045–1105), a friend and disciple of Su Tung-p'o, writes that if the artist has the conception of bamboo (for example) already formed before he begins to paint, then the brush and ink "transform" it (cause it to grow into full existence) just as natural objects are "transformed," matured by the forces of nature. "When one takes up the brush and ink, one's achievement is the same as that of natural creation."[68] Tung Yu writes in a colophon on a painting, "The sage transforms [or creates, *hua*] through movement of his spirit; his skill is identical with that of Heaven and Earth."[69]

Once more, the ideas underlying such statements are to be found in Confucian thought. The person who is possessed of "complete sincerity," says the *Chung yung,* "can assist the transforming and nourishing operations of Heaven and Earth . . . he can form a trinity with Heaven and Earth." And also: "It is only he who is possessed of the most complete sincerity under heaven, who can transform."[70] The leap from transformation as the moral betterment of the world (as the *Chung yung* intends it) to transformation as the creation of artistic form is a broad one, but not too broad for the agile-minded *wen-jen hua* theorists. Both kinds were seen as analogous to creation-transformation in nature, and so to each other.

An important element in the analogy between cosmological and artistic creation is the regulation of both by *li,* that "principle" or "natural order" which, in the words of Fung Yu-lan, "prevents the creative process from proceeding haphazardly."[71] Su Tung-p'o, in an often quoted colophon dealing with *li* in painting, distinguishes some things which have constant forms (people, animals, buildings) from others which have only constant *principle* (rocks, trees, water, clouds). Any deviation from "truth" in the former is easy to spot, he says, whereas only the most perceptive will detect a lack of *li* in the latter. The bamboo paintings of Wen T'ung, he goes on, "are in accord with natural creation, and also satisfying to human conceptions. Truly, they are embodiments [lodgings] of [the mind of] a man of complete wisdom."[72]

Tung Yu, in a colophon on a "Playing Dogs" painting, claims that a painter who catches the outer form and likeness of such things as dogs and horses is not necessarily skillful; to be called skillful, he must also capture their *li.*[73] Huang Kung-wang, in the Yüan dynasty, goes so far as to speak of *li* as "the most urgent necessity in painting."[74]

We need not expend any space here in establishing the importance of *li* in later Confucianism. *Li-hsüeh,* the "study of *li,*" is in fact one of the Chinese terms for Neo-Confucianism. *Li,* for the Sung philosophers, was "that which is above form"; for the Sung *wen-jen hua* theorists, as well as for the philosophers, it was what guided the creation of form; for the artists, one may suppose, it was that sense of "rightness" which preserved the forms they produced from seeming "perverse and willful."

The virtue of concealment. Nothing was more vociferously abhorred by the literati critics than showiness—the deliberate display of brilliance, beauty, or skill. However admirable it may appear to the person capable of penetrating its seeming plainness, the painting must be unassuming always. We need not, when we observe this quality of plainness in the works of literati artists, attribute it directly to their Confucian background; it is more likely to be simply a manifestation of the more reserved and subtle taste of the cultivated man. But the statements applied to these works by the critics, especially their words of praise for "blandness" (*p'ing-tan*), certainly call to mind the Confucian disapproval of ostentation. The virtues sought in a painting corresponded closely to those which the *Chung-yung* assigns to the *chün-tzu,* the princely or superior man:

It is said in the *Shih-ching,* "Over her embroidered robe she puts on a plain, single garment," intimating a disinclination to display the elegance of the former. Just so, it is the way of the superior man to prefer the concealment [of his virtue] . . . It is characteristic of the superior man, though he appears bland, never to produce satiety . . .[75]

P'ing-tan, "blandness," came to be the quality most highly prized in human personality. Liu Shao, Wei dynasty author of the *Jen-wu Chih* ("Notices of Personalities"), writes:

In the character of a man, it is *balance* and *harmony* which is most prized; and for a character to have this balance and harmony, it must have blandness [*p'ing-tan*] and flavorlessness [*wu-wei*]. . . . Therefore, when one observes a man in order to inquire into his character, one must first see if he has blandness and only later seek for his cleverness and brilliance.[76]

One must hasten to add, as the Chinese writers frequently do, that the "blandness" was only apparent; a semblance of impoverishment in a painting should conceal an inner richness, serve as the plain garment which covers the embroidered robe. "Blandness" is not to be equated with dullness, either in the art work or in the man it reflects.

The preference for "awkwardness." Another attribute admired by the literati critics was *cho,* "awkwardness," the opposite of *ch'iao,* "skill." An admirable kind of "clumsiness" was held to be more difficult to achieve than technical competence, and to be the natural outcome of a truly spontaneous act of creation. That an element of Confucian morality is involved in this preference is suggested by Chou Tun-i's pronouncement on skill and awkwardness, which begins in a Taoist vein but ends in a Confucian one:

Someone said to me, "People call you awkward." I responded: "Skillfulness is what I detest. Moreover, it grieves me to see so much skill in the world." I was then pleased to make a poem:

> "The skillful talk much,
> The awkward keep silent.
> The skillful exert themselves,
> The awkward are more retiring.
> The skillful are the thieves,
> The awkward are the virtuous.
> The skillful bring misfortunes upon the people,
> The awkward bring them happiness."

Ah! if only all people in the world were awkward! Harsh government would be discontinued; there would be tranquillity above and obedience below; customs would be purified, and abuses ended.[77]

Skillfulness in painting carried the additional stigma of professionalism, and was always suspect of indicating a desire to please. Tung Yu writes:

The artisan-painter makes his work salable by his skillful craftsmanship; by giving pleasure to the vulgar ones of his time, he hopes to make his pictures easier to take. He is afraid only that the world will not want his pictures because they are different.[78]

Like all actions of the proper Confucian, painting must be motivated by a worthy aim—or, ideally, by no rationalized aim at all. In any event, desire to win the favor and patronage of others was decidedly *not* a worthy aim. The literatus could paint for either (or both) of two reasons: as a pastime in the intervals between scholarly pursuits, an outlet for excess energy; or as a means of presenting to the understanding of others something of his own nature, feeling, and thought.

The scholar who was equipped with only a moderate technical facility in painting, but who had practiced the self-cultivation and acquired the classical education of the ideal literatus, was thus considered to be better prepared to produce worth-while paintings than the professional who had concentrated upon learning the technique of the art. Feng Shan, an eleventh-century scholar and author of a commentary on the *Spring and Autumn Annals*, writes these lines in a poem about landscape painting:

> Creation by means of brush and ink is not an
>   achievement in itself;
> In essence it is the overflow of literary activity.
> Thus, true [painting] skill, in our time, is
>   the property of us Confucians.[79]

"Set your heart upon the Tao, support yourself by its power, follow the dictates of loving-kindness, and seek delight in the arts." With this quotation from the *Analects* of Confucius,[80] the anonymous author of *Hsüan-ho Hua-p'u*, writing in the early twelfth century, opens his first chapter. "Art," he goes on, "is a thing which the gentleman whose heart is set on the Tao cannot neglect; but he should only 'seek delight' in it, and no more"—that is, it must not be his chief concern in life, but only an avocation. "Painting is also an art," the passage concludes. "When it attains the highest point, then one does not know whether art is Tao, or Tao art."[81]

Such a statement—even more, the occurrence of it at the beginning of the imperial catalog of an emperor, Hui-tsung, who was not especially sympathetic to the *wen-jen hua* ideal—indicates the standing which painting had by this time attained within the Confucian community. Painting had joined literature, calligraphy, and music as an activity suitable for the literatus; and a responsiveness to the subtler qualities of painting, as well as to those of the other arts, was expected of the cultivated man. It was the formulation of *wen-jen hua* theory as a Confucian doctrine for the creation and evaluation of paintings, and the practice of painting by an increasing number of scholars, which had brought about this adoption of painting into the group of "polite arts," those with potential moral value to the individual and to society. The statement in the last quotation about painting and Tao is quite similar to what Chu Hsi writes of literary art: "The Tao is the root of literary art, and literary art the branches and leaves of the Tao . . . literary art *is*, in fact, Tao. Su Tung-p'o, in our time, has put it thus: 'What I call literary art has to be at one with *Tao*.' "[82]

We may conclude by observing how completely this same philosopher adheres to what was, by this time, the orthodox viewpoint for one of his class, when he comes to write about painting and calligraphy. Chu Hsi had no very profound interest in either art, and was no connoisseur; on one occasion, writing on a painting of oxen, he was guilty of echoing the eternal axiom of the philistine: "I don't know anything about painting, but I know that this is a *real ox* in this picture!"[83] Elsewhere, with no greater originality of thought but in better accord with prevailing views, he writes the following:

On a letter from Tu K'an (978–1057) to Ou-yang Hsiu (1007–72): "When I scrutinize and enjoy these 'delineations of his mind,' it is as if I could see the man."

On a landscape by Mi Fu: "These must be the most beautiful scenes from the hills and valleys within the breast of this old man, which at that moment he all at once spewed forth, to give lodging to his genuine enjoyment."

On the calligraphy of Huang T'ing-chien: "It cannot be judged in terms of skill and awkwardness. Rather, when I look at it I think back to all the loyal and worthy men of that age, and reflect how sad it is that they should have met with failure."

On an "Old Tree and Strange Stone" painting by Su Tung-p'o: "This piece of paper by the late master Su is the product of a moment's sport, the overflow of a playful spirit. He did not set out to do it with any special deliberation; and yet his proud bearing, revealed in it, reverberates through ancient and modern times. It serves to let us see in imagination the man himself."[84]

It would have distressed Chu Hsi deeply to be told that the paintings he admired, and the attitudes toward them which he accepted, were really expressions of Taoist or Buddhist mysticism. Fortunately for him, no one of his time was likely to tell him anything of the sort; for, so far as we can ascertain from surviving writings, nobody thought so. The assignment of a large part of what is vital and interesting in Chinese art to the opponents of Confucianism did not take place until very recent times. It rests, I think, on the flimsiest of foundations or on none at all; and it demands a strict reexamination. It may well prove in other cases, as in that of *wen-jen hua,* to have been an obstacle rather than an aid to our understanding.

Robert Ruhlmann

TRADITIONAL HEROES
IN CHINESE POPULAR FICTION

Heroes in literature and art express more than the personal opinions and dreams of particular authors. They also embody current values and ideals, and convey a powerful image of the conflicting forces at work in the society of their time. Superhuman yet human, these prestigious personalities inspire and encourage imitation, initiate or revive patterns of behavior, and thus play a significant role in shaping history.

Some are created by writers and artists in a definite time and place; others are passed on from ages immemorial by continuous or intermittent traditions. Some are myths which in the course of time were given a historical character; others are figures from history transformed into myths.[1] Stable eras tend to mirror themselves in a "classical" type of hero, a healthy and reasonably happy man who is successfully adapted to his circumstances; dynamic tensions and crises of an age of change, in contrast, are usually embodied in a "romantic" hero, a younger man, often the victim of tragedy—a misfit, a rebel, a defender of the old order or founder of a new one. Study of heroes, of their genesis and mutations, has much to contribute to the understanding of social and intellectual history.

For this purpose fictional literature is of exceptional interest; the novel, the drama, and some forms of narrative poetry all have a broader appeal and offer more direct and explicit means of expression than non-fiction, music, and visual arts. Indeed, students of European and American literature have for some time been mining fiction for historical data relating to the economic, the religious, and other aspects of the past. Leo Lowenthal, in his brilliant book *Literature and the Image of Man*,[2] extracts from texts of European dramas and novels—from Vega and Cervantes to Ibsen and Hamsun—elements for a picture of three centuries of social change.

Scholarly studies of Chinese fiction for the history of Chinese thought and institutions are relatively few and recent,[3] primarily because the novel and the drama have until this century traditionally been disdained by Chinese literocrats[4] as inferior genres and, when written in the colloquial language, as altogether unworthy of the name of literature. It is becoming clear that Chinese fiction may well be the only available source for the study of certain values and attitudes that have influenced the course of Chinese history. Chinese fiction offers an indirect but fruitful approach precisely where direct research into motivations is difficult—among the illiterate and semiliterate common people of China.

In Chinese fiction there are popular heroes, scholarly heroes, and also those resulting from the interaction between the first two types. This paper seeks to analyze some of the specific attributes of these heroes, some of the political, moral, and sentimental values they stand for, some of the reasons for their appeal to men's hearts, and some of their effects on human behavior at particular periods.

POPULAR FICTION AND CONFUCIAN SCHOLARS

Mencius distinguishes, in a famous formula, between "those who labor with their minds" and "those who labor with their physical strength," adding that the former govern the latter and are supported by them.[5] This formula could hardly ever have applied literally to China, but it is reflected to some extent in the more or less permanent division of Chinese society into two distinct strata—the peasantry and a small and proud elite based on land, office, and literacy. It was the elite that produced for its own consumption the bulk of Chinese literature and Chinese historiography. All formal works, such as commentaries on the Classics, poems, technical treatises, and documents of an ideological or administrative character were written by scholar-officials for other scholar-officials, and remained inaccessible to the illiterate masses. The same is true of the anecdotes and parables, the "tales of the marvelous" (ch'uan ch'i), the "occasional notes" (pi chi), the short stories, and the other kinds of fiction composed by scholars in the classical language across a span of more than two thousand years. Ming and Ch'ing novels, though written in colloquial language and patterned in form after popular fiction, were obviously intended to be read only by the educated.[6] One should no more assume that these scholar-writings accurately expressed the beliefs and feelings of the masses than that the thoughts of the two communities coincided at any given time.

These genres, however, are only a part of Chinese fiction. The remainder is basically oral and addressed to a motley audience—mostly peasants, artisans, shopkeepers, and merchants, and often their womenfolk too, who throng the marketplace or the teahouses to listen to storytellers, puppeteers, and singing girls, crowd around stone stages of temples at festival times, or gather before crude wooden platforms of open-air theaters to watch the actors. Singing girls are seldom found outside big cities. But storytellers and theatrical troupes are everywhere, and often wander from place to place, even into out-of-the-way villages[7] and the secluded women's quarters of large mansions.[8] Then, those who have heard stories and plays retell them for those who have not.

Chinese oral literature also includes innumerable songs, proverbs, children's rhymes, work chanties, and dialogues of all sorts. Different degrees of elaboration can be found among them, from pure folklore, if such a thing exists, to the most sophisticated prose and poetry. And, while many of these forms are peculiar to their own province or district (the number of local schools of theater runs into hundreds), there is a constant exchange of themes and techniques among them.

These forms of entertainment have proved to be very enduring. From a comparison of contemporary observations with T'ang and Sung documents,[9] it is clear that most of them have been thriving for more than a thousand years with few changes in form. Their regular audiences in today's Peking and those of Ch'ang-an during the T'ang, of Kaifeng and Hangchow during the Sung, seem to be, *mutatis mutandis*, of closely comparable social level and occupation. The language they use is the colloquial speech of their time, with only a few passages in formal style. The subjects of Sung storytellers fall into six traditional categories: ghosts and supernatural manifestations; Buddhist miracles and reincarnations; love and aspects of daily life; crimes and their detection; feats of strength and courage; and historical tales commemorating exploits of great men or the founding and collapse of dynasties. Each of these themes was handled by a specialized guild, among which the guild of *chiang-shih*—"raconteurs of history"—enjoyed the most dignity. As a result of this specialization, each group of stories long retained its distinctive character while apparently losing nothing of its popularity and vitality.

Many texts have been preserved to this day, some only recently rediscovered and lately published. Among these are dozens of pre-T'ang and T'ang "popularizations" or *chantefables* (*pien-wen*), three Sung plays of the Southern tradition (*hsi-wen*), several Sung dramas in narrative form (*chu-kung-tiao*), and more than two hundred Yüan plays (*tsa-chü*). From Yüan times on, there are a number of "ballads" which were partly recited and partly sung (*ku-tz'u, t'an-tz'u*), novels (*yen-yi, ts'ai-tzu-shu*), hundreds of short stories (*p'ing-hua, hsiao-shuo*), and thousands of plays (*hsi, ch'ü*).[10] These are, however, only a small fraction of the total.[11] Some performers used promptbooks, but most could not read or write: the transmission of the repertory from fathers to sons or from masters to apprentices was more often than not entirely oral. Of the extant texts, many are anonymous or of collective authorship, and some, products of cumulative authorship spread over several centuries, were long passed on in oral form before being transcribed.

Texts available for research, though only a portion of the rich oral repertory, are a valuable means of access to the thought of the illiterate population whom narrators and actors not only entertained but also educated. For centuries, Chinese with little or no formal schooling have derived from theatergoing an amazing knowledge of, and concern for, the history of their country. More important still, storytelling and the theater provided channels of expression for feelings that had little or nothing to do with elite influence; they describe not only the life and routine circumstances of the common people, but also "heterodox" beliefs, immoral conduct, and political activities directed toward subversion or revolt.

Actually, the very existence of a fiction of this sort has always been a challenge to Confucians. Some authors of fiction were literati who refused to take official posts, or who retired under the influence of "heterodox" (Taoist or Buddhist) ideas or out of personal frustration and disenchantment. Others had successful careers as Confucian administrators while writing fiction surreptitiously; they regarded their penchant for these despised genres as a weakness and tried to hide it behind pseudonyms and outward conformity.

The outward conformity, of course, was to the code of the Confucian elite. For the best part of twenty centuries, most Confucians were agreed on certain basic attitudes about the issues of life and on every man's duty to cultivate corresponding inner values and to organize society accordingly. Literature's function and *raison d'être* in this perspective were to teach truth and virtue: it must contribute to uplifting men by attracting them emotionally toward approved ideals.

Storytelling and drama fell far from these standards. Primarily interested in entertaining, not in improving morals, free to improvise as the occasion might dictate, performers were often indecorous and sometimes indulged in irreverent or even subversive satire. Some of their heroes conform to established social and ethical standards; others, however, belong to mythologies which Sung Confucianism wanted to suppress, or exemplify chivalric values altogether foreign to Confucian orthodoxy. Many tales and plays take pains to caution the public explicitly against violating the Confucian codes, and illustrate their point by punishing evil and rewarding good. But this moralizing appears often as superficial and superimposed, a mere sop to would-be censors. The

picture of sin, represented vividly and with warm human understanding, engraves itself more deeply upon the consciousness than the moral
exhortations.

It is essentially fiction's indifference to conventional morality that
explains the Confucian attitude toward it and the efforts of Confucian
bureaucrats to restrict its influence. During the Ming and Ch'ing
dynasties, the government repeatedly tried to ban "seditious plays,"[12]
and "novels and licentious works" (*hsiao-shuo yin tz'u*), calling them
"frivolous, vulgar and untrue."[13] Even so unconventional and nonconformist a man of letters as Chin Sheng-t'an (*ca.* 1610–61) saw fit to alter
and truncate the text of the *Water Margin* in order to discourage ban-
ditry: in his 1644 edition, no honorable surrender is possible for the
outlaws; they must all be executed.[14] Further evidence of the effort to
keep the theater under control is found in the low legal status given to
actors; all law codes denied them the designation of "normal commoners" (*liang-min*). They were classified with slaves, prostitutes, and
yamen-runners in the lowest class of the population, as "vile subjects"
(*chien-jen*). This discrimination worked hardship, since offenses committed by *chien-jen* were more severely punished than those committed
against them.[15] Again, local magistrates, responsible for maintaining
public morals, checked theatrical performances in town and countryside,
and insisted that every time romantic stories like *Hsi Hsiang Chi* were
staged, actors should also perform plays stressing fidelity, filial piety,
chastity, and charity. This way of injecting moral elements into the
repertory (and so have the Devil spread a Confucian gospel) is comparable to the technique the Buddhists had used for centuries, that of
making their doctrine palatable by coating it in colorful adventures of
rebirths. Why not present to the "inferior men" and "selfish and money-
motivated" tradespeople, through the best mass medium available, examples of pious sons, devoted subjects, and other virtuous heroes?

Study of popular fiction, as it was appreciated by common folk and
manipulated by officialdom, can help us to a variety of understandings:
of the ambivalent attitude of the literati toward popular media; of their
own differences of view on Confucian principles; of the attitudes of the
common people—always drawn to and always resistant to the culture
of their betters. We shall here explore these problems through one of
the many possible approaches: a consideration of the heroes of popular
literature.

FACT AND FANCY

Historiography purports to describe events as they really happened;
it takes pains to ensure unbiased, impersonal observation. Fiction, on

the other hand, connotes the invention of characters and situations by a creative mind for audiences seeking entertainment or escape. To absorb and move is the storyteller's and the playwright's aim; their livelihood is at stake, and they cannot afford the dry matter-of-fact tone of police files or official statistics. They can and do "falsify" history for dramatic effect. Yet the very nature of dramatic effect usually limits the extent to which such falsification is possible, bound as it is by the mental habits of authors and audiences alike.

Paradoxically, the Chinese official histories may be less reliable than pure fiction. They

report everything as seen from the imperial court, generally neglecting the viewpoint of the provinces. . . . And they are naturally prejudiced in favor of the established institutions and beliefs—the Chinese type of monarchy, the Confucian code of ethics, etc. Also, the historiographers as a body are generally hostile to certain groups of people, such as eunuchs, merchants, monks, foreigners, and soldiers.[16]

The historiographer had often to use a "crooked brush" (*ch'ü pi*) in favor of family or clique, of the reigning house, and of powerful individuals. The reader can never be sure that statements of "historical fact" were not in reality calculated moves in some literary or political dispute, or selections of particulars meant to drive home a moral lesson, to encourage the good and warn the evil.[17]

Chinese novelists and playwrights, by contrast, are not tied by all these intentions, conventions, pressures, and prejudices. They bring the common people and the local interests into the picture, and throw a colorful light on minor events omitted by histories. They deal with techniques, tools, food, and dress, with institutions, customs, and psychology. Largely free from didactic and missionary purpose, they show man as he is or would like to be, not as the rules say he should be. They offer a candid and intimate view of the society of their time:

Without resorting to abstract discussion, they let us understand the conscious and unconscious assumptions of a society. . . . They indicate what has happened to religious and ethical ideals after they have been popularized and perhaps diluted, or as they are reflected through the novelist's individual mind; they reveal the imperfect ways in which social institutions operate in ambiguous and refractory human situations. The novel stands at the point where social history and the human soul intersect.[18]

Love stories, ghost stories, and Buddhist tales seek the moving and the sensational, but their narrations and dialogues are commonly realistic: the motions may be unnatural but the furniture is real. Detective stories give us a welcome view from below of the administrative process and help us visualize the lives of lesser officials and their aides.

As for specifically historical tales, romances, and plays, their method is what an expressive Chinese phrase calls *ch'i shih san hsü,* "70 per cent truth and 30 per cent falsehood," which might here be paraphrased as "70 per cent unreliable history and 30 per cent revealing fiction"; they add to the historical record a wealth of pithy anecdotes and appealing details, suggest motivations, reconstruct conversations, and accomplish "the infusion of the spirit of life into figures of the past, and the re-creation of the circumstances which surrounded them."[19] For this imaginative 30 per cent, authors rely on their own knowledge and experience, and all falsifications, adornments, and rationalizations, whether spontaneous or due to official pressure, all shifts of emphasis and of sympathy detectable in their writings, throw precious light on ideas and beliefs current in their time.

The writer of fiction seldom alters the broad outline of past events as represented in the histories; his fictional touches are limited to well-defined episodes. Nor does fictitious embroidery often affect the spirit of the sources. For example, stories and plays about the agrarian reformer Chia Ssu-tao (d. 1275) unquestioningly adopt the prejudiced views of the *History of the Sung,* which was written by Chia's political opponents. According to this official account, Chia rises to high office on the recommendation of his sister, a favorite of the emperor, becomes notorious for his luxury and many iniquities, and finally betrays the country to the Mongols. Fiction adds some highlights to this portrait of a typical "bad last minister," in particular a description of Chia's ordering one of his concubines beheaded for a minor offense: she had watched two young men boating and whispered, "How handsome they are!"[20]

In other cases, there are interesting differences of outlook between history and fiction. In moral standards and political legitimacy, there was no great disparity among rival protagonists of the Three Kingdoms (A.D. 220–80). Their first historiographer, Ch'en Shou (233–97) handles them impartially. But the later novels *San-kuo chih P'ing-hua* and *San-kuo chih Yen-i,* as well as numerous ballads and plays, strongly favor one kingdom over the other two: Shu is right and good, Wu wrong and bad, Wei very wrong and very bad. This emotional preference expresses a popular prejudice already current in Sung times,[21] and an opinion of political theorists, including the illustrious Chu Hsi, who eventually determined that Shu-Han was the legitimate dynasty.

One consequence of this is that the great Ts'ao Ts'ao (A.D. 155–220), founder of Wei, appears in fiction as an unregenerate and sometimes slow-witted villain, probably because he had been the most powerful opponent of the "right side" in the civil war. The horror felt by audiences for him and his machinations was matched by their sympathy for his adversaries.

Clearly fictional literature, while a help in correcting biases of histories, has biases and distortions of its own. Sophisticated novels like *Chin P'ing Mei* and *Hung Lou Meng*, as well as related stories and plays, are best suited to describe subtle nuances and to suggest more elusive aspects of a complex society. But the peculiar optics of historical and heroic storytelling and drama require, as medieval theatricals and modern television bear out, that, in a way, all must be good in one camp and bad in the other, and most characters must be either 100 per cent black or 100 per cent white.

Some specifically Chinese factors may have accentuated this Manichean pattern; one is the high degree of formalization in Chinese behavior. Despite the sweeping alternations of peace and war, order and anarchy, and the deep but slow changes effected by urbanization, technical progress, and the evolution of juridical and political structures, society remained for centuries "embedded in the cake of custom."[22] Education relied mostly on imitation of one's elders, and moral excellence was thought to lie rather in the proper fulfillment of established *social* roles in family and community living than in individual accomplishments (as in Western civilization). The concept of "roles" was more stereotyped than in other societies, and the *right* and *wrong* ways to play these roles were more sharply defined.

This is confirmed and reiterated in Chinese biographical writing, which classifies its subjects not only by status or role, but also by ethical judgment of performance; hence such categories of biographies as "principled officials" (*hsün li*), "oppressive officials" (*k'u li*),[23] "filial sons and faithful friends" (*hsiao yu*), "traitors" (*chien ch'en*), and "virtuous women" (*lieh nü*).[24]

Popular fiction does not speak of nondescript fathers and sons, but of "good" and "bad" fathers and "filial" and "ungrateful" sons. Good characters say and do exactly what is expected of them, invariably with identical phrases and attitudes; evil ways inspire a somewhat freer invention and more colorful details, but their depiction remains very stereotyped. To give a few examples: the typical bad stepmother has her stepsons dressed in light clothes during the winter, and the father discovers it by accident. Ruthless ambition is portrayed in an ever-recurring cliché: a young married man passes his examinations, is thereupon offered an official post and a rich marriage to a minister's daughter, claims to be a bachelor in order to be free for the flattering alliance, and forgets his wife back home or drowns her.[25] There seem to be only two kinds of courtesans: the heartless one who squanders all a man's money and then has him thrown out into the cold a beggar;

and the tender, generous one who helps her penniless lover through his studies.[26]

Critics have classified the subject matter of Yüan opera into a small number of stock characters and situations;[27] the rich variety of human experiences in the rest of fictional literature may be similarly classified.

There is the myth of the wicked prime minister, as conventional and stereotyped as the bad last ruler. From Chao Kao of the Ch'in to Yen Sung of the Ming, there are many representatives of this type, all carbon copies of each other, villains appearing on stage with face conventionally whitened, wearing the regulation jade belt and long-winged court hat, each with his contemptible offspring—typically a daughter in the imperial harem who spies for her father, and an idle and lustful son who roams around the capital with his bodyguards, on the lookout for young women to seize. These wicked prime ministers promote worthless men, dismiss good officials or have them put to death, and often plot for the throne. They double-cross hard-pressed generals on the frontiers, deprive them of supplies and reinforcements, then accuse them of losing battles deliberately. Sometimes they even conduct treacherous negotiations with the enemy.

The hero's role in all these cases is to unmask the villain, to awaken the emperor ot his duties, and, if not heeded, to face death resolutely. Variations occur in details,[28] but the over-all treatment of the theme is a cliché.[29]

Names of great men readily turn into common names, synonymous with specific attributes or virtues. An incorruptible judge will be called "a Pao Kung"; "a Chang Fei" will mean a man of impetuous and reckless courage. Ch'ü Yüan becomes the symbol of the loyal minister misunderstood by an unworthy prince, Kuan Yü the symbol of unwavering fidelity to his lord. On these prototypes are molded a whole series of characters who display the same qualities and resemble each other physically.[30]

Skillful use of the stereotyped technique is made in the play *Hsiao Yao Chin*, in which Ts'ao Ts'ao puts to death the Empress Fu and the two sons of Hsien-ti, the last Han emperor, almost before his eyes. The villain does not know that the dynasty he is about to found will end in a similar way; that his own great-grandson Ts'ao Fang, Emperor Fei of Wei, is going to suffer the same fate at the hands of his prime minister, Ssu-ma Shih (this is the subject of another play, *Ssu-ma Pi Kung*). Nor does he dream that the grandfather of this future agent of divine retribution is Ssu-ma I, his silent lieutenant, who stands right now by his side. History repeats itself: the familiar irony of a theme that has become a staple of the literary craft here ushers in a masterpiece of pathos.[31]

Despite intriguing literary effects of this kind, individualization is generally sacrificed to the emphasis on heroic traits. The hero emerges as a rather ingenuous, obvious, and single-minded fellow who makes his decisions without qualms or hesitations and demonstrates little psychological growth. Yet once this literary convention is accepted, each reader or theater-goer fills in the stereotypes with his own emotions.

In China as elsewhere, in fiction as well as in historiography, yesterday's hero may become tomorrow's villain when he represents the ideals or interests of specific groups in society. Witness the Taipings and their adversary Tseng Kuo-fan (1811–72), or the Yellow Turbans, the robbers of Mount Liang, Li Tzu-ch'eng (1605?–45) and Chang Hsien-chung (*ca.* 1605–47), the Boxers.[32] Hero worship is a touchstone for the social historian: "Tell me who your hero is, and I'll know who you are."

EXEMPLARY HEROES

Moral teaching around the world has traditionally emphasized temperance and moderation; a distrust of excess and a cult of perfection understood as a golden mean were ideals of both Hellenic and Confucian thought, and of many other cultures as well. On the other hand, poetry and fiction everywhere traditionally glorify extreme virtues and accomplishments. Ordinary people behave with circumspection, avoid head-on clashes whenever possible, fear men in power, accept and propose all kinds of compromises. Heroes are made of sterner stuff; scorning vulgar formulas for success and looking beyond the dilemmas and vacillations that defeat more scrupulous and fearful souls, they satisfy our yearning for an existence that is self-transcending and meaningful in the deepest reaches of the imagination.

The Chinese equivalents for "hero" include *ying-hsiung* ("male," "outstanding man"), the archaic phrase *ta-chang-fu* ("great man"), and the plebian *hao-han* ("good fellow"); also widely used in fiction texts are the term *fei-ch'ang jen* ("extraordinary man") and the epithet *ch'i* ("remarkable," "strange"). These words most often connote unusual physical or moral strength, energy and purposefulness, devotion to a great cause—good or bad—unconventional behavior, and sometimes striking traits of physiognomy and stature.

Liu Pei, Kuan Yü, and Chang Fei, meeting for the first time and by coincidence, are mutually attracted by each other's size and distinctive features: Liu Pei "is eight feet tall, the lobes of his ears touch his shoulders, his hands hang down below his knees; his eyes are set so that he is able to see his ears." Chang Fei is also eight feet tall; "he has the head of a leopard, round eyes, the chin shaped as the tail of a swallow, the whiskers of a tiger, a voice like thunder and the strength of a horse." Kuan Yü is even taller, nine feet, with a two-foot-long beard.

"His face is as brown as dates, his lips as red as seal-ink; he has the eyes of the phoenix and his eyebrows resemble sleeping silkworms." "Clearly," each remarks of the others, "this is no ordinary man!"[33]

Physical details are all signs;[34] they signify and reveal inner greatness even before words and deeds prove it. Passionate and sensitive, the heroes possess "outstanding gifts of personality and talent, and the resolution to behave on a level higher than that of the sages and the wise."[35] They are kind, generous, and refuse rewards; for duty and ideal, they sacrifice their dearest and closest attachments. This is "supramoral."[36] A general orders his son beheaded for a breach of discipline, even though he realizes that his son had to do what he did, and served the country best by doing so.[37]

Here appears the fundamental difference between the heroic and the "sublunary"[38] genres in popular fiction. Tales of love and crime, novels of manners, and other stories, ballads, and plays belonging to the sublunary genre describe the world as it is, with little or no idealizing. Protagonists of their comic or tragic plots are often evil people, who enjoy money, sex, and power, even if this means early death, or they are common cowards, weaklings, or no-nonsense realists. Sometimes the leading role is played by virtuous men cast from the Confucian mold, men who walk with cautious prudence mostly along paths of compromise chosen as lesser evils. These characters, while being true to ordinary life, are petty and weak when seen from the "supramoral" level of heroic fiction. True heroes are "more than life-size."[39]

And heroic actions are exceptional and extraordinary. Critics continuously debate their credibility in literature.[40] But is heroism unnatural? Every man secretly cherishes the ambitions of his youth, and ascribes to conflict and compromise the failure of his high aspirations. He sees in heroes strong persons able to do what he hoped to do, overcome all obstacles and handicaps, withstand all compromise. Thus, heroic behavior expresses human nature and its desires more truly than nonheroic behavior.

In China, as elsewhere, the hero and the ordeal he experiences and surmounts are often viewed as a symbol of man's spiritual ordeal. There are several classic types of ordeal. Hercules, Chu-ko Liang, and Wu Sung perform superhuman labors assigned to them. Su Wu, Pao Ch'eng, and Joan of Arc remain faithful to voices heard in their youth. Hector and Achilles, Kuan Yü, Chang Fei, and Yüeh Fei sacrifice their lives in service to their king, their country, their cause. Theseus and Jason, Ulysses and Alexander, Mu-lien, Hsüan-tsang, and San-pao confront the mysterious dangers of the other world, or of distant countries; not all come back alive, but all win everlasting glory.

Along this lonely path, so high above his fellow men and utterly isolated from them by his own greatness and the uniqueness of his trials, the hero often experiences the tragic despair of Vigny's Moses:

> O Seigneur! j'ai vécu puissant et solitaire,
> Laissez-moi m'endormir du sommeil de la terre![41]

But this anguish does not stop him any more than other obstacles or conditions do: driven by passion and faith, he gives himself entirely to his goal, resolved to persevere against all odds. Death itself does not deter him. Thus he knows no failure: his venture succeeds on a moral plane, for all of us; we re-experience it and gain new dimensions. The hero thrills the imagination because he proves what so many respectable citizens secretly doubt—that virtue ultimately triumphs over vice.

The popularity of military heroes and of the upright judge Pao Ch'eng during the Sung and Yüan dynasties, an era when people were distressed by centuries of misery, military defeat, and wounded pride, is to be understood in these terms. The poor and downtrodden could find little to console and uplift them in the traditional advice of those in power, that they should reconcile themselves peaceably to their lot (an fen). More appealing was the image of a savior who would come to relieve their suffering, and to rescue them from invasion, natural catastrophes, and abuses of authority. Such hopes were nourished not only in meetings of secret societies but in the relaxed and escapist atmosphere of theatrical performances. Playgoers could watch Pao Ch'eng redressing wrongs, regardless of the wrongdoer's eminence, and ordering the execution of a murderous brother-in-law of the Emperor despite the pleas and threats of Princess and Empress Dowager.[42] They were even afforded in Hung Tsung Lieh Ma ("Lady Precious Stream") the spectacle of a beggar marrying the prime minister's daughter, winning battles and becoming emperor, after which he sentences the villains who conspired against him and rewards the deserving.[43]

If love for fictional heroes were in proportion to their visible triumphs or to their power of inspiring optimistic dreams, the most popular tales would be those of the marvelous, which draw upon the heterogenous body of popular religious beliefs and weave elaborate plots that revolve around the workings of Heaven and Hell and feats of divination and magic. Chains of reincarnations lead virtuous men upward through successive rebirths—for example, from official to monk, and finally to emperor—while the wicked are gradually degraded to the status of animals.[44] Worthy youths receive from venerable immortals heavenly books containing secrets of warfare that enable them to win battles and establish empires.[45] Ghosts hound their murderers, and by dreams and miracles engineer their conviction and punishment.[46] Snakes and vixens appear in the shape of comely maidens to bewitch scholars and drain them of their vital substance.[47] The well-known novels *Feng Shen Yen-i* and *Hsi Yu Chi* are rich in supernatural episodes.

Though protagonists of these tales are heroes in a sense, the sphere of their activities is as naïve in conception as a child's fairy story. The marvelous seems to be exploited for its own sake, catering to popular delight in the mischievous, quaint, and comical antics of demons and gods in whose world laws of gravity and rules of common sense are suspended. The victor in these tales is not the most virtuous man, or the strongest, or the most courageous, but the one with the showiest bag of tricks; and this is hardly a valid criterion of heroism.

By contrast, historical romances and plays[48] tell mostly of actions that really took place in the past, or still happen regularly, or at least belong in the sphere of the plausibly human. Here the notion of heroism is more genuine; reduced to their own resources and facing critical situations, men show what they are really worth. Psychological evaluations reappear; heroes emerge against a credible background.

This is not always true, however, and the line dividing the heroic and the magical is hard to draw. There is no single and clear-cut answer to whether popular imagination conceived its heroes as gods, genii, or just superior men. The use of the word "divine" (*shen*) in fiction is suggestive: Wu Sung lightly tosses about a stone pedestal, and enthusiastic onlookers cheer, "This is no common man! Truly he is a god!" (or, "divine man!" *T'ien shen, shen-jen*). But obviously this record-smashing champion is considered part of the human race.[49]

If it remains possible to distinguish between the heroic and supernatural classes of fiction, the difference lies in the relative number of marvels and other-world events. Kuan Yü has been worshipped for centuries as the warriors' God of Loyalty, but most of his deeds, even in fiction, are those of an exemplary man, not of a deity. Heroes display human or suprahuman rather than supernatural strength and energy: this is true of the famous captains, knights-errant, outlaws, statesmen, and diplomats of the Warring States, and of their emulators in all periods of Chinese history; of the Lady Mi who kills herself to save her son, and of Mu-lan, so devoted she joins the army to free her aged father from conscription.[50]

Most characteristic of heroic fiction are the unyielding patriots, Su Wu and Yüeh Fei. Sent by the Han Emperor Wu as ambassador to the Hsiung-nu, Su Wu was held prisoner by them for nineteen years. First thrown into a pit to die of hunger, he managed to keep himself alive by eating snow; after a few days the Hsiung-nu relented and sent him to the frontiers of their land, near the "Northern Sea" (probably Lake Baikal), where he lived as a shepherd. Several times the Hsiung-nu offered him honorable posts, but he always refused, to the discomfiture of his countryman Li Ling, who had been captured in battle by the Hsiung-nu and had accepted high office at their court. Su Wu, set off against the traitor Li Ling, becomes the symbol of refusal to collaborate with the enemy.[51]

Psychologically similar to Su Wu is Yüeh Fei, leader of the twelfth-century resistance war against the Chin. Whatever may have been the facts of the long strife between the War and Peace parties at the Sung court and at Yüeh Fei's camp—and the circumstances are far from clear —his motto, "Give us back our rivers and mountains!" (*huan wo ho shan*), has remained a battlecry of Chinese patriots through the centuries. (It was often chalked on walls in areas occupied by the Japanese during World War II.) One play shows Yüeh with his mother before he leaves for a critical campaign; he is asking her to tattoo on his back the vow "A perfect fidelity to repay our Country!" (*ching chung pao Kuo*). Yüeh Fei's tragic death is the subject of another play. It begins with the treacherous intrigues of Ch'in Kuei and the recall of Yüeh Fei from his front-line camp to the capital. On his way, the hero stops at the Chin-shan monastery, where the abbot warns him not to proceed to the court and to retire at once from public life. Yüeh ignores this advice, moves on, and is arrested and put to death, along with his two sons, in the Dungeon of Wind and Waves. The execution takes place in the middle of the night, two days before the New Year (1142); outside a monotonous drizzle falls, "as though Heaven were shedding bitter tears at the injustice."[52]

The preceding pages make clear that the division of popular fiction into realistic, supernatural, and heroic genres cannot be clear-cut. Few novels, stories, ballads, or plays lend themselves to tidy classification; "sublunary" tales, for instance, often include some heroic or supernatural episodes. But even so, heroic fiction may be seen to exist by itself, between the two other genres, and to embody values and ideals in a way which is both exalted and attractive: this explains the influence it exerts on human behavior. Su Wu and Yüeh Fei are dedicated to aspirations untarnished by concern for gross, mundane hindrances. Yet, their achievements do not discourage imitation because they appear humanly possible, not divinely miraculous.

To teach by imitation has long been the practice in China, where, traditionally, education has relied on models and precedent more than on rules. When youngsters studied the *San Tzu Ching* and the *Erh-shih-ssu Hsiao,* they did not memorize a precept, "Honor thy father and mother." Rather, they read of (Huang) Hsiang, who "aged nine, knew how to warm the bed of his parents."[53] A well-known passage of the *Li Chi* makes its point simply by describing in everyday detail the filial piety of King Wen as a young crown prince.[54]

Buddhist preachers used the same technique very early, proposing Buddhas and Bodhisattvas as models of altruistic self-denial. Even the Taoist free ideal of conformity to nature and noninvolvement is illustrated by exemplary drunkards, poets and hermits—oblivion-bent heroes whose heroism is tested against the blandishments and threats of temporal powers that seek to enlist their services.

Some heroes of popular fiction conform closely to Confucian, Buddhist, or Taoist patterns; others demonstrate original ways of playing human roles, ways that reveal the impact of the "little traditions" of thought alive within the common people and sometimes indigenous to a particular province or district.

Chinese of all classes are accustomed from childhood to seeing the hero as exemplar, to persuading each other when necessary by references to historical or legendary precedents.[55] This fact gives an added dimension of interest to our consideration of three heroic types: the prince, the scholar, and the swordsman.

PRINCES

Kings and emperors of fiction reveal much about popular sentiment toward Chinese monarchy and toward individual rulers of the past. The popular imagination was fascinated by their prestige, their apparently arbitrary exercise of power for good or evil, and their leisurely and luxurious life in palaces "of gold and jade."

Analyzing in this volume the life of Sui Yang-ti in history and in fiction, Arthur Wright describes the wide possibilities offered to popular fiction by the stereotype of the "bad last ruler," a political formula exploited by incipient dynasties for almost two thousand years.[56]

Another popular stereotype, predominant from the T'ang onward, was the bad last minister, upon whom the fall of the Sung and of the Ming was blamed, as the fall of the Han had been for centuries. Hsien-ti, the last Han emperor, is helpless. In the play *Hsiao Yao Chin*, those he loves most have just been massacred by Ts'ao Ts'ao; foreseeing his own abdication and years of captivity, he sings the poignant lament well known to opera lovers, in which the words, "How he humiliates Us!" (*ch'i kua-jen* . . .) are fifteen times repeated, each time with a comparison: ". . . like a mouse in a cat's paws," ". . . like a bird in a cage," ". . . like a little boat on the Yangtse." Victim and no real hero, placed on the Dragon Throne when a child, Hsien-ti remains in his last years what he has always been, a pawn in the hands of his crafty ministers: first Tung Cho, and later Ts'ao Ts'ao. Aware of their crimes, he has been incapable of curbing them. Still, in this play, his rank as legitimate holder of the Mandate gives him the audience's sympathy.[57]

One degree higher is the last Ming emperor: his suicide lends him the aura of a tragic hero. In the play *Mei Shan Hen*,[58] his armies having been defeated, he is abandoned by all except a faithful eunuch, and hangs himself from a tree in the imperial park after having first killed his wife and his daughter. He leaves the rebel leader a letter, written in his own blood, asking protection for his subjects: "My life I give up without regret, but do spare my people." A palace maidservant, moved by this cruel spectacle, disguises herself as the princess, hoping to attract the rebel and then murder him. Her plan almost works: she slays his lieutenant, the Tiger General Li Hu. This play pictures the rebels as odious and idealizes loyalist devotion to the fallen dynasty.

Other rulers are dismissed with some condescension as "muddle-headed" (*hun chün*). A typical example is the spineless Liu Ch'an, second and last ruler of Shu in the time of the Three Kingdoms, who leads an indolent life in his harem while his men defend hard-pressed frontiers, and who thinks only of surrender when the enemy approaches.[59] The remonstrances and noble suicide of his fifth son are not enough to open his eyes.[60] Later, a captive at Wei, he "listens to music and forgets his country."[61]

Popular fiction also considers as muddle-headed T'ang Hsüan-tsung and Sung Hui-tsung, two "rather bad" rulers who did not lead their dynasty to final ruin but weakened it significantly. Romantic figures, remarkable for their artistic tastes and talents, they lack moral integrity. They exhibit primarily the *passive* features of the Wright characterology: neglect of upright officials, favoritism toward corrupt officials, drunkenness, sloth, lack of personal virtue, addiction to sorcery and "heretical" religious practices, etc. They do not show the *violent* characteristics: abuse of officials, exactions, harsh punishments, cruelty, sadism. Their self-indulgence and licentiousness escape condemnation by most authors.

Hsüan-tsung appears in *Ch'ang-sheng Tien*[62] as a patron of the arts, the Maecenas to the poet Li Po and to the musician Li Kuei-nien, and the founder of the Pear Garden, the first theater school in Chinese history; but driven to exile by rebellious forces, he cannot save his beloved Yang Kuei-fei from the cruel fate he himself has brought on her by entrusting to her brother the powers of state. The *Water Margin* describes Sung Hui-tsung's passion for rare stones and art objects, his skill in painting and calligraphy, and his love of football. But, blind in his choice of ministers, the aesthete is unable to keep peace and order in the empire and to secure its frontiers: the corrupt administration which causes Sung Chiang's and Fang La's revolts and invites the encroachments of the Chin is a consequence of the artistic ruler's ineptitude.

Average emperors, not being endowed with any such gifts and tastes, reveal better what seems a fundamental outlook of popular fiction since Sung times: the concept of a transcendent but outwardly passive ruler. He has the Mandate of Heaven, but takes no direct part in government and lets his ministers and generals act for him. He lives in secrecy, surrounded only by women and eunuchs; men in his government are admitted to his presence once a day at most, unless a crisis necessitates an extraordinary audience. On the stage, he appears preceded by a retinue of young court ladies. His behavior suggests that he is far above the cares and hurly-burly of the world and administrative routine. This concept of monarchy is related to the Taoist ideal of *wu-wei*, "no intervention against Nature," and to the Confucian theory that the ruler ensures order and harmony merely by the emanation of his Virtue, without stepping out of his palace, or even taking his hands out of his sleeves. The dramatic possibilities of such a role are obviously limited.

Founders of dynasties are more spectacular figures, closer to the type of the European hero-king. The rise of an outsider, from a farm or a bandit's lair, through constant challenges and dangers up the ladder to imperial majesty, will cover, of course, a wider range of events and provide the setting for a more colorful show than the flat career of a spoiled porphyrogenite. Here are bold spirits, men who at one point decided to burn their bridges and to plunge into the great adventure of outlawry and rebellion. They measured the stakes: success meant the glorious inauguration of a new dynasty; failure, a cruel and ignominious death, and the name (perhaps forever accursed) of rebel and usurper. They gambled.

Such are Liu Pang, Liu Pei, Li Shih-min, Ch'ien Liu, Chao K'uang-yin, Chu Yüan-chang, and a few others. While drawing the individual features of such a man, the novel and the drama commonly give a stereotyped account of the principal stages of his climb to power: he starts out as a strong man charged with the protection of a local community in a period of anarchy and disorder; his tiny band of followers snowballs into an army, and he eventually takes over provinces and perhaps the whole country, in part by battles and negotiations, but also in part by a mysterious charisma which wins him the spontaneous support of all who meet him.

The crimes and the amoral opportunism of these dynasty-founders are sometimes glossed over in fiction, but they are not concealed. Liu Pang ungratefully permits the execution of Han Hsin, to whom, above all others, he owes his throne.[63] Four centuries later, he will be punished by the disintegration of his empire into the Three Kingdoms.[64] In the play *Ta Tao*,[65] young Chao K'uang-yin, a reckless bully, is shown killing the two smiths who forged his sword; later, when on the throne, in a fit of drunkenness, he orders the beheading of Cheng En, his loyal friend and supporter, because of a well-meant remonstrance.[66] These examples, and many more, illustrate the concept of the corrupting influence of supreme power. But more than crimes and corruption, popular fiction emphasizes the fundamental passivity, if not weakness, of the rulers. The founding of a dynasty is credited to Heaven's protection of the challenger, but is directly brought about by the exploits and sacrifices of his men. Liu Pang's army is besieged in a fortress by Hsiang Yü and on the verge of surrender because of lack of food; Liu Pang sends a double disguised as himself to Hsiang Yü's camp, ostensibly to negotiate a surrender, while he himself escapes in humble attire through another gate when the ruse makes the enemy less vigilant. By the time Hsiang Yü discovers his mistake, Liu Pang is already far away and safe. His double is put to a cruel death. The idea that saved Liu Pang on this occasion was not even his, but an adviser's.[67] Another play shows him as Han Kao-tsu a few years later, with his "Three Heroes," Han Hsin, Chang Liang, and Hsiao Ho, shortly after his enthronement. To their congratulations he replies: "Without you I would never have succeeded." And he is right.[68]

His descendant Liu Pei does not love books or serious learning, but dogs, horses, and fine clothes. He lacks initiative and his chief resource when faced with danger is tears. For some time he has been prudently devoting himself to gardening in order to appear harmless; Ts'ao Ts'ao suspects him, nevertheless, and one stormy day, to search out his character and intentions, starts a discussion about heroes. Presently he states: "The only heroes in our time are you and I!" Shocked, Liu Pei lets his chopsticks drop to the floor. He is saved by luck: at that very moment there is a clap of thunder and he pretends to have been frightened by it, not by Ts'ao's words.[69] He would never dream of challenging Ts'ao to his face.

In battles, he lets his men plan and fight for him; he is critically defeated in an expedition undertaken after the death of his old companions and against the advice of his strategists.[70] Not his own wits, but those of his adviser Chu-ko Liang, allow him to escape from the Yellow Crane Tower in which Chou Yü thought he had safely imprisoned him, and from the Sweet Dew Temple, where soldiers were lying in ambush to kill him. The play *Huang Ho Lou* emphasizes his pusillanimity almost to the point of farce: he foresees danger and refuses repeatedly to leave; prodigies of eloquence from Chu-ko Liang are needed to convince him; then, he learns that he is supposed to proceed alone with only one bodyguard, and he refuses again.[71] When his adviser's prophetic resourcefulness has turned the ambush at the temple into a fortunate and satisfying marriage, Liu Pei forgets all his duties to his country and stays with his bride for months on end, wholly intoxicated by her charms, never leaving her apartments, and barely listening to his good captain Chao Yün's admonitions. Escaping finally, he owes the success of his flight to the ingenuity of his bride, who deceives the pursuers: he is too frightened to think.[72]

Dynastic founders seldom take the decisive step of claiming the throne; they are usually pushed by their followers and refuse several times before finally accepting. Moreover, refusal is not a pure formality.[73] Chao K'uang-yin's men dress him in yellow robes and cap during his drunken sleep; terrified, when he wakes up, by the *lèse-majesté* situation he finds himself in, he has but one way open: to accept.

Yet these seemingly weak men climb to and stay in power. They attract and keep devoted followers. The inhabitants of Ching-chou follow Liu Pei in his retreat when Ts'ao's army attacks; a pitiful column of refugees, they have voluntarily abandoned homes and possessions to cast their lot with the humane ruler.[74] In this episode we see three elements: the Mencian image of people flocking to a sage king, an echo of the terror and mass flight induced by the Mongol conquest, and the power of attraction exercised by a ruler's passivity.

This power is partly explained when the passivity is viewed not as a weakness, but as wily scheming. "Cry-baby Liu Pei" ("*K'u Liu Pei*" is a Chinese proverb), and Sung Chiang, the "uncrowned king" of Mount Liang, rely constantly on subtle diplomacy to keep balance among their men, to play one against another, and to check strong personalities indirectly rather than openly opposing them. Liu Pang is a monument of hypocrisy compared with his straightforward, noble, artless rival Hsiang Yü. Liu Pei, on his deathbed, slyly tests his loyal Chu-ko Liang, saying, "My son is a weakling. . . . You are a genius. . . . If he proves incapable, then take the throne yourself." He does this only to elicit Chu-ko's public and formal protest.[75]

A rational explanation does not suffice, however. In popular fiction, a supernatural atmosphere surrounds the founders. At the time of their birth, their mothers have prophetic dreams. The prince's high destiny is announced by omens and portents: balls of fire or dragons appear in the air above him, or a red snake crawls in and out of his mouth, ears, and nostrils while he sleeps.[76] As a boy he already shows promise of leadership: the round tree near which the young Liu Pei plays soldiers with his peasant playmates resembles the canopy of a nobleman's carriage and is taken by neighbors for a sign that a great man will some day come forth from that house.[77] Later the prince is miraculously protected in danger and war: Liu Pei's horse leaps across a torrent impassable to his pursuers; Chao Yün rescues an infant prince from a pit while a flash of light frightens the enemy;[78] a goddess hides Sung Chiang from the police who search for him, gives him a heavenly book on strategy, and later appears in a dream to advise him.[79]

Apparently writers and actors of fiction represent the typical ruler as helpless in order to underline his transcendent character, to demonstrate that human ability needs supplementing by a mysterious charisma. This suggests a comparison between the princely hero and the conventional romantic hero of love tales. The lover, too, shows an almost morbid lack of initiative, and depends on others for the success of his suit. If villains or ill luck separate him from his beloved, he will languish for months without stirring to fight for his happiness, and he depends on a savior for release from his troubles:

[He] is generally a quite unheroic person, . . . a scholar, with all a Chinese scholar's disdain of physical prowess, who naturally leaves to his inferiors such matters as the rescue of fair maidens. . . . Well-educated, handsome, lacking experience of the world, often weak in character, and endowed with sensibility to a high degree, he is seldom capable of thinking or acting for himself and for the protection of his lady. . . . In place of the knight of western story and legend, whose life was spent in rescuing maidens in distress, there is in many Chinese tales a secondary hero whose business it is to solve the problems and difficulties of the situation and make everything easy for the hero and his lady.[80]

A hero's ability to attract devotion without apparent effort or spectacular action is the best measure of his merit and prestige. When Wu Tzu-hsü flees, pursued by an evil king's horsemen, a boatman and a girl who have helped him on his way commit suicide before his eyes to assure him that his secret will not be betrayed.[81] True lovers do not need to take active steps toward each other, because they are marked by predestination (*yüan*). Similarly, the true prince does not need to act: he and his people are also destined for each other, and the success of the men in his service is proof enough he holds the Mandate. His essential gift is the ability to choose and administer men well, to distribute responsibilities appropriately. He must also show his men proper respect, treating his adviser as a teacher (*hsien-sheng*) and his swordsman as a friend. These test his will and character before tying their destiny to his.[82]

To sum up, popular fiction often represents its typical prince as fundamentally a weak personality, dissolute and hypocritical, and something of a figurehead. Sometimes exaggerated, this picture is probably well meant, drawn thus to enhance the prestige of ministers and fighters, and also to suggest the necessarily mysterious charisma which flows from a prince. On the stage, the prince has a noble countenance, a low-pitched voice, and the discreet gesture that traditionally belong to the kingly way.

To many princely heroes of Chinese fiction, Donald Keene's description of Genji would apply:

Genji has no need of his fists to prove his status as a hero. . . . He is a superman who breathes no fire. . . . His capacity to love, his beauty, wit and talent mark him as a hero, though he performs no heroic deeds.[83]

SCHOLARS

The apparent passivity of the ruler leaves the front of the stage to his men. In the imperial courts, literature finds not only some of its greatest heroes and worst villains, but also a mirror for the psychology of ordinary mankind. There the fevers of ambition, jealousy, and hatred run highest, intensified by constant proximity to fortune and ruin.

An important distinction immediately appears among the rulers' men, between the advisers and musclemen: the brains that conceive, and the arms that execute. In Chinese opera performances, these two functions have been developed into a pair of dramatically contrasted psychological types.

The difference is definitely not a generic one between the man of peace and the man of war, the "soft" intellectual and the "violent" man of action. Both are men of action and of violence, normally involved in strife. They are fighters who use different weapons: the one would kill his enemy with the point of his sword, the other with the tip of his tongue or, better, of his brush. Both are equally daring and courageous, the swordsman on the battlefield, the scholar usually in court and council.

Both also play indispensable and complementary parts in the great civilian enterprise of organizing society and ensuring its survival, while bringing or restoring peace and order in the world (*chih kuo, p'ing t'ien-hsia*). The adviser assesses situations, maps out plans, advises the ruler; his formalized behavior embodies norms of an orderly state and society. The muscleman is called upon when brute force has to be applied, when normal patterns must momentarily be discarded under pressure of some emergency; once "unleashed" by the ruler into his natural element, the free-for-all of a battlefield, he rushes forth with his troops and kills untiringly.

To their different vocations correspond different psychologies and attitudes: the impetuous, rash, outspoken, and candid ways of the one set off the suave, inscrutable, and considered manner of the other. The swordsman speaks his mind, without concern for the "face" of people around him, who appreciate, and sometimes resent, his frankness. The scholar manages to use men smoothly for his own ends while diplomatically letting them think they are deciding matters for themselves. Before committing himself, the scholar takes time for reflection; the swordsman's nature is to "kill first and talk later."

The scholar-heroes are the Chinese equivalent of our "polytropos Odysseus." Classical anecdotes, often rewritten into popular tales or plays, revolve around the ingenuity of these heroes and the ruses they invent to extricate themselves from dangerous predicaments and turn defeat into victory: Lin Hsiang-ju "returns to Chao with the jade disc unbroken" and "gets the king of Ch'in to beat the drum";[84] Su Ch'in, an itinerant politician of the fourth century B.C., cleverly intrigues for the "international" alliance of the Six States against Ch'in;[85] Yen-tzu the Dwarf enters the capital of Ch'u through the main gate, shames into silence a rude king, and "with two peaches kills three giants."[86]

One of the most important characters in the *Water Margin* is another scholar, the strategist Wu Yung, nicknamed "the star of much wisdom." Never dismayed by difficult situations, he always has a plan—simple, elegant, efficient, and, if need be, treacherous. He traps enemies in snow-covered pits, tricks all kinds of useful people into joining his band, and is a master in tactics and the use of spies and fifth columnists.[87] One of his lesser triumphs is maneuvering a caravan of pseudo-merchants, ostensibly laden with dates but actually with drugged wine, through a mountain pass to meet escorted wheelbarrows en route to the capital with the prime minister's birthday presents. The day is hot and the escorters happily drink themselves senseless; when they awake, the presents are gone.[88]

"Young people should not read the *Water Margin*, old people should not read the *Three Kingdoms*"; thus runs a Chinese proverb, meaning that the young are disposed enough to rash behavior, and the old to intrigues. The *Three Kingdoms* is a mine of all tricks and stratagems (*chi ts'e*) needed in war and politics. By using a pretty girl—this is the *mei-jen chi* ruse ("ruse de la Belle") that worked so well for Hsi Shih[89]— Wang Yün arouses jealousy and hatred between the dictator Tung Cho and Lü Pu, Tung's adopted son and devoted henchman, in order to secure Lü's support in murdering Tung.[90] Ts'ao Ts'ao rashly beheads his able admirals after his enemy, young Chou Yü, has cunningly encouraged a spy to steal a forged letter that fraudulently implicates the admirals in an imaginary plot.[91]

Without doubt, the keenest and most clever is Chu-ko Liang, whose name is still used proverbially as a synonym for intelligence. His career begins when, at the age of twenty-seven, he conceives a tripartition of China by exploiting the rivalry between Wei and Wu which would allow Szechwan to exist as an independent "third force" and later, hopefully, to restore the Han dynasty a second time. He goes to ask the advisers of Wu to commit their ruler's strength against Ts'ao Ts'ao. In a "battle of tongues" with twelve experienced and self-confident politicians, in the presence of twenty others, all hostile, the young debater, alternately moralistic, provocative, disdainful, persuasive, and ironic, always superbly aware of each opponent's background and character, refutes all objections and shatters the opposition.[92]

Chu-ko is a master of all the old tricks of war and diplomacy, and ingenious at inventing new ones. He fails in his major enterprise—to reunify China—but through no fault of his own. For he anticipates his enemies' every move, and by flattery and provocation gets the best from his warriors. He founds military farms, invents "the wooden oxen and the rolling horses,"[93] uses doubles and, when necessary, blackmail. In a campaign against the aborigines in the fever-ridden mountains of the Southwest, he captures their chieftain seven times. Six times the chief claims that he has been cheated or caught by surprise; each time Chu-ko releases the chief. The seventh time, the chief surrenders, overcome more by Chu-ko's "psychological warfare" than by his battalions.[94]

Most spectacular and full of suspense are the episodes in which Chu-ko faces opponents as subtle as himself. His resentful young ally, the jealous Chou Yü, cannot be happy as long as Chu-ko is alive, but Chu-ko escapes his repeated snares. Chu-ko promises to bring 100,000 arrows within three days; Chou Yü, believing that Chu-ko is merely boasting and will never be able to deliver the arrows, makes him pledge his head, and goes to bed charmed by the prospect of Chu-ko's impending death. But, at dawn of the third day, a thick fog covers the Yangtze River, and Chu-ko launches twenty boats covered with straw mats toward the opposite bank where their common enemy Ts'ao Ts'ao is encamped. Ts'ao, fearful that he is being attacked, orders his archers to shoot at these boats which are vaguely outlined in the fog. The arrows stick in the straw, and Chu-ko returns to camp triumphant.[95]

Years later, because of a subordinate's defeat, Chu-ko finds himself trapped in an almost defenseless fortress, with only a few old and wounded soldiers to face a huge enemy army. He quickly sees that his only hope of salvation, at least until the expected arrival of reinforcements, lies in making the enemy believe that the fortress is full of troops. He orders the four gates opened wide and the ground in front of each swept clean as if to welcome the enemy. Standing himself on the wall, he drinks wine and plays on his lute with apparent unconcern. When Ssu-ma I appears at the head of his thousands, Chu-ko invites him to enter, and states repeatedly that the fortress is empty. The trick works: Ssu-ma suspects a snare and refuses to take the risk. Chu-ko's masterly lute playing impresses and misleads Ssu-ma because it seems to imply perfect self-control and ease of mind: "I know music! These notes would not ring so pure if he had a single care!"[96]

The scholar-hero has no nerves. Neither good news nor bad news affects his composure; he displays neither hatreds nor affections. He has infinite patience. He can prepare and wait twenty years to take revenge, and, in the meantime, he smiles and talks courteously to the man on whom he intends to wreak vengeance. Knowingly, he watches and interprets others' actions, but he seldom reveals his own feelings. Lifelong concentration helps him to hide his quick and intense sensitivity under a mask of relaxed self-confidence. The impassivity which he exemplifies is a virtue traditionally ascribed to fathers, judges, and administrators in this country where uncontrolled emotional outbursts even within the family are exceptional and considered childish and uncivilized.

Scholar-heroes, however, have more than intellectual strength and self-control; they are also endowed with supernatural powers. They interpret dreams, deal with the other world, and master the forces of nature. The Pao Ch'eng of fiction is in daytime a judge of the Sung court; at night, he may have to sit in Hades to decide a difficult case for King Yen, the Chinese Yama.[97] In his black robe embroidered with eight Trigrams in white, waving a white feather fan, Chu-ko Liang appears on the stage with some features of a Taoist magician, almost like an Immortal (*shen-hsien*): by performing a mysterious ceremony in front of a black altar, he is able to conjure an east wind that will propel his incendiary boats against the enemy fleet;[98] he reads in the stars the day set for his death and, through another black mass, almost succeeds in averting Fate.[99] Although he may not have manufactured the providential, life-saving fog on the river,[100] his ability to forecast weather accurately appears supernatural.

Some scholar-heroes encourage belief in vulgar superstitions, even though they themselves are unbelieving: Chu-ko Liang orders his old soldiers to open the gates of the empty fortress, notices their fright, and reassures them: "I have twenty thousand 'celestial troops' (*shen ping*) hidden inside."[101] The first Ming emperor also exploits the credulity of simple souls, telling the two princes who planned to poison him that he knows of their plot because Heaven has warned him in a dream. In reality, he was informed by a spy.[102] These statements are readily believed since the supernatural powers of both heroes are taken for granted.

Imperfect heroes such as Chou Yü and Shen Lien, and villains such as Wang Lun and Ts'ao Ts'ao, set off the perfection of a Chu-ko Liang.[103] Chou and Shen are nervous and impulsive. Wang is neurotic, unsure of himself, overly suspicious. Ts'ao Ts'ao has been built up into a monster of evil: he murders people in cold blood, terrorizes court and state by periodical mass killings, plots for the throne, torments and humiliates the emperor.[104] With blatant partiality, traditional fiction charges him with "low cunning" and "treacherous perfidy," while his rival Liu Pei is credited with "skillful dissimulation"; theatrical audiences roar with delight at the "clever stratagem" of Huang Chung who, in order to provoke the enemy to battle, shoots a poisonous arrow into the back of a newly released prisoner.[105]

The Ts'ao of fiction lacks intelligence as well as virtue. Although his army is larger than the combined armies of the other two kingdoms, time and again he is defeated by the smaller forces, and falls into his enemies' traps.[106] Here can be seen a distinctive idea often found in Chinese tradition: moral superiority is more important and essential for success, in war as well as in other endeavors, than technical skill; that is, skills cannot be acquired until one earns them through moral cultivation.

It must be observed, however, that novels and plays which condemn Ts'ao also find in him a certain greatness. The first few chapters of the *Romance* describe him as a clear-sighted and responsible young statesman who acts while the intellectuals only speak.[107] And it is interesting to note that on stage Ts'ao is played by a large-framed actor of imposing presence, whose face is chalk white except for two long black slits indicating half-closed eyes, who speaks in a low and powerful voice and suggests boundless energy and vitality. This "perverted hero" (*chien hsiung*)[108] might be said to be "perverted, but a hero."

The seventeenth-century commentator Mao Tsung-kang recognizes the ethical value of his open defiance of convention:

The killing [by Ts'ao] of [Lü] Po-she's family resulted from a mistake and is excusable. But his killing of Po-she is a crime odious to the extreme, and his statement, "Rather hurt others than allow anyone to hurt me!" is even worse. All readers at this point hate him, swear at him, even wish to kill him. They do not realize that here resides [Ts'ao's] superiority [*kuo jen*]. I wonder who on earth does not feel as he does; but who dares to voice it? Our moralizing worthies turn this sentence the other way around and say: "Rather have others hurt me than to have me ever hurt others." This sounds nice indeed, but check their behavior: every step is a covert imitation of [Ts'ao's] motto. He is despicable, but at least his heart and mouth are in accord. The hypocrisy of that bunch is worse than his carefree directness.[109]

Scholarly heroes and villains, of which the Chu-ko Liang and the Ts'ao Ts'ao of fiction represent two extremes, are at home in both the literary and the popular literatures of China. Their superior mental capacities and, once in a while, their supernatural talents satisfy both the sophisticated tastes and the primitive needs which coexist in illiterate as well as in learned minds. They express some of the ideals and dreams of the authors who are usually scholars themselves; they also reveal the common people's imaginings about life in court and government, and their mixed feelings toward the "father-and-mother officials." Sometimes honest, like Pao Ch'eng, more often elegantly rapacious, like magistrate T'eng,[110] frighteningly impassive as they sit in their yamen tribunal and decree beatings and torture, always skilled in the noble art of speech and clever at arranging compromises, these representatives of law and power, who know the books so well, appear to the humble as a different human species, refined and formidable.

SWORDSMEN

The swordsman-hero's primary attribute is great bodily strength. There are times of crisis which require the use of force, and in a war the most astute planning will lead nowhere if officers and men are unable to fight better than the enemy. But the swordsmen are not merely useful auxiliaries of the princely and scholarly heroes. Their powerful muscles immediately attract attention and command respect. Kuan Yü, Chang Fei, and the heroes of the *Water Margin* and of more modern novels of adventure, such as *Ch'i Hsia Wu I* and *Erh Nü Ying-hsiung Chuan*, are able to lift stones weighing several hundred pounds. They are not flushed or out of breath after these exertions, and their hearts do not beat faster. Little Hsüeh Chiao is only twelve but he can hoist the stone lions standing outside his house, each weighing half a ton.[111] Wu Sung, when his stick breaks in two, kills a tiger with his bare hands after a fierce struggle; it takes sixty or seventy punches on the head to knock the beast out.[112]

Good fighters have trained for years in "military arts" (*wu-shu*), i.e., boxing and wrestling, fencing and the use of various weapons. These arts remain their favorite pastime. They also jump and climb high walls, walk on roofs, and so on, with exceptional agility. Some know how to walk under water.[113]

Novels abound in detailed descriptions of fights, calling the various blows by all their technical names. The theater stages long and spectacular battles and displays great skill in changing weapons from one scene to another in order to avoid any possible monotony. And the audiences' enthusiasm for a good "military" actor (*wu-sheng* or *wu-ch'ou*) has some of the features of authentic hero worship.

Not content to fight well and bravely, the true swordsmen-heroes add to their prowess the spice of an often humorous bravura, crowning serious action with an aura of playful art. Kuan Yü in a war volunteers to kill the enemy general, rushes out and decapitates him, then brings the head back to camp, all in such a short time that the cup of wine he left there is still warm.[114] Chang Fei with twenty scouts patrols a walled city occupied by the Yellow Turbans, intent on provoking them into battle; when he grows tired of waiting under the hot sun for them to come out, he takes a bath in the moat with his men under a barrage of arrows falling like rain.[115] Another time, left behind with a rear guard to cover the retreat of Liu Pei, he destroys a bridge and stands alone, fiercely defiant, facing Ts'ao's troops. His dark face shines, his bulging eyes blaze, his hair and bushy beard stand on end as he shouts, "Here is Chang I-te! Who wants a fight to the death? Come on! Come on!" At this the enemy flees in terror.[116] Chang's twelfth-century counterpart Li K'uei, to save the life of his chieftain Sung Chiang, on the very day set for his public beheading in Chiang-chou city, gives the signal to his companions hidden in the crowds by leaping, stark naked, from a roof into the execution square, brandishing two battle axes.[117]

These heroes show the same courage in resisting pain as in fighting battles. Suffering from an old wound, Kuan Yü accepts his surgeon's decision to cut open his arm and scrape the bone: the bloody operation is performed during a drinking feast and Kuan Yü continues talking and playing chess as if nothing were happening.[118] And Wu Sung, when he is to receive the "customary" hundred blows on entering prison, refuses to be held down during the punishment and boasts that he will not utter one cry. He even challenges the jailers to strike harder.[119]

Outspoken bluntness and a volcanic temper characterize most swordsmen-heroes in popular fiction. They are obtuse, guileless, childish, belligerent, tempestuous, irascible, devoid of manners, and completely uninhibited. They boast and quarrel as a pastime, and occasionally kill by mistake. Chang Fei stubbornly refuses to open the city gate to his sworn brother coming back from years of captivity because he suspects him of treason, and he will let the poor man perish under the arrows of his pursuers without giving him a chance to explain his innocence.[120] Li K'uei too readily believes slanderous reports against his chieftain Sung Chiang and rushes to kill him forthwith.[121] An ever-present menace to the neighborhood, the swordsman indulges in a kind of behavior that is frowned upon among ordinary men. He eats and drinks to excess, threatening to break everything in the house if more wine is not forthcoming. Once intoxicated, he brawls like a thug, often on the silliest pretexts. Lu Ta bullies monks into eating meat against their vows.[122] Drunk one winter night, Wu Sung takes a dislike to a dog and pursues it, knife in hand, along a brook, stumbling and falling twice into the icy water, where he is caught by some men he has previously insulted and beaten.[123]

Why are these raving bullies still so loved by their companions and by the devotees of fiction? First, because they are honest and straightforward in a world in which persons officially vested with authority prefer the devious approach. With them one knows where one stands. Their friendships, born in the street, in wineshops, or in other humble places, are disinterested, spontaneous alliances of congenial souls. They are totally indifferent to money and will not take a penny of what is not theirs. They do not fawn and flatter, and nothing can make them shift their loyalty. All deserve the nickname "Do-or-die," bestowed on Shih Hsiu, one of their number. They are resolute men, always ready to lay down their lives for their friends, never willing to surrender or to let themselves be curbed or humiliated. Muscle play brings them a natural exhilaration, their strength and courage lead to a careless self-confidence, their crude jokes reveal a robust sense of humor, and their whole manner exudes *joie de vivre*. They have all the companionable qualities that are subsumed in the phrase *hao-han*, "good fellow."

Impulsive generosity is their most likable trait. One day Chang Fei, with angry curses, orders a prisoner beheaded. "All right! Have me put to death," says the prisoner calmly, "but why get nervous about it?" Delighted by this *sang-froid*, Chang Fei sets the man free and asks him to join his staff.[124] Often a crafty scholar takes advantage of a swordsman's big-heartedness. Spectators look up to the former, but give their sympathy to the latter. They love Chang Fei and Li K'uei as one loves children, admiring their open defiance of authority and regretting that real life gives adults so few opportunities to act as they do.

As might be expected, the *hao-han* are little interested in women. "They waste no time in amorous dalliance, but conserve their energies for feats of valor."[125] Following traditional theories on *yin-yang* and on cultivating one's vitality (*yang-sheng*),[126] they believe their training in boxing to be incompatible with other claims on their energy. One of the unfaithful wives in the *Water Margin* starts an affair with a monk because her husband, too interested in gymnastics, spends his nights at the yamen barracks and leaves her alone.[127]

Outlaws and rebels are potential heroes in all literatures: even without a just cause, they have a glamour of their own when they are daring and true to themselves; and if they are victims of official injustice, or represent the right against oppressive government, the prestige of ethical justification is added to their glamour. Their controversial situation and the immediate danger in which they involve those who help them (or who merely fail to report them to the authorities) force the common people to take sides: no neutrality or indifference remains possible. Everybody is concerned; outlaw and rebel become consummate heroes *or* villains. This division of public opinion into two camps may separate friends or members of the same family—a splendid source of dramatic interest for poetry, novels, and the theater.

Chinese fiction has no inherent predisposition against the government and in favor of rebels, or vice versa. The "three musketeers" and the "five rats"[128] who help put down the revolt of the Prince of Hsiang-yang, as well as Huang T'ien-pa, who catches bandits for his detective master Shih Kung,[129] are well-loved heroes of law and order; but no less admired are the 108 robbers whose case the *Water Margin* presents so convincingly:

Unscrupulous, defiant, stern as the fates, but true in covenant and brave in conflict, these men and women are not of the smiling, temperate, human sort; they are terrible: beings of the cave and the mountain den. Their implacable demand . . . for a justice which the law is too feeble and too corrupt to give underlines the cruelties and oppressions of an age when right is defenseless and authority takes the side of the wrong-doer.[130]

The *Water Margin* is a classic text for motivational research into Chinese revolutionary movements. Its heroes are not asocial or maladjusted psychopaths. They had no desire to rebel in the first place, and would have been happy members of a normal community. Some of them are the innocent victims of frame-ups; others have run to the defense of the weak without reflecting how heavy their fists could be; most go spontaneously to face trial at the official yamen. They only repair to the "greenwood," to the "rivers and lakes" (Chinese terms corresponding to the Corsican "maquis"), when a bitter experience convinces them that there is no other way to survive. Many rebels in Chinese history, successful and unsuccessful alike, claimed the right, implicitly asserted by Mencius, to revolt against an evil ruler. It may seem timid of the *Water Margin* to hold the administration, not the emperor, responsible for the prevalence of corruption, but the novel is truly radical in its assumption that the society of the outlaws is more authentically Confucian than orthodox society[181]—indeed, that in the sorry circumstances of the time the mountain lair of the robbers is the *only* place men can behave like Confucian gentlemen (*chün-tzu*). In this light their motto, "Accomplish the Way for Heaven!" (*T'i t'ien hsing tao*), a typical rebel slogan, is a proud challenge to imperial authority and a claim to interpret the will of Heaven—in short, to act on absolute standards. Against a system that is looked upon as betraying the fundamental "Confucian" values, the outlaws of Mount Liang have recourse to an inner truth and a higher allegiance.

Their common purpose is symbolized by the oath of brotherhood they all take. The day after they first meet, the three heroes of the *Three Kingdoms* take a similar oath: "We were not born the same year, the same month, the same day, but we swear to die the same year, the same month, the same day."[132] Instead of the normal types of loyalties between prince and subject, lord and vassal, father and son, which can be called *vertical*, the oath of brotherhood, found in all secret societies, establishes between swordsmen a bond of *horizontal* loyalties. These brotherhoods of swordsmen have always, as have the "parties" and "cliques" (*tang, p'eng*) among scholars, been resented by the monarchy as an intolerable threat to itself.[133] Liu Pei, Kuan Yü, and Chang Fei themselves were standing on the side of the law at the time of their oath, and their common will was to fight the Yellow Turbans, a rebel movement; yet their oath as recorded in fiction has made them patrons of illegal societies for centuries. It would be farfetched to regard the *Three Kingdoms* as a novel of rebellion, cleverly camouflaged by its Yellow Turbans episode into a tale of devotion to the Han throne. But the fact remains that the very formulation of the heroes' solemn vow indicates its priority over other loyalties, including those professed at the same time, and therefore contains the germ of rebellion. The novel is from the beginning spun around the founding of a new dynasty.

The *hsia*, or "adventurer," does not openly challenge the government as the rebel does. His calling is to break laws, not to question their validity. By killing or other unconventional means, he acts where legal action is bound to fail, for example in cases when his adversaries have won immunity by bribery or intimidation. He puts loyalty to his friends above all, to the extent of ignoring his natural duties toward state and ruler as well as toward his parents: he is a virtual rebel against the established order. Bold and self-reliant, he is prepared to sacrifice his peace and happiness and, if necessary, his very life. He can also, thanks to his extraordinary strength and agility, escape capture repeatedly and live for years in the wilderness with the wind and rain as his companions.

Traditional fiction, however, requires somewhat more of him before his lawbreaking can be idealized into chivalric heroism. The wicked acrobats who break into people's houses at night to steal their valuables or seduce their daughters[134] do not seem to qualify as genuine *hsia*, nor do the perverted prizefighters who impose their unwanted "protection" on tradespeople[135] or who rob travelers on deserted highways, sometimes killing them, slicing them up, and selling their flesh in the form of what might be called "manburgers" (*jen-jou pao-tzu*).[136] Directing one's skill toward criminal ends can be an overpowering temptation, but victimizing the helpless is all too easy a job. The "good" swordsman is tested through tougher trials and fights adversaries whose strength at least matches his. Moreover, he is not hired or paid for his prowess, and does not expect personal profit or advantages out of it. The typical *hsia* is depicted as a savior of the weak, a man who embraces their cause when they cannot or dare not defend themselves, and does it gratuitously, solely for the sake of justice (*cheng-tang*). The people he saves are not his relatives, and they may well be total strangers; he thus deserves the appellation "chivalric" (*i*), which signifies behavior beyond the limits of strict duty. Playful thefts, robberies committed against the rich and the mighty, flogging of corrupt officials,[137] and other such deeds are winked at by fiction in direct proportion to the selflessness of the perpetrator's motive; murder itself is judged by the same standard. Storytellers and playwrights reserve their full blessing for violence on behalf of unknown victims,[138] and for disinterested vengeance pursued for the benefit of others, such as the assassination of Wang Liao, "tyrant" of Wu, by Chuan Chu,[139] and the unsuccessful attempt of Ching K'o against the life of the First Emperor, then King of Ch'in. In each of these two instances, the *hsia* has been noticed by a prince in distress who has treated him as an equal and convinced him of the justice of his cause: these are further examples of "horizontal" loyalty.

The themes underlying their stories in fiction of recent centuries have their roots in very ancient times. In his chapter on "wandering adventurers" (*yu-hsia*, often translated "knights-errant") and in other chapters of his history, Ssu-ma Ch'ien[140] describes the peculiar status of political assassins and the armies of "guests" kept by certain feudal lords of the Warring States period. He notes that the true *hsia* cannot be bought for money, but that one meets them on a footing of equality and must convince them of the importance, patriotic or other, of the crime expected of them.

While pointing out how much the *hsia's* achievements shocked Confucians and Legalists alike, Ssu-ma underlines the honorable side of the "have sword, will travel" specialists of ancient China: "The words are reliable, their deeds effective; once they have given their word, they stick to it."[141] Scholars, it is implied, are more skilled at diplomatic compromises and at cautious evasions.

No society leaves its members wholly free to question its basic rules and to act according to their own judgment. Yet folklore all over the world glorifies noble-hearted outlaws such as Robin Hood, Rozsa Sandor, the "bandits corses," or the Chinese *hsia*. The place of rebels and *hsia* in Chinese fiction is to be understood in relation to a recurrent, if unofficial, institution, that of the private guards hired by merchants and village notables for escorting goods and for help in other businesses requiring *manu militari* handling. Called "guests" and enjoying a status above that of servants or employees, these boxers and fighters rise, with their "hosts," to positions of local importance each time that insecurity of any kind threatens the peace in the vicinity: wars, foreign invasions, natural catastrophes, or economic and social collapse cause the common people to turn toward local strong men for protection against bandits, plundering troops, and rapacious officials. Holders of these incipient lordships and their "guests" thus constitute power nuclei with which the authorities have to reckon, and which may grow to august proportions: some dynasties have begun with far fewer than 108 men! The *Romance of the Three Kingdoms* realistically shows Chang Fei, a well-to-do farmer (a butcher in some plays) offering a feast to the young men of his village in order to enroll them into his sworn brothers' band. The band is then given horses, gold, and iron by traveling merchants.[142] A bid for the empire begins in this way!

A private guard turned into a soldier of the government by accidents of disorder and war found himself feared by the average peasant at the beginning and at the end of his typical career, but experienced in between, when greater dangers made him appear as a protector instead of a menace, a time of popularity. The *hsia* of fiction, nonprofit champion of the underdog, is, I suggest, an idealized image of this intermediate-stage swordsman.

After Ssu-ma Ch'ien, no official history contains a chapter on the *hsia*. Since the virtues of the *hsia* are seen as appropriate for times of disorder and aberrant in times of peace and good government, it is in direct proportion to national disunity and public unrest that the *hsia*'s prestige grows in literature and that his distance from the common robber widens. Government pressure, as reflected in the banning or edulcorating of subversive books and plays, is also most effective in periods of maximum law and order. Typical instances in Ch'ing dynasty works concern the tamed swordsmen who serve on the side of the law.[143]

Here the sympathies of fiction and of its consumers go rather to the cops than to the robbers: that was not the case with the *Water Margin*.

KUAN YÜ, A COMPOSITE HERO

The fact that the *hsia* and the rebels in literature are so easily admired sets up a critical moral dilemma. On the one hand, heroic stories and hero worship make virtue attractive; on the other hand, stories that exalt heroism encourage strong personalities to ignore the laws, to seek the autonomy of the hero, and to espouse his unorthodox ways. Confucians in particular felt strongly that the heroic code of honor was detrimental to respect for family ties and for authority. As administrators and judges, they were bound to resent stories such as those of Hsiao En taking justice into his own hands by killing the local squire, of the Mount Liang robbers banding together against the government. Of course they recognized the deep-rooted popularity these stories enjoyed and knew from experience that suppressing them was an impossible task. Besides, there was an advantage in letting dissatisfied souls discharge their aggressive energies in the imaginary arena of the heroes' misfortunes and revenges. But as men responsible for raising and refining the people's ethical standards, the Confucians at the same time recognized some of the basic values which inspired this kind of fiction, and sympathized to a large extent with the aspirations it expressed. After all, the Confucians themselves were not immune to conflicts of loyalty; they often sought guidance on such questions as what to do when duty to father and ruler came into conflict.

Moreover, the most enlightened Confucians probably realized that, despite appearances, the *hsia* of fiction contributed more to social stability than to subversion. *Hsia* commonly flourished in troubled times, when the normal, vertical relationships were upset in any case, and their moral transgressions amounted to no more than a daring readiness to cope with issues beyond the immediate power of the established hierarchies. Finally, they set in motion new political constellations which organized local peasantry for work and taxation along more or less traditional lines, and which could ultimately be brought back into a lawful framework through the legitimation process which novels call *chao-an* ("calling to peace"), i.e., letting rebels rally to the side of the government and admitting them into the regular army.[144]

It was easier, of course, for Confucians to accept the "good" heroes—men explicitly committed to values such as *i* ("selflessness," "generous behavior beyond duty") and *chung* ("loyalty")—than to accept wild, uninhibited bandits whose example could exercise a dangerous influence on public mores. Loyalty of almost any description could be interpreted as exemplifying the virtue of loyalty to the emperor and the proper authorities. This explains the evolution of the official worship of Kuan Yü, a hero of popular tradition, and his build-up into a universally accepted paragon of virtue.

The biography and the character of the historic Kuan Yü emerge clearly in the *History of the Three Kingdoms,* written about fifty years after his death,[145] and in the fifth-century commentary to this history. First an outlaw, then a bodyguard of Liu Pei, he became a general and governor of a province, and died in battle after an eventful career of adventure and war. He was haughty, extremely brave, unshakably faithful to his lord. Ts'ao Ts'ao once captured him in a battle and tried vainly to win him over with lavish presents. Beginning in T'ang times, poetry and fiction magnify the historic facts into mythical proportions, and add many hues to an already colorful picture: a story of righteous homicide rationalizes his outlaw origins, and vivid details enrich various moments of his life, especially his now naïve, now ingenious resistance to the temptations engineered by Ts'ao,[146] his "lone sword" meeting with the men of Wu,[147] and his tragic death.[148]

As Kuan Yü's stature grows in storytelling and drama, he assumes an increasing importance both in popular religion and in the official cult. Miracles and apparitions mark his high rank in the Other World. He becomes the most potent aide in evoking spirits and exorcizing devils, and becomes the god protector of actors, who call him, with a respectful familiarity, *Lao-yeh* ("our old Lord") and honor him with a backstage shrine. His role is played with unique and spectacular solemnity, as a god and not as a man. Meanwhile, he has been awarded posthumous titles—ducal, princely, and imperial—by Sung and Ming edicts, and, from Yüan times on, he has replaced Chiang T'ai-kung as the official god of warriors. Ch'ing emperors order him worshiped in thousands of temples (*Kuan Ti Miao*) and, in the midst of their struggle against the Taipings (1856), decree him the equal of Confucius. From the K'ang-hsi reign onward, official committees of scholars compile successive editions of his hagiography.[149] They hold him up as the incarnation of loyalty (*chung*) and stress his undeviating devotion to his lord in a period of anarchy when it would have been easy for him to set up a kingdom for himself as others did.

The obvious political intent of these efforts was to indoctrinate the populace in loyalty and submission to authority, even as the "Twenty-four Filial Sons"[150] were used to inculcate submission to the head of the family. Kuan Yü literature reveals many of the ways in which Neo-Confucians sought to couple "loyalty" (*chung*) and "filial submission" (*hsiao*). Yet it also exemplifies the conflicts which arise between the two moral imperatives. In times of crisis loyalty to one's prince may conflict with loyalty to principle or to country as well as with one's obligations to one's parents. Kuan Yü's example could encourage hesitating officials and soldiers to serve an apparently doomed dynasty against attractive challengers. But perplexing tensions also emerge from his hagiography. The hero once spares a fallen enemy who defects to his side and thereafter remains loyal.[151] Is this sort of generosity in war always to be approved by those responsible for the state? Another time, Kuan Yü captures Ts'ao Ts'ao and releases him unmolested.[152] Does this not mean that by settling a personal debt in this way, he has allowed the archenemy of his prince to fight on and continue to menace the state which Kuan Yü serves? The resourceful panegyrists of Kuan Yü do not deny this episode: they find involved explanations and excuses to justify it.

The story of the warrior hero Kuan Yü—part swordsman, part scholar, with princely characteristics[153]—illustrates the interaction of folklore and institutionalized religion. It demonstrates how fiction was affected by the state worship of one of its heroes and, conversely, how the popularity of a hero of fiction encouraged his officially managed apotheosis as a model of exemplary behavior.

But the primary virtue—loyalty—that Kuan Yü is supposed to exemplify soon appears as a knot of multiple loyalties, a knot that easily becomes an impossible tangle. Kuan Yü's story shows how difficult it is to serve simultaneously parents, friends, prince, country, and justice. Despite the efforts of official hagiographers, this heroic figure has all the complexity of life.

The heroes we have considered seem reducible to three types: the impetuous, uninhibited, and generous Swordsman, a lovable and explosive "good fellow"; the Scholar, of outstanding intelligence, resourcefulness, eloquence, and self-control, "knowing all knowable things and some others," whose powers of reading minds, of seeing into the future, of influencing the forces of nature have a supernatural cast; and the Prince, holder of Heaven's mandate, who does nothing spectacular himself, but is skilled in judging men and in choosing the Scholars and Swordsmen who will enable him to fulfill his destiny.

To what extent are they Confucian? Some of them behave like saints in the Books, and exemplify the correct Confucian ways of playing various roles in society; others carry to extremes the selfish ways of ordinary men, subtle or brutal, with an instinctive disdain for the weakling "give-in" (*jang*) morality of the herd, with a passion for avenging offenses despite the law. One will find, among the first group, sage rulers and loyal subjects, loving parents and filial children, devoted friends, who promote the Confucian ideals of an enlightened humanism and of the general welfare of society. One also finds, on the other hand, tyrannical emperors whose rule reeks of Legalism and self-indulgence. Among the scholars there are cynics and hypocrites who use their cleverness to flaunt common morals. There are gangs of robbers in the woods, rebellious masses, and men whose passions lead them into orgies of indiscriminate killing and destruction.

We have noted the officially managed apotheosis of one hero, and we can see the effects of Confucian indoctrination in countless situations and characters. We have mentioned the pressure of censorship on writers, publishers, and actors, particularly in the later dynasties. It is not surprising, therefore, that no novel or play directly challenges the privileged position of the "gentry" or ventures to idealize the merchant, the immemorial object of Confucian scorn and discrimination. But factors were at work which limited the effort to make fiction an instrument of social control, a servant of an official orthodoxy. One was simply the demand of audiences and readers for verisimilitude — for believable human situations and conflicts. Such a demand meant that fiction had to be peopled with recognizable characters and not simply with positive and negative exemplars. The second factor is more complex. The Confucian tradition itself sanctioned behavior in periods of crisis that it would heavily censure in an age of peace. The swordsman-hero in particular had the moral right to lead others in revolt against corrupt government. His behavior suggested that wisdom and goodness is present in all people and that the difference between a Confucian gentleman (*chün-tzu*) and a common person (*hsiao-jen*) was a moral, not a social one. Once his moral *raison d'être* is established, the swordsman, in the hands of novelists, storytellers, and playwrights, takes on characteristics which make him the object of delighted admiration on the part of the common folk, and disdain or alarm on the part of staid conformist Confucians.

Thus all efforts to "Confucianize" fiction remained only partly successful. It is this relative freedom that keeps fiction close to the common life of China through many centuries, thus providing us with vivid insights into the hopes, the desires, the hates and affections of innumerable generations. The scholarly use of fiction for the purposes of social history will help us penetrate the veil of myth perpetuated in the vast corpus of official historical writing.

David S. Nivison

PROTEST AGAINST CONVENTIONS
AND CONVENTIONS OF PROTEST

Students have often been found to complain about what they are required to learn and how they are held accountable for their lessons. Often their complaints follow a time-worn pattern. But if we look behind the pattern and if the students are serious, we may find that their complaints are both penetrating and important. This has been true even in China, that land of exemplary students, where teachers were respected as nowhere else, and where the emperor himself was the chief examiner.

Let me begin by telling some stories.

I

Shortly before 1060, Ou-yang Hsiu, the early Sung historian, official and man of letters, wrote a short essay, as was often done by Chinese literary men, in the back of a particularly treasured old book from his personal library. The book was an early print, from Ssu-ch'uan, of the collected prose of the ninth-century writer Han Yü. In this essay, Ou-yang Hsiu relates that as a young man, being of a poor family, he had had no books; but, finding this book discarded in the house of a friend, he begged for it and read it with fascination, not fully understanding it but nonetheless aware of its worth. In his own time, regular, so-called "modern" prose (*shih wen*) was preferred over the free style or "ancient" prose (*ku wen*) of Han Yü. "People who were skilled in it," writes Ou-yang Hsiu, "passed the examinations and were the only persons who had any reputation; no one ever talked about the writings of Han Yü." Just at this time, Ou-yang Hsiu himself had attempted the examinations unsuccessfully, and this failure had strengthened his dissatisfaction with the literary standards of his age. "I took my copy of Han Yü," he continues, "and, rereading it, I sighed and said, 'Scholars ought to go no farther than this!' And I marveled that people of the present day were so misguided." Admitting to himself that he must study for the examinations now, to obtain an official position and so be able to support his parents, he nevertheless had resolved that after he had succeeded he would turn back to what he really valued. "Later," Ou-yang Hsiu continues, "learned men throughout the world all turned their attention gradually to the past, and Han Yü's writings eventually became well known. Thirty-odd years have passed since that time, and people now study nothing but Han Yü."[1]

Ou-yang Hsiu clearly feels that his values as a young student were right and the officially sanctioned and conventionally approved ones wrong, and that he has been vindicated, inevitably, by time. Furthermore, he is able to assure himself, his pursuit of learning has been motivated only by the purest interest in learning itself—"It was simply that I was devoted to the past," he says—and not by hope of fame or material advantage. In him, as in other Confucians of his time, conservatism, a love of antiquity, is actually a protest against an ignoble conventionality. But did not Ou-yang Hsiu capitulate? He did study for the examinations, and with conspicuous success. Further, he did this, as he admits, precisely in order to qualify for a salaried official post. The intensity of this conflict, between devotion to higher ideals and the practical necessity of coming to terms with the world, can be seen in the fact that the ultimate Confucian social duty, that of filial piety, had to be invoked to set matters right.

Yet the reasonableness of the appeal can hardly be gainsaid. It is indeed the duty of a Confucian to provide for his parents; and so here is another conflict, now between two values, both of which were Confucian: one social, one intellectual; on the one hand family duty, on the other one's own personal development.

It will be instructive to turn, for a slightly different sort of case, to the early part of the T'ang period, when the modern examination system first became important. The historian Liu Chih-chi in the early eighth century wrote, in an autobiographical essay in his *Shih T'ung* ("General Principles of History"), that when he was a child it had been determined that he should specialize in the third of the Confucian Classics, the *Shang Shu*. But, he writes, "I was always bothered by the difficulty of its language, and . . . although I was frequently beaten, I got nowhere in my study. But when I happened to hear my father teaching my elder brothers the *Spring and Autumn Annals* and the *Commentary of Tso*, I always put aside my books and listened . . . and sighing to myself, I said, 'If only all books were like this, I would no longer be lazy!'" Liu's father was surprised at his son's independence of inclination, and, surprisingly, relented; Liu was allowed to read the *Tso Chuan*, and finished his study of it rather quickly. But now, his father would have him specialize in the *Tso Chuan* alone, going on to read all the existing commentaries to that text. To understand the father's point of view, we need to be aware that an intense study of one or two Classics served a man well in the T'ang examinations: the *chin-shih* and *ming-ching* examinations were probably the two most frequently taken even in Liu's time; and in offering for the first of these, one had to prepare one Classic, and be prepared further to find the questions dealing with commentaries rather than with the text itself. For the latter, one had to prepare somewhat less intensively in two or three Classics.[2]

But although his father's wishes in view of this situation may have been sensible, Liu fought free again. He had wanted to read the *Tso*, not because it was an examination text but because it was history; he now wanted to read more history—not because it would get him somewhere but because it was interesting, and because he thought he had insights into it worth having. Eventually he turned aside from his interests for a few years to learn to write in the poetry and essay forms required in the examinations. He does not indicate that he was bitter about this interruption, but he makes it perfectly plain that it was an interruption in his work.[3]

Both Liu Chih-chi and Ou-yang Hsiu, it is evident, found themselves as young men pursuing conflicting goals. The interest of Ou-yang's and Liu's experience and of their attitudes toward it would be slight, if this experience and these attitudes were unique; but we shall see that, far from being unique, they are so common among Chinese writers of the past thousand years as to seem stereotyped. This surely makes the matter of great interest; for people worry about conflicts, in whatever mode of life they are in; and when people worry, they think.

There exist, I suggest, recognizable conventions of protest against the educational mold into which a student felt himself forced. (1) There is the tendency, perhaps found in any aristocratic social order, to suspect values which are popular and modish of being shallow. Consider the curious feeling often encountered that only a very few people are likely to appreciate a really good painting or book. Surely we see something of this in Ou-yang Hsiu's conviction as a youth that only he saw matters rightly, and that generally accepted literary standards were "misguided." There is much more of this, offered with delicious frankness, in Han Yü himself. And whenever the relative merits of "ancient" and "contemporary" prose come up, no matter how *de rigueur* it may be for a critic to come down on the side of *ku wen*, or in favor of a "devotion to the past," he will usually in doing so manage to think of himself as alone in a Philistine wilderness (for Ou-yang Hsiu's conviction that only he appreciated Han Yü is surely nonsense). (2) But there is another motif which is simply the uncomplicated rebelliousness of a man of original temper when forced to do something distasteful, a motif likely to be found wherever such pressure exists. This was the sort of reaction we found in Liu Chih-chi. Yet, if these two modes of protest are not peculiar to Chinese culture, they certainly arise very naturally in a culture like China's which has been authoritarian—for Liu's independence was a reaction against a strict parental authority—and which has always had the persuasion that there are "superior" men, capable of perceiving values to which ordinary men are obtuse.

These two styles of self-assertion and protest may be seen in the lives and recollections of other writers, even very recent ones; and often we have the impression that specific literary models are playing a role. To cite two modern examples, the contemporary historian Ku Chieh-kang, like Liu Chih-chi, says he wanted, as a boy, to study the *Tso chuan* despite the objections of his parents and his teacher (his *bête noire* was the *Book of Odes,* not the *Shang Shu*), and surprised his mentors with his ability when finally allowed to study it.[4] Hu Shih writes in his autobiography that he happened, while in a neighbor's house, to discover a dilapidated copy of *Shui Hu Chuan,* which he was allowed to keep. This was the beginning of Hu's interest in popular literature, which he championed successfully against the established values of *his* day.[5] I assume that this incident happened; and it may even have had the importance ascribed to it. But the fact that it was worth relating surely owes something to Ou-yang Hsiu.

Wang Yang-ming, in the year 1518, wrote a letter of advice to two young men who were preparing for the examinations:

Since your home is poverty-stricken and your parents are old, what else can you do but seek emolument and official position? If you seek emolument and official position without studying for the examinations, you will not be able to carry out your duties as men, and will pointlessly find fault with fate. This is hardly right. But if you can firmly fix your aim, in all your pursuits fully express the Tao, and be influenced in thought neither by desire for success nor by fear of failure, then, though you study for the degree, this will be no real hindrance to your learning to become virtuous men.[6]

Wang, like Ou-yang Hsiu, here justifies the pursuit of worldly ends by appeal to the obligation of *filial duty.* There is more, of course, to Wang's attitude than this. He reveals himself highly suspicious of the influence the examinations had on a young man's mind. It may be possible, he reluctantly concedes, for a man to study for the degree of *chü-jen* or *chin-shih* without detriment to his self-development; all too many, however, through "lack of a fixed aim," as Wang puts it, "have come to think exclusively of honor, gain and literary style"; and as a result "they cannot avoid cherishing the desire for small advantages and quick results."

A young man must always resist this temptation the examinations present to him to succumb to vulgar values and to let his desires be involved in what he is doing.

One of the most intriguing cases of the use of these conventions of protest and self-assertion in a man's appraisal of himself is to be found in Chang Hsüeh-ch'eng (1738–1801). Chang, like Liu Chih-chi (and Ku Chieh-kang) was interested in the *Tso Chuan* when he was a boy, to the point of starting a project of rewriting it in standard history form, a project which he carried on in secret and which was sniffed at by his teacher when discovered—for it was in fact a rebellion against his routine study of examination essays and Classics. Chang's dislike of this training was expressed forcefully in early letters, in which we find him complaining that the examination form of essay (*shih wen*) is a worthless waste of time; yet he must study it in order to pass and get a position, "for my family is poor and my parents are old."[7]

One specific youthful episode about which Chang wrote is especially curious. In his seventeenth year, he recalls, he bought a copy of Han Yü; but his teachers had forbidden all extracurricular reading—lest Chang acquire literary habits which would injure his chances in the examination halls—and as a consequence Chang read his new purchase in secret, not fully understanding it, he confesses, yet with such great delight that he could not bear to let the book out of his hands. It is interesting to find here again that a young man would normally have his access to books and his choice of studies rigidly controlled. But more interesting, it looks very much as if Chang had been reading Ou-yang Hsiu; and indeed he had. Ou-yang Hsiu's reflections were set down in an essay on an old edition of Han Yü, and as in Chang's case, they deal with events in his seventeenth year. Chang's remarks are made in an essay on another old edition of Han Yü, Chu Hsi's *Han Wen K'ao-i*. Ou-yang Hsiu had remarked that he was writing of happenings thirty years past. Chang's own essay concludes, "As I fondle this book, the scenes of thirty years ago come back as though I were living them again."[8] Apparently Chang wrote because he had reached the appropriate time of life to express sentiments in just this way.

A few examples cannot establish the point that the individual writer's subjective protests against the examinations and the sort of training they required follow a fascinating pattern of stereotyped detail. But they may lend this point a plausibility which ensuing discussion will strengthen.

II

We have not been dealing merely with a curious but meaningless set of literary conventions. The civil service examinations have been called the hallmark of the "Confucian state." Preparing for them in order to seek an official career was a basic duty to family and to the world. Their existence as an institution more than anything else signalized the ascendancy of the man of learning and culture in society. Yet, almost from the beginnings of this institution in the later empire, the examinations, and the educational standards they produced, were resented and criticized. Students resented being fettered and constrained. Statesmen found the institution wanting as a means of "nurturing talent" and recruiting the best men for public service. Literary critics and moral philosophers bewailed its influence on the quality of letters and on the state of public and private virtue. This polyphony of protest may be found in every generation. And the surprising fact is that throughout all this we find the examination-education complex, the function and effect of which was to ensure the dominance of the Confucian classical tradition, criticized precisely by appeal to *Confucian* moral, aesthetic, and political values.

This is not a situation we would have expected. Its oddity may help to explain the fact that, for all of the attention scholars have given to the imperial examination system and its ramifications, the long tradition of protest against this system has been almost completely ignored. In what follows I shall attempt to open the matter up. My attempt will of necessity be extremely superficial, for the volume of relevant literature is enormous: in this literature we must include innumerable personal letters and essays, novels (such as *Ju-lin Wai-shih* by Wu Ching-tzu, 1701–54) on the life of the literati, as well as many official and unofficial treatises on public policy. Simply to relate the history of reforms and proposed changes in the system would require volumes. But an analysis of some of the ideals and motivations which perpetually generated this criticism may be more feasible.

The motive of Liu Chih-chi's self-assertion was his wish to pursue an easily comprehended interest—namely, in history and in the traditions of historical writing; and for this interest he has little compulsion to offer any further justification (though there is ample Confucian justification for it). With Ou-yang Hsiu the case is different. He admired the writing of Han Yü, yes; but this was not all. He was also "devoted to the past," and he scorned present-day styles, mastery in which served others in the mere pursuit of gain. We are inclined to ask, On behalf of just what ideals is this disinterestedness urged? Ou-yang Hsiu does not say, but it is fair to note that this very disinterestedness, the claim that the quest for gain and fame for oneself is unworthy of a writer, is itself an ideal of a higher order. Why should it seem appropriate to Ou-yang Hsiu to link this attitude with an esteem for Han Yü?

The reason may be that Han Yü has given this ideal for the literary man in China perhaps its most beautiful and intensely moving expression. In a letter "In Reply to Li I," Han, for the benefit of his correspondent (who apparently had asked questions about literary art, and perhaps had sent some writings), describes his own earlier efforts to learn to write. First, Han Yü says, he buried himself in the writings of the Han and of pre-Han antiquity, uncritically admiring all that he found. He was oblivious to the world around him and quite unaware of the criticism or amusement of others. At this stage, he says, in what he wrote he tried to keep out "hackneyed phrases," but the going was very difficult; the words that came to him just didn't fit. At a later stage in his progress, he began to be more critical of ancient writers, seeing the good and the bad in their writings distinguished "as clearly as black and white." When he tried to write himself, words now came much more freely; and he tested the results by observing reactions of others to his literary efforts: "If people were amused at my work, then I was happy; if they praised it, then I was worried, since then I knew that other people's ways of talking must still infect it." Now, words came in a flood; but this imposed a severe task of self-examination on him. He must hold up the flow of language, make sure that it was all "pure," by "cultivating" it, "guiding it into the path of goodness and right, reinvigorating it in the springs of the *Shih* (*Book of Poetry*) and the *Shu* (*Book of History*)."

The task of learning to write is not at all one of learning verbal tricks and forms; it is a task of self-cultivation, a *moral* exercise, a matter of nourishing one's *ch'i* or spirit; *ch'i* is like water, words the mere objects that "float" in it; if *ch'i* is adequate, there will be no trouble with words. This literary ideal is found everywhere in Chinese critical thought since T'ang (it is surely related to the ideal of the "gentleman painter" described by Mr. Cahill elsewhere in this volume) and has had the effect of making literary criticism in China a variety of moral philosophy. "If you hope to grasp the ancient ideal of writing," Han tells his reader, "then do not hope for quick success, do not be tempted by power and advantage; nourish your roots and wait for the fruit; add the oil and wait for the light . . ."

A person who does this will come close to perfection. But, Han stresses, he will be largely unappreciated; he will "seldom be used by others," i.e., employed by those in power. Setting out to be a good writer is not to be advertised as a good way to get a position. Han closes by saying that it is just because he realizes his friend is not interested in "gain" that he is willing to speak to him frankly. "If you wait to be employed by others, you will be like a mere utensil; your being used or neglected will depend on others. The superior man is not like this. In ordering his mind, he has the Tao. In conducting himself, he is upright." Rank and position mean nothing to him. "When he is employed, he applies his Tao to others. When he is unemployed, he transmits it to his disciples, commits it to writing and creates a model for later generations."[9]

For anyone taking Han's view of writing really seriously, it is difficult to see how studying for the literary examinations—deliberately seeking the road to "gain" and preferment—could be anything but a stumbling block on the path of self-cultivation. And we should notice in particular how Han Yü associates not only writing, but also teaching, with indifference to mundane success or failure. The good man does not seek office. If it comes his way, he does his best. If it does not, he writes and teaches. In both modes of life he serves and is devoted to the Tao.

But was the literary and moral ideal expressed in the letter to Li I actually related in this way to the problem of the examinations in Han Yü's mind? Han has answered this question explicitly in a letter to another friend named Ts'ui Li-chih.

At the time of writing, Han had for the second time failed to obtain office through the placing examinations offered under the Board of Civil Office, and Ts'ui had written to urge him not to lose heart. Han replied with a long *apologia*:

> When I was sixteen or seventeen, I had no knowledge of the realities of the world. I read the books of the sages, and thought to myself that when a man enters official service, he is acting only for others with no advantage for himself. When I reached twenty, I was distressed by the poverty of my household; I consulted with members of my family and came to understand that official service is not just to the advantage of persons other than oneself.

Han went to the capital, noted that men who became *chin-shih* were highly honored, and set out eagerly to acquire the skill to become one of them. He was shown examples of questions that had been used in the examinations administered by the Board of Ceremonies—calling for pieces of rhymed prose, poetry, and essays, and considered that he could write these things without studying, so he tried at the examinations; but the examiners' standards were purely subjective: Han tried four times before succeeding, and even then was not given a post. Following this he tried twice at the placing examination, excited by the idea of the fame he would gain by passing—though he noticed with surprise when he looked at successful essays that they were of just the kind required by the Board of Ceremonies. He set to work, like an actor learning his lines, for several months; again, however, he was disappointed in his quest for office.

Then, Han says, he took stock of himself, and realized that the standards he was following and those of the examiners were utterly different. If Ch'ü Yüan, Mencius, and Ssu-ma Ch'ien were to find themselves competing for these honors they would be ashamed; they simply would not push themselves forward in this way;

but if they did take part in this abysmal competition, they would surely fail. Yet, if these men were living today, though their Tao were not recognized by the world, would this shake their confidence? Would they be willing to have their worth decided in competition with mere time-servers by the rating of one dunce of an examiner, and be pleased or distressed at his decision?

Han then realized that the most he could hope to gain from success in the examinations would be advantages of a paltry material sort.

He concluded by assuring Ts'ui (and himself) that he was not (as Ts'ui had suggested) to be compared to Pien Ho in Han Fei-tzu's story, who had twice tendered his "uncut jade" to the King of Ch'u only to have a foot cut off on each attempt. He has offered no "jade" to his ruler—yet. But he can. The times are troubled; the world has fallen short of ancient ideals; the dynasty is militarily insecure; the emperor and his ministers are worried; Han can analyze these difficulties and offer his views. Perhaps he will be recognized and rewarded with a high post; but if not, Han said, he can tend his sequestered plot in quietness, and search out the details of the history of the dynasty, the lives of its great men, and write a "classic" on the T'ang, which will condemn villains and sycophants and praise examples of concealed virtue. This he will pass on to posterity forever.[10]

A really good man, apparently, is above playing the ordinary game, and will refuse to accept the judgment meted out to the many. If the court has the wisdom to use him, good; if not, he is not hindered in his devotion to the Tao. His position approaches that of the recluse described by Professor Mote in this volume, and the writing of history—traditionally a critical exercise—appears as a peculiarly suitable occupation for the man who withdraws.

Han's concern with the examinations in relation to his own literary ideals suggests that in his time the examination system was an active political issue. This seems indeed to have been the case. In the later T'ang empire, as Mr. Pulleyblank's study in this volume indicates, profound (and as yet inadequately understood) social changes were taking place. The great aristocratic families of the north, which had been powerful in an earlier era, were declining or breaking up, and "new men" from outside this closed elite were coming on the scene. The availability of office to members of different social or regional groups was therefore a matter of intense interest, and the question was raised whether the examinations brought into office men who truly deserved it.

A prominent criticism was that the examinations rewarded the man who merely happened to have a good memory, though he might have no grasp of the "essential meaning" of the Classics—their relevance to current moral and political issues. Another persistent issue was the propriety of requiring of the candidate a facility in highly artificial literary forms such as the *fu* ("rhymed prose") and *p'an* ("decision") which could have nothing to do with his performance in office. Yüan Chen in 806, for example, in an essay submitted at the Palace Examination, made a revolutionary proposal that chief emphasis in the examinations be placed on knowledge of contemporary law and history, and that the competition be opened to all ranks of society (he would have abolished the examination on which Han Yü foundered, the placing examination, which required a candidate to prove that his father was neither an artisan, nor a merchant, nor a criminal).[11]

But such criticisms do not question the value of the examination system in principle. One important kind of criticism did do just this. Curiously, we find this criticism brought out with special clarity in a somewhat backhanded justification of the literary requirements. This appears in the "Monograph on Examinations" of the *Hsin T'ang Shu*. The authors observe that although in the *chin-shih* examination "the choice is made on the basis of literary compositions written in a vague style and on subjects of little practical value," still the successful candidates do perform well in office. They continue:

In later ages (i.e., after classical antiquity), customs became more and more corrupted, and superiors and inferiors came to suspect each other. Hence it came to be thought that the correctness of a candidate's use of rimes would allow examiners to judge his merits objectively. Whenever this procedure was abandoned, . . . no stable standard could be established. And consequently, it has never been possible to change anything. Alas, it is clear therefore that the method used in the Three Dynasties of antiquity, whereby local districts presented men to the sovereign because of their virtuous conduct, is one which cannot obtain except under a perfect government.[12]

Here eleventh-century historians are picking up ideas from a proposal made in 763 to "restore" certain features of a system for the direct recommendation of "virtuous" men to the court. Nonetheless, they are editorializing; and we might bear in mind that the editor who directed the compilation of this part of the *Hsin T'ang Shu*—in all probability writing parts of it himself—was Ou-yang Hsiu.

The idea of doing away with the examinations entirely, and of filling the ranks of government servants by recommendation of "virtuous" men from below, was resurrected again and again.[13] It bears witness to an almost incredible extreme of political idealism in Sung and Ming China. The vision was of a perfect society supposed to have existed in antiquity, a government of perfect virtue, in which there would be complete mutual trust and harmony between men of high and low estate. Inferiors would know their station and have no desire to rise beyond their merits, while those above would be motivated only by the purest love of virtue itself. In such a world order, the best man would always be chosen (and those not chosen would have no resentment), for it would always be the best who would come to the attention of the rulers, and the rulers would always be able to recognize the best. Examinations would not only be superfluous in such a state of affairs, they would be incompatible with it, for they would excite a spirit of striving and of selfish competition among the people. This is just what the examinations do; and for many Sung and Ming philosophers this corrupting and disturbing influence exercised upon the mind, preventing men from "fixing their aim" on ultimate moral values instead of short-term gains, is the greatest fault of the system.

The utopian picture of an ancient, prebureaucratic, perfect Confucian society was a basic element underlying and shaping opinion about educational policy and examination practices in the factional politics of the Sung; indeed this utopian conception seems to be central in all reformist and counterreformist thought in that period. Here I cannot take up the details of these policy struggles, save to note that these questions were always important. Examination requirements were changed constantly, and this must have resulted in much anxiety, leading in turn to an intensification of concern over these problems.[14] Basically, the call for ending the examinations and turning back to some earlier and presumably better method of bringing good men into government—easily combined with a Mencius-inspired concern for the reform of local schools—was of a piece with Mencian "well-field" utopianism in economics and land policy. Essentially it was part of an idealistic regret that the "Confucian" bureaucratic state, with its contamination of Legalism and its (real or fancied) attendant moral corruption in official life, had come into existence at all.[15]

Two illustrations will bear this out, both from Sung philosophers of first rank. Ch'eng I (1033–1107), in a long discussion of examinations as conducted in the "three colleges" of the Sung Imperial Academy, expressed the usual regrets: the formal, detailed, legally prescribed literary requirements were not of use in evaluating the moral worth of the students, while the atmosphere of competition turned their minds to a love of "profit," and made them actually forget their parents. The trouble is that the government relies on "detailed regulations" for appraising candidates for the civil service, rather than on whatever ability those in high places may have to recognize "virtue." But are "detailed regulations" really dispensable?

Someone may say, "If the right men are obtained for the highest positions, then all is well. But if not, it is better to have many detailed regulations to guard against wrongdoing, so that there will be a clear course to follow." Such a person fails entirely to realize that the ancient rulers devised laws in the expectation that there would be suitable men to carry them out. I have never heard that they made laws for the case in which capable men could not be found. If the high officials are not good men, and do not understand the principle of education, but merely adhere to the empty letter and the minute details of the law, surely they will not be able by these means to lead men to perfect their talents.[16]

Ch'eng's reply is a standard Confucian rejoinder to quasi-Legalist recipes: the law cannot effect its own implementation; at best it is a guide for the judgment of good men.

But Ch'eng did not proceed very far with these anti-bureaucratic regrets. Another philosopher, Chang Tsai (1020–77), however, was so repelled by the spectacle of vulgar competition for positions that he praised, in contrast, the giving and holding of hereditary offices, which had persisted in the later bureaucratic empire as a not very significant and rather artificial continuation of ancient feudal forms.

The distinction of hereditary office is the way a ruler gives recognition to those who achieve great things and honors the virtuous, cherishing them and being generous to them, displaying his boundless grace. Their heirs therefore ought to be happy with their duties and be encouraged to achievement . . . excelling in purity and abstaining from the pursuit of profit.

But in these times, Chang complained, "descendants of high dignitaries like to compete with ordinary people, working at the craft of verse-making and selling their wares to the authorities," i.e., sitting for the examinations in the hope of getting appointments, "not realizing that actively seeking for office is wrong."[17]

Chang Tsai's feeling that it is unseemly for a man of quality to engage in the common scramble for advantage is here perhaps reinforced by another persuasion: that the gentleman will not push himself forward. This is the conduct one expects of a social climber; the true "superior man" waits until his prince calls him. But this is not for excess of humility; on the contrary, he may be deeply offended if it be thought that his merits are open to question. An amusing story told of "the philosopher Ch'eng" (either Ch'eng I or his brother Ch'eng Hao, 1032–85) shows how ingrained these attitudes were.

Hsieh Chi passed through Loyang on his way from Shu to the capital and saw Ch'eng-tzu. The master asked him, "Why have you undertaken this trip?" He answered, "I am about to take the examination for a post in the Bureau of Education." The master did not reply. Chi said, "What do you think of it?" The master said, "Once when I was buying a servant-girl I wanted to test her. Her mother became angry and would not permit it, saying, 'My daughter is not one who may first be tried out.' Today you want to become a teacher of men and want to undergo a test for this purpose! You would certainly be laughed at by that old woman." Chi subsequently did not go.[18]

Dignity is a precious thing indeed! Clearly, a dignified and lofty refusal to compete, a high-minded protest that one is not interested in advancement and will leave this matter to fate, and the cherishing of a picture of society in which the poisonous craving for "profit" is absent, are all attitudes which fit closely together.

In considering the bearing of Neo-Confucian ethical thought upon the examination problem, we cannot neglect the most famous of Sung philosopher-statesmen, Chu Hsi (1130–1200). Chu, describing the idealized ancient practice of recruiting officials by direct recommendation without examinations, says that as a result of it "men's minds were composed and they had no distracting desires. Night and day they were diligent, fearing only lest they be wanting in virtue, and not caring whether rank and salary came their way." Clearly he too shared the common Neo-Confucian nostalgic utopian ideal.[19]

Chu Hsi made the foregoing statement in an essay which in its day was famous—a "Private Opinion on Schools and Examinations," which, the "Monograph on Examinations" in the *Sung Shih* tells us, "was read by the whole world."[20] In it he was bitterly critical of examination standards and practices in his day. He proposed at least a limited use of direct recommendation, and an end to practices of favoritism; in particular he called for fairer geographical distribution when allocating quotas of candidates to be passed. The main part of his proposal, however, would have had the effect of making the examinations very different in content and tone: he would change the subject matter of the examinations through a twelve-year cycle, guaranteeing that the state would have at its disposal men with a wide variety of specialized backgrounds. Examinations in poetry and *fu* would be suppressed. Chu wanted his candidates to think, and to know how to think for themselves; in studying the Classics, they should study not only the classical texts but also the commentaries of different schools of interpreters, and in answering a question should be prepared to cite different opinions, concluding with their own judgment. Chu went on actually to list commentaries he would have examinees required to read; somewhat surprisingly, commentaries by Wang An-shih are included for all the most important Classics, although Chu was in general opposed to Wang's policies. Chu expected much if his proposals were acted upon. If they were adopted, "men's minds would be composed and there would be no spirit of hustling and striving; there would be actual virtuous conduct and none of the corruption of empty words; there would be solid learning and no unusable talent."[21]

Chu in this essay was flailing away at the system, and doing so, at least in part, in terms of his ideal of a perfect social and political order. But this ideal of a perfectly virtuous world was ambiguous. It could be used, not to criticize the edifice of requirements, standards, pressures, or unfair practices which confronted the student, but rather to upbraid the student himself. For one can say that in a perfectly virtuous society the government would not make the mistakes the examination system embodied; but, by the same argument, students would not exhibit the qualities of restless self-seeking and anxiety that these mistakes induced. Chu has a rather often-quoted remark that "it is not that the examinations are a vexation to men, but simply that men vex themselves about the examinations." And he continues,

A scholar of lofty vision and broad understanding, when he reads the books of the sages, will produce writing which reflects what he grasps, and all considerations of gain and loss, advantage and disadvantage, are set aside. Even though he constantly works at preparing for the examinations, he is undisturbed. If Confucius were to come back to life now, he would not avoid the examinations; but surely they would not disturb him.[22]

Chu goes on to admit that as a young man he himself had a certain disdain for the examinations, but this feeling was not, he argues, based on any understanding of the matter. The situation could be compared to that of one who has a natural dislike for the taste of wine or for a certain color, this natural and unreasoned reaction being of no importance.

The foregoing remarks, along with much more of the same sort, are preserved in a systematic anthology of Chu's sayings and writings on various subjects compiled by the Ch'ing government in the early eighteenth century, the *Chu Tzu Ch'üan Shu*, edited by Li Kuang-ti. The *Ch'üan Shu* was intended as an orthodox presentation of Chu's philosophy from the official point of view; and in the section presenting Chu's opinions on the examination problem, remarks by Chu are culled out of his writings and put together so as to justify the system against typical complaints made by students. Needless to say, in these pages the editors do not even hint at the existence of Chu's "Private Opinion." We do not need to regard the *Ch'üan Shu* as purely a Ch'ing document, however. It illustrates not only the way in which Neo-Confucian idealism could be turned about to justify the status quo, for the student complaints which Chu is shown to have answered in the *Ch'üan Shu* must after all have been complaints actually brought to him by his contemporaries. They are quite possibly as typical of student dissatisfaction in the twelfth century as in the seventeenth.

Let us see how some of the complaints and answers go. Notice that in the remarks just reproduced Chu preaches that a really worthy scholar would "set aside" considerations of "gain and loss." This sounds like Han Yü. But there is an important difference; namely, in the one case we have a defiant scholar bravely telling himself and the world that he will not be moved by the temptations to "fame and profit" that the state and the pressures of society create; whereas here we have a teacher pontifically telling students that they ought not to be so moved, and adding that if they are not, they can have no reason to complain of what is expected of them.

In this same passage there is another element worth noting. Chu says that he himself as a young man found examination studies naturally distasteful to him, but argues that this natural disinclination was of no significance. The plain implication in this is that Chu was approached by unhappy students who also found their examination studies distasteful, who felt that the guidance of their own inclinations was valuable, and who found themselves, like Ou-yang Hsiu and Liu Chih-chi, inclined to spend their time on other lines of study and self-improvement. Chu is shown by the *Ch'üan Shu* editors to have dealt with this plaint in various ways. Sometimes he simply pooh-poohs all the fuss about the matter:

Concerning study for the examinations, there is really nothing very important to be said. When a man of worth devotes himself to it, he will presumably have some energy to spare. If he has understood the true philosophy, then in the course of his daily activities, whatever their degree of importance, he will not need to divide his attention: if he always first understands "this," he will succeed at "that."[23]

In other words, see that you cultivate yourself properly and study the right point of view, and there will be no conflict—you will automatically do well in the examinations. As Han Yü had said, a good man will naturally write well. Chu's friend and rival philosopher Lu Chiu-yüan picked up the same idea when, in 1181, he was guest lecturer at Chu's White Deer Grotto Academy. Cultivate yourself circumspectly, says Lu, instill in yourself a devotion to right, and learn to have no impulses toward selfish expediency. "When one who conducts himself in this way approaches the examination halls, his writing will always express the learning and self-cultivation in which he is constantly engaged and the richness stored up within himself, and he will not offend against the sages."[24]

What if a young man self-importantly and loftily says that he has better things to do with himself than study examination essays? Chu offers the following dash of cold water:

Not taking the examinations is really only a small matter. But nowadays when someone says he is not going to take the examinations it is treated as something surprising and extraordinary. As I see it, as soon as one devotes one's thought to understanding the Tao, one takes a bit of respite from this sort of thing (i.e., the examinations), and there is obviously nothing of importance in this fact. I don't know why, but [when people begin to understand the Tao] they automatically look down on all sorts of wealth, honor, and attainment . . .[25]

This is less interesting as an example of Chu's attitude than it is as a negative image of a point of view which must have been prevalent among students.

Chu recognizes the common rationalization of students that they must study for the examinations in order to support their parents, and he condemns it. Such an attitude merely indicates that the student's mind is not composed—that he still feels a conflict between studying for the examinations and "real learning."[26] Sometimes, however, Chu admits by implication that there can be such a conflict, and attempts to deal with it or resolve it by some argument or stratagem. On one occasion, a disciple named Huang Ch'ien was ordered by his father to go to the prefectural school and study for the examinations, a course the young student was much disinclined to take. Huang laid his situation before Chu, who replied, "You can study for the examinations in the daytime and read the books you want to at night!" and added that if Huang refused to follow his father's wishes, father and son would become estranged, a situation which, he implies, would be as detrimental to Huang's program of "study" (i.e., self-cultivation) as the examinations course could ever be.[27]

As we might expect, Wang Yang-ming shared the Neo-Confucian vision of a perfect, strife-free society. Writing in 1525, he gives this idyllic picture of antiquity:

The man at the village well or in the rural district, the farmer, the artisan, the merchant, everybody had this (the true) learning . . . and looked only to the perfecting of character as important. How is this to be accounted for? They were not subject to the confusion inherent in much hearing and seeing, nor to the annoyance of remembering and reciting, nor to extravagance of speech and composition, nor to the striving and gaining of honor and advantage. The result was that they were filial toward their parents, respectful to their elders, and faithful toward their friends.

In this remote age, "the government schools were devoted to perfecting virtue, . . ." and "the people of the empire, with clear, resplendent virtue, all viewed one another as relatives of one home. . . . They did not strive for exalted position," each being content with his station. People at this time were not envious of others' accomplishments: "They did not distinguish between themselves and others. . . . They can be compared with the body of a single person . . ." and as one's eyes are not ashamed because they cannot hear, likewise no man was ashamed or was thought ill of for lack of the intellectual attainments found in the great.[28]

If this is noteworthy, it is chiefly as an intense (if dreamy) re-expression of a common Neo-Confucian political ideal. It is obvious, at least, that the addition of an examination system would seriously mar Wang's pretty scene. If there is a novel emphasis in what he says, it is found in his almost Taoist feeling that the purity of men's minds will be injured by too much "seeing and hearing," "remembering and reciting," or by "extravagance of speech and composition." For it is typical of Wang that he has a rather wholesale distrust of the verbal, conceptual side of man's mental existence. His distrust of mere "words" fits into a growing intellectual trend which became very important in the Ch'ing.

This attitude can be more easily understood if we examine the character of the district and metropolitan examinations during the Ming (to a large extent the description will fit the Ch'ing also). The Ming examinations followed, with some modification, the form of the Sung examinations as revised in 1071 when, as a result of one of the reforms of Wang An-shih, the *ming-ching* examination was abolished and certain features of it incorporated into the *chin-shih* examination. As it ultimately took shape, the Ming examination scheme (for both *chin-shih* and *chü-jen* degrees) consisted of three sittings or tests several days apart. The first test consisted of "essays on the meaning of the Classics" (*ching-i*)—three on the Four Books, and four on texts from other Classics. The second test was given over to *lun* ("essays") and *p'an* ("decisions," a T'ang examination form) and to questions on imperial "instructions"; the third, to *ts'e* ("dissertations") on history and current problems.[29] As far as this description goes, such an examination might be quite comprehensive. Actually, as Ku Yen-wu points out, the only test given any careful attention by the examiners was the first, on the meaning of the Classics and the Four Books.[30] Further, although all candidates had to answer questions on the Four Books, it was possible to get by with specialization on just one other Classic. This was certainly very far from what Chu Hsi had wanted in his "Private Opinion."

But this was not all. Where Chu had wanted candidates to have a knowledge of many different schools of criticism, the Ming system required candidates to prepare themselves in the views of just one school, ironically the school of Chu Hsi himself. After the official publication, in the Yung-lo reign, of the compendium of the opinions of this school, the *Ssu-shu Wu-ching Ta-ch'üan*, even the standard T'ang commentaries were dispensed with. In consequence, less and less came to depend on wide learning or genuine understanding, even of the Classics themselves; more and more it came to be crucially important for the candidate to excel in the style of his essays on the meaning of classical texts in the first test.[31]

What of the form of these essays? A form for the *ching-i* essay had been fixed by the Board of Ceremonies shortly after Wang An-shih's reform; and as such official forms will, it evolved over successive reigns and dynasties. By the Ming, it had come to be fixed in eight sections (hence its popular name, *pa-ku*, "eight legs"). The number of words to be used in the essay was also fixed from time to time. A typical specimen takes the announced topic—a passage from one of the Classics—and analyzes it into two subthemes. The essay then moves into a more and more elaborate treatment of these two themes. In the main body of the essay, an extended sentence or group of sentences will be put forward on one of the themes; these are in loose, "ancient prose" style, but they are at once followed by an exactly similar sentence or set of sentences on the other theme, which mirror the earlier ones character for character. This game will be played several times before the essay reaches its close. In tone, the entire piece can effectively be compared with a sermon on a text from sacred scripture.[32]

The total effect is not at all displeasing, if one is merely browsing through a few of these curios, and surely some value must be acknowledged in any literary form which required the Chinese literati to write well-constructed and systematically organized pieces of prose. But if one had to read and imitate such essays as if one's life depended upon it for the years needed to acquire sufficient skill to satisfy the examiners, one can readily imagine that ennui would soon give way to intense distaste. The necessity of finding antitheses in the theme in order to carry the essay through was particularly galling, since it was a purely formal requirement which took precedence over whatever meaning the classical passage might contain. Candidates had to be prepared to distort, or even invent, meaning in the assigned text, and had by long practice to learn this art thoroughly.[33]

Worse, the examiners over the centuries not unnaturally developed a little tradition of playing a game with the candidates, by choosing texts which would be difficult to handle in the required way, or which were chopped out of context in the most misleading fashion possible, with the natural phrasing and breaks in meaning of the original text largely ignored. An example, given by Chu Hsi (who excoriated the practice in his "Private Opinion") is a Sung examination question consisting of three lines from the *Shih ching*, viz.,

> Shang t'ien chih tsai
> Wu sheng wu ch'ou
> I hsing Wen Wang[34]

Legge's translation is as follows:

> The doings of high heaven
> have neither sound nor smell.
> Take your pattern from King Wen, . . .[35]

The second half of the second pair of lines, which is dropped, is approximately "and all countries will give you their confidence." But of course much more context even than this would be required if one were to make sense out of the passage. Still, Chu Hsi's example is tame compared to what sometimes happened. Imagine yourself writing an essay on the following five words:

Kou wei wu pen ch'i[36]

These words correspond approximately to the italic words in the following passage from *Mencius*:

> The disciple Hsü said, "Chung-ni often praised water, saying, 'O water, O water.' What did he find in water to praise?" Mencius replied, "There is a spring of water; how it gushes out! It rests not day nor night. It fills up every hole, and then advances, flowing on to the four seas. Such is water having a spring! It was this which he found in it to praise.
>
> "*But suppose that* the water *has no spring.—In the seventh* and eighth months when the rain falls abundantly, the channels in the fields are all filled, but their being dried up again may be expected in a short time. So a superior man is ashamed of a reputation beyond his merits."[37]

In the *pa-ku* as part of the examinations, clearly, we have a prime example of violation of the classical principle that "one must not let words injure meaning." The term *pa-ku* came widely to connote an exercise in mere verbal cleverness with utter disregard for content. Reflect that every schoolboy had to struggle with this form, and that often all possible social, family, and pedagogical pressure was put upon him to master it. And consider that in order to master it he had to develop by long practice at least a hypothetical sort of taste for it, and thus condition himself in a device for which he was likely to have both philosophical and aesthetic disgust. The bitter complaints about *shih wen* (this term now had come to mean *pa-ku*) in the letters and reminiscences of seventeenth- and eighteenth-century writers are not hard to understand.

Ku Yen-wu, in the seventeenth century, was one of several now famous men who meditated and wrote on the reasons for the decline and fall of the Ming Dynasty. Much of his *Jih-chih Lu* has this sort of point, and in particular the parts of that book dealing with examinations and schools, though treating these subjects in great historical depth, are pointed up into a criticism, often extremely biting, of the character and operation of the Ming examination system. In many of these critical sections, however, he writes as though he were talking of contem-

porary conditions, and we probably must assume that at the time he
wrote conditions had not greatly changed.

Ku insists that writing, to be worth anything, must say something,
and the writer must be unencumbered by formal restrictions in the
saying of it:

Writing can have no fixed form. When a form is set for people to follow in
their writing, the writing will not be worth talking about. The T'ang selected
its officials on their skill in writing *fu*, and the *fu* became utterly decadent.
The Sung selected men on their skill in composing essays and dissertations
(*lun ts'e*) and these genres likewise decayed. The Ming selected men on the
basis of their essays on the meaning of the Classics (*ching-i*, i.e., *pa-ku*), and
this form of writing became worse than anything that had been seen before.
The reason in each case was that writing was required to follow a fixed form,
and as a result the writing continually became worse. The reason the examination replies of Ch'ao Ts'o, Tung Chung-shu, and Kung-sun Hung are outstanding in history is that in their day there was no fixed form for writing. If
we wish to invigorate the writing of the present day we must not fetter it with
forms, and then outstanding talent will make its appearance.[38]

In Sung, Yüan, and Ming, the characteristic objection to the examination system had been its tendency to induce a fever of competition.
Ku's indictment of *pa-ku* suggests that the characteristic objection was
now to the examinations' bad influence on writing and thinking. By
stressing purely formal, merely verbal inducements to stagnation, the
examinations actually deprived the state of a supply of good men. The
situation has become so bad, Ku thinks, that the only remedy is to
suspend the examinations altogether for a time, and teach people anew
how to study. Ku also attacks the brainless orthodoxy which he feels
the examinations propagate, and recommends that examination questions on the Four Books deal with "doubtful" matters, questions which
will probe into embarrassing contradictions. Ku cites the *p'an* genre
on the T'ang examinations as exemplifying what he intends, but it is
likely that some of the examination questions prepared by Wang An-
shih would have served him even better. Ku, however, had a rather
low opinion of the Sung reformer.[39]

Ku reserves his strongest language for a somewhat different matter,
however. Just because the examinations place so much emphasis on
formally correct essay writing, they do nothing to recognize or encourage really solid scholarship. Instead, the examinations are so contrived
as to allow mere know-nothings to pass. Ku's exposé of the abuses by
which this can occur is one of the bitterest and most interesting parts
of his treatise. The trick consists of a practice Ku calls *ni t'i*, or "making
up questions." There is, he says, no evil greater than this in the whole
system. It works as follows: In the crucial first test, when a candidate

has to write essays on the Classics he has chosen as a specialty, there will usually be only a few dozen questions likely to be asked.

Rich families and powerful clans engage well-known scholars and install them in their family schools. The scholar then takes these few dozen themes and writes an essay for each, receiving pay according to the number of essays he writes. The sons and younger brothers in the family, and servant boys who are especially clever, are then made to memorize and study thoroughly these essays. When they go to the examination halls, eight or nine out of every ten themes announced will correspond to the themes they have studied, and they need only copy down the writings they have memorized.[40]

This procedure, Ku observes, is incomparably easier than the examinations as they are traditionally pictured; for plainly, the son of a rich family might in this way pass without having read through the text of even one Classic. "The same procedure," Ku writes, "is used for the Four Books. And when the grades are announced, these fellows turn out to be at the top. Many who are mere pretty-faced youths are selected for official appointments."

Ku then adds that from time to time parts of the Classics have ceased to be drawn upon for examination themes, so that what a young man has to contend with in his preparation has become less and less, and the trick of "making up likely themes" becomes that much easier. As a result,

What men in former times needed ten years to accomplish can now be finished in one; what once required a year to learn can now be finished in a month. . . . But if by chance you ask someone about a Classic he has not read, there are those who will be so confused they will not know what book you are talking about. Therefore, I say that the injurious effects of *pa-ku* are as great as the effects of the Burning of the Books, and the ruination of talent that it brings about is worse than the result of the Burial of the Scholars. . . .

Ku then recommends, citing Chu Hsi's "Private Opinion," that candidates be examined on passages in the Classics that would call for some original thinking, and that in studying one Classic they be required to gain a general acquaintance with the rest; that they be required to become familiar with conflicting interpretations, and that in their answers they be required to render their own judgment. Further, themes used in the examinations should not be so standard that they can be guessed at in advance. "Then their essays will have to be written in the examination halls, and it can really be determined whether a scholar understands the Classics or not, and his ability to write can really be tested."[41]

Not the least interesting part of what Ku says is his conviction that it is characteristically the rich who are most easily able to get away with murder. But the substance of his plea is that solid scholarship should be demanded of a candidate at the examinations and should be the criterion of his worth. In this plea Ku perhaps had real influence, for his prestige as a classical scholar mounted enormously in the next century. Successive generations of scholars grew up who looked back to him with reverence, and many such men, of course, served frequently as examining officials. One can well imagine that one of Ku's "pretty-faced youths" would have scant chance of passing under such an examiner as, say, Juan Yüan.[42]

But this same prestige of Ku as a classical scholar, and the philological *zeitgeist* which developed in the eighteenth century, had eventually another and very different effect on examination standards. For although the tendency occasionally improved the caliber of examining officials, still, in any given case, the chances were that an examiner would find himself in the situation of passing judgment on a candidate or candidates who knew more philology than he did. Examiners caught in this sort of situation tend to look for a simple and foolproof line of defense into which to retreat. The examiner's recourse in the present case was to limit his inspection once again to mere questions of form: not, now, to the formal correctness of the candidate's essays, but to the form of the individual characters he wrote—to his calligraphy. By the second and third decades of the nineteenth century, it was a ritual perfection in the handling of the brush which was the mark of the candidate most likely to succeed.

Needless to say, this new situation provoked protests appropriate to it. Such an expression of protest is to be found in a bitterly sarcastic essay by Kung Tzu-chen, an intense, brilliant, and erratic scholar-official, philologist, poet, and friend of Wei Yüan and Lin Tse-hsü, who attempted the examinations repeatedly before attaining the *chin-shih* degree in 1829, failing, however—as he believed, because of poor handwriting—to pass the palace examination which a successful *chin-shih* normally took. Kung's essay pretends to be a preface to a book he has written on calligraphy. He describes first, with mock reverence, the ritual of the palace examination in which he failed. The examining officers, "in court robes, face the throne and kneel thrice, touching their heads to the floor nine times. All the candidates do likewise, respectfully taking their positions. When the examination is over, the eight examiners then respectfully make a selection of ten papers in which the elevation of characters is according to form and in which even and deflected tones have been properly used, and which exhibit a formal calligraphic style which is especially sparkling and delicate, presenting these for the emperor's perusal. . . ."

Kung describes more examinations—the preliminary examination before the palace examination, and the examination following it, both,

again, turning on the candidate's skill in calligraphy. He misses no
chance to dwell on the grave and weighty importance of success which
turns on so trivial a matter. "Those who place high in all three examinations are appointed to the Han-lin Academy. In our dynasty, the highest officials invariably arise from among members of the Han-lin, and
more than half of the assistant ministers at court and of the governors
of provinces are chosen in the same way." To be chosen for a clerkship
in the Grand Council is likewise a great honor; for "in time of war the
function of the Grand Council is to assist the throne in making plans
by which victory is decided, while in time of peace it provides advice
based on the records of earlier emperors in the issuance of edicts affecting the imperial household." But, "when one is recommended to the
Grand Council there is an examination, in which selection is made as
before on the basis of calligraphic skill." Kung goes on to explain to us
how other important posts are filled, and always with the same final
twist.

Finally Kung tips his hand:

I, Kung Tzu-chen, passed the examination in the Board of Ceremonies; three
times I went up for the palace examination and three times I failed. I was
not assigned to the Han-lin Academy. I was examined for the Grand Council
but was not given a post there. . . . So I have withdrawn to my home and
have reproached myself, and have written a book in self-criticism. Its contents consist of twelve sections discussing the principles of selecting a fine
brush-tip, five sections on the proper method of grinding the ink and im-
pregnating the brush, . . . one hundred and twenty sections on fine points
in the drawing of the dot and in the execution of the sweeping down-stroke,
twenty-two sections on the framing of characters, twenty-four sections on the
spacing of characters in column, three sections on quality of spirit; and seven
sections on natural temper. Having finished the work, I have entitled it *A New
Treatise on Gaining Office,* and am entrusting it to my descendants.

Kung dates his "preface" the fourteenth year of Tao-kuang (1834).[43]

Needless to say, Kung's *Treatise* was never written or even seriously
contemplated. Kung's bitterness about calligraphy, it should be stressed,
was provoked by a situation peculiar to his time. We find a very different
attitude in Ku Yen-wu. Ku would have his candidates know how to
write characters well, and no nonsense. He cites in this connection, and
with evident approval, a practice in court examinations in the Northern
Ch'i Dynasty. In those high and far-off times, it seems, if a candidate's
writing was sloppy, he was required as a penalty to drink a pint of ink.[44]

The Chinese civil service examinations were not discontinued until
1905. The remainder of the story, however, would be a study in itself,
and I lack both the space and the knowledge to enter upon it. But it

does seem plain that it would be hasty to ascribe the Chinese state's rejection of the examination system simply to a Westernizing fever, or to say that the Chinese did away with that system merely in order to be rid of a conservative institutional force. Perhaps it will turn out that what the "impact of the West" accomplished was to tip the balance in favor of persuasions which were centuries old, but which had not been strong enough radically to alter the set institutions of a bureaucratic state. The complaint that the examinations failed to nourish talents of practical use to the state was not a new and radical idea in the nineteenth century; on the contrary, it was a familiar criticism in the ninth. The complaint of Ku Yen-wu (and Chu Hsi) that the examinations fostered a cult of "empty words" and dead forms was an argument repeated with force in memorials preceding the system's abolition. The idea of a Confucian utopia, in which Neo-Confucian philosophers lodged their moral objections to the system, was an idea which was by no means dead in the late nineteenth century. Perhaps it is not dead yet.

The examination system must certainly be called Confucian. It gave form to the ideal that the ruler should select the best men as his officials, and it provided in most periods a fixed if narrow and difficult avenue to prestige and position for that social group who had a special interest in reading and cherishing the Confucian classical texts. And yet the bitter regrets the Chinese have had about the system must also be called Confucian. The Neo-Confucian utopian ideal, and the "anti-formalist" and moral criteria of literary value enunciated by Han Yü in the ninth century and by Ku Yen-wu in the seventeenth are essential parts of the idealistic side of the Confucian tradition which has its roots in Mencius.

When we consider the position of the individual student or candidate, we see that he was pushed in two directions at once. He must do the right thing for his parents and family; the *ipsissima verba* of the Master could be cited in abundance to assure him of this; also it was the duty of a Confucian to take office and "put his Tao into practice" if he could. In the later empire, the only apparent way to perform these duties was to prepare for the examinations and seek official position thereby.

Yet the Confucian also had a duty to cultivate himself and to respect his own dignity. Entry into the competition for office obliged him, it seemed, to place "profit" ahead of "right" in his own personal ordering of values, and at least to seem to be seeking the approbation of persons, whether gossiping townspeople or examining officials, whom he might regard as vulgar or petty-minded. If we read reflectively a novel such as *Ju-lin Wai-shih,* we suspect that the scorn measured out to examiners and examination writing is, so to speak, but the exposed part of an iceberg whose bulk is the pervasive revulsion of independent-minded men against social pressures to conform, to accept the vulgar conventions and values, to chase after the pretty tags of so-called success, to court favor with the "best" families in town. Beneath this disposition was always the conception of the Superior Man, who cannot be moved by mere things.

A Chinese who thought seriously about himself and his society did not live in a placid intellectual world in which all his questions had ready answers. He lived in a world of tensions, both social and intellectual—tensions such as those I have been describing; and if we are to understand his politics, his literature, his philosophy, we must measure these tensions and their effect upon him. We must see him as he was.

Frederick W. Mote

CONFUCIAN EREMITISM
IN THE YÜAN PERIOD

The Mongols conquered North China in the early 1230's, and completed their conquest of the rest of the country in the years 1275–79. The North already had been held for a century by the Chin Tatars, another alien and (in Chinese eyes) barbarian conquering people from beyond China's northern frontiers. The wounds caused by this long division between alien-ruled North China and Chinese-ruled South China were further aggravated by the attitudes and policies of the Yüan dynasty, as the Mongol government of the newly reunited Chinese world was called.

The Mongols themselves faced a difficult adjustment when, as nomadic tribesmen, they suddenly became the rulers, or at least the holders of power within the ruling group, of a vast sedentary population. Moreover, with each of the first few generations of their rule the role they assigned to China in their world empire shifted and changed. Only gradually did these Mongol rulers come to see themselves as the successors to earlier Chinese dynasties, and as Chinese emperors. The Chinese, on their part, often were moved to fierce resentment of the Mongols, not so much by the fact of alien rule itself as by the lack of regard in which these barbarian rulers, beyond all others in their history, held their ancient and revered way of life. Those things which the Chinese held to be the essentials of civilization—their Confucian ethical and social principles; their theories and forms of civilian-administered, bureaucratic government; their humanistic culture—suffered serious decline, and seemed to many to face the danger of extinction. An incipient racism made brief appearance, contradicting in its spirit the traditional patronizing Chinese attitude toward "barbarian" neighbors.

Of all the rulers in China's history, the Mongols were perhaps the least well-equipped to deal with Chinese problems and the least concerned about dealing with them. Moreover, the Yüan period was a period of instability, in which many kinds of new forces were at work. In some respects this was beneficial, but in many respects it was not, and in almost all respects it alarmed and grieved the educated, thinking Chinese of the time. The magnificent achievements of the Mongols in such matters as military organization and technique scarcely impressed their Chinese subjects, who saw only the low quality of Mongol government and the deterioration of social order. By the same token, the developments in literature and painting for which we now value the Yüan period offered little solace to the Chinese literatus of the time. The times were hard; as the Yüan dynasty wore on, they became harder, and China sank deeper into pessimism, frustration, and apathy. The intellectual climate and moral tone of the Mongol era in China cannot be described in greater detail here,[1] but must be kept in mind; they are essential to an understanding of what follows.

VARIETIES OF EREMITISM

Even in the Yüan period some persons remained zealously devoted to Confucian ideals—to an active life in the service of the Yüan, and to heroism as Confucianism defined it. Far more of the literate turned in despair to the other extreme: to various forms of escapism, and *fin de siècle* frivolity. There is a third group which renounced both state service and extreme self-indulgence and chose instead some variety of withdrawal.

Recluses, or hermits, are often called *yin-i* in historical writings, and usually referred to themselves as *ch'u-shih* or *chü-shih*. All these terms are customarily translated "recluse" or "hermit"; in Chinese society they signified withdrawal from the active public life in the service of society that Confucian ethics prescribed as the most suitable course for all whose abilities, cultivation, and learning qualified them for it. To bar one's gates and earn one's own living without reliance on the emolument of office, to display a lack of regard for the social status which could be attained only by entering officialdom, and to devote one's life to self-cultivation, scholarship or artistic pursuits made one a recluse. By the mores of Confucian society, this was a step which set one apart, which justified the special appellation.

The distance to which one withdrew, the firmness with which one barred the gate, and the seriousness with which one cultivated oneself all admitted of wide variations, even among those whose motivations in withdrawing were sincere. (We are not concerned here with the many who became recluses when it suited their purpose to do so, and returned to public life at their convenience.) The variations, however, were of only secondary importance; the degree of a man's commitment to withdrawal had no effect on his status. It was the renunciation of office-holding—either at the outset or after a period of public life—that defined the recluse.

Nemoto Makoto's recent book, "The Spirit of Resistance in Authoritarian Society: A Study of Chinese Eremitism," is the first full-scale study of the recluse in Chinese civilization, and more particularly in the "middle period" of imperial history.[2] Nemoto sees eremitism, especially the kind suggested by the title of his book, as a reflection of some of the deepest problems afflicting authoritarian society. He is at his best in describing the special character of Chinese eremitism, its contrast with Indian and Christian European eremitism, and the relation of the Chinese recluse to the rest of Chinese society. He describes well the significance of the renunciation of the official life, which as we have seen is the keystone of Chinese eremitism, and which distinguishes it from the connotations of the word in other civilizations (e.g., religion, solitude, eccentricity) and also from the really unrelated general problem of Buddhist monasticism in China.

This is not to imply that Buddhist eremitism is altogether foreign to our subject. Actually, some potential scholar-officials did become Buddhist or Taoist, rather than Confucian, recluses. The three types of eremitism, although distinct in character, are all more or less congenial to each other. The Buddhist, for example, may have become a monk, or may merely have become a lay-associate (*chü-shih* also has the specific meaning of a Buddhist lay-associate who has taken certain vows; both this meaning and that of a non-Buddhist recluse were and still are current for the term). The Buddhist recluse might continue to live with his family in normal conjugal life, or he might withdraw to celibacy and seclusion. In most cases we may assume that Buddhist thought had an intellectual appeal, and that the Buddhist literatus-recluse retained the respect and the acquaintance of his non-Buddhist friends. Such learned Buddhists, both monks and lay-associates, some of them as famous as their more worldly friends in the fields of poetry, painting, literature, and scholarship, are known in all ages, and were particularly numerous in the Yüan period.

The Taoist recluse likewise may have taken up the dress and hairdo of the professed Taoist adept, or may have maintained a looser connection with religious and popular Taoism. In either case he typically withdrew to a rural place, had a small following of apprentices, and practiced some more-or-less obscure Taoist art such as medicine or alchemy. He was likely to be at least slightly eccentric, if not awesomely unfathomable, but usually not to the point of losing the respect of the conventional intellectual community on whose fringes he lived.

It is the Confucian recluse, however, who interests us the most.

Usually he was less cut off from the normal pattern of life in society than the Buddhist or the Taoist. He cultivated nothing as metaphysically profound as Buddhism, or as mysteriously incommunicable as Taoism. If, beyond literature and the arts, he cultivated anything in the realm of the spirit, it was Confucian thought, which—unless one becomes wrapped up in the study of the *I-ching*—cannot take one far from the everyday world of man. He might indeed be somewhat eccentric, or he might be simply what we would call a retired gentleman of leisure, perhaps even one of great means living in elegant fashion. More often he was a man of modest means, living by teaching or working his own land, or a scholar living in poverty. The Confucian recluse might double as a devotee of the poetry-and-wine type of escapism; the serious life is not demanded of him, although it is more common. These various types of recluse, including the Buddhist and Taoist, had only one thing in common: they had withdrawn voluntarily from active participation in public life.

Although the pattern of the recluse has existed for millennia in China, it became an alternative way of life of particular importance in times of disorder and impending doom, when thoughtful pessimism seemed more attractive to educated men than the normal pattern of life. The Yüan period was preeminently such an age.

Many of the Yüan literati, we must presume, wanted office. Some would have accepted it but lacked ambition or energy; some did accept it and served the dynasty, even loyally. For the many who did not obtain office, the pose of a righteous indifference may have been an easy solace. But there can be little doubt that, for an important and influential number, withdrawal was genuine—an honest expression of protest prompted by their Confucian ideals.

But were there no literati who were neither recluses, nor scholar-officials loyal to the Yüan, nor passive idlers—no group, however small, who saw the inevitability of the Yüan dynasty's downfall and actively sought to hasten it? In the last generation of Yüan rule it is possible to discern the outlines of such a group. Dissociation with Mongol interests usually was their first step. Some merely became recluses, or scholars in retirement, who thought and sometimes wrote about social and political problems of their age, awaiting opportunities to become active. Some participated in the creation of local or regional forces which assumed some governmental responsibilities, but which made no open break with Yüan rule. Others lived by choice in territories under rebel rule, waiting to evaluate the rebellion's chances of success before openly joining it, but in their own minds condoning rebellion. Still others (few until the very end) openly served rebellious movements, movements which originated with and represented non-literati social forces but which could not begin to function on the level of government without the technical assistance of the literati. It must be emphasized, however, that activists and potential activists of this sort were few, scattered, and without much influence. The vast majority of the literate remained passively loyal to Yüan rule, and most of the educated members of society hoped for nothing more than improvement in the effectiveness of the legitimate government and a restoration of social order.

THE ORIGINS OF CONFUCIAN EREMITISM

Confucianism is normally and properly associated with the ideology of participation, of public service. In fact, however, there is an equally valid aspect of Confucianism, apparent in the thought of Confucius and Mencius, which justifies withdrawal from public life and official service under some conditions. Withdrawal is not to be preferred to the active life: it is not to be regarded (as by Taoism) as intrinsically valuable; but in some circumstances it is necessary and laudable. To Confucius and Mencius it was clear that a man should serve when he could maintain and actively promote his principles, and that he should withdraw when the conditions of public service were degrading, or when his principles were threatened. A man's personal ethical standards were to determine the decision.

It is a commonplace that this early Confucian thought is often at variance, in matters of specific detail and in tone and emphasis, with the "imperial Confucianism" of the Han and subsequent ages. The reasons for this are clear: the political and social realities of an authoritarian state could scarcely have been fully anticipated by Confucius and Mencius, two unemployed thinkers reflecting on an age of decaying feudalism. There are significant differences even between Confucius and Mencius, and still greater ones between Mencius and Hsün-tzu, reflecting both the development of Confucian thought and the changing conditions of successive ages. If early Confucian thought had not centered so heavily on the ethics of political and social situations, the ever-changing conditions of the political and social worlds would have borne less relevance to it, and the discrepancies between earlier and later Confucianism might have figured less importantly in the history of Chinese thought. If, for example, Confucius had been concerned primarily with religious or metaphysical concepts, his followers in later ages would have had less trouble adjusting to changing times, for they would have felt less compelled to become involved in government and practical affairs. But Confucianism, by its nature, demands action, or at least commitment. Moreover, there exists within it the roots of possible tension between the individual's observance of his ethical standards and the demands of society and state. To Confucius and Mencius, it was comparatively easy to draw the line between when a man should serve and when he should not, although in fact both were criticized by some of their own followers for apparent inconsistencies in such decisions. But, Confucius and Mencius discussed the motives of men who did or did not serve, and fixed their evaluations of them accordingly. Often those who did not serve received high praise.

Hsün-tzu, as might be expected, was harder on the recluse. Although a Confucian and a believer in the ethical foundations of society, in his insistence on the importance of ruler and state, he left little room for a man to maintain any private and personal moral standards that might under any circumstances conflict with the primary duty of serving the ruler. The later Legalists, among them especially Hsün-tzu's pupil Han Fei-tzu, were still more severe. Legalist writers pronounced the hermit guilty of a crime meriting death; in his eremitism he was "ungovernable" and "disloyal," and his existence could not be tolerated by the authoritarian state.

Legalist principles and practices exerted a significant influence on the character of imperial Confucianism. In fact, during the formative Han period Legalist and Confucian principles were in some measure mixed and blended together; the resulting amalgam, though it continued to be called Confucianism, was not the Confucianism of old. Fung Yu-lan, adopting the terminology of William James, refers to the materialistic, realistic Hsüntzian trend in Confucianism as the "tough-minded" side of it, as opposed to the "tender-minded" idealism of the Mencian tradition, and he sees the dominant Ch'eng-Chu school of Neo-Confucianism as the heir to the tough-minded tradition.[3]

Eremitism fared better with the tender-minded. It is clear that eremitism of all kinds was tolerated to a much greater degree in earlier history, and in particular that the nobly motivated eremitism of the uncompromising man of principle was highly praised.[4] Gradually, in the early imperial period, it lost favor, perhaps in part because it was associated with the religious eremitism of Taoism and Buddhism, but primarily, it would seem, because of the increasingly authoritarian character of the state.

Devaluing eremitism meant reinterpreting the words of Confucius and Mencius, and a perhaps unconscious acceptance of the attitudes of Hsün-tzu. Even the Neo-Confucianists, who ostensibly ranked Mencius highest among the followers of the Sage, bowed to this necessity. As Hsiao Kung-ch'üan has pointed out, the Sung Neo-Confucianists held the very un-Mencian idea that the servitor had the duty of absolute and unswerving loyalty to the ruler and his dynasty, even at the price of death or forced retirement. Moreover, they held this principle to be based on the teachings of Confucius himself, despite certain explicitly contradictory teachings of Confucius and Mencius.[5] Living in an age when the need to strengthen the state was apparent, they came to look upon even the most idealistically motivated refusal to serve the state as morally suspect. Ultimately they demanded absolute loyalty to the ruler and his dynasty, and looked upon one man's successive service to two ruling houses as being incompatible with morality. On the one hand, refusal to serve in ordinary times came almost to imply sedition; on the other, willingness to serve a new dynasty after serving the old implied moral degeneracy.

From various kinds of evidence, but in particular from that found in the dynastic histories, it becomes clear that the concept of Confucian-sanctioned eremitism underwent a remarkable transformation, the results of which can be seen most clearly with the emergence of Neo-Confucianism in the Sung period. Two kinds of Confucian eremitism, distinct in character and very differently evaluated, had come into being.

One of these I will call "compulsory" eremitism. It was imposed as a moral duty in the name of *chung*, or loyalty, and theoretically it was binding on all servitors of a fallen dynasty. Its usefulness to the holders of power was so great that even newly founded dynasties, which suffered from it during the first years of their rule, nonetheless promoted and praised it. They even honored those who practiced it against them, and have been known to censure those who did not.[6] The roots of this kind of eremitism do not go deeply into the thought of Confucius and Mencius, where in fact its ideological foundations are at least implicitly denied, but stems from Hsün-tzu and the Legalists. And it did not assume its later significance until Neo-Confucian thought promoted a new concept of loyalty consonant with its exaltation of the ruler and the state.

The second I shall call "voluntary" eremitism. It has valid roots in the thought of early Confucianism. However, by Sung and Yüan times it was slightly stressed if at all, and where mentioned in the official histories, greatly de-emphasized.

No work of the time known to me contains an explicit statement of the two aspects of eremitism, the one compulsory and approved of, and the other voluntary and of doubtful worth. Only the *Hsin Yüan Shih*, a product of the early twentieth century, views the eremitism of the Yüan period with this division in mind, albeit without reference to its philosophical and historical implications.[7] Yet both the division and its implications are clearly reflected in the writings of the men of the time, especially those who practiced some form of eremitism, as we shall see in the following pages.

VOLUNTARY EREMITISM OF PROTEST

Refusal to serve on moral grounds is clearly an expression of protest against impossible conditions of service, and more or less directly a protest against the ruler and his government. Eremitism so motivated is essentially voluntary, for although a person may feel morally compelled to refuse to serve, the problem of recognizing the evil conditions is his individual problem; his decision is a matter of his own conscience and is made on his own initiative, commonly in the teeth of personal and social pressures. A decision to withdraw usually led to hardship, and sometimes, when it was irritating to a jealous tyrant, to danger. To most of the recluse's contemporaries, even to his own family, it might well appear foolish, impractical, eccentric. Nemoto notes that honor and praise were accorded such hermits, because their eremitism was vaguely felt to be an expression of the otherwise unarticulated feelings of protest and of resistance that authoritarianism engendered in society. This to a certain extent must have been true, and personal satisfaction was an additional compensation. But to most recluses, these compensations must have appeared less than adequate for the sacrifice of the official career, the career their society valued above all others.

On the one hand, Confucian ethics put the highest possible premium on the maintenance of ethical standards; on the other, they demanded that a man serve society, not only for social but also for family reasons. A man should achieve prominence for the sake of the family name and fame, to win respect and honor (in some instances, posthumous ranks and titles) for his ancestors, and for the material benefit of his living parents and family members. To many persons these noble-sounding reasons may have carried less weight than baser motives, such as the lust for power and wealth, but that is inconsequential. The important thing is that such Confucian principles existed, and strengthened the demands on men to serve. In this conflict of values, with Confucian principles seemingly supporting either decision, the factors favoring office-holding were real, positive, practical, and immediate. Those favoring withdrawal were abstract, negative, difficult to maintain and to defend. Thus a kind of open choice remained. It is for this reason that I call this kind of eremitism "voluntary" and Nemoto refers to it as "subjectively determined."[8]

Evidence of the Neo-Confucian impatience with dissent can be traced in historiography, and particularly in the historical writings of

Ou-yang Hsiu, who did more to form the intellectual and ethical standards of the Sung period than any other figure of his time. Ou-yang used history as Confucius had used it in editing the *Spring and Autumn Annals,* to promote morality by praising the good and blaming the unworthy. The influence of his historiography on the writing of history in the Yüan and Ming periods (particularly the official dynastic histories) was enormous.

In his *Wu-tai Shih Chi* ("Historian's Record of the Five Dynasties"), Ou-yang departs from several precedents of historiography, among them the precedent of including a chapter devoted to biographies of recluses. He confines himself to commenting on certain aspects of eremitism of which he approved, thereby avoiding any all-inclusive approval of the concept of withdrawal, and particularly of the eremitism of protest. He mentions noble scholars who withdrew from public service in the chaotic and degenerate times of the Five Dynasties, to be sure, but he discusses them in his introduction to the chapter of biographies of persons of "singular conduct" ("I-hsing Lieh-chuan," ch. 34)—his version of the "Tu-hsing" ("unique conduct") or "Cho-hsing" ("extraordinary conduct") chapters of earlier historiography whose subjects were men of heroic virtue, and characteristically martyrs, often in the public service. The implication is that voluntary eremitism is commendable only when it becomes extraordinary, and that even at its most commendable it is merely one kind of extraordinary devotion to moral principles. Ouyang's recluses, moreover, are by no means typical of the Confucian literati patterns. Two are Taoist adepts, one is a military man who sacrificed his life in blind loyalty to an unworthy ruler, and one is presented as an extraordinary example of filial piety. Only one is a Confucian scholar-official who refused to continue to serve under humiliating conditions.

The pattern is fairly clear. Ou-yang wished to devalue the behavior of the recluse. In his mind it was possible to justify voluntary eremitism only as one of the varieties of extraordinary conduct, and even then as something possible only in the most degenerate of ages. By merging it with extreme acts of devotion to other specific moral principles, such as filial piety, he sought to gloss over its political significance. By grouping true recluses with Taoist adepts, he sought to dim the luster of eremitism for the Confucian literati. His introduction to *chüan* 34 reads in part as follows:

Alas! The Five Dynasties period reached the extreme limits of chaos. It was a period like that referred to in the [*I-ching, Wen-yen*] *chuan,* where it states: "Heaven and Earth are closed; the worthy man withdraws." It was an age when servitors murdered their rulers, sons killed their fathers, and scholar-officials of high rank and position placidly accepted their emolument and took their places at court, unabashed and with no appearance of integrity or shame. All were thus!

I have always said that, since antiquity, loyal servitors and righteous scholars have appeared in large numbers in times of disorder, yet I am surprised that, in that age, those who merit mention are so few. It cannot be that there really were no such persons. Even when we grant that warfare had arisen and schools had been destroyed, so that propriety and righteousness were in decline and the people's practices had degenerated accordingly, yet never in history has there been a time when in all the world there were no worthy men. I mean that there must have been upright and uncompromising scholars who resented their world and kept themselves far distant from it, and thereby became lost to our view. Since antiquity there always have been able and worthy men who have cherished their noble principles within and not made them visible without, living in poverty in lowly lanes or hiding themselves in the wilds. Even such a man as Yen Hui would not have become known if he had not met Confucius. How much more likely it is that such a man should remain unknown in an age of decline and disorder, when the *tao* of the superior man was on the wane. Therefore I maintain that there must have been able and upright persons who simply sank out of sight, disappearing so completely that we can know nothing of them. When we seek for them in the records and annals, we find that the written records of that age of chaos and collapse are scanty and incomplete, and such persons are not recoverable. Thus I have have been able to find only four or five such persons . . .

Here the "loyal servitor" and the "righteous scholar" are discussed together. To be sure, "worthy men who withdraw into seclusion" are praised, and unworthy men who serve in office, condoning if not committing crimes of regicide and parricide, are scorned. But the outlines of the concept of voluntary Confucian eremitism are somewhat blurred by subsuming it under the more general rubric of "singular conduct"; and the scope of its application has been greatly narrowed to times that merit total condemnation.

The decision to withdraw, as praised by Ou-yang Hsiu, is less a personal one, less a matter of individual choice; it is one that objective conditions make necessary, without reference to a man's private ethical standards. Significantly, the recluse is warned that probable obscurity will be his only reward for withdrawing from the world. In all ways the value of the independent act of protest is deemphasized, and its clear definition is obscured.

Nonetheless, Ou-yang preserved a certain indestructible basis for withdrawal to which the voluntary recluse of the Yüan dynasty could still appeal. He could not proclaim himself a righteous recluse without taking a stand openly inimical to the authority of the state and the person of the ruler, but he was fairly safe if he limited his protest to veiled sentiment and indirect expression. In the Yüan dynasty the recluse was

actually safer than in the following two dynasties, because of the wall
that separated the Chinese people from the alien court, and the lack of
close communication and real concern from the one side of that wall to
the other. People could say with impunity in the Yüan period things
that it would have cost them their lives merely to hint at under Ming
T'ai-tsu. But even so, after the passage of seven centuries, the rediscovery of the true feelings of a recluse of the time is no simple, straightforward matter.

With this background in mind, we shall now consider a representative recluse of the Yüan period, Liu Yin.

LIU YIN AND EREMITISM

Liu Yin (1249–93) was one of the most eminent scholars and teachers
of the age of Kubilai Khan. His biography in the *Yüan Shih*[9] tells us
that he was a native of Jung-ch'eng in Pao-ting prefecture, in what
would be modern Hopei, and that his forebears for generations had been
scholars. His father, Liu Shu, is described as a scholarly, unambitious
man who refused an appointment to a magistracy in a nearby prefecture on the excuse of illness. According to the *Yüan Shih*:

At the age of forty, he still had no son. He sighed: "If Heaven indeed causes
me to have no son, so be it. But should I have a son, I would surely make him
a scholar." On the evening when Yin was born, Shu had a dream in which a
divine being came riding a horse and bearing a child to his house, saying to
him: "Rear him well!" When Shu awoke, Yin was born.

Such circumstances surrounding the birth of talented persons are common enough, as are the descriptions of Liu Yin's youthful precosity.
Perhaps we cannot take too literally the statement that at the age of
two or three

. . . he could recognize characters, and each day could memorize passages of
a hundred or a thousand characters. He need pass his eyes over something
but once to memorize it. At the age of five he could write poetry and at six
prose. Whenever he set his pen to paper he amazed people by what he produced. By the time he reached the age of twenty his genius had fully flowered.

Liu Yin, beyond doubt, was a brilliant young scholar of whom great
things were expected. His father was a student of the Neo-Confucian
theories of human nature, and Liu Yin also studied near his own home
under Yen Mi-chien (ca. 1204–ca. 1281), a southern scholar who had
been brought to the North during the conquest of the South. Liu Yin is
said to have been impatient with mere lexical and philological studies
of the exegetical works, wanting to know the "true essence of the Sages'
teachings." The *Sung-yüan Hsüeh-an*, both in the biography of Liu Yin

and in that of Yao Shu, makes it clear that Liu felt he had really encountered the new Sung learning only when he went to Mount Su-men in Honan to study under Yao Shu.[10] This is what his biography in the *Yüan Shih* is referring to when it states:

Subsequently, when he encountered the writings of Chou Tun-i, Ch'eng I, Chang Tsai, Shao Yung, Chu Hsi, and Lü Tsu-ch'ien, he was able to expound their subtleties on first reading. "Ah!" he exclaimed, "I always said that this must exist!" Commenting on the best points of each, he said: "Shao is the most comprehensive, Chou the most intensive, and Ch'eng the most correct. Master Chu achieved the limit in comprehensiveness, exhausted intensiveness, and made it all concrete with correctness." His insight and profound perception were customarily of this order.

Struck with admiration for Chu-ko Liang's (A.D. 181–234) phrase "Quiescence wherewith to cultivate the self," he adopted the name Ching-hsiu or "Quiescent Cultivation" for his studio. This well suits the description of his personality given in his biography:

By nature Liu Yin was not gregarious; he did not enter lightly into association with other people. Although his family was very poor, he would accept nothing if it did not accord with his principles. He lived at home and taught there, maintaining rigid observance of the teacher's role. Students who came to him were taught in accordance with their native abilities, and all showed progress. High officials in great number passed through Pao-ting and hearing of Liu Yin's fame, often went to call on him. Yin usually hid himself and would not come forth to meet them. People who did not know him took this for arrogance . . .

Liu Yin had no son and heir. He died at the early age of 45 *sui* in the summer of 1293, probably at home and of some illness.

These scanty biographical data include very little that contributes to our understanding of Liu Yin as a recluse. For this we must turn to his own writings. A preface by the late sixteenth century writer Shao Pao to a reprinting of Liu's works[11] states that in Liu's essay " 'Hsi Sheng' chieh" ("An Explanation of 'Aspiring to Become a Sage' "), written when he was only eighteen, "his purpose in life is already more or less apparent." A partial translation of it follows:

It was the year *ting-mao* [1267], at the end of the . . . month. The autumn scene was as if freshly bathed. The Milky Way was bright and sparkling white. Heaven was high and the air clear. All life was at rest. At that time I, Liu Yin of I-ch'uan, was sitting in my central court. I had a goblet of wine, but on drinking it, I found it tasteless. I had a lute, but when I strummed it, no music came forth. I had a book, from the hand of Master Chou Tun-i. Called the *I-t'ung*, it is subtle of meaning and difficult to grasp. Looking aloft seeking its meaning, I found it as lofty as the blue Heavens. Taking it up again to pursue its ideas, I found it as deep as the Yellow Springs. So I took it up and read it under the stars and moon, until I came to the sentence: "The scholar aspires to become a Worthy, the Worthy aspires to become a Sage, the Sage aspires to become Heaven." This I could not comprehend, and I said with a sigh: "What vacuous words! How vast and all-enfolding is Heaven, that lofty intelligence, that divine wisdom. Who can aspire to that? Does this not deceive us who belong to later ages? How vacuous are these words!" Then I hummed a poem to the pure wind, and enjoyed the bright moonlight. I grasped at Existence, and drank of the Great Harmony. I chanted the words of the song "T'ai Ku Ts'ang Lang" ["How Vast and Empty the Primordial Beginnings"]. I raised my head to Heaven and whistled; I sighed as I sang: "How pure is the Great Void, wherein life dwells! How brilliant is the Great Source, wherein the power of creation is lodged! The Emperor Fu-hsi is remote; whom shall I acknowledge my sovereign? The age of Confucius is far away; whom shall I take as my guide and companion?" So I hummed and chanted unceasingly. I sat and dozed, and only after a long time again arose, when suddenly my courtyard was overwhelmed with an auspicious air; I seemed to hear the sound of feet on the steps, and when I looked about, saw three old men. . . . [In his dream Liu converses with the three old men, who identify themselves metaphorically as the forces governing the universe. They discuss philosophical concepts, and one of the three asks Liu why he doubted the validity of the sentence of Chou's *I-t'ung*, claiming it as his own words. This dialogue follows; Liu speaks:] I replied to him, asking, "Can Sagehood then be aspired to?" He answered, "It can." "Is there some important prerequisite for attaining it?" He replied, "There is." I asked him what this was, and he replied, "The important thing is singleness." "What is singleness?" He said, "It is the absence of desire." When I asked who can be without desire, he replied, "All the people in the world can be without desire." Then I asked if all the people in the world could not become Sages, and he replied. "They can." "In that case, this student's confusion of mind is great indeed, and I do not understand you."

The master said: "Sit down. I shall discuss it with you. You have heard that in all of Heaven and Earth, there is but one Principle [*li*] and nothing else, and through interactions it dispersed to become all things. In the end, it again comes together, again becoming one principle. Heaven and Earth are man, man is Heaven and Earth. Sages and Worthies are I, I am the Sages and Worthies. That of *li* which is present in man is perfect and penetrable. That of *li* which material things receive is imperfect and nonpenetrable. Being imperfect and nonpenetrable, there is no way by which it can be transformed. But in the case of man, the perfect and the all-penetrable can indeed be penetrated. Then what can it not achieve?

"The Sage aspires to be as Heaven. When he succeeds, he becomes one with Heaven; when he does not succeed, he is a Great Sage. The Worthy aspires to be a Sage. Surpassing that, he becomes one with Heaven; not achieving it, he is a Great Worthy. The Scholar aspires to become a Worthy. Surpassing that, he becomes a Sage; not achieving it, he still does not fail to become a man of renown. This is what makes a Sage a Sage, and what makes a Worthy a Worthy. You have been given a nature midway between Heaven and Earth, and are endowed with a physical nature that is blemish-free and submissive to the Five Constants. Your nature is the same substance of which the Sage is made; the teachings you study are the same as that which constitute the Sage's achievement. You are the same as the Sages; the Sages are the same as you. You would challenge this, at the same time thinking my words vacuous. Are you vacuous? Or is your teacher vacuous? If you pursue self-cultivation to achieve quiescence, exert yourself to achieve tranquillity, satisfy the design of your bodily organization, and fulfill your nature, from the level of mere thought you will proceed to that of divine wisdom. Being enlightened, you will possess sincerity. Do you aspire to be a Sage, or do the Sages aspire to be you? You would cast this truth aside, thinking I have cheated you! Do you cheat your teacher? Or does your teacher cheat you?" . . . [At this, Liu confesses his stupidity and his stubborn foolishness, and humbly thanks the divine visitor for his instruction. As the three take leave of him, they pat his shoulder and say encouragingly:] "Apply yourself diligently. There will come a day when we shall hear of a man of purity in the world; and that man will be you."[12]

Dominant in this interesting essay is the idea, stressed by Mencius, that anyone who works hard enough at perfecting his basically good nature can become a Sage or a Worthy. More immediately, Liu takes his language and concepts from Chou Tun-i's (1017–73) *I-t'ung* (also known as the *T'ung-shu*), or "Explanatory Text on the *Book of Changes*."[13] Liu's presentation of these concepts is somewhat naïve and impressionistic, evidence of his youth and also perhaps of the primitive state of philosophic and scholarly studies in the Mongol-ruled North China of that time. Of greatest interest to us, however, is the three sages' encouraging prediction that Liu will become known as a man of purity (*ch'ing-ts'ai*), and that he applies to himself here this term that Confucius reserved for two praiseworthy recluses: "It may be said of Yü-chung and Li-i that while they hid themselves in their seclusion, they gave a license to their words; *but in their persons they succeeded in preserving their purity, and in their retirement they acted according to the exigency of the times.*"[14]

At this age Liu did not regard purity and the official career as necessarily incompatible. In fact, many of his poems show that his devotion to purity complemented his natural desire to seek fame as a scholar and a writer and to win high position in recognition of his undoubted talents. An example is an undated poem called "Overcome with Thoughts on an Autumn Evening,"[15] the second half of which reads:

> In this life, the years of youth
> Are so fleeting. How sad it is!
> Beside the humble scholar's window, when one is old—
> How petty that life; what good comes of it?
> Learn swordsmanship, and win with it a princedom!
> With martial valor face every enemy.
> If man's ambition is to serve men,
> What use has this devotion to book and sword?
> My mind is bright and clear,
> It holds within it ways to rule the world in peace.

> If someday I encounter recognition and opportunity,
> And on all sides worthy routes open,
> I shall mount to the highest power and rank,
> Soaring aloft, borne up by strong wings.[16]
> I shall bring all the universe to order,
> Thereby establishing my name for a thousand years.

Many of these sentiments are rather conventional clichés, but the message is clear and forceful. The sword and the book, representing ability in war and peace, symbolized the ambitious young Confucian scholar's equipment and aspirations. But Liu has a mind of a higher order, enough so that sword and book are no longer needed. He feels he can "conquer the world" without sword and book, and speaks of his great ambition. He implies, however, that the times are not auspicious, and says that he must wait for "worthy routes" to open to him.

His attitude toward eremitism is set forth rather explicitly in his brief essay "An Explanation of the Sui-ch'u ["Following the Original"] Pavilion":[17]

The original mind of the superior man is to do good, and not to do evil; it is to be a superior man, and not to be a petty man. This is all there is to the matter. If a person acts in a way that is good, and does what the superior man does, then his original mind has been followed [i.e., fulfilled]. For *tao* is everlasting and omnipresent.

Hence if one wants to do what is good and be a superior man, there is no time or place in which one cannot do so. Hence there is no time and no place in which our original natures cannot be followed.

Suppose that one were to say: "My original mind-nature is to go forth and devote myself to the affairs of the world. If the times do not permit this to me, then throughout my life I shall not succeed in following my original mind-nature." That would be to say that *tao* is all on the side of coming forth to serve, and that withdrawal is in no sense ethically permissible.

Suppose that one were to say: "My original mind-nature demands that I withdraw and follow my own interests. If the times do not give me freedom for this, then throughout my life I shall not succeed in following my original mind-nature." That would be to say that *tao* is all on the side of withdrawal, and that there is nothing to be said for the life of active service.

Is *tao* in truth like that?

The *chan-shih*,[18] Mr. Chang Tzu-yu, is a man whose mind I know most intimately. He is a man who takes delight in doing what is good, and whose only fear is that he will not act as a superior man should. Recently he has built a pavilion to which he has given the name "Following the Original." His inclination is to enjoy ease and to pursue his own interests. Yet the gentlemen who have composed poems and essays about his pavilion have all stressed that since he is a man of whom great things can be expected, and since he is greatly endowed with talent and learning, he should devote himself to assisting the state and succoring humanity.

Both are wrong. His ideal principles lead him to leisurely pursuit of his interests, yet the times demand assistance and succor. Both are things of which we can approve. Yet, of his original nature, we cannot say that it has predetermined him to either of these before it can be said to have been followed. If his nature is thus—and nothing is beyond the scope of man's nature—then it is because he has sequestered himself in a sheltered corner. For *tao* is by nature omnipresent, and when it is forcibly confined to one small area, the harmful consequences can be great. If Chang Tzu-yu will think about my words, he will eventually understand my meaning.

Written in the year *jen-ch'en* of the reign period *chih-yüan* (1292), by Liu Yin.

Liu's friend Chang not only refuses to serve, but evidently refuses to take a broad interest in life and current problems as well. He has returned to his villa and built his Sui-ch'u pavilion to proclaim to the world that it is in keeping with his original nature to withdraw. Liu writes this essay not to urge him to come forth and serve, but to correct his thinking. Chang's attitude smacks of Taoism; Liu provides a Confucian corrective. He says, in essence, what Confucius meant when he stated that there was nothing for which he is predetermined and nothing against which he is predetermined. Liu wrote this in 1292, shortly before his death, and after repeatedly refusing calls to office. Clearly, then, Liu himself does not regard withdrawal as intrinsically superior to active service. There is another reason.

The same attitude toward office-holding is presented, though from a slightly different angle, in a very brief essay called "An Explanation of the Tao-kuei ["Tao-noble"] Hall." The circumstances are similar: a friend has named a hall in his home and has asked Liu for an essay explaining the name. The name comes from a poem by Shao Yung (1011–77), an outstanding Neo-Confucian of thc Northern Sung who never held any office, who lived an idyllic if austerely simple life, and who was a fine poet. Liu evidently admired Shao Yung and felt close in spirit to him; his works contain frequent references to Shao's writings. In this brief essay he is as concerned about representing Shao's idea correctly as he is about gratifying his friend. He writes:

> In Shao K'ang-chieh's poetry we find:
>> "Though lacking office, he is of himself lofty;
>> But how could one lack *tao*, and be of himself noble!"

This is not intended to relate *tao* to office, but rather is to say that the presence of *tao* is not to be decided in terms of whether or not one holds office.

If one were to understand *tao* and office as correlative, then the meaning of the two lines would be shallow and narrow, forced and strained. Not only would this interpretation display lack of knowledge of what it is that makes *tao* the *tao*, it also would display envy for superficial externals, and would be too full of errors for me to name them all. Mr. Li of Ho-chien has taken words from Shao's poetry as a name for his study, calling it Tao-kuei and has asked me to write an explanation of it, hence this.[19]

Tao here, as in the last essay quoted, means ethical principles. There are two ideas here: first, that there is no necessary correlation between the ethical evaluation of a man and the kind of a career he follows; second, that a man who lacks ethical principles is not a laudable person regardless of his career and status.

Office-holding, then, can be a good thing, but it is not the greatest good thing in the world, and it confers no glory on a man with moral deficiencies. Liu was not of course admitting moral deficiencies in himself. On the contrary, as he saw it, the chief threat to ethical principles in his time lay precisely in office-holding; hence his consistent refusal to hold office. This was undoubtedly his reasoning when he chided his contemporary, Hsü Heng, for his alacrity in accepting appointment to office.[20] When Hsü replied that unless one were eager to serve the state one could not serve the *tao*, Liu remarked that to serve the state was to fail to show proper respect for the *tao*.

Liu could have held any kind of office he might have wanted. He was offered very high and honorable positions in the Confucian Academy and the Chi-hsien Yüan (roughly equivalent to the Han-lin), and educational posts. His letter to the government official who recommended him for office the last time, in 1291, is included in his biography in the *Yüan Shih* presumably as being a work representative of his character. It reads, in part:

I have since my early youth been engaged in study, and thus have acquired some knowledge of the discourses of great persons and superior men. Though I may have learned nothing else, I can say that at least I have a very clear and thorough conception of what is meant by the moral principle of "the duties that should be observed between ruler and minister."[21] Nor need the general meaning of this be discussed; let me rather talk only in terms of its daily application in actual affairs. For by whose power do all of us of the people have the opportunity to live in peace and plenty, and thus to multiply and prosper in happiness? This is all bestowed by our ruler. And accordingly all of us who live must give either of our strength or our knowledge and abilities, but in any event each must contribute something in order to discharge his responsibility. The truth of this principle is obvious: from the most ancient times it has been unvaryingly so. This is what Chuang Chou meant when he said that "There is no escaping [the duties that should be observed between sovereign and minister] anywhere in the whole wide world."[22] I have lived forty-three years, and have not yet contributed the least bit of my strength toward repaying the nation's beneficence to me in nurturing and sustaining me. Moreover, the imperial grace has repeatedly favored me with appointments to office. Could I dare to secrete myself and not come forth to serve, to court a reputation for lofty nobility as a form of self-indulgence, thereby repudiating my nation's gracious favor in recognizing me, and still have received the most excellent and righteous teaching of the Sage? On the contrary, from my early youth onward, in my mind I have never for even one day dared to be in any way aloof and superior, eccentric or deviant from the usual course. All my friends, if they know me at all, know that this is the true state of my mind. However, it may be that rumors exist about me which fail to represent the truth of the case. Seeing only what my actions might seem to indicate, some have labeled me a proud and lofty recluse. However, you, sir, know that I have never so considered myself. Please permit me to explain the circumstances of my repeated refusals to serve item by item . . . [There follows a detailed résumé of his illnesses, the illness and death of his mother, and the like.] I am in truth a most remote and humble servitor. My case is different from that of the many gentlemen who hold office, for their coming to accept office and retirement from it seems to present no difficult problems for them. I am always dependent on your excellency's assistance to me.[23]

This letter was addressed to an unnamed chief minister who had been responsible for recommending Liu's appointment. It was not a simple matter to decline such an appointment; the government of Kubilai Khan had been known to bring persons forcibly to the capital, and it might not accept mere disinclination to serve without satisfactory reasons. Liu's closing sentence is an appeal for assistance in prevailing upon the court to accept his refusal. The court did not subject Liu to further pressure to serve, and the Emperor Kubilai Khan on hearing of the matter is said to have remarked: "In antiquity there were the so-called 'servitors who could not be summoned.' They must have been of the same type as this person!"

The remark about servitors who cannot be summoned, of course, is a reference to Mencius. Liu was forced to counter rumors that he was arrogant and critical of the government; his illness at the time was probably real, but it was not the real reason for his refusal. The real reason was known to Kubilai Khan, for in using Mencius' phrase he must have been conscious of the context in which Mencius used it. The passage reads:

Mencius said: ". . . The philosopher Tseng-tzu said, 'The wealth of Ch'in and Ch'u cannot be equaled. Let their rulers have their wealth—I have my benevolence. Let them have their nobility—I have my righteousness. Wherein should I be dissatisfied as inferior to them? Now shall we say that these sentiments are not right? Seeing that the philosopher Tseng-tzu said them, there is in them, I apprehend, a real principle. In the Empire there are three things universally acknowledged to be honorable. Nobility [i.e., noble or royal rank] is one of them; age is one of them; virtue is one of them. At the court, nobility holds the first place of the three; in villages, age holds the first place; and for helping one's generation and presiding over the people, the other two are not equal to virtue. How can one who possesses only one of these presume to despise one who possesses the other two? Therefore a prince who is to accomplish great deeds will certainly have *ministers whom he cannot summon.* When he wishes to consult with them, he goes to them. The prince who does not honor the virtuous, and delight in their ways of doing, to this extent, is not worth having to do with."[24]

Mencius here establishes the ideal of the proud and independent scholar, the man of ability and virtue, who sets his own standards for service and who need not consider himself in any way inferior to the ruler himself. It is to the credit of Kubilai Khan's intelligence that he labeled Liu Yin correctly, and to the credit of his magnanimity that he let the matter rest with an amused remark, which incidentally contained a gracious compliment to Liu.

It should be pointed out that Liu's refusal to serve did not spring from any sense of loyalty to another dynasty. Liu was born under Yüan rule. Moreover, he evidently felt no sense of attachment to the Sung as a dynasty, to judge from his poems, which include a *fu* "On the Crossing of the Yangtze" celebrating the progress of the Mongol forces against the collapsing Southern Sung in 1275.[25] Much less was he attached to the Chin dynasty, which fell in 1234, fifteen years before his birth.[26] On the other hand, that he strongly endorsed the virtue of absolute loyalty to one dynasty is clear from his poem ridiculing Feng Tao, who served four dynasties in succession in the Five Dynasties period. Ou-yang Hsiu's history of the period, in discussing Feng, served to make him a symbol of the unrighteous servitor wanting in every virtue, but particularly in the virtue of loyalty.[27] Liu concurred completely with this judgment; his four short lines on Feng are even more devastating than Ou-yang's long and vehement discourse.[28] Elsewhere, too, Liu shows himself to be completely in harmony with the Neo-Confucian concept of loyalty, notably in his admiration for the recluse T'ao Yüan-ming (also known as T'ao Ch'ien, A.D. 372–427), whose eremitism Liu considered to have been motivated by loyalty to the Eastern Chin dynasty (317–419).[29]

LIU YIN AND TAOISM

We have seen that Liu Yin was devoted to the principle of loyalty and all of the Neo-Confucian connotations of the word and that he felt no sense of attachment to any dynasty other than the Yüan. Accordingly, we must look further for a clear expression of his reasons for refusing to serve the Yüan government.

It should be clear by now that Liu felt himself to be completely within the Confucian fold, and that Taoism, with its self-centered lack of concern for the world of affairs, could not have appreciably influenced his decision to withdraw. To be sure, there was, and there continued to be, a natural tendency to associate eremitism with Taoism; and later writers, seeing Taoist terms used in Liu's poetry, have accused him of promoting Taoist concepts.[30] But if any doubt remains, it is easily dispelled by Liu's specific and emphatic statements of his attitude toward Taoism.

Liu was not bigoted toward Taoism, but he was convinced that it was unreasonable, in some ways fundamentally unethical, and in many ways inferior to the Confucian teachings. In a long essay outlining what a man should study and why it merited study, Liu mentions the Taoists first under the "various schools of philosophy":

After studying history, one can go on to read the various schools of philosophy. *Lao-tzu, Chuang-tzu, Lieh-tzu,* and the *Yin-fu Ching*[31]—these four works are all of one kind. Although they are classified as Taoist writings, within them are contained some things which are quite in accord with principle. One does well to take from them merely those things which accord with principle, and ignore their [misleading] metaphors . . .[32]

Perhaps Liu's attitude toward Taoism is best seen in his essay on a painting of Chuang-tzu dreaming that he was a butterfly, portions of which follow:

Chuang Chou's theories are a development from those of the Diplomatists.[33] They represent the thought of persons whose ambitions have been frustrated by the conditions of their age, and who seek only safety in a world of chaos. Nonetheless his genius was great, and his concepts are very broad. There are persons who cannot be self-sustaining. They see how vast the world is, and how great the span of time from the past to the present. They observe how comprehensive and how abundant are the achievements of the Sages and Worthies, and how tiny and insignificant they themselves are, how they are as if adrift among all the innumerable and motley things of this world for but a brief moment of time. Thus they say "right" and "wrong," "permissible" and "not permissible," are things which should be left beyond our concern, while they concern themselves with matters of gain and loss, long life or short. They do not admit the relevance of righteousness to their problems. They fall back on adopting the manners and attitudes of the unlettered common people, seeking to achieve by this means a kind of temporary security, but they do not achieve it. It is all vague fancy and specious ramblings. They take some real object or event and transfer it to the realm of fantasy, and having achieved a simile, they enlarge on it in the most unrestrained and unwarranted fashion. Blindly they proclaim themselves to be beyond the present realities of Heaven and earth and all creation. Seen in this light, even though they themselves speak of fantasy, they do not perhaps see wherein the fantasy really lies. It is a fantasy which they do not recognize as fantasy.

Hence they can scarcely apprehend what I mean when I speak of "equalizing"; they can hardly be expected to fathom what I mean when I speak of "no end that cannot be reached." What I refer to when I speak of "equalizing," when I speak of "no end that cannot be reached," are things which are subject to *tao* [i.e., ethical principle], and therefore one can lead the most active of public lives without increase of it, and one can live in the extremity

of withdrawal without loss of it. It accommodates itself to times and situations, it fits its form to the reality about it. Where does one go that there is
not equalization? Where would one go that one cannot? This is what I mean
by "equalizing" and "the possible." For [in philosophy] it is necessary to follow step by step and to exhaust the limits of reason; only in that way can one
talk about a thing.

But Chuang Chou does not proceed in that fashion. He starts by recount-
ing some tale in the realm of fantasy, and insists that somewhere in the dark
and vague confusion of it all there lies what he calls *tao*. What careless person with no patience for details is not delighted by such simplicity, and anxious to adopt it? And as for persons who find themselves rebuked by the strict
principles of morality and propriety, or whose ambitions have been frustrated
by the conditions of their time, how many of them feel benefited by such
theories and drawn to them! Of course it is unnecessary to mention those who
felt this way among the *Cheng-shih* and *Hsi-ning* factions.[34] But even among
men known in the world as leading Confucians there are frequently encountered those who, on suffering setbacks, fall back on such ideas, seeking
solace and diversion. In short, it can only be said that none of them know the
meaning of righteousness . . .[35]

Liu's argument here is entirely directed against the central ideas of the
chapter "Ch'i-wu lun" in *Chuang-tzu*, which closes with the anecdote
illustrated in the painting on which he wrote this essay. Chuang-tzu,
awaking after dreaming he was a butterfly, asks: "Am I Chuang Chou
who dreamed I was a butterfly, or am I really a butterfly dreaming I
am Chuang Chou?" This chapter sums up the Taoist concept of the
relativity of truth and falsehood, right and wrong, and all the other
distinctions which Confucianism meticulously maintained. To Chuang-
tzu, such distinctions are essentially inconsequential. Liu states in the
beginning of his essay that he simply does not know what Chuang-tzu
meant by the butterfly metaphor. If Chuang-tzu chooses to speculate
that there are no distinctions or restrictions in the realm of fantasy, he
has the right to do so, but fantasy after all is not reality. Real equalization and power can come only through recognizing the omnipresence
of an *ethical Tao*.

Throughout this essay we see Taoism rejected on several grounds.
First, it is irrational; it relies on "dark and vague confusion." Second,
it ignores the fundamental ethical questions. The repudiation of true
and false, of right and wrong, is self-deception that has evil social consequences. Selfish concern solely with one's own immediate good is
both evil and impractical to Liu. Taoists fall back on primitive ways,
rejecting civilization, but the security they seek is not to be had in that
way. Liu's faith is in a Confucian concept of security to be gained
through the application of human intelligence in ordering society and
maintaining standards of morality.

Third, and of most interest here, Taoists in Liu's mind are weak defeatists; they are frustrated persons seeking easy solutions. Taoism is to them a respectable-sounding cover for their inability to meet the problems of life, to maintain their integrity and to do what society expects of them. This aspect of Taoism he rejects most positively. He rejects it for himself, and he warns others to avoid confusion which may result from careless use of terms that are capable of a Taoist interpretation. Note in this connection his "Explanation of 'The Studio of Stupidity' ":

Scholars and gentlemen in recent ages have often selected words meaning ignorance and stupidity and lack of refinement—things in themselves not at all laudable—as their studio names. Such persons are not necessarily really like that, nor are they intentionally making a mere gesture of humility. There is, to be sure, some reason in it; their intent can be of two kinds.

It may be that they are distressed by the great departure from ethical standards as evidenced in the lack of integrity and the low public morality. In this case their intent is to cling to fundamental values as a kind of self-corrective. Thus they adopt such names with the feeling that it is necessary to do so, and their intent is as if to say: "Rather than err in that direction, I would prefer to err in this one." Having this kind of attitude, they are guilty of no moral fault.

Or it may be that some are expressing the ideas of Lao-tzu and Chuang-tzu, in which case it is quite a different matter. They feel that the whole world, past and present, must inevitably revert to such a state [of ignorance and lack of refinement] in order to approach the *Tao* with no expenditure of effort. They retain all their resources in order to keep themselves whole. They adopt such names as a matter of preference, and not because they feel compelled to do so. Their purpose is to benefit themselves, and nothing more.

Should the former theory be generally practiced, it would cause everybody to uphold the basic values, and would not be without benefit to the world at large. But if the latter should come to be widely accepted, then all the people in the world would take to crude rusticity and would flee from the world; how far its harmful effects would spread! Alas! Even in so small a matter the subtleties of intent and method and the distinction between righteousness and selfishness can be so great as this! One cannot be careless in such things . . .[36]

In another essay written on a similar theme and with a similar purpose in mind, Liu again states this idea very forcefully. He grants that Lao-tzu's concept of the *Tao* has certain admissible features, but condemns its practical manifestations as self-centered individualism, as incompatible with ethics, and as potentially disastrous to the nation and the people. This is in an essay explaining the name of "The Studio of Withdrawal." The use of such a Taoist-sounding name is permissible, Liu feels, if it is used in the self-corrective sense, but not if it is used in the Taoist sense. "I am delighted," he says of his friend, "about Chung-li's withdrawal, but at the same time I want him to be most careful about his own reasons for having chosen to withdraw."[37]

To sum up, Liu Yin evidently was very clear-minded about Taoist thought and its implications. That is not to say that he was conscious of Neo-Confucian borrowings from Taoism, i.e., that he would have explained them as such, or that he wished to rout them from the canon. But he was very conscious of a gulf between his own Confucian orthodoxy and what he and like-minded Confucians called Taoist heterodoxy. He was particularly sensitive to the fact that withdrawal seemed to imply the acceptance of Taoist principles and emphatically denied the implication. Thus we must look beyond Taoism for the explanation of Liu's withdrawal.

LIU YIN AS A VOICE OF PROTEST

The real reason for Liu's eremitism is by now clear. "To serve under such conditions would be to show lack of respect for *tao*." Times were hard. Liu's teacher Yao Shu withdrew to a life of seclusion and teaching at Mount Su-men in protest against the corruption of government and the sense of defilement he felt on participating in it. Liu's fellow scholar at Su-men, Hsü Heng, whose sense of responsibility led him repeatedly to serve in high positions at court, nonetheless was frequently overcome with despair, and frequently resigned out of a sense of frustration and protest. Throughout the Yüan period it became increasingly difficult for men of integrity to remain in office. Liu had no less desire than others to achieve fame and honor, but he had a clearer perception of the extent of the compromise that office-holding would demand of him. Moreover, having early fixed for himself an ideal of purity, he was more than usually sensitive in ethical matters, with the result that his personal bent reinforced his objective conclusions. Only one decision was possible. He stubbornly refused to serve, devoted himself to teaching others the same moral standards by which he lived (most of his students refused appointments), and by implication rebuked those who did serve, especially those who served dishonorably. In addition, as we have seen, he occasionally gave vent to his feelings in his writings, above all in his poetry.

If one reads Liu's poetry with care, one finds in it much that can be taken as the expression of his resentment. There is nothing explicit or dramatic; nothing of the ringing accents of a Tom Paine or the incisive satire of a Voltaire. No precedent for either existed in the China of Liu Yin, and nothing in Liu Yin's life is without precedent. Yet the protest is there. Its influence can only be estimated, but it must have been significant.

Consider the following stanza:

When one is born in a degenerate and disorderly age
And there is no one worthy of being called a ruler, who would want
to serve?
If one must drift and float like a cross-current in a measureless ocean,
Is it because one would have chosen to do so?

This stanza is quoted out of context. Does it really mean what it seems here to mean, or is there perhaps some less subversive explanation? As it happens, the above stanza is the first four lines in a poem of fourteen lines; the remaining lines speak of the pleasures of peaceful rural existence, and the poem ends with an expression of the people's cause for rejoicing in the good fortune of having an emperor whose might assures their peace and happiness. Moreover, the poem is one of a collection written to the rhyme patterns and poetic forms of T'ao Yüan-ming.[38] It is usually possible to construe these poems as poetic extensions of the mood of T'ao's originals, thereby making them Liu's conception of the voice of T'ao, rather than the voice of Liu himself. In their poetic ambiguity, it is also often possible to see them as philosophic reflections on theoretical rather than on actual conditions. It is precisely this poetic ambiguity that Liu relied on as a veil for his true intent, a veil that could protect him without obscuring his meaning from those readers by whom he wanted to be understood. Ch'ien Mu, the modern scholar and historian of Chinese thought, has quoted the above stanza as an expression of Liu Yin's true feelings about his own environment and his own fate;[39] I wholly concur with this interpretation. However, in bald translation and out of context, the poem's essential ambiguity is lost, and no problem of interpretation seems to exist. The degree to which translation represents interpretation and eliminates the ambiguity which is a consciously-employed element in the original must be kept in mind.

If I am right about Liu Yin's intentions, it is in this collection of poems written on the model of T'ao Yüan-ming's poetry that we find the most profound expression of Liu's protest. Liu's seven poems written matching the form and rhyme of T'ao's "Ho Yung P'in Shih ("In Praise of Poor Scholars") are of interest here, because Liu has adopted T'ao's subject as well as his form. The fourth is as follows:

Sticks and stones can bear being spit upon,
Minister Lou Shih-te is not alone in that.
And if spitting were as rain,
Not even the most intemperate man would react to it.
To be without preconceptions is the "upright way."
To suppress one's natural feelings is in truth the way of Chuang Chou.
"What is beyond my own self is of no concern to me."

"What does it matter to me if one stands by my side with breast and
    arms bare!"
Po I looked upon the whole world
And wished that all men might stand with him.
I say that it was Liu-hsia Hui who was narrow-minded;
Let the reader himself find my reasons for saying so.

The allusions in this poem are to a historical figure of the T'ang dynasty,
and to two officials-turned-recluse who are discussed and compared
both in the *Analects* and in *Mencius*. Lou Shih-te (630–99) of the T'ang
was a man whose forbearance was so great that he did not approve of a
man's so much as flickering an eyelid if someone spat in his face. When
someone asked him, "Do you mean you would just wipe it off and nothing
more?" he replied that he would not even bother to wipe it off; he would
be so unmoved that he would let the spittle dry by itself.[40] This, says
Liu, is unnatural in humans, but comes naturally to sticks and stones,
if there is any virtue in men's adopting the standards of sticks and stones!
Liu extends this idea, and applies it to his comparison of the two figures
of antiquity. To be without preconceptions is bad; it implies being
without ethical standards, since ethical standards must be fixed in advance so that they can be adhered to under all conditions. The "upright
way" is the way in which Confucius described the conduct of Liu-hsia
Hui, and it is not unqualified praise; it implies a kind of straightforward
integrity without any sensitivity to higher moral principles. Lou Shih-te
and Liu-hsia Hui, Liu feels, were alike in unnaturally suppressing their
feelings, in insensitivity to feelings of defilement. This is Taoistic (line
6); the Taoist has his whole world within himself, hence cannot be defiled or revolted by his surroundings or by what people do to him
(line 7).

    The poet's real intent is seen in his comparison of Liu-hsia Hui and
Po I in the last lines. Line 8 quotes Liu-hsia Hui in the anecdote told
in Mencius, from which the poem takes its text. Mencius says of Po I
that he

"would not serve a prince whom he did not approve, nor associate with a
friend whom he did not esteem . . . He thought it necessary, if he happened
to be standing with a villager whose cap was not rightly adjusted, to leave
him with a high air, as if he were going to be defiled."

Liu-hsia Hui, on the other hand,

. . . was not ashamed to serve an impure prince, nor did he think it low to be
an inferior officer. When advanced to employment, he did not conceal his
virtue, but made it a point to carry out his principles. When neglected and
left without office, he did not murmur. When straitened by poverty, he did
not grieve. Accordingly, he had a saying, "You are you, and I am I. Although

you stand by my side with breast and arms bare, or with your body naked, how can you defile me?" Therefore self-possessed, he companied with men indifferently, at the same time not losing himself. When he wished to leave, if pressed to remain in office, he would remain. He would remain in office, when pressed to do so, not counting it required by his purity to go away. Mencius said, "Po I was narrow-minded, and Liu-hsia Hui was wanting in self-respect. The superior man will not follow either narrow-mindedness, or the want of self-respect."[41]

Liu wished to present Po I in a better light. He sees Po I as identifying himself with the will of the people, and hence insistent on standards of ethics which benefited all of the people. Thus he would not serve, and thus no doubt Liu saw himself, for to serve a ruler who commanded no respect, or to serve side by side with persons of whom one could not approve, would require that one unnaturally curb one's spontaneous reactions to them, and this to Liu would have been Taoistic.

We can well imagine that Liu saw Hsü Heng as the very type of a contemporary Liu-hsia Hui. Hsü responded eagerly to calls to serve at the Yüan court under what to Liu must have seemed most defiling conditions, yet undeniably served with uprightness. It is pertinent to recall that Liu criticized Hsü as being superficially Confucian, but Taoistic at heart. Confucius gives qualified praise to Liu-hsia Hui for being upright (*Analects*, XVIII/2), but elsewhere criticizes him for having "surrendered his will and submitted to taint his person" (*Analects*, XCIII/8/3). This is Liu Yin's criticism of Liu-hsia Hui, and by implication he extends it to all men who serve, however honestly and uprightly, in evil times like his own. Mencius intended to point out a middle course of action, between Po I's extreme insistence on personal purity and Liu-hsia Hui's utter lack of self-respect. Liu Yin feels that the Mencian judgment fails to do justice to Po I, and he makes a strong defense of his ideal of purity.

In another poem in the same collection, Liu says:

> Those who uphold *tao* (i.e., ethics) frequently are led to follow a solitary course.
> This practice has existed since Chou and Ch'in times.
> The solitary course of the recluse moreover merits approval;
> What kind of person would weakly submit to defiling himself?
>
> . . . .
>
> In a degenerate final age,
> Is it not meaningless to possess Confucian rank and office?[42]

And in another:

> Is not this life of man a life of toil?
> Through all antiquity it has been so declared.
> Who can be idle and unproductive?

Rise early, and only at dusk return and sleep.
To live such a life is not what I most honor,
But neither is having to till my own land what I sigh about.
However, if I can but attain my desire,
How gladly I'll surrender the glories and comforts of high station.

There follow allusions to worthy recluses of history who suffered want and discomfort in maintaining their high principles, and Liu ends by invoking their decisions as a justification for his own.[43] Praise of the recluses of antiquity is frequently seen in Liu's poetry; in particular, he refers several times to the "four white-haired ones" (*ssu hao*), and wrote two poems in praise of them. They were four old men who, having fled the terrors of Ch'in, ignored repeated calls to come forth and serve the founder of the Han dynasty. At last Han Kao-tsu's chief minister Chang Liang (d. 192 B.C.) used a ruse to get them to appear at court in the retinue of the heir-apparent. The emperor, astonished at their appearance, reproached them: "I have sought you for many years, and you have always fled from me and concealed yourselves. How is it that you are now in the service of my son?" They replied: "You, sire, despise scholars and are given to reviling them. It is contrary to our principles to submit to insult, and we accordingly fled and concealed ourselves. But we have heard that the crown prince is benevolent and filial, respectful and reverent, and venerates scholars. All the world would strain to die in the crown prince's service, hence we too have come forth."[44] Liu's praise of these four inevitably calls to mind this famous conversation, recorded in the *Shih Chi*. The implications are obvious.

Many other passages from Liu's poetry could be cited to the same effect, but it is perhaps best to spare the reader further translations, which (in my hands, at least) do far less than justice to the originals.

It remains to consider the extent to which Liu Yin spoke for the literati of his time, and the extent of his influence. The more one reads in the writings of the period, the clearer it becomes that Liu in his eremitism represents a large and growing segment of the Yüan literati. Read the biographies of recluses, of persons in residence away from their native places, and of local worthies and literary figures in the local gazetteers of the Yüan, or in the sections devoted to the Yüan in the much more numerous extant gazetteers of the Ming. Particularly in the less troubled areas of the South, where such persons tended to gather, you will find a disproportionately large number of persons who are presented as recluses, or as former officials who had been forced to retire from the official career, and were living in seclusion or eking out a living by teaching. Or look through Ku Ssu-li's comprehensive anthology, the *Yüan Shih Hsüan*, and note the large number of pessimistic poems written by persons to whose names is added the comment "lived as a recluse, and would not serve in office."

Many other sources could be cited. All that can be learned of the period reinforces the belief that it was one in which ambitious Confucian scholars found official appointments both hard to come by and unattractive on ethical grounds. Both those who like Liu refused to serve, and those who tried to serve only to become disillusioned, suffered feelings of resentment and frustration. Their Confucian training led them to hold the ruler and his government responsible for their own and the country's sorry plight. Most, like Liu, expressed some resentment, but generally accepted the situation as a matter of fate. Few indeed were spurred to rebellion. This passivity, this inclination to blame fate and wait for a better day, is yet another problem, and one whose explanation goes beyond the scope of this study. But can it not be said that this low potential for defiant political action was in part the result of the Neo-Confucian stress on loyalty, and its acceptance in principle of extreme authoritarianism exercised by an unapproachable and unreproachable emperor?

COMPULSORY EREMITISM

As we have seen, the Neo-Confucian concept of loyalty demanded that the loyal official of a fallen dynasty withdraw into lifelong retirement on the fall of the dynasty under which he first took service. This concept of loyalty, which one looks for in vain in the thought of Confucius and Mencius, gradually took form in the imperial period, and in fact assumed its later importance only in the Northern Sung period, when the concept of unlimited despotism was reaching its theoretical heights. Unlimited despotism demanded theoretical adjustments. The position of the ruler had to be elevated, and the gulf between ruler and servitor had to be deepened. Ssu-ma Kuang (1019–86), an influential spokesman and theoretician for this position, went so far as to repudiate the Mencian theory that the virtuous servitor was entitled to oppose the wishes of the tyrannical ruler. Mencius had said that of the three most honored things—age, noble rank, and virtue—virtue is by far the most valuable to state and society, thereby giving the virtuous servitor a kind of equality with the ruler. Ssu-ma Kuang found this wholly unacceptable.[45]

In the spurious "Classic of Loyalty" (*Chung-ching*), a work whose text and commentary are falsely attributed to Ma Jung and Cheng Hsüan, respectively (both of the Han period), there exists a most interesting expression of this new extreme in Confucian authoritarian thinking. This work is now regarded as a forgery of the period from the late T'ang to the early Sung, but was widely accepted as genuine in the Sung and later periods.[46] Similar in form and style to the *Hsiao-ching*, or "Classic of Filial Piety," it develops at length the theme that *hsiao* (filial submission) and *chung* (loyalty) are parallel virtues, different only in the area of their application and equally fundamental to all morality. However, *chung* here is not the ancient reciprocal loyalty of Confucius and Mencius, but is redefined as a one-way, utterly blind devotion to the sacrosanct ruler by all of his servitors. To be sure, the servitors of an erring ruler are required to censure and guide him in a humble and respectful manner, but they must remain obedient and loyal whether or not he heeds their censure. They must look upon death as a small matter as compared to compromise of virtue. The concept of loyalty embodied in this work became general among Neo-Confucianists of the rationalist school; hence it is not surprising to find it echoed by Chu Hsi, who wrote: "Father and son, ruler and servitor—herein lies the fixed principle of the universe. There is no escaping it anywhere in the whole wide world."[47] The second sentence is straight from the *Chuang-tzu*, where it is used to disparage what the Taoists considered to be the Confucian error of overstressing the duty of loyalty. In applying it to both *hsiao* and *chung*, Chu Hsi not only reflects the attitudes of the "Classic of Loyalty," but accepts as correct Confucianism a statement about loyalty that originated not in Confucianism, but in Taoist ridicule of Confucianism.

The unity of the Ch'eng-Chu or orthodox school of Neo-Confucianism on the subject of compulsory loyalty can be further illustrated by referring again to the case of Feng Tao (d. A.D. 954), the high official of the Five Dynasties period who served four dynasties in succession. Feng Tao by objective standards was anything but an evil man. Originally the historians dealt favorably with him, reporting factually that in his youth he had displayed unusual filial piety, that as a high official he had served ably and energetically, and that as a man he was cultivated, humane, and possessed of literary talent, albeit a trifle conceited. Ou-yang Hsiu was the first to reverse this judgment. In his vehement comments on Feng's biography in the *Wu-tai Shih-chi*, Ou-yang makes Feng the very symbol of the immoral servitor; for all his virtues, his incredible readiness to transfer his allegiance convicts him of an utter lack of integrity and of the sense of shame. Ssu-ma Kuang, in his *Tzu-chih T'ung-chien* (ch. 291), repeats Ou-yang's condemnation:

Heaven and Earth have their fixed positions; the Sage takes them as his models in determining the social norms [*li*] and establishing laws [*fa*]. Within, there is the relationship of husband and wife; without, that of ruler and servitor. The wife follows her husband, and to the end of her days will not remarry.

The servitor serves his ruler, and will die in preference to serving another. This is the great standard of human ethics. Should it be abandoned, no greater chaos could be imagined. . . . If a servitor is not loyal, even though he be possessed of abundant ability and intelligence and have an excellent record in administration, he is not to be highly valued. Why is this? It is because he lacks the most fundamental aspect of integrity. . . . Rulers rose and fell in succession; Feng Tao continued to hold wealth and high position as if nothing had happened. This is indeed the extreme example of the treacherous official. I believe that the servitor can lose his life thereby preserving his virtue complete, but cannot seek to preserve his life thereby destroying his virtue; how then can we call a man worthy who specializes only in preserving his life and fending off dangers to himself? . . . Moreover, this is not solely the crime of Feng Tao; the rulers of the time must also assume some of the responsibility.

Chu Hsi takes the same line. The *T'ung-chien Kang-mu*, while only in small part directly from Chu Hsi's pen, was produced under his supervision and can be considered as expressing his sentiments. In its comments on the death of Feng Tao (ch. 59), the criticisms originating with Ou-yang Hsiu and developed by Ssu-ma Kuang are further extended. Feng's objective virtues and abilities are again recorded (as they are throughout this period, to the credit of Chinese historiography), but they are explicitly said to have been completely negated by his one great failing, and he is once again presented as the most sinister kind of moral leper. By this time his symbolic value had come completely to overshadow the objective truth about him. Even Chu Hsi, astute critic of history that he elsewhere showed himself to be, had no thought of setting this matter straight. For him it was "straight" as Ou-yang Hsiu presented it. For him, too, the symbolic value outweighed the objective facts.

In contrast with earlier moral thinking, Neo-Confucianism laid greater stress on formalized patterns of behavior; moral principles now came to require rigid observance of strict rules. The virtues of chastity and filial piety and the observance of mourning all became increasingly rigid and severe; and the same was true of "loyalty."

For example, the concept of chastity, prior to the Sung Neo-Confucian redefinition of it, had little of the harsh and unnatural character it subsequently acquired. Relations between the sexes were relatively free in T'ang and earlier times, and the re-marriage of widows was commonplace, even in the highest levels of literati society. Subsequently, however, upper-class women were ever more rigorously confined, and the re-marriage of a widow, or even of an affianced girl who had never seen her husband-to-be, became a shameless and even a legally punishable act. And there was a similar transformation in many of the other virtues of earlier Confucianism. Filial piety came to mean the utter subservience of younger to elder. A strict and unreasoning observance of mourning became obligatory, at times to the complete extinction of its humane content. These extremes, which were witnessed and commented on by nineteenth and twentieth century Westerners in China so much that we have come to think of them as typical expressions of the spirit of Chinese civilization, are in fact late developments quite out of keeping with the entire atmosphere of earlier China.

A forced and unnatural withdrawal from life, in the name of morality, was demanded of widows. Filial submission, when extreme, intruded unnaturally into both family and public life. At least a temporary withdrawal was demanded of persons in mourning for their parents, overriding the duty of the official to the state, and disrupting unnaturally the life of the family. Thus both family and state, the twin foci of Confucian emphasis, suffered from the dehumanizing effects of Neo-Confucian morality, a morality which in fact strove to strengthen the authoritarian character of both family and state. Ultimately, this morality was detrimental to both; in a word, it was irrational.

Demanding absolute loyalty to a fallen dynasty of its servitors was equally irrational. In theory, it imposed a lifetime of uselessness on countless proven and experienced statesmen, and denied a career to many young men who had only just launched their careers under the old dynasty, men who were in no sense personally responsible for their misfortune. Of course this moral prohibition was never fully effective; some found ways to evade it, and some flouted it. But by and large it was precisely those persons who could not bring themselves to evade or flout moral prohibitions who were potentially the most valuable servants of state and society, and whose services successor dynasties were denied.

EXAMPLES AMONG SUNG LOYALISTS

The active career of the famous Sung loyalist Hsieh Fang-te[48] (d. 1289) began in the 1250's, some twenty-five years before the fall of the Sung. From the very beginning of his career he was noted for his penetrating criticism of Sung government and officials. He courageously disputed with powerful ministers, and repeatedly got into trouble. He was deprived of his official posts for several years, was demoted, rebuked, and punished. A participant in the military disaster at the time of the Mongol conquest, when Sung armies would not fight, he saw at first hand the incompetence of the Sung forces and the inevitability of the Sung collapse. Hsieh knew Sung government from the inside, saw its faults and weaknesses, and was sternly critical of it. After the fall of Hangchow in 1276 he returned to his home in Fukien, where he lived in retirement as a teacher.

The Yüan court thought such a man might be willing to serve, and offered him a number of attractive posts. He refused every one, not because he considered the Yüan government inferior to the Sung (though he doubtless did), not because he had any expectation that the Sung might rally and return to power, not primarily because of his distaste for the crude and cruel Mongol conquerors, but from his emotional devotion to the principle of loyalty itself. As far as can be seen, Hsieh was a clear-headed and practical-minded man up to the year of the disaster, 1276; his irrational behavior commenced in that year. When the Yangtze Valley bastions were falling rapidly to the Mongol forces in the winter of 1275–76, many of them without a fight, Hsieh (in disguise and wearing mourning robes) went into the newly occupied areas and wept in the market places, making a display of his grief on the passing of the dynasty as a rebuke to those who had surrendered. Throughout the remainder of his life—until he finally starved himself on being taken to the Mongol capital in the hope he could be made to accept office—he displayed unwavering loyalty to the fallen Sung, refusing to use the new Yüan calendar, referring to the former emperor as if he were still reigning, reproaching Chinese who had accepted the Mongols as their legitimate rulers, and doing his best to incite resistance to the new dynasty (albeit without any real program or organization). Moreover, for this irrational behavior he was so generally praised that even the Mongol court was obliged to recognize a kind of moral correctness in his defiance. As for the Chinese literati class, Mongol-servers and Mongol-haters alike made a hero of him.

Very similar was the case of Hsieh's most famous fellow Sung loyalist, Wen T'ien-hsiang. Wen was a brilliant scholar turned military leader, a heroic and upright man, and an entirely sympathetic character. The comments appended to his biography in the *Sung Shih* (ch. 418) praise him above all for working tirelessly at his military effort to turn back the Mongols after the fall of Hangchow when he and everyone else could see that it was doomed to failure. A Ming writer, in a colophon to Wen's collected works, praises him on the same grounds:

At the fall of the Sung those righteous and unyielding servitors who died in the service of their dynasty were very numerous. But of all of those who died maintaining their moral principles, there were none whose heroic qualities equaled Wen's. . . . The Sung dynasty, by the *Te-yu reign* [1276], was ended; the Mandate of Heaven had left it. It was a situation that no one scholar could save. Nor was Wen unaware of this . . .[49]

Wen T'ien-hsiang earned the praise of eight hundred years of Chinese writers, not for showing stubborn faith in victory which would have to be earned against great odds, but for remaining loyal to the principle of loyalty when he knew his cause was hopeless, even lacking the sanction of Heaven.

Perhaps the extreme of such irrational behavior in a national hero is seen in the case of a third Sung loyalist, Cheng Ssu-hsiao. Cheng was in his twenties at the time of the fall of Hangchow. He had passed the first examinations, but had had no career as an official in the Sung government. He nonetheless spent the rest of his life expressing his implacable hatred of the Mongols and his intense devotion to the fallen Sung. In his writings, which may have circulated in manuscript during the Yüan period (they were not published until they were rediscovered late in the Ming),[50] he calls the Mongols inhuman beasts and uncivilized trespassers on China's soil. But his devotion to the Sung cause was far less a matter of racial antagonism than of attachment to what he regarded as the tenets of Confucian morality, among them the oneness of the virtues of filial subservience, of the faithfulness of wives to one husband, and of loyalty to one dynasty. He wrote:

I have heard my father say: "To live or to die is a small matter, but a moral lapse is a great matter. The servitor of one ruler will die in preference to serving another." Moreover, he told me: "The family teaching that I received from my father and grandfather, and that sustained the family, has consisted purely of filial piety and loyalty. I pass it on to you. Do not forget your father's words!" Often I have sat through the night, alone and forlorn, overcome with grief and choking with sobs, turning over and over in my mind these thoughts of country and of family. Ruler and teacher alike have instructed and nourished me with these same principles. My father and mother have taught me and reared me the same way. Yet today I am forced to be otherwise. How can I bear it![51]

His idealization of Sung rule, a constant theme of his writings, is seen in his poem "Thinking about the Men of the Past Generation":

In the past, in the age of the former emperor,
Who faced the sun for forty years,[52]
The bright light of learning and refinement flooded the world,
And superior and heroic men stood before their ruler.
But once the barbarian soldiers invaded,
With sudden shock, Han rule was toppled.
To this day the proper ways of men are in chaos.
To lonely mountain valleys have fled all the worthies of the former
    age.
In that age of peace, the ways of the superior man flourished,
Men of talent appeared who were models of human achievement.

With open hearts they looked on the sun and moon,
From their mouths flowed words of lofty and noble import.
The auspicious atmosphere was almost that of the Three Dynasties of
    antiquity,
Literary standards were taken directly from the Six Classics.
Today the likes of it are not to be seen.
As I look about there is darkness on all sides.[53]

Cheng himself was faced with the necessity of reconciling conflicting demands of the Confucian morality which he so venerated. In his "Song Written on Falling into Captivity," written in the winter of 1275–76 after the fall of Soochow, where Cheng was living, he first describes the treachery by which Soochow was surrendered and his chagrin at seeing others associating with the conquerors, and then reflects:

As I remember my father's teachings
Day and night I shed tears of blood, and am nearly mad with grief.
There is my old mother, ill with her old illness,
Dependent on me to keep her alive a bit longer.
I want to die, but cannot die and be a filial son.
I must live, but cannot live and be a loyal servitor.[54]

Because of his duty to his mother, Cheng did not commit suicide on coming under Mongol rule, but he spent the remainder of his life regretting his decision, hating the new dynasty, praising fellow loyalists like Wen T'ien-hsiang, and heaping scorn on Chinese who served the Mongols. The bitter intensity of his feelings can only be appreciated by reading his poetry and essays.

Why did the Mongols tolerate such a trouble-maker? There were several reasons. First, the Mongols were relatively insensitive to the attitudes of the Chinese. Second, Cheng was not a threat, not the leader of any organized rebellious movement. Third, his actions were an extreme expression of a moral principle that all Chinese acknowledged. And finally, his agitation was more or less clandestine—noticeable, perhaps, but in the circumstances not obtrusive enough to disturb an unconcerned government.

Cheng Ssu-hsiao, to be sure, is an extreme example. But a definite element of the irrational is obvious in the actions of all the Sung Loyalists, and they were a large group. They refused to make any formal acknowledgment of the fact of Mongol rule, and some even went so far as to avoid standing, sitting, or lying facing the north, the position assumed by the servitor acknowledging his prince. They avoided the use of the Yüan reign-period titles. They developed a secret language of complex allusions to the Sung, and gathered together to write poetry in this language.[55] There could be no question of rebellion: they were a large group, but they were not an army, and no army could be rallied to a cause so plainly lost. Their political influence was greatest as a restraining force on others who would have been willing to serve the Mongol government but for the fear of being labeled shameless and immoral traitors. Some who braved this scorn suffered greatly from it.

THE CASE OF CHAO MENG-FU

Chao Meng-fu (1254–1322) was one who suffered. His defection to the Mongols was a double enormity, for not only had he held office under the Sung, but he was a lineal descendant of one of the Sung emperors, a member of the imperial clan, and an official under the Sung. When his move became known, many of his friends refused to speak to him, and some members of his own clan refused to recognize him as a clan member and wrote strong criticism of him. Remarkably enough, however, Chao's ability was so impressive that he largely succeeded in rising above this criticism, and he became in many ways the great figure of his age.[56] His biographers, unable to deny his accomplishments, can only observe sadly that it was Chao's unfortunate fate to have been a man of one dynasty whose great talents could only be employed in the succeeding dynasty.

Chao did not rush to seek office under the Mongols. In his twenties at the time of the conquest, he retired to intense study and self-cultivation for some years, and only accepted office ten years later in 1286. He immediately attracted the attention of the aging Kubilai Khan, and held positions of high trust under Kubilai's successors. He made many constructive contributions to government. He was a competent scholar, but is best known as a poet, artist, and calligrapher (he has been called the last of the "eight princes of calligraphy"). He was a man of facile genius, akin to Li Po of the T'ang and Su Shih of the Sung, to whom he was compared by the Mongol Emperor Jen-tsung (1312–20). An imaginative and romantic figure and a forceful personality, he gives the Yüan period much of its color and interest.

Nonetheless, later writers found it hard to forgive his "treason." He himself was uneasy about his position, as we can see from his poem on a painting depicting T'ao Yüan-ming's return to his recluse home after resigning his official position (T'ao, it will be recalled, was thought of as a man forced into the recluse life by loyalty to a fallen dynasty):

> Each person lives his life in this world according to his own times;
> Whether to come forth and serve, or to retire in withdrawal, is not a
>   fortuitous decision.
> Consider T'ao Yüan-ming's poem "On Returning";

The excellence of his course is not easily explained.
Subsequent ages have much admired him,
Closely imitating him, sometimes well and sometimes crudely.
And in the end, themselves unable to withdraw,
They remain, irresolute, in this dusty world.
But this man T'ao truly possessed *tao*.
His name hangs aloft like the sun and moon.
He followed his lofty way, noble as the green pines.
He was like a chrysanthemum, touched by the frost and still bright.
How readily he gave up his official position.
And bore poverty, dozing contentedly by his north window.
Rolling up this painting, I sigh repeatedly;
How long since the world has known the likes of this Worthy!

T'ao was a difficult subject for Chao to write about. He acknowledges the correctness of Tao's motives and admires his noble character as seen in his withdrawal and his uncomplaining acceptance of the humble life which that imposed on him. Yet he suggests that this is a matter in which each person must make his own decision, according to his own times.

This his contemporaries and writers of subsequent ages would not grant. A Ming writer, discussing the poem, wrote: "From this poem we can see that Tzu-ang [Chao] had the greatest admiration for T'ao Yüanming. Yet he himself served the barbarian court, inviting the derision of later ages. In truth he was one who knew how to speak but whose own actions did not measure up to his words."[57] Thus Chao Meng-fu, who could not be brushed aside so easily as a man like Feng Tao, has remained not an evil villain in Chinese history, but a guilty man, a great man upon whom there is an ineradicable blemish that later ages must not be permitted to overlook.

It has been noted above that the concept of loyalty was so generally accepted, and potentially so useful to a new dynasty, that the new ruler had to seek a course between two possible dangers. By promoting the concept too zealously, he might lose the service of valuable officials and conceivably strengthen the potential forces of rebellion; by condemning it, he might antagonize equally valuable officials and weaken a useful buttress of his own authoritarian power. The Yüan government, and particularly the Emperor Kubilai Khan, who reigned at the time of the conquest of Sung, played this game skillfully. On several occasions he publicly rebuked prominent persons who had too readily abandoned the Sung, but he did not do so until the conquest was assured. He praised certain hold-out Sung loyalists, particularly after the immediate period of the conquest had passed. He and his successors knew the value of the concept of loyalty, and if they failed to promote it as well as the Sung, it was only because of the general inefficiency of their administration.

COMPULSORY EREMITISM AT THE FALL OF THE YÜAN

The forces making for involuntary eremitism in the name of loyalty never again functioned so effectively as they had on the fall of the Sung, except, perhaps, on the fall of the Ming in 1644, when an intensely felt, emotional kind of loyalty to the fallen dynasty served to create a serious problem for its successor. The Manchus were neither as confident in their military superiority, as willing to try and rule without integrating the Chinese into their administration, nor as insensitive to the feelings of their Chinese subjects, as were the Mongols. Hence the disaffection of a large portion of the leading class in the society of the newly conquered country created a much greater problem in 1644 and the generation thereafter than it had in 1276.

The comparison is instructive. The Sung was a revered dynasty; the Ming, although fallen on evil days, still offered the ambitious scholar-official the possibility of a satisfying career in its service. Both were succeeded by fierce and barbaric aliens. It seems almost certain in the circumstances that in both instances the literati's resentment and fear of the conquerors reinforced their righteous feelings of loyalty to the old dynasty, and to the old world which threatened to pass with it.

The fall of the Mongol dynasty bears out the hypothesis that the workings of the loyalty concept varied with varying circumstances. In 1368 an unloved government, which for nearly a century had frustrated and alienated the literati class, and which for a generation had failed to maintain order and command obedience, at last was expelled and replaced. The new government had exceptional credentials: not only had it brought peace and order to the realm, but it was a Chinese government and it had just succeeded in expelling the first alien conquest dynasty ever to rule all of China. Rules or no rules, it could scarcely be considered shocking for a person to transfer his loyalty from the Mongols to the Ming. In any event, the fall of the Yüan was accompanied by no such wave of loyalty as had attended the fall of the Sung. Chao I, the Ch'ing period historian, in an item entitled "Many Literary Figures of the Early Ming Refused to Hold Office,"[58] discusses a long list of men who refused to come forth and serve because of the uncertainties and dangers of service under the vicious and unpredictable Ming tyrant, but notes that only two of those on his list refused out of loyalty to the old dynasty. Certainly no figures comparable to Wen T'ien-hsiang, Hsieh Fang-te, and Cheng Ssu-hsiao appeared, to be made national heroes for their spirit of resistance to the successor dynasty.

Other names can be found to add to the list of Yüan loyalists (many others, of course, had resisted the rebel movements prior to 1368, when they still had the character of local or regional bandit operations); they were respected for their principles, but attained no prominence either in their own time or later.[59]

Disloyalty to the Yüan, however damnable in theory, was in practice at worst a minor offense. Sung Lien (1310–81), Liu Chi (1311–75), and many others among the leading officials of the court of the Ming founder all had held office under the Yüan, yet suffered no scorn from their contemporaries and but little and mild criticism from historians. The *Ming Shu* argues their case as follows:[60]

. . . Moreover, the rightness of Ming T'ai-tsu's assumption of rule over the nation surpasses that of any other ruler's since antiquity. That all of the servitors of the Yüan followed and served him was in accord with Heaven and in response to mankind. Neither did they thereby violate the righteous principle set forth in the *Spring and Autumn Annals*. They are not to be put in the category of P'ei Chü, who transferred his loyalty to the T'ang, or Chao Meng-fu, who was a traitor to the Sung. How can they be criticized? Nevertheless, when the news of victory over the Yüan was received, Ming T'ai-tsu forbade all servitors who had previously served the Yüan to submit congratulatory memorials. Moreover, he had memorial shrines constructed to honor the memory of Yü Ch'üeh and Li Fu,[61] bestowed a posthumous title on Fu Shou,[62] each year despatched officials to conduct sacrifices in his honor, and appointed Fu Shou's son Ch'en-kung, who was but a minor prefectural military official, to the high post of *T'ai-p'u-ch'ing*. And when [Fu Ch'en-kung was] later implicated in the Hu Wei-yung faction treason case, [the emperor] specially excused his guilt. When T'ai-tsu heard the shuffling sound of the old servitor's shoes, he rebuked him by reminding him of Wen T'ien-hsiang, and he went away and died.[63] His practice of instructing [his court in the virtue of loyalty] was indeed profound and far-reaching. Therefore, I am taking as my model Ou-yang Hsiu's "History of the Five Dynasties" in setting up here the category of Miscellaneous Biographies, selecting those who had previously served the Yüan specially for inclusion here, arranging them in sequence according to the rank of their official position held under the Yüan. . . .

Here we see Ming T'ai-tsu following the same practices as Sung T'ai-tsu and Yüan Shih-tsu before him. Of greater interest, however, is the historian's attitude: he is not very critical of officials disloyal to the Yüan cause, and argues that they are not to be compared with the likes of Chao Meng-fu, who was, in his eyes, really guilty of treason. He is prepared to honor T'ai-tsu's technical distinction to the extent of relegating all officials who had served the Yüan to a special category of biographies, but he makes it clear that he regards them as being morally without fault. A similar defense of the same figures can be found wherever the problem of their breach of loyalty is discussed.

It seems evident that the concept of loyalty itself underwent no change between 1276 and 1368, and that its importance remained undiminished. Rather, other elements, which the Chinese historian would describe as the "rightness" or the "justice" of the rise to power of a new dynasty, but which we might call the natural consideration given to other factors, operated to affect its workings. Even the most rigidly upheld standards of Neo-Confucian morality were not absolute; even its most central tenets could not command assent when they conflicted with the overwhelming sentiment of the times.

Yuji Muramatsu

SOME THEMES IN
CHINESE REBEL IDEOLOGIES

In this paper the origin and development of certain themes which appear in Chinese rebel ideologies of the eighteenth and nineteenth centuries will be examined. The themes available to would-be rebels against the established order steadily increase in number and variety as time and change alter the settings, composition, and objectives of rebel movements. Some themes persist through the whole history of rebel movements. Among all these themes—some constant, others peculiar to certain periods and circumstances—we shall give particular attention to the following:

1. Non-Confucian religious beliefs—Shamanist, Taoist, and Buddhist—which were important in inspiring and solidifying mass rebellions.

2. Respect or awe among the rebels for the Confucian notion of the mandate of Heaven, or for those who allegedly held such a mandate.

3. An ethnocentric notion of China as the "central cultural florescence," especially against alien dynasties such as the Ch'ing.

4. Demands for equal distribution of property, including land, either by sporadic mob plundering or by more systematic measures.

We shall consider the themes in order, beginning with the first and second. In doing so, we shall encounter certain recurrent sequences of events and patterns of behavior which may be briefly outlined by way of introduction.

Rebel leaders often rationalized their uprisings by referring to portents, rumors, children's songs, and so on, which were commonly faked or planted and then interpreted as showing a supernatural power's support of their uprising.

Sometimes the ringleaders who actually led revolts against local authorities later made their peace with the central government and accepted invitations from the emperor to fight foreign invaders, or sometimes even other rebels.

Rebel leaders often tried to establish their legitimacy by claiming to be descendants of an emperor of a former dynasty or members of a former imperial clan. Sometimes they claimed that they were the only truly loyal servants of the throne and were fighting against a disloyal clique of flatterers who dominated and misled the emperor. At any rate, the rebels made repeated references to Heaven. Some rebels, for example, carried banners bearing the phrase *T'i t'ien hsing tao,* "Realize the Way for Heaven," as well as *Kuan pi min pien,* "The officials oppress and the people rebel."[1]

Some Chinese rebels were strongly influenced by Taoism and Taoisized Buddhism. At the same time, they seem to have shared with the emperors and literati a reliance upon the benevolence of Heaven, and in this way they were drawn into the historical constellation of Confucian ideas. Most of the rebels openly expressed hatred of the local government, or, more exactly, of the local officials—who were usually alleged to be hopelessly corrupt and hard on the common people. These denunciations did not exclude the possibility of compromise with the emperor as long as he was acknowledged to hold a residue of the "mandate." Rebel groups rarely severed relations altogether with a reigning dynasty and proclaimed their own new mandate until circumstances left them no alternative; only then did they become radically and totally rebellious against the reigning emperor and his dynasty.

It is clear, even from these preliminary observations, that one cannot associate Confucian orthodoxy solely with Confucian rulers, or rebel ideologies solely with non-Confucian heterodoxy. To do so would be to oversimplify what is obviously a far more complex relation between class and ideology.

The Marxist view now dominant on the Chinese mainland is also too simple. The view that the lack of a proletarian leadership forced Chinese rebels to acquiesce century after century in the rule of "feudal oppressors" prevents us from seeing the historical variety that characterizes rebel movements and their ideologies.[2]

Vincent Shih's recent study of nine rebellions between 209 B.C. and the end of the Ming dynasty is useful in stressing the constant and recurring elements in rebel ideologies.[3] K. A. Wittfogel and Wolfram Eberhard both emphasize, in different ways, certain stable and constant characteristics of Chinese society.[4] But, despite certain constants, there was also a kind of cumulative change that took place in rebel ideologies over the centuries. In an effort to get at the nature of this change, we shall address ourselves to the following questions: How were Chinese rebel ideologies affected by the importation of Buddhism, Manicheanism, and other foreign religions, and by the growth of popular Taoism? What was the actual relation between these new elements and traditional Confucian ideas of political change? How was it that many elements of ideology were shared by peasant rebels and their natural antagonists, the ruling dynasties? What other non-cyclical developments introduced new elements into rebel ideologies?

THE INTRODUCTION OF ALIEN BELIEFS

It is only natural that the introduction of religious beliefs and customs from abroad should have a powerful effect on rebel behavior and rebel thinking. It may be noted, however, that as early as the rebellion of Ch'en Sheng and Wu Kuang against the Ch'in in 209 B.C.—considered by Shih and others as the first genuine rebellion—Chinese rebels were apparently deeply influenced by a belief in a supernatural spiritual power, a power from which they derived confidence, discipline, and a rationale for their deeds.

Ch'en and Wu were among a party of recruits dispatched by the Ch'in ruler to the border region for military service. While they were passing through the "Village of the Great Marsh," a heavy rain made it impossible for them to reach their destination by the appointed time. Aware that delinquency in such matters was punishable by death, Ch'en and Wu, both doubtless ambitious and reckless, decided to launch a rebellion. First, however, they asked the advice of a fortuneteller, who encouraged them with a vague promise of success in their plot and enjoined them to consult the "spirit" (*kuei*). They thereupon proceeded publicly to worship the Spirit, and soon afterward faked the famous fish and fox omens, giving their comrades to believe that they had been chosen for greatness by some unseen god and that Ch'en would be a king. All this was done before they killed a Ch'in officer and openly declared their intention to rebel.

Whether these two former farm laborers were cynical impostors or whether they really believed in the Spirit and the Spirit-worship cult is difficult to say. Some degree of genuine belief seems likely, for when Ch'en later assumed the title of king and established a provisional government, he gave a diviner named Chou Wen the seal of a general and put him in command of the main force to attack the Ch'in capital. Chou Wen's expedition ended in complete failure, his army being destroyed in the eastern suburbs of the capital.[5]

There seem to have been three indigenous beliefs in the background of Ch'en Sheng's and Wu Kuang's behavior: (1) a belief in a Spirit (or spirits) whose will governed social and political events; (2) a belief in omens and portents that reflected the will of the Spirit and foretold the future course of events; and (3) a belief in the power of a human intermediary to decipher the concealed meaning of such omens. Some remarks on the tradition of the Spirit-worship cult, omens, and the important role played by such human intermediaries as the *wu* (shaman priests) and *pu* (diviners) will be made later in this paper.

With the Yellow Turban rebels, who rose in revolt under the leadership of Chang Chüeh in A.D. 184, we find a few new elements, including some from Taoism as a popular religion. Chang Chüeh was a native of Chü-lu in southern Hopei. He was influenced by a Taoist book, the *T'ai-p'ing Ch'ing-ling Shu*, one of the earliest documents of religious Taoism, allegedly written by Yü Chi (died *ca.* A.D. 200), a native of Lang-yeh in southern Shantung. Chang Chüeh amassed a following by claiming the ability to cure illnesses. He put his patients in quiet rooms and ordered them to reflect and to confess their past misdeeds, to kneel and worship before the Spirit, to eat papers inscribed with spells, and to drink charmed water; his successes were many, and his fame spread. In a little more than ten years, he acquired fame, wealth, and several hundred thousand followers in eight provinces covering the North China Plain. In 184, judging the time to be ripe, he divided his followers into thirty-six divisions (*fang*) and rebelled. His rebellion was suppressed in the same year, but the chronic political disturbances of the time continued, leading ultimately to the collapse of the Han Empire and its dismemberment into the Three Kingdoms.[6]

In the same year another rebellion was plotted in Hanchung (southern Shensi and northern Szechwan) by Chang Heng, known also as Chang Hsiu. His father, Chang Ling, known also as Chang Tao-ling, a native of what is now northern Kiangsu, went to Szechwan and founded a Taoist sect called *Wu-tou-mi-tao* ("The Way of the Five Pecks of Rice"). He cast spells and made charms, worshiped spirits, cured people, collected five "pecks" of rice from each convert, and became very influential. His practices seem much like those of Chang Chüeh and the Yellow Turbans, though no actual relationship between them has been traced. Chang Ling died in A.D. 178, and his son rebelled six years later. No details are available concerning Chang Heng's rebellion or his death, but the rebellion must have been suppressed only superficially, if at all, because Chang Heng's son, Chang Lu, soon made his presence felt as the ruler of a powerful semi-independent state in the same western provinces. The Han central government could do nothing but condone Chang Lu's status; it even gave him an official title, in return for which it managed to extract some tribute from his domain. When Chang Lu finally surrendered his territory to Ts'ao Ts'ao in A.D. 212, his power in western China had been a source of concern to the rulers of the Three Kingdoms for nearly thirty years.[7]

Chang Lu's power was based on the political and religious system he built up in his territory, in which he was spiritual "master" (*shih-*

chün) of the "Rice" sect as well as secular ruler. The newly converted commoners were supervised by priests and grand priests, who served also as local officials in the civil administrative system. The people were taught to believe in the Way of the Spirit (*kuei-tao*) and to worship the Spirit. The population was controlled through a well-organized penal system. Persons guilty of misdeeds were punished by being assigned to road-building and similar tasks. "Public cottages" (*i-she*) were established along the highways and free food was supplied to travelers.[8] The five pecks of rice, which under Chang Ling and Chang Heng had been occasional payments for cures, presumably later became regular taxes collected on fixed dates.[9]

Popular Taoism, with its collectivist cults, prospered at almost the same time in the eastern and western parts of China at the end of the second century A.D., and seems to have added important elements to the theory and practice of Chinese rebels, notably: (1) the idea of a direct, causal relationship between deeds and future happiness or misery, which had been vaguely present but never explicitly set forth in traditional spirit beliefs and medium cults; (2) the idea that self-control and self-cultivation were required of men by their unseen and all-seeing supervisors, a belief offering a basis for strong discipline and group cohesion among religiously organized rebels; (3) the notion of a popular "church" or organization of convert groups, with certain religious and social functions, which could at any time be turned into a military force or a system of rebel cells. Lesser practices such as incense burning, the prohibition of drinking, and the prohibition of hunting in the spring may in some cases be traced to Buddhist influence.[10]

The area of what is now northern Kiangsu, southern Shantung, and Hopei was one of the first in China where Buddhism took root. The fact that all the founders of the early Taoist religion were born in or near this area suggests the strong possibility of Buddhist influence on the formation of their cults.[11]

From the third century A.D. to the fifth, new ideas were introduced into China by Buddhist missionaries and monk-translators. Influencing rebel thinking were the notion of the indestructibility and transmigration of the spirit, the idea of a causal connection between men's deeds and happy or miserable rebirths, and the idea of sweet heavens and wretched hells. The repeated translation of the Maitreya sutras fostered popular belief in the Buddha's prophecy that after a *kalpa* or Buddhist eon, a Maitreya or *Mi-lo*, a Buddha of the Future, would appear on earth and an apocalyptic change would occur.[12]

The eschatological notion of a *kalpa* was quickly adopted by the Taoists. The *Wei Shu* even states that Chang Ling had already preached

on the *kalpa*, and had prophesied that after the "longest duration" of
time a cataclysm would occur, destroying Heaven and earth.[13] A later
Taoist statement on the *kalpa* explains that after 4,100 million years the
kalpa will be "opened" by Heaven, that the Heavenly book of only
eight enormous characters will appear, and that a "truly imperial man
of Heaven" will be born to interpret its meaning.[14]

In both cases the wording is vague, but there can be no doubt of
the importance of the notion of the *kalpa* and its use in rebel ideologies.
The question of whether or not the truly imperial man of Heaven is a
simple Taoist version of the Confucian idea of the true mandate holder
(*chen ming t'ien tzu*) is still a problem. The idea of the opening of a
kalpa, and of having the revelation explained by a *superior man*, shows
the influence of both Buddhism and Confucianism on popular Taoism.
Thus foreign ideas—for example, the idea of the *inevitability* of cataclysm, which never existed in traditional Confucianism—were introduced
and became part of the common stock of ideas on which rebel leaders
drew in developing their ideologies.

The influence of these ideas of the apocalypse and of the future
Buddha are to be seen in several rebellions in the Northern Wei period,
a number of which were plotted by Buddhist monks.[15] Although many
of the rebel monks were also fortunetellers or sorcerers, they were clearly
influenced by Maitreya Buddhism. For instance, the monk Fa-ch'ing
rose in 515 with the cry, "A new Buddha has appeared! Get rid of the
old devils!" His followers destroyed Buddhist temples, burned sutras,
and killed many local officials. Liu Ching-hui, a nine-year-old child,
was alleged to be an incarnation of Yüeh-kuang t'ung-tzu (who, the
Buddha had predicted, would be a ruler of China) and was used as a
puppet in a rebellion of 516. The new faith probably helped to consolidate the rebels.

Many Maitreya and other Buddhist cults practiced vegetarianism.
One official memorialized Hsiao Wen-ti of the Wei, warning him of
the political danger of such vegetarian groups (*chai hui*), which were
spreading very rapidly and in which the people not only worshiped
and ate together but also often publicly criticized the government.[16]

Under the Sui, the T'ang, and the Sung many Buddhist rebel leaders
arose, each claiming to be Maitreya, destined to fulfill the Buddha's
prophecy. Among these were Sung Tzu-kuei, who held a great communion gathering (*Wu-che ta-hui*) in 613 at Kao-yang, in Hopei, and
plotted to attack Sui Yang-ti; the monk Hsiang Hai-ming, who in the
same year claimed to be Maitreya and rebelled at Fu-feng, in Shensi;
Wang Hui-ku, who called himself a "New Buddha" and rebelled against
T'ang Hsüan-tsung in the K'ai-yüan era (713–41); and Wang Tse, who

organized a rebellion by mobilizing a mass of Maitreya believers in 1047.[17] Understandably enough, popular belief in Maitreya was the object of repeated governmental suppressions.

As an object of popular devotion Maitreya was gradually eclipsed from the early T'ang onward by O-mi-t'o-fo (Amitābha),[18] though the Maitreya theme lingered in the ideologies of the White Lotus Society and similar movements. The cult of Amitābha emphasized the effectiveness of chanting the Buddha's name (*cheng ming*). The chanting, combined with the vegetarian requirement, strengthened the existing tendency of these believers to organize compact groups. Since they usually met at night and sometimes secretly, their meetings often provided fertile ground for rebellious plots.

Some sects and secret societies such as the Pai-yün (White Cloud) and Pai-lien (White Lotus) included a mystic cult of sexual intercourse. Moreover, although joining such a group meant the renunciation of family ties, the convert to a secret society now had recourse to a pseudo-familial organization that protected his interests. For example, whenever an adherent came into conflict with an outsider, he could count on the strong support of his fellow-converts.[19]

The famous White Lotus Society, which played an important role in the fourteenth-century rebellion of the Red Turbans, grew from among such chanting and incense-burning groups under the Southern Sung. Mao Tzu-yüan, a Buddhist monk in Su-chou, founded the White Lotus Society at the beginning of the Shao-hsing reign-period (1131–62) as a branch of T'ien-t'ai Buddhism. The sect was accused of heresy and was proscribed; Mao was exiled, but his doctrines were secretly propagated and attracted many followers.[20] Elements of White Lotus ideology and cult practices persisted in rebel movements of the Yüan, Ming, and Ch'ing periods, and even in the Boxer Rebellion of 1900.[21]

Manicheanism was introduced into China no later than 694.[22] The original Manichean belief that all history represented the course of a struggle between two fundamental elements, Light and Darkness, and that the whole process could be divided into three inevitable stages—the absorption of Light by Darkness, the struggle between them, and the promised victory of Light over Darkness—was greatly modified by traditional Chinese beliefs. Converts, however, were required to obey very strict commandments. They had to follow a purely vegetarian diet, they were forbidden to worship idols or to take part in the ancestor cult, and they were required to repeat their prayers regularly, theoretically seven times a day. Vegetarianism was so important to the Manicheans that they became known as "vegetable eaters" or "vegetable-eating demon-worshipers" (*ch'ih-ts'ai shih-mo*).[23] From the repeated prohibitions against the gatherings of vegetarians, we can surmise that Manichean prayer-communion groups—as well as Buddhist vegetarian cults—must have been quite effective in gathering together the most impoverished members of the agricultural population. The terms *chai* (a vegetarian diet, abstinence from animal foods) and *ts'ai* (vegetables and food) appear often in the names of rebel groups throughout the Sung and post-Sung periods; for example, the Pai-lien-ts'ai, the Pai-yün-ts'ai, and the Shih-ti-chai.

Similarly, many later bands of rebels were known by names which suggest specific religious cults; for example, the Jan-teng-fei (Light Offerers) and the Hsiang-fei or Hsiang-chün (Incense Burners). The introduction of various foreign sects and sectarian modes of organization was cumulative. Modes of organization and ideological elements derived from several foreign religions were intermingled, until by the end of the Yüan dynasty both the organization and the ideology of the typical rebel group were enormously complex.[24] To this complexity there was added, beginning in the Southern Sung period, an element of racial ethnocentrism, which developed against a background of foreign invasion and conquest. For example, Liu Fu-t'ung, who led an uprising in 1351, was a member of the White Lotus Society, but he was also one of the officers of Han Shan-t'ung who claimed to be an eighth-generation descendant of the Sung emperor Hui-tsung and who also claimed that his son, Han Lin-erh, was Maitreya. Both the Maitreya rebels and the White Lotus rebels wore red cloths on their heads and were generally called "Red Turban forces" (*Hung-chin chün*). Chu Yüan-chang, founder of the Ming dynasty, was originally a Buddhist beggar-monk, a member of the White Lotus Society, and an avowed racialist bent on delivering China from Mongol rule.[25]

Although there were cumulative changes in rebel ideologies as different thought systems and religions were introduced, there remained a substratum of indigenous tradition which was modified but not radically changed by these accretions. It is to this substratum that we now turn.

CONTINUITY IN REBEL BELIEFS AND IDEOLOGIES

As we have seen, the changes in Chinese rebel ideologies were essentially accretions rather than thoroughgoing transformations that swept out the old and replaced it with the new. Chinese rebels from the most ancient times seem to have shared some fundamental beliefs with their natural antagonists, emperors and officials. Two salient facts should be noted in this connection:

1. Both Confucian orthodoxy and rebel heterodoxy shared as their

common origin a vague but firm belief in a spirit-ruler of the world and in the mystic effectiveness of certain skilled or specially qualified human intermediaries.

2. Rather than being essentially independent, the monks and priests, who spread the new beliefs introduced from abroad, were always dependent on court or government patronage and thus were usually ready to make an ideological compromise with established authority.

Both of these propositions should be examined; let us begin with the first. We have already encountered the fortuneteller who encouraged Ch'en Sheng and Wu Kuang to consult the Spirit, and Ch'en's fortunetelling, Spirit-worshiping general, Chou Wen. Both men were believed to possess some special genius in reading the hidden meanings of omens sent by some supernatural will. They were thus respected and regarded with awe, and became influential not only among the common people, but also with kings and lords. Similar cases can be pointed out, going back to pre-Ch'in times.

The Shang, of course, had their state cult of divination by means of oracle bones, combined with a system of divining by lots. They consulted the spirits on all important matters of state, war, peace, hunting, rain, travel, dates of worship, and so forth, through the agency of "priests" who specialized in putting queries on the oracle bones and interpreting the "answers." These specialists were also influential ministers of the state. And the Shang kings were originally the highest-ranking of the divining priests.[26]

The Chou, too, in spite of their ethnic difference from the Shang, believed in spirits and spirit intermediaries. Kaizuka regards the *Ta-kao* section of the *Book of History* as a record of divination sentences, which should be read to mean that the Chou treasured a great sacred tortoise shell inherited from Chou Wen-wang; that they also had ten diviners or *wu*, who originally belonged to the Shang state; and that their reading of the tortoise shell showed that Heaven's mandate had been bestowed on the Chou and that Heaven specifically supported the Chou king against the Shang rebels, who rose up against the Chou rulers not long after the Chou conquest.[27] The *Book of Changes* may also be regarded as a handbook of divination.

As early as the Warring States period, there were numerous official or state diviners as well as the unofficial diviners who lived in the towns and villages and were consulted by commoners. At the same time there appeared from among the literate but powerless strata of intellectuals the philosophers of the "Hundred Schools," men who tried in various ways to rationalize and systematize current knowledge and beliefs into elaborate theories. They often criticized the older teachings in the books they wrote for their kings, their noble masters, and their pupils, but their writings in no sense eliminated the original beliefs. A considerable part of the older beliefs and ideas came down to later generations in the form of popular traditions, crude but firmly rooted and independent of what philosophers thought and wrote.

In the Ch'in and Han periods, there were many fortunetellers, sorcerers, and professional spirit worshipers. These roles were sometimes performed by one and the same person, commonly a private townsman or villager caring for the needs of his community on an offertory basis. As we have seen, men of this profession—even under the highly centralized empire of Han—often achieved local and regional prominence. Not a few became rich by their labors, and some used their money to buy the protection and support of ruthless youngsters, brigands, and local officials, or to establish friendly connections with influential people.[28] Their profession, however, was not considered a respectable one, and they were treated as undesirable and underprivileged members of society. Their close connection with feudal kings rendered them suspect to the rulers of the emerging unified and centralized state. In spite of public watchfulness and official suspicion, popular faith in their effectiveness persisted, and they continued to become rich and influential.

The Chinese empire, as established by the Ch'in and consolidated by the Han, is often referred to as a Confucian state. It is too often forgotten that imperial Confucianism had only a tenuous relation to the thought of Confucius and his disciples. Confucius lived in an age when a centralized empire was not yet conceived, much less established; he was one of a group of early philosophers whose modest aim was to rationalize the ideas which had come down from an earlier and simpler day, and to coordinate these ideas in the interest of a reformed society. Yet if there was a considerable discrepancy between the intellectual map of the world as he drew it and the world he lived in, there was a still greater difference between his intellectual map and the actual situation in Chinese society of the Han empire. The great problem facing the so-called "Confucianists" of Imperial China was to reconcile the insights and dicta of Confucius with the interests of the centralized state and its emperor. The result was a compromise and a vulgarization of the founder's thought. A parallel process may be observed in the development of Taoism.

As for what these Confucian literati actually did, Ku Chieh-kang once wrote that they did exactly what the emperors demanded. Among other things, they created an elaborate system of imperial rituals and ceremonies designed to make the emperor's mandate evident to his subjects.[29] The proper colors, dates, and calendar for major ceremonies were determined by the number mysticism of the "five element" theory. This theory was applied to dynastic changes, and the succession of elements was held to reflect and to influence transfers of power. Such ritual-symbolic usages proliferated as time passed. Confucian intellectuals became more and more subservient to the throne; as a result their thinking became increasingly formalistic rather than humane, and inclined more toward the magic-mystic than the rational. When the Confucianists began to use various omens and portents and to interpret them in the interests of the emperors, and when they sought support for their ideas in various apocryphal documents, they stood very near the point where their forerunners—the sorcerers (*wu*) of the pre-Ch'in period—had stood, and served in a similar way the rulers who had already acquired the throne.

Taoist alchemists and sorcerers originally served emperors in a personal, rather than a political, capacity. Their alchemical efforts were directed at finding the elixir of life, and they developed various techniques of respiration and diet, of successfully having heirs, and of replenishing a man's strength by sexual contacts with women. But as soon as these Taoists acquired the throne's patronage, they began publicly to worship Heaven, Earth, and T'ai I, or the Great One; and they gradually instituted a complicated system of formalistic rituals that rivaled its Confucian counterpart. The Taoists also used the "five elements" theory, which was so widely accepted that no one dared deny or resist it.[30]

The difference between elite and popular Taoist practices has been stressed,[31] but the two groups and the Confucianists all seem to have had at least one strong tendency in common: their concern with magic. Adepts in all three creeds typically sought relief from emotional, political, or social stress not by trusting in some sacred and divine being, not by rational socio-legal measures, but in mystic spells and magical practices. The old belief in the supernatural will of the Spirit, and in the effectiveness of human intermediaries, survived under various disguises.

It is always difficult to draw a clear line between ready credulity and shrewd deception. We only know that Confucianists and Taoists, emperors and rebels, repeatedly "discovered" omens which could be interpreted as evidence that the supernatural powers were on their side: e.g., the fish and fox of Ch'en Sheng and Wu Kuang; the white snake and the black dragon (replaced by a yellow dragon when a new interpretation of the "five elements" system was introduced) of the Han; the rumor or prophecy in the time of the Yellow Turbans that the "blue Heaven" would die and the "yellow Heaven" would succeed.

During the period of rapid political change from the Three Kingdoms (A.D. 221) to the reunification by the Sui (589), the frequent succession of dynasties nearly always took place peacefully. In almost all such cases the aspirant to power arranged for some friendly official to recommend that the emperor renounce the throne "voluntarily" and invite the usurper to accept it. The transfer of authority to the new "mandate-holder" was carried out with elaborate ceremony and an external show of courtesy. It was always preceded by the discovery of omens, which were given appropriate interpretations, and by formal petitions from officials supposedly representing the general desire of the subjects, calling for the emperor's abdication in favor of the new "chosen" man. After formal repetition of the invitation and formal refusals by the emperor and the emperor-to-be, the nine symbols of imperial power were finally awarded, and the ceremony of ascending the throne was performed. At first it was customary for the former emperor to be treated as a noble but powerless guest of the court, or at least to be held alive as a prisoner, but it later became the custom, after all the necessary ceremonies had been accomplished, to kill ex-emperors, either by arms or by poison.[32]

From our point of view, the important points are that aspirants to power always used omens to demonstrate their eligibility for the Heavenly mandate, and that in spite of increasing perfunctoriness, the procedure cannot be understood as a mere formality; Confucian scholars and scholar-officials were always ready to serve this process, especially by interpreting omens and drafting the speech in which the former emperor awarded the nine symbols and welcomed his successor.

Theoretically, peaceful abdication and "revolution" by force were regarded as two different ways of replacing a discredited emperor, and since Confucianism was basically pacifistic, the relatively bloodless method of "voluntary" abdication was considered morally superior to the use of arms. With respect to supernatural sanctions, however, there was no essential difference between abdication and revolution: in both cases favorable omens were essential to the success of the process. Two of a variety of omens used by rebel leaders to "rationalize" their conduct are Han Lin-erh's one-eyed stone figure in the fourteenth century and the inscribed stone tablet excavated by Boxer sympathizers in 1899.

The Confucian notion of the Heavenly mandate and rebel claims of supernatural patronage both originated from the same source, the ancient folk belief in the potency of the Spirit. Moreover, the fact that Confucianism, although committed to the image of a "chosen" culture, lacked the idea of a "chosen" tribe or a "chosen" dynasty permitted diverse and sometimes contradictory interpretations of Heaven's mandate. Rebellious interpretations were accommodated partly because Confucianism had originally been a doctrine not only for the rulers but also for the ruled; it had early sought not dynastic stability, but equilibrium in a multi-tribal state; at the beginning of the imperial order it had been remade to serve the needs of a monarch who had newly assumed broad powers. Whatever its uses and modifications, there remained associated with it a hard core of belief in the spirit and the supernatural.

There is no doubt that ancient beliefs, with some inevitable changes, survived to a very late period among the lower layers of Chinese society, and to a significant extent among the upper classes as well. Many emperors and empresses were devotees of magic; and at least during the Han and the Six Dynasties periods, professional fortunetellers and mediums were engaged by lords, generals, and emperors to assist them not only in personal matters but also in statecraft. When the fourth-century ruler Sun Ts'e of Wu was planning to kill Yü Chi, a founder of popular Taoism, Sun's mother tried in vain to dissuade him on the grounds that Yü could "help the army and bring luck in war."[33]

The esteem of emperors and nobles, however, was not readily acquired; Buddhists and Taoists carried on elaborate campaigns and ruthless rivalries among themselves, or between themselves and the Confucianists, for the support and patronage of the throne. Many Buddhist monks and Taoist adepts proved their usefulness to the throne as the Confucians did, by serving as consultants in military and political matters, and by "discovering" omens favorable to the dynasty's prospects. Buddhist monks and Taoist adepts were as ready as the Confucians to reconcile their doctrines with the interests of the throne.

An excellent example of the adjustment of such Taoists and Buddhists to the needs of the "Confucian" ruler, and of their strong campaigns for court patronage, is to be found in the Wei dynasty, which patronized Buddhism at first, suddenly turned Taoist in the reign of T'ai-wu-ti (424–51), and then returned to Buddhism again under the latter's son and grandson. The sudden switch to Taoism, accompanied by the killing of Buddhist monks, the destruction of temples, and the burning of sutras, was carried out in 446 by the order of T'ai-wu-ti, under the strong influence of a vigorous Taoist priest, Kou Ch'ien-chih, and a Taoist-Confucian literatus-official, Ts'ui Hao, who supported Kou in order to fight the overwhelming influence of Buddhism in the court at the time.[34]

Kou Ch'ien-chih had spent more than thirty years as a hermit, and on two occasions, in 415 and in 423, had produced various scriptures allegedly conferred upon him by Lao-tzu and other Taoist immortals.

On the basis of such authority, he accused popular Taoism of spreading
heretical teachings, and proclaimed his desire to purify Taoism of such
irregular practices as the collection of taxes by priests, and the teaching
of the way of sexual intercourse.

The "taxes" or offerings collected by the Taoist priests were indeed
often unduly heavy; and secret ceremonies involving sexual relations,
originally intended to secure heirs and increase longevity, had gradually degenerated into obscene performances. From the purely religious
viewpoint, Kou's move for reform was reasonable.[85] But Kou was also
striving to gain the patronage of the throne. In his "purified" doctrine,
he not only charged the Taoist priests to reform, but also encouraged
the people to be loyal to the government and dutiful to their parents,
and prophesied that soon, in North China, an "Immortal Prince of
Great Peace" (*T'ai-p'ing chen chün*) would appear, obviously referring
to T'ai-wu-ti of the Wei. Of course he produced some omens to prove
this prophecy, and his campaign, with Ts'ui Hao's support and some
Buddhist indiscretions, led to the famous persecution. T'ai-wu-ti, in
accordance with Kou's prophecy, changed his reign title to *T'ai-p'ing
chen chün*, and the conspirators became very powerful, Kou as a teacher
to the emperor, and Ts'ui as the highest minister.[36]

Buddhist monks were no less scheming, and no less disposed to
flatter emperors. The *Wei Shu* informs us of their repeated attempts
to persuade the Wei emperors that they were Buddhas, both before
and after Kou's intrigue. The monks' activities help to account for the
Wei court's patronage of Buddhism, its shift for a brief time to Taoism,
and its subsequent return to Buddhism.[37] Under the Sui and T'ang
dynasties (whose favor also fluctuated between Taoism and Buddhism),
the Buddhists faked various evidence to show that Sui Yang-ti and
the Empress Wu were both incarnations of the Buddhas, the latter
being Maitreya. The monks edited an apocryphal sutra, *Ta-yün Ching*,
or "sutra of the Big Cloud," and inserted into it a prophecy of the
Buddha to the effect that the Empress Wu, as Maitreya, would some
day rule the whole universe.[38]

In their struggle for imperial patronage, the Buddhists and Taoists
had to adjust themselves to the fundamental interests and desires of
successive rulers. These adjustments altered the original doctrines and
led to an intermingling of elements from Taoism, Buddhism, and Confucianism. During the competition for official support, heated discussions about the superiority of the one or the other belief went on; both
Taoists and Buddhists produced faked evidence of their superiority,
the Taoists insisting on the derivative nature of Buddhism, the Buddhists
claiming the converse, and each side supporting its stand by producing
apocryphal scriptures.[39]

From the middle of the T'ang period, a ceremony was held at each enthronement of a new emperor, in which a debate was held among spokesmen of the "three religions." These debates between creeds were gradually formalized, and further intermixing of the three beliefs was promoted.[40] In a later period it became popular and common practice to worship the three founders of these beliefs, Confucius, Buddha, and Lao-tzu, in one and the same local shrine, and this syncretic cult was frequently given official encouragement.[41] Rulers and officials became increasingly indifferent to doctrinal matters. Those in power disapproved of any disputes that might lead to political disturbances, but the emperors continued to be more interested in the monks' and adepts' magical power than in their doctrines.

To the common people differences between doctrines became more and more blurred. It is often said that popular beliefs became increasingly Taoistic, but it is more accurate to say that the people held to their original magico-spiritual beliefs with accretions from Buddhism, Taoism, and Confucianism.

The historical developments just reviewed suggest some possible hypotheses:

First, the common people as well as their rulers played an important role in maintaining certain common traits in popular beliefs in general, and rebel ideologies in particular.

Second, between the two main strata of Chinese society—the ruling class, including the emperor and his officials, and the common people, including peasant farmers, merchants, and artisans—there seems to have been a third or middle layer of literate but originally powerless intellectuals: monks, priests, jobless lower-degree holders, and the like, including such pseudo-intellectuals as fortunetellers and sorcerers. This socially rather unstable group came partly from hermits of upper-class origin and partly from the more enterprising members of the lowest social classes. They had no power to tax, as did the rulers, nor theoretically any means of economic support, as did the commoners; thus they were a sterile, dependent class. Their dependence on patronage was not absolute, however. The Buddhist monks and Taoist adepts, for example, could levy tax-like imposts; their temples were wealthy within the bounds permitted by the government. But no templemaster could become truly independent without actually rebelling against the state. On the other hand, the central government was always anxious to absorb any congenial (or potentially dangerous) intellectuals into its own camp, by giving them official posts through examination. The number of examinees and official candidates who passed the examination grew rapidly in the later dynasties. But the government was increasingly unable to include all the unemployed and unsteady literates into its ranks, and so the middle layer always remained, unstable and often discontented.

As a dependent group, they had to depend either on the upper, ruling layer of society, or on the lower layer, the commoners. If there had been a clear-cut difference between the rulers and the commoners in fundamental outlook, perhaps this middle layer might accordingly have split into two distinct groups, or perhaps a third set of values might have developed, as happened in the West. However, with the original similarity in thought patterns between the rulers and commoners, who shared the ancient proto-Confucian belief, the intellectual efforts of the third group served to strengthen and stabilize the existing ideology rather than to disturb it.

Moreover, the fundamentally magical basis of the original thought patterns worked the same way. Rather than choose one doctrine and reject its competitors, it was prudent to reject none and partake of the magic of all.

SOCIO-ECONOMIC AND ETHNOCENTRIC THEMES

We have considered the process of change in Chinese rebel ideologies as certain core elements of native origin were interwoven with a sequence of imported elements. In this discussion we have been mainly concerned with developments up to the end of the ninth century. After that time certain new themes appear in rebel ideologies. Some of these are strongly racialist; others reflect new economic conditions and new, often egalitarian demands on the part of the rebels. Without attempting a full explanation of why these particular themes became prominent, we may note some contributing causes. First, there is evidence of widespread social and economic change beginning in the late T'ang. Second, large-scale foreign invasions and the establishment of dynasties of conquest affected the whole tone and fabric of Chinese life. Third, and consequent on these developments, there was a marked increase in social mobility.

It is only after the middle T'ang that the so-called egalitarian slogans of the rebels were explicitly proclaimed. Mainland Chinese scholars have been working on the socio-economic causes of rebellion for several years, and it is noteworthy that they have not discovered a single slogan of this kind before the T'ang. From the ninth century, by contrast, it was common practice for rebels to declare their aim of remedying some social inequality. A few examples may be in order.

Wang Hsien-chih, a salt smuggler, and Huang Ch'ao, an unsuccessful official candidate and also a salt smuggler, rose in 874 against the T'ang. Wang called himself a "Heaven-Commissioned Great General to Equalize Inequality" (*T'ien-pu p'ing-chün ta-chiang-chün*).[42]

Wang Hsiao-po and Li Shun, who rebelled against the Northern Sung dynasty in Szechwan in 993, simply proclaimed that they "were sick of the inequality which exists between the rich and the poor, and wanted to level it off for the benefit of the people." Directly after his uprising, Li Shun assembled the rich and influential people of the area, registered their grain supplies, confiscated any surplus above their immediate needs, and distributed it to the poor.[43]

Fang La, who is generally believed to have been under the influence of Manicheanism, rose against Sung Hui-tsung at Ch'ing-chi in Chekiang in 1120, proclaiming that under his new dispensation there should be no distinction at all between the high and the low, or the rich and the poor.[44] Similarly Chung Hsiang and Yang Yao, who revolted in 1130, declared: "The law that discriminates between the common and the noble is not a good law. If we promulgate a law, ours shall make the noble equal to the commoner, and the poor man equal to the rich."[45] And Liu Fu-tung, one of the White Lotus leaders who rebelled against the Yüan in Anhwei in 1351, announced to his red-turbaned followers: "Heaven has dispatched a spiritual army to wipe out inequality (*pu p'ing*)."

Great differences between rich and poor were never deemed desirable by the dynastic rulers. Many Confucian classics, including the *Analects*, declared that wealth should be distributed evenly among the people; that everybody should possess enough resources to live peacefully; and that each man should be independent of all others save in his relations with the government. According to one generally accepted Confucian view, the very rich and the very poor were equally undesirable: the very rich because they were independent and could not be controlled through government patronage; the very poor because their desperation often led to violent and uncontrollable outbreaks. These views were reflected in the land and tax policies of successive dynasties.

Even in the Han period some demanded that limits be placed on private landholding (*ming-t'ien*), and during the first period of disunion, under both the Northern and Southern dynasties some efforts were made to check the concentration of land in the hands of the privileged few. Subsequently the Sui and the T'ang both attempted redistributions of land in accordance with the "equal-field" system. This system, accompanied by the per capita *tsu-yung-t'iao* tax system, was based on the fundamental assumption that both the land and the tax burden should be distributed evenly among the people. Every able-bodied male (and adult female in some cases) theoretically received the same amount of land, was taxed the same amount of grain, silk, etc., and rendered the same number of days of labor to the state.

This system gave way in 780 to the "two-tax" (*liang-shui*) system of the T'ang, under which the existence of inequalities in landholdings was admitted and the tax was made proportionate to the area of land actually owned. The goal of "equal fields" was dropped and replaced by the goal of "equal tax" or "equal corvée." There can be little doubt that this change in the fiscal system reflected and further developed the idea of private ownership of land, and encouraged the concentration of land in the hands of influential families.[46] There appears to be a casual connection between this socio-economic change and the appearance of the motifs of socio-economic egalitarianism in rebel ideologies.

The appearance of egalitarian slogans cannot, of course, be attributed exclusively to the impoverishment of the peasants and their separation from the land. Actually, few if any of the "egalitarian" leaders who rebelled under the T'ang and Sung came from impoverished peasant families; most that we know of were from well-to-do landowner families or from the merchant class.

The leaders who came from the new "middle class" of landlord-merchants and entrepreneurs were quite capable of oppressing the peasantry, but they themselves were subject to pressure from government officials. Under the late T'ang and Sung governments, this pressure often took the form of fiscal controls and restrictions on private business.

The smuggling of salt and tea was a result of state control of these commodities and the subsequent rise in their prices from the middle T'ang period onward. State control of salt was reinstituted with new vigor in the middle T'ang as a measure to repair the fiscal structure after the rebellion of An Lu-shan; it continued through the Ch'ing period.[47]

A heavy tax was levied on the tea trade under the T'ang dynasty; and under the Sung, in 990–94, tea was made an object of government monopoly. The Sung government also controlled many other products, such as silk and lacquer, by charging a very heavy tax in kind, or rather by confiscating a certain part of the product in return for trifling compensation.

After the middle of the ninth century, armed bands of salt or tea smugglers and bandits became bolder and increasingly active. Bandits from the northern provinces often invaded the Central Plain, exchanged booty for tea in the Yangtze Valley, and then smuggled the tea to the north. When the government increased its surveillance and made punishments for smuggling harsher (it prescribed, for instance, the death penalty for anyone who illegally traded more than two pecks of salt),[48] the smugglers simply increased their precautions and their armed strength.

There are many examples of leaders who came from this new "middle class." The late tenth-century rebel leaders Wang Hsiao-po and Li Shun were both tea traders in Szechwan; they lost their businesses when the Sung government took control of the tea trade.[49] Fang La had been fairly well off as the owner of a lacquer-producing sumac plantation and a shop, but he, too, was forced to close his shop because of government controls under Sung Hui-tsung.[50] Huang Ch'ao and Wang Hsien-chih were both wealthy salt smugglers; they formed a strong armed band of petty salt smugglers to fight the government troops dispatched to suppress the "private salt."[51] Chung Hsiang and Yang Yao, mentioned above, were Taoist-Manichean preachers and sorcerers, but they were also wealthy and influential landlords who could collect thousands of militiamen for the Southern Sung government.[52] Thus what made these rebel leaders revolt was fiscal or military pressure from the government rather than social and economic pressure from wealthier, more influential exploiters.

Most of the rank-and-file followers of these rebel leaders were recruited from among the peasants. But the "egalitarian" slogans appear to reflect less the leaders' honest sentiments than their shrewdly conceived propaganda efforts to rouse the peasantry and secure their loyalty and support.

The accelerated process of land concentration after the middle of the T'ang abetted the rebel leaders' efforts to rouse the disaffected peasantry. Estates or manors (*chuang* or *chuang-yüan*) were owned in increasing numbers by warlords, imperial family members, officials, Buddhist and Taoist temples, and schools.[53] These holdings were increased by the opening of new land, by the purchase of land (which became legal after the introduction of the "two-tax" system), by imperial gifts of land to officials, and by private and imperial donations to temples and schools.[54]

From the beginning of the Sung, the *kuan-hu*, or official families, became increasingly important as parvenu possessors of large *chuang*; their position was strengthened, under newly invigorated bureaucratic rule, by their legal exemption from the *corvée* (and later from *corvée* money) and by their ability to evade taxes.[55] Because local officials were responsible for collecting a fixed amount of tax from a certain area, the expansion of such privileged landholdings inevitably increased the burden on the common farmer. Many hard-pressed farmers sold their land at a nominal price to the *kuan-hu* and became tenants; some registered their land under the *kuan-hu*'s name, after paying a fee for the privilege;[56] *t'ou k'ao*, "seeking protection," became more and more popular, and many farmers fled from their homes to become tenants or hired hands on the large estates. Still others joined outlaw bands.

Some of the farmers who gave up or lost their own land attached themselves to big families as *nu-pei* (slaves and maids), *t'ung-p'u* (servants), or *kuo-chi-tzu* (nominally adopted sons), and served as slaves, farm laborers, domestic servants, secretaries, or accountants. This made such official families powerfully dominant in the countryside, and increased the numbers of the dispossessed and disaffected.[57]

Further abuses arose as a result of the concentration of land. Since the large landowners usually purchased—or took by foreclosure—scattered parcels of land, they were often obliged to allow their slaves and servants to manage the land and collect the rent and taxes. These people often became rich and powerful in a local area and oppressed the tenants while defrauding their masters.[58] As a result of these developments, rebellions of new types appeared in the countryside: (a) revolts of tenants against landlords, under the slogan of refusing payment of rent; (b) revolts of commoners against tyrannical gentry or country-based official families; (c) revolts of landlords, farmers, tenants, and slaves in unison against the government, refusing the payment of taxes, or at least demanding humane consideration in the collecting of them. The role of the new "middle-class" leadership in these revolts remains to be explored.

Tenant uprisings against rent collection (*k'ang-liang*) took place as early as the Southern Sung era. In one case discussed by Sudō, rent collectors in Chekiang had the local police and military forces arrest and imprison tenants who were either too poor or too independent to pay rent regularly. This drove the tenants to form bandit groups and attack the rent collectors and local government officers.[59] Similar contretemps occurred frequently under all later dynasties. The landlords or their agents always tried to use official power to force rent payment, and the local officials, under pressure to meet their tax quotas, were all too willing to cooperate with the landlords.

In 1442 Teng Mou-ch'i, a *tsung-chia* (head of a mutual responsibility unit) in Fukien province, demanded abolition of the offering of various customary additional gifts by the tenants, such as chickens and fagots. He also demanded that landlords share the expense of transporting the rent grain paid by the tenants. The local officials supported the landlords in rejecting these demands and dispatched a few bowmen to bring Teng to the county seat. Teng refused and killed the men. Three hundred soldiers sent after Teng were defeated, almost annihilated. Thereupon Teng's band sacrificed a white horse, drank each other's blood, swore an oath to Heaven, and rebelled.[60]

Attacks by commoners on unpopular gentry families were frequent, and then often developed into local disturbances. The family of Tung

Ch'i-ch'ang, the famous painter, calligrapher, and art collector, was very wealthy and influential in the later Ming period. Tung, a *chin-shih* of 1577, eventually rose to be President of the Board of Ceremonies before retiring to his home as a landlord. The family established a vast landed estate, built a large mansion, evaded taxes, lent both land and money, and accepted protection-seekers whom it employed as agents to collect rent. Various abuses and injustices were rumored, especially on the part of Tung's brother and his head slave, but the family had too much influence with the local government to be brought to account. In 1616, however, popular indignation against the family burst out when the brother publicly insulted an old lady from a less influential scholar family. Anonymous vernacular documents hinting at the incident and accusing the family were circulated. Placards were posted on the streets. Finally a mob attacked Tung's house, set fire to it, and watched while the magnificent structure burned down with all its treasures.[61]

A similar case occurred in 1593 in the small town of Nan-hsün in the prefecture of Su-chou. Tung Fen, another former president of the Board of Ceremonies, established an enormous estate in the Nan-hsün area, invested in pawnshops and other commercial enterprises, speculated in the rice market, and of course lent both money and land to his neighbors. Later, Tung's family set about acquiring nearby plots of land as cheaply as possible, either by exerting its influence or by foreclosing its mortgages. The people protested and then rioted, and the government dispatched an official from the capital to investigate. He was greeted by a petition of protest against the Tung family. Many of the petitioners were slaves of the family, and others were members of less influential scholar families; the accused were Tung family members and powerful slave-clerks. Unrest mounted and involved other families of the lower Yangtze Valley. A rebellion was averted when the government at last ruled that almost fifty per cent of the land held by the Tung family was to be returned to its original owners.[62] Other efforts to check the gentry's abuse of power were made, but had little effect.[63]

Riots by tenants against landlords and attacks by commoners against gentry families were especially frequent in the Yangtze delta and the southern provinces of the Ming. But in the nation-wide disturbances which finally led to the collapse of the Ming government at Peking, and to the forty days' occupation of the capital by Li Tzu-ch'eng in 1644, another cause of rebellion—opposition to taxation—was also important. Disturbances based on tax grievances began in 1627 in Shensi, when a certain Wang Erh incited the peasants to attack and kill the county magistrate who was pressing them for taxes. And in 1628 an-

other peasant leader, Wang Chia-yang, first attacked and robbed the
wealthy gentry families of provisions, and then rebelled when the government moved against him. Tax disturbances soon spread over the
whole province of Shensi; they expanded into Shansi in 1630, and into
Honan and Hu-kuang in 1633.[64] The whole of north and central China
was thrown into the turmoil from which Li Tzu-ch'eng and Chang
Hsien-chung ultimately emerged as rebel leaders.

Both of these men were born in 1606 in northern Shensi, and both,
according to legends, grew up with some resentment against the gentry
class. Chang was reportedly a son of a cotton cloth dealer in Yenan,
and had followed his father to Szechwan. His father once was insulted
and beaten severely by a member of the gentry.[65] Li came from a prosperous farm family, whose members served as village elders and collected taxes for the government. On one occasion some villagers could
not pay their taxes, and Li borrowed the amount on their behalf from
a member of the gentry. When Li could not pay the interest regularly,
the creditor had him arrested and chained in the street without food
or water. A mob rescued him and he fled the village.[66]

In 1640, when Li and his small band entered Honan, the province
was in a convulsion caused by the famine of 1639–40; food prices were
sky-high, and the starving populace were being forced to leave their
villages because they had no way to pay their taxes or their rent. Li
Tzu-ch'eng, abetted and advised by a certain Li Yen, struck a note in
exact accord with the temper of the people by putting forward two
slogans: equalization of land (*chün-t'ien*) and abolition of the land tax.
He even composed a song to encourage peasants not to pay any tax
to the local officials. His followers grew from about thirty in 1640 to
more than a hundred thousand in 1649.[67] He called himself *Fen-t'ien
ch'ang-i ta-yüan-shuai* ("Great General Claiming Justice for Heaven")
and maintained a very strict discipline in his army, a practice that
assured him of strong popular support and enabled him to occupy many
cities and towns with the blessing of the townsmen and, in some cases,
help from defecting Ming officials.

After he entered the capital in 1644 and established his short-lived
government in Peking, he issued no edict to equalize the land of the
realm—possibly because his period of power was too short—nor did
he levy any tax. He raised money by confiscating the private wealth
of princes, officials, gentry families, and merchants.[68]

Chang Hsien-chung, like Li Tzu-ch'eng, used the appeal of abolishing the land tax,[69] and he and his army were also usually supported and
guided by dissidents who resented the overbearing gentry and could
not pay the intolerably heavy taxes.[70] After he occupied Chengtu in

1644, enthroned himself, and established the new state and dynasty of Ta Hsi ("Great West"), he confiscated the bronze curios and Buddhist figures from the princes' residences and temples, coined cash, persecuted the gentry, and temporarily was very popular.[71]

The Ming rebel ideology would appear to show clearly the strong influence of the socio-economic changes in the post-Sung period. But did the former rebels establish any new form of government, or any new principles of government? The answer must be that they did not. The first thing both Li and Chang did, directly after their enthronements, was to call in cooperative officials of the defunct dynasty and give them official posts. Both soon announced the holding of official examinations to recruit new lower officials; and both publicly worshiped Heaven to demonstrate that they had been favored with the mandate.[72] The government structure of Li Tzu-ch'eng was almost the same as that of the Ming, and all the heads of his six boards were former Ming officials. In the Chengtu government of Chang Hsien-chung almost half of the department heads were holders of Ming *chin-shih* degrees, and the examination subjects were chosen from the Confucian canon. The themes announced for Li Tzu-ch'eng's examinations included such classical tags as "The whole world will turn to one who is benevolent."[73] One may be sure that if Li Tzu-ch'eng had remained in power, his government would soon have begun to collect taxes in the traditional manner.

In these cases we see once again the attempt by erstwhile rebels to restore a traditional stable government with the same machinery and the same sort of officialdom against which they had revolted. In their slogans and ideologies as rebels they had shown sensitivity to the hardships of the common people under such a system. Why then this reversion?

Even before they assumed power, the rebels' concern for popular hardship and other social conditions was always expressed in the form of a good ruler's benevolent attitude toward the people. The rebel leader pretended to be "good" according to traditional standards of monarchal and official behavior: he inveighed against the aggressiveness and economic privileges of the gentry, the shortage of necessities, soaring prices, and heavy taxes, not as evils in themselves but as deviations from Confucian principles. Famines and other disasters were interpreted, by the rebel masses and leaders alike, as warnings to those who violated such principles.

These beliefs, so widely shared, proved useful to the rebel leaders of the late Yüan and the late Ming. Their rebellions began as scattered uprisings in hundreds of localities. The task of a major rebel leader such as Chu Yüan-chang or Li Tzu-ch'eng was to knit together these scattered dissidents into a unified and powerful force. The "Confucian" critique of the existing regime was the most widely understood and accepted, and thus best served the unifier's needs. Further, the examination system of Sung and after had steadily enlarged the corps of Confucianist literati, many of whom failed to find official employment and thus were potential dissidents. Some scholars, such as Li Tzu-ch'eng's aide Li Yen, helped to strengthen the Confucian strain in these rebel ideologies.

RACIALIST THEMES

Foreign invasions of "China" and Chinese conquests of "barbarians" began at least as early as Chou times and were the dominant feature of Chinese political history from about A.D. 300 to 589. The distinction between "Chinese" and "barbarian" was established in early times, and figured in the thought and behavior of many generations. Nevertheless, it was not until the Southern Sung dynasty that racial and ethnocentric motifs found explicit popular expression in rebel ideologies.

The Southern Sung government would not admit to being another "southern dynasty" like the many short-lived Chinese dynasties at Nanking between 317 and 589. Rather the Sung insisted that it was the rightful and legitimate government of all China, and that the regimes in the north were nothing but invaders and usurpers. Patriotic, often chauvinistic sentiments were common to elite and masses alike, and the idea of the rightfulness of Chinese rule over Chinese gradually became a fixed value. The rapid economic development of the south from the T'ang onward now made it possible for peasant and scholar official families alike to flee from the north and rally to the "legitimate" and "Chinese" government in the south. Bands of loyalists called the "loyal and chivalrous" (*chung-i chih-shih*) were formed from among these refugees, some by government recruitment, others voluntarily for self-defense. Such resistance groups often turned into "rebellious" bandits, rebellious not only against the dynasty of conquest in the north but also against the "legitimate" government of China.

In rebellions against alien dynasties, ethnic differences and racial prejudice often played an important role in creating and spreading hostility. For example, the Chin (Juchen) in the twelfth century, like the Manchus in the seventeenth, ordered the Chinese populace under their rule to shave off their long hair. The Mongols superimposed a racial stratification on Chinese society and put Chinese and southern Chinese at the two bottom layers of it. Rebels against these masters made the most of such discriminations. Racialist slogans were especially useful when leaders attempted to unify diverse local rebel movements into a single formidable force.

Rebels against surviving Chinese governments, such as that of the Southern Sung, often railed against the dynasty for its unwillingness or inability to resist "barbarian" incursions. Local gentry families mobilized militia ostensibly to help the government resist the invaders, but often primarily to maintain order in their own districts. To this end the local militia was sometimes used to fight both the invaders and disorderly government troops. It is clear that such militia could easily be transformed into local rebel forces.

Local rebels sometimes described themselves as "loyalist" guerillas, and used racialist and patriotic slogans to rationalize their predatory activities. The central government was usually too weak and beleaguered to check these movements or refuse their "patriotic" offers of assistance.

Often bands of local militiamen, loyalist guerrillas, and bandits fought side by side. The head of one such heterogeneous coalition was Sung Chiang. He was one of the *hao-chieh*, or "chivalrous" leaders of ethnocentric dissidents, and subsequently became the popular hero of the famous vernacular novel *Water Margin*. As a fictional hero he greatly influenced the behavior of a number of later Chinese rebels.[74]

A typical case of such "resistance bandits," independent of both the alien and the native dynasty, is the band known as the "Red-coat Loyalists" (*Hung-ao chung-i-chün*), led by Li Ch'üan, an ex-cattle dealer, and Li T'an, his son. This band fought a guerrilla war over a vast area of the North China Plain from 1205 to 1262, attacking and burning local government offices, and robbing and killing officials and collaborators of both the Juchen and the Mongols. They held their mountain fort near Wei-chou in Shantung for more than sixty years, keeping it independent of both the northern dynasties and the Southern Sung, as long as the latter survived.

Li T'an let his followers call him "Emperor" and his fort an "imperial castle," issued paper currency, and seized the land and salt-tax revenues of the northern governments. He collaborated with the Sung in fighting the Chin, and occasionally received financial support and provisions from the southern government. But he always remained at least semi-independent of the Sung. The Sung government in turn, fearful of the growing power of such leaders and the danger of their turning totally rebellious, made serious efforts to keep Li in check. The Sung court on one occasion put pressure on this band by delaying the delivery of promised provisions and by bribing several low-ranking "Red-coats" to kill Li Ch'üan's brother and wife, send their heads to the capital, and join the government army with their followers.[75]

Appeals to the desire for racial independence or ethnic integrity, though powerful under dynasties of conquest, were insufficiently strong to provide a complete ideology of rebellion. Therefore appeals of this sort were combined with other ideological elements: with the belief in supernatural spirits and the efficacy of chosen human intermediaries, with other elements from popular Taoism. For example, one of the officers of the Red-coat Loyalists was called Wang Hsien, "Wang the Immortal."[76] Again, Chung Hsiang and his disciple Yang Yao, who rebelled in 1130 and maintained their independence of both the Chin and the Sung until 1135, were, as we have seen, Taoist-Manichean sorcerers. A popular belief spread that Chung's followers would become rich because of their unusual luck, with supernatural support, in rice cultivation and silkworm breeding. Chung, whose home and area of influence were the Tungting Lake region of present-day Hunan, was originally a subject of the Southern Sung. When the Southern Sung court began to recruit militia to fight the Chin invaders, Chung dutifully sent one of his sons and several thousand of his followers. But under the peaceably inclined Emperor Kao-tsung, the mobilized militiamen were ordered back to their home provinces, and Chung at this point decided to keep the men returned to him as his own private army. In 1129–30, after a large band of the defeated and demoralized Southern Sung army passed through and devastated the province, Chung Hsiang declared the independence of his territory from both the North and the South.[77]

Ethnocentrism was also often mixed with Buddhist ideas. Many rebel leaders at the end of the Yüan dynasty were members of the White Lotus sect, and Han Shan-t'ung, the central figure of this enormous rebel group, came from a family steeped in White Lotus doctrines: his father and grandfather had been White Lotus preachers. Han accumulated a following and a fortune at Chao-chou, in Hopei. He sought to extend his popularity and enforce his claim to the mandate not only by proclaiming himself a descendant of the last Northern Sung ruler Hui-tsung, but also by alleging that Han Lin-erh, his son, was an incarnation of Maitreya. Chu Yüan-chang, a former Buddhist beggar monk who served for a time as an officer under the banner of Han Shan-t'ung and Han Lin-erh, erected big yellow banners with slogans proclaiming a restoration of the Sung dynasty as soon as he had occupied the castle of Wu-chou, his first important military success against the Mongol army.[78]

One possible reason ethnocentrism was not by itself a strong enough motive for rebellion even under alien dynasties was that no such dynasty ever succeeded in establishing a durable super-stratification of Chinese society. The Mongols, directly after the establishment of the Yüan dynasty, decreed a clear system of social stratification, placing themselves at the top, Westerners (*se mu*) second, northern Chinese next, and southern Chinese at the bottom. But they were never able to translate this order into a social or economic class system. Political measures, such as reserving for Mongols almost all the highest government and military posts and instituting a penal code which strongly favored Mongols, had a certain effect; but they could not abolish the influence of rich Chinese families or prevent the masses of Mongols from becoming rapidly impoverished and sometimes even being bought and sold as slaves by the Chinese.[79] Very much the same thing happened under the Manchus: a rapid impoverishment and weakening of the Manchu military, and their increasing economic dependence on wealthy and influential Chinese.[80]

Of course, some Mongols and Manchus were rich and powerful, and it is not surprising to find racial or ethnic hostility against them intermingled with other motives, especially socio-economic discontent. Thus Han Shan-t'ung accusingly compared "the extreme poverty south of the Yangtze" with "the fabulous wealth north of the Great Wall" (*Ch'iung chi chiang-nan, fu ch'eng sai-pei*), and the Taipings combined anti-Manchu feeling with socio-economic egalitarianism.[81]

The Western invasion of China in the nineteenth century brought heightened resentment against foreigners. The Boxer Rebellion of 1900 reflects in its ideology the increased importance of anti-foreignism as a rallying point for rebellion. The Boxers' main slogan was "Exterminate the foreigners and support the dynasty." Yet at the same time, they invoked the support of Buddho-Taoist divinities and made the age-old claim of special invulnerability to the weapons of their enemies.

This was perhaps the last time that an amalgam of traditional rebel ideological elements appeared in the program of a rebel movement. New methods in war, new ideas from the West, and new means of influencing the masses combined with the fragmentation of the old order and its value system to bring a sharp break with traditional patterns. When the Ch'ing dynasty collapsed, the long, complex history of Chinese rebellions and their ideologies came to an end, and the age of "revolution" began.

Joseph R. Levenson

ILL WIND IN THE WELL-FIELD:
THE EROSION OF THE CONFUCIAN
GROUND OF CONTROVERSY

Don't chop that pear tree
Don't spoil that shade;
Thaar's where ole Marse Shao used to sit,
Lord, how I wish he was judgin' yet.

> from the *Shih-ching*, version of Ezra Pound[1]

A square li covers nine squares of land, which nine
squares contain nine hundred *mâu*. The central
square is the public field, and eight families, each
having its private hundred *mâu*, cultivate in common the public field.

> Mencius[2]

In 1919, a classic year for Chinese free-thinkers, whose
"May Fourth Movement" laid the whole range of old verities under
fire, Mencius was brought into controversy. Hu Han-min (1879-1936),
in a journal article, accepted the ancient existence of ching-t'ien
("well-field"), a system of landholding originally described and recommended by Mencius in the fourth century B.C. Early in 1920 Hu
Shih responded in the same journal with a denial that ching-t'ien had
ever been. Liao Chung-k'ai (1877-1925), Hu Han-min again, and
others made rebuttals, and in fact the skeptics have not won out: today
ching-t'ien turns up regularly in the writings of Chinese Communist
historians, not as a fable but as something there in history. This hardly
means, however, that Marxists are back on the *tao*, that Confucianism
has somehow withstood the modern temper. Instead, that temper's
very emergence can be divined in the persistence of the ching-t'ien
idea. For the latter, after centuries of having a literal Confucian significance, as simply a social system which Mencius described, recommended, and challenged his heirs to deal with, turned into metaphor.
It *stood* for things, values or social theories which were not Confucian

at all. This transformation of ching-t'ien in the twentieth century was effected by all men who in any way—as traditionalists, radical idealists, or materialists—defended its historicity.

The account of the ching-t'ien system in Mencius, with its refinements in the *Chou-li* (the latter ostensibly pre-Mencius, but actually late and derivative), makes up the most symmetrical story ever told. Mencius' *"ching"* unit of land was so-called because it was laid out regularly like the character *ching*, or "well," for his eight families' fields and a ninth, their common field. In the *Chou-li* nine *fu* ("cultivators," here units of cultivation), comprised a *ching*, and *kou* ("drains") four feet wide and deep marked off one *ching* from another; a square of ten *ching* by ten was a *ch'eng*, and between *ch'eng* there were *hsü* ("ditches") eight feet wide and deep. This pattern was built up with strict regularity to larger and larger blocks of space and wider and deeper waterworks.[3] Nothing could be more precise and tidy, more literal a statement of design. And nothing, accordingly, could be more vulnerable to the Hu Shih sort of dismissal, as a transparently contrived Confucian ideal of harmony, with nothing of the odor of historical social reality. It was simply, he said, a case of *t'o-ku kai-chih*, an appeal to (imagined) antiquity as a sanction for change.[4] As a like-minded scholar observed later, ching-t'ien had no history: it was only a species of social thought, an aspiration, an ideal.[5]

Yet, the ching-t'ien theory's weakness to Hu was its strength to his opponents—which is only to say that all of them were modern men together. For, really, the literal ching-t'ien was scrapped by just about all hands, and Hu Shih's denial of ching-t'ien's literal, material existence was countered by a triumphant assertion of its ideal character; there was a subtle difference, however, in the nature of the idealism, a displacement of emphasis from ideals ("what would be best") to ideas ("what really *is*, beneath diverse appearances"). The anti-Hu Shih factions, that is, extricated the ching-t'ien system from its old allotted particular spot in a single national history and made it a universal. The ching-t'ien system, in the eyes of its defenders, became a type.

For some, the more sentimental radicals and some traditionalists, too, it became a sort of divine ground of socialism. For others, more developmental thinkers on the whole, Communist or otherwise, it became a form whose content was a transnational universal stage. In either case, ching-t'ien ended up not as its literal self, pinned to time and place in history, but as a free-floating metaphor alluding to something not explicitly stated. When ching-t'ien was read as the "socialist goal of man," or as "primitive communism" or "feudalism," this was a modern *translation* of an ancient text, translation in just the spirit of Ezra

Pound assigning an Uncle Remus vernacular to a Chinese poem of some millennia past. A time, a place, an idiom—individual historical bearings—these are only phenomena, Pound intimates, concealing the noumenal eternity from men of other times or places. And the literal idiom of Mencius, too, is spirited out of history, metaphorized into a formal suggestion of one or another implicit ideal content.

CHING-T'IEN AND CONFUCIAN REFORMISM

When Hu Shih took the *ching-t'ien* system as nothing more than fantasy, men who rejected his skepticism charged him, in effect, with being too literal-minded. The argument had an interesting dialectic, in that Hu's opponents, defending a Classic, were clearly far from the traditional view of the Classic which Hu attacked. They preserved ching-t'ien for history in their way by deploring literal-mindedness; but pre-modern Confucianists had taken Mencius at face value and his ching-t'ien description literally.

For some two thousand years, from the Han dynasty down to Ch'ing, there were officials and scholars who recommended a return to the ching-t'ien system or who denied the possibility of return. Yet, no professedly orthodox Confucianist, whatever he thought of the prospects of ching-t'ien in a later age, denied that here as elsewhere the Classics were history. Han Ying (fl. 150 B.C.) took over the full Mencian idyll of mutual aid on the *ching* (not only on the eight families' common land but in all their social relationships), and used it as Confucianists always used classical-sage history, as a bar of judgment for a lesser posterity.[6] The literal ching-t'ien, in such a fashion, became a standing reproach to less deserving ages; though to some Confucianists it was a ground for moral pessimism, to others a challenge to moral fervor for a noble climb backward and upward.

In comparing these implications, we would probably do well to avoid psychological conjecture. Doubtless Chinese thinkers have had a random variety of temperaments, some more sanguine than others, but throughout Confucian dynastic history a more accessible set of alternatives was posed in philosophical and political terms—inner and outer (*nei* and *wai*), bureaucracy and monarchy—and angles of approach to ching-t'ien may be fairly sighted from these poles.[7] There was conflict among Confucianists and indeed within them—between their social, outer commitment to strive for perfect governance (a commitment coinciding with the monarchy's interest in curbing private aggrandizement in land), and the inner commitment to morality, as against the force that would have to be used to wrest the land, in an egalitarian spirit, from such hierarchically ordered possessors as the bureaucrats themselves. To say that ching-t'ien could not be revived was as much as to say that the outer world, the province of kingly government, was too badly flawed to accept a perfect institution unless, perhaps, it was forced to. And to that side of Confucianism leaning to inner morality, the outer application of force (proof that an emperor was falling short of a sage's emanation of virtue) must compromise the value of the effort. But to the side of Confucianism leaning to ethical obligation out in society, such quietist defeatism was uncongenial, and action, necessarily imperial, was recommended. Su Hsün (1009–66),[8] Chu Hsi (1130–1200),[9] and Ma Tuan-lin (thirteenth century),[10] were some of the major figures who believed the ching-t'ien irredeemably past. Wang Mang (d. 23) and Wang An-shih (1021–86), a would-be emperor and an imperial protegé, active ching-t'ien enthusiasts and much more noted for their outer mark than their inner metaphysics, were prime targets of the pessimists' recriminations.[11]

Wang An-shih referred to the *Chou-li* as a model for political reform; ching-t'ien came in with the rest as sacrosanct.[12] The unpopular Wang's self-identification with the *Chou-li* made some literati doubt its authenticity, until Chu Hsi reaffirmed it.[13] The doubters, of course, were right, but for what Hu Shih and the moderns would consider the wrong reasons.

Rather than being critical of a text, primarily, they were critical of centralization, though ambiguously so; for as Confucian literati they, too, had an "outer" strain, and as Confucian officials they, too, needed a state while resisting the state's pretensions to interfere with private accumulation. In this condition of tension between the poles, there were naturally Confucianists who tried to make things easier by dismissing the *Chou-li* from the canon, and thus dismissing, too, the menace of a Classic which could lend itself to the exegesis of an activist like Wang. Chu Hsi scorned this expedient, lived with the *Chou-li* in its troublesome place of authority, and simply, frankly emphasized the inner over the outer, morality and metaphysics over political activism. This was consistent with a point of view for which not just the *Chou-li* but *Mencius*, especially *Mencius*, was a true and commanding text. It was necessarily a view, then, which included the ching-t'ien ideal, but sadly renounced it for these latter days on grounds of social degeneration from the age of sages: to bring back ching-t'ien would require force, the inadmissible.

There were seventeenth-century scholars who felt that Chu Hsi's *li-hsüeh* philosophy, with its non-empirical metaphysic of reason, was far too much concerned with "inner" ideas and too little with tangibles. Quite appropriately, they parted from Chu on the ching-t'ien issue.

Huang Tsung-hsi (1610–95) believed firmly that ching-t'ien could be revived.[14] For Chu, ching-t'ien was a lost Eden to any people even a little lower than the sages, but Ku Yen-wu (1613–82) commended the system with a less austere counsel of perfection. Citing, as Mencius had, the *Shih-ching* poem asking for "rain on our public field and then on our private fields," he saw this as a symbol of the relation of the empire to the family; the sage-kings, said Ku, knowing the primacy of the empire, yet knew, too, that man's original nature had a private impulse. Far from ruling this out, they sympathized with it, conferred lands in the ching-t'ien system, and so joined communal and private in the empire.[15]

Yen Yüan (1635–1704), another who preferred activism to speculative philosophy, felt an attendant obligation to press for a modern ching-t'ien. He offered detailed plans, with all manner of measurements, for a literal restoration of the system, the key to *wang-tao*, the kingly way. Propriety was violated, he felt, if human feelings were sacrificed to the spirit of wealth, whereby the product of the labor of masses of men leaves one man unsatisfied. "To have one man with some thousands of *ch'ing* (each a hundred *mou*, or about fifteen acres) and some thousands of men with not one *ch'ing* is like a parent's having one son be rich and the others poor."[16] He agreed with Chu Hsi that the classical *san-tai*, the "three eras," whose crowning excellence was ching-t'ien, had set a standard of sageliness which no subsequent dynasty had ever approached. For Yen Yüan, however, the destruction of ching-t'ien caused or comprised the falling off, and this could be reversed, the ching-t'ien re-established; while for Chu Hsi the end of ching-t'ien was a sign of the fact of decay, not the fact, a remediable fact, itself.[17] Yen Yüan could enter completely into Su Hsün's sorrow at a world without ching-t'ien: "The poor cultivate, but cannot escape starvation; the rich sit at their ease and are sated with enjoyment."[18] But Su, like Chu, took the classical past as past (and for Chu, anyway, the ching-t'ien's aim had not been social equality, but proper discrimination).[19]

Actually, of course, the pessimists were right. As long as thinkers were unequivocally Confucian and took ching-t'ien literally (not metaphorically, as the spirit of something or other), the system could not be legislated. Either it was an immediate fiasco for one who tried to make it general, like Wang Mang, or it was a toy set up in a small corner of a society which ignored it. Such was the short-lived "eight-banner ching-t'ien," established in 1724 in two counties of Chihli, the metropolitan province, as a tentative effort to solve the problem of livelihood for the Ch'ing's growing number of parasitical bannermen. Some 2000 *mou* from lands attached to the Board of Revenue and the Imperial Household were allotted to 50 Manchu, 10 Mongol, and 40 Chinese families. There were private fields, with eight families working a public field; the *Hui-tien* says that the *Chou-li* was supposed to be followed. In 1729 lands in two more counties were brought into the system, but the public-field idea was a failure, and in 1736 Ch'ien-lung abolished the baby ching-t'ien.[20]

What, then, could be the recourse of men who acknowledged both the primacy and the hopelessness of ching-t'ien? Chu Hsi was more gloomy or more high-minded than most, and felt that even an approximation of ching-t'ien was unattainable after the sages' era.[21] Ma Tuan-lin and Su Hsün, however, who shared his views on ching-t'ien, were prepared to try something as near to it as possible. If in ching-t'ien times there were no very rich or very poor, the emperor and his officials should still see to it that these extremes were banished.[22] *Hsien-t'ien* ("limiting the fields") should be put into practice, to share out the land and check aggrandizement, "to get the benefit of ching-t'ien without using the ching-t'ien system."[23]

The sponsors of *hsien-t'ien* in Chinese history (or *chün-t'ien,* field equalization, as it was often called, since limitation was meant to prevent imbalance) always saw their efforts as at least a pale reflection of ching-t'ien. Actual ching-t'ien advocates like Chang Tsai (1020–77) and Wang An-shih identified *chün-p'ing,* equalization, as the essence of ching-t'ien,[24] and statesmen with somewhat lower sights could still call for *chün* as a compensation, a derivative of *ching.*[25] Where authorities who took ching-t'ien seriously as a practical matter were liable to be stigmatized as ruthless (and pure scholars of a like persuasion apt to be thought extravagant), *chün-t'ien* could sometimes satisfy a Confucianist's "outer" and "inner" predilections, his concern for the empire and at the same time his implicit rebuke to emperors.

Yet the rebuke (the accepted belief that *chün-t'ien* was second to ching-t'ien, which was not viable with the emperor's imperfect virtue) was surely muted, and *chün-t'ien* was largely an interest of the emperor, not the bureaucracy. It was the emperor, that is, his dynasty depending on effective centralization, who was most concerned with curbing power that might eventually drain the state and goad a slipping peasantry to riot. The *chün-t'ien* effort with the ching-t'ien inspiration was a natural expedient. Why, then, should we find the archmonarchical Ch'in state universally charged with destroying the ching-t'ien system and outraging thus, as in other ways, the Confucian sense of what was right?

The facts appear to be these. The pre-Ch'in period, a time to which Confucianists later consigned ching-t'ien, was a feudal period, with political fragmentation and restrictions on the alienability of land. Establishing the free right of buying and selling land (which indeed would be subversive of a hypothetical ching-t'ien system of regular, fixed al-lotments), Ch'in spread its vital power to tax throughout its domain, and bequeathed this ideal to subsequent dynasties.[26] But to preserve that power, so hard won from a previous feudal age, dynasties every now and then tried to resort to measures of land equalization, infringing on rights of property so as to save the imperial system which had secured them in the first place. Thus, *chün-t'ien* programs with their ching-t'ien aura were attempts to prevent a reversion, via private aggrandizement, to "ching-t'ien" conditions (i.e., pre-Ch'in conditions) of land not bought and sold under state aegis and accordingly not in the state's power to tax.[27]

What dynasties needed was the poetry of ching-t'ien; it covered their *chün-t'ien* efforts to stop recurrence of the truth that had passed as ching-t'ien. And Confucian landowners, hurt by *chün-t'ien* pressures, often decried the latter as quasi-Ch'in or Legalist, recalling the infamous liquidators of the ching-t'ien system. Either way, whether as the state's excuse or the gentry's shaming of the state's force, ching-t'ien came down as the highest ideal of polity. The "Ming History" records a schol-ar's unequivocal statement that, for ultimate peace in the Empire, ching-t'ien had to be put into practice: *hsien-t'ien*, field limitation, would not do; *chün-shui*, tax equalization, would not do.[28] And at the end of Ch'ing, when foreign ideals insistently claimed attention, it was for the most part ching-t'ien, with merely its faint classical intimations, not the amply documented *chün-t'ien*, which Chinese thinkers identified with Western egalitarianisms. It may have been precisely the elusive histori-cal status of ching-t'ien which made it so adaptable. It was so much better a metaphor—the distillation of "socialism," for example—when historically, prosaically, it could not be just itself.

THE SOCIALISM–CHING-T'IEN CLICHÉ

The weakening of ching-t'ien as a denotative term began with K'ang Yu-wei's "modern text" Confucianism around the turn of the twentieth century. K'ang (1858–1927) and his followers made specific statements about ancient ching-t'ien.[29] K'ang, for instance, in one of his typically profuse tributes to Confucius (whose achievements he inflated beyond the traditional estimate) maintained that Confucius had devised the ching-t'ien system, which gave land to every man, and therefore ban-ished slavery from any real place in ancient China. But however modern thinkers like K'ang stated their premises, they were involved in a totally new sort of Confucian interpretation, an effort to keep Confucius im-portant. To restless Chinese intellectuals the appeal of Western ideas and values had become compelling, and Confucius faced oblivion unless

Confucianists could put him in tune with Western authority. For Chu Hsi and Yen Yüan indiscriminately—opposites though they were on the ching-t'ien issue in its older context—ching-t'ien's value had been self-evident and *sui generis*; now it was forced to be something shared and identified with an eminent foreign value. "China's ancient ching-t'ien system stands on the same plane as modern socialism," said Liang Ch'i-ch'ao (1873–1929) in 1899,[30] and even the martyred T'an Ssu-t'ung (1865–98), with his deep though eclectic Confucian faith, may be seen to have taken ching-t'ien as a passkey to the modern world as much as for itself. "With the ching-t'ien system the governments of the world can be made one"—"ching-t'ien makes the rich and the poor equals"—and then, touchingly, "Westerners deeply approve of China's ching-t'ien system."[31]

Here, inspiration still flows from a Chinese institution. An air of prophecy shrouds it, in a good "modern-text" way, as though the real meaning, esoteric but always there, were unmistakable now. ("Modern-text" thinkers in early Han as in late Ch'ing, near the beginning as at the end of the long dynastic sequence, had taken a more allusive approach to the Classics than the literalists of the ultimately orthodox "ancient-text" school.) Still, its meaning rises not from the exuberant native vision alone, but from a foreign vision: ching-t'ien is its poetic image. "Westerners deeply approve . . ."—in a "modern-text" Confucianist, is this a sign of nothing more than passionate universality? It seems to concede that Europe decides what enters the universal.

As recently as the T'ung-chih period (1862–74) a scholar had wondered, with dogged literalness, how one could count on the *ching's* eight families to have but one son of the house, so that the system might not be fatally committed to infinite expansion.[32] Yet, in the space of a generation the classic conception of the ching-t'ien system, in its literal details, had ceased to compel attention. Connotations were what was wanted, relating to problems not of Confucian implementation but of adjustment to the West.

On the whole, the "modern-text" school of K'ang Yu-wei was the end of the line in Confucian history, showing the last shreds of authentic dependence on Confucian sources. The reaction that killed T'an Ssu-t'ung in 1898 killed Confucian reformism, and from then on the main authorities in Chinese thought were from the outside. Accordingly, ching-t'ien ceased to inspire political views, but only gave a familiar gloss to something new and seemingly important. Socialism might be vaguely thrilling, as it sometimes was for Sun Yat-sen and some of his followers, or it might be unappealing, but in either case, in rashes of statements from 1900 to now, it invaded Mencius, dissolved his literal meaning, and made a sentimental metaphor of ching-t'ien. Banality proved a spur to repetition. Socialism, over and over again, was claimed for China (with priority over the West) in triumphant allusions to ching-t'ien.

PARADISE LOST AND REGAINED: FROM CLASSICAL UNIQUENESS TO THE COMMON LOT IN HISTORY

A concentrated dose of these socialism–ching-t'ien commonplaces has an altogether soporific effect now (I have rolled a few pills for the notes).[33] But for Hu Shih in 1920, exposed to writings in this vein which were not a part of the academic record but presumably living thoughts, the effect was irritant. For one thing, he felt that scientific moderns (and to be modern was to be scientific: Hu had his own clichés) had no reason to coddle Mencius but should question him severely. One should not start reverently with a Classic and simply assume that the historical facts must fit; rather, one should look at the text coolly, and try to find out whether it fits the facts or distorts them for ideological reasons.[34] And for another thing, out of this same scientific commitment, Hu suspected the ching-t'ien verbiage which clogged discussions of socialism; it suggested a lingering slavishness to classical authority. Science demanded two things, correction of authority and release from authority. Hu did not believe that the ching-t'ien system had ever existed; and he believed that even if it had, it should not affect decisions on socialism one way or the other.[35]

Hu deals at the end of his basic ching-t'ien essay (actually a composite of published exchanges) with an interesting part of the argument, the suggestion that ching-t'ien is communist in the sense that "primitive society" is communist. He declines to acknowledge that a politically organized people could have a whole long span of history down to the alleged Ch'in destruction of ching-t'ien, and still be in "primitive society."[36] This makes a nice debating point, and others take it up,[37] but Hu drops the argument just where the ching-t'ien question really comes to life as an issue for the post-Confucian temper.

Hu, that is, never analyzed the argument he was in. He kept essentially to his brief—as someone described it fifteen years later, he denied only the ching-t'ien of the *ju*, the old Confucianists. "Hu engages only in *k'ao-cheng*, criticism of ancient texts, but he does not study history. . . . He has only negative doubts, not positive explanations."[38] Hu, in short, satisfied himself that no one could prove a literal ching-t'ien from Mencius and his successors. But most of the other controversialists were busy establishing a metaphorical ching-t'ien from materials of comparative history, and shifting the base of the argument right under his feet. When Hu looked backward and argued the case for modern assumptions, he was lecturing into an almost empty hall. His real opponents were out in the modern world themselves, and confounding Hu with ching-t'ien systems almost untouched by all his blows at the Classics.

The most straightforward opposition came from the Hu Han-min materialist wing. Hu Han-min had long given up the easy equation of ching-t'ien and a socialist ideal. As a matter of fact, as a seriously anti-Communist Kuomintang ideologue he had no desire to glorify socialism; men who paired off ching-t'ien and socialism usually did it with such an intention.[39]

"Modern socialism stems preponderantly from the industrial revolution," he said unequivocally. Of course, he went on, "socialism" has a general aura of freedom and equality, such aspirations are familiar enough in history, and so people have invoked the Greek polis, or Christianity, or Chinese antiquity for the origins of socialism. But ancient methods cannot apply to the present, nor can modern European socialist prescriptions apply to China. All that Hu Han-min will say is that vaguely humanitarian ideas and objectives are common to Chinese and foreign and ancient and modern.[40]

The later Hu Han-min, then, never larded ching-t'ien into policy statements for the future, even when dealing with subjects, like Sun Yat-sen's "equalization of landed power," which were meltingly receptive to cliché treatment (as Sun himself was dispensing it just then).[41] And in statements about the past, he kept his ching-t'ien firmly fixed in the past. His historical materialism demanded it, in the sense that ching-t'ien's equivalence with modern socialism or communism could only be established by an antihistorical utopianism (Hu Han-min admired Marx for his conclusion, contrary to Plato and all the utopians through Owen and Saint-Simon, that communist society must come from the womb of capitalism).[42] The discovery of socialism was Marx's, not Mencius'.

But the rediscovery of ching-t'ien was a little bit Marx's, too. Although Hu Han-min took what Marxists might criticize as rather too Malthusian a line on the breakdown of ching-t'ien,[43] his discussion of ching-t'ien in its prime was socially evolutionary, of a sort not originated by Marx or restricted to Marxists, but owing much of its current persuasiveness to Marx's powerful influence. For ching-t'ien Hu Han-min read "society of primitive communism,"[44] a term with more than classical, more than Chinese, significance. And into the breach poured a host of scholars, ready to hang the ching-t'ien label on one world-historical phase or another.

Not all of them were "primitive communist" partisans. Mencius (IIIA, iii, 9) had quoted the *Shih-ching*, the "Eook of Poetry": "May the rain come down on our *kung-t'ien* / And then upon our *ssu[t'ien]*." *Ssu* was clearly "private." But was *kung-t'ien*, which had such priority, "public field"? Was *kung-t'ien* "lord's field"? Was the age of the ching-t'ien system, then, "primitive communist" or "feudal"? Yet, whatever answer they chose, these periodizers in the wake of Hu Han-min were beyond the reach of classical authority. Though opposed to Hu Shih, they would have brought no joy to Mencius. To them, as to Hu Han-min, ching-t'ien was not an ideal in the sense of something to aspire to. Mencius was not a sage, but Mencius' favorite institution could be soberly referred to, as a Chinese translation, one might say, of something universal. Ching-t'ien had to be retained; it made it seem possible to document a general phase of history from famous Chinese sources. Sage-kings depart but ching-t'ien remains, shining through other lineaments.[45]

Christianity has had its vicissitudes, too, in modern culture (though suffering nothing like the attenuation of Confucianism); a Christian comparison may indicate just what it was that Hu Han-min portended for Confucianism. For many centuries, particular revelation had been at the heart of the Christian claim to supreme religious value. But in recent times, comparative anthropology of the Frazer "Golden Bough" variety came to insist on the universality of myth and ritual patterns (the ubiquity of death-and-resurrection figures, etc.), so that the Christian drama began to seem just one of many that had long been dismissed as pagan. There was a way to accommodate this in a Christian view, but only through an unmistakable drift in Christian conviction, from Christianity as a historically unique ideal, to Christianity as a universal idea, an archetype out of depth psychology. Then the Christian claim might seem to be warranted (as something primordially, *mythically* true, as the Oedipus story has been said to be true), not confounded by its apparent repetition.

Yet, this triumphant transformation of a rationalistic objection into a mystical confirmation may be more gaudy than final. One may, of course, be satisfied that some universal pattern of divine kingship was fulfilled in the Christian myths; but there always remains, never really dismissed by the fanfare of "perennial philosophy," the original question raised by the perception of parallels. Are ancient Near Eastern myth and ritual patterns reflected in Christian soteriology because they were mystically, perennially fulfilled in it, or because they prosaically, historically suggested it? When Christianity is considered a "universal idea," it may be vindicated, or it may be shaken.[46]

We have already suggested that the ching-t'ien system, once accepted as an ideal part of a uniquely valuable Confucianism, was salvaged by many moderns as a universal idea, confirmed for China by its parallels abroad. This confirmation, too, was bought at the price of a drift in conviction, to a point where Confucianism was undermined by such comparative anthropologizing. For Confucian China was properly the acme of Culture, not a respecter of cultures, and its institutions were certainly not supposed to be avatars, merely local versions of universal things. The ching-t'ien of the Confucianists was unique. But if it was the "pattern" that guaranteed ching-t'ien, then even though moderns might conclude that ancient China had known that Confucian experience, it lost its traditional meaning. And this had its compensation for Chinese anti-traditionalists: they were cheerfully impervious to an attack on their ching-t'ien convictions which was directed (as Hu Shih directed it) against these willfully abandoned old associations. Unlike still-committed Christians, for whom pattern-thinking was potentially a double-edged weapon, post-Confucianists, having nothing Confucian left exposed, had nothing to fear from the inside. Christians depending on parallels and universals for their affirmations of Incarnation or Resurrection had to be, however slightly, uneasy: the status of the Bible had somehow become ambiguous. But Chinese depending on parallels and universals for their affirmations of ching-t'ien could be calmly unconcerned: for them, the status of the Classics was not ambiguous but perfectly clear and acceptable. The Classics were not classics any more, but sources for the Chinese branch of universal history.

SENTIMENTAL RADICALISM

Hu Shih was left in a somewhat embarrassing stance. Here was the scientific critic of outworn fancies immobilized with his literal Mencius, while sophisticated rebuttalists danced round him (for years), raising a fog of Russian *mirs* and German *marks*, Japanese *shōen* and French demesnes and English manors, something Inca and something Welsh, all to shield a ching-t'ien that he had never meant.[47] But in this bewildering debate there were degrees of license, and from Hu Shih's standpoint the sentimental radical idealism of Liao Chung-k'ai must have been much more exasperating than Hu Han-min's at least internally consistent historical materialism. Having discovered his ching-t'ien as a historical idea, immanent in China and almost everywhere at a stage in history, Hu Han-min had the grace to leave it there, instead of setting it up as a beacon for modern times. But Liao gave an almost unexampled display of intellectual double-entry. Trading on the materialism which posited an ancient ching-t'ien era, one which had to be superseded as history made its way, Liao claimed it as well for social-ism, man's last best hope. Conjectures which others had made to estab-lish ching-t'ien as the primitive-communal or feudal idea, of merely historical and no normative significance, Liao diverted to his own end of nonhistorical idealization.

Liao, as a socialist enthusiast rather than anything a Marxist would call a "scientific socialist," embraced a modern ideal and, in the trite fashion long established, found its earlier Chinese model. He wanted to believe in ching-t'ien, to see a Chinese version of a norm that crossed the ages, and he almost pleaded with Hu Shih, in their published cor-respondence on the great question, not to disillusion him. Hu Shih had said there was no Santa Claus: Hu Han-min said there was. But of course there was a discrepancy, though the name was the same. Hu Shih was denying a model of blissful harmony. Hu Han-min was affirming an iron age of shared but meager satisfactions. Liao used Hu against Hu, then slipped the jolly image of his own fancy in the place of the worn-out ancient. "Primitive communism," somehow more credi-ble than Mencius' idyll of settled communities (with their mulberry trees everywhere, and women nourishing silkworms, and each family with its five brood hens and two brood sows), assured Liao that there was a ching-t'ien after all. Then the "primitive" slipped away—at least the "primitive" of the relativistic materialists, "primitive" in the sense of rudimentary or first in the stages of progress—and a Rousseauistic "primitive" supervened. Ching-t'ien became the natural, the true value, out of history, and prototype of the true value (release from struggle to mutual aid and unrestrained fulfillment) of the modern western world.

Liao Chung-k'ai, then, ran the approved course through the land-scape of collective ownership and collective use, signposted on the right by familiar proof-texts from the Classics (especially the *Shih-ching*'s hard-worked "rain on our public fields"—no "lord's-field" *kung-t'ien* for socialist Liao), and on the left by Marx, Maine, and Emile de Laveleye, Guizot, Vinogradoff, and Henry George. Communal land-holding was each people's original system, ching-t'ien marked the pass-ing from a pastoral to agricultural stage. Consider primitive Germany. Contemplate Anglo-Saxon England. Reflect on ancient Italy, Wales, Java, and the Russian *mir*.[48]

Most of the literature which Liao used, especially de Laveleye (*De la propriété et de ses formes primitives*, Paris, 1874), was ten-dentious. Its *tendenz* was the discrediting of contemporary inequality by reference to early (i.e., natural, fundamental) communal institu-tions.[49] This was Liao's polemical purpose, too, and he had to be pulled up short in his utopist-historicist garble. Chi Yung-wu gave him the weary counsel that communism was communism and the equal-field concept the equal-field concept—they should never be mixed in one discussion—and that communal land-holding in a tribal society was not the realization of "ultimate communism."[50] Another writer, attacking half-baked Westernization, struck Liao at least a glancing blow. He scorned the travesties of Western ideas which Chinese made when they imagined Yüan Shih-k'ai to represent the American presidency, Tuan Ch'i-jui the French cabinet system, or Chou dynasty ching-t'ien Marxist communism.[51]

THE CONTEMPORANEITY OF HU SHIH, HU HAN-MIN, AND LIAO CHUNG-K'AI

The three main shades of opinion in the ching-t'ien controversy of the 1920's were equally modern. How, in summary, did they relate to one another?

The question of the existence of ching-t'ien had to be asked by Hu Shih, because he meant, by claiming its nonexistence, to reveal it as merely Confucian utopianism. With the Classics thus stripped of credit as history, minds might then be liberated and decisions made on a modern pragmatic basis, without any stress on conformity to unchallenged tradition. But the question, once put, lent itself to answers irrelevant to his issue, and the air was filled with answers to Hu Shih which did *not* avow what he challenged, Confucian authority, but merely asserted the social plausibility of the existence of something which could have been the wraith of Mencius' creation. Thus Hu Han-min, while accepting the existence of ching-t'ien or some facsimile, had none of the attitudes which Hu Shih saw bound up in the ching-t'ien affirmation. Hu Shih's anti-Confucian scholarship was matched by a post-Confucian scholarship, i.e., one in which the question of the validity of Confucian ideals scarcely occurs.

With Liao Chung-k'ai, on the other hand, Hu Shih had a closer confrontation. Liao treated Mencius as though he mattered intensely. He treated ching-t'ien, that is, not just as though it characterized an early phase of Chinese history (though he did that, too) but as though it lived metaphorically in the latest. He obviously saw it as metaphor, a concept sharing its spiritual content with a modern ideal, though differing in form, material embodiment: when it came to actual prescriptions for China's needs, Liao's great concerns were industrialization and the nationalism which he hoped would protect it against foreigners' obstruction.[52] Any literal conception of ching-t'ien, a system of land distribution, had nothing to do with this.

Under these circumstances, Hu Shih and Liao Chung-k'ai were like critic and exegete. Neither critic nor exegete takes a text at face value, but they differ in what they do to it. The critic has an air of detachment and uncommitted intellect, and tends to see opaqueness in a text or unintelligibility as a likely sign of corruption. The exegete feels challenged by the text and moved by its problems to draw out of it a truth which the words only partly expose, a truth or essential content which could take form in other words. The critic of Mencius asks what he says, and sees unauthentic history. The exegete of Mencius asks what he means, and sees Marx.[53]

Perhaps, if Liao's exegesis be compared with rabbinic exegesis of the Hebrew Bible, the nature of Liao's relation to his classical tradition can be made clearer. By the rabbis of the Mishnah and the Talmud, it was taken for granted that any truths which a dedicated student of Torah could disclose were already made known to Moses on Sinai. Oral traditions were believed implied in biblical revelation from the outset. It was held that they could be reconstructed by "hermeneutic" reinterpretation, methods of rigorous reasoning, as in the ancient and medieval "seven modes of Hillel," the thirteen modes of R. Ishmael, or the thirty-two modes of R. Eliezer.[54]

Rabbinical Judaism thus relates later values to an original revelation, which lends the later values their absolute validity. Confucianism characteristically had no such revelation (as it had no such infinite and transcendent God, directing and law-giving, on the far side of an abyss from finite man). K'ang Yu-wei's "modern-text" radicalism, which would have brought Confucianism nearer than orthodox scholars brought it to the status of religion, came closer to a rabbinical feeling for exegesis; Confucian texts (in appropriate versions) were given a strained authority and modern particulars deduced from them. But Liao Chung-k'ai was a good deal past the "modern-text" influence, and his "validation" of socialism by reference to Mencius and ching-t'ien was quite a different proposition. There was no "hermeneutic" interpretation of the text. Socialism was just made, hopefully, "Chinese" and authorized *as such*, not as a deduction from absolute ancient authority. This was emotive rhetoric, not rigorous reasoning. The authority flowed backward, not forward.

The connection Liao made between socialism and ching-t'ien was analogous not to rabbinic extension of biblical revelation forward but to the modern rhetorical extension of Marx backward, as in statements that Marxist history is secular messianism or that Marxism is the reflection of the "prophetic passion for social justice." If this analogy lets us move for the moment wholly to the Western scene, we may be able to set at its true quality a post-Confucian protestation of devotion to a Classic. For no one could more explicitly disavow rabbinic tradition than Karl Marx; and perhaps we may permit him to be his own judge in this, without injecting a "mere form" demurrer to his insistence on genuine change in content. Dealing high-handedly with Liao, we should have to decline to let him be his own judge: he saw himself in relation to the past as some others so sentimentally and superficially have seen Marx. But Liao was a modern man, with industrial predilections and socialist sympathies that were something more than classical ching-t'ien attachments, merely formally changed. His ideas, like Marx's—unlike the ideas of Talmudists—had intellectual antecedents eccentric to the classics of their respective ancestral traditions.

THE CHANGING STYLE OF CONSERVATISM

It may be easy to accept that Liao Chung-k'ai, a prominent radical of the Kuomintang left, should be beyond the Confucian tradition, even if he did sound loyal to Mencius. Less obviously, perhaps, but just as conclusively, Chinese conservatives of the May Fourth period and after have been just as new. As we have seen, Hu Han-min, though politically of the Kuomintang right, was unindulgent to Confucianism and remarkably detached about Marxism. When he said that Marxism was "not new," he did not say it in the spirit of other conservatives, for whom ching-t'ien anticipated Marx. Hu Han-min made no mention of ching-t'ien here; he was merely referring to the lapse of seventy years since Marx developed his theories, and suggesting that progress had passed him by. And when Hu Han-min said that Marxism was "not adequate," he did not invoke a Chinese spirit which this alien creed could never satisfy. Rather, he spoke of Marx's devotion to scientific method (of which Hu approved), but mentioned the limitations of his circumstances which made his conclusions scientifically incomplete— his study of only one phase of the economic process (said Hu), with economic data from only one or two European countries.[55]

What of the other conservatives, however, the ones who seemed opposed to modernization in an unequivocal way? When they spoke of industrialism it was with utter distaste,[56] and when they spoke of ching-t'ien they treated it with the literalness of the old believers. There was unblushing use of the traditional vocabulary, no resorting like Liao Chung-k'ai to the language of social science. Mencius and the *Chou-li* were cited without a murmur, and ching-t'ien was traced in good fundamentalist fashion to the sage-kings, called by name, and not with euhemerist intent.[57] Hu Shih might never have written.

Or is that a wrong conclusion? For these traditionalists, ostensibly so literal in their approach to the texts, may well have been no less metaphorical in their treatment of ching-t'ien than Liao. Ching-t'ien spoke to the latter as socialism. The traditionalists took him at his word. They associated ching-t'ien with socialism, too, and ended up with a ching-t'ien which was not important as its traditional literal self, but as a traditionalistic (a modern) symbol of the mortally threatened traditional way of life. When they agreed that socialism had a Chinese precedent, of course they were not recommending it. They were calling attention to Chinese verities not to encourage new thought but to preclude it; they meant to show the absurdity of cultural apostasy. What they were doing was putting ching-t'ien forward (and *chün-t'ien*, too, to some extent) as the proto-socialist (and superior) guarantors of equality and social harmony, and as standing reproaches, therefore, to the shallow pursuers of "new culture."[58]

Taking ching-t'ien really in a metaphorical sense, as representing the culture to which Chinese owed commitment, and thereby fostering tradition in the "national essence," non-Confucian way, these conservatives were not remote from the modern point of view. When they used the ching-t'ien–socialist argument to confound genuine radicals, they were talking the radicals' language. But in monarchical days, when centralizing officials like Wang An-shih preached ching-t'ien to the conservatives, they were talking the conservatives' language. These old conservatives could charge their foes with hypocrisy in invoking tradition, with seeking really anti-Confucian ends under a guise of fidelity to Confucianism. But modern radicals could charge their foes—*new* conservatives—with hypocrisy in invoking radicalism, with calling ching-t'ien the original socialism as an antisocialist tactic in a battle for tradition. What made these conservatives new was a change in the tactical situation: unlike Wang An-shih's antagonists, modern traditionalists did not set the rules of the game. They were no longer the ones who owned the ideas whose prestige their opposite numbers had to acknowledge.

Other modern conservatives of a more practical political turn were just as new as these—ostensibly old but in just as illusory a way. Chiang Kai-shek, for example, also handled ching-t'ien in a pseudo-traditional fashion. His particular tradition was that of the ching-t'ien pessimists, like Chu Hsi, who considered it too disruptive to try to make ching-t'ien work. Chiang wrote (or signed) a discussion of land ownership which purported to prove from history (the failure of Wang Mang's ching-t'ien order of A.D. 9, etc.) that compulsory equalization was bound to fail.[59] But this was not really traditional either; there was none of the poignancy of a Chu Hsi's or a Su Hsün's feeling that one *should* be restoring a perfect institution. Chiang repeated a long-established pragmatic conclusion against ching-t'ien, without the premises, the "inner" and "outer" poles, that gave it the Confucian pathos. For Chiang as for the more contemplative new conservatives, ching-t'ien stood for something—in their case Chinese culture, in his, social disorder. The literal meaning had long been overlaid.

CONFUCIAN SOUND IN A MARXIST SENSE

The social disorder which Chiang deplored came his way. The victorious Communists, however, interpreted history as progress, and had no intention of seeing the "spirit" of their movement in an ancient institution. Chiang Kai-shek might array himself with the Confucian foes of ching-t'ien optimists like Yen Yüan, but the Communists, true to the dialectic, were as far from Yen Yüan as Chiang really was from Chu Hsi. A Communist's appraisal of Yen Yüan, while generally friendly (Yen is seen as a "progressive" in his day, with popular affinities and patriotic intent), nevertheless gives short shrift to his ching-t'ien propositions; this zeal for renewing the "feudal system," the Communist biographer writes, was a great error, a sin against social progress, out of place in the newly emerging world of capitalist and working classes.[60] And Wang Mang, one of the solidest ching-t'ien enthusiasts of all time, and one of the most roundly condemned by Confucianist and Kuomintang alike, nevertheless fails to impress another Communist scholar with these credentials; he sees Wang as a selfish plunderer, and Hu Shih's references to Wang as a "socialist emperor" meet with contemptuous rejection, as an attempt, allegedly, to discredit socialism by fastening the hated usurper on its back.[61]

Given these premises, the Communists were quite distinct, too, from sentimental radicals of the Liao Chung-k'ai variety. Although Liao's widow, in a memoir published in Peking in 1957, wrote loyally of his feelings of nearness to Communists whom he knew in Canton in the early '20's—Mao Tse-tung, Chou En-lai, and Li Ta-chao, among others —she could only bring him near, not within, that circle.[62] He was not a Communist in fact, and his ching-t'ien views show him not a Communist in theory, in his mode of interpreting history.

Liao once spoke of the stability of Chinese society and Chinese values from Ch'in unification to Western invasion, roughly twenty-two centuries. He granted that there were great changes, social and economic, during the Chou transition from the communal ching-t'ien to a feudal private property system, but after the feudal system met its end in the Ch'in-Han centralization, there had been fixity, a dead balance in a self-sufficient economy. This stasis was shattered by the West. "The invasion of imperialist capitalism is the source of the ten thousand evils."[63]

Liao could be a good enough Nationalist with such a picture of Chinese history, but Chinese Communism said something else again. The Communists yielded to none in vituperation against imperialism. Yet, in their eyes, Liao's view of the matter could only seem hyper-emphasis. It seemed to have as a corollary the deemphasis of domestic evil, exploitation by "feudalists"—whom the Communists did *not* see expiring at the end of the classical era. Rather, as both revolutionaries and Chinese, seeking their place in synthesis between a rejected Confucian China and a resisted modern West, the Communists needed "feudal exploitation"; it was something to weigh off even-handedly against foreign exploitation. In itself, Liao's anti-imperialism (anti-Westernism of a sort) was quite all right. Without it, one might be revolutionary but alienated from China. Yet, if one were only anti-imperialist, one might be at home in China but too much at home, alienated from modern revolution.

Thus, when Liao cut off feudalism at the triumph of Ch'in, he cut out the heart of the Communist version of Chinese history, a version composed with just that even-handedness: China developed *on its own* through *universal stages*, and accordingly indigenous capitalism would still have emerged (from feudalism, as in the West) had there been no influence of foreign capitalism, no Opium War and aftermath.[64] And a theory like Liao's, which seemed to abort the historical process, naturally (and to the Communists, unacceptably) included the view of ching-t'ien timelessly linked with socialism by identity in essence. This was far from the Communist view of ching-t'ien's place in the midst of historical process, and ching-t'ien's link with socialism only by a thread of intervening time.

For ching-t'ien has its place in Communist histories. Few indeed are the mainland scholars who dismiss it as Mencius' fantasy.[65] After all, Hu Shih was the original powerful exponent of that view, a fact which makes it filth by association, since Hu has decided to absent himself from felicity. More than that, while deep down the Communists know that they and the May Fourth liberals like Hu Shih have a common bond in antitraditionalism (antifeudalism in the Communist lexicon), the Communists' matching commitment to anti-imperialism also carries weight; therefore Hu's Ju-baiting, which in isolation no Communist would think unreasonable, comes under the heading of colonialism, mere surrender to cultural aggression. It is not approved as anti-Confucianism but condemned as anti-Communism. And so the Communists denounce "Ching-t'ien Pien," Hu's original contribution of 1920 to the controversy, as "reactionary poison," a "wild treatise," anti-scientific. Impugning the system of communal production on public land, it denies the existence of primitive communism in China, and thus denies the objective laws of social development, and thus attacks Communism.[66]

Under the circumstances, one may wonder whether certain literati may not be keeping their powder dry for a blast at Kuo Mo-jo, Vice-minister of Culture. Kuo, long ago, by his publication of *Chung-kuo Ku-tai She-hui Yen-chiu* ("Researches into Ancient Chinese Society") (Shanghai, 1930), laid himself open to identification with Hu Shih on the ching-t'ien issue.[67] Sun Li-hsing, who was so harsh with Hu Shih, did not fail to note in the same invective that Kuo had once been similarly unsound, finding the textual evidence for ching-t'ien very dubious. After the Liberation, Sun noted (perhaps with innuendo: opportunism?), Kuo set aside his skepticism; after the Liberation, historians grasped the laws of social development.[68]

This is to say that (for both generally Communist and specially Chinese Communist reasons) history as progressive and ordered development became the rule, and the ching-t'ien issue, which had long ago won its way into almost any polemic on ancient history, became enmeshed in the problem of periodization. Ching-t'ien existed. But did this mark the Chou period as slave or feudal?[69]

That is where ching-t'ien rests, in the middle of a question really about something else. Its evocative power, so vivid to centuries of Confucianists and decades of sentimentalists, seems almost gone—to the extent that a Chinese can blandly identify ching-t'ien with that primitive communal ownership which is attributed in *Das Kapital* to ancient Rumania and Poland—hardly the obvious Chinese choices for centers of civilization.[70] What passion still attaches to ching-t'ien per se seems to come from the Hu Shih anathema, and one of Hu's pursuers is even so hot in the chase that he strays into a sticky thicket. The ching-t'ien system must have existed, he says, because we know from the *Chou-li* its connection with irrigation, in the *kou-hsü* network. And Marx (continues the argument) has pointed out the high importance of waterworks in ancient oriental agriculture.[71]

Caveat Sun Li-hsing. We may shake our heads at finding him near these deep Wittfogelian waters. Still, though the example may be unusual, there is a nuance here we can well accept as standard Chinese Communist: the *Chou-li* suggests a link between irrigation and ching-t'ien—but Marx is the Classic, not *Chou-li*, which dictates that irrigation must have anciently existed. And where Marx and Mao judge no Shao is judging yet, no Mencius and no Confucius. *Les poiriers sont coupés.*

Tse-tsung Chow

THE ANTI-CONFUCIAN MOVEMENT
IN EARLY REPUBLICAN CHINA

One of the major political and intellectual controversies in recent Chinese history has concerned the new ideas of democracy and science and their relation to Confucianism. As understanding of the West increased, the attitude of Chinese intellectuals toward science and democracy changed. In the late Ch'ing period the majority of the literati stoutly rebuffed science and democracy on the grounds that these had not been mentioned by ancient Chinese sages (certainly not by Confucius), that they were foreign, and that China had flourished in antiquity without them. Most of the literati thought the traditional Confucian way of life was quite adequate to the new world situation. Had not Mencius advocated "changing the barbarian foreigners with Chinese ways" instead of "having the Chinese changed by barbarians"?[1] But as a number of foreign wars ended in defeat and increasing humiliation, Chinese intellectuals, after the mid-nineteenth century, were forced to re-examine their attitudes toward Western ideas. Their first step was the claim by pioneering reformers that the concepts of science and industrial technology had appeared in the Chinese Classics but had been lost during the book burning of 213 B.C.; that Westerners had merely improved upon ideas they had learned from China.[2] Such men as Feng Kuei-fen, Cheng Kuan-ying, Ch'en Li, Ch'en Chih, T'ang Chen, Hsüeh Fu-ch'eng, Wang Jen-chün, and Chang Chih-tung used this idea to justify the study of science and technology.

After China's defeat by Japan in 1894–95, some of these men, and a few of the younger men who were just beginning to write, urged the Chinese to study not only the science and technology of the West but also its laws and political institutions. They were still claiming, however—some from conviction, some to comfort themselves and their readers—that the principles of modern Western social science could be found in the Confucian Classics. Writers like Ch'en Chih, K'ang Yu-wei, and Liang Ch'i-ch'ao contended that the *Mencius* and other Classics advocated the parliamentary system. K'ang even maintained that the *Spring and Autumn Annals (Ch'un-ch'iu)* was in effect a Chinese constitution drafted by Confucius.[3] In the opinion of Ch'en Chih, the *Record of Rites (Li-chi)* and *Book of History* contained legal principles similar to those of the West. According to Chang Chih-tung, modern economic theories appeared in the *Record of Rites* and the *Great Learning.* Other writers suggested that certain Western religions, languages, and musical forms also originated in Chinese antiquity.[4] All these theories were expounded at the turn of the century to justify the study of Western social science and to provide a Confucian foundation for political reforms. As Wang Chih-ch'un remarked, "Western learning does not belong to the Westerners alone. With its name 'Western learning,' the Confucians feel ashamed to accept it since it seems to be foreign; but if they knew that it was derived from China, they would feel ashamed of not learning it."[5] This line of reasoning did serve in part to encourage studies of the West; it also had a different effect among conservative Chinese for it seemed to heighten the prestige of Confucianism.

These early efforts to reconcile Chinese and Western ideas were closely related to the controversy between the Ancient Text and Modern Text schools on the nature of Confucianism. The Ancient Text scholars regarded the Six Classics as historical material and Confucius himself as a great teacher, historian, and editor of the Classics. According to them, the Master had merely adhered to the Classics and preserved the tradition. They believed it was the Duke of Chou and not Confucius who had created most Chinese institutions. The Modern Text scholars held the significantly different view that Confucius himself was the author or reviser of the Six Classics, which were not primarily historical material but imaginative descriptions of antiquity written to explain Confucius' own political thought and to promote the institutional reforms in which he believed. The watchword of the Modern Text school was "Make use of antiquity to change institutions." This was of course no down-grading of Confucius; rather, it made him a great philosopher, statesman, educator, and even an "uncrowned king" with the "Mandate of Heaven."

The fervent study of the Classics earlier in the Ch'ing period had evolved to a gradual revival of the Modern Text school. Its emphasis on "explicit ideas and subtle expositions" (*ta-i wei-yen*) and its concern with political and social problems appealed to reformers at the turn of the century, for by that time the long-dominant Ancient Text school was devoted mainly to textual criticism. The prestige of the Modern Text school was further enhanced when K'ang Yu-wei in 1891 published his "Study of the Classics Forged during the Hsin Period"

(*Hsin-hsüeh wei-ching k'ao*) and "Study of Confucius' Institutional Reforms" (*K'ung-tzu kai-chih k'ao*) in 1897. By claiming Confucius as a reformer and as the founder of a religion (*chiao-chu*), and by finding a Confucian precedent for Western laws and political institutions, K'ang and his followers were beginning to undermine the ideological fortress of their opposition.

K'ang was not merely using Confucianism for political reform; he made of it a saving faith for China. As early as 1898 he proposed to the throne that Confucianism be proclaimed the state religion, that a Confucian department be attached to the central government, and that Confucian "churches" be established throughout the country. According to this plan, government officials and citizens would worship Confucius in the "churches" every week and the head of the "Church" would have charge of education for the whole nation. Following the Christian custom, K'ang also proposed that the national calendar be based on the birth date of Confucius.[6] This plan was part of the abortive program of the Hundred Days' Reform.

Since the issues of reform were argued within a Confucian framework common to all, there were certain important points on which the reformers and their opponents agreed. Both wanted to strengthen the monarch's power, and thus both appealed to the first part of a Confucian doctrine—"Respect the emperor and resist the barbarians" (*tsun-wang jang-i*). To counter these groups, the nationalist revolutionaries —Chang Ping-lin, for example, who also used Confucianism, but to justify a proposed revolution—invoked the last half of the same hallowed phrase to oppose the reigning Manchu rulers as "barbarians."

The conservatives' use of the doctrine was clear in the policies of the court after it threw the reformers out of the government. The first two of the five new educational principles proclaimed in 1906 by the Empress Dowager were "loyalty to the emperor" and "reverence for Confucius." At the same time Confucius was promoted to enjoy the highest sacrificial rites, the "Great Sacrifice," hitherto reserved for Sage Emperors.

After the 1911 Revolution, the nationalist revolutionaries might have been expected to continue a Confucian justification for their program. In fact, however, they did not emphasize Confucianism again for many years. When the republican government was established, sacrificial rites to Confucius were suspended in many places and a number of Confucian temples were converted into school buildings. This anti-Confucian stance probably resulted from the fact that, on the one hand, the still active monarchists could make more of Confucianism than revolutionaries could, and, on the other, in the early years there were important anarchist and iconoclastic influences within the nationalist movement.

Other groups than the nationalist revolutionaries, however, remained staunchly Confucianist,[7] and the "reverence for Confucius" controversy started in the first days of the Republic. In the Provisional Educational Conference held in Peking on July 13, 1912, the nationalist revolutionaries defeated a Confucianists' resolution to revive the sacrifices to Confucius. After this, the Confucianists carried their campaign into the provinces and cities through the organization of Confucian societies with such names as *K'ung-chiao hui*, *K'ung-tao hui*, and *K'ung-she*. Most of these organizations were inspired by K'ang Yu-wei and his followers. In 1912, K'ang's disciple Ch'en Huan-chang, together with Shen Tseng-chih, Chu Tsu-mou, Liang Ting-fen, and others, founded in Shanghai a Confucian Society (*K'ung-chiao hui*). In February 1913, K'ang established in the same city a one-man magazine, "Compassion" *(Pu-jen)*, to promote the idea of a Confucian state religion. For that purpose of the society published the same month in Peking the "Journal of the Confucian Society" (*K'ung-chiao hui tsa-chih*).

To win support—especially from conservatives—President Yüan Shik-k'ai soon became an enthusiastic patron of the Confucian movement. On June 22, 1913, he ordered the restoration of sacrifices to Confucius. On July 15 Ch'en Huan-chang, with the nominal support of Liang Ch'i-ch'ao, proposed to Parliament that a Confucian state religion be provided for in the forthcoming constitution. At the end of August, representatives of the Confucian Society, including Ch'en Huan-chang, Wang Shih-t'ung, Yen Fu, and Liang Ch'i-ch'ao, petitioned Yüan's office with a similar proposal.[8] A resolution in Parliament to adopt Confucianism as the state religion was opposed by the Kuomintang members but supported by Yüan's followers and some members of the Chinputang (Progressive Party). After long arguments, the issue was temporarily settled by a compromise. In Article XIX of the Draft Constitution of the Republic of China, known as the "Temple of Heaven Draft," the following provision was made by the Constitutional Commission: "Confucius' principles shall be the basis for the cultivation of character in national education."[9]

Early in 1914 Yüan's Political Council resolved to restore sacrifices to Confucius. As an inaugural gesture he attended on March 6 a grandiose sacrificial rite. This was one of Yüan's first steps toward the realization of his monarchical ambitions, which reached their climax a year later and by which his increasing reliance on Confucian trappings became obvious to all. Yüan's death in 1916 seriously weakened the position of the Confucianists. However, a year later K'ang Yu-wei became the principal adviser to the military governor, Chang Hsün, who succeeded in restoring, very briefly, the Manchu boy-emperor to the throne. The conservative Confucianists' hopes to use this development to advance their own cause were quickly dashed.

THE RISE OF THE ANTI-CONFUCIAN TIDE

As we have seen, the Confucianists' reaction to Western learning evolved from total rejection, through acceptance within the framework of the Confucian tradition, to the use of Western sanctions for a "modernized" Confucianism. In consequence of this paradoxical interaction between Western learning and Confucianism, as science gained a firmer foothold in China the movement to make Confucianism the state religion also gathered momentum; at the same time that the Chinese were talking about democracy, legal principles, and modern political institutions, a new monarchical movement was developing and supporting Confucianism. But there was a further paradox of opposite import. The emerging Confucianist movement, stimulated by the challenge of Western ideas in a national crisis, had within it the seeds of its own destruction, for it was a reform movement and those who supported it had absorbed too much from the West. Only the anti-reformists took a truly traditionalist attitude toward the problem of modernization, and they had been discredited by the collapse of the empire and the old order.

The contrived and false justification of Western learning by identification with Confucian principles, and later the justification of Confucianism by Western learning, were vulnerable to attack. At first the objection was primarily to the treatment of Confucianism as a religion. In 1898 Yen Fu insisted that although Confucianism had been treated as a state religion for two thousand years, it actually was a humanist philosophy.[10] Chang Ping-lin also protested against the ideas that Confucius was the creator of a religion and that Confucianism should be taught as one.[11] Liang Ch'i-ch'ao reversed in 1902 his earlier position and rejected the idea of a Confucian religion on the ground that this would impede independent thought: "I love Confucius, but I love truth more." Liang also now denied that Western ideas were latent in early Confucian writings.[12]

All this was limited criticism within the system. A strong, total attack on Confucianism, from a Westernized point of view, did not take place until the period of the May Fourth Movement, roughly between 1917 and 1921.[13] Modern criticism of Confucianism, however, could be traced back at least to the fall of 1915. By this time Western ideas had become rather well known, if only in outline, to Chinese intellectuals. By the end of the nineteenth century, Western philosophy and political and social theories were introduced into China and popularized by translators and writers. Social Darwinism and utilitarianism were expounded by Yen Fu; French liberalism was spread by Liang Ch'i-ch'ao's passionate writings.

The all-out attack on Confucianism began when Yüan Shih-k'ai was preparing to set himself up as emperor. From the first issue (September 1915) onward, Ch'en Tu-hsiu's monthly "New Youth" or "La Jeunesse" *(Hsin ch'ing-nien)* published articles attacking the whole framework of the Chinese traditional ethics, customs, and institutions; he based his arguments on science, human rights, and democracy. In the February 1916 issue of the magazine an article appeared by Yi Pai-sha (1886–1921). Entitled "A Critical Discussion of Confucius" *(K'ung-tzu p'ing-i)*, this article traced the history of the use of Confucianism by Chinese monarchs as a tool to rule the people, and pointed out certain features of the doctrine that lent themselves to such abuse. Yi argued further that the official orthodoxy was by no means the whole of the Confucian tradition, that Confucius and some of his disciples were in a sense revolutionaries, and that despite its claims the Confucian tradition was not the whole of Chinese thought.[14]

In the same issue Ch'en Tu-hsiu took even a stronger stand than Yi and set a keynote for the next few years of Chinese intellectual controversy. Ch'en believed the time had come for the Chinese to have an "ethical awakening" along with their political awakening after the 1911 Revolution. In effect, this meant a re-evaluation and rejection of Confucian ethics.[15]

The call to a criticism and rejection of Confucian ethics met with widespread response in the fall of 1916, when the controversy over the provision for a Confucian state religion in the Draft Constitution recaptured the attention of Parliament. By then, because of Yüan Shih-k'ai's downfall, Parliament and the administration were inclined to abolish the provision for "Confucian principles" in Article XIX of the draft. In protest against this measure, K'ang Yu-wei wrote a letter to President Li Yüan-hung and Premier Tuan Ch'i-jui renewing his proposal for a Confucian state religion. Ch'en Tu-hsiu responded with a series of articles which began to appear in October 1916.[16]

The anti-Confucian campaign gained further support from Wu Yü (1871–1949), a scholar who had studied law and political science in Tokyo. Early in 1917 he sent to "New Youth" a number of critical essays on Confucianism which he had written earlier but had found no favorable circumstances for publishing. Wu criticized the Confucian philosophy both in the abstract and in its application to morals, law, institutions, customs, and the evaluation of historical events. He compared the traditional Confucian arguments in judicial cases with the theories of the Taoists, and with those of Montesquieu, Jenks, John Stuart Mill, Herbert Spencer, Endō Ryūkichi, and Kubo Tenzui, as well as with the principles of the constitutional, civil, and criminal laws of Europe and America. His criticism was therefore more provocative than that of others at that time. Later, referring to these articles of Wu's, Hu Shih hailed Wu as "the old hero from Szechwan Province who beat Confucius and Sons single-handed."[17] The slogan "Overthrow Confucius and Sons" thereafter became a widespread anti-Confucian battle cry.

Meanwhile, the polemics of the "literary revolution" greatly stimulated the anti-Confucian movement. The October 1, 1916, issue of "New Youth," which carried Ch'en Tu-hsiu's retort to K'ang Yu-wei's letter to the President and the Premier, also published a letter from Hu Shih to Ch'en, urging a revolt against the old literature. The proposal was enthusiastically supported by Ch'en, and attacks on the old literature from a humanitarian, naturalistic, or romantic standpoint poured from the magazine. And since most traditional literature had been used as a vehicle for the promotion of Confucian principles or morality (*wen i tsai tao*), the new polemics struck at the very heart of Confucianism.

Following the emergence of vernacular literature, a fiercer and more effective fighter against the traditional ethics and customs appeared, Lu Hsün. His attack on Confucian ethics was directed at the whole of traditional society and life, at the Chinese character itself. Armed with a superb style and wit, and occasional flashes of irony, Lu Hsün wrote short stories and short essays which won him many readers and dealt a serious blow to the Confucian moral tradition. In his first short story, "The Diary of a Madman," published in May 1918, Lu Hsün challenged the entire Chinese ethical system by saying through the madman that the Chinese had "unconsciously practiced cannibalism for four thousand years." Wu Yü later interpreted this to mean that, in the extremes of the filial piety cult, cannibalism was demanded in the name of Confucian morality.[18]

The attacks on Confucianism by Ch'en Tu-hsiu, Wu Yü, and Lu Hsün had gone far, but in the hands of the young people they often went even further. The anti-Confucian campaign was in fact only one aspect of a broader intellectual trend, which the young men and women at the time called "the new thought tide" (*hsin ssu-ch'ao*). From the first decade of the twentieth century Western ideas enjoyed wider circulation and greater esteem than before. Nationalism and socialism were vigorously promoted by such Kuomintang writers as Chang Ping-lin, Sun Yat-sen, Wang Ching-wei, and Chu Chih-hsin; anarchism and nihilism were spread by Li Shih-tseng, Wu Chih-hui, Ts'ai Yüan-p'ei, and Liu Shih-fu; in literary criticism Nietzsche's and Schopenhauer's views were adopted by Wang Kuo-wei. John Dewey's pragmatism, which was introduced to China chiefly through Hu Shih, and Bertrand Russell's neo-realism and logic were in vogue. At the same time that the Russian Revolution of October 1917 stimulated socialist zeal in China, a new hope for more democracy and national independence, generated in Europe at the end of World War I, captured the imagination of young Chinese intellectuals. All these factors contributed to a new intellectual ferment calling for a radical re-evaluation of tradition. In the circumstances, it was not surprising that the Confucianist activities were considered to be the main obstacle to the furious intellectual "flood" (*hung-shui*), to use a metaphor of Ts'ai Yüan-p'ei's.

From 1917 to the spring of 1919 this anti-Confucian ferment of the new thought movement and the new literature movement was centered at the National University of Peking, where Ts'ai Yüan-p'ei was Chancellor, Ch'en Tu-hsiu, Dean of the School of Letters, and Hu Shih and many other liberal scholars and writers were on the faculty. Men of this stamp attracted a wide following among young intellectuals and students. With the establishment early in 1919 of the monthly "New Tide" or "Renaissance" (*Hsin ch'ao*) by students of the university, the anti-Confucian campaign, especially its opposition to the big family system and to the ethic of filial piety, was spread to colleges and middle schools in other cities.

The fierce attack on Confucian ethics alarmed the conservatives. In March 1919 the famous translator Lin Shu published a letter to Ts'ai Yüan-p'ei, accusing the professors at the university of "attempting to overthrow Confucius and Mencius and to destroy the five virtues and five ethical relationships." Ts'ai replied in defense of the professors' position. Jokes were circulated to the effect that Ch'en Tu-hsiu had changed the old proverb "Adultery is the first of all sins, and filial piety, the first of all virtues" into a new dictum, "Filial piety is the first of all sins, and adultery, the first of all virtues." The conservative old gentry tried to persuade the government to intervene, and social and political pressure on the university was so strong that in March Ch'en Tu-hsiu had to resign as Dean.[19]

The progress of the anti-Confucian campaign might have been temporarily checked had not the May Fourth Incident taken place. On May 4, 1919, over three thousand college students in Peking held a demonstration against the resolution of the Great Powers in the Paris

Peace Conference on the Shantung question and against the Peking government's weak policy toward Japan; the demonstration resulted in the burning of a cabinet member's house. With unprecedentedly strong support of the students from the public, the incident brought down the cabinet sustained by the Anfu clique.

The significance of the young intellectuals' victory over the Peking government, as far as the anti-Confucian campaign was concerned, lies in the fact that many of the students and teachers behind the student protest were vigorous and active promoters of the new thought and new literature movements, whereas the zealous Confucianists often maintained close relations with the government. In the months following the incident, students in all the major cities carried on a vigorous campaign against the government's foreign policy. More than 400 new magazines, mostly student publications and all in the vernacular, helped to spread, besides patriotism, criticism of the Chinese tradition and its major ideological foundation, the Confucian ethic. These efforts at reform and rejuvenation of the Chinese civilization, known as the New Culture Movement (*Hsin wen-hua yün-tung*), were at first promoted mainly under the banner of science and democracy, but later leaned more and more to nationalism and socialism.

The intellectual upheaval following the May Fourth Incident led to more destructive criticism of Confucian ethics than ever before. At the same time, the new skeptical spirit of the progressive intellectuals forced more critical study of the Confucian Classics by modern Western methodology, and as a result, disputes over Confucianism were intensified.

THE ARGUMENTS FOR AND AGAINST A CONFUCIAN STATE RELIGION

Among the Confucianists, those who advocated a Confucian religion were the most zealous and were regarded by the anti-Confucianists as an obstacle to intellectual reform. Consequently, the anti-Confucian movement in its early stage was directed at the issue of Confucian religion.

K'ang Yu-wei was the principal supporter of Confucianism as a religion. Educated by his Neo-Confucian grandfather, his childhood ambition had been to become a sage. Later he was influenced both by the Modern Text studies and by Western books in translation.

Though he was one of the first to urge economic and material reconstruction, K'ang, like most Confucianists, held morality to be the most important factor in saving China. Traditional morality was discredited when the Ch'ing Empire collapsed, and no substitute was at hand. Confucianists and non-Confucianists alike felt that the nation was deteriorating. K'ang thought a state religion would be the most effective means of improving the morality of the nation, since certain areas of human behavior, as far as the majority of the people were concerned, could not be effectively governed by philosophical principles or by law. Fear of a supernatural power or unquestioning obedience to ethical rules, he believed, might provide moral restraints.[20] The proposal for a Confucian state religion, therefore, was from the beginning motivated by utilitarian considerations.

Furthermore, K'ang argued that religion was a requisite for modern civilization. "Now all countries have religion except the barbarian tribes," said K'ang; "if the Chinese are not going to worship a religious leader, do they concede to be atheists and accordingly barbarous tribes?"[21] By saying this, K'ang denied without factual justification the existence of religions both in primitive tribes and in China. All these were easily disproved by the anti-Confucianists. The historical argument of religion was also used by the latter group, but with a reversed conclusion. They argued that in Western history the evolution from Catholicism to Protestantism and Unitarianism proved only the decline of religion.[22]

The main issues in the Chinese controversy were whether or not Confucianism was a religion, whether at least it had functioned as a religion and might be made to serve as such in a modernized China. K'ang Yu-wei gave an affirmative answer. Citing the *Record of Rites* and the *Book of Changes*, he maintained that Confucius had paid reverence to Heaven and had testified to the existence of spirits and gods; consequently Confucianism had with reason been treated in China as a religion for more than two thousand years.[23] But, according to Chang Ping-lin, a writer of the Ancient Text school, who referred with confidence to the *Analects* and *Mencius,* Confucius often refused to discuss Heaven and death, only "assuming" that God "existed" (*tsai*).[24] Ch'en Tu-hsiu thought that the essence of religion was a quest for the salvation of man's soul and that Confucianism, not dealing with the problem, was only a philosophy concerned mainly with man's life on earth.[25] This view was shared by many other prominent intellectuals; some, however, took the position that since the Han period Confucianism had, though unjustifiably, been looked on as a religion. But even when it was conceded that Confucianism had functioned as a religion, the twentieth-century Confucian religious movement could not develop if it were found that Confucius' own teachings were not a religion. So the battle still had to be fought over the question of whether Confucius' teachings themselves truly constituted a religion.

The answer to this question depended on the answers to two others:

who wrote the Six Classics, and, what is religion? The results of new
studies, as we will show, challenged most of the opinions on authorship
the orthodox Confucianists took for granted; and K'ang Yu-wei, with
a few others, used a broader definition of religion than did most Chinese of the time. To K'ang, *tsung-chiao*, the Chinese term for religion,
possibly derived from the Japanese, did not mean merely a system of
thought dealing with superhuman power or the way of the gods (*shen-
tao*), but also, especially in the sense of a modern and advanced religion,
a system for the quest of the ideal life or the ideal human way (*jen-
tao*).²⁶ Those who subscribed to K'ang's view argued that under this
definition, Confucianism, which the populace had since the fifth century been calling *K'ung-chiao*, was clearly a religion. Since the character
chiao here could be interpreted as a reduced form of either *tsung-chiao*
(religion) or *chiao-hua* (teachings or cultivation), Ch'en Tu-hsiu insisted on the latter interpretation, that is, that *K'ung-chiao* meant "Confucian teachings" instead of "Confucian religion."²⁷ Even so, if one
accepted K'ang's broad definition, Confucianism would still be a religion,²⁸ but it became difficult to distinguish religion from ethics or a
philosophy of life.

The question of whether or not Confucianism had been a religion
remained unanswered, but it became part of a sharper controversy: did
China need a state religion? The Confucianists, as we have said, maintained that a state religion would furnish an effective moral standard
for the ordinary people. They insisted that Confucianism as a state
religion had long existed and was embodied in every aspect of Chinese
life. To give it up meant to give up the whole of Chinese culture.²⁹
Official disparagement of the religion of the people would be an en-
croachment on their customary rights and their freedom of belief.³⁰

But in the opinion of the anti-Confucianists, the Confucian moral
principles belonged to the dead past and could not be applied to the
twentieth century. They argued that Confucianism did not represent
the whole of Chinese culture, that to reject it as a state religion would
not deny its past contribution but rather would give Confucius' teachings their proper place in Chinese history.

The anti-Confucianists found the argument for people's rights and
freedom of belief more to their advantage. As Ch'en Tu-hsiu maintained, to proclaim Confucianism a state religion was to deprive other
religious groups such as the Buddhists and Christians of their freedom
of worship. Admitting that these religions might be judged foreign and
Confucianism the "national quintessence" of China, he asked how to
consider Taoism, Mohism, and all other philosophical schools developed
in ancient China. The Confucian Society had its right to promote Con-

fucianism, but it should not ask the government to "force the people to espouse a religion."[31] To reprove K'ang Yu-wei, Ch'en also pointed out that if Confucianism was to be proclaimed a state religion, then no non-Confucians would be allowed the opportunity to be elected president of the republic or appointed to other public offices.[32] On this point the anti-Confucians were supported by the Christians, Moslems, and other religious groups. Indeed, in the winter of 1916, a Society for the Freedom of Religion (*Hsin-chiao tzu-yu hui*) was organized in Peking. Adding to his own arguments, Ch'en further demonstrated, albeit in sharp contrast to his later support for a state political ideology, that official support for Confucian principles in education interfered with freedom of thought and teaching, for no theory could be accepted as the sole truth; this would halt the free development of thought and civilization.[33]

K'ang's reply to the arguments based on concern for freedom of belief showed that he had not meant to propose a totalitarian theocracy. He acknowledged the coexistence of various religions in China and insisted that the establishment of a state religion was not intended to exclude the free development of other religions. Confucianism had been a state religion for more than two thousand years in China, he argued, and it still allowed the spread of such religions as Taoism and Buddhism. Confucianism was and would be the most tolerant religion. The other religions, according to him, were not qualified to be state religions because they were intolerant. In fact, the proposed Draft Constitution provided both for a state religion and for freedom of religion. The establishment of a state religion, as K'ang saw it, would not mean that every citizen had to accept it but merely that the government recognized the fact that Confucianism had been accepted by the majority of the people as the most valuable system of thought. K'ang pointed to Britain and other nations to show that state religions need not restrict freedom of religion.[34]

This argument satisfied most of K'ang's opponents, including Ch'en Tu-hsiu, who retracted some of his previous points, and Chang Tung-sun, who was a great admirer of Confucianism. Chang, however, went on to argue that since Confucianism was indeed already a state religion in this sense, there was nothing to be gained by enacting political measures to support it.[35] Most important, Ch'en Tu-hsiu pointed out, the government's revenue was contributed by the people without reference to religious belief. Therefore, even if religious freedom was preserved, state support of Confucianism alone would be a denial of financial equality to other religions. Ch'en then suggested that all the Confucian temples and their sacrificial functions be abolished.[36]

This radical proposal to abolish the visible symbols of Confucianism appealed strongly to many young intellectuals of the time. There were men like Ch'en Tu-hsiu himself who took a naturalistic and materialistic stand, believing that all religions would be abandoned in the future and be replaced by science, because, in the long run, all mankind's problems could be solved by science.[37] Others took an agnostic viewpoint. Still others tended to be pragmatic or positivistic, to search for reasons to exclude or find a substitute for religion. Broadly speaking, during the years from 1912 to 1917 when Confucianism as a religion was disputed, an anti-religious intellectual climate was developing. The failure of the monarchical restoration in the summer of 1917 cast the Confucian religion movement into oblivion. Then, from 1919 to the early twenties, mainly through the efforts of the Young China Association (*Shao-nien Chung-kuo hsüeh-hui*), anti-religious feelings spread among the youth.

The debate on the problem of Confucian religion, however, did not merely have negative effects on Chinese youth. The argument by both sides for freedom of belief and people's rights seems to have fostered the growth of a spectacular liberal revolt in the May Fourth Movement.

CONFUCIANISM AND THE DEMOCRATIC WAY OF LIFE

When the political reformers of the late Ch'ing period attempted to justify their policies in Confucian terms, they were compelled to reinterpret Confucianism. The abolition of the monarchy was inconceivable according to the conventional interpretation of the Confucian doctrine, and daring reinterpretation was required if sanctions were to be found for a constitutionally limited monarchy. It was no wonder that T'an Ssu-t'ung, an iconoclast and anti-monarchist, had no use for Confucius until he became acquainted with K'ang Yu-wei's reinterpretations.[38]

K'ang seized upon a hint from the Classics in the Modern Text and elaborated a theory which influenced the Confucian movement for decades following. This was what might be called the Confucian theory of periodization: "to link up the Three Dynasties [i.e., Hsia, Shang, and Chou] and to unfold the Three Ages" (*t'ung san t'ung, chang san shih*). According to this theory, Confucius divided human history into three ages: (1) the Age of Government in Tumult (*chü-luan shih*), exemplified by Confucius' own time; (2) the Age of Rising Peace (*sheng-p'ing shih*) or Minor Peace (*hsiao-k'ang*), covering the Three Dynasties, Hsia, Shang, and Chou; according to K'ang, this sequence depended on reform and had characterized all periods of good government from the time of Confucius to the late nineteenth century; (3) the Age of Universal Peace (*t'ai-p'ing shih*), or One World (*ta-t'ung*), a utopia with the characteristics of a republican democracy, economic communism, and anarchism, in which human beings would at last become demigods. Each of the three ages is in turn broken down into three subperiods, which are labeled with the same terms as in the first gross periodization. And these nine are similarly divided and redivided, making a total of eighty-one ages. In K'ang's interpretation, the "Confucian Magna Charta," i.e., the *Spring and Autumn Annals,* provided a "written constitution" for the Age of Tumult in the form of "explicit ideas," whereas the unwritten constitutions for the other two ages were contained, in order to prevent possible persecution by political rulers, in an esoteric tradition of interpretation (i.e., "subtle expositions") of the Classics passed on orally from Confucius to his followers, then to Mencius, and finally to the Modern Text Confucians. The principles for one age, K'ang maintained, should not be mistakenly applied to other ages.[39]

Whatever its intrinsic merits, this theory certainly permitted the flexible application of Confucian principles. In 1898 the reformers argued that needed reforms should be carried out under a monarchy instead of a republic because they were living in an Age of Rising Peace which had become corrupt. A republic was not to be realized until the remote third age. Later, during the Republic, the Confucianists used the same theory to blame the republicans and revolutionaries for all evils, saying that the republican system had been established prematurely. Naturally the Confucianists supported the 1916 movement to restore the monarchy. When this failed, they could still insist on Confucianism as a doctrine for all times and a panacea for all ills. In idealistic appeal, they could outdo not only the republicans but also the socialists and anarchists—and in later times, the communists—for they pointed out that Confucius had anticipated and planned not only a democracy or a classless society, but a death-free world.[40] Those Confucian principles obviously contrary to modern ideals could be explained away as applicable only to the Age of Tumult, or as forgeries.[41]

The anti-Confucianists would not accept the "periodization" of Confucianism, though they seemed to have their own argument based on social periodization. Ch'en Tu-hsiu and Wu Yü took the position that Confucianism was a product of a feudal and autocratic society, that it was created to support that order, and that its principles were obviously incompatible with republican and democratic life. Confucius, they argued, had consistently supported autocratic monarchy and the principle of unconditional loyalty of ministers and subjects to a sovereign. How could all this be applied to an age without monarchs? Wu Yü pointed out that although Mencius had remarked, "In a state, the people are of primary importance, the shrines of the state gods come next, but the monarch is least important," Mencius had also said, "Those who reject their monarchs and fathers are beasts."[42] According to Ch'en, Confucianism and monarchy were indissolubly bound.[43] In a letter of 1916, which K'ang Yu-wei wrote to President Li Yüan-hung and Premier Tuan Ch'i-jui praising Li as a great leader and soliciting his support for the Confucian religion, Ch'en found cause to attack the Confucianists with their own theories. "Confucius' *Annals* intended to reprove and condemn or to 'execute by words and pen' usurpers and rebels; now we have a criminal case: The president whom you are praising so highly is the general who was the very first to raise the rebel flag in 1911 to overthrow the Manchu monarchy. At that time you denounced him as a 'wicked rebel.' How would you now pass judgment according to your Confucian 'constitution'?"[44]

As a reply to Ch'en, the Confucianists might have been able to cite several cases in which Confucius and Mencius approved of justifiable rebellions and the fact that early Confucians even took part in rebellions. According to K'ang's interpretation, Confucius had his ideal of One World wherein there would be no monarch. But the difficulty was that the monarchical movement itself, supported by K'ang Yu-wei's group, seemed clear proof that Ch'en was right. When such Confucian apologists as Ku Shih and Ch'ang Nai-te suggested that the autocrats, with the aid of Han and Sung scholars, had distorted and misused Confucius' teachings, Ch'en scored a good debating point by asking why they chose Confucianism and not some other philosophy to fashion into a support for their tyrannies.[45]

According to the anti-Confucianists, there were a number of other Confucian principles which were incompatible with the modern democratic way of life. For example, free choice of political affiliation was essential to constitutional government (whether monarchical or republican); sons and wives must be able to join political parties other than those of their parents and husbands; but according to Confucianism, sons must accept their parents' belief, at least until three years after the latter's death, and women must obey their fathers, husbands, and sons.[46]

A more fundamental question was whether even the remote ultimate ideals of Confucianism were compatible with modern democratic principles. In the chapter "The Operation of Li" "Li yun" from the *Record of Rites*, Confucius was represented as opposed to the inheritance of political power and to private ownership of property. The authorship of this passage had been in dispute for centuries. The early Confucians had rejected it mainly because they thought it heretical and consequently attributed it to Taoist or Mohist sources.[47] But Ch'en Tu-hsiu claimed it was of little consequence to whom this passage was attributed; even the ideal of One World now proudly ascribed to Confucius was also inconsistent with democratic principles. In the ideal world a sovereign freely chose his successor, selecting, it is true, virtuous and able men rather than his blood descendants, but still transmitting power from ruler to ruler without recourse to popular elections.[48]

The anti-Confucianists held the Confucians responsible for all the despotic practices in Chinese history. They claimed that Confucianism was a natural tool of despotism, and that Confucius himself, when in government, pursued a harsh and intolerant policy toward his opponents. Such accusations were no more true than the eulogies of the Confucianists.[49] The essential questions were: What were the political philosophies, institutions, laws and customs rightly or wrongly attributed to Confucius, and what were their effects? Did the Confucian idea of "benevolent monarchy" (*jen-cheng*) provide a check to the autocratic power, and if so, to what extent? Such questions were debated in a polemical spirit by partisans on one side or the other of monarchy or state religion. There was much inconsistency in the views expressed. For example, in his above-mentioned letter proposing a state religion to President Li and Premier Tuan, K'ang Yu-wei modified his earlier proposal when he suggested that the government should "follow and carry out, as before, those [Confucian principles] which are not contradictory to the conditions of a republic."[50] This paradoxical proposal shows clearly why the periodization theory had to be employed as a *deus ex machina*. On the other side, the main argument of the anti-Confucianists was certainly that, if Confucianism were to be re-established as an official doctrine, the same intellectual stagnation would recur which, they maintained, China had already suffered for over two thousand years. They sometimes went so far as to reject Confucianism as a whole, whereas they conceded at other times that it was not without certain merits.[51]

THE ATTACK ON THE OLD ETHICS

The Confucian social theory and ethics, popularly known since the early Republic as *chiu li-chiao*, became the major target of attack from the young intellectuals for a few years following 1918. Under the influence of Western thought and following the liberation from monarchical control, and as the new economy and urban life developed and expanded, the Chinese intellectuals began to feel a great need for individual freedom. Nationalist sentiment was growing, intensified by China's failure in diplomatic relations. Now it seemed clear that a strong nation-state must be established to resist foreign aggression. It was further argued that a society based on the family ideal and clan system and regulated by Confucian ethics constituted a great obstacle to this end. Though the two demands—for greater individual freedom and for a strong nation-state—appeared incompatible, both led to attacks on the traditional social organization and its ethics.

Modern exponents of Confucianism often emphasized Confucius' teachings of *jen* (benevolence) and *i* (righteousness). But these are abstract ideas with little behavioral force. Historically more weight had been attached to *li* (propriety), as interpreted by Han scholars and systematized in later centuries, which prescribed social roles and obligations for a stable hierarchical society. *Li* specified the proper attitudes and modes of behavior which should obtain between old and young, noble and base, near and distant kin, members of upper and lower social groups.[52]

These traditional social and ethical principles were vigorously attacked by such writers as Ch'en Tu-hsiu and Wu Yü. They charged that these rules amounted to a caste system, which should not be retained in a democratic republic.[53] As long as such ethical and social principles governed the family and clan systems, neither personal nor economic independence of the individual was possible. In accordance with Confucian theory, grown-up children could not own private property until the death of their parents, and in normal cases women were without economic rights.[54] Furthermore, *li* demanded a one-sided female chastity, and prescribed many irksome taboos in relations between the sexes.[55]

The basis of the old *li-chiao* was, as Wu Yü pointed out, the traditional paternalistic family system. The system's principle of "filial piety" (*hsiao*) out of which grew the principle of absolute "loyalty" (*chung*) to the sovereign, formed the theoretical foundation of despotism. Originally, in Confucius, the father's authority was limited by his obligation to be kind, and the child's piety was supposed to spring from natural affection. However, when *li* was elaborated and institutionalized in later times, filial piety was regarded more as a duty than affection, and, in practice, moral checks to parental authority were ineffective. Similarly, in the original Confucian sense, *chung* meant loyalty or honesty toward others, whether of monarch to minister, minister to monarch, or friend to friend.[56] But after Confucius' time (as Mr. Mote shows elsewhere in this volume) *chung* was often interpreted as a one-way obligation of ministers and subjects toward the monarch. From the Han period onward, filial piety was identified with loyalty to the sovereign; the state was compared with the family and the sovereign with the father. These interpretations were set down definitively in the *Classic of Filial Piety (Hsiao-ching)*, a work of the late Warring States or early Han period, the authorship of which is in doubt. The *Classic of Loyalty (Chung-ching)* appeared during the early Sung period. It imitated the *Classic of Filial Piety* and was attributed to a Confucian scholar of the later Han period. With these late interpretations of *hsiao* and *chung*, the subjects' absolute obedience to their sovereign became an unequivocal duty.[57] Further, through the theory of the "three bases of *li*" (*li san pen*), developed by Hsün-tzu, the sovereign, father, and teacher were linked together with Heaven and Earth.[58] If these theories were observed literally, then an individual had no existence outside of the family and the emperor's court. Consequently, Wu Yü remarked, "The effect of the idea of filial piety has been to turn China into a big factory for the production of obedient subjects."[59]

This whole body of legal and ethical principles was effectively challenged by the young intellectuals during the May Fourth period. Hu Shih, Lo Chia-lun, and many other writers fired the youth to demand with increasing vehemence the individual's freedom and woman's emancipation. In the student demonstrations and strikes following May 4, 1919, boy and girl students started to meet and work together, a practice not allowed by traditional Confucian proprieties. Subsequently coeducation was established in China. Among the young intellectuals, arranged marriages were being abandoned in favor of "love marriages." Young men and women rose to rebel against their parents. Family resistance, which sometimes led to matrimonial tragedies, helped to stir up defiance among the youth against Confucian ethics and fortified the older generation's impression that the morals of the young were deteriorating and a restoration of Confucian moral authority was desirable.[60]

The May Fourth Movement was by no means the first revolt against the Confucian institution of filial piety, and its spokesmen drew on ancient Taoist, Legalist, and Mohist arguments to attack this value.

The fact that criticisms from such divergent and contrasting points of view were reiterated to support the new anti-Confucianism was an indication of the ideological heterogeneity of the modern anti-Confucianists. The young intellectuals, with their inclination toward liberalism and anarchism, and their desire for the emancipation of the individual, found Taoism more appealing than the established conventions. With their new nationalism in the face of foreign threats they responded to the Legalist advocacy of a strong state.[61] They saw in Mohism ideals similar to those of Western socialism whose influence in China was increasing.[62]

By contrast, original Confucianism preached moderation and adaptation. Young intellectuals of the early Republic apparently felt that this doctrine was too passive for the militarist threat from outside and for international power politics: Wu Yü argued that even the souls of Confucius and Mencius, and the Thirteen Classics, could not save the two sages' birthplace, Shantung, from Japanese occupation, and that the living members of the Confucian Society with their old ethics could not resist Japan.[63]

Central to all discussion of morals is the problem of the relation between the individual and organization. Unlike either individualists or totalitarians, early Confucians, who possibly descended from a subjugated tribe with a philosophy for exploiting the virtue or strength of weakness, tried to solve the problem in a middle way, that is, by a relative and humanistic solution achieved gradually, by degrees. This idea of degree and gradualness dominated Confucian educational principles and was easily extended to apply to the relation of the individual to his family and that of the state to the people. In Confucian theory, there seems to be no concept of the public good except that based on familial relations.[64] Although the Confucians tried to temper their doctrine of duties by emphasizing relations of natural affection, their paternalism was sometimes distorted to an extreme point, illustrated by the legend of a man's attempt to bury his son alive for the sake of filial piety to his mother.[65] This is probably why young men in the early Republic went so far as to describe the old family system and ethics as "sources of all evils."[66]

Defending the Confucian ethics, the old literati showed as much passion as the young intellectuals. That stubborn moralist Lin Shu, in a letter of 1919 to Ts'ai Yüan-p'ei, listed his reasons for defending Confucian ethics: "Confucius was," said he, citing the *Mencius*, "a sage adjustable to any time in which he might have lived."[67] In other words, he would always have adapted himself to the times. To attribute the present weakness of China to him or to the traditional ethics was, according to Lin, "as if a sick child should refuse to see a good doctor to cure itself, but instead should denounce the 'latent disease' of its parents and drive them away." Lin maintained that the essence of Chinese ethics was also observed by the Westerners. "Of late," Lin said, "the new reformers have propounded the so-called 'new ethics.' They denounce filial piety on the ground that children are produced by parents only because of the parents' sexual passion, not as an act of parental grace. This absurd statement comes from 'the head of a man with the speech of a beast.' There is no use arguing with him." Lin also accused them of judging as good the lustful women and disloyal ministers of history.[68] In this argument Lin, like his Confucianist contemporaries, seems to have missed the point: the problem was not whether Confucius could have adjusted himself to modern times but whether the people of modern times should adjust themselves to Confucius' teachings and even to the pseudo-teachings forged by later writers.

CONFUCIAN ISSUES REDEFINED

In support of his theory that Confucius had promoted institutional reforms by means of an imaginative description of antiquity, K'ang Yu-wei argued that there had really been no reliable record of Chinese antiquity.[69] This idea could be taken to mean that the antiquity described in the Classics was merely a forgery and Confucius' account of antiquity had no factual support. K'ang's theory therefore backfired when the anti-Confucian movement gained strength.

Meanwhile, K'ang's position was supported and reinforced by his follower Ts'ui Shih (1851–1924), a scholar who taught at Peking University in the early Republic. After 1917 Ts'ui's disciple Ch'ien Hsüan-t'ung, a fervent supporter of the Modern Text school who was influenced by both K'ang and Ts'ui, also taught at the University. At that time, Hu Shih introduced pragmatic "genetic method" into the study of ancient Chinese philosophies. By 1920 another student of Ts'ui, Ku Chieh-kang, inspired by the Modern Text School and pragmatism and encouraged by the then rising new-thought and new-literature movements, started his research on the Chinese Classics and antiquity. Since Ku and Ch'ien took a very skeptical attitude in their studies, they were known in China as "Antiquity-Doubters" (*I-ku-p'ai*). Mainly through their efforts, the Chinese view of Confucius' relation to the Six Classics was greatly altered.

The complicated problem of the authorship of the Classics is not yet completely solved, but we are here concerned with the changing attitudes toward the problem, not its solution. Since the Sung period, scholars had been in doubt about the authorship of several of the Six Classics; but generally it was accepted that Confucius had participated in writing or revising some or all of them. The "Antiquity-Doubters" in the 1920's and after took a wholly different view. They suggested that the term "Six Classics" was created after Confucius' time, probably at the end of the Warring States period. In their opinion, these were only the names of six subjects Confucius taught his disciples. The original *Shih, Shu, Li, I,* and *Ch'un-ch'iu* were five unrelated books, while the alleged lost *Book of Music* (*Yüeh*) had never existed. Confucius only read and used the five works as textbooks, and in some cases might have interpreted them, but never wrote or revised them.[70] Although these views were disputed by some scholars, many writers, especially in the twenties and early thirties, accepted them. Consequently, from the late Ch'ing to the early Republic, Confucius' position was, generally speaking, reduced from that of an "uncrowned king" and religious founder to that of an "old teacher" (*chiao-shou lao-ju*). As Ku Chieh-kang remarked, "Confucius was regarded in the *Ch'un-ch'iu* period (722–481 B.C.) as a gentleman, in the time of the Warring States (403–221 B.C.) as a sage, in the Western Han (202 B.C.–A.D. 9) as a religious founder, after the Eastern Han (A.D. 25–220) again a sage, and now is about to be regarded once more as a gentleman."[71] This evolution was, however, not entirely unfavorable to the Master. Stripped of the old mystery, he was also rediscovered. Many writers came to see him as the Socrates of the East—China's first popular educator and great philosopher.[72]

In the 1920's, along with the new studies of the Classics, came a new group of Confucian defenders, some of whom had previously been associated with K'ang Yu-wei. Distressed by the tragic World War, such Chinese thinkers as Yen Fu and Liang Ch'i-ch'ao began to feel that the materialistic civilization of the West could only lead the world to disaster, and that the Eastern civilization, of which Confucius' teachings were a central part, should prevail in the world. With the publication in 1921 of Liang Sou-ming's "Eastern and Western Civilizations and Their Philosophies" (*Tung Hsi wen-hua chi ch'i che-hsüeh*), this view was strengthened in spite of subsequent criticisms from the Westernizers such as Hu Shih. Meanwhile, Liang Ch'i-ch'ao's now pessimistic view of science, expressed at the end of World War I, was echoed in Carsun Chang's speech in 1923 provoking the famous polemic on "science and view of life." While the two great debates were not carried on entirely in terms of Confucianism, the major challengers of Western civilization and science were to a degree committed to Confucian or Neo-Confucian philosophies. In many cases, Confucian ideas were brought into the controversies to be compared with Western ideas.

In their theoretical aspects, the debates over Confucianism after the twenties differed from the earlier ones. Few writers in the later period defended all of Confucius' ethical and political principles; only some major Confucian themes were considered. Meanwhile, as a result of the radical approach of the "Antiquity-Doubters," many Classics, which had previously been offered with unhesitating confidence as bases in the defense and criticism of Confucianism, could not now be cited without supporting testimony.

The sentiments stirred up among the populace and in the government by the early Confucianist and anti-Confucianist campaigns existed even two decades later, and resulting clashes between the two groups continued into the thirties and forties. "Reverence for Confucius," "Read the Classics," and "Overthrow Confucius and Sons" still remained popular slogans, although they were not the serious intellectual problems they had been a generation before.

CONCLUSION

The anti-Confucian movement in the early Republic, viewed in historical perspective, might be considered on the one hand the manifestation of a desire, fed by Western ideas, for intellectual liberation from an imposed state ideology or religion. On the other hand, and probably more important, it should be seen as an attempt by the Chinese intellectuals to jettison a time-honored ideology and way of life in order to save China from the weakened international position in which she found herself at the end of the nineteenth century. These two reactions were apparent, as we have pointed out above, in the demands for greater individual freedom and for a strong modern nation-state.

But the demand for individual freedom was from the beginning very weak. Without a strong middle class, the argument advanced by a few liberals in the May Fourth period that a powerful state would be achieved when its citizens became free individuals had never gained wide support among the Chinese. In their attack on Confucian ethical and socio-political principles, the young intellectuals made individual freedom, equality, and independence some of their major themes. Student writers even proposed during the May Fourth period that individualism based on the consideration of self-interest should be adopted as a substitute for the old ethical teachings.[73] Many of them, however, also cited collectivistic theories to underscore the ineffectiveness of Confucianism as a way to strengthen the nation. Indeed, the desire for a strong state to resist foreign aggression became so intense that it soon drowned out the argument that the nation could be saved only when its individuals lived as free and independent beings.

Though the early anti-Confucian movement showed a tendency toward attack on authoritarianism in general, this trend did not develop. Starting in the late Ch'ing period when Confucianism was used as authority to justify divergent political programs, appeals to one orthodoxy or another continued. The challenge to authoritarianism in the early Republic, albeit often in the name of liberalism, was actually advanced as much under the influence of anarchist ideas as by liberalism and individualism. With the decline of anarchism and liberalism in China in the twenties, the anti-authoritarian drive soon ran out of steam.

On the other hand, it is clear that the thinking of both the Confucian-

ist and anti-Confucianist groups had been biased by a kind of nationalistic sentiment and complicated by undiscriminating attitudes toward
tradition. Justification by tradition soon became an expedient. This was
well exemplified by the attitude of the traditionalistic Confucianists
toward the modernization of China, which was caustically and incisively
summarized by Lu Hsün: "There is a favorite technique used by those
who know the old literature. When a new idea is introduced, they call
it 'heresy' and bend all their efforts to destroy it. If that new idea, by its
struggle against their efforts, wins a place for itself, they then discover
that 'it's the same thing as was taught by Confucius.' They object to all
imported things, saying that these are 'to convert Chinese into barbarians,' but when the barbarians become rulers of China, they discover
these 'barbarians' are also descendants of the Yellow Emperor."[74] But
Lu Hsün only told one side of the story. As we have shown, the "favorite
technique" was also adopted by the reformers, and to a lesser degree by
the nationalist revolutionaries and later the leftists. With this technique,
K'ang Yu-wei and other reformers easily won the sympathy of the young
intellectuals and undermined the opposition of such people as Chang
Chih-tung and Ku Hung-ming. Nationalist writers such as Hu Han-min
declared in 1919 that socialist ideas could be found in Confucianism,[75]
while leftist writers such as Kuo Mo-jo in later years often followed the
example of the early Nationalists and described Confucius as a revolutionary.[76]

The anti-Confucianists during the early Republic, however, presented a unique case. They emphasized the basic differences between
Confucian principles and modern Western ideas of science and democracy, and insisted on uncompromising renunciation of the former. In
this respect, they might be considered the extreme opposition to the
ultraconservative group, represented by Chang Chih-tung, Ku Hung-
ming, and others. During the May Fourth period, Lin Shu and Yen Fu
almost retreated to this latter group. Unlike K'ang Yu-wei, these late
ultraconservatives believed that Chinese tradition, so different from
Western civilization, had supreme merit in its own right and for its own
sake. With these arguments, they might once have provided a strong
opposition to the young intellectuals, but the power of Western learning
as the means of reinvigorating China was by now widely accepted.
Many young Chinese intellectuals could not preserve confidence in
their own tradition unless they identified strands of that tradition with
the values of modern Western civilization.

In the contention that the ideas of Confucius and his disciples had
prefigured modern ideas, the question remained as to what Confucian
principles really meant. This was the question that precipitated the anti-

Confucian movement, and the point at which the Confucianists defeated themselves. According to K'ang Yu-wei, almost all the Western ideas cherished by the younger intellectuals had been recommended by Confucius. Thus democratic republicanism was a Confucian ideal (but the boy emperor was to be restored to the throne); in the ideal Confucian society the family system and private ownership of property would be completely abolished (but the attack on these institutions by the younger generation was premature and immoral); and so on. And yet, as K'ang saw it, it was proper that Confucianism should be established in the constitution as a state religion.

Given the above arguments, the course of the anti-Confucianists' campaign was in a sense predetermined. The anti-Confucianists lost no time in putting together a list of all the principles expressed in the Classics which they considered contradictory to modern ideas. As a result, in most of the debates for and against Confucianism in the first decade of the Republic, Confucius was presented either as God or as Satan.

One may ask why the issue was charged with so much emotion, and why the reformers and revolutionaries failed to appropriate certain strands of Confucianism or other traditions to consolidate a modern state. Attempts to do this had been made throughout the late Ch'ing period. The failure to do so now did not necessarily prove that the Confucian tradition was anachronistic. It was rather that China lacked the necessary political, social, and economic prerequisites to make such an appropriation successful. Meiji Japan made a successful appropriation, but the interpretation and application of Confucianism in modern Japan and China were not the same. Further, the Chinese were more emotionally attached to Confucian teachings than the Japanese were. More important, the educational and social background of the young Chinese anti-Confucianists, with their sympathies for radical liberalism, anarchism, or socialism, set them apart from the older generation and distinguished them sharply from the Japanese elite of the Meiji period.

Finally we may ask how the anti-Confucian movement affected the Confucian Chinese tradition and Chinese society. Unquestionably the iconoclasm of the "angry youth" had devastating effects on the old dogmas. After these protests and criticisms Confucianism as a coherent body of thought was never the same again. The high illiteracy might appear to have prevented the spread of criticism of old ways and old values among the masses. But the May Fourth Movement was in a sense a popular movement, and the youths' campaign for the "new culture" and patriotism soon reached all the major cities, at least two hundred in twenty-two provinces. The struggle of youth against the family and traditional social relations consequently was carried throughout the land. Furthermore, the high rate of illiteracy gave unusual power and prestige to intellectuals, and their ideas therefore carried proportionately greater weight among the populace. The institutionalizing of new ideas was of course a long process, but even in the beginning it influenced the life of ordinary people. The authority of Confucianism suffered serious attacks, even as the society it had long dominated underwent great change.

These changes in ideology and afterwards in a way of life did not mean the complete elimination of the influence of Confucianism. Nor did it mean that after such attacks certain Confucian principles were not reinterpreted to suit modern needs. While the disintegration of the old ethics probably emancipated the individual somewhat from the bond with his family and clan, it also cleared the way for placing the individual in bondage to state, party, or other social and economic organizations.

NOTES

NOTES TO INTRODUCTION

1. Marvin Meyers, *The Jacksonian Persuasion* (Stanford, Calif., 1957), p. 6.

2. *Yen-shih Chia-hsün*, Wan-yu Wen-k'u ed. (Shanghai, 1937), ch. 1, p. 14. The second part of the quotation echoes the *Lü-shih ch'un-ch'iu*, ch. 7, p. 41 (Ssu-pu Ts'ung-k'an ed.), and reflects the compromise with Legalism which the Confucians first made in the Han dynasty.

3. Jacques Gernet, *Les Aspects économiques dun Bouddhisme dans la société chinoise du Ve au Xe siècle* (Saigon, 1956), pp. 288–92.

4. Passage from the county gazetteer (*hsien-chih*) of Anking, Anhwei, translated in John K. Shryock, *The Temples of Anking and Their Cults* (Paris, 1931), pp. 132–33.

5. Cyril Birch, *Stories from a Ming Collection* (London, 1958), p. 8. Translated from the Preface to the *Ku-chin Hsiao-shuo* of Feng Meng-lung.

6. *Shih-chi* (T'ung-wen edition of 1884), ch. 99, p. 6b.

NOTES TO THE CONFUCIANIZATION OF SOUTH CHINA

Abbreviations Used in the Notes

The following Standard Histories are cited from the Po-na-pen texts:

CS	Chin Shu	HTS	Hsin T'ang Shu	SC	Shih-chi
CTS	Chiu T'ang Shu	LS	Liang Shu	SKC	San-kuo Chih
HHS	Hou Han Shu	NCS	Nan Ch'i Shu	WS	Wei Shu
HS	Han Shu	NS	Nan Shih		

Geographical descriptions:

CHTC   *Chiang-hsi T'ung-chih*, by Chao Chih-ch'ien and Liu K'un-i (1881). 180 ch.

FCTC   *Fu-chien T'ung-chih*, by Ch'en Shou-ch'i and Liu Erh-chien, revised ed. (1871). 278 ch.

HNTC   *Hu-nan T'ung-chih*, by Li Han-chang and Tseng Kuo-ch'üan (1885). 288 ch. Commercial Press ed., Shanghai, 1934.

KTTC   *Kuang-tung T'ung-chih*, by Juan Yüan and Chiang Fan (1822). 334 ch. Commercial Press ed., Shanghai, 1934.

YNTC   *Yun-nan T'ung-chih*, by Ts'en Yü-ying (1894). 262 ch.

1. Toshisada Naba, *Chūka shisō* ("Sinocentric Thought") (Tokyo, 1936).

2. Henri Maspero, *Le Taoisme* (Paris, 1950), pp. 15–16.

3. *The Analects*, ch. 3, par. 5, James Legge, *The Chinese Classics*, I (Oxford, 1893), 156.
4. *The Analects*, ch. 14, par. 18. Legge, *op. cit.*, p. 282.
5. *The Analects*, ch. 5, par. 13. Legge, *op. cit.*, p. 174.
6. *The Analects*, ch. 9, par. 13. Legge, *op. cit.*, p. 221.
7. *The Analects*, ch. 12, par. 5. Legge, *op. cit.*, p. 253.
8. *The Analects*, ch. 13, par. 19. Legge, *op. cit.*, p. 271.
9. *The Analects*, ch. 15, par. 5. Legge, *op. cit.*, p. 295.
10. Matthew 10:16.
11. *The Analects*, ch. 15, par. 38. Legge, *op. cit.*, p. 305.
12. *Meng-tzu*, Book 3, part 1, sec. 4. Legge, *The Chinese Classics*, II, 253–55.
13. *Meng-tzu*, Book 1, part 2, sec. 11. Legge, *op. cit.*, p. 171.
14. *Meng-tzu*, Book 3, part 2, sec. 9. Legge, *op. cit.*, p. 284.
15. LS, ch. 54, pp. 39a–40b; WS, ch. 101, pp. 22b–26a; *Chou Shu*, ch. 50, pp. 10b–13a; NS, ch. 79, pp. 14a–15a; *Sui shu*, ch. 83, pp. 6a–8a; CTS, ch. 148, pp. 3b–5b; HTS, ch. 221, pp. 4a–5b; *Sung-shih*, ch. 490, pp. 8a–12b.
16. SC, ch. 110, pp. 15b–17a.
17. Hisayuki Miyakawa, *Rikuchōshi Kenkyū* ("A Historical Study of the Six Dynasties Period") (Tokyo, 1956), pp. 144 ff.
18. SC, ch. 97, pp. 6a–7a.
19. YNTC, ch. 11, p. 7b.
20. *Kuang-chou Hsien-hsien Chuan* ("Lives of Former Worthies of Kuang-chou"), cited in KTTC, ch. 268, pp. 4644–45.
21. HHS, ch. 86, pp. 20b–21c. YNTC, ch. 11, p. 31b. Also the *Hua-yang Kuo-chih* ("A Topography of Southwest China") by Chang Ch'ü, a fourth-century writer.
22. SC, ch. 31, p. 1b.
23. CHTC, ch. 134, p. 4b.
24. Y. Hisamura, "Kodai Shisen ni Dochaku seru Kamminzoku no Raireki ni Tsuite" ("The Origin of Chinese Letters in Ancient Szechwan"), *Rekishi-gaku Kenkyū*, No. 204 (1957); N. Kano, "Gokan matsu no Sesō to Ha-Shoku no Dōkō," ("Conditions at the End of the Later Han and Tendencies in the Pa-Shu Region"), *Tōyōshi Kenkyū*, Vol. XV, No. 3 (1957).
25. HHS, ch. 76, pp. 3a–4b; KTTC, ch. 231, p. 4066.
26. HHS, ch. 76, pp. 6a–6b.
27. SKC, ch. 53, p. 9a.
28. The *T'ao-shih Chia-chuan* ("History of the T'ao Family"), as quoted in the commentary to *Chin-shu Chiao-chu* (Peking, 1928), ch. 120, p. 10b. Also KTTC, ch. 268, p. 2648.
29. Unlocated.
30. See note 5.
31. HHS, ch. 76, p. 17a; KTTC, ch. 231, p. 4067.
32. HS, ch. 89, pp. 2b–3a.
33. HHS, ch. 57, pp. 3a–3b.
34. HHS, ch. 36, p. 26a.
35. *T'ai-p'ing Kuang-chi*, ch. 173; HNTC, ch. 160, p. 3176.
36. HHS, ch. 180, p. 25a.
37. HHS, ch. 86, p. 14a.
38. HHS, ch. 76, pp. 4a–4b.

39. Yü Fu, "Chiang-piao Chuan," cited in *SKC*, ch. 46, pp. 14b–15a.

40. Fukui Kōjun, "Dōkyō no Kisoteki Kenkyū" ("A Basic Study of Taoism") (Tokyo, 1952), Appendix, pp. 375–76; *SKC*, ch. 49, p. 10a.

41. Chang Kuan-ying, "Liang Chin Nan-pei-ch'ao Shih-ch'i Min-tsu Tapien-tung chung ti Lin-chün Man" ("The Lin-chün Man Tribes in the Great Migration in the Periods of the Chin and the Southern and Northern Dynasties"), *Li-shih Yen-chiu*, No. 2 (1957), pp. 67–85.

42. *Chou Shu*, ch. 35, pp. 23a–24a; *Pei shih*, ch. 36, pp. 19b–20a.

43. *CS*, ch. 120, p. 2a.

44. Chang Kuan-ying, *op. cit.*, pp. 70, 83.

45. *SKC*, ch. 35, p. 8b, commentary.

46. Wang Shu-wu, "Kuan yü Pai-tsu Tsu-yüan Wen-t'i" ("On the Origin of the Pai Tribe"), *Li-shih Yen-chiu*, No. 4 (1957), pp. 1–17.

47. *SKC*, ch. 45, p. 4b.

48. *SKC*, ch. 43, p. 7b.

49. *SKC*, ch. 35, p. 8b, commentary.

50. *LS*, ch. 22, p. 6b; *NS*, ch. 52, p. 2a.

51. *LS*, ch. 52, p. 3a.

52. *FCTC*, ch. 55, pp. 1b, 30b–31a; ch. 56, p. 1a.

53.

The T'ao Family

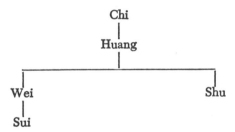

The Shih Family

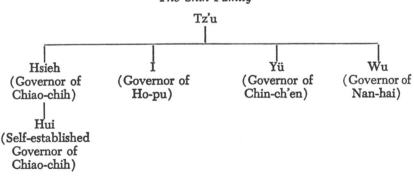

54. *Sui-shu*, ch. 80, p. 4b; *Pei-shih*, ch. 91, p. 12b; *KTTC*, ch. 268, pp. 4651–52.

55. Also *FCTC*, ch. 170, p. 8a.

56. *CTS*, ch. 177, pp. 9b–10a; *HTS*, ch. 182, p. 6b.

57. *Ch'üan T'ang-wen,* ch. 81. An Edict of Hsüan-tsung (847–59).
58. *KTTC,* ch. 233, p. 4103.
59. *HTC,* ch. 163, p. 2a.
60. *HTS,* ch. 150, p. 3a; ch. 203, p. 7a.
61. *HTS,* ch. 197, p. 7b.
62. *Liu Pin-k'o wen-chi.* (Ssu-pu Ts'ung-k'an ed.)
63. *CTS,* ch. 187A, pp. 7a–7b; *HTS,* ch. 112, pp. 1a–1b; *KTTC,* ch. 262, p. 4536.
64. *CTS,* ch. 174, p. 2a.
65. *CTS,* ch. 192, p. 11b.
66. *Tung-tu shih-lüeh* ("A Brief History of K'ai-feng"), by Wang Ch'eng (S. Sung), ch. 3, p. 4a.
67. *Sung-shih,* ch. 300, p. 15a.
68. *FCTC,* ch. 56, p. 2b.
69. *Chia-ch'ing Shan-yin Hsien-chih,* by Hsü Yüan-mei (1803), ch. 11, p. 2a.
70. *Hsia-men Chih,* by Chou K'ai (1839), ch. 15, p. 9a.
71. *Ch'eng Hsien-chih,* by Yen Ssu-chung (1870), ch. 20, p. 3a.
72. Herold J. Wiens, *China's March Toward the Tropics* (New Haven, 1954), chap. vii, "Frontier Policy and Tribal Administration: The T'u Ssu System," pp. 201–66.
73. Inō Yoshinori, *Taiwan Bunkashi* ("A Cultural History of Taiwan") (1928), II, 1–180.
74. *Chih T'ai Pi-kao Lu* ("Essential Information for Taiwan Administration"), by Ting Yüeh-chien (1867), ch. 1, pp. 30a, 64b–65a.
75. Inō, *op. cit.,* II, 181–211.
76. Inō, *op cit.,* I, 507–12.

NOTES TO SUI YANG-TI

1. I have dealt in some detail with this in "The Formation of Sui Ideology," in John K. Fairbank, ed., *Chinese Thought and Institutions* (Chicago, 1957), pp. 71–104. Peter A. Boodberg's study of the house of Yang in "Marginalia to the Histories of the Northern Dynasties," *HJAS,* IV (1939), 253–70, is of prime importance for any study of the Sui ruling house.
  In the notes that follow, editions cited are Ssu-pu Ts'ung-k'an unless otherwise noted. The histories are cited in the edition of the T'ung-wen Shu-chü, 1884. In the writing of this paper I have benefited greatly from talks with my colleague Dr. K'ai-yu Hsü and, on Yang-ti's poetry, with Professor Jinichi Konishi. The comments of participants in the Third Conference on Chinese Thought have also proved enormously helpful.
2. Cf. Boodberg, *op. cit.,* p. 266. Boodberg was the first to point to the various symptoms of a sense of hubris in the behavior of Wen-ti and to relate that sense to the speed with which the Sui rose to power—a speed which precluded the usual ritual-symbolic preparations for usurpation which Chinese political ideology demanded.
3. Her biography from *Sui-shu,* ch. 36, pp. 4–6, exists in the pioneer

translation of August Pfizmaier, *Darlegungen aus der Geschichte des Hauses Sui* (Vienna, 1881), pp. 25–29.

4. For characterizations of northern women of the period in contrast to southern, see *Yen-shih Chia-hsün*, ch. 1, p. 18, and Moriya Mitsuo, "Nanjin to Hokujin" ("Northerners and Southerners"), *Tōa Ronsō*, VI (1948), 36–60.

5. Cf. Chao I, *Nien-erh Shih Cha-chi* (photolithographic ed. of the Wen-jui Lou, Shanghai, n.d.), ch. 15, p. 13b.

6. Yang Kuang's childhood name was A-mo, a transliteration of the Sanskrit *ambā* ("mother"), often used as a title of respect. The feminine overtones of such a name suggest that it might have been chosen to confuse the evil spirits which prey on male children.

7. The Buddhist activities of the Sui princes are discussed in Yamazaki Hiroshi, *Shina Chūsei Bukkyō no Tenkai* ("The Development of Medieval Chinese Buddhism") (Tokyo, 1942), pp. 291–94.

8. *Sui-shu* (hereafter SS), ch. 3, pp. 1a–1b.

9. *Tzu-chih T'ung-chien* (hereafter TC), ch. 176, p. 6, commentary. The edition cited, including Hu San-hsing's commentary, is that of Yamana Zenjō (Tokyo, 1882).

10. For the biography of Yang Kuang's wife, née Hsiao, see SS, ch. 36, pp. 7–9. TC, ch. 175, p. 14b, places the marriage in 582. The bride's father was the Emperor Ming of the Later Liang—a small state in Hupeh which was successively a satellite of the Western Wei, the Northern Chou, and the Sui. It was abolished by the Sui in 587. The girl, in her upbringing, had been the victim of a southern superstition that children born in the second moon are a threat to their parents and must be adopted out. The SS text may here have the character for "two" as a mistake for "five," since other sources specify fifth-month children as the unlucky ones. Cf. *Feng-su T'ung-i* (ed. of the Centre Franco-chinois, Peking, 1943), ch. 2, p. 20.

11. For a detailed study of the differences in human relations, manners, festivals, ceremonies, food, and customs in general, see Moriya Mitsuo, *op. cit.*

12. Among monarchs of northern origin Frederick II, Hohenstaufen and Christina of Sweden are among those who "took up" Mediterranean culture with full-blooded zeal. The tradition of sentimental lyricizing about the dulcet ways of the south begins in China at this time, and there are many Chinese analogues to Goethe's

> Kennst du das Land, wo die Zitronen blühn,
> Im dunkeln Laub die Gold-Orangen glühn, . . .

13. SS, ch. 3, pp. 1b–2.

14. Cf. Tsukamoto Zenryū, "Zui no Kōnan Seifuku to Bukkyō" ("The Sui Conquest of the South and Buddhism"), *Bukkyō Bunka Kenkyū*, III (1953), 8–9. Tsukamoto makes extensive use of the valuable documents on the relations between Yang Kuang and Chih-i to be found in the *Kuo-ch'ing Pai-lu* by the monk Kuan-ting (561–632). Cf. *Taisho*, XLVI, 793–823. Mr. Leon Hurvitz is making an exhaustive study of this text. Yang Kuang's Buddhist name was drawn from Seng-chao's commentary to the *Vimalakīrtinirdeśa*. It signifies absolute control, the embodiment of thought, meditation, and wisdom.

15. *Kuo-ch'ing Pai-lu*, ch. 3, p. 807b.

16. Cf. Tsukamoto, *op. cit.*, pp. 16–17.

17. SS, ch. 45, p. 4.

18. For the testament, see *Kuo-ch'ing Pai-lu*, ch. 3, pp. 809–10.

19. See Harold D. Lasswell, *Psychopathology and Politics* (Chicago, 1930), p. 50.

20. Boodberg, *op. cit.*, p. 267, was the first to stress the importance of the completion of the sixty-year cycle.

21. Yamazaki Hiroshi, "Yōtei no Shi Dōjō" ("Yang Ti's Four Temples"), *Tōyō Gakuhō*, XXXIV (1952), 22–35, includes a study of the new Jih-yen Ssu. Yamazaki observes that of the total complement of monks in the temple, nearly one-third came from Yang-chou, and all but three came from either the Huai or Yangtse valley areas. This is one of the ways in which southern Buddhism was brought north to dominate the religious life of the capital.

22. *Kuo-ch'ing Pai-lu*, ch. 3, p. 813c. All the allusions are to the Lotus sutra, which was, of course, the supreme scripture of the T'ien-t'ai. Candrākadīpa is the title of the 20,000 Buddhas who succeeded each other preaching the Lotus. The eight are the mortal sons of the last of this series; all became Buddhas. The second Buddha is the fabulous begetter of sixteen sons, including Sakyamuni, all of whom became Buddhas after hearing their father preach the Lotus. For a similar pious salute to his parents, see ch. 2, p. 803b.

23. *SS*, ch. 3, p. 2.

24. *Hsü Kao-seng Chuan*, ch. 11, in *Taishō*, L, 110b.

25. *TC*, ch. 179, p. 13.

26. *SS*, ch. 3, p. 2.

27. See particularly the biography of the lady Hsüan-hua, *SS*, ch. 36, pp. 6–7, and the collection of accounts discussed in Hu San-hsing's commentary to *TC*, ch. 180, pp. 2–2b. A full analysis of all accounts must await a later study.

28. See Etienne Balazs, *Le Traité économique du 'Souei-chou'* (Leiden, 1953), p. 10, note 1.

29. See *SS*, ch. 75, pp. 2b–3, introduction to the biographies of Confucians (*ju-lin*). The account of the revival of Confucian learning by Yang-ti is in marked contrast to the remarks on the Confucians' sad fate in the latter years of Wen-ti's reign. The authors of the *Sui-shu* sense a conflict in historical interpretation here: Wen-ti was indifferent or hostile to Confucianism, yet left the empire strong and prosperous; Yang-ti favored Confucianism, yet brought the empire to ruin. Two explanations of this are offered: (1) the disintegrating effect of struggles against the barbarians; (2) the theory that Yang-ti's Confucian revival was more apparent than real. "There was the empty name of organizing Confucian studies, but there was no reality of spreading Confucian teachings."

30. Yang-ti was furious with official compilers of a new gazetteer who had referred to the inhabitants of the Wu area in the lower Yangtse valley as "eastern barbarians (*tung-i*) who trespass against the rites and the principle of righteousness." Yang-ti chastised them and expatiated on the brilliant culture of the area as far back as the Han, its prime importance as the very center of Chinese culture during the period of disunion, and its incomparable contribution of Confucian scholars, literary figures, and men of talent since the incorporation of the area into the Sui empire. Cf. *Sui-shu Ching-chi-chih K'ao-cheng*, ch. 21, in *Supplements to the Twenty-five Histories*, IV, 5413.

31. Yamazaki, *Chūsei*, pp. 278–79, estimates that only 26 per cent of

all top-ranking Sui officials were of non-Chinese origin, as against 65 per cent under the Northern Chou. He also notes that non-Chinese officials under the Sui tended to be concentrated in the Board of Works and the Board of War. Yamazaki's recent and detailed study "Zuichō Kanryō no Seikaku" ("The Character of Sui Officialdom") in *The Bulletin of the Tokyo Kyōiku University Literature Department*, VI (1956), suggests at several points the trend toward a greater share of power for southerners during the reign of Yang-ti. "The Treatise on Geography," SS, ch. 31, p. 14, remarks that the worthy people of the Kiangsu-Chekiang area subsisted on their official stipends. Cf. Balazs, *op. cit.*, p. 317.

32. I am inclined to reject the account in *TC*, ch. 180, p. 8, which sees the move to a new capital simply as a reaction to advice from oracle-takers.

33. Cf. SS, ch. 24, pp. 17–17b, and Balazs, *op. cit.*, pp. 165–66.

34. Cf. Balazs, *op. cit.*, p. 226, note 182.

35. Cf. SS, ch. 24, p. 18, and Balazs, *op. cit.*, p. 168.

36. One of two poems commemorating the Liao-tung campaign. Cf. *Yüeh-fu Shih-hsüan*, ch. 79, p. 54. The term translated "monstrous beast" is literally "great whale," a metaphor for evil men, here the emperor's enemies; "ancient capital" is literally Hao-ching, said to have been the capital of the Chou conqueror Wu-wang. The term *wu yüan*, "the five plains," refers to the area of Ch'ang-an.

37. For useful materials on the increase of domestic rebellion during and after the Koguryō campaigns, see Woodbridge Bingham, *The Founding of the T'ang Dynasty* (Baltimore, 1941), pp. 37–58, 130–41, and Maps IIa and IIb.

38. For the text, see SS, ch. 22, p. 24.

39. *Chen-kuan Cheng-yao* ("Essentials of Government of the Chen-kuan Period"), compiled by Wu Ching (670–749), ch. 1, pp. 17b–18a. Contains the political views of the great T'ang T'ai-tsung and his ministers, arranged topically. Much of the material is thought to have been drawn from the *shih-lu*, the "veritable record" of T'ai-tsung's reign, a contemporary source that no longer exists. The *Chen-kuan Cheng-yao* was read in both China and Japan for many centuries, and its judgments of Yang-ti were widely influential.

40. *Ibid.*, ch. 3, pp. 1b–2a.

41. Franke, *Geschichte des chinesischen Reiches*, II (Berlin, 1936), 328–29, attributes Yang-ti's patronage of Confucian learning and revival of the examination system to vanity and love of ostentation. The historical reasons for these activities are likely to be found on the level of interpretation I have suggested.

42. I do not consider the *Shu-ching* accounts of the bad-last ruler of the Hsia dynasty; these seem to me to be Chou fabrications designed to lend the persuasion of "historical precedent" to their own ideological interpretation of the supplanting of the evil Shang by the virtuous Chou.

43. Cf. John Weakland and Ruth Bunzel, "An Anthropological Approach to Chinese Culture" (dittographed, Columbia University, 1950), and Warren Muensterberger, "Orality and Dependence: Characteristics of Southern Chinese," *Psychoanalysis and the Social Sciences*, III (1951), 37–69.

44. Cf. Chavannes, *Les Mémoires historiques de Se-ma Ts'ien*, II, 242.

45. Cf. *ibid.*, pp. 235–36, 243; also the speech in his own defense by

Li Ssu from *Shih-chi*, ch. 87, as translated by Derk Bodde in *China's First Unifier* (Leiden, 1938), p. 49.

46. Cf. *SS*, ch. 2, pp. 1–3, and *TC*, ch. 176, pp. 12b–13.

47. Cf. *SS*, ch. 41, p. 3.

48. This accusation is drawn verbatim from the *Shu-ching,* "The speech of Kan." Cf. Legge's translation, p. 153. The translation of *san-cheng* is in doubt. I can only guess how contumely toward the five elements may have manifested itself in the Ch'en emperor's behavior.

49. Cf. *Ch'en-shu*, ch. 6, pp. 15b–16.

50. Text I is *SS*, ch. 4, pp. 16b–18. Text II is *SS*, ch. 70 (comment on the biographies of rebels against the Sui). Text III is *SS*, ch. 5, p. 4 (comment on the reign of the shadow emperor K'ung-ti, Yang-ti's grandson, who "ruled" as a pawn in the struggle for dynastic succession from June 24, 618, to May 25, 619). Cf. Balazs, *Traité économique*, p. 231, note 208. Estimates in the *Pei-shih* differ only in detail, giving further evidence that, in respect to the Sui, this "private history" deviated only slightly from the *Sui-shu*.

51. Cf. *SS*, ch. 22, p. 24.

52. Cf. Etienne Balazs, *Le Traité juridique du 'Souei-chou'* (Leiden, 1954), pp. 89–90.

53. Text II offers a point-by-point comparison between Yang-ti and his father designed to highlight the folly and vice of the son. This exaltation of Wen-ti is strikingly at variance with the historians' judgments on many separate aspects of his reign and his character.

54. *Nien-erh Shih Cha-chi*, ch. 28, pp. 13b–15a. Chao I has a quantitative approach to the judgment of evil which he shares with other Chinese political moralists. This attitude deserves a separate study.

55. Cf. J. R. Hightower, *Topics in Chinese Literature* (Cambridge, Mass., 1950), pp. 92–93. In this whole section I find myself on unfamiliar ground, and answers to many of the questions raised must await intensive research.

56. *Ssu-k'u Ch'üan-shu Tsung-mu* (photolithographic ed. of the Ta-tung Shu-chü, Shanghai, 1930), ch. 143, p. 2a.

57. The first three works are discussed in *ibid.* They are usually listed as anonymous and of T'ang date, but they show signs of later reworking, probably in Sung times. The *Ta-yeh Shih-i Chi* is often attributed to Yen Shih-ku (581–645), but this seems to me doubtful. For the first three texts I have used the editions of the Wu-ch'ao Hsiao-shuo Ta-kuan (Shanghai, 1926). For the fourth I have used *Shuo-fu*, ch. 110.

58. This characterization is never fully developed, but Empress Hsiao as the *femme fatale* appears in the moral-pointing introduction to a story, probably of Ming date, entitled "Hsin-ch'iao-shih Han-wu Mai Ch'un-ch'ing," in *Ku-chin Hsiao-shuo* (Peking ed., 1955), Vol. I, ch. 3, p. 1b. There the author cites two historical examples of women who brought men to ruin: Empress Hsiao and Yang Kuei-fei, favorite of Emperor Hsüan-tsung of the T'ang. Since Yang Kuei-fei is the most famous of all the *femmes fatales* of Chinese history, the stereotyping of Empress Hsiao in this context is complete.

59. The *Sui Yang-ti Yen-shih* was written under the pseudonym of "Ch'i-tung Yeh-jen," and is in eight *chüan* and forty incidents (*hui*). The

copy consulted was from the East Asiatic Library of the University of California, and this appears to be a late run-off—minus illustrations—of the plates used for the 1631 edition described in Sun K'ai-ti, *Chung-kuo T'ung-su Hsiao-shuo Shu-mu* ("Bibliography of Chinese Popular Fiction") (Peking, 1932), p. 46. [Stanford University has acquired what appears to be a complete copy of the 1631 edition. I shall publish a note on this in the near future.] There is a 1946 edition by the Chung-yang Shu-chü, Shanghai.

60. Cf. Li Hua-ch'ing, *Sung-jen Hsiao-shuo* ("Fiction of the Sung") (Taipei, 1956), ch. 2, p. 26.

61. I use the 1956 edition of the Ku-tien Wen-hsueh Ch'u-pan She, Shanghai. The author, Ch'u Jen-hu, is said to have flourished ca. 1681. The publishers' preface cites the author's acknowledgment of his indebtedness to the standard histories and to informal writings concerning the Sui and T'ang, but it goes on to say that the author's own area of invention was very wide and that the novel is to be regarded as a work of creative fiction.

62. Kuo Chen-i in his *Chung-kuo Hsiao-shuo Shih* ("History of Chinese Fiction"), II (Ch'ang-sha, 1939), 262, suggests that the *Sui Yang-ti Yen-shih* was written under the influence of the famous *Chin-p'ing Mei*, and that the *Yen-shih* was one of the principal sources drawn upon by Ch'u Jen-hu in writing the *Sui T'ang Yen-i*. A limited comparison of the two texts suggests that whole sections were taken from the earlier novel with certain deletions and rearrangements.

63. This novel, a biography of the god Chen-wu which is of Ming date, is known under seven different titles. The quotation is from Willem A. Grootaers, "The Hagiography of the Chinese God Chen-wu," *Folklore Studies*, XI (1953), 157.

64. Cf. Ssu-ma Kuang's *T'ung-chien K'ao-i*, ch. 8, pp. 56–59.

65. Cf. Edwin G. Pulleyblank, "Chinese Historical Criticism" (mimeographed, London, 1956), p. 15. This important paper will shortly appear in a symposium volume on Far Eastern historiography edited by Professor William Beasely.

66. Hsü Li-ch'un, *Chung-kuo Shih-hua*, pp. 76–78. The work was first published in Yenan in 1942 and appeared in a revised (!) edition in Peking, 1950.

67. Han Kuo-ch'ing, *Sui Yang-ti* (Changsha, 1957), p. 92. We are indebted to the same author for *Sui-ch'ao Shih-lüeh* ("Brief History of the Sui Dynasty") (Shanghai, 1954). This work is similar in composition to his life of Yang-ti: uncritical acceptance of all data from the standard histories plus random and meaningless injections of Marxist liturgical phrases.

68. The *Yüan-shih Chi-shih* ("Record of Yüan Dynasty Poetry"), compiled under the Republic by Ch'en Heng, remarks: "When a dynasty falls, there must be 'a person who was negligent in state affairs' whom people can point to and look at, one who will appear in songs. . . . For the fall of the Sung, Chia Ssu-tao [d. 1276] was this person." Cf. Commercial Press edition, p. 76. I am indebted to Professor Mote for this reference. An exception to the more recent treatment of last rulers might be Shun-ti of the Yüan, who was given many of the qualities suggested in our paradigm of the "bad last" ruler. Cf. Herbert Franke, "Some Remarks on the Interpretation of Chinese Dynastic Histories," *Oriens,* 3 (1950), 117–20.

NOTES TO NEO-CONFUCIANISM AND NEO-LEGALISM IN T'ANG
INTELLECTUAL LIFE

Abbreviations:

CTS: *Chiu T'ang shu* (*Ssu-pu pei-yao* edition).

CTW: *Ch'üan T'ang wen* (1814 edition).

HTS: *Hsin T'ang shu* (Po-na edition).

SPTK: *Ssu-pu ts'ung-k'an.*

TCTC: *Tzu-chih t'ung-chien.* References are given to *chüan* and date. The punctuated edition of The Ku-chi ch'u pan she, 1957, has been used.

TFYK: *Ts'e-fu yüan-kuei* (1642 edition).

THY: *T'ang Hui-yao* (*Kuo-hsüeh chi-pen ts'ung-shu* edition).

TT: *T'ung-tien* (*Shih-t'ung* edition).

The *Yin hua lu, T'ang kuo-shih pu, T'ang chih-yen* are quoted from the *Chung-kuo wen-hsüeh ts'an-k'ao tzu-liao hsiao ts'ung shu* (Shanghai, 1957).

1. *HTS*, ch. 217A, p. 7b; *TCTC*, ch. 224 (Ta-li 7/1/chia-ch'en, 7/7/kuei-ssu, 8/7/hsin-ch'ou); ch. 225 (Ta-li 9/9/jen-yin, 10/9/wu-shen, 14/7 keng-ch'en). [Dates are here given as: Era name, year of the era, month of the year, followed by the cyclical term indicating the day. Ed.]

2. For example, see *TCTC*, ch. 227 (Ch'ien-yüan 3/11/—), proposal for an alliance between certain of the Chieh-tu shih.

3. Cf. E. G. Pulleyblank, *The Background of the Rebellion of An Lu-shan* (London Oriental Series, Vol. 4, 1955), p. 100.

4. *Ibid.*, p. 144, n.24.

5. On the origins of the Shu-mi Yüan see Sun Kuo-tung, "T'ang tai san sheng chih chih fa-chan yen-chiu" ("Development of San Sheng System of the T'ang Dynasty"), *Hsin-ya hsüeh-pao*, III (1957), 112–16.

6. On the beginnings of the *chien-chün* system see *The Background of the Rebellion of An Lu-shan*, p. 74.

7. *TT*, ch. 11, p. 63.1.

8. See J. Gernet, *Les aspects économiques du bouddhisme dans la société chinoise du Ve au Xe siècle* (Publications de l'Ecole Française d'Extrême-Orient, Saigon, 1956), pp. 50–51, and E. G. Pulleyblank in *Journal of the Economic and Social History of the Orient*, I (1957), 155.

9. S. Balazs, in "Beiträge zur Wirtschaftsgeschichte der T'angzeit," Part 2, *MSOS*, XXXV (1932), 30. Note that the rebels also were forced to the expedient of issuing token coinage at the ratio of 1:100 ordinary cash. *HTS*, ch. 54, p. 7a.

10. *TCTC*, ch. 222 (Shang-yüan 2/1/—).

11. *TCTC*, ch. 222 (Pao-ying 1/chien-yin month/wu-shen, 1/8/chi-ssu); *CTS*, ch. 11, p. 2b; ch. 110, p. 5a.

12. Biographies of Liu Yen are in *CTS*, ch. 123, *HTS*, ch. 149. Cf. also the eulogy by Ch'en Chien, "Liu Yen lun," in *CTW*, ch. 684. Chü Ch'ing-yüan, *Liu Yen p'ing-chuan* ("A Critical biography of Liu Yen") (Shanghai, 1937), is an important study of his economic policies. See also D. C. Twitchett, "The Salt Commissioners after An Lu-shan's Rebellion," *Asia Major* IV (1954), 64ff.

13. Cf. Balazs, *op. cit.*, Part 1; *MSOS*, XXXIV (1931), 82–92. Chü Ch'ing-yüan, *T'ang tai ts'ai-cheng shih* ("History of Government Finance in the T'ang Dynasty"), 1940 (Japanese translation by S. Nakajima, Tokyo, 1944) pp. 49–94; T'ao Hsi-sheng and Chü Ch'ing-yüan, *T'ang tai ching-chi shih* ("Economic History of the T'ang Dynasty") (Shanghai, 1936), pp. 152ff. A number of studies of this reform have recently been published by Hino Kaisaburo.

14. Cf. Wei Ch'u-hou, "Ch'ing ming ch'a Li Feng-chi p'eng-tang shu" ("Memorial Requesting the Investigation of the Faction of Li Feng-chi"), *CTW*, ch. 716.

15. Kanai Yukitada, *Tōdai no shigaku shisō* ("T'ang Dynasty Historiographical Thought") (Tokyo, 1940), pp. 105ff. Cf. Chü Ch'ing-yüan, *Liu Yen p'ing-chuan.*

16. See below.

17. Cf. Li Chao, *Han-lin chih*, in *Han-yüan ch'ün shu*, 2 ch. (Chih-pu-tsu chai ts'ung-shu); Sun Kuo-tung, "T'ang tai san sheng chih chih fa-chan yen-chiu," as cited in note 5, pp. 108–12.

18. Besides the examples referred to in this article, there are very many more in biographies, epitaphs, etc., of the period and after. There are also references of a more general kind to the migration. Cf. *HTS*, ch. 194, biography of Ch'üan Kao.

19. Biography in *HTS*, ch. 143. See also the excellent *Yüan Tz'u-shan nien-p'u*, by Sun Wang, first published in *Chin-ling ta-hsüeh wen-hsüeh yüan chi-k'an* in 1935, revised 1948 and reprinted in Shanghai, 1957.

20. *HTS*, ch. 143. Eight pieces by him are included in *CTW*, ch. 377. Note especially his "Ts'ao t'ang chi" ("Record of the Thatched Hall") written in 767, in which he says, "I have made my home above the Hsiu River (near Hsiu-shui hsien in Kiangsi) for ten years. This land is distant and remote; war has not reached it. Yet I still daily see the wrong of poor people being sold . . ." The freeing of people sold into bondage is a meritorious act recorded of several persons sent to govern southern prefectures at the end of the eighth century and the beginning of the ninth, including both Han Yü and Liu Tsung-yüan. There were, moreover, imperial decrees trying to stop the practice. Previously traffic in "southerners" (*nan-k'ou*) seems to have been regarded as quite legitimate. It is striking that this antislavery movement should have coincided with the Confucian revival.

21. *CTS*, ch. 130, biography of Ts'ui Tsao. Cf. also Han Yü's epitaph of Lu Tung-mei in *Han Ch'ang-li chi*, ch. 24. The *k'uei* is best known as a mythological one-legged creature mentioned in *Chuang-tzu*, the *Shan-hai ching*, etc., but it is also the name of one of the ministers of Yao and it is in this sense that it was applied to Han Hui and his companions. Cf. "Yao tien," ch. 35, "The emperor said: K'uei, I charge you to be Director of Music, to teach the descendant sons, [to be] [apprehensive:] careful, [hard:] firm and yet not tyrannical, great and yet not arrogant. Poetry expresses the mind . . ." Karlgren, *Book of Documents* (Stockholm, 1950), p. 7: The appellation thus aptly fits the ambition to serve in ministerial capacity and the ideal of using literature as a means of reforming the world. *T'ang Kuo-shih pu*, ch. 3, p. 58, refers to Han Hui's singing ability as a reason for the sobriquet, but this may well be anecdotal invention. *T'ang chih-yen*, ch. 4, ascribes the name "Four K'uei" to four other persons, one of whom was Li Hua. Chu Hsi,

no doubt rightly, rejects this (*K'ao-i* to *Han Ch'ang-li chi, loc. cit.*), but it shows that the name was current.

22. *Li T'ai-po ch'üan-chi* (Chung-hua Press, Peking, 1957), p. 29.

23. Han Yü, who was born in 768, lost his father at the age of three (*sui*), therefore in 770. See his biography with commentary by Chu Hsi appended to *Han Ch'ang-li chi.*

24. The earliest express statement of this seems to be by Hung Hsing-tsu in his *Han-tzu nien-p'u* (*Han Wen lei p'u*, ch. 3, p. 9a, in *Han Liu nien-p'u*, 8 ch.) reprint of Hsiao Ling-lung shan kuan (1875). It is not clear whether this is based on an unnamed separate source of information or whether it is inferred from references to his living in Chiang-nan with his sister-in-law around 781 and to members of his family living there around 820. Even if only the latter, it seems very probable. See the commentary on "Shih Shuang shih" ("Poem Shown to [Han] Shuang") in *Han Ch'ang-li shih hsi-nien chi-shih*, XII, 565–66 (Shanghai, 1957), edited by Ch'ien Chung-lien.

25. *TCTC*, ch. 225 (Ta-li 12/4/kuei-wei). Cf. Hung Hsing-tsu, *Han-tzu nien-p'u* in *Han Wen lei-p'u*, ch. 3, p. 7a.

26. *CTS*, ch. 130, biography of Ts'ui Tsao. Cf. Kanai Yukitada, *Tōdai no shigaku shisō*, p. 105.

27. Han Hui wrote a piece called the "Wen heng" ("Balance of Literature"), which is quoted *in extenso* in a short biography of him written by the Sung writer Wang Chih. It shows him to have been an advocate of *ku-wen* in the same extreme way that we find in Li Hua. That is, he considers that the decline in letters set in with Chuang-tzu and Lao-tzu in philosophy, with Ch'ü Yüan and Sung Yü in poetry, and with Ssu-ma Ch'ien and Pan Ku in narrative. Wang Chih remarks that it showed how much Han Yü resembled his elder brother. Recently Ch'ien Mu has quoted this to show that Han Yü derived his interest in *ku-wen* from his own family, not from Tu-ku Chi and Liang Su as stated in his biography, a fact which would explain the absence of references to Tu-ku and Liang in his works. It seems clear that Han Yü did look back to his brother and uncle for inspiration, but it is also true that, as one would expect, both in philosophy and in ideas on literature he shows the influence of the evolution in thinking that had taken place through Tu-ku Chi, Liang Su, *et al.* For Han Yü accepted all Chou and early Han literature and held the western Han writers Yang Hsiung and Ssu-ma Hsiang-ju in particularly high regard; and though his rejection of Buddhism represents a sharp contrast to Liang Su—and is probably sufficient to account for his failure to say much about him—his emphasis on the *Chung-yung, Ta-hsüeh*, and *I-ching* is in the Liang Su tradition. Cf. Ch'ien Mu, "Tsa-lun T'ang tai ku-wen yün-tung" ("The Classical Prose Reform Movement in the T'ang Dynasty"), *Hsin-ya hsüeh-pao*, III (1957), 123–68.

Wang Chih's *Han Hui chuan* originally formed part of the *Han Wen lei-p'u*, in 10 *chüan*, edited by Wei Chung-chü and appended to the *Hsin-k'an wu-pai-chia chu yin-pien Ch'ang-li Hsien-sheng wen-chi*, published in 1200. Later reprints of this edition omit the supplementary material, and the separate edition of the *Han Wen lei-p'u* in 7 *chüan*, forming the major part of the *Han Liu nien-pu*, 8 *chüan*, omits the *Han Hui chuan*. (The *Han Liu nien-p'u* was separately constituted in 1730 by Ch'en Ching-yün. I have consulted it in the reprint of the Hsiao Ling-lung shan kuan, 1875.) A facsimile reproduction of the edition of Han Yü's works of the year 1200 was published by the Commercial Press in 1912, but I have been unable to consult it. The *Han Hui chuan* is, however, also included in *Ch'üan T'ang wen chi-shih*, ch. 39, pp. 10a ff. Cf. also Kung Shu-chih, *Han Yü yü ch'i ku-wen yün-tung* ("Han Yü and His 'Ancient Style' Movement") (Chungking, 1945), p. 14.

It should also be noted that Han Hui's name appears among Liu Tsung-yüan's list of the friends of his father. Hui is said to have been good at philosophical conversation (*ch'ing yen*) and famed for his literary ability. See *Liu Ho-tung chi*, ch. 12 (ts'e 2, p. 89, edition of the *Kuo-hsüeh chi-pen ts'ung-shu*).

28. On the beginnings of this movement, see *inter alia*, Kung Shu-chih, *op. cit.;* Kuo Shao-yü, *Chung-kuo wen-hsüeh p'i-p'ing shih* ("History of Chinese Literary Criticism") (rev. ed., Shanghai, 1955); Lo Ken-tse, *Chung-kuo wen-hsüeh p'i-p'ing shih* (new ed., Vol. II, Shanghai, 1957); Ch'ien Chi-po, *Han Yü chih* (rev. ed., Shanghai, 1957); Ch'ien Mu, *loc. cit.*

29. Biographies in *CTS*, ch. 190C; *HTS*, ch. 203. Preface to his collected works by Tu-ku Chi, *CTW*, ch. 388, p. 11b. See also Ch'ien Chi-po, *op. cit.*, pp. 12–16.

30. *CTW*, ch. 388.

31. Biographies in *CTS*, ch. 190C; *HTS*, ch. 202. See also Ch'ien Chi-po, *op. cit.*, pp. 5–12; Hiraoka Takeo, *Keisho no dentō* ("The Tradition of the Confucian Canon") (Tokyo, 1951), pp. 92–139.

32. *HTS*, ch. 202; *Yin hua lu*, III, 89–90; *Han Ch'ang-li shih hsi-nien chi-shih*, p. 525. Cf. Ch'ien Chi-po, *op. cit.*, p. 12.

33. *CTS*, ch. 102; *HTS*, ch. 135; Li Hua, "San hsien lun," *CTW*, ch. 317, p. 3b; *T'ang kuo-shih pu* 1, p. 15.

34. *Op. cit.*, vol. 2, pp. 113–14.

35. *HTS*, ch. 162. Cf. the *hsing-chuang* by Liang Su, *CTW*, ch. 522, p. 3b; preface to his works by Li Chou, *CTW*, ch. 443, p. 16a; *shen-tao pei* by Ts'ui Yu-fu, *CTW*, ch. 443, p. 16a. The dates of his taking office at Hao-chou, Shu-chou, and Ch'ang-chou can be inferred from his memorials expressing thanks for his appointments at Hao-chou and Ch'ang-chou in *CTW*, ch. 385.

36. *Op. cit.*, pp. 125–30.

37. Edited by K'ung Ying-ta in 180 *chüan* and completed in 653. See Nagasawa Kikuya, *Shina gakujutsu bungeishi* (Tokyo, 1938), pp. 145 ff. (trans. P. Eugen Feifel, *Geschichte der chinesischen Literatur*, Peking, 1945, pp. 176ff.).

38. There is only a brief mention of Tan Chu in *CTS*, ch. 189B. The biography in *HTS*, ch. 200, is based, rather inaccurately, on Lu Ch'un's "Ch'un-ch'iu li t'ung hsü" ("Preface to the Compendium of Rules of the *Spring and Autumn Annals*"), *CTW*, ch. 618, p. 3b. This piece also appears as *p'ien* 8 in Lu Ch'un, *Ch'un-ch'iu chi chuan tsuan li* in the *Ku ching chieh hui han*.

39. Besides brief mentions of him in *CTS*, ch. 189B, and *HTS*, ch. 200, and in Lu Ch'un's preface cited in note 38, we know that he (later?) became Prefect of Yang-chou (Shensi). Cf. *TT*, ch. 17, p. 97.

40. *CTS*, ch. 189B; *HTS*, ch. 200; *mu-piao* in *Liu Ho-tung chi*, p. 9. His name was changed from Ch'un to Chih (Mathews' number 1009) to avoid a taboo in the name of the Emperor Hsien-tsung. Although this was not

homophonous with the name of Lu Chih (Hsüan-kung) (Mathews' number 980), it was sufficiently similar that there is occasionally confusion between them. See note 64.

41. No separate works by Tan Chu were listed in the bibliographical chapter of the *Hsin T'ang shu* or of the *Sung shih*. He was extensively quoted by Lu Ch'un, and these quotations together with one or two others from Sung and Yüan commentators of the *Ch'un-ch'iu* have been collected by Ma Kuo-han and published under the title *Ch'un-ch'iu chi chuan* in the *Yü-han shan fang chi-i shu*. Chao K'uang was the author of the *Ch'un-ch'iu ch'an-wei tsuan-lei i-shu* in 10 chüan, which is not listed in the *HTS* "I-wen chih" but is found in the *Sung shih* "I-wen chih," as well as bibliographies from the Sung period such as the *Chung-hsing kuan-ko shu-mu*. It is no longer extant, but quotations from Chao K'uang in the works of Lu Ch'un, together with one or two more from Sung and Yüan works, have been collected under this title by Ma Kuo-han and published in the above-mentioned collection. Three works by Lu Ch'un on the *Ch'un-ch'iu* still exist, namely, (1) *Ch'un-ch'iu chi-chuan tsuan-li*, 10 ch., (2) *Ch'un-ch'iu wei chih*, 3 ch., (3) *Ch'un-ch'iu Tan Chao erh hsien-sheng chi-chuan pien-i*, 10 ch. They are all reprinted in the *Ku-ching-chieh hui-han*.

On their ideas and influence see, *inter alia*: P'i Hsi-jui, *Ching-hsüeh t'ung-lun* (Shanghai, 1938), pp. 56ff.; Nagasawa Kikuya, *Shina gakujutsu bungeishi* (Tokyo, 1938), pp. 152ff. (trans. E. Feifel, *Geschichte der chinesischen Literatur*, pp. 185–86); Takeuchi Yoshio, *Chūgoku shisōshi* (Tokyo 1954; 1st ed., 1936), p. 238; Honda Nariyuki, *Chung-kuo ching-hsüeh shih* (Chinese translation by Sun Liang-kung) (Shanghai, 1935), p. 235; Kanō Naoki, *Chūgoku tetsugaku shi* (Tokyo, 1953), pp. 340–43.

42. See *Shih-t'ung*, especially ch. 13, "Suspicions about Antiquity"; ch. 14, "Doubts about the Classics"; ch. 15, "Preferring Tso." Cf. E. G. Pulleyblank, "Chinese Historical Criticism—Liu Chih-chi and Ssu-ma Kuang," to be published shortly in a collection of papers on the historiography of East Asia by the School of Oriental and African Studies, London.

43. P'i Hsi-jui, *op. cit.*, p. 59, quotes praise of Tan Chu and his followers from Shao Yung, Ch'eng Tzu (one of the Ch'eng brothers), Chu Hsi, and Wu Ch'eng (of Yüan). Honda, *loc. cit.*, also refers to praise by Lu Chiu-yüan.

44. Hung Yeh (William Hung), "Ch'un-ch'iu ching-chuan yin-te hsü," pp. i–cvi in *Ch'un-ch'iu ching-chuan yin-te* (4 vols., Peking, 1937).

45. See Tsukamoto Zenryū, *Tō chūki no Jōdokyō* ("Chinese Buddhism in the Middle Period of the T'ang Dynasty, with Special Reference to Fa-chao and the Doctrine of the Pure Land"), Kyōto, 1933 (with English summary).

46. On the general development of Buddhism in this period, see Arthur Wright, "Buddhism and Chinese Culture," *JAS*, 17 (1957), 17–42, especially pp. 31–38.

47. Chan-jan has a biography in *Sung Kao-seng chuan*, ch. 6 (*Taishō Tripitaka*, 2061, L, 739; see also the biography of his disciple Yüan-tsao, *ibid.*, p. 740). According to his biography, Chan-jan resolutely declined all invitations to go to Ch'ang-an, but Wei Ch'u-hou's epitaph for the Ch'an monk Ta-i (important for its account of the four schools of Ch'an after the death of Hui-neng) relates that Chan-jan was in Ch'ang-an shortly before his death, engaged in disputes over doctrine with Ta-i in the Nei Shen-lung-ssu within the palace in the presence of the future Shun-tsung. There is clearly

much more to be investigated about the influence of Buddhism on Shun-tsung and the people around him. (*CTW*, ch. 715.)

48. *Sung Kao-seng chuan, loc. cit.*; *Fo-tsu t'ung-chi,* ch. 10 (*Taishō Tripitaka,* 2035, XLIX, 203C).

49. *Fo-tsu t'ung-chi, loc. cit.*

50. *CTW*, ch. 388, p. 16b. The Han Yu-shen mentioned in this *hsü* is the financial expert Han Hui who was involved, along with the other Han Hui, Han Yü's brother, in the downfall of Yüan Tsai. (See n. 25.) This style is not given in his biographies in *CTS*, ch. 129, and *HTS*, ch. 126, but is mentioned in his *hsing-chuan* by Ch'üan Te-yü (*CTW*, ch. 507, p. 4a).

51. *CTS*, ch. 119. Cf. *HTS*, ch. 142; *TCTC*, ch. 225 (Ta-li 14/4/kuei-mao).

52. See below.

53. I refer to him by his title, by which he is well known in China, instead of his name because of the possibility of confusion with Liu Chih (see below). Biographies in *CTS*, ch. 139; *HTS*, ch. 157. See also preface to his works by Ch'üan Te-yü in *CTW*.

54. Biography in *HTS*, ch. 203. See also Ch'ien Chi-po, *op. cit.,* pp. 60–64.

55. Biography in *HTS*, ch. 203. See also Ch'ien Chi-po, *op. cit.,* pp. 58–60.

56. Biographies in *CTS*, ch. 164; *HTS*, ch. 152.

57. Biographies in *CTS*, ch. 159; *HTS*, ch. 165.

58. *THY*, ch. 57, p. 979.

59. Biography in *HTS*, ch. 202 (appended to Su Yüan-ming). Epitaph by Ts'ui Yüan-han, *CTW*, ch. 523, p. 26a. Preface to his works by Ts'ui Kung, *CTW*, ch. 480. Cf. Ch'ien Chi-po, *op. cit.,* p. 26.

60. *CTW*, ch. 523, p. 26b.

61. *CTW*, ch. 517, pp. 16a ff.

62. *Taishō Tripitaka,* 2061, L, 740 (appendix to biography of Chan-jan).

63. See note 59.

64. Biographies in *CTS*, ch. 137; *HTS*, ch. 160. Eulogy (*lei*) by Liu Tsung-yüan, *Liu Ho-tung chi,* ch. 9 (*ts'e* 2, p. 49). Preface to his works by Liu Yü-hsi, *CTW*, ch. 605, p. 10b states that he studied the *Ch'un-ch'iu* under Lu Chih (Lu Hsüan-kung), but this must be a mistake for Lu Ch'un (see note 40), as stated in the *HTS*. Lü Wen refers to the importance of *Ch'un-ch'iu* studies in a letter to a cousin (*CTW*, ch. 627, pp. 15a ff.). Ch'ien Mu ranks him above any of his contemporaries as a thinker. (*Hsin-ya hsüeh-pao* 3/1, pp. 163ff.).

65. *CTS*, ch. 160. T'ang chih-yen, ch. 7, p. 80, has an anecdote about Liang Su and four of the candidates he recommended to Lu Hsüan-kung in 792, in which he is said to have made predictions about their future careers. Ch'ien Mu (*loc. cit.,* p. 131) shows that it could not have happened.

66. "Yü Tz'u-pu Lu Yüan-wai shu" ("Letter to Lu San"), *Han Ch'ang-li chi,* ch. 17 (*ts'e* 4, p. 75). See also "Ou-yang sheng ai-tz'u" ("Lament for Ou-yang Chan"), *ibid.,* ch. 22 (*ts'e* 5, p. 45). A letter of Li Ao also mentions Li Kuan as having recommended the poet Meng Chiao, who was also a close friend of Han Yü, to Liang Su (*CTW*, ch. 635, p. 19b).

67. Cf. A. Waley, *The Life and Times of Po Chü-i* (London, 1949), p. 23.

68. *HTS,* ch. 162.

69. *CTS*, ch. 147; *HTS*, ch. 165. Cf. Waley, *op. cit.*, pp. 18, 23.

70. *CTS*, ch. 148; *HTS*, ch. 165.

71. "If the words of those who recommended scholars to him were worthy of credence, [these scholars] did not fail to find employment because they were commoners; if the words were not worthy of credence, then even though high officials and men of influence interceded, he did not in the slightest degree alter his opinions." Ch'üan's epitaph in *Han Ch'ang-li chi*, ch. 30 (*ts'e* 6, pp. 47–49).

72. *CTS*, ch. 137; *HTS*, ch. 160.

73. *CTS*, ch. 160; *HTS*, ch. 168. See also his autobiographical sketch, "Tzu Liu-tzu chuan" (*CTW*, ch. 610, pp. 13b ff.).

74. *CTS*, ch. 171; *HTS*, ch. 81. He was the author of a criticism of Mencius (*Meng-tzu p'ing*). See note 83. He also seems to have had connections with Han Yü's circle, for Li Ao couples his name with that of Chang Chi in a recommendation to the Military Governor of Hsü-chou, Chang Chien-feng (letter cited in note 66 above). A later incident in his rather colorful career is referred to by Waley, *op. cit.*, p. 138.

75. *HTS*, ch. 168 (appended to the biography of Wang P'ei). He belonged to the true Ch'ang-li Han clan. (Although Han Yü is referred to, and referred to himself as from Ch'ang-li, from which the most ancient and illustrious Hans came, his family did not in fact come from there. See Chu Hsi's commentary to the biography in *Han Ch'ang-li chi*.) He was related, in the next generation to the two brothers Han Huang and Han Hui, who were both financial experts (*CTS*, ch. 129; *HTS*, ch. 126; see note 50 above). The genealogical table of Chief Ministers in the *HTS* calls him the son of Han Hui (*HTS*, ch. 73A, p. 15a), but *CTS*, ch. 129, refers to him only as the *tsu-tzu* of Han Huang.

76. *HTS*, ch. 168 (brief reference appended to Wang P'ei's biography). According to *HTS*, ch. 73A, p. 9a he belonged to the same clan as Han Yüan, a chief minister under Kao-tsung (*CTS*, ch. 80; *HTS*, ch. 105). Han Yü later recommended him to replace himself as prefect of Ch'ao-chou in 820. After the collapse of the Wang Shu-wen party, Han Yeh had been banished to Ssu-ma of Ch'ien-chou (Kan-hsien in Kiangsi). In 815, when the exiled members of the party were given a partial reinstatement, he was made Prefect of Chang-chou (Lung-ch'i hsien in Fukien). Han Yü was banished to be Prefect of Ch'ao-chou (Hai-yang hsien in Kuang-tung) in 819 on account of his famous memorial on the bone of Buddha. Since both Chang-chou and Ch'ao-chou were prefectures of the lowest grade and Ch'ao-chou was actually farther south, it is not obvious what superiority the one had over the other. Possibly in recommending Han Yeh, Han Yü was trying to enable him to enter the stream of regular promotion, since Yeh had already been at Chang-chou for five years, much longer than the normal length of time. In any case it is interesting to find Han Yü endeavoring to help victims of the downfall of Wang Shu-wen. (See *Han Ch'ang-li chi*, ch. 39, *ts'e* 7, p. 43.)

77. *HTS*, ch. 168, after the biography of Wang P'ei. There are six pieces by him in *CTW*, ch. 684, including an essay in praise of Liu Yen, on whose staff he had once served.

78. Letter to Wu Wu-ling in *Liu Ho-tung chi*, ch. 31, *ts'e* 4, pp. 101–2.

79. Letter in answer to Yüan of Jao-chou in *Liu Ho-tung chi*, ch. 31, p. 98. See also his epitaph on Lu Ch'un, *ibid.*, ch. 9, *ts'e* 2, p. 45.

80. See the essays on these books in *Liu Ho-tung chi,* ch. 4.

81. *Ibid.,* ch. 44–45.

82. *Ibid.,* ch. 31, *ts'e* 4, p. 100. The character *chih* (Karlgren, *Grammata Serica,* no. 804e) is not given the meanings "attack" or "destroy" in dictionaries but it is occasionally found in texts where it evidently has such a sense. See *P'ei-wen yün-fu* under *chih-hui* (G.S., no. 356a) and *ch'iung* (G.S., no. 1006g) *chih.*

83. *Ibid., pu i, ts'e* 6, p. 86.

84. *CTW,* ch. 627, pp. 15a ff.

85. "Shih shuo," *Han Ch'ang-li chi,* ch. 11, *ts'e* 3, pp. 75–77.

86. Letter in reply to Wei Chung-li, *Liu Ho-tung chi,* ch. 34, *ts'e* 5, pp. 3–5.

87. Su Mien's *Hui-yao* was in 40 *chüan. THY,* ch. 39, p. 660, appears to say that it was presented to the throne in Chen-yüan 19 (803), but as this merely forms an addition to an item recording the presentation of the *T'ung-tien* (which was moreover probably presented in 801, not 803—see note 103), this is not to be relied upon. In any case, the book was probably completed toward the end of the Chen-yüan period.

88. Su Pien has biographies in *CTS,* ch. 189B, and *HTS,* ch. 103, and Su Mien is mentioned in both, but little is said of him besides the fact that he wrote the *Hui-yao.* He also edited the literary works of Chia Chih, who had been a friend of Li Hua and Hsiao Ying-shih. This may indicate that Su Mien had an interest in the *ku-wen* movement—like the majority of his contemporaries. (*HTS,* ch. 60, p. 8a.)

89. Cf., for example, his comment on the development of the practice of appointing special commissioners (*shih*) (*THY,* ch. 78, p. 1438, translated in *The Background of the Rebellion of An Lu-shan,* p. 133).

90. *CTS,* ch. 102; *HTS,* ch. 135. Funeral address (*chi-wen*) by Li Hua in *CTW,* ch. 321, p. 17a.

91. *THY,* ch. 47, p. 830, includes his discussion on "feudalism" (*feng-chien*) from the *Cheng-tien.* It is also reasonable to assume that the discussion (*lun*) on examinations ascribed to him and included in *TT,* ch. 17, is from the *Cheng-tien.*

92. *Tōdai shigaku shisō,* pp. 90 ff.

93. Yang Kuo-chung, who was widely blamed for having been responsible for the rebellion, feared the proximity to the capital of the large, immobile army of Ko-shu Han defending the western end of the T'ung-kuan. He therefore used every effort to have Ko-shu Han ordered to advance, against his better judgment, on the rebels camped at the eastern end. When, as a result, Ko-shu Han did advance, his army was completely routed, leaving the road to Ch'ang-an undefended. *TCTC,* ch. 218 (Chih-te 1/ before 6/kuei-wei). The part played by Li Hua, Fang Kuan, and Liu Chih in trying to prevent Ko-shu Han from being forced to advance is not mentioned in the *TCTC* and has been largely overlooked by historians. Li Hua describes it in his funeral address on Liu Chih (see note 90), and there is an obscure reference to unaccepted memorials in Li's biography in *HTS,* ch. 203, p. 1a, which seems to refer to it. There seems no reason to doubt the truth of Li Hua's statement, which would give additional reason for the extraordinary trust placed in Fang Kuan by both Hsüan-tsung and Su-tsung thereafter.

94. *TCTC,* ch. 218 (Chih-te 1/7/ting-mao).

95. A brief account of Prince Lin's adventure is given by Waley in *The Poetry and Career of Li Po* (London, 1950), pp. 78–79.

96. *TCTC*, ch. 219 (Chih-te 1/10/kuei-wei and hsin-ch'ou). See Kanai, *op. cit.*, p. 91. In spite of these disasters, Fang Kuan, who represented the literatus element at a court dominated otherwise largely by eunuchs and military men and was a friend of the poet Tu Fu as well as such men as Li Hua and Liu Chih, has retained his reputation as a paragon of Confucian virtue. This is reflected in the accounts of him by Florence Ayscough and William Hung in their biographies of Tu Fu

97. The *Chih ko chi*, 7 ch., and the *Chih-te hsin i*, 12 ch., both now no longer extant. See *CTS*, ch. 102, p. 7a, and *HTS*, ch. 59, p. 15a. Cf. Kanai, *op. cit.*, p. 91.

98. *TCTC*, ch. 220 (Ch'ien-yüan 1/6 wu-wu).

99. See Li Hua's funeral address (note 90). This document is not dated, but it says that Liu Chih died in his place of banishment, just when he was about to be promoted to a more important place.

100. Biographies in *CTS*, ch. 147; *HTS*, ch. 166; inscriptions, etc., about him by Ch'üan Te-yü in *CTW*, ch. 496, pp. 4a ff., ch. 505, pp. 4a ff., ch. 509, pp. 14a ff. On Tu Yu as a thinker, see Naitō Torajiro, "Ni ts'e i tao," in *Kanō kyōju kanreki kinen Shinagaku ronsō* ("Chinese Studies in Honor of Professor Kano"), pp. 5–8, and Kanai Yukitada, *op. cit.*, pp. 96 ff. Cheng Ho-sheng, *Tu Yu nien-p'u* (Shanghai, 1934), is useful but not very thorough.

101. Biography in *CTS*, ch. 115.

102. See Wu T'ing-hsieh, *T'ang fang-chen nien-piao*, p. 134.2 (*Erh-shih-wu shih pu-pien*, Shanghai, 1936, p. 7416.2).

103. The date of presentation of the *T'ung-tien* is given as Chen-yüan 17 (801), in *CTS*, ch. 13, p. 18b, and as both Naitō (*op. cit.*) and Tamai Zehaku ("Daitō rikuten oyobi Tsuten no Sō kampon ni tsuite," *Shina shakai keizai shi kenkyū* (Tokyo, 1942, pp. 429–63) have shown, there are good reasons for accepting this date in preference to the date 803 given in *THY*, ch. 39, p. 660 (see note 87) or the date Chen-yüan 10 (794) given in the text of the memorial of presentation as recorded in some editions of the *T'ung-tien*. In this memorial he states that he has worked on the book for thirty-six years, which would mean that he had begun it around 765 or 766. This in turn is consistent with an earlier preface to a preliminary draft of the work, written by Li Han, printed at the front of modern editions of the *T'ung-tien*.

The Ch'ing historian Wang Ming-sheng, who was hostile to Tu Yu, minimized his achievement by pointing out that he had had Liu Chih's text as a basis and that the bulk of the additional material consisted of the *Ta T'ang K'ai-yüan li* incorporated bodily into the text. It is impossible to tell how much of the *T'ung-tien* is in fact taken over from the *Cheng-tien*, but the prefaces and author's discussions, as well as much of the double-line commentary, are unquestionably his, and it is there that we have the basis for assessing his stature as a historian and thinker. (*Shih-ch'i shih shang-ch'üeh*, ch. 90, pp. 10a ff. *Kuang-ya shu-chü ts'ung-shu.*)

104. This is shown by quotations from it in Wang Ying-lin, *K'un-hsüeh chi-wen*, ch. 5, p. 20b; ch. 6B, p. 20b; ch. 14A, p. 1b; ch. 14B, p. 7a (*SPTK*). Tu Yu's preface and memorial of presentation are quoted in *Yü hai*, ch. 51, p. 28b. There we learn that it had 33 *p'ien* distributed among the 10 *chüan* under the following headings: ch. 1–3, Shih-huo ("Economics"); ch. 4, Chü,

ming-kuan ("Examinations, Appointment of Officials"); ch. 5, Li chiao ("Rites and Instruction"); ch. 6, Feng-chien, chou-chün ("Feudalism," "Administrative Geography"); ch. 7, Ping hsing ("Military Affairs, Criminal Law"), ch. 8, Pien-fang ("Frontier Defense"), ch. 9–10, Ku-chin i-chih i ("Discussions on the Differences in Institutions Between Ancient and Modern Times"). This is similar, though not identical, to the arrangement of the *T'ung-tien*. Cf. Naitō, *op. cit.*

105. *TT*, ch. 12, p. 71.3. Cf. Arthur Wright, "The Formation of Sui Ideology," in *Chinese Thought and Institutions* (Chicago, 1957), p. 81.

106. *TT*, ch. 12, p. 68.1.

107. See especially the section entitled "Mo-ni" ("Imitation") in *Shih-t'ung*, ch. 8.

108. Letter to Wei Chung-li, *Liu Ho-tung chi*, ch. 34, *ts'e* 5, p. 4.

109. Quoted in *Yü hai*, ch. 51, p. 29a.

110. *TT*, ch. 185, p. 985. Compare also *TT*, ch. 48, p. 279; ch. 58, p. 337. Cf. Naitō, *op. cit.*, Kanai, *op. cit.*, pp. 127–31.

111. *TT*, ch. 1, p. 9.1.

112. *TT*, ch. 31, p. 177.

113. *Liu Ho-tung chi*, ch. 3. In the Sung period Liu's essay was generally considered to be the best discussion on the question. Among those who expressed approval were Sung Ch'i, in the historian's *tsan* at the end of *HTS*, ch. 168; Su Shih in "Shih-huang lun, Chung," *Ching-chin Tung-po wen-chi shih-lüeh* (Peking, 1957), ch. 24, p. 201; and Fan Tsu-yü, in *T'ang chien*, ch. 4, p. 27 (*Ts'ung-shu chi-ch'eng*). A certain Mr. K'ung also praised the "Feng-chien lun" as being something to which there was nothing comparable in Han Yü's works. See the commentary to the title in *Liu Ho-tung chi, loc. cit.*

114. R. des Rotours, *Le traité des examens traduit de la Nouvelle Histoire des T'ang* (Paris, 1932).

115. *TT*, ch. 18, p. 104.

116. *TT*, ch. 17, p. 97.

117. *TCTC*, 234/5/jen-tzu.

118. E. A. Kracke, Jr., *Civil Service in Early Sung China (960–1067) with Particular Emphasis on the Development of Controlled Sponsorship to Foster Administrative Responsibility* (Cambridge, Mass., 1953).

119. *TCTC, loc. cit.* There was of course nothing new in the idea that high officials should recommend people for office and that they should be held responsible for misdemeanors of those whom they had so recommended. It is the institutionalizing of this as a part of the regular procedures for appointing officials which seems to be an innovation of the post-rebellion period. Lu Hsüan-kung's proposal is not the first time we hear of it; it appears to be only a more extensive use of a procedure that was already being introduced. We find decrees on the subject from 766 onward. See *TFYK*, ch. 630. pp. 13a, 14b, 15a, etc.

120. *CTW*, ch. 465. Translation by Balazs, *op. cit.*, Part 3; *MSOS*, ch. 36 (1933), pp. 1–41.

121. *TCTC*, ch. 235 (Chen-yüan 10/11/jen-shen, 12/jen-hsü).

122. *TT*, ch. 7, p. 42.2.

123. *TT*, ch. 7, p. 41.1. Tu Yu's favorable treatment of Yü-wen Jung is in marked contrast to that of Su Mien in the *Hui-yao* and of the official histories. See *The Background of the Rebellion of An Lu-shan*, pp. 30 ff.; Suzuki

Shun, "Ubun Yū no kakko ni tsuite," *Wada Hakushi kanreki kinen Tōyōshi ronsō* ("Oriental Studies Presented to Professor Wada") (Tokyo, 1951), pp. 329–44.

124. *TT*, ch. 7, p. 42.3.

125. *TT*, ch. 4, p. 25.

126. See Esson M. Gale, *Discourses on Salt and Iron* (Leiden, 1931).

127. *TT*, ch. 11, p. 63.1.

128. *TCTC*, ch. 227 (Chien-chung 3/4/chia-tzu).

129. *Han Ch'ang-li chi*, ch. 40, *ts'e* 7, p. 55. Cf. *TCTC*, ch. 242 (Ch'ang-ch'ing 2/4/chia-hsü).

130. The *Shun-tsung shih-lu*, which deals with these events, has been translated by Bernard S. Solomon as *The Veritable Record of the T'ang Emperor Shun-tsung* (Cambridge, Mass., 1955). It purports to be by Han Yü but is certainly not now in the form which finally left his brush. As I have shown elsewhere, there is some reason to think that it may be only the preliminary draft by Wei Ch'u-hou which Han Yü revised and enlarged (*BSOAS*, XIX, 1957, 336–44). The question is not unimportant, for inferences about Han Yü's attitudes have frequently been made from it.

131. Biographies in *CTS*, ch. 135; *HTS*, ch. 168.

132. Biographies in *CTS*, ch. 135; *HTS*, ch. 168.

133. Biographies in *CTS*, ch. 135; *HTS*, ch. 168. In the writings of Li Te-yü there is a sacrificial piece (*chi-wen*) to Wei Chih-i. There is a difficulty about the date, since it begins, "In the fourth year of Ta-chung (850)" and according to the histories Li Te-yü died in the twelfth month of Ta-chung 3 (*CTS*, ch. 18B, p. 8a; ch. 174, p. 11b; *TCTC*, ch. 248 [Ta-chung 3/12/chi-wei]). Assuming it to be genuine, however, it is a very interesting document. Since Li Te-yü was in exile on Hainan island, the victim of factional attack, it may be no more than an expression of sympathy for someone who had suffered a similar fate. Possible implications for the nature of the feud between Li and the Niu faction cannot be gone into here.

134. Solomon, *op. cit.*, p. 56.

135. *TCTC*, ch. 239 (Yüan-ho 10/3/i-yu).

136. *CTS*, ch. 135, p. 12a. It is noteworthy that Liu Tsung-yüan said that his own association with the "guilty men" had gone on for ten years before they came to power. *Liu Ho-tung chi*, ch. 30, *ts'e* 4, p. 69.

137. See note 47 above.

138. *HTS*, ch. 202, p. 16a.

139. *Jung-chai hsü-pi*, p. 7.4b (*SPTK*).

140. *Tu T'ung-chien lun*, p. 25.1a ff. (*SPPY*).

141. *Shih-ch'i shih shang-ch'üeh*.

142. See, for instance, Shigezawa Junrō, "Ryū Sōgen ni mieru Tōdai no gōri shugi" ("Rationalism in the T'ang Dynasty as Seen in Liu Tsung-yüan"), *Nihon Chūgoku gakkai hō*, III (1951), 75–84; Huang Yün-mei, *Han Yü Liu Tsung-yüan wen-hsüeh p'ing-chieh* ("A Critical Introduction to the Literary Works of Han Yü and Liu Tsung-yüan") (Chinan, 1957), first published in *Wen-shih-che*, 1954; Shimizu Shigeru, "Ryū Sōgen no seikatsu taiken to sono sanzuiki," *Chūgoku bungaku hō*, II (1955), 45–74.

143. David S. Nivison, "Ho-shen and His Accusers" in David S. Nivison and Arthur F. Wright, eds., *Confucianism in Action* (Stanford, 1959), pp. 209–43.

144. Solomon, *op. cit.*, p. 53.

145. *Ibid.*, p. 19.

146. See the commemorative inscription set up on Tu Yu's departure from Yang-chou in 803 (*CTW*, ch. 496, p. 7a) and also his epitaph (*CTW*, ch. 505, p. 5a). The latter passage is quoted as by Ch'üan Te-yü, but without mention of the particular piece it comes from, in *Yü hai*, ch. 33.

147. Letter to Yüan of Jao-chou discussing government, *Liu Ho-tung chi*, ch. 32, *ts'e* 4, pp. 104 ff.

148. The only means of dating the "Yüan tao" and its companion pieces, the "Yüan hsing," etc., appears to be what is very probably a reference to them in a letter to Li Sun in 805 (*Han Ch'ang-li chi*, ch. 15, *ts'e* 4, p. 44). See Chu Hsi's commentary to the title of the "Yüan hsing" (*ibid.*, ch. 11, *ts'e* 3, p. 63); also J. K. Rideout, "The Context of the Yüan Tao and the Yüan Hsing," *BSOS*, XIX (1948), 408. This gives only a *terminus ante quem*, and it is of course possible that he had written these pieces somewhat earlier, but I am inclined to think they were produced during his period of exile. Rideout believed that the "Yüan hsing" in particular was a reaction to Li Ao's "Fu hsing lun," which he convincingly dates in 799–800 (*op. cit.*, p. 406 n. 4). It seems to me to be possible to accept this and still leave room for the possibility that an additional stimulus may have come from contacts with Liu Tsung-yüan and Liu Yü-hsi in 803, and possibly also from Tu Yu's writings.

149. *Liu Ho-tung-chi*, ch. 16, *ts'e* 3, p. 63.

150. Shih Tzu-yü, *Liu Tsung-yüan nien-p'u* (Wu-han, 1958), p. 15.

151. Biography with commentary by Chu Hsi, *Han Ch'ang-li chi*, *ts'e* 8, pp. 30–31.

152. *CTW*, ch. 607 (see also *Liu Ho-tung chi*, ch. 16). That this was written when the two Lius were no longer together is indicated by the fact that Liu Yü-hsi sent his "T'ien lun" to Liu Tsung-yüan by letter and Liu Tsung-yüan wrote a letter back to him about it (*Liu Ho-tung chi*, ch. 31, *ts'e* 4, p. 97). Shih Tzu-yü is no doubt right in assigning this letter to the period of exile and he may also be right in putting the actual writing of the "T'ien shuo" after Liu Tsung-yüan had gone to Yung Chou, though it is merely a subjective judgment. (*Op. cit.*, pp. 83–84.)

153. See note 158 below.

154. See note 12.

155. *Han Ch'ang-li chi*, ch. 15, *ts'e* 4, p. 42. Cf. Chu Hsi's note on Han Yü's biography, *ibid.*, *ts'e* 8, p. 31. Ch'ien Chi-po, in his *Han Yü chih*, p. 33, besides referring to this letter, quotes another letter to a certain Li Shang-shu (*Han Ch'ang-li chi*, ch. 19, *ts'e* 5) to show that Han Yü retained his friendship and regard for Li Shih. Chu Hsi's commentary, however, argues that the Li Shang-shu in question in the latter case is Li Chiang, not Li Shih, and this must be correct. Li Chiang was made prefect of Hua-chou in 815, but there is no record of Li Shih's having held this post. On the other hand, the severe criticism of Li Shih in the *Shun-tsung shih-lu* need not mean that Han Yü was deliberately showing ingratitude, or alternatively being vindictive. In the first place, it is doubtful whether he was in any way responsible for the existing version of the *Shih-lu*, and in any case he was working on the basis of an existing draft which he would hardly have dared to alter for personal reasons.

156. *TCTC*, ch. 236, Chen-yüan 19/12/–; *Han Ch'ang-li chi, ts'e* 8, pp. 31–32.

157. *Han Ch'ang-li chi*, ch. 37, *ts'e* 7, pp. 18–19.

158. Han Yü's biographies in the histories attribute his dismissal to a memorial criticizing the abuses in purchasing for the palace in the markets of the capital, but there is no such memorial in his works. Li Ao's *hsing-chuang* (*CTW*, ch. 639, pp. 22a ff.) says that he "was hated by a favorite of the emperor." A memorial inscription by Huang-fu Shih mentions the memorial about famine conditions and says that he was in consequence hated by those in charge of the government (*CTW*, ch. 687, pp. 14a ff.). Han Yü's epitaph for Chang Chien, one of the men who was banished with him, also says they were slandered by a "favorite" (*Han Ch'ang-li chi*, ch. 30, *ts'e* 6, pp. 41–43). It is a natural inference that the person offended was Li Shih. (Cf. Hung Hsing-tsu in *Han Wen lei-p'u*, ch. 2, pp. 4a ff.). On the other hand, in a long poem written at the end of 805, Han Yü refers to his memorial but says that it was appreciated both by the emperor and Tu Yu and wonders if his words have been reported to his enemies by his friends the two Lius (*Han Ch'ang-li shih hsi-nien chi-shih*, ch. 3, pp. 132 ff.). His hostility to Wang Shu-wen and Wang P'ei is made abundantly clear in other poems written shortly afterward (*ibid.*, pp. 151 ff., pp. 171 ff.). See Ch'ien Chi-po, *op. cit.*, p. 32; cf. Solomon, *op. cit.*, pp. xiii, xiv.

159. *TCTC*, ch. 236 (Chen-yüan 19/9/chia-yin); Solomon, *op. cit.*, p. 54.

160. Lu T'ung's collected poems are extant (*Yü-ch'uan tzu shih-chi*, 2 ch., *wai-chi*, 1 ch., *SPTK*). He lived as a recluse in Lo-yang, and Han Yü visited him when he was Magistrate of Ho-nan in 810–11. Han Yü liked his long satirical poem "On an Eclipse of the Moon" and wrote an imitation, which, however, has been less admired than the original by the critics (*Han Ch'ang-li shih hsi-nien chi-shih*, pp. 324 ff.). He also wrote another poem to him, which is a principal source of information about him (*ibid.*, pp. 340 ff.). The brief notice about Lu T'ung in *HTS*, ch. 176, is based on this and appended to Han Yü's biography. Lu T'ung wrote a commentary on the *Ch'un ch'iu* in 4 chüan, which survived into Sung. Fragments have been collected in the *Nan-ching shu-yüan ts'ung shu.*

161. Letter in reply to the Censor Yin, *Han Ch'ang-li chi*, ch. 18, *ts'e* 4, pp. 81–82.

162. Cf. Chu Hsi's comment on "Tu Ho-kuan-tzu," *Han Ch'ang-li chi*, ch. 11, *ts'e* 3, p. 73.

163. Han Yü's point of view is expressed in "Shih shuo," *Han Ch'ang-li chi*, ch. 11, *ts'e* 3, pp. 75–77. Liu Tsung-yüan's is most fully given in his letter in reply to Wei Chung-li, *Liu Ho-tung chi*, ch. 34, *ts'e* 5, pp. 3–5.

164. *CTW*, ch. 794, pp. 6b ff. Sun Ch'iao, in a letter to a friend (*CTW*, ch. 794, pp. 14a ff.) describes himself as a disciple of Han Yü through Huang-fu Shih and a certain Lai Tse (style Wu-tse)—cf. *Teng-k'o chi-k'ao*, ch. 20, p. 4b (*Nan-ching shu-yüan ts'ung-shu*), and *HTS*, ch. 50, p. 9a.

165. See Lü Chen-yü, *Chung-kuo cheng-chih ssu-hsiang shih* (Peking, 1955), pp. 397 ff., 413 ff.

166. Ts'en Chung-mien, *Sui T'ang shih* (Peking, 1957), chap. 45. Cf. Ch'en Yin-k'o, *T'ang tai cheng-chih shih shu-lun kao* (Shanghai, 1947), pp. 53–93.

NOTES TO CONFUCIAN ELEMENTS IN THE THEORY OF PAINTING

I am indebted to a number of people for corrections and suggestions, especially to Professor Kai-yu Hsü of San Francisco State College and Professor David S. Nivison of Stanford University.

Citations from the early treatises on painting, unless otherwise noted, are from the Wang-shih Hua-yüan edition.

1. W. Theodore de Bary, "A Reappraisal of Neo-Confucianism," in Arthur Wright, ed., *Studies in Chinese Thought* (Chicago, 1953), p. 82. This is not, of course, de Bary's own opinion.

2. Ernest Fenollosa, *Epochs of Chinese and Japanese Art* (London, 1912), I, 29.

3. Arthur Waley, *Zen Buddhism and Its Relation to Art* (London, 1922), p. 22.

4. Joseph R. Levenson, "The Amateur Ideal in Ming and Early Ch'ing Society: Evidence from Painting," in John K. Fairbank, ed., *Chinese Thought and Institutions* (Chicago, 1957), p. 326.

5. The same parallel has been drawn in the Sung period between two tendencies in poetry and the schools of Ch'an; see Yen Yü, *Ts'ang-lang Shih-hua* (Ts'ung-shu Chi-ch'eng ed.), pp. 1a ff. Since Yen Yü was referring to poetry produced before the rise of Ch'an in China, there is certainly no suggestion of a Ch'an aesthetic being involved. The author, in fact, ends his discussion with the statement that in determining the schools of poetry, he has merely "borrowed Ch'an as an analogy." Tung Ch'i-ch'ang only applied the same analogy to painting.

6. Alexander Soper, "Standards of Quality in Northern Sung Painting," *Archives of the Chinese Art Society of America*, XI (1957), 13.

7. Victoria Contag, *Die Beiden Steine* (Braunschweig, 1950), pp. 13–51: "Versuch einer Erklärung des Begriffs Ch'i Yün Sheng Tung"; also "The Unique Characteristics of Chinese Landscape Painting," *Archives*, VI (1952), 45–63. Two other exceptions to my generalization about the failure of recent writers on Chinese art to take sufficient note of Confucianism may be cited: Osvald Sirén's discussion of the Six Laws of Hsieh Ho (*A History of Early Chinese Painting* [London, 1933], I, 31–36); and Laurence Sickman's excellent short presentation of the Confucian and Taoist poles of Chinese thought and their effect upon art, in Sickman and Soper, *The Art and Architecture of China* (London, 1956), pp. 22-24.

8. Alfred Forke, trans., *Lun-Heng*. Part II. "Miscellaneous Essays of Wang Ch'ung" (Berlin, 1911), pp. 250, 352; adapted from Forke's translations.

9. Chang Yen-yüan, *Li-tai Ming-hua Chi*, ch. 1. See William Acker, *Some T'ang and Pre-T'ang Texts on Chinese Painting* (Leiden, 1954), pp. 72–75. Acker's translation. For the parts of *Li-tai Ming-hua Chi* not included in Acker's book, I have used the Chi-ku-ko edition of Mao Chin. See also F. S. Drake, "Sculptured Stones of the Han Dynasty," *Monumenta Serica*, VIII (1943), 286–93, for translations of Han dynasty literary references to painting, some of which contain this same concept of the function of painting. For example, p. 292, the *Lu Ling-kuang Tien Fu*, speaking of portraits of ancient rulers and ministers: ". . . the wise and the foolish, victors and vanquished,

there were none that were omitted; the evil to warn the world, the good to teach posterity."

10. Acker, *Texts*, p. 151. Acker's translation. Quoted also in many other books. The same observation is attributed to the painter Ku K'ai-chih, among others.

11. De Bary, "Reappraisal," p. 84.

12. Chow Yih-ching, *La Philosophie morale dans le néo-confucianisme* (*Tcheou Touen-yi*) (Paris, 1954), pp. 32–33 and 181; Chinese text on pp. 196–97. The Chinese text of Chou Tun-i's works is included in this book, which I cite hereafter as *Chou Tun-i*. The translations are my own.

13. The fragmentary essay by Wang Wei (not to be confused with the T'ang dynasty poet-painter) is included in ch. 6 of *Li-tai Ming-hua Chi*.

14. Tsung Ping, "Hua Shan-shui Hsü"; contained, along with the Wang Wei essay, in ch. 6 of *Li-tai Ming-hua Chi*. I have translated these and other passages from these essays, and discussed them at greater length, in the introduction to an unpublished study, "The Theory of Literati Painting in China." In that study I treat more fully some of the questions dealt with in the present paper, and provide more thorough documentation than I can introduce here.

15. See Fung Yu-lan, *A History of Chinese Philosophy*, trans. Derk Bodde (Princeton, 1952), Vol. II, chap. 5; also Arthur Wright's review of A. A. Petrov, *Wang Pi (226–249): His Place in the History of Chinese Philosophy*, in *HJAS*, X (1947), p. 86, for Wang Pi's concept of "images."

16. Fung Yu-lan, *A Short History of Chinese Philosophy*, chap. 20, "Neo-Taoism: the Sentimentalists."

17. Liu Hsieh, *Wen-hsin Tiao-lung* (Kuang Han Wei Ts'ung-shu ed.), section 46: ch. 10, p. 1a.

18. Acker, *Texts*, p. 61. Acker's translation, except that I have altered the opening phrase and removed the parentheses enclosing explanatory matter introduced by the translator. I have removed parentheses and brackets, in the interest of smooth reading, in some other quotations as well.

19. Acker, *Texts*, Introduction, p. li.

20. *Li-tai Ming-hua Chi*, ch. 8, p. 4a.

21. Acker, *Texts*, p. 153. Acker's translation.

22. *Li-tai Ming-hua Chi*, ch. 10, p. 4b.

23. Quoted from the "Yüeh-chi" ("Record of Music") section of the *Li-chi*, part III, par. 5; see Legge's translation (*Sacred Books of the East*, Vols. XXVII–XXVIII, *The Li Ki*), II, 116.

24. Quoted from the *Lun-yü*, Part VII, par. 6. Cf. Alexander Soper, *Kuo Jo-hsü's Experiences in Painting* (Washington, D.C., 1951), p. 15 and note 181. Adapted from Soper's translation.

25. *Li-tai Ming-hua Chi*, ch. 8, p. 1b.

26. Acker, *Texts*, p. li.

27. Forke, *Lun-Heng*, p. 229. Adapted from Forke's translations.

28. Chung Jung, *Shih P'in* (Kuang Han Wei Ts'ung-shu ed.), ch. 2, p. 4b.

29. *Wen-hsin Tiao-lung*, section 48: ch. 10, p. 8b.

30. *Chou I*, "Hsi-tz'u" part I, section xii; Legge's translation (*Sacred Books of the East*, Vol. XVI, *The Yi King*), pp. 376–77. The words are ascribed to Confucius.

31. From his preface to the *Lun-yü*; see *Sung Yüan Hsüeh-an* (Kuo-hsüeh Chi-pen Ts'ung-shu ed.), ch. 24, p. 11a.

32. Legge, *The Shih King* (*The Chinese Classics*, vol. IV), p. 34.

33. Legge, *The Li Ki*, II, 131.

34. "Shih Chi-chuan Hsü," in *Min-an Hsien-sheng Chu Wen-kung Wen-chi* (Ssu-pu Ts'ung-k'an ed.), ch. 76, p. 3a. Chu Hsi is speaking of the *Shih-ching* poems in particular, but surely intends his words to have a more general application to other poetry.

35. See the "Yüeh-chi," section 2; pp. 105–14 in Legge's translation. The pertinent statements are too long to be quoted in full. See also Chou Tun-i's statement of the moralizing power of music (*Chou Tun-i*, p. 176; Chinese text, p. 198).

36. Chu Hsi, "Shih Chi-chuan Hsü"; see note 34 above.

37. *Mencius*, Book V, Part 2, ch. 8. Translation adapted from that of Legge, *The Chinese Classics*, II, 391–92.

38. Forke, *Lun-heng*, p. 102. Forke's translation.

39. Acker, *Texts*, p. lvi. Acker's translation.

40. Wei Heng, "Ssu-t'i Shu-shih," in *P'ei-wen-chai Shu-hua P'u*, ch. 1, p. 4b.

41. The essay is included in *Fa-shu Yao-lu* (comp. by Chang Yen-yüan), ch. 4.

42. Fung, *History of Chinese Philosophy*, I, 342. Bodde's translation.

43. Quoted in *Pei-wen-chai Shu-hua P'u*, ch. 6, p. 5b.

44. The practice never seems to have gone so far as the theory; subject matter was never entirely neglected, however close the paintings' approach to abstraction. This question of the role of subject matter is a complex one, which we cannot take up fully here.

45. Carsun Chang, *The Development of Neo-Confucian Thought* (New York, 1957), pp. 75, 236.

46. *Chou Tun-i*, pp. 25–26.

47. *Sheng-hua Chi*, comp. by Sun Shao-yüan, ch. 2, p. 1a. The *Sheng-hua Chi* is a twelfth-century compilation of poems written as inscriptions for paintings.

48. See note 24.

49. *T'u-hua Chien-wen Chih*, ch. 1, p. 12a. Adapted from Soper's translation (see note 24).

50. There is a possibility that it is not *shuo*, "discourse," but the other reading of the character, *yüeh*, "pleasure," which is intended here. Painting is sometimes spoken of, in the literati school, simply as an enjoyable occupation. In the present context, however, *shuo* seems more likely.

51. *Shan-hu Mu-nan*, comp. by Chu Ts'un-li (1444–1513), ch. 3, p. 24b. An inscription on a landscape.

52. *Fa-yen* (Kuang Han Wei Ts'ung-shu ed.), ch. 4, p. 3a.

53. *T'u-hua Chien-wen Chih*, ch. 1, p. 12b.

54. *Hsüan-ho Hua-p'u* ("Imperial Catalog of the Collection of the Emperor Hui-tsung"), ch. 20, p. 8b.

55. *Hua-chi*, ch. 3, p. 15a, on Fan Cheng-fu.

56. Quoted in *P'ei-wen-chai Shu-hua P'u*, ch. 6, p. 14b.

57. *Chung-yung*, ch. I, sec. 4. Legge's translation (*Classics*, I, 384).

58. Fung, *History*, I, 374.

59. *Kuang-ch'uan Hua-pa*, ch. 1, p. 11a.

60. *Tung-p'o Wen-chi Shih-lüeh* (Ssu-pu Ts'ung-k'an ed.), ch. 53, p. 3a. I have abbreviated the passage.

61. *Kuang-ch'uan Hua-pa*, ch. 1, p. 12a–b.

62. Cf. Li Ao: "When the mind is calm and not in action, the corrupted thoughts will stop naturally. As long as one's nature is enlightened, no corruption can be produced." (Carsun Chang, *Development*, p. 110.)

63. *Chou Tun-i*, Chinese text, p. 204. Beginning of section 2, of his "T'ung Shu."

64. In the Addenda to Wen T'ung's collected literary works, *Tan-yüan Chi*, p. 32a.

65. *Hai-yüeh T'i-pa*, ch. 1, p. 1a.

66. From his essay "Ting Hsing"; see *Sung Yüan Hsüeh-an*, ch. 13, pp. 11–12.

67. *Chung-yung*, ch. 20, sec. 18. Legge's translation (*Classics*, I, 413).

68. Huang T'ing-chien, *Shan-ku T'i-pa*, ch. 3, p. 18a.

69. *Kuang-ch'uan Hua-pa*, ch. 6. Tung is referring, perhaps more as a loyal subject than as a candid critic, to the painting of the Emperor Hui-tsung, who "transformed" less than most, being a relatively realistic painter.

70. *Chung-yung*, chs. 22, 23. Translations adapted from Legge, *Classics*, I, 415-17, and Derk Bodde, "Harmony and Conflict in Chinese Philosophy," in Wright, ed., *Studies in Chinese Thought*, p. 55.

71. Fung, *History*, II, 523.

72. *Tung-p'o Wen-chi*, ch. 54, p. 9a.

73. *Kuang-ch'uan Hua-pa*, ch. 2.

74. *Hua Shan-shui Chüeh*, section 29.

75. *Chung-yung*, ch. 33, sec. 1; adapted from Legge's translation (*Classics*, I, 430-31).

76. *Jen-wu chih* (in *Kuang Han Wei Ts'ung-shu*), beginning of ch. 1.

77. *Chou Tun-i*, p. 23; Chinese text, p. 191.

78. *Kuang-ch'uan Hua-pa*, ch. 3.

79. Quoted in *P'ei-wen-chai Shu-hua P'u*, ch. 50, p. 58a.

80. See note 24. I have used Waley's translation (*The Analects of Confucius* [London, 1938], p. 123) for the first half, but prefer Soper's "seek delight in the arts" to Waley's "seek distraction in the arts" for *yu yü i*.

81. *Hsüan-ho Hua-p'u*, ch. 1, p. 1a.

82. "Chu-tzu Lun Wen," in *Chu-tzu Ch'üan-shu*, ch. 65, p. 6a.

83. "Hui-an T'i-pa" (in *Chin-tai Pi-shu*), ch. 2, p. 7a. Chu Hsi was probably alluding to a famous story (related by Kuo Jo-hsü, among others; see Soper, *Kuo Jo-hsü's Experiences in Painting*, p. 96) about a rustic who was caught laughing at a famous painting of fighting oxen. Asked to explain himself, he said: "I know nothing about paintings; I only know what cattle are really like when they are fighting."

84. *Ibid.*, ch. 3, p. 5a; ch. 3, p. 27b; ch. 3, p. 37a.

NOTES TO TRADITIONAL HEROES IN CHINESE POPULAR FICTION

1. See Joseph Bédier, *Les Légendes épiques* (Paris, 1914), 4 vols.; Marcel Granet, *Danses et légendes de la Chine ancienne* (Paris, 1926), 2 vols.; H. M. Chadwick and N. K. Chadwick, *The Growth of Literature* (Cambridge, England, 1932), 3 vols., especially III, 697–772; F. R. S. Raglan, *The Hero* (London, 1936); Max Kaltenmark, "Le Dompteur des Flots," *Han Hiue*, III (Peking, 1948), 1–113; R. A. Stein, *L'Epopée tibétaine de Gesar* (Paris,

1956); Rufus Mathewson, *The Positive Hero in Russian Literature* (New York, 1958), especially pp. 5–6, 265.

2. Published in Boston, 1957. See the neat synthesis on pp. 4–5 of the Introduction ("Social Meanings in Literature").

3. Abbreviations:

CKCK: *Chin Ku Ch'i Kuan*, a Ming collection of 40 short stories (Shanghai, 1888), 6 *ts'e*.

CPC: *Chui Po Ch'iu*, collection of libretti of *K'un-ch'ü* operas (preface, 1770, re-ed., Shanghai, 1955), 12 vols.

KCHS: *Ku Chin Hsiao Shuo*, a Ming collection of 40 short stories (Peking, 1958 ed.), 642 pp.

KP: *Ku Pen Yüan Ming Tsa Chü* ("Yüan and Ming Dramas in Rare Editions") (Peking, 1957), 4 vols.

KTH: Chao Ching-shen, *Ku Tz'u Hsüan* ("Anthology of Drum Ballads") (Shanghai, 1957), 164 pp.

SH: *Shui Hu Chuan* ("Water Margin") (Peking, 1954 ed.), 1,834 pp.

SKPH: *San Kuo Chih P'ing Hua* ("Narration of the Three Kingdoms"), a Yüan novel (Shanghai, 1955 ed.), 145 pp.

SKYI: *San Kuo Chih Yen I* ("Romance of the Three Kingdoms"), a Ming novel (Peking, 1953 ed.), 990 pp.

YCH: *Yüan Ch'ü Hsüan* ("Anthology of Yüan Operas"), Wan Yu Wen K'u ed. (Shanghai, 1930), 48 vols.

Collections of libretti of Peking operas:

CCHP: *Ching Chü Hui Pien* (Peking, 1957), 27 vols.

CCTK: *Ching Chü Ts'ung K'an* (Shanghai, 1958), 958 pp.

HC: *Hsi Chien* (Shanghai, 1948), 4 vols.

HK: *Hsi K'ao* (Shanghai, 1918), 30 vols.

The Histories are cited in the Po-na-pen edition (Shanghai, 1930–36).

4. This word has been aptly coined by C. C. Wang: see "Chinese Literature," *Chambers' Encyclopaedia*, III (New York, 1950), 491.

5. *Meng-tzu Chu-shu* (Ssu-pu Pei-yao ed.), ch. 5B, pp. 1b–2a. See Ch'ü T'ung-tsu, "Chinese Class Structure and Its Ideology," in J. K. Fairbank, ed., *Chinese Thought and Institutions* (Chicago, 1957), pp. 235–50.

6. See Wang, "Chinese Literature," pp. 492–96, and the outlines and bibliographies in J. R. Hightower, *Topics in Chinese Literature* (Cambridge, Mass., 1950), pp. 14–21, 72–79, 95–102. See also W. Eberhard, *Die chinesische Novelle* (Ascona, 1948).

7. See Lu Hsün, "She-hsi" ("Village Opera"), *Na-han* (Shanghai, 1926), pp. 235–53.

8. See *Hung Lou Meng*, chaps. 18–19, 22–23, 43, 53–54.

9. Especially detailed are, for the Northern Sung, Meng Yüan-lao, *Tung-ching Meng Hua Lu* (twelfth century), and for the Southern Sung, three works of the thirteenth century: Nai Te-weng, *Tu-ch'eng Chi Sheng;* Wu Tzu-mu, *Meng Liang Lu;* Chou Mi, *Wu Lin Chiu Shih.* See J. Prusek, "Researches

into the Beginnings of the Chinese Popular Novel," *Archiv Orientalni*, XI (1939), 91–132; J. L. Bishop, *The Colloquial Short Story in China* (Cambridge, Mass., 1956), pp. 7–12; and J. Gernet, *La Vie quotidienne à l'époque des Song* (Paris, 1959), pp. 240–45.

10. See Wang, pp. 494–97, and the outlines and bibliographies in Hightower, pp. 84–102, and in R. G. Irwin, *The Evolution of a Chinese Novel* (Cambridge, Mass., 1953), pp. 1–8, 213–23. See also *YCH, KP, CPC, KTH, HK, HC, CCTK, CCHP*.

11. For instance, 737 Yüan dramas are mentioned in lists, but the texts of only 217 have been preserved.

12. See L. C. Goodrich, *The Literary Inquisition of Ch'ien-lung* (Baltimore, 1935), pp. 194–97.

13. See Yao Chin-kuang, *Ch'ing-tai Chin-hui Shu-mu Ssu Chung* ("Four Lists of Books Banned under the Ch'ing Dynasty"), Wan Yu Wen K'u ed. (Shanghai, 1937); and A-ying, "Kuan-yü Ch'ing-tai ti Ch'a-chin Hsiao-shuo" ("On Novels Banned under the Ch'ing Dynasty"), in *Hsiao-shuo Erh T'an* ("More Talks about Novels") (Shanghai, 1958), pp. 136–42. See also Goodrich, p. 261; W. Fuchs, *Monumenta Serica*, III (1937–38), 305; and Cheng T'ien-t'ing and Sun Yüeh, eds., *Ming-mo Nung-min Ch'i-i Shih-liao* (Shanghai, 1952), pp. 355–56.

14. See Irwin, *Evolution of a Chinese Novel*, pp. 87–90.

15. See Ch'ü, in *Chinese Thought and Institutions*, p. 249.

16. H. H. Frankel, "Objektivität und Parteilichkeit in der offiziellen chinesischen Geschichtsschreibung vom 3. bis 11. J." ("Objectivity and Bias in Chinese Official Historiography from the Third to the Eleventh Century"), *Oriens Extremus*, V (1958), No. 2, p. 134.

17. *Ibid.*, pp. 133–44; see also Frankel's authorities, from the *Ch'un-ch'iu* on.

18. Y. T. M. Feuerwerker, "The Chinese Novel," in Wm. Theodore de Bary, ed., *Approaches to the Oriental Classics* (New York, 1959), p. 172.

19. C. Birch, "*Ku-chin Hsiao-shuo*, A Critical Examination," manuscript thesis (London, 1954; hereafter Birch, Thesis), p. 295.

20. *KCHS*, ch. 22, pp. 333–54, esp. 335, 339. See Uchida Michio, " 'Kokon-shōsetsu' no Seikaku ni Tsuite" ("On the Nature of the *KCHS*"), *Bunka*, XVII, No. 6 (1953), pp. 26–45, and H. Franke, "Die Agrarreformen des Chia Ssu-tao," *Saeculum*, IX, No. 3/4 (1959), pp. 345–69. See also the play *Hung Mei Ko*, in *HK*, XIV, ch. 20. On the term "bad last minister," see above, pp. 155–56.

21. Found in the well-known text of Wang P'eng quoted by Su Shih, *Tung-p'o Chih-lin*, ch. 1, p. 7b, trans. Prusek, in *Archiv Orientalni*, p. 111, and Irwin, *Evolution of a Chinese Novel*, p. 23.

22. J. I. Crump, "The Elements of Yüan Opera," *Journal of Asian Studies*, XVII (1958), 419.

23. See J. T. C. Liu, "Some Classifications of Bureaucrats in Chinese Historiography," in David S. Nivison and Arthur F. Wright, eds., *Confucianism in Action* (Stanford, 1959), pp. 170–72.

24. See *Shih Chi*, chs. 119–20, 122; *Han Shu*, chs. 89, 90; *Hou Han Shu*, chs. 106, 107, 114; *Chiu T'ang Shu*, chs. 185, 186, 188, 193; *Hsin T'ang Shu*, chs. 195, 197, 205, 209, 223–25; *Sung Shih*, chs. 426, 460, 471–77; *Ming Shih*, chs. 281, 301–3, 308.

25. *KCHS*, ch. 27, trans. C. Birch, "The Lady Who Was a Beggar," in *Stories from a Ming Collection* (London, 1958), pp. 17–36; *CKCK*, ch. 32; *Hung Luan Hsi, HK*, II, ch. 19.

26. *Ch'ing Lou Meng: HK*, XX, ch. 10. *Ching Shih T'ung Yen*, ch. 32; *CKCK*, ch. 5; *HK*, VIII, ch. 8. *Yü T'ang Ch'un: HC*, I, 316–17; *CCTK*, p. 97; L. C. Arlington and H. Acton, *Famous Chinese Plays* (Peiping, 1937), p. 414.

27. See this traditional list in Crump, in *Journal of Asian Studies*, XVII, 420.

28. As when the loyal censor Sun An brings nineteen coffins with him to memorialize to the Wan-li emperor, in *Chia Chin P'ai, HK*, XVII, ch. 3.

29. Chao Kao: in *Yü-chou Feng, HK*, II, ch. 14, *CCTK*, pp. 279–83. Ts'ao Ts'ao: see p. 165. Ssu-ma Shih: see p. 149. On Kao Ch'iu, one of the arch-villains in *Water Margin*, see also *Pao Chien Chi*, by Li K'ai-hsien (1501–68), and *Yen Yang Lou, HK*, XI, ch. 9. Ch'in Hui: in *Feng Seng Pao Ch'in, CCTK*, pp. 928–34. Chia Ssu-tao: see p. 147. Li Liang: in *Ta Pao Kuo, HK*, IV, ch. 8, and *Erh Chin Kung, HK*, V, ch. 7. Yen Sung: in *KCHS*, ch. 40, and *Ta Yen Sung, HK*, III, ch. 9, *HC*, I, 280–99, *CCTK*, pp. 700–714.

30. One can draw the following equations between heroes of the *Three Kingdoms* and of the *Water Margin*:

$$\text{Kuan Yü} = \text{Kuan Sheng} = \text{Chu T'ung}$$
$$\text{Chang Fei} = \text{Li K'uei}$$
$$\text{Chu-ko Liang} = \text{Wu Yung} + \text{Kung-sun Sheng.}$$

31. *Hsiao-yao Chin, HK*, IV, ch. 1; *HC*, I, 564–83. *Ssu-ma Pi Kung, HK*, XIII, ch. 1. Compare *SKYI*, chs. 66, 119. The play *Li Ling Pei* (*KP*, 93; *HK*, XI, ch. 1; *HC*, I, 352–58) builds up another dramatic parallelism.

32. The rebels Li Tzu-ch'eng and Chang Hsien-chung, now glorified by the Communists as revolutionary leaders, were the villains of two traditional plays, *Tz'u Hu* and *Feng Huo Mei* (see above, p. 156), which were focusing sympathy on the two "Judiths" who attempt to kill them. On the Kuomintang's switch of feelings, in the late twenties, from the Taipings to Tseng Kuo-fan, see Mary C. Wright, *The Last Stand of Chinese Conservatism* (Stanford, 1957), pp. 304–5. Similarly the respect for Confucius in the twentieth century is a barometer of change in the Chinese intellectual climate.

33. *SKPH*, pp. 10–11; *SKYI*, ch. 1, pp. 3–4. The Han foot was shorter than ours.

34. Fortune-tellers read Ts'ao Ts'ao's destiny and evil genius from the bones of his face: *SKYI*, ch. 1, p. 6.

35. Thus is Thirteenth Sister judged by her father-in-law: *Erh-nü Ying-hsiung Chuan*, quoted by Fung Yu-lan, *Hsin Shih-lun* (1940), p. 78, trans. Yang Lien-sheng, "The Concept of Pao," in *Chinese Thought and Institutions*, p. 296.

36. Fung, *Hsin Shih-lun*, p. 78.

37. *Yüan Men Chan Tzu: HK*, III, ch. 6. *Chen T'an-chou: HK*, XIX, ch. 12.

38. This word, used by Bishop (*The Colloquial Short Story in China*, p. 15), characterizes this kind of fiction more aptly than the word "realistic."

39. Birch, Thesis, p. 272.

40. See a polemic against Hu Shih about a novel of Maupassant and

Chinese heroic fiction: Jen Fang-ch'iu, "Stereotyping and Humor in Classical Literature," in *Ku-tien Wen-hsüeh Yen-chiu Chi* ("Studies on Classical Literature") (Wuhan, 1956), pp. 109–11.

41. Alfred de Vigny (1797–1863), "Moïse," *Poèmes antiques et modernes* (Paris, 1822).

42. In the play *Cha Mei An, HK,* VII, ch. 3, pp. 7–8, *HC,* II, 759, *CCTK,* p. 753.

43. *HK,* V. ch. 1, VIII, ch. 5, and XI, ch. 3; *HC,* I, 416–28, 521–32, II, 234–40; *CCTK,* pp. 256–71; *CCHP,* XXI, 1–119; trans. S. I. Hsiung (London, 1936).

44. *KCHS,* chs. 31, 37.

45. Chang Liang, for example, in *I Ch'iao Chin Lü, KP,* 12.

46. *Wu P'en Chi, HK,* XIII, ch. 6, *HC,* I, 583–600.

47. *Pai She Chuan, HK,* X, ch. 11, XXIII, ch. 10; *CCTK,* pp. 688–700; *KTH,* pp. 155–59. *Ch'ing Shih Shan, HK,* IX, ch. 12. Eberhard, *Die chinesische Novelle,* pp. 94–98.

48. Both stem from the *chiang-shih* storytelling (see p. 143). The best known of the romances are the *Tung Chou Lieh Kuo Chih,* 108 ch., the *Tung Hsi Han Yen I,* 18 ch., the *San Kuo Chih Yen I,* 120 ch., the *Ying Lieh Chuan,* 34 ch., whose titles speak for themselves, then the *Shuo Yüeh Ching Chung Chuan,* 80 ch., which deals with Yüeh Fei and the founding of Ming. The *Shui-hu Chuan,* 120 ch., the *Ch'i Hsia Wu I,* 120 ch., the *Hsiao Wu I,* 120 ch., the *Erh Nü Ying-hsiung Chuan,* 54 ch., and the various *kung an,* very popular detective novels, can be classified with the romances.

49. *SH,* ch. 28, p. 443.

50. Lady Mi: *SKPH,* pp. 73–74; *SKYI,* ch. 41, p. 346, and *Ch'ang Pan P'o, HK,* IX, ch. 6, pp. 6–7, *CCTK,* pp. 74–77, trans. Acton, *Famous Chinese Plays,* pp. 31–32. Mu-lan: *HK,* XXIX, ch. 3, *HC,* II, 37–71.

51. *CPC,* I, 1–25, VII, 66–80, XII, 180–88; *HC,* III, 289–312. See E. Chavannes, *Mémoires historiques* (Paris, 1895), I, xxxvii–xxxix, and K. P. K. Whitaker, "Some Notes on the Authenticity of the Lii Ling Su Wuu Letters," *Bulletin of the School of Oriental and African Studies,* 1953, pp. 113–37, 566–87, especially "The Story of Su Wuu and Lii Ling," pp. 113–16.

52. *Yüeh Mu Tz'u Tzu: CPC,* VI, 65–71; *CCTK,* pp. 243–47. *Feng Po T'ing: HK,* XVII, ch. 1; *HC,* IV, 70–99.

53. See *San Tzu Ching,* attributed to Wang Ying-lin, 1223–96 (Chang Ping-lin ed., pp. 2b–3a), and Baba Harukichi, *Wa-Kan Nijushikō Zusetsu* ("The Japanese and Chinese 24 Examples of Filial Piety, with Illustrations and Commentaries") (Tokyo, 1941).

54. *Li Chi* (Ssu-pu Ts'ung-k'an ed.), ch. 6, pp. 12a–b: trans. J. Legge, *Li Ki,* I (Oxford, 1926), pp. 343–44.

55. That is how Shen Lien seeks to imitate Chu-ko Liang (in *KCHS,* ch. 40; *CKCK,* ch. 13), how the emperor Hsien abdicates (in *SKYI,* ch. 80, pp. 653, 655–56; *HK,* XXVI, ch. 2), how Meng Ta justifies his desertion (in *SKYI,* ch. 79, pp. 648–49).

56. See pp. 47, 58; see also *Chao-ko Hen, HK,* XVIII, ch. 1, and Granet, *Danses,* pp. 394–97.

57. *HK,* IV, ch. 1, p. 13; *HC,* I, 580–81.

58. *HK,* XVIII, ch. 6; XXII, ch. 4.

59. *SKPH*, pp. 135, 143–44; *SKYI*, ch. 115, pp. 945–46; ch. 116, pp. 952–53; ch. 118, pp. 967–69.

60. *SKYI*, ch. 118, pp. 967–68; *HK*, XXII, ch. 2.

61. *SKYI*, ch. 119, pp. 976–77.

62. The famous play by Hung Sheng (1645–1704), and its modern popularizations such as *Ma Wei P'o* (*HK*, XV, ch. 1).

63. *Wei Yang Kung, HK*, XVI, ch. 5. See also *Chuan K'uai T'ung, YCH*, III, and *Chang Liang Tz'u Ch'ao, HK*, XVII, ch. 10.

64. *SKPH*, pp. 3–6; *KCHS*, ch. 31.

65. *HK*, XXII, ch. 9; *CCHP*, II, 77–106.

66. *Chan Huang P'ao, HK*, III, ch. 11; *HC*, IV, 267–87.

67. *Ch'ü Jung-yang, HK*, IV, ch. 7.

68. *CCHP*, X, 2–3.

69. *SKYI*, ch. 21, pp. 178–79.

70. *SKYI*, ch. 81, pp. 661–63; ch. 84, pp. 686–90; *Fa Tung-Wu, HK*, XIII, ch. 11; *Lien Ying Chai, HK*, VI, ch. 1; *HC*, I, 615–33; *CCTK*, pp. 951–58.

71. *KP*, ch. 22; *HK*, I, ch. 12; *HC*, II, 282–301. Acton, *Famous Chinese Plays*, pp. 230–51.

72. *SKYI*, chs. 54–55; *HK*, XVIII, ch. 9; V, ch. 11; *CCTK*, pp. 438–58.

73. Ts'ao P'ei and Liu Pei in *SKYI*, ch. 80, pp. 655–56, 657–59. See Granet, *Danses*, p. 79, n.2, and pp. 86–87: "modération rituelle."

74. *SKYI*, ch. 41, pp. 340–41.

75. *SKYI*, ch. 85, pp. 695–96.

76. *KCHS*, ch. 21, pp. 298, 307; ch. 37, p. 557. *HK*, XVIII, ch. 7, p. 2; XXV, ch. 8; *CCHP*, XXI, 4. *Mo Fang Ch'an Tzu, HK*, XXVIII, ch. 5. Writers of historical romances found much material of this kind in the standard Histories. See *Shih Chi*, ch. 3, p. 1a; ch. 4, p. 1a; ch. 8, pp. 2a–b, 4b, 6a; *Han Shu*, ch. 1, pp. 1a–2b.

77. *SKPH*, p. 12; *SKYI*, ch. 1, p. 3. From *San Kuo Chih*, ch. 2, pp. 1a–b.

78. *SKYI*, ch. 34, p. 290; ch. 41, p. 347. Chao's horse changes suddenly into a dragon in the play *Ch'ang-pan P'o, HK*, IX, ch. 6, pp. 7–8, trans. Acton, *Famous Chinese Plays*, pp. 34–35.

79. *SH*, ch. 42, pp. 677–80; ch. 88, pp. 1,445–47.

80. E. D. Edwards, *Chinese Prose Literature of the Tang Period*, II, 22, 26. See also Birch, Thesis, pp. 176a, 185. The story of *Hsi Hsiang Chi* illustrates the point well.

81. *Wan Sha Chi: YCH*, XX, 27–40; *Tung Chou Lieh Kuo Chih*, chs. 72–73; *CCTK*, pp. 152–56.

82. On Chu-ko Liang testing Liu Pei, see *SKPH*, pp. 65–68; *SKYI*, chs. 37–38; *HK*, XIX, ch. 3; *CCTK*, pp. 55–67; see also *San Kuo Chih*, ch. 5, p. 9b.

83. Donald Keene, "The Tale of Genji," in de Bary, ed., *Approaches*, p. 194.

84. *Wan Pi Kuei Chao, HK*, XI, ch. 1. *Sheng-ch'ih Hui, KP*, ch. 8.

85. *YCH*, XIV. See H. Maspero, "Le Roman historique dans la littérature chinoise de l'Antiquité," in *Mélanges posthumes*, III (Paris, 1950), 53–62.

86. *KCHS*, ch. 24, pp. 384–90. *Tung Chou Lieh Kuo Chih*, ch. 69, p. 633.

87. *SH*, chs. 14–16, 39–40, 48–50, 61, 77, and others.

88. *SH*, ch. 16, pp. 225–26, 232–36.

89. *HC*, II, 1–37.

90. *SKPH*, pp. 33–34; *SKYI*, chs. 8–9, pp. 62–72. *Lien Huan Chi, YCH*, XLIII; *CPC*, X, 204–13; *HK*, XVII, ch. 12; *HC*, II, 560–90; *CCTK*, pp. 407–23; Acton, *Famous Chinese Plays*, pp. 353–59.

91. *SKYI*, ch. 45, pp. 378–80; *HK*, III, ch. 2, pp. 7–8; *HC*, II, 440–47; *CCTK*, pp. 167–73.

92. *SKYI*, chs. 43–44, pp. 356–68, trans. J. Steele, *The Logomachy* (Shanghai, 1907); *HK*, XIX, ch. 4.

93. *SKPH*, pp. 134, 138–39; *SKYI*, ch. 102, pp. 849–53.

94. *SKYI*, chs. 87–90.

95. *SKYI*, ch. 46, pp. 383–86; *HK*, III, ch. 2, p. 14; *HC*, II, 450–51, 453–56; *CCTK*, pp. 175–81; Acton, *Famous Chinese Plays*, pp. 202–6; *KTH*, pp. 148–51.

96. *HK*, I, ch. 1; *HC*, I, 401–16; *CCTK*, pp. 1–11; *SKYI*, ch. 95, p. 787 (less detailed).

97. *T'an Yin Shan, HK*, II, ch. 6. *Cha P'an-kuan, CCHP*, Vols. XXIV and XXV.

98. *SKPH*, pp. 84–85; *SKYI*, ch. 49, pp. 404–5; *HK*, XV, ch. 7; Acton, *Famous Chinese Plays*, pp. 208–9.

99. *SKPH*, p. 142; *SKYI*, ch. 103, pp. 860–61.

100. See p. 163.

101. *HK*, I, ch. 1, p. 4; *HC*, I, 411; *CCTK*, p. 7.

102. *Ying Lieh Chuan* (Shanghai, 1955), ch. 24, pp. 127–28.

103. Shen Lien, whose biography is in *Ming Shih*, ch. 209, is the hero of a patriotic story in *KCHS*, ch. 40 (*CKCK*, ch. 13). He models his behavior on Chu-ko Liang; see above, n. 55. Wang Lun is the first leader of the Mount Liang lair; see *SH*, chs. 11–19.

104. Eloquent lists of Ts'ao's crimes are the climaxes of the plays *Chi Ku Ma Ts'ao* (*HK*, I, ch. 5; *HC*, I, 254–66; Acton, *Famous Chinese Plays*, pp. 39–52), and *Hsü Mu Ma Ts'ao* (*HC*, II, 178–86). See similar lists in *SKYI*, chs. 23–24, 36. On the real Ts'ao, see E. Balazs, "Ts'ao Ts'ao, Zwei Lieder," *Monumenta Serica*, II (1936–37), 410–20.

105. *SKYI*, ch. 71, p. 588; *Ting Chün Shan, HK*, VI, ch. 7, p. 10.

106. See pp. 161, 164.

107. *SKYI*, chs. 4, 5.

108. "In a time of peace and order, you are to be an able subject [or minister: *ch'en*]; in a time of disorder, you are to be a perverted hero," a physiognomist tells him: *SKYI*, ch. 1, p. 6.

109. *Ti-i Ts'ai-tzu-shu* (other name of *SKYI*) with the commentaries of Mao Tsung-kang, published by Chin Sheng-t'an, 20 *te'e* ch. 1, 27b. Mao comments here on Ts'ao's first alleged crime, as told in *SKYI*, ch. 4, pp. 32–33, and staged in the play *Cho Fang Ts'ao, HK*, I, ch. 6, pp. 8–10; *HC*, I, 600–615.

110. *KCHS*, ch. 10.

111. *Shuang Shih T'u, HK*, XXIII, ch. 2.

112. *SH*, ch. 23, pp. 345–47; *HK*, XVII, ch. 11; *CCTK*, pp. 659–60. Favorite episode of storytellers.

113. Chiang P'ing, one of the Five Rats of *Ch'i Hsia Wu I*, can remain days in the water: *T'ung Wang Chen, HK*, XVII, ch. 5.

114. *SKYI*, ch. 5, p. 40.

115. *SKPH*, p. 18.

116. *SKPH*, p. 75, *SKYI*, ch. 42, pp. 349–50; *HK*, IX, ch. 6, pp. 9–10; Acton, *Famous Chinese Plays*, p. 25.

117. *SH*, ch. 40, p. 646.

118. *SKPH*, p. 116; *SKYI*, ch. 75, pp. 615–16; from *San Kuo Chih*, ch. 6, pp. 2b–3a.

119. *SH*, ch. 28, p. 448.

120. *Ku Ch'eng Hui, HK*, XV, ch. 2. See *SKYI*, ch. 28, pp. 236–38.

121. *Li K'uei Fu Ching, YCH*, XLIII, 14–30. *SH*, ch. 73.

122. *SH*, ch. 4, p. 73.

123. *SH*, ch. 32, pp. 495–96.

124. *SKPH*, p. 111; *SKYI*, ch. 63, p. 526; from *San Kuo Chih*, ch. 6, p. 5a.

125. Birch, Thesis, p. 294.

126. See H. Maspero, "Les Procédés de nourrir le principe vital," *Journal Asiatique*, CCXXIX (1937), 380–81.

127. *SH*, ch. 45. *Ts'ui-p'ing Shan: HK*, III, ch. 7, pp. 1–2; *HC*, II, 538–39. Acton, *Famous Chinese Plays*, pp. 364–66.

128. In the novels *Ch'i Hsia Wu I* and *Hsiao Wu I*.

129. *Shih Kung An, passim*, and *HK*, VI, chs. 9–10 and XX, ch. 5.

130. G. T. Candlin, *Chinese Fiction* (Chicago, 1898).

131. See the eloquent sentences in Li Chih's preface to *SH*, translated by Irwin, *Evolution of a Chinese Novel*, p. 86; also the remarks in Y. Muramatsu's article, pp. 264–65 below.

132. *SKPH*, p. 12; *SKYI*, ch. 1; *KP*, ch. 65; *HK*, XXVI, ch. 8.

133. See the imperial dissertations about cliques in D. Nivison, "Ho Shen and His Accusers," *Confucianism in Action*, pp. 222–32.

134. Such as Hua Yün-lung in *Chao Chia Lou, HK*, XV, ch. 13, and Hsieh Hu in *Yi Chih T'ao, HK*, XVII, ch. 14.

135. Such as Chiang "the Gate-God": *SH*, ch. 29; *CCTK*, pp. 672–73.

136. Such as Chang Ch'ing and his wife Sun Erh-niang: *SH*, chs. 27–28, pp. 426–37, and ch. 31, pp. 478–84. *CCTK*, pp. 667–72.

137. See Chang Fei flogging Tu Yu: *SKYI*, ch. 2, pp. 12–13.

138. Kuan Yü: *SKYI*, ch. 1, p. 4. Lu Ta: *SH*, ch. 3, pp. 50–51.

139. *YCH*, XX, 46–52. *Tung Chou Lieh Kuo Chih*, ch. 73. *Yü Ch'ang Chien, HK*, II, ch. 9, pp. 2–4; *CCTK*, pp. 157–58.

140. *Shih Chi*, ch. 124 (Yu-hsia Chuan), ch. 75 (Meng-ch'ang Chün Chuan), chs. 76–78, and others. See an analysis of the *hsia* institution and of the *"jen hsia* temperament" in Tatsuo Masubuchi, "The Yu Hsia and the Social Order in the Han Period," *Annals of the Hitotsubashi Academy*, III, No. 1 (1952), pp. 84–101. On the *hsia*, see also Lao Kan, in *T'ai-ta Wen-shih-che Hsüeh-pao*, I, 1–16, and Yang Lien-sheng in *Chinese Thought and Institutions*, pp. 294–96, 305–8.

141. *Shih Chi*, ch. 124, p. 1b.

142. *SKYI*, ch. 1, p. 4; *San Chieh I, HK*, XXVI, ch. 8.

143. For instance, Huang T'ien-pa: see above, n. 129.

144. See Chang Fei calling the Yellow Turbans to rally in *SKPH*, pp. 15–20, and the campaigns of the *Water Margin* robbers against the Liao and the rebels T'ien Hu and Fang La in *SH*, chs. 83–119.

145. *San Kuo Chih*, ch. 6, pp. 1a–4a. See above, p. 167.

146. *SKPH*, pp. 51–62; *SKYI*, chs. 25–28; *Ch'ien Li Tu Hsing, KP*, ch. 27; *HK*, XL, ch. 13, XXI, ch. 3, XIII, ch. 3 and XIX, ch. 2; *CCTK*, pp. 350–72.

147. Kuan Han-ch'ing, *Tan Tao Hui, KP*, ch. 2; *SKPH*, pp. 116–17; *SKYI*, ch. 66, pp. 546–49; *HK*, XVI, ch. 3; *CCTK*, pp. 464–71.

148. *SKYI*, chs. 76–77. *Tsou Mai-ch'eng, HK*, XX, ch. 1. *Hsien Sheng, HK*, XXII, ch. 3.

149. See, for instance, the *Kuan Sheng-ti-chün Sheng-chi T'u-chih Ch'üan-chi* ("Complete Collection of Writings and Illustrations Concerning the Holy Deeds of the Saintly Sovereign Kuan"), 5 *ts'e*, published in 1693, and its successive re-editions in 1756, 1824, 1899, 1921 (all in the Harvard-Yenching Library).

150. See n. 53.

151. *SKYI*, ch. 53; *Chan Ch'ang-sha, HK*, VI, ch. 2.

152. At Hua-jung Tao: *SKYI*, ch. 50; *HK*, XI, ch. 13.

153. His appearance on the stage is more prestigious than any emperor's.

NOTES TO PROTEST AGAINST CONVENTIONS AND CONVENTIONS OF PROTEST

I wish especially to thank Mr. Fang Chao-ying of the East Asiatic Library, Berkeley, and Mr. Conrad Schirokauer of Swarthmore College, for the many helpful suggestions with which they have assisted my work on this paper.

1. Ou-yang Hsiu, "Chi Chiu Pen Han Wen Hou" ("An Essay Attached to an Old Edition of Han Yü"), *T'ang Sung Pa Chia Wen*, Vol. I (in *Kokuyaku Kambun Taisei*, Ser. 2, Vol. 7), ch. 12, pp. 135–36.

2. Robert des Rotours, *Le Traité des Examens, traduit de la Nouvelle Histoire des T'ang*, Bibliothèque de l'Institut des Hautes Etudes Chinoises (Paris, 1932), II, 147.

3. P'u Ch'i-lung, *Shih T'ung T'ung Shih* (Wang Family reprint, published by Han-mo-yüan, no date), ch. 10, p. 11b.

4. Ku Chieh-kang (A. W. Hummel, trans.), *The Autobiography of a Chinese Historian*, Sinica Leidensia Vol. I (Leiden, 1931), pp. 8–10.

5. Hu Shih, *Ssu-shih Tzu-shu* ("Autobiography at Forty") (Shanghai, 1940), pp. 46 ff.

6. F. G. Henke, *The Philosophy of Wang Yang-ming* (Chicago, 1916), p. 453 (my translation differs slightly from Henke's).

7. Hu Shih, Yao Ming-ta, *Chang Shih-chai Nien-p'u* (Shanghai, 1931), pp. 7, 18.

8. *Chang Shih I-shu* (Chia-yeh-t'ang edition, 1922), Vol. 2, ch. 13, pp. 19a–b.

9. *Chu Wen-kung Chiao Ch'ang-li Hsien-sheng Chi* (Ssu-pu Ts'ung-k'an edition), ch. 13, pp. 9a–10a.

10. *Ibid.*, pp. 7a–9a.

11. Arthur Waley, *The Life and Times of Po Chü-i, 772–846* (London, 1949), pp. 27, 40–41.

12. Rotours, *Traité*, pp. 185–86.

13. This idea, basically a piece of Confucian feudal utopianism, should not be confused with the system of promotion by recommendation actually in use in the Sung period. The Sung recommendation device, as Kracke makes clear (E. A. Kracke, Jr., *Civil Service in Early Sung China, 960–1067*, Cambridge, Mass., 1953, pp. 58, 75–76, 119, 190) was essentially a means of promoting and assigning officials rather than a means of recruitment into

the civil service. It was a practice which evolved gradually in the early Northern Sung period. For recommendation practices prior to the T'ang, cf. Donald Holzman, "Les Débuts du système médiéval de choix et de classement des fonctionnaires: les neuf catégories et l'impartial et juste," en l'Institut des Hautes Etudes Chinoises, *Mélanges,* tome premier (Paris, 1957), pp. 387–414.

14. Ch'en Tung-yüan, *Chung-kuo Chiao-yü Shih* ("History of Chinese Education") (1934), pp. 271–72.

15. For further description of this attitude, see my introduction to *Confucianism in Action* (Stanford, 1959), especially pp. 4–9.

16. Chu Hsi, *Chin-ssu Lu,* Ts'ung-shu Chi-ch'eng edition, p. 250; Olaf Graf, *Dschu Hsi, Djin-si Lu, Die Sung konfuzianische Summa* (Tokyo, 1953), II, p. 564. I am indebted to Mr. Conrad Schirokauer for bringing this and the following two items from *Chin-ssu Lu to* my attention.

17. *Chin-ssu Lu,* p. 220; Graf II, pp. 497–98.

18. *Chin-ssu Lu,* p. 216; Graf II, p. 491. The translation is Mr. Schirokauer's.

19. *Chu Tzu Wen-chi* (Commercial Press, Kuo-hsüeh Chi-pen Ts'ung-shu edition), p. 471.

20. *Sung Shih* ("History of the Sung"), ch. 156, K'ai-ming edition 4851.1–2.

21. *Chu Tzu Wen-chi,* pp. 473–75, 472.

22. *Chu Tzu Ch'üan Shu* (compiled by imperial order under the editorship of Li Kuang-ti, in 66 *chüan;* memorial of submission dated 1714), ch. 65, p. 26, a, b. The "disturbance" which for Chu is to be avoided here is concern about worldly success and failure, emotional involvement in events affecting oneself; his attitude (he seems to assume anyone would have it) is perhaps a Neo-Confucian transformation of the Buddhist ethic of non-attachment. For a similar point of view in Ch'eng I, see *Chin-ssu Lu,* p. 219; Graf II, pp. 495–96. Li Kuang-ti's essays in *pa-ku* form were highly recommended as models to students preparing for the examinations. For his political views, see my "The Problem of 'Knowledge' and 'Action' in Chinese Thought since Wang Yang-ming," in A. F. Wright, ed., *Studies in Chinese Thought* (Chicago, 1953), p. 133.

23. Chu Hsi, "Reply to Sung Shen-chih," in *Chu Tzu Ch'üan Shu,* ch. 65, p. 28b.

24. *Chu Tzu Ch'üan Shu,* ch. 65, pp. 30b–32b.

25. *Ibid.,* ch. 75, p. 27b.

26. *Ibid.,* ch. 65, p. 25b.

27. *Ibid.* The Ch'ien-lung Emperor of the Ch'ing Dynasty made skillful use of the side of Chu's thought represented in the *Chu Tzu Ch'üan Shu* when he addressed an edict of moral instruction to the students in the Imperial Academy in 1740, urging them to avoid being too much concerned with passing the examinations and to make it their primary aim to become better men. See my "Ho-shen and His Accusers: Ideology and Political Behavior in the Eighteenth Century," in *Confucianism in Action,* p. 223.

28. Henke, pp. 328–30.

29. *Ming Shih* (Palace edition), ch. 70, pp. 1b–2a.

30. Ku Yen-wu, *Jih-Chih Lu* (Kuo-hsüeh Chi-pen Ts'ung-shu edition, 1933 [1935]), Vol. 1, Bk. 6, p. 46.

31. *Ming Shih,* ch. 70, p. 2a.

32. Liu Lin-sheng, *Chung-kuo P'ien-wen Shih* (*Chung-kuo Wen-hua-shih Ts'ung-shu,* Ser. I, Commercial Press, Shanghai, 1936 [1937]), pp. 117–18. Many Ming prose writers, notably Kuei Yu-kuang (1506–71), are recognized as masters of this form. Cf. *Chang-shih I-shu,* ch. 2, p. 36a.

33. This feature of the *pa-ku* was also characteristic of the *ching-i* of Chu Hsi's day, and he complained about it strongly: "Not only does it not result in classical scholarship; it does not even result in acceptable writing." (*Chu Tzu Wen-chi,* p. 476.)

34. *Chu Tzu Wen-chi,* p. 476.

35. James Legge, *The Chinese Classics* (1895 edition), Vol. VI, p. 431.

36. Liu Lin-sheng, p. 120.

37. Legge, II, 324–25.

38. Ku, *Jih-chih Lu,* Vol. 1, Bk 6, p. 52.

39. *Ibid.,* pp. 45, 49; Williamson, I, 333–35.

40. *Ibid.,* p. 47.

41. *Ibid.,* pp. 47–48.

42. In this and the following paragraph, I am indebted to Mr. Fang Chao-ying for some useful suggestions.

43. Kung Tzu-chen, "Kan Lu Hsin Shu Tzu Hsü," *Ting-an Wen-chi* (Kuo-hsüeh Chi-pen Ts'ung-shu edition, 1936), pp. 138–39.

44. Ku, p. 54.

NOTES TO CONFUCIAN EREMITISM IN THE YÜAN PERIOD

1. As originally presented to the Committee on Chinese Thought in the conference held at Stockbridge, Massachusetts, in September 1957, this paper included a long introductory chapter entitled "The Intellectual Climate of the Yüan Period," in which the character of the age was discussed in detail. It has been deleted here in order to reduce this paper to a more suitable length. In revised form it will be published elsewhere as an essay on the intellectual history of the Yüan period.

2. Nemoto Makoto, *Sensei Shakai ni okeru Teikō Seishin* (Tokyo, 1952).

3. Cf. Fung Yu-lan, *A History of Chinese Philosophy* (tr. D. Bodde), I, 281.

4. As originally presented at the Stockbridge conference, this paper also contained a lengthy digression into the ideological foundations of Confucian eremitism, in which this point was explored in considerable detail. A revised and expanded treatment of this subject will be published as a separate study.

5. Hsiao Kung-ch'üan, *Chung-kuo Cheng-chih Ssu-hsiang Shih* ("History of Chinese Political Thought") (reprint, Taipei, 1954), esp. pp. 66, 102. This modern classic contains, in passing, the most useful remarks on Chinese eremitism in relation to Chinese thought that have come to my attention, and in many places the present study draws directly or indirectly on Professor Hsiao's work.

6. A striking example of the censure of officials who displayed insufficient loyalty to the fallen dynasty by the ruler of the succession dynasty is referred to in the prefatory remarks to the chapters of biographies of loyal officials in the *Hsin Yüan Shih,* K'ai-ming ed., ch. 230, p. 7038.

7. *Ibid.*, p. 7056.

8. Nemoto Makoto, *Sensei Shakai ni okeru Teikō Seishin*, pp. 51–54.

9. *Yüan Shih*, ch. 171. The *Hsin Yüan Shih* biography in ch. 170 is roughly the same, slightly shorter through the omission of some details. The information about Liu in Giles, *Bio. Dict.* (No. 1370), is inaccurate and misleading, as is that in Giles, *A History of Chinese Literature*, Book the Sixth, Part I.

10. Yao Shu (1203–80), a very young man serving in the secretariat of a high Chinese official in the Mongol expeditionary forces at the time of the Mongol conquest of Chin North China in the early 1230's, saved the life of the famed Southern Sung scholar Chao Fu, who had been taken prisoner. Chao was taken to the North, and Yao became his pupil. In this first scholarly contact between North and South China in over a century, the Neo-Confucian synthesis of Chu Hsi was spread to the North and propagated there chiefly by men like Yao and other pupils of Chao Fu. See also p. 224.

11. I.e., Liu-TSCC. Liu's works are quoted here in two standard editions: (1) The *Ching-hsiu Hsien-sheng Wen-chi* (poetry and prose), in the Ssu-pu-ts'ung-k'an 1st series, quoted here as "Liu-SPTK"; this is the 22-*chüan* edition of 1330. (2) The Chi-fu Ts'ung-shu edition, reprinted in the *Ts'ung-shu Chi-ch'eng* (Vols. 2076, 2077, and 2078) in 12 *chüan*; this will be quoted here as "Liu-TSCC." The government-sponsored edition of 1350 in 30 *chüan* referred to in ch. 166 of SKTY may be no longer in existence. A large selection of Liu's poetry and prose also is included in the *Yüan Wen Lei* ("Classified Anthology of Yüan Literature") compiled by Su T'ien-chüeh (1294–1352); this is referred to hereafter as YWL. A brief selection of Liu's poetry with biographical data and comment of later writers appears in *chüan* 5 of the *Yüan-shih Chi-shih* by the late Ch'ing scholar Ch'en Yen; this will be referred to hereafter as YSCS.

12. Translated from Liu-TSCC, ch. 1; not included in Liu-SPTK.

13. Cf. Fung Yu-lan, *History*, II, 443–51, and bibliographic note, p. 731. I have drawn on Professor Bodde's work, adopting his translations of many philosophic terms, here and elsewhere.

14. *The Analects* (Legge), XVIII/8/4, italics mine.

15. "Ch'iu-hsi Kan Huai," Liu-TSCC, ch. 6, p. 116. Expressions of this mood and attitude are numerous in Liu's poetry. Much of his poetry is more personal and more revealing than his prose, if at the same time more easily misinterpreted. I have not translated more of it for inclusion here because its highly allusive nature demands that it be burdened with bulky footnotes and explanations in order to be intelligible in translation. Hence the reader is referred directly to Liu's poetry for a more accurate presentation of his thought and feelings.

16. The translation of this line is tentative. The reference seems to be to the *Chou Li* ("The Ritual of the Chou Dynasty"), *incipit* "yü jen" in ch. 4, "Ti-kuan," p. 37b of the SPTK edition. The term appears also in the "Song of Ch'u" which Han Kao-tsu recited, as quoted in the *Shih Chi*, ch. 55, in roughly the meaning in which it is translated here.

17. Liu-SPTK, ch. 20, p. 3a; Liu-TSCC, ch. 1, p. 21.

18. Chang Tzu-yu has not been identified. He apparently had at one time held the office of *chan-shih*, an office in the retinue of imperial princes frequently given to persons of learning and exemplary conduct and carrying little or no official responsibility.

19. "Tao Kuei T'ang Shuo," Liu-SPTK, ch. 20, p. 3b; Liu-TSCC, ch. 1, p. 20.

20. Hsü Heng (1209–1281), the outstanding Confucian of the Mongol-ruled North China in the time of Liu Yin, is more important as an upright and conscientious official who sought to promote a Confucian revival in the North than as a scholar or thinker. His name is often coupled with that of Liu Yin, although Liu disapproved of him. See also pp. 224 and 227.

21. Cf. *The Analects* (Legge), XVIII/7/5.

22. *Chuang-tzu*, ch. 4, "Jen Chien Shih," where it is attributed to the Confucians and quoted disapprovingly. Cf. also Hsiao Kuang-ch'üan, *Chung-kuo Cheng-chih Ssu-hsiang Shih*, p. 66.

23. The text of this letter is to be found in both the *Yüan Shih* and the *Hsin Yüan Shih* biographies, as well as in Liu-SPTK, ch. 21, p. 1a; Liu-TSCC, ch. 3, p. 52; and YWL, ch. 37.

24. *Mencius*, "Kung-sun Ch'ou," part II, II/6–7. This translation is altered but slightly from Legge; the italics are mine.

25. I.e., the "Tu-chiang fu," Liu-TSCC, ch. 5, p. 94.

26. Note, for example, the critical tone of his comments on the Chin, as in his preface to "Chai Chieh-fu Shih," Liu-SPTK, ch. 1, p. 8b; Liu-TSCC, ch. 6, p. 105; and YWL, ch. 3.

27. Ou-yang Hsiu, *Wu-tai Shih-chi* ("Historian's Record of the Five Dynasties"), a preface to ch. 54, and comments in the biography of Feng Tao in the same *chüan*. Cf. Giles, *Bio. Dict.* No. 573.

28. This poem is quoted with interesting comment in YSCS, ch. 5.

29. Note in this connection particularly the poems "Ts'ai-chü T'u" and "Kuei-ch'ü-lai T'u" in Liu-SPTK, ch. 4, p. 3b; Liu-TSCC, ch. 7, p. 122; and YWL, ch. 5. The legend that loyalty prevented T'ao from serving or even from acknowledging the new Liu Sung dynasty (420–78) is one that came to be widely accepted in the later imperial age, reflecting the mores of that age (and one that has been disproved by modern scholarship).

30. See the comments appended to the poem "Yung Tseng Tien" in YSCS, Commercial Press Kuo-hsüeh Chi-pen Ts'ung-shu edition, ch. 5, pp. 49–50. The comments refer to the use of the term *tso wang* ("sitting and forgetting"), although in the version of the poem printed there the parallel (Taoistic) term *hsin chai* is used in place of *tso wang*. Other editions, such as Liu-SPTK, ch. 13, pp. 3a–b, have *tso wang* for *hsin chai*. These comments show but a shallow understanding of Liu's thought.

31. For the *Yin-fu Ching*, see SKTY, ch. 146, first and second entries; also Liu's preface, dated 1271, to a new edition of the work, in Liu-TSCC, ch. 2, p. 26. This is a Taoistic work forged in the T'ang period. Liu's interest in this work is one he shared with Chu Hsi and many other Neo-Confucian scholars.

32. This long essay, "Hsü Hsüeh," Liu-TSCC, ch. 1, pp. 3–8, merits study as a document expressing attitudes toward all fields of thought and learning.

33. I.e., *tsung-heng chia*—this translation of the term is Bodde's, as used in his translation of Fung Yu-lan.

34. Cheng-shih (A.D. 240–48) and Hsi-ning (A.D. 1068–77) were reign-periods which from the strict Confucian point of view represented the triumph of heterodoxy: the former is associated with the Taoist-inspired *ch'ing-t'an* episode in intellectual history; the latter is the period when the arch-villain in Neo-Confucian history, the reformer Wang An-shih, was in power.

35. "Chuang Chou Meng Tieh T'u hsü"; see Liu-SPTK, ch. 19, pp. 5a–b; Liu-TSCC, ch. 2, p. 27; and YWL, ch. 33.

36. "Ch'un-chai Shuo," Liu-SPTK, ch. 20, p. 2a; Liu-TSCC, ch. 1, p. 21.

37. "T'ui-chai Chi," dated 1276; see Liu-SPTK, ch. 18, p. 7a; Liu-TSCC, ch. 1, p. 42; YWL, ch. 28.

38. I.e., "Ho T'ao Chi," Liu-SPTK, ch. 3; Liu-TSCC, ch. 12.

39. Ch'ien Mu, *Sung-Ming Li-hsüeh Kai-shu* ("A General Account of Sung and Ming Neo-Confucianism") (Taipei, 1953), p. 180.

40. Lou Shih-te's biography appears in the *Chiu T'ang Shu*, ch. 93, and in the *Hsin T'ang Shu*, ch 108. This anecdote appears only in the latter. This became a famous anecdote, and it was much discussed by writers of the Yüan period, some of whom praised Lou, and some of whom like Liu found nothing praiseworthy in such conduct.

41. *Mencius* (Legge), "Kung-sun Chou," Part I, IX/2–3.

42. Lines from the poem "Jen Chün T'ien-hsia Shih," in the *Ho T'ao Chi*, No. 20 of the "Ho 'Yin Chiu' " poems.

43. This poem is not in the *Ho T'ao Chi*, but is composed of lines taken from T'ao Yüan-ming's poetry and reassembled by Liu to make a new poem. It therefore bears the title "Chi T'ao Chü" ("Assembled Lines from T'ao"), and appears in Liu-SPTK, ch. 1, p. 4b, and Liu-TSCC, ch. 6, p. 100.

44. This famous anecdote appears in Ssu-ma Ch'ien's *Shih Chi*, ch. 55, " Liu Hou Shih Chia."

45. Hsiao Kung-ch'üan, *Chung-kuo Cheng-chih Ssu-hsiang Shih*, pp. 482–84.

46. This work is discussed by Hsiao, *ibid.*, pp. 506–7. References to the work here are to the edition of the late Ming scholar Mao Chin, in his collectanea, the *Chin-tai Pi-shu*.

47. Chu Hsi, *Chin-ssu Lu*, ch. 2, pp. 19a–b, in the photolithographic reprint of the Commercial Press in the collectanea *Ssu-k'u Ch'üan-shu Chen-pen Ts'ung-shu*; here the work bears the title *Chin-ssu Lu Chi-chu*. Cf. also the translation of this passage in Olaf Graf, *Djin Sï Lu* (Tokyo, 1953), II (Part I), 151. The discussion of the remonstrating but loyal servitor in the *Chin-ssu Lu*, esp. ch. 10, p. 6b, seems to reflect both the wording and the general meaning of the passage in the *Chung Ching*, section 15, pp. 10a–b. Otherwise also there seems to be *no* evidence that Chu Hsi, in summing up the Neo-Confucian rationalist position that was to become the orthodox one, differed with what have been described here as the Neo-Confucian connotations of the concept of loyalty, or with the intensified authoritarianism in political philosophy in general. It should be noted that in his reply to Ssu-ma Kuang's essay "I Meng" ("Doubts about Mencius"), Chu Hsi does not defend Mencian liberalism against Ssu-ma Kuang's authoritarian-minded attack on it. Rather, he tries to harmonize what he considers to be Mencius' real intent with Ssu-ma Kuang's philosophic position. Thus he sums up one of his arguments by saying, "Seen in this way, Ssu-ma's argument really reinforces Mencius' position"; and in several other places he says, "If Ssu-ma Kuang had only understood that this is what Mencius really meant, he would have had no reason to doubt him." However, the whole subject of the relation of Neo-Confucian rationalism to Mencius is a complex one, and one that merits fuller study. Cf. also Hsiao Kung-ch'üan, *Chung-kuo Cheng-chih Ssu-hsiang Shih*, pp. 482–83, discussing Ssu-ma Kuang's rejection of Mencius.

48. Hsieh's biography is in *Sung Shih*, ch. 425.

49. A portion of the colophon by P'an K'an, dated 1575, appended at the end of the SPTK edition of Wen T'ien-hsiang's collected literary works, the *Wen Wen-shan Ch'üan-chi.*

50. Some doubt has existed about the authenticity of the collection known as *Hsin-shih,* or *T'ieh-han Hsin-shih,* recovered in 1638 in an iron box (i.e., *t'ieh-han*) in a well in Soochow where Cheng is purported to have concealed it 350 years earlier. It appeared at a time when its racist sentiments and its appeal to loyalty were of potential use in stiffening Ming resistance to the Manchu threat. However, these doubts have been dealt with by several modern scholars, and I am inclined to accept the authenticity of the work. See the various prefaces and colophons to the recent edition of the work published in the *Min-tsu Cheng-ch'i Ts'ung-shu,* one of the several portions of a new collectanea being published by the World Book Company under the title *Ssu-pu K'an-yao,* Series I, Taipei, 1955. This edition is cited here.

51. "Hou Ch'en-tzu Meng hsi," *Hsin-shih,* pp. 76a–b.

52. I.e., tang yang, to face the sun, or the south, in the position of the ruler. The reference is to the Emperor Li-tsung, who reigned 1225–64.

53. "I Ch'ien-pei," *Hsin-shih,* p. 44b.

54. "Hsien Lu Ko," *Hsin-shih,* pp. 25a–b.

55. One such society of Sung loyalists was the famous Yüeh-ch'üan She, prominent throughout the last quarter of the thirteenth century. For some idea of its size and importance, note the number of poets listed as its members in YSCS, especially ch. 6, pp. 96–105, and pp. 596 ff. (in the edition of this work cited in note 11 above).

56. Chao Meng-fu is the subject of a study by Herbert Franke entitled "Dschau Mong-fu," in *Sinica* (Frankfort), XV, 25 ff.

57. YSCS, ch. 8, p. 125, quotes this poem, entitled "T'i T'ao Ch'ien Kuei-ch'ü-lai T'u," with comment, portions of which are translated here. Note in the same work, p. 124, the comment of later writers on the poem which Kubilai Khan commanded Chao to write ridiculing Liu Meng-yen, a high Sung official who quickly transferred his allegiance to the Yüan and took service under the Mongols. A later writer, expressing a common opinion, states that even the Mongol emperor, although an alien to Chinese civilization, knew enough to despise Liu Meng-yen's character, and the poem he commanded Chao to write ridiculing Liu actually becomes self-ridicule of Chao as well.

58. Chao I, *Nien-erh Shih Cha-chi,* ch. 32, "Ming-ch'u Wen-jen To Pu Shih."

59. K'o Shao-min in his *Hsin Yüan Shih,* ch. 230, prefatory remarks to the biographies of loyal officials, says that the number of Yüan loyalists at the end of the dynasty was very great, but his comparison is with the end of the Liao and the Chin, and not with the Sung loyalists of ninety years earlier. Moreover, in this place he is moralizing about the virtue of loyalty and the beneficial effects of Kubilai Khan's maintenance of it. The facts do not bear out his statement that the literati were enthusiastically and devotedly loyal to the doomed Yüan cause and anxious to die for it.

60. Fu Wei-lin (died 1667), *Ming Shu,* introductory remarks to ch. 143. Here again the influence of Ou-yang Hsiu's historiography is attested to, for the *Ming Shu* follows the example of his *Wu-tai Shih-chi,* which had created the classification of *tsa chuan,* "miscellaneous biographies," for persons who had served more than one dynasty and thus were more or less tainted with

immorality. Despite the tone of the remarks translated here, Fu was not a Ming loyalist.

61. Yü and Li were famous Yüan period figures who died in the bandit movements of the late Yüan, loyally defending the Yüan cause.

62. Fu Shou was a Tangut, a military leader under the Mongols defending Nanking when Ming T'ai-tsu led his small bandit army to capture it in 1356. Fu alone among the Yüan officials on the scene died defending the city. See his biography in *Yüan Shih*, ch. 144, and *Hsin Yüan Shih*, ch. 217.

63. The "old servitor" whose shuffling shoes aroused T'ai-tsu, and prompted the conversation between them referred to here, was Wei Su (1295–1372). The *Ming Shu's* indirect reference to the anecdote here uses the same words with which it is told in Wei's biography in the same work, ch. 144.

NOTES TO SOME THEMES IN CHINESE REBEL IDEOLOGIES

1. There was, for instance, the generally accepted myth of T'ien-ti Hui (The Heaven and Earth Society), the most rebellious of the Ch'ing secret societies. The society originated from a sworn brotherhood first formed in the K'ang-hsi period by six Buddhist monks and several dissidents. The six were among the 118 warrior-monks from the Shao-lin temple in Fukien who fought bravely for the Manchu dynasty and expelled the Hsi-lu invaders, only to be falsely charged with rebellion and cut down (save for the six) by government troops. The survivors fled from Fukien to Kiangsu, where they discovered an omen, a strange incense burner with an inscription to the effect that the Manchu government would be overthrown and Ming rule restored. They were joined by a young man who allegedly was a descendant of the last Ming emperor; whereupon they drank each other's blood and took an oath of brotherhood. Cf. Hsiao I-shan, *Chin-tai Chung-kuo Mi-mi She-hui Shih-liao* ("Materials on the history of modern Chinese secret societies") (Pciping, 1935), I, 1a–17b; II, 1b–19a.

2. Chao Li-sheng and Kao Chao-i, *Chung-kuo Nung-min Chan-cheng Shih Lun-wen-chi* ("A Collection of Essays on the History of Chinese Peasant Wars"), hereafter referred to as CALC (Peking, 1955), pp. 9–17. Also see *Chung-kuo Nung-min Ch'i-i Lun-chi* ("A Collection of Essays on Chinese Peasant Rebellions"), compiled by the Li-shih Chiao-hsüeh Yüeh-k'an She (Peking, 1954), hereafter referred to as CILC. According to Chao and Kao, "peasant wars," or rebellions, were repeatedly directed against "feudalistic rule," and "promoted to some extent the development of social productive power." As a result, new dynastic rulers inevitably were benevolent at first. But the benevolent government had a meager margin, and its exploitation of productive capacity was usually heavy, so no radically new "productive relationship" resulted. Without any leadership and encouragement from a "proletariat," the naturally conservative peasant class could not but acquiesce in the continuance of feudalism.

3. Vincent Y. C. Shih, "Some Chinese Rebel Ideologies," *T'oung-pao*, XLIV (1956), 151–226.

4. Cf. K. A. Wittfogel, *Oriental Despotism* (New Haven, Conn., 1957), pp. 324–69, 413–43, and Wolfram Eberhard, *Conquerors and Rulers* (Leiden,

1952), pp. 13–17, 52–64. Cf. also Eberhard, *Das Toba-Reich Nordchinas* (Leiden, 1949), pp. 240–69.

5. *Shih-chi,* ch. 48, pp. 2b, 4b. The *Shih-chi* and other histories cited in this paper are in the Po-na-pen edition.

6. Fukui Kōjun, *Dōkyō no Kiso-teki Kenkyū* ("A Basic Study of Taoism") (Tokyo, 1952), pp. 2–36. See also Lien-sheng Yang, *"Lao-chün Yin-sung Chieh-ching* Chiao Shih" ("Collation and Annotation of the *Lao-chün Yin-sung Chieh-ching"*), *Bulletin of the Institute of History and Philology of the Academia Sinica,* XXVIII (Taipei, 1956), pp. 17–54; Henri Maspero, *Le Taoisme* (Paris, 1950), pp. 43–57, 148–56.

7. Fukui Kōjun, "Dōkyō seiritsu Izen no Nisan no Mondai" ("Several Problems Concerning the Period Preceding the Formation of Taoism as a Religion"), *Tōyō-shisō Kenkyū* Vol. I (Tokyo, 1937), pp. 59–147.

8. *San-kuo Chih,* Wei chih, ch. 8, pp. 22b–25b.

9. Lien-sheng Yang, *op. cit.* (note 6), pp. 24–26.

10. Maspero, *Le Taoisme,* pp. 15–24; Joseph Needham, *Science and Civilization in China* (Cambridge, England, 1956), II, 33–64.

11. Northern Kiangsu was held as a fief by Prince Ying of Ch'u, a son of Kuang Wu-ti of the later Han and one of the earliest and most noted Chinese Buddhist converts. He lived near the present Hsü-chou from A.D. 52 to 70. Fukui Kōjun, *Dōkyō no kisoteki kenkyū,* pp. 93–103. Also Henri Maspero, "Les Origines de la communauté Bouddhiste de Lo-yang," *Journal Asiatique* CCXXV (1934), 87–107.

12. *Wei Shu,* ch. 20, pp. 2a–2b, 3b, 6a–9b, etc. See Leon Hurvitz, "Wei Shou, Treatise on Buddhism and Taoism, An English Translation of the Original Chinese Text of Wei-shu CXIV and the Japanese Annotation of Tsukamoto Zenryū," in Seiichi Mizuro and Toshio Nagahiro, *Yün-kang, The Buddhist Cave-Temples of the Fifth Century* A.D. *in North China,* Vol. XVI, Supplement (Kyoto, 1956), pp. 33, 39.

13. *Wei Shu,* ch. 20, p. 32b.

14. *Sui Shu,* ch. 35, pp. 26b–27a.

15. Tsukamoto Zenryū, "Hoku-Gi no Bukkyō-hi" ("The Buddhist Bandits in the Northern Wei"), included in his book *Shina Bukkyō shi Kenkyū, Hoku-Gi-hen* ("Studies in the History of Chinese Buddhism, the Northern Wei") (Tokyo, 1942), pp. 243–91. See also Eberhard, *Das Toba-Reich Nordchinas,* pp. 240–69.

16. *Wei Shu,* ch. 47, pp. 4a–b.

17. Shigematsu Toshiaki, "Tō Sō Jidai no Miroku Kyōhi" ("The Maitreya Bandits of the T'ang and the Sung"), *Shien,* No. 3 (1931), pp. 68–103.

18. Tsukamoto, "Ryūmon Sekkutsu ni arawaretaru Hoku-Gi Bukkyō" ("Buddhism under the Northern Wei, Seen from the Lungmen Buddhist Caves"), in *Shina Bukkyō-shi Kenkyū, Hoku-Gi-hen,* pp. 377–78; Shigematsu, "Sō-Gen Jidai no Kōkin-gun to Gen-matsu no Miroku Byakuren Kyōhi ni tsuite" ("On the *Hung-chin-chün* of the Sung and Yüan, and the Maitreya and White Lotus Bandits at the End of the Yüan"), *Shien,* No. 24 (1940), p. 82.

19. Shigematsu, "Sō-Gen Jidai no Haku-un Shūmon" ("The *Pai-yün* Sect in the Sung and Yüan"), *Shien,* No. 2 (1930), pp. 39–55, especially p. 46.

20. Shigematsu, *op. cit.* (note 18), p. 81.

21. On the White Lotus sect in the Ming, see Li Shou-k'ung, *Ming-tai*

Pai-lien-chiao K'ao-lüeh ("A General Consideration of the White Lotus Sect in the Ming Period"), National Taiwan University, *Wen-shih-che Hsüeh-pao,* No. 4 (1955), pp. 151 ff.; and on the famous White Lotus Rebellion in the Chia-ch'ing period, see Suzuki Chūsei, *Shinchō Chūki-shi no Kenkyū* ("A Study of the History of the Middle-Ch'ing Period"). On the Boxers, see Chester Tan, *The Boxer Catastrophe* (New York, 1955).

22. Ch'en Yüan, "Mo-ni-chiao Ju Chung-kuo K'ao" ("On the Introduction of Manichean Belief into China"), *Kuo Hsüeh Chi-k'an,* I (1923), 203–40; see also Shigematsu, *loc. cit.* (note 17).

23. Shigematsu, "Tō-Sō Jidai no Mani-kyō to Ma-Kyō Mondai" ("Problems of Manicheanism and Other Heretical Religions of the T'ang and the Sung"), *Shien,* No. 12 (1936), pp. 85–143.

24. Shigematsu, "Sō-Gen Jidai no Kōkin-gun to Gen-matsu no Miroku Byakuren Kyōhi ni tsuite," Part 2, *Shien,* No. 26 (1941), pp. 138–54; Part 3, *Shien,* No. 28 (1942), pp. 107–26; Part 4, *Shien,* No. 32 (1944), pp. 81–123.

25. Wu Han, *Chu Yüan-chang Chuan* ("Biography of Chu Yüan-chang") (Shanghai, 1949), pp. 11–22, 36–40, 114–23.

26. Kaizuka Shigeki, *Chūgoku Kodaishi no Hattatsu* ("The Development of Ancient Chinese History") (Tokyo, 1948), pp. 271–74.

27. Kaizuka, "Kiboku to Zei" ("Tortoise Shell and Lot Divination"), *Tōhō Gakuhō* (Kyoto), Vol. XV, No. 4 (June 1947), pp. 25–86.

28. Masubuchi Tatsuo, "Kandai no Fu to Kyō" ("*Wu* and the Chivalrous in the Han Period"), in Mikami Tsuguo and Kurihara Tomonobu, eds., *Chūgoku Kodaishi no Shomondai* ("Problems of Ancient Chinese History"), (Tokyo, 1954), pp. 233–55.

29. See Ku Chieh-kang, *Han-tai Hsüeh-shu Shih-lüeh* ("A Short History of the Doctrines and Thought of the Han Period"), (Shanghai, 1936), reprinted in Peking in 1955 under a new title, *Ch'in Han Chi Fang-shih Yü Ju-sheng* ("Taoist Practitioners and Confucian scholars in the Ch'in and Han"). On the Confucian effort of adjustment from a more sympathetic viewpoint, see E. Balazs, "La Crise sociale et la philosophie politique à la fin des Han," *T'oung-pao,* XXIX (1949), 83–131.

30. Ku Chieh-kang, *Han-tai Hsüeh-shu Shih-lüeh,* pp. 24–47.

31. Maspero, *Le Taoisme;* Sun Tso-min, "Chung-kuo Nung-min Chan-cheng ho Tsung-chiao ti Kuan-hsi" ("The Relation between Chinese Peasant Wars and Religion"), in his book *Chung-kuo Nung-min Chan-cheng Wen-t'i T'an-so* ("Studies concerning the Problem of Chinese Peasant Wars") (Shanghai, 1956), pp. 73–95.

32. Miyakawa Hisayuki, "Zenjō ni yoru Ōchō Kakumei no Kenkyū" ("A Study of Dynastic Change through *Shan-jang* [Voluntary Abdication]"), in his book *Rikuchō-shi Kenkyū* ("Studies in the History of the Six Dynasties") (Tokyo, 1956), pp. 73–172. See the detailed case study of the ascension to the throne of Wei Wen-ti (Ts'ao P'ei) (*ibid.,* pp. 89–99) and of the ex-emperors who were assassinated (*ibid.,* pp. 104, 124, 132, 148, etc.).

33. *Wei Shu,* ch. 1, pp. 14b–15a. Also cf. Leon Hurvitz, *op. cit.* (note 12), pp. 56, 64–66, and *passim.*

34. Tsukamoto, "Hoku-Gi Taibu-tei no Hai-Butsu Ki-shaku" ("Buddhist Persecution by Tai-wu-ti of the Northern Wei"), in *Shina Bukkyō-shi no Kenkyū,* pp. 99–130.

35. Lien-sheng Yang, *op. cit.* (note 6), pp. 21–38.

36. Tsukamoto, *op. cit.* (note 34), pp. 111–30.

37. *Wei Shu,* ch. 20, pp. 8b–9a, 16b. Tsukamoto Zenryū, "Shamon Don Yō to Sono Jidai" ("The Monk T'an Yao and His Time"), in *Shina Bukkyō-shi Kenkyū,* especially pp. 141–43. On additional cases of Buddhist cooperation with secular power, see Itano Chōhachi, "Ryu Yū Jumei no Bukkyō-teki Zuishō" ("The Buddhistic Good Omen Predicting the Enthronement of Liu Yü), *Tohō Gakuhō* (Kyoto), Vol. XI, No. 1 (April 1940), Pt. 1, pp. 72 ff., and Ōcho Enichi, "Shina Bukkyō ni Okeru Kokka-ishiki" ("The Notion of the State in Chinese Buddhism"), *Tohō Gakuhō,* XI, 152 ff.

38. *Chiu T'ang Shu,* ch. 183. See also Shigematsu, "Tō-sō Jidai no Miroku-kyōhi," *Shien,* No. 3 (1931), pp. 68–70, 75–80.

39. Tokiwa Daijō, *Shina ni Okeru Bukkyō to Jukyō, Dōkyō* ("Buddhism, Confucianism, and Taoism in China") (Tokyo, 1930), pp. 23–138, 577–626.

40. Shigematsu, "Shina San-kyō-shi Jō no Jakkan no Mondai" ("Several Problems in the History of the Three Beliefs in China"), *Shien,* No. 21 (1939), pp. 125–39.

41. *Ibid.,* pp. 142–55.

42. Yang Chih-chiu, "Huang Ch'ao Ta Ch'i-i" ("The Great Rebellion of Huang Ch'ao"), CILC, pp. 66–75. The biography of Huang Ch'ao has been translated by H. S. Levy; see *The Biography of Huang Ch'ao,* University of California Dynastic History Translation Series, No. 5 (Berkeley, Calif., 1955).

43. Ting Tse-liang, "Kuan-yü Pei-Sung Ch'u-nien Wang Hsiao-po Li Shun Ch'i-i Chi-ko Wen-ti" ("Some Problems Regarding the Rebellions of Wang Hsiao-po and Li Shun in the First Years of the Northern Sung"), CILC, pp. 76–84. See also Shigematsu Toshiaki, "Sō-dai no Kinsan-ikki to Sono Keitō" ("The Egalitarian Bandits in the Sung Period and Their Origin"), *Shigaku zasshi,* Vol. XLII, No. 8 (1931), p. 11. See also W. Eichhorn, "Zur Vorgeschichte des Aufstandes von Wang Hsiao-po und Li Shun in Szechuan (993–995)," *Zeitschrift der deutsche morgenländische Gesellschaft,* CV (1955), 192–209.

44. Ch'ien Chün-hua and Ch'i Hsia, "Fang La ti Ch'i-i" ("The Rebellion of Fang La"), CILC, pp. 109–19.

45. Teng Kuang-ming, "T'an Chung Hsiang Yang Yao ti Ch'i-i" ("Remarks on the Revolt of Chung Hsiang and Yang Yao"), CILC, pp. 120–29; and Chao Li-sheng and Kao Chao-i, "Nan-Sung Ch'u ti Chung Hsiang Yang Yao Ch'i-i" ("The Revolt of Chung Hsiang and Yang Yao at the Beginning of the Southern Sung"), CILC, pp. 97–108. See also Shigematsu, *loc. cit.* (note 43).

46. See Sudō Yoshiyuki, "Chūgoku Tochi Seido Kenkyū Josetsu" ("An Introduction to a Study of the Chinese Land System"), in his book *Chūgoku Tochi Seido Shi Kenkyū* ("Studies in the History of the Chinese Land System") (Tokyo, 1954), pp. 1–6. See also Edwin G. Pulleyblank, *The Background of the Rebellion of An Lu-shan* (Oxford, 1955), pp. 24–39.

47. Saeki Tomi, *Shin-dai Ensei no Kenkyū* ("A Study of the Salt System in the Ch'ing Period") (Tokyo, 1956), pp. 3–4.

48. Hori Toshikazu, *Kō Sō no Hanran* ("The Revolt of Huang Ch'ao") in *Tōyō Bunka Kenkyūsho Kiyō* ("Memoirs of the Institute for Oriental Cultures"), No. 13 (1957), pp. 28–33.

49. Ting Tse-liang, *op. cit.* (note 43), pp. 76–84.

50. Ch'ien Chün-hua and Ch'i Hsia, *op. cit.* (note 44), pp. 101–15; and

Chao Li-sheng and Kao Chao-i, "Pei-Sung Mo to Fang La Ch'i-i," CALC, pp. 86–96.

51. Yang Chih-chiu, *op. cit.* (note 42), p. 61.

52. Chao Li-sheng and Kao Chao-i, "Nan-Sung Ch'u ti Chung Hsiang Yang Yao Ch'i-i," CALC, p. 101; and Teng Kuang-ming, *op. cit.* (note 45), p. 121.

53. Sudō Yoshiyuki, "Tō-matsu Go-dai no Sōen-sei" ("The *Chuang-yüan* System in the Late T'ang and Five Dynasties"), *op. cit.* (note 46), pp. 9–40; see also his "Sō-dai Sōen-sei no Hattatsu" ("On the Development of the *Chuang-yüan* System in the Sung Period"), *ibid.*, pp. 208–22.

54. Katō Shigeshi, "Tō no Sōen-sei no Seishitsu oyobi Sono Yurai ni tsuite" ("On the Attributes of the *Chuang-yüan* System in the T'ang and Its Origin"), in his *Shina Keizai-shi Kōshō* ("Studies in Chinese Economic History") (Tokyo, 1952), pp. 208–30; and his "Tō-Sō Jidai no Sōen no Soshiki narabi ni Sono Shūraku to shite no Hattatsu ni tsuite" (On the Organization of *Chuang-yüan* in the T'ang and the Sung and Their Development as Villages"), *ibid.*, pp. 231–60.

55. Sudō, "Sō-dai Sōen-sei no Hattatsu," *op. cit.* (note 46), p. 280.

56. Miyazaki Ichisada, "Sō-dai igo no Tochi Shoyū Keitai" ("The Demesne in China in the Sung Period and After"), *Tōyōshi Kenkyū*, XII, No. 2 (December 1952), p. 15.

57. See note 53.

58. Miyazaki, "Sō-dai igo no Tochi Shoyū Keitai." Also see Saeki Yūichi, "Min-matsu no Tō-shi no Hen" ("On a Riot against the Tung Family at the End of the Ming"), *Tōyōshi Kenkyū*, XVI, No. 1 (June 1957), pp. 47–49.

59. Sudō, *op. cit.* (note 46), pp. 154, 159, 264–65.

60. Miyazaki, "Chūgoku Kinsei no Nōmin Bōdō—Tokuni Tō Mo-shichi no Ran ni tsuite" ("Peasant Riots in Modern Chinese History—with Special Reference to that of Teng Mou-ch'i"), *Tōyōshi Kenkyū*, X, No. 1 (December 1947), pp. 6–7.

61. Hsieh Kuo-chang, "Ming-chi Nu-pien K'ao" ("Remarks on the Slave Riots in the Later Ming Period"), in his book *Ming-Ch'ing Chih-chi Tang-She Yün-tung K'ao* ("*Tang* and *She* Movements in the Late Ming and Early Ch'ing Periods") (Shanghai, 1934), and Miyazaki, "Min-dai So-Shō Chihō no Shidaifu to Minshū" ("The Literati and the Common Populace in the Suchou-Sungchiang Area in the Ming Period"), *Shirin*, XXXVII, No. 3 (1954), pp. 19–20.

62. Saeki Yuichi, *op. cit.* (note 58), pp. 38–41.

63. Miyazaki, *op. cit.* (note 61), pp. 16–20, 26–30.

64. Li Wen-chih, *Wan-Ming min-pien* ("Rebellions in the Late Ming Period") (Shanghai, 1948), pp. 26–32, 33–34.

65. *Ibid.*, p. 72.

66. *Ibid.*, pp. 97–99.

67. *Ibid.*, pp. 102–8.

68. *Ibid.*, pp. 141–43, 216–20.

69. *Ibid.*, p. 89.

70. *Ibid.*, pp. 77, 86, 89.

71. *Ibid.*, pp. 91–92.

72. *Ibid.*, pp. 85–92, 135–40.

73. *Ibid.*, pp. 91, 139. On Chang Hsien-chung see also James B. Parsons,

"Overtones of Religion and Superstition in the Rebellion of Chang Hsien-chung" *Sinologica,* IV (1954), 170–76.

74. Chang Cheng-liang, "Sung Chiang K'ao" ("On Sung Chiang"), CILC, pp. 85–100.

75. Chao Li-sheng and Kao Chao-i, "Nan-Sung Chin Yüan Chih-chi Shan-tung Huai-hai Ti-chü Chung ti Hung-ao Chung-i-chün" ("The Red-Coat Loyalists in Shantung and the Huai-hai Area in the Southern Sung, Chin, and Yüan Periods"), CALC, pp. 109–24.

76. Chao Li-sheng and Kao Chao-i, "Chi Lu Chien-san T'ung-chih Kuan-yü Hung-ao-chün I-ch'i ti Lai-hsin" ("On Comrade Lu Chien-san's Letter Concerning the Relics of the Red-Coat Loyalist Army"), CALC, pp. 125–27.

77. See note 45.

78. Shigematsu, "Sō-Gen Jidai no Kōkin-gun to Gen-matsu no Miroku Byakuren-kyo-hi ni tsuite," Part 4, *Shien,* No. 36, p. 81.

79. Meng Ssu-ming, *Yüan-tai She-hui Chieh-chi Chih-tu* ("Social Classes in China under the Yüan Dynasty") (Peiping, 1938), pp. 25–170.

80. Sudō Yoshiyuki, *Shin-dai Manshū Tochi Seisaku no Kenkyū* ("A Study of the Land Policy of the Ch'ing Period in Manchuria") (Tokyo, 1944).

81. Meng Ssu-ming, *op. cit.* (note 79), pp. 206–16.

NOTES TO ILL WIND IN THE WELL-FIELD

I am indebted to Mr. George Yu for bibliographical assistance.

1. Ezra Pound, *The Classic Anthology Defined by Confucius* (Cambridge, Mass., 1955), p. 8.

2. James Legge, trans., *The Chinese Classics,* Vol. II, *The Works of Mencius* (Oxford, 1895), p. 245.

3. For the *kou-hsü* system, see *Chou-li* (Ssu-pu Ts'ung-kan ed.) (Shanghai, 1942), *ts'e* 6, ch. 12, p. 18b, and Edouard Biot, trans., *Le Tcheou-li ou Rites des Tcheou* (Paris, 1851), II, 566.

Chu Hsi, it is true, maintained that the *Chou-li* made a distinction between the ching-t'ien and *kou-hsü* systems. It was the rival Yung-chia school of Chekiang (oriented more to questions of "rites" and "music" than to his own great concerns of "mind" and "human nature"), he said, which was currently amalgamating the two systems in its discussion of land problems; see Chu Hsi, "Li I: *Chou-li*" ("'Rituals' #1: *Chou-li*"), in *Chu-tzu Ch'üan-shu* ("Complete Works of Chu Hsi"), ed. Li Kuang-ti (1714), *ts'e* 15, ch. 37, p. 12b. For a modern expression of skepticism about the link between ching-t'ien and *kou-hsü,* see Tazaki Masayuki, *Shina Kōdai Keizai Shisō oyobi Seido* ("Economic Thought and Institutions in Chinese Antiquity") (Tokyo, 1925), pp. 495–511. But, notwithstanding Chu Hsi's disclaimer and his presentation of the issue as a matter of contemporary polemic, ching-t'ien and *kou-hsü* were generally linked together in Confucian scholarship, e.g., in the Sung works, Su Hsün, "T'ien-chih" ("Land Systems"), in *San Su Wen-chi* ("Collection of Writings of the Three Su Worthies") (Shanghai, 1912), *ts'e* 1, ch. 6, p. 6a; and Ma Tuan-lin, *Wen-hsien T'ung-k'ao* (Che-chiang Shu-chü ed., 1896), *ts'e* 2, ch. 1, pp. 4a–9a, 33b–34b, 36b–37a. Su Hsün and Ma Tuan-lin wrote, respectively, before and after Chu Hsi's time.

4. Hu Shih, "Ching-t'ien Pien" ("The Ching-t'ien Dispute"), in *Hu Shih Wen-ts'un* ("Selected Essays of Hu Shih") (Shanghai, 1927), p. 249.

5. Kao Yün-hui, "Chou-tai T'u-ti Chih-tu yü Ching-t'ien" ("The Chou Period's Land System and Ching-t'ien"), *Shih-huo*, I, 7 (1935), 12. See Ting Tao-ch'ien, "Yu Li-shih Pien-tung Lü-shuo tao Chung-kuo T'ien-chih ti Hsün-huan," ("From Theories of Legal Change in History to 'Recurrence' in Chinese Land Systems"), *Shih-huo*, V, 3 (1937), 46, for a modern comment on Ssu-ma Ch'ien's (145–90 B.C.) often-quoted assertion that Shang Yang (390?–338 B.C.), Legalist minister of the Ch'in state, destroyed the ching-t'ien system; Ting maintained that there had never actually been any ching-t'ien in Ch'in, either in form or in fact. He distinguished between ching-t'ien as a system (nonexistent) and as a socio-political conception, and saw only the latter reflected in any remarks about traces of ching-t'ien in Ch'in.

6. James Robert Hightower, trans., *Han Shih Wai Chuan: Han Ying's Illustrations of the Didactic Application of the Classic of Songs* (Cambridge, Mass., 1952), pp. 138–39.

7. For these dichotomies, see Benjamin I. Schwartz, "Some Issues in Confucianism," and Joseph R. Levenson, "Confucianism and Monarchy at the Last," in David S. Nivison and Arthur F. Wright, eds., *Confucianism in Action* (Stanford, 1959).

8. Faithful to the letter of the Classics, he felt that *kou-hsü* complexity would be one of the factors aborting a ching-t'ien revival: Su Hsün, *ts'e* 1, ch. 6, p. 6a.

9. For Chu's denunciation of an opinion that at least some post-classical monarchs had governed like the sage-kings, see Shōji Sōichi, "Chin Ryō no Gaku" ("The Thought of Ch'en Liang"), in *Tōyō no Bunka to Shakai* ("Far Eastern Culture and Society"), V (1954), 98.

10. For Ma lamenting the *"san-tai,"* the heroic ages of ching-t'ien, of classical Hsia, Shang, and Chou, "when there were no very rich or very poor" see Ma Tuan-lin, *Wen-hsien T'ung-k'ao, ts'e* 1, Preface, pp. 5a–5b; see also Chen Huan-chang, *The Economic Principles of Confucius and His School* (New York, 1911), II, 528.

11. In A.D. 9 Wang Mang, damning the Ch'in dynasty for "destroying the institutions of the sages and abolishing the ching-t'ien," proclaimed the latter's restoration, with land made public (royal) and inalienable by sale or bequest, and families of fewer than eight males restricted to one *ch'ing* of holdings. He threatened (and to some extent carried out) deportations of opponents of his ching-t'ien system. See C. Martin Wilbur (translating from *Ch'ien-Han Shu*), *Slavery in China During the Former Han Dynasty, 206 B.C.–A.D. 25* (Chicago, 1943), pp. 452–53.

For Wang An-shih's view of ching-t'ien as a possible cure for maladministration, see his poem, "Fa-lin" ("Distribution of Grain"), translated in H. R. Williamson, *Wang An Shih* (London, 1935), I, 27: "Even ministers buy their posts/This is more than loyal hearts can stand/For the nine-plot system I long." See W. Theodore de Bary, "A Reappraisal of Neo-Confucianism," in Arthur F. Wright, ed., *Studies in Chinese Thought* (Chicago, 1953), pp. 103–4, and Carsun Chang, *The Development of Neo-Confucian Thought* (New York, 1957), p. 188, for discussions of the tension between adherence to Mencius' prescription of ching-t'ien (the stance of Chang Tsai, 1020–77, and Wang An-shih) and revulsion from coercion (Ch'eng Hao, 1032–85; Ch'eng I, 1033–1107; and Chu Hsi).

12. See Wang An-shih, *Chou-kuan Hsin-i* ("New Interpretations of the Government System of Chou") (Shanghai, 1937), I, 84 (deriving from *Chou-li, ts'e* 2, ch. 3, pp. 23a–23b; Biot, *Tcheou-li*, I, 226–27) for his elaborate formal pyramid of units of administration, beginning with "nine *fu* make a *ching,*" up to "four *hsien* make a *tu*"—which also appears elsewhere in *Chou-li*; see note 3, above.

13. Williamson, *Wang An Shih*, II, 301. See *Chu-tzu Ch'üan-shu, t'se* 15, ch. 37, p. 10a, for Chu Hsi's arguments against a father and son named Hu, who maintained that Wang Mang ordered Liu Hsin (d. A.D. 23) to compose it. Chu Hsi reaffirmed the orthodox tenet that it was handed down by the Duke of Chou.

14. W. T. de Bary, "Chinese Despotism and the Confucian Ideal: a Seventeenth-Century View," in John K. Fairbank, ed., *Chinese Thought and Institutions* (Chicago, 1957), pp. 188–89.

15. Ku Yen-wu, *Jih-chih Lu* ("Record of Knowledge Day by Day") (Shanghai, 1933), I, ch. 3, p. 12; *Mencius*, IIIA, iii, 9 (Legge, p. 242).

16. Yen Yüan, "Ts'un-chih Pien," in *Yen Li Ts'ung-shu* (1923), *ts'e* 4, pp. 1b–4b. Li Kung (1659–1733) explicitly echoed Yen, his master and colleague, on reinstitution of ching-t'ien; see Li Kung, *Yüeh-shih Hsi-shih* (Shanghai, 1937), ch. 4, pp. 47–48.

17. Yen Yüan, *Hsi-chi Chi-yü* (Shanghai, 1936), ch. 1, p. 10.

18. Su Hsün, *ts'e* 1, ch. 6, p. 5.

19. See Chu Hsi, "Meng-tzu Chi-chu" ("Annotation of Mencius"), in *Ssu-shu Chang-chü Chi-chu* ("Piecemeal Annotation of the 'Four Books'") (Shanghai, 1935), ch. 5, p. 67, where he discusses *Mencius, IIIA, iii, 15* (Legge, p. 244): "I would ask you, in the remoter districts, observing the nine-squares division, to reserve one division to be cultivated on the system of mutual aid, and in the more central parts of the kingdom, to make the people pay for themselves a tenth part of their produce." Chu Hsi says that this method of land division and of payment is the means whereby the countrymen (*yeh-jen*) are governed and the superior men (*chün-tzu*) supported. Here the concern is very much for the gentleman who toils not, and ching-t'ien is a regularized system providing for his thoroughly proper support; cf. *Mencius*, IIIA, iv, 6 (Legge, pp. 249–50): "Hence there is the saying, 'Some labour with their minds, and some labour with their strength. Those who labour with their minds govern others; those who labour with their strength are governed by others. Those who are governed by others support them; those who govern others are supported by them.' This is a principle universally recognized." On the last part of *Mencius*, IIIA, iii, 19 (Legge, p. 245: "And not till public work is finished may they presume to attend to their private affairs. This is the way by which the countrymen are distinguished *from those of a superior grade*"), Chu Hsi emphasizes that the *kung-t'ien*, "public field," provides the *chün-tzu's* emolument, and that the priority of public field over private field marks the distinction between *chün-tzu* and *yeh-jen*.

20. "Rinji Taiwan Kyūkan Chōsakai Dai-ichi-bu Hōkoku" ("Temporary Commission of the Taiwan Government-general for the Study of Old Chinese Customs, Report of the First Section"), in *Shinkoku Gyōseihō* ("Administrative Laws of the Ch'ing Dynasty"), kan 2 (Kobe, 1910), p. 232.

Wang An-shih had provided the precedent for this agricultural military ching-t'ien effort. In 1070 he had established a militia system with ching-t'ien assumptions of collective responsibility. According to T'ao Hsi-sheng, Wang saw ching-t'ien and his *nung-ping* ("farmer-soldier") systems as inseparably tied together. See T'ao Hsi-sheng, "Wang An-shih ti She-hui Ssu-hsiang yü Ching-chi Cheng-ts'e" ("The Social Thought and Economic Policies of Wang An-shih"), *She-hui K'o-hsüeh Chi-k'an* ("Social Sciences Quarterly"), V, 3 (1935), 126.

For a modern expression of dogged confidence in ching-t'ien—an insistence that the Yung-cheng ching-t'ien was not merely a Confucian archaism but a plausible specific for a social ill, which failed to cure not because of ching-t'ien's inherent hopelessness but because of the defective class-character of the bannermen—see Wei Chien-yu, "Ch'ing Yung-cheng Ch'ao Shih-hsing Ching-t'ien Chih ti K'ao-ch'a" ("A Study of the Ching-t'ien Experiment during the Yung-cheng Reign of the Ch'ing Period"), *Shih-hsüeh Nien-pao* ("Yenching Annual of Historical Studies"), I, 5 (1933), 125–26.

21. Chen Huan-chang, *Economic Principles of Confucius*, II, 526.

22. Ma Tuan-lin, *Wen-hsien T'ung-k'ao*, *ts'e* 2, ch. 1, p. 39a, quoting another Sung scholar and concurring with him.

23. Su Hsün, *ts'e* 1, ch. 6, p. 6a.

24. For Chang Tsai, who believed like Wang in the viability of the *Chou li* and who saw no ultimate peace if the empire were not governed on the basis of *ching* landholding, which he defined by saying, "The way of Chou is only that of *chün-p'ing*," see Ch'ien Mu, *Kuo-shih Ta-kang* ("The Main Outlines of the National History") (Chungking, 1944), II, 415, and Ting Tao-ch'ien, (note 5, above) p. 49 (citing his biography in *Sung-shih*). For Wang An-shih's *chün-p'ing* objective as the main emphasis in one of his *Chou-li* ching-t'ien discussions, see Wang An-shih, *Chou-kuan Hsin-i*, I, 98.

25. E.g., Tung Chung-shu to the Han Emperor Wu (134–86 B.C.): "Although it would be difficult to act precipitately [in a return] to the ancient land system ching-t'ien, it is proper to make [present usage] draw somewhat nearer to the old [system]. Let people's ownership of land be limited in order to sustain [the poor] . . . ," in Nancy Lee Swann, *Food and Money in Ancient China: Han Shu 24* (Princeton, 1950), p. 183; and a *chün-t'ien* memorial to Emperor Ai (6 B.C.–A.D. 1): "Of the ancient sage-kings, there was none who did not establish ching-t'ien, and henceforward their governing made for peace . . . ," in Teng Ch'u-min, "T'u-ti Kuo-yu Wen-t'i" ("The Question of Land Nationalization"), *Tung-fang Tsa-chih* ("The Eastern Miscellany"), XX, 19 (1923), 14. For testimony to the modern coupling of *chün-t'ien* with ching-t'ien, from a scholar who sees *chün-t'ien* as originally a tax system with "leveling" connotations for later men but who sees ching-t'ien as a purely feudal exploitation of serfs by nobles, and who criticizes his contemporaries for what seems to him a widely believed error—the characterization of ching-t'ien as a Confucianist prototype of egalitarian *chün-t'ien*—see Liang Yüan-tung, "Ku-tai Chün-t'ien Chih-tu ti Chen-hsiang" ("What the Ancient *Chün-t'ien* System Was Really Like"), *Shen-pao Yüeh-k'an* ("The Shun Pao"), V, 4 (1935), 65–66; and "Ching-t'ien chih Fei T'u-ti Chih-tu Shuo" ("Exposition of the Ching-t'ien System as Not a Land System"), *Ching-chi-hsüeh Chi-k'an* ("Quarterly Journal of Economics of the Chinese Economic Society"), VI, 3 (1935), 51–53.

26. Almost all discussions of ching-t'ien history accused the minister Shang Yang (fourth century B.C.) of this policy of destruction; see note 5

above. Yen Yüan put the responsibility on Ch'in Shih Huang-ti himself, the "First Emperor," who united the empire in 221 B.C.

27. For emphasis, in the ching-t'ien discussion of the 1920's and later, on *chün-t'ien* as the concomitant of private ownership, see Hu Han-min, "Hu Han-min Hsien-sheng Ta Hu Shih-chih Hsien-sheng ti Hsin" ("Hu Han-min's Answer to Hu Shih's Letter"), 1920, in Chu Chih-hsin, *et al.*, *Ching-t'ien Chih-tu Yu-wu chih Yen-chiu* ("A Study of Whether There Was or Was Not a Ching-t'ien System") (Shanghai, 1930), p. 45; Liu Ta-tiao, "Chung-kuo Ku-tai T'ien-chih Yen-chiu" ("An Investigation of Ancient Chinese Land Systems"), *Ch'ing-hua Hsüeh-pao* ("The Tsing Hua Journal"), III, 1 (1926), 85; and Liang Yüan-tung, "Ching-t'ien chih Fei T'u-ti Chih-tu Shuo," p. 51. For a corollary identification of ching-t'ien with the *feng-chien* ("feudal") system, which had yielded to Ch'in establishment of general alienability of land and unification of the empire—so that Ch'in Shih Huang-ti, his triumph inseparable from these policies, could not have a ching-t'ien revival (which the author poses as a hypothetical wish), since this would have to occur in isolation from its former and necessary context—see Hu Fan-jo, "Chung-kuo Ching-t'ien chih Yen-ko K'ao" ("On the Overthrow of the Ching-t'ien System in China"), *K'o-hsüeh* ("Science"), X, 1 (1925), 139–40. On the other hand, for a Communist identification of *chün-t'ien* not with a post-ching-t'ien regime of private ownership but precisely with the very ching-t'ien system allegedly destroyed by the expansion of private ownership, see Fan I-t'ien, "Hsi-Chou ti She-hui Hsing-chih—Feng-chien She-hui" ("The Nature of Western Chou Society—Feudal Society"), *Chung-kuo Ku-shih Fen-ch'i Wen-t'i Lun-ts'ung* ("Collection of Essays on the Question of the Periodization of Ancient Chinese History) (Peking, 1957), p. 234.

28. *Ming-shih*, ch. 226, quoted in Ch'en Po-ying, *Chung-kuo T'ien-chih Ts'ung-k'ao* ("General Survey of Chinese Land Systems") (Shanghai, 1935), p. 233.

29. See Laurence G. Thompson, trans., *Ta T'ung Shu: The One-World Philosophy of K'ang Yu-wei* (London, 1958), pp. 137, 211. For essentially the same statement on slavery by a disciple of K'ang, see Chen Huan-chang, *Economic Principles of Confucius*, II, 374 (though, more conventionally, he attributed ching-t'ien to sage-kings and the Duke of Chou; *ibid.*, I, 82).

30. Liang Ch'i-ch'ao, "Chung-kuo chih She-hui Chu-i" ("China's Socialism"), *Yin-ping-shih Ho-chi* (Shanghai, 1936), "chuan chi," 2:2, p. 102.

31. T'an Ssu-t'ung, "Jen-hsüeh" ("Study of Benevolence"), in *T'an Ssu-t'ung ch'üan-chi* ("Collected Works of T'an Ssu-t'ung") (Peking, 1954), p. 69.

32. Wang K'an, *Pa-shan Ch'i-chung*, quoted in Ch'en Po-ying, *Chung-kuo T'ien-chih Ts'ung-k'ao*, p. 18.

33. (a) Hu Han-min, with Sun Yat-sen's endorsement, wrote in *Min-pao* (1906) that socialism would be easy enough for China, since her ancient ching-t'ien system was a socialist model long in the Chinese mind: quoted in Robert A. Scalapino and Harold Schiffrin, "Early Socialist Currents in the Chinese Revolutionary Movement: Sun Yat-sen versus Liang Ch'i-ch'ao," *Journal of Asian Studies*, XIII (1959), 326.

(b) Sun called ching-t'ien ("the best land system of Chinese antiquity") essentially the same as his own socialist principle of equalizing land rights— "similar in idea (*i*) but different in method (*fa*)": Ch'en Cheng-mo, "P'ing-chün Ti-ch'üan yü Chung-kuo Li-tai T'u-ti Wen-t'i" ("Equalization of Land

Rights and the Land Question Through Chinese History"), *Chung-shan Wen-hua Chiao-yü Kuan Chi-k'an* ("Quarterly Review of the Sun Yat-sen Institute for Advancement of Culture and Education"), IX, 3 (1937), 889–90, 911. Note that the *i-fa* dichotomy, an old one in Chinese rhetoric, always implies the "mereness" of *fa*, which, as "method," is tantamount to the empirically observable historical event; while *i*, "principle," is precisely the essence which metaphor shadows forth.

(c) In 1906, in *Hsin-min ts'ung-pao*, Liang Ch'i-ch'ao wrote condescendingly of Sun that the latter failed to understand that his "socialism" was only ching-t'ien, not the real thing (Scalapino and Schiffrin, p. 337). At this time Liang was no longer a "modern-text" Confucianist and was reacting against his own former practice of finding classical precedents for the latest things. But in 1916 Liang was bromidic again: "Socialist economic theories, which the West thinks so advanced, were foreshadowed by the ching-t'ien system"; see Liang Ch'i-ch'ao, "Lun Chung-kuo Ts'ai-cheng-hsüeh Pu Fa-ta chih Yüan-yin chi Ku-tai Ts'ai-cheng Hsüeh-shuo chih I-pan" ("On the Reason for the Lack of Progress in Chinese Study of Finance, and a Miscellany of Ancient Financial Theories"), *Yin-ping-shih Ho-chi*, "wen-chi," ch. 12, pp. 33, 92–93.

(d) Feng Tzu-yu, old Kuomintang stalwart, while acknowledging that the socialism at issue today came from modern European thought, held that the ching-t'ien system, "practiced by ancient sages and famous monarchs of high antiquity," was early Chinese socialism: Feng Tzu-yu, *She-hui Chu-i yü Chung-kuo* ("Socialism and China") (Hong Kong, 1920), p. 2.

(e) "Although modern socialism stems from Europe, yet there were early shoots of this type of thought in ancient China . . . Western missionaries of the seventeenth and eighteenth centuries brought ancient Chinese thought to Europe, and this may well have been one of the sources of modern socialist thought . . . Mencius' intellectual spirit was such that he ought to be regarded as a very great unveiler to latter-day socialists": Leng Ting-an, *She-hui Chu-i Ssu-hsiang Shih* ("History of Socialist Thought") (Hong Kong, 1956), pp. 9–13.

34. See Hu Shih, in *Hu Shih Wen-ts'un*, pp. 248–49, for his call to a scientific attitude on ching-t'ien. He suggests that the ancient Chinese feudal system (which should be compared with the European and Japanese) was not what Mencius and the *Chou-li* described. He feels that to a scientific, modern mentality the burden of proof is on the ancients; he does not so much prove the ching-t'ien account false as reject as too slight such affirmative proofs as the *Shih-ching* offers (again, p. 265). Mencius himself offers no proof (p. 269). For *Kung-yang Chuan, Ku-liang Chuan*, Ho Hsiu commentary, *Ch'un-ch'iu*, and *Wang-chih* section of *Chou-li* (all traditional sources for corroboration of ching-t'ien) as being late dependents on a tainted common source or simply crudely misapplied to the problem, see pp. 271–72, 278–81.

35. See *Hu Shih Wen-ts'un*, p. 270, for his impatience (irrespective of the question of the historical validity of texts) with those who take the ching-t'ien of Mencius' description as having anything to do with communism.

36. *Ibid.* p. 281.

37. Viz., *Ching-t'ien Chih-tu Yu-wu chih Yen-chiu*, Appendix I, p. 83, where Chi Yung-wu concurs with Hu in doubting that the Chinese, with their long experience in history well into Chou, should not have developed private ownership of land. Also, Kao Yün-hui, *op. cit.* (note 5), p. 13, where the

author notes that one cannot have it all ways: if the *Shih-ching* is cited to prove the existence of ching-t'ien (as, following Mencius, every ching-t'ien apologist cites it), and ching-t'ien is equated with "primitive communism," we must note that the *Shih-ching* reflects a culture obviously long evolving to sophistication. It hardly represents the rude culture which must be supposed to characterize primitive communism.

38. Kao Yün-hui, *op cit.*, p. 12.

39. Liang Ch'i-ch'ao also, as a settled anti-Communist in the post-War period, did not revert to his earlier occasional practice of grouping ching-t'ien and socialism together (as in note 33, above). He called the ching-t'ien question a dead issue, pertaining to the Chou dynasty, not to modern times; see Liang, "Hsü-lun Shih-min yü Yin-hang" ("Supplementary Discussion of Citizens and Banks"), *Yin-ping-shih Ho-chi*, "wen-chi," chs. 13, 37.

For Hu Han-min's role as a spokesman for the uniqueness of Sun Yat-sen's "three people's principles" and their superiority to Communism as well as their distinction from Communism, see Hu Han-min, "P'ing-chün Ti-ch'üan ti Chen-i chi T'u-ti Fa Yüan-tse ti Lai-yüan" ("The True Meaning of Equalization of Landed Power and the Provenance of the Basic Rule of the Land Law"), in Shih Hsi-sheng, ed., *Hu Han-min Yen Hsing Lu* ("Biography of Hu Han-min"), Part III, pp. 119–21; and Hu Han-min, "San-min-chu-i chih Jen-shih" ("Knowledge of the Three People's Principles"), in Huang-p'u Chung-yang Chün-shih Cheng-chih Hsüeh-hsiao T'e-pieh Tang-pu ("Special Kuomintang Party Council, Whampoa Academy"), ed., *Chiang Hu Tsui-chin Yen-lun Chi* ("Most Recent Collected Discourses of Chiang Kai-shek and Hu Han-min") (Canton?, 1927), Part II, pp. 1–12, esp. pp. 5–6, where the three principles are explained as defining one another, in such fashion as to be superior to the three envisioned alternatives, nationalism (i.e., *kuo-chia chu-i*, not the Sun principle of *min-tsu chu-i*), anarchism, and communism.

40. Hu Han-min, "Meng-tzu yü She-hui Chu-i" ("Mencius and Socialism"), in *Wei-wu Shih-kuan yü Lun-li chih Yen-chiu* ("A Study of the Materialist Interpretation of History and Ethics") (Shanghai, 1925), pp. 155–56.

41. Hu Han-min, "P'ing-chün Ti-ch'üan . . . ," pp. 117–28. For Sun in 1921, maintaining that the principles of the ching-t'ien system coincided with the intentions of his "equalization of landed power," see Hsiao Cheng, "P'ing-chün Ti-ch'üan Chen-ch'üan" ("The True Interpretation of Equalization of Landed Power"), *Ti-cheng Yüeh-k'an* ("The Journal of Land Economics"), I, 1 (1933), 10.

42. Hu Han-min, *San-min-chu-i ti Lien-huan-hsing* ("The Cyclical Character of the Three People's Principles") (Shanghai, 1928), pp. 65–66.

43. See Hu Han-min, "Chung-kuo Che-hsüeh chih Wei-wu ti Yen-chiu" ("Chinese Philosophy from the Materialist Standpoint"), in *Wei-wu shih-kuan yü lun-li chih yen-chiu*, p. 74, for his discussion of the critical population factor; Hu bases it on Han Fei-tzu (cited in very "Malthusian" vein, emphasizing the geometrical rate of natural increase). Hu considers also the factor of the development of exchange and the power of merchants relative to farmers.

44. Hu Han-min, *ibid.*, p. 73.

45. Western scholarship on ancient China, naturally unaffected by the emotional overtones of the ching-t'ien controversy, and accordingly more directly concerned with construction of a history than destruction of a text, tends toward this view, which metaphorizes the ching-t'ien of Mencius. See Henri Maspero, *La Chine antique* (Paris, 1927), pp. 108–10. (Among others

following Maspero, J. J. L. Duyvendak, *The Book of Lord Shang: a Classic of the Chinese School of Law* (London, 1928), pp. 41–44, declines to follow Hu Shih in dismissing ching-t'ien as mere utopianism. They see it as a system of dependents and lord in a time of slash-and-burn cultivation, before individual property was possible. As soon as families became more settled on more or less definitely allotted land, say Maspero and Duyvendak, the tendency to develop individual property began.

According to a notice in *T'oung Pao*, XXIX (1932), 203–4, a serious Russian work, M. Kokin and G. Papayan, *"Czin-Tyan," agrarnyi stroi drevnego Kitaya* ("The Ching-t'ien Agrarian System of Ancient China") (Leningrad, 1930), also follows Maspero closely.

For early modern Japanese scholarship on this subject, see Hashimoto Masuyoshi, "Shina Kodai Densei Kō" ("Examination of the Land System of Chinese Antiquity"), *Tōyō Gakuhō*, XII (1923), 1–45, 481–94; XV (1925), 64–104. Hashimoto relates the Chinese factions to Japanese schools of interpretation: Hu Han-min, Liao Chung-k'ai, and Chu Chih-hsin with Katō Shigeru in the pre-private-property school, Hu Shih and Chi Yung-wu with Fukube Unokichi in the school critical of Mencius. See Part I, p. 15.

46. For this question, see S. G. F. Brandon, "The Myth and Ritual Position Critically Considered," in *Myth, Ritual, and Kingship: Essays on the Theory and Practice of Kingship in the Ancient Near East and in Israel*, ed., S. H. Hooke (Oxford, 1958), p. 280.

47. Examples from pre-1949 period (official Communist scholarship to be treated below):

(a) For ching-t'ien as "primitive communism" or "communal village society" or "natural socialism" (the ching-t'ien age being characterized by small population, no economic exchange, no free competition, no capital, and an institution of landownership either tribal or village-based or nonexistent; the ching-t'ien system being analogous in social organization and technical development with early "Gemeineigentum" and systems of collectivist organization elsewhere, being established by the ontological necessity of something in the real historical past to account for Mencius' idea of it, and not deserving Hu Shih's sweeping skepticism, see successively, Pang Li-shan, "She-hui Chu-i yü She-hui Cheng-ts'e" ("Socialism and Social Policy"), *Tung-fang Tsa-chih*, XXI, 16 (1924), 20; Ni Chin-sheng, "Ching-t'ien Hsin-ch'eng Pieh-lun" ("Another Discussion of New Clarifications of Ching-t'ien"), *Shih-huo*, V, 5 (1937), 22, 25; Chang Hsiao-ming, *Chung-kuo Li-tai Ching-ti Wen-t'i* ("The Land Question in Chinese History") (Shanghai, 1932), pp. 20–22, 365; Chu Hsieh, "Ching-t'ien Chih-tu Yu-wu Wen-t'i chih Ching-chi Shih shang ti Kuan-ch'a" ("Examination from the Standpoint of Economic History of the Question of the Existence of the Ching-t'ien System"), *Tung-fang Tsa-chih*, XXXI, 1 (1934), 187–90; Yü Ching-i, "Ching-t'ien Chih-tu Hsin-k'ao" ("New Examination of the Ching-t'ien System"), *Tung-fang Tsa-chih*, XXXI, 1 (1934), 163–65, 168–72; Cheng Hsing-sung, "Ching-t'ien K'ao" ("Examination of Ching-t'ien"), Part I, *Ching-chi-hsüeh Chi-k'an*, V, 2 (1934), 58–59, 61; Hsü Chung-shu, "Ching-t'ien Chih-tu T'an-yüan" ("An Inquiry into the Ching-t'ien System"), *Chung-kuo Wen-hua Yen-chiu Hui-k'an* ("Bulletin of Chinese Studies"), IV, Part 1 (1944), 153–54—these studies, like the ones which follow, often incapsulating other studies of the 1920's and later.

(b) For ching-t'ien as feudal or affiliated with feudalism (*kung-t'ien* being "noble's field," not "public field" as anachronistically later understood; the system idealized by Confucianists but with rough outlines of actual feudal system behind it; a servile basis of land-cultivation (the peasantry being the lord's "oxen and horses"), rather than an egalitarian or "public-ownership" basis; ching-t'ien as possibly a fossil form of Shang communalism in a Chou feudal context; *Chou-li* suggesting manorial practice; Japanese affinities; "mutual aid" as corvée), see Niu Hsi, "Tzu Shang chih Han-ch'u She-hui Tsu-chih chih T'an-t'ao" ("Inquiry into Social Organization from Shang to Beginning of Han"), *Ch'ing-hua Chou-k'an* ("Tsing Hua Weekly"), XXXV, 2 (1921), 26–27; Liu Ta-tiao, *op. cit.* (note 27), p. 683; Chao Lin, "Ching-t'ien Chih-tu ti Yen-chiu" ("Investigation of the Ching-t'ien System"), *Shih Ti Ts'ung-k'an* ("History and Geography Series"), No. 1 (1933), pp. 7–9, 17; Lü Chen-yü, "Hsi-Chou Shih-tai ti Chung-kuo She-hui" ("Chinese Society in the Western Chou Period"), *Chung-shan Wen-hua Chiao-yü kuan Chi-k'an*, II, 1 (1935), 120–26; Wang I-sun, "Chung-kuo She-hui Ching-chi–shih shang Chün-t'ien Chih-tu ti Yen-chiu" ("Investigation of the *Chün-t'ien* System in Chinese Social and Economic History"), *Tung-fang Tsa-chih*, XXXIII, 14 (1936), 53–54; Kao Yün-hui, *op. cit.* (note 5), pp. 12, 15–17; Hsü Hung-hsiao, "Ch'in Han She-hui chih T'u-ti Chih-tu yü Nung-yeh Sheng-ch'an" ("Land Systems and Agricultural Production in Ch'in and Han Society"), *Shih-huo*, III, 7 (1936), 13; Ch'i Ssu-ho, "Meng-tzu Ching-t'ien Shuo-pan" ("Mencius' Theory of Ching-t'ien"), *Yen-ching Hsüeh-pao* ("Yenching Journal of Chinese Studies"), No. 35 (1948), pp. 107, 120–21, 127; Shao Chün-p'u, "Ching-ti Chih-tu K'ao" ("On the *Ching* Land System"), Ling-nan Hsüeh-pao ("The Lingnan Journal"), IX, 2 (1949), 199–200. This last study, p. 200, and Wei Chü-hsien, "Ching-t'ien ti Ts'ai-liao" ("The Character of Ching-t'ien"), *Hsüeh-i* ("Wissen und Wissenschaft"), XIV, 5 (1935), 17, are among the few to inject a note of historical geography into the essentially textual argument for the feudal origins of some actual ching-t'ien land arrangement; they note the present-day topographical character of certain villages, with their regular dimensions in diked fields and waterways—persisting, it is suggested, notwithstanding changes in the economics of land tenure, from feudal antiquity.

48. Liao Chung-k'ai, "Ta Hu Shih chih Lun Ching-t'ien Shu" ("In Answer to Hu Shih's Writings on Ching-t'ien"), in *Liao Chung-k'ai Chi* ("A Liao Chung-k'ai Collection") (Taiyuan, 192?), pp. 87–93.

49. Harold J. E. Peake, "Village Community," *Encyclopaedia of the Social Sciences* (New York, 1935), XV, 253–54.

50. *Ching-t'ien Chih-tu Yu-wu chih Yen-chiu*, Appendix I, p. 103.

51. Chien Hu, " 'Ou-hua' ti Chung-kuo" ("Europeanized China"), *Tung-fang Tsa-chih*, XX, 4 (1923), 1.

52. Liao Chung-k'ai, "Chung-kuo Shih-yeh ti Hsien-chuang chi Ch'an-yeh Lo-hou ti Yüan-yin" ("The Present Condition of Chinese Industry and the Root Cause of Backwardness in Production"), in *Chung-kuo Kuo-min-tang Shih-yeh Chiang-yen* ("Chinese Nationalist Party Lectures on Industry") (Shanghai, 1924), p. 54.

53. For this distinction between critic and exegete, see Arthur A. Cohen, *Martin Buber* (New York, 1957), p. 60.

54. Salo W. Baron and Joseph L. Blau, *Judaism: Postbiblical and Talmudic Period* (New York, 1954), pp. 101–2.

55. Hu Han-min, "San-min-chu-i chih Jen-shih," *op. cit.* (note 39), p. 7.

56. E.g., Hsü Shih-ch'ang, *Ou-chan Hou chih Chung-kuo: Ching-chi yü Chiao-yü* ("China After the European War: Economics and Education")

(Shanghai, 1920), pp. 58–59: Hsü praised the "Chinese national spirit," based on agriculture and education in *tao* and *te*, held tenaciously for thousands of years, incomparable in the world. He saw commerce and industry as "captivating" but very thinly based; they were the rivals of agriculture, as "practical education" was the rival alternative to cultivation of *tao* and *te*. But Europe's flourishing was just a matter of a recent century or two, while Chinese culture was early and rich. Hsü resented the vaunting of science and material efficiency against *tao-te* and the slur on agriculture as a "feudal" association. He only knew, he said, that the ancients revered virtue and laid stress on agriculture.

57. For references to ching-t'ien as the "golden age" land regime of the *san-tai*, founded by the Yellow Emperor, reconstituted by Yü the Great after the great flood, etc., see *ibid.*, p. 56; Tsou Cho-li, "She-hui Chu-i p'ing-i" ("A Balanced Consideration of Socialism"), *Hsüeh-heng* ("The Critical Review"), No. 12 (1922), p. 6; Teng Ch'u-min, "T'u-ti Kuo-yu Wen-t'i" ("The Question of Land Nationalization"), *Tung-fang Tsa-chih*, XX (1923), 13–14; Hsiang Nai-ch'i, "Tzu Ma-k'o-ssu Nung-yeh Li-lun chih Fa-chan Lun tao Wo Kuo T'u-ti Wen-t'i" ("A Discussion of the Land Problem in China from the Standpoint of the Development of Marxist Theories on Agriculture"), *She-hui K'o-hsüeh Chi-k'an*, V (1930), 15.

One would be hard put to distinguish these accounts of the origins and nature of ching-t'ien from such a traditional account as that of Ch'ien T'ang (1735–90) in "Kai-t'ing Shu-ku Lu," *Huang-Ch'ing Ching-chieh* (1829), *ts'e* 195, ch. 718, p. la. Cf. Ch'en Chao-k'un, "Chung-kuo Ku-tai T'ien-fu Hsing-ko Lun-lüeh" ("An Outline of Land-tax Innovation in Ancient China"), *She-hui K'o-hsüeh Chi-k'an* (new series), II (1943), 1–2, for a euhemerist identification of the Yellow Emperor's establishment of ching-t'ien (cited from the *T'ung-tien* of Tu Yu, 735–812) with transition in Chinese history from successive hunting and pastoral stages to the agricultural stage, the latter having delimitation of land as its novel requirement.

58. Hsü Shih-ch'ang, *op. cit.* (note 56), p. 58; Tsou Cho-li, *op. cit.* (note 57), pp. 1, 6, 10; Teng Ch'u-min, *op. cit.* (note 57), p. 16; Hsiang Nai-ch'i, *op. cit* (note 57), pp. 14–15.

59. Chiang Kai-shek, *China's Destiny* and *Chinese Economic Theory*, ed. Philip Jaffe (New York, 1947). The reference is from the latter work, published in 1943.

60. Yang P'ei-chih, *Yen Hsi-chai yü Li Shu-ku* ("Yen Yüan and Li Kung") (Wuhan, 1956), pp. 84–85.

61. Li Ting-fang, *Wang Mang* (Shanghai, 1957), pp. 50, 52. Hu Shih published articles on "China's socialist emperor" in 1922 and 1928.

62. Ho Hsiang-ning, *Hui-i Sun Chung-shan ho Liao Chung-k'ai* ("Recollections of Sun Yat-sen and Liao Chung-k'ai") (Peking, 1957), p. 33.

63. Liao Chung-k'ai, "Nung-min Yün-tung So Tang Chu-i chih Yao-tien" ("Important Points Which the Peasant Movement Should Take into Account"), in Cheng Wu, ed., *Tang Kuo Hsien-chin Yen-lun Chi* ("Discourses of Kuomintang Elders") (Changsha, 1938), p. 144.

64. Joseph R. Levenson, "History Under Chairman Mao," *Soviet Survey*, No. 24 (1958), pp. 32–37.

65. One such is Li A-nung, *Chung-kuo ti Nu-li Chih yü Feng-chien Chih* ("Slave Regime and Feudal Regime in China) (Peking, 1954), p. 75.

66. Sun Li-hsing, "P'i-p'an Hu Shih ti 'Ching-t'ien Pien' chi Ch'i-t'a"

("Criticism of Hu Shih's 'The ching-t'ien dispute', etc."), in *Hu Shih Ssu-hsiang P'i-p'an* ("Critique of Hu Shih's Thought"), VI (Peking, 1955), 160–64. Similarly, for an insistence that "science" (i.e., precisely the "objective laws of social development") demands rejection of the idea that ching-t'ien was simply a utopian vision of Mencius', see Kao Heng, "Chou-tai Ti-tsu Chih-tu K'ao" ("On the Chou Land-tax System"), in *Chung-kuo Ku-shih Fen-ch'i Wen-t'i Lun-ts'ung*, p. 30.

67. For a description of Kuo Mo-jo as using arguments similar to Hu Shih's against the actual existence of ching-t'ien, with rich and seemingly convincing evidence from bronze inscriptions, showing among other things that land could be given away in the Chou period, see Wolfram Eberhard, "Zur Landwirtschaft der Han-Zeit," *Mitteilungen des Seminars für Orientalische Sprachen zu Berlin*, XXXV, Part I (Ostasiatische Studien) (1932), 81.

68. Sun Li-hsing, *op. cit.* (note 66), pp. 166–67.

69. The literature on this question is already enormous. Sun Li-hsing, *ibid.*, records the agreement of the great majority of scholars that some system of communal production on public land (and it seems to have come down to the alternatives of calling this ching-t'ien or something else of the same name) existed in Chinese antiquity. Kao Heng, *op. cit.* (note 66), pp. 63–64, concludes that the Chou period was feudal, but (p. 29) he deems a ching-t'ien system compatible with any of the possible definitions of pre-Ch'in society. However, two interpretations, by and large, have divided the field, (a) that this system was one of a village agricultural communal society, and (b) that it was a feudal manorial system. If (a), then Chou was a slave society (on the authority of B. K. Nikorsky's *History of Primitive Society*, which said that agricultural village communal society is the backwash of primitive society in the first class society, i.e., slave); if (b), then Chou was feudal.

Kuo Mo-jo, in *Nu-li chih Shih-tai* ("The Slave Era") (Shanghai, 1952), p. 23, showed his conversion to acceptance of ching-t'ien by repeating as a statement of fact the famous *Shih-chi* description of the influence of Shang Yang, to the effect that in 350 B.C. Ch'in Hsiao-kung "did away with ching-t'ien, opened public roads." And in *Shih P'i-p'an Shu* ("Ten Critiques") (Peking, 1954), p. 324, Kuo wrote that in Shang Yang's period Ch'in society was in a transitional phase from slave to feudal. Thus Kuo Mo-jo sees ching-t'ien ultimately in a context of slave society; see Jan Chao-te, "Shih Lun Shang Yang Pien-fa ti Hsing-chih" ("On the Nature of Shang Yang's Reforms"), *Li-shih yen-chiu* ("Historical Research") (1957), No. 6, p. 44. Hou Wai-lu, likewise, in "Lun Chung-kuo Feng-chien Chih ti Hsing-cheng chi Ch'i Fa-tien Hua" ("On the Form of the Chinese Feudal Regime and Its Legal Development"), *Li-shih Yen-chiu* (1956), No. 8, p. 24, called the Ch'in Hsiao-kung action against ching-t'ien (above) a "shoot" of feudalism, thus relating it and Chou society to slavery.

Other writers, e.g., Fan Wen-lan, interpret Shang Yang (hence ching-t'ien as well) differently, seeing his day as transitional from one sort of feudalism to another; see Jan Chao-te, p. 43. Like Yang Hsiang-k'uei, "Shih Lun hsien-Ch'in Shih-tai Ch'i-kuo ti Ching-chi Chih-tu" ("Tentative Discussion of the Economic System of the Pre-Ch'in State of Ch'i"), in *Chung-kuo Ku-shih Fen-ch'i Wen-t'i Lun-ts'ung*, p. 88, Wang Yü-che, "Yu Kuan Hsi-Chou She-hui Hsing-chih ti Chi-ko Wen-t'i" ("Some Problems Relating to the Social Character of the Western Chou Dynasty"), *Li-shih Yen-chiu* (1957), No. 5, pp. 87–88, notes that the famous *kung-t'ien—ssu-t'ien* ("public fields" and "private fields") distinction of the *Shih-ching* and Mencius is a "characteristic of the first phase of feudalism," hence should not be dismissed. However, he notes further (an old observation: see note 47 above) that *kung* in the *Shih-ching* signifies not "public" in the sense of belonging to the collectivity but only in the sense of belonging to the nobles, the governing class. Indeed, according to Ch'en Meng-lin, who was a slave-society theorist not on "village-communal" grounds but on grounds of skepticism about servile land-tenure, *ssu-t'ien* as well as *kung-t'ien* was nobles' land. The *kung-t'ien* was distinguished by being, after the fall of Shang, royal domain retained by the ruling house during the process of infeudation; by extension of this principle of classification down through the system, progressively minor nobles' land was known as *kung-t'ien* when it was retained by the superior during the process of sub-infeudation. See Ch'en Meng-lin, "Kuan-yü Hsi-Chou She-hui Hsing-chih Wen-t'i" ("Questions Relative to the Character of Western Chou Society"), in *Chung-kuo Ku-shih Fen-ch'i Wen-t'i Lun-ts'ung*, p. 208.

As is natural in a Communist exposition, for which feudalism—whatever the permissible dispute about the date of its inception—must not be assumed to have been superseded until fairly recent times, there is no interpretation of this semantic problem here like that in Fung Yu-lan, *A History of Chinese Philosophy: the Period of the Philosophers, from the Beginnings to circa 100 B.C.*, tr. Derk Bodde (Peiping, 1937), pp. 118–19 (first published in Chinese, Shanghai, 1931); Fung saw the original ching-t'ien system as contrived to benefit the noble class. Mencius, in a typically Confucian act of creation by transmission of traditional forms, converted it into an "economic institution having socialistic implications," *kung* shifting in connotation from "noble" to "public."

70. Ho Tzu-ch'üan, "Kuan-yü Chung-kuo Ku-tai She-hui ti Chi-ko Wen-t'i" ("Some Questions Relating to Ancient Chinese Society"), in *Chung-kuo Ku-shih Fen-ch'i Wen-t'i Lun-ts'ung*, pp. 135–36.

71. Sun Li-hsing, *op. cit.* (note 66), p. 162.

NOTES TO THE ANTI-CONFUCIAN MOVEMENT IN
EARLY REPUBLICAN CHINA

1. *Mencius*, Bk. III, Part I, Chap. 4, Sec. 12. See also Ch'üan Han-sheng (Chüan Han-seng), "Ch'ing-mo fan-tui Hsi-hua ti yen-lun" ("Opinions against Western Culture at the End of the Ch'ing Period"), *Ling-nan Hsüeh-pao*, V, 3–4 (Canton, Ling-nan Ta-hsüeh, December 20, 1936), pp. 122–66; Ch'en Teng-yüan, "Hsi-hsüeh lai Hua shih kuo-jen chih wu-tuan t'ai-tu" ("The Chinese Dogmatic Attitude toward Western Knowledge When It Was First Introduced into China"), *Tung-fang Tsa-chih*, XXVII, 8 (April 1930), pp. 61–76.

2. Ch'en Chih, *Yung-shu* ("Book of Utility") (edition of Hsi-cheng ts'ung-shu, first published 1897), "Wai p'ien" and author's preface. Also Ch'üan Han-sheng, "Ch'ing-mo-ti 'Hsi-hsüeh yüan ch'u Chung-kuo' shuo" ("Research on the 'Theories of the Chinese Origin of Western Sciences' at the End of the Ch'ing Dynasty"), *Ling-nan Hsüeh-pao*, IV, 2 (June 15, 1935), pp. 57–102.

3. K'ang Yu-wei, "K'an-pu *Ch'un-ch'iu* pi-hsiao ta-i wei-yen k'ao t'i-tz'u" ("Introduction to a Study of the Explicit Ideas and Subtle Expositions of the

Spring and Autumn Annals") (written in Suma, Japan, 1913), *Pu-jen* ("Compassion"), No. 8 (Shanghai, Kuang-chi Shu-chü, November 1913), "Chiao-shuo," pp. 1–4. See *infra*, n. 39.

4. Ch'üan Han-sheng, "Ch'ing-mo-ti 'Hsi-hsüeh yüan ch'u Chung-kuo' shuo," *loc. cit.*, pp. 86–89.

5. Wang Chih-ch'un, *Li-ts'e chih-yen* ("My Humble Opinions"), (m.p., n.d.) "Kuang hsüeh-hsiao" ("On Education").

6. K'ang Yu-wei, "Tsou ch'ing tsun K'ung-sheng wei kuo-chiao li chiao-pu chiao-hui i K'ung-tzu chi-nien erh fei yin-ssu che" ("A Memorial Urging the Throne to Proclaim Confucianism a State Religion, to Establish a Religious Department and Confucian Churches, to Base the National Calendar on the Birth Date of Confucius, and to Abolish Improper Sacrifices"), *Pu-jen*, No. 7 (August 1913), "Wen," pp. 1–8.

7. The term "Confucianist" I use here and in the following to describe or denote someone who attempts to promote a Confucian movement or to advance enthusiastically a Confucian cause, whereas the term "Confucian" I use only to mean someone who accepts Confucius' basic teachings or their later interpretations. Therefore, not every Confucian is a Confucianist, and a Confucianist such as K'ang Yu-wei might be challenged as to how Confucian he really was both in his thinking and in his career. The same distinction holds for the terms "traditional" and "traditionalist."

8. Ma Chen-tung, *Yüan shih tang-kuo shih* ("A History of Yüan Shih-k'ai's Administration") ([Shanghai?] Chung-hua Yin-shu-chü, 1930), Part I, Chap. XIV, Sec. 3, pp. 392–95. For the Chinese Confucian movement, see Shih Yung-chang, ed., *Tsun K'ung shih* ("A History of the Reverence-for-Confucius Movement"). See also Joseph R. Levenson, *Confucian China and Its Modern Fate, the Problem of Intellectual Continuity* (Berkeley, California, 1958).

9. Kuo-hsien ch'i-ts'ao wei-yüan-hui ("Committee for the Drafting of the National Constitution"), ed., *Ts'ao hsien pien-lan* ("A Guide to the Constitutional Drafting") (Peking, 1925), Part III, pp. 2–4; Part IV, p. 28.

10. Yen Fu, "Pao chiao yü i" ("A Further Discussion of the Preservation of Religion"), in *Yen Chi-tao shih wen ch'ao* ("Collected Essays and Poetry of Yen Fu") (Shanghai, Kuo-hua Shu-chü, 1922), ch. 2, pp. 8a–10b.

11. Chang Ping-lin, "Po chien-li K'ung-chiao i" ("A Rebuttal to the Proposal for a Confucian Religion"), in *Chang T'ai-yen wen ch'ao* ("Collected Essays of Chang Ping-lin"), ch. 3, pp. 43a–45b.

12. Articles by Liang Ch'i-ch'ao published in 1902 and 1914, cited in his *Ch'ing-tai hsüeh-shu kai-lun* ("An Outline of the Scholarship of the Ch'ing Dynasty"), Chap. 26, in *Yin-ping-shih ho-chi*, "chuan-chi," *ts'e* 25. English translation by Immanuel C. Y. Hsü, *Intellectual Trends in the Ch'ing Period* (Cambridge, Mass., 1959), pp. 102–7. For Liang's thought, see Joseph R. Levenson, *Liang Ch'i-ch'ao and the Mind of Modern China* (Cambridge, Mass., 1953), Chaps. III, IV, V, VI; and Ting Wen-chiang (V. K. Ting), ed., *Liang Jen-kung hsien-sheng nien-p'u ch'ang-pien* ("A Draft Chronological Biography of Liang Ch'i-ch'ao") (Taipei, Shih-chieh Shu-chü, 1958), 3 vols. See also Sanetō Keishū, *Shin Chūgoku no jukyō hihan* ("Criticism of Confucianism in New China") (Tokyo, 1948), V, 61–76.

13. For the definition of the movement see Chow Tse-tsung, "May Fourth Movement," in the *Encyclopædia Britannica* (Chicago, 1960).

14. For an analysis of this article and other problems of the anti-Confucian

movement see Chow Tse-tsung, *The May Fourth Movement: Intellectual Revolution in Modern China* (Cambridge, Mass., 1960), pp. 300–317.

15. Ch'en Tu-hsiu, "Wu-jen chih tsui-hou chüeh-wü ("Our Final Awakening"), *Hsin Ch'ing-nien (Ch'ing-nien Tsa-chih, "New Youth"),* I, 6 (Shanghai, February 15, 1916), pp. 1–4.

16. See *New Youth,* II, 2 (October 1, 1916), to III, 6 (August 1, 1917).

17. Hu Shih, "*Wu Yü wen lu* hsü" ("Preface to the *Collected Essays of Wu Yü*"), written on June 16, 1921, in Wu Yü, *Wu Yü wen lu* (Shanghai, Ya-tung T'u-shu-kuan, 1921), p. vii. Hu's remark on Wu was an allusion from the Chinese novel *Shui hu chuan.*

18. Lu Hsün, "K'uang-jen jih-chi" ("The Diary of a Madman"), *New Youth,* IV, 5 (May 15, 1918), pp. 414–24; reprinted in *Na-han* ("Cries") (1923), pp. 13–22. Wu Yü, "Ch'i-jen yü li-chiao" ("Cannibalism and the Teaching of *Li*"), *New Youth,* VI, 6 (November 1, 1919), reprinted in *Wu Yü wen lu, chüan* 1, pp. 63–72.

19. For an outline translation of Lin Shu's letter to Ts'ai Yüan-p'ei and Ts'ai's reply, and the opposition to the new thought, see Chow Tse-tsung, *The May Fourth Movement: Intellectual Revolution in Modern China,* pp. 61–72.

20. K'ang Yu-wei, "Chung-hua chiu-kuo lun" ("On Saving the Chinese Nation"), *Pu-jen,* No. 1 (February 1913), "Cheng lun," pp. 15–16.

21. K'ang Yu-wei, "Chih Tsung-t'ung Tsung-li shu" ("Letter to President Li Yüan-hung and Premier Tuan Ch'i-jui"), cited in Ch'en Tu-hsiu, "Po K'ang Yu-wei chih Tsung-t'ung Tsung-li shu" ("Refutation of K'ang Yu-wei's Letter to the President and the Premier"), *New Youth,* II, 2 (October 1, 1916), p. 1.

22. *Ibid.,* pp. 1–2.

23. K'ang Yu-wei, "A Memorial to the Throne," *op. cit.,* p. 5; also "K'ung-chiao hui hsü" ("Introduction to the Confucian Society"), No. 1, written in September 1912, *Pu-jen,* No. 1 (February 1913), "Chiao-shuo," pp. 1–10.

24. Chang Ping-lin, *Kuo-hsüeh kai-lun* ("An Introduction to Chinese Classical Studies") (Shanghai, 1922; Hongkong, 1953), Chap. I, Sec. 1, pp. 6–7. James Legge translated the word *tsai* in the passage as "were present" (*Confucian Analects,* Bk. II, Chap. 12, in *The Chinese Classics,* Vol. I). But considering the same word in Bk. I, Chap. 11, one may accept Chang's interpretation.

25. Ch'en Tu-hsiu, "Refutation of K'ang Yu-wei's Letter to the President and the Premier," *op. cit.,* p. 2.

26. K'ang Yu-wei, "Kung-chiao hui hsü ("Introduction to the Confucian Society"), No. 2, in *K'ang Nan-hai wen ch'ao* (Collected Essays of K'ang Yu-wei), ch. 1, pp. 20b–21a; also "On Saving the Chinese Nation," *op. cit.,* p. 15.

27. Ch'en Tu-hsiu, "Refutation of K'ang Yu-wei's Letter to the President and the Premier," *loc. cit.;* see also *New Youth,* III, 1 (March 1, 1917), "Letters to the Editor," pp. 20–24; and III, 3 (May 1, 1917), "Letters to the Editor," pp. 10–13, Yu Sung-hua's correspondence with Ch'en Tu-hsiu.

28. It seems to me that recent studies on the problem prove no more than that Confucius accepted some of the prevailing religious ideas. We cannot deny that in many cases he merely dismissed the problem of the supernatural, and that the absolute majority of his arguments were based on his consideration of human affairs supported by moral justification rather than by superhuman forces. We may of course find many of his ideas to be religious; but

cannot we find as much in Socrates, who was labeled as the "maker of new gods"? The argument has been advanced that since Confucianism had been installed as a religion, then it must have been a religion. One could counter this with a similar postulate: Since Confucianism has in modern times been treated as a secular doctrine, then it must be secular. For this problem see C. K. Yang, "The Functional Relationship between Confucian Thought and Chinese Religion," in John K. Fairbank, ed., *Chinese Thought and Institutions* (Chicago, 1957), pp. 269–90.

29. K'ang Yu-wei, "Chung-kuo hsüeh-hui pao t'i-tz'u" (Introduction to the Journal of the Society for Chinese Studies), *Pu-jen*, No. 2 (March 1913), "Chiao-shuo," pp. 2–3.

30. K'ang Yu-wei, "I-yüan cheng-fu wu kan-yü min-su shuo" (Parliamentary Government Has No Right to Interfere with Folkways"), in *ibid.*, "Cheng-lun," pp. 1–14.

31. Ch'en Tu-hsiu, "Hsien-fa yü K'ung-chiao" ("The Constitution and Confucianism"), *New Youth*, II, 3 (November 1, 1916), p. 2.

32. *Ibid.*

33. Ch'en Tu-hsiu, "Letter in Reply to Wu Yü," in *ibid.*, II, 5 (January 1, 1917), p. 4; also in *Wu Yü wen lu, chüan* I, p. 13.

34. K'ang Yu-wei, "On Saving the Chinese Nation," *op. cit.*, pp. 49–51, 54–55. Also "I K'ung-chiao wei kuo-chiao p'ei-t'ien i" ("A Proposal to Proclaim Confucianism a State Religion and to Worship Confucius Together with Heaven"), *Pu-jen*, No. 3 (April 1913), "Chiao-shuo," pp. 8–11. For the argument of "the majority of the people," see also Joseph R. Levenson, "The Suggestiveness of Vestiges: Confucianism and Monarchy at the Last," in David S. Nivison and Arthur F. Wright, eds., *Confucianism in Action* (Stanford, Calif., 1959), pp. 247–51.

35. See Ch'en Tu-hsiu, "Tsai lun K'ung-chiao wen-t'i" ("More Discussion on the Confucian Religion Problem"), *New Youth*, II, 5 (January 1, 1917), p. 3; Chang Tung-sun, "Yü-chih K'ung-chiao kuan" ("My View of the Confucian Religion"), *Yung-yen* ("The Justice"), I, 15 (July 1, 1913), "T'ung lun" II, 1–12.

36. Ch'en Tu-hsiu, "More Discussion on the Confucian Religion Problem," *op. cit.*, p. 4.

37. *Ibid.*, p. 1.

38. See Liang Ch'i-ch'ao, "Wu-hsü cheng-pien chi" ("An Account of the 1898 Coup d' État") and his biographical sketch of T'an Ssu-t'ung printed in T'an's *Jen-hsüeh*.

39. The theory of *san-t'ung* was based on Tung Chung-shu (*ca.* 179–104 B.C.) (*Ch'un-ch'iu fan-lu, chüan* 7, Chap. 23, "San-tai kai-chih chih wen"); *san-shih* was based on Ho Hsiu (A.D. 129–182) (*Ch'un-ch'iu Kung-yang chieh-ku*, "Yin-kung yüan-nien" [722 B.C.]). For K'ang's interpretation see his "Introduction to a Study of the Explicit Ideas and Subtle Expositions of the *Spring and Autumn Annals*," *loc. cit.*; "Meng-tzu wei," *ibid.*, No. 6 (July 1913), pp. 1–18. See also Derk Bodde, "Harmony and Conflict in Chinese Philosophy," in Arthur F. Wright, ed., *Studies in Chinese Thought* (Chicago, 1953), pp. 32–36.

40. In his *Ta-t'ung shu*, K'ang attributed all human agonies to the existence of the "nine boundaries or conditions" (*chiu-chieh*), i.e., country, caste, race, sex, family, class, oppression, species, and agony itself. In the ideal world of his *Ta-t'ung*, being released from all these agonies, man will become

immortal and attain the greatest happiness, as described in Taoist and Buddhist works.

41. For this see Ch'ien Mu, *Chung-kuo chin san-pai nien hsüeh-shu shih* ("History of Chinese Scholarship in the Last Three Hundred Years") (Shanghai, 1937), pp. 704–9.

42. See Wu Yü, "Hsiao-chi ko-ming chih Lao Chuang" ("The Passive Revolutionists Lao-tzu and Chuang-tzu"), *New Youth*, III, 2 (April 1, 1917), pp. 1–3.

43. *Ibid.*, also Ch'en Tu-hsiu, "Chiu ssu-hsiang yü kuo-t'i wen-t'i" ("The Old Thought and the Problem of State Structure"), a speech delivered at the Peking Shen-chou hsüeh-hui, *New Youth*, III, 3 (May 1, 1917); "Fu-p'i yü tsun K'ung" ("The Monarchical Restoration and Reverence for Confucius"), *ibid.*, III, 6 (August 1, 1917), pp. 1–4.

44. Ch'en Tu-hsiu, "Refutation of K'ang Yu-wei's Letter to the President and the Premier," *loc. cit.*, p. 3.

45. Ku Shih, "She-hui chiao-yü chi kung-ho kuo-hun chih K'ung-chiao lun" (Social Education and Confucianism as the Spirit of the Republic), *Min-i Tsa-chih*, No. 2 (1916); Ch'en Tu-hsiu, "The Constitution and Confucianism," *loc. cit.*, pp. 3–5; Ch'ang Nai-te's letter to Ch'en Tu-hsiu and Ch'en's reply in *New Youth*, II, 4 (December 1, 1916), "Letters to the Editor," pp. 4–7.

46. Ch'en Tu-hsiu, "K'ung-tzu chih tao yü hsien-tai sheng-huo" ("Confucius' Principles and Modern Life"), *New Youth*, II, 4 (December 1, 1916), pp. 1–7.

47. Wu Yü, "Ju-chia ta-t'ung chih i pen-yü Lao-tzu shuo" ("On Lao-tzu's Being the Origin of the Confucian Conception of One World"), *ibid.*, III, 5 (July 1, 1917), pp. 1–3; also Wu's letter to Ch'en Tu-hsiu and Ch'en's reply in *ibid.*, pp. 4–5.

48. *Ibid.*; and Ch'en Tu-hsiu's letter in reply to Ch'ang Nai-te, in *New Youth*, II, 6 (February 1, 1917), "Letters to the Editor," p. 10.

49. See Liang Ch'i-ch'ao, "Ku shu chen wei chi ch'i nien-tai" ("The Genuine and Forged Ancient Books and Their Dates"), in *Yin-ping-shih ho-chi*, "chuan-chi," *ts'e*, 24, Part 104, pp. 5–6.

50. Cited in Ch'en Tu-hsiu, "Refutation of K'ang's Letter to the President and the Premier," *loc. cit.*, p. 4.

51. Ch'en Tu-hsiu, "Letter in Reply to Ch'ang Nai-te," *New Youth*, II, 6 (February 1, 1917), "Letters to the Editor," pp. 9–10; also Ch'en's letter in reply to Yü Sung-hua, in *ibid.*, III, 1 (March 1, 1917), "Letters to the Editor," pp. 23–24.

52. For a preliminary study of the Confucian theory of *li*, see Chow Tse-tsung, "Hsün-tzu li yüeh lun fa-wei" ("Introduction to Hsün-tzu's Theory of *Li* and *Yüeh*"), *Hsüeh-shu Shih-chieh* (Academic World), II, 3 (Shanghai, January 1937), pp. 69–71; II, 4 (April 1937), pp. 61–66.

53. See Wu Yü, "Li lun" ("On Li"), *New Youth*, III, 3 (May 1, 1917), pp. 1–8; also his "Ju-chia chu-chang chieh-chi chih-tu chih hai" ("The Harm in Confucians' Advocacy of Caste System"), *New Youth*, III, 4 (June 1, 1917), pp. 1–4; Ch'en Tu-hsiu, "The Constitution and Confucianism," *loc. sit.*, pp. 3–5.

54. Ch'en Tu-hsiu, "Confucius' Principles and Modern Life," *loc. cit.*, pp. 3–4.

55. *Ibid.*, pp. 4–5.

56. See, for example, *Analects*, Bk. I, Chap. IV; English translation by

James Legge, in *The Chinese Classics* (Hong Kong and London, 1861–72), I, 139, and that by Arthur Waley, *The Analects of Confucius* (London, 1938), p. 84; *Tso chuan,* "Huan-kung liu nien" (706 B.C.); see French translation by Fr. S. Couvreur, *Tch'ouen Ts'iou et Tso Tchouan* (Ho Kien Fou, China, 1914), Vol. I, p. 87; English translation by James Legge, *The Chun Tsew with the Tso Chuen,* Vol. V, Part 2 of *The Chinese Classics,* pp. 47–48; also Ch'ang Nai-te, "Wo chih K'ung-tao kuan" ("My Views on the Confucian Principles"), *New Youth,* III, 1 (March 1, 1917), "The Readers Forum," p. 9.

57. The authorship of the *Classic of Filial Piety* was attributed to Tseng Ts'an by *Shih-chi,* to Confucius by *Han shu,* and to Confucius' or Tseng Ts'an's disciple by Ssu-ma Kuang and Yao Kung-wu. Since Chu Hsi, many scholars have considered it the work of early Han Confucians. There was also an Ancient Text *Classic of Filial Piety* (*Ku-wen hsiao-ching*), which was probably forged in the Han period ofter the Modern Text edition. The *Classic of Loyalty* was first mentioned in the eleventh century with its author listed as Ma Jung, a famous Confucian scholar of the second century.

58. See *Hsün-tzu,* "Li lun p'ien"; Wu Yü, "Tu Hsün-tzu shu-hou ("A Note after Reading *Hsün-tzu*"), *New Youth,* III, I (March 1, 1917), p. 1; also Chow Tse-tsung, "Introduction to Hsün-tzu's Theory of *Li* and *Yueh,*" *op. cit.,* II, 4 (April 1937), pp. 61–63. Wu Yü held Hsün-tzu responsible for the theory of the absolute power of a sovereign. While this may be partly true, we must remember that Hsün-tzu, like Mencius, believed that the people were more important than the sovereign, that the latter held his position only to serve the former, and that certain revolutions were justifiable. See "Ta-lüeh," "Fu-kuo," "Cheng-lun," "Wang-chih," and "Wang-pa," trans. by Homer H. Dubs, *The Works of Hsüntze* (London, 1928); also his *Hsüntze, the Moulder of Ancient Confucianism* (London, 1927), pp. 257–58.

59. Wu Yü, "Shuo hsiao" ("On Filial Piety"), in *Wu Yü wen lu, chüan* I, p. 15.

60. *Mencius,* Bk. IV, Part I, Chap. 26. The old family system was attacked by many student magazines; see for example Ku Ch'eng-wu, "Tui-yü chiu chia-t'ing ti kan-hsiang" ("My View of the Old Family System"), *New Tide,* I, 2 (February 1, 1919), pp. 155–68; and the following issues.

61. *Tao te ching, chüan* I, Chap. 18; English translation by Arthur Waley, *The Way and Its Power* (London, 1934), p. 165. See also *Analects,* Bk. XIII, Chap. 18; English translations, Legge and Waley; also Giles, *Confucianism and Its Rivals* (London, 1915), p. 86; Wu Yü, "Tao-chia Fa-chia chün fan-tui chiu tao-te shuo" ("On Taoists and Legalists Being Opposed to the Old Morality"), in *Wu Yü wen lu, chüan* I, pp. 23–46.

62. *Ibid.;* also Wu Yü, "Mo-tzu ti lao-nung-chu-i" ("Mo-tzu's 'Workers and Peasants' Doctrine"), in *Wu Yü wen lu, chüan* II, pp. 66–85. The Chinese term *Lao-nung chu-i* was customarily used in the early Republic as a translation of "Bolshevism" or "Communism." Wu probably did not use the term in this particular sense. Possibly he only meant "socialism" in general or a doctrine for the workers and peasants.

63. Wu Yü, "On the Taoists and Legalists Being Opposed to the Old Morality," *op. cit.,* p. 45.

64. *Analects,* Bk. XIII, Chap. 18, Legge's translation.

65. The legend appears in *Sou shen chi,* a book of mystic stories attributed to Kan Pao of the fourth century.

66. See Fu Ssu-nien, "Wan o chih yüan" ("The Source of All Evils"), *New*

Tide, I, 1 (January 1, 1919); see also a similar article in the organ of the anarchist organization Shih-she ("Practice Society"), *Tzu-yu lu* ("Record of Liberty").

67. See *supra,* No. 19; also *Mencius,* Bk. V, Part II, Chap. 1.

68. *Supra,* No. 19. The reference to the problem of the birth of children was probably provoked by Wu Yü's article on filial piety and Hu Shih's poem "My Son."

69. The first chapter of K'ang's *K'ung-tzu kai-chih k'ao* has the subject: "A Study on the Lack of Knowledge of the Remote and Obscure [Chinese] Antiquity."

70. See Ku Chieh-kang, ed., *Ku-shih pien* ("A Symposium on Ancient Chinese History"). I (Peiping, P'u she, 1926), pp. 7, 56, 76–78.

71. Ku Chieh-kang, "Ch'un-ch'iu shih-tai ti K'ung-tzu ho Han-tai ti K'ung-tzu" ("The Confucius of the Ch'un-ch'iu Period and of the Han Period"), in *ibid.,* II (1930), p. 139.

72. Fung Yu-lan, "K'ung-tzu tsai Chung-kuo li-shih chung chih ti-wei" ("Confucius' Place in Chinese History"), *Yen-ching Hsüeh-pao,* No. 2 (December 1927), pp. 233–47.

73. See for example Wu K'ang, "Lun wu kuo chin-jih tao-te chih ken-pen wen-t'i" ("The Fundamental Problem of Morality in China Today"), *New Tide,* I, 2 (February 1919), pp. 327–33; Ch'ang Nai-te, "Chi Ch'en Tu-hsiu chun yen-chiang tz'u" ("A Record of Mr. Ch'en Tu-hsiu's Speech"), *New Youth,* III, 3 (May 1, 1917), pp. 1–3.

74. Lu Hsün, "Lao tiao-tzu i-ching ch'ang wan" ("The Old Tune Is Finished"), a speech delivered in Hong Kong on February 19, 1927, adapted from the translation by Lin Yutang, in *Chinese Wit and Wisdom* (New York, 1942), p. 1089.

75. Hu Han-min, "Meng-tzu yü she-hui-chu-i" ("Mencius and Socialism"), first published in the *Chien-she tsa-chih* ("The Construction") in 1919, reprinted in *Wei-wu shih-kuan yü lun-li chih yen-chiu* ("A Study of the Materialistic Conception of History and Ethics") (Shanghai, Min-chih Shu-chü, 1927), pp. 155–78.

76. Kuo Mo-jo, "K'ung Mo ti p'i-p'an" ("A Critical Study of Confucius and Mo-tzu"), in *Shih p'i-p'an shu* ("Ten Critiques") (Shanghai, Ch'ün-i Ch'u-pan-she, 1945, 1950), pp. 76–129.

Index

No attempt has been made to include Chinese characters for names found in Arthur W. Hummel, ed., *Eminent Chinese of the Ch'ing Period* (Washington, 1943–44).